Acclaim for Robert Wright's

THE EVOLUTION OF
GOD

"In his brilliant new book, Robert Wright tells the story of how God grew up.... Wright's tone is reasoned and careful, even hesitant, throughout, and it is nice to read about issues like the morality of Christ and the meaning of jihad without getting the feeling that you are being shouted at. His views are provocative and controversial. There is something here to annoy almost everyone.... For Wright, it is not God who evolves. It is us—God just comes along for the ride. It is a great ride, though."   —Paul Bloom, *New York Times Book Review*

"Straddling popular science, ancient history, and theology, this ambitious work sets out to resolve not only the clash of civilizations between the Judeo-Christian West and the Muslim world but also the clash between science and religion.... Wright's core argument, that religion is getting 'better' with each passing aeon, is enthralling."   —*The New Yorker*

"On any list of nonfiction authors that many people may not know but should, Robert Wright would rank high.... Taken together, *The Moral Animal, Nonzero,* and *The Evolution of God* represent a powerful addition to modern thought. If biology, culture, and faith all seek a better world, maybe there is hope."
        —Gregg Easterbrook, *Wall Street Journal*

"The faith versus reason debate has gone on for years.... *The Evolution of God* is about to reframe this.... Wright gives relief and intellectual ballast to those believers weary of the punching bag."
        —Lisa Miller, *Newsweek*

"The possibility of a reasonable engagement between faith and reason, between doctrine and biblical scholarship, between a mature theology and a golden age of scientific research—all this seems very distant right now. And that's why *The Evolution of God* gives me hope. It reminds us that if you take a few thousand steps back from our current crisis, the long-term prognosis is much better than you might imagine....The tone of the book is dry skepticism with a dash of humor; the content is supple, dense, and layered. What makes it fresh and necessary is that it's a nonbeliever's open-minded exploration of how religious doctrine and practice have changed through human history—usually for the better."
— Andrew Sullivan, *The Times* (London)

"*The Evolution of God* is a big book that addresses a simple question: Is religion poison?...Wright rejects that assumption. No religion is in essence evil or good, he writes. Scriptures are malleable. Founders are betrayed. At least for historians, there is little provocation here. The provocation comes when Wright claims that religious history seems to be going somewhere, as if guided by an invisible hand. Judaism, Christianity, and Islam all appear to have a 'moral direction,' and that direction is toward good....*The Evolution of God* offers the sort of hope even unbelievers can believe in: that we can somehow learn to talk about religion."
— Stephen Prothero, *Washington Post*

"As a lively writer, supple thinker, and imaginative synthesizer, Wright is bound to attract attention. His sprightly style deprives his subject of any solemnity."   —Dan Cryer, *Boston Globe*

"Across 567 remarkably lively pages, Wright argues that our current globalized, highly interdependent culture may well produce versions of Christianity, Islam, and Judaism that worship a less prickly and more empathetic god than ever before."
—David Van Biema, *Houston Chronicle*

"The book is filled with richly observed details about the Bible and the Qur'an, though Wright wears his learning lightly as he guides us through several thousand years of religious history."

— Steve Paulson, Salon.com

"It's not God, of course, who evolves in Robert Wright's provocative new book — it's our ideas about him.... Wright ably synthesizes the work of other scholars into an original and highly readable account of the origins and historical changes in Judaism, Christianity, and Islam.... The tone of Wright's volume is lively.... Religion might be capable of dividing us, but in its more mature forms, it's also capable of reminding us of what we have in common, and it plays a role, Wright argues, in allowing us to transcend our sense of ourselves as separate creatures and tap into our shared welfare."

— Margaret Quamme, *Columbus Dispatch*

"*The Evolution of God* is a remarkable book, engaging, audacious, and provocative in an open-ended way.... There are, it seems, two Robert Wrights — a tough-minded Robert Wright and a tender-minded Robert Wright — who have collaborated on a book about religion.... This collaboration works."

— Peter Steinfels, *American Prospect*

"While the diatribes of the 'new atheists' — Richard Dawkins, Sam Harris, and company — have made headlines in recent years, Wright takes a decidedly more friendly approach to human religiousness.... Wright's approach will appeal to a broad range of readers turned off by the 'either/or' choice between dogmatic atheism and religious traditionalism."   —*Library Journal*

"God works in mysterious ways, as the saying goes. How mysterious? Well, as Robert Wright, a nonbeliever, argues in his new book, God can save the world even if he doesn't actually exist."

— Jerry Adler, *Daily Beast*

"Wright asks big questions.... By providing an evolutionary history of God as presented in the religious texts of Christianity, Judaism, and Islam, Wright attempts not only to bridge the philosophical gaps but also to show how they can address the challenges presented today.... Wright's argument is undeniably optimistic."

— *Kirkus Reviews*

"Fully seduced, I started reading and, for all its weight, couldn't stand to put it down.... The hefty 500-pager starts to feel like a breezy, concise charge through the most titillatingly inversionary historical-critical readings of Hebrew and Christian and Muslim scripture. It's stuff that many people don't know is out there and available for hanging one's cosmic hat on: a vast anti-narrative provided by the wonders of modern scholarship."

— Nathan Schneider, KillingtheBuddha.com

" 'Can religions in the modern world reconcile themselves to one another, and can they reconcile themselves to science?' Robert Wright — journalist, philosophy professor, and author of the acclaimed books *Nonzero* and *The Moral Animal* — ardently believes the answer is yes. In this meaty account, the result of ten years of scholarly research, he attempts to do so, drawing on evolutionary psychology, archaeology, and game theory to trace a common pattern in the world's monotheistic faiths. It's a thoroughly materialist account of religion and yet is ultimately allied with one of religion's basic goals: to provide guidance and comfort in a chaotic world."

— *Seed*

THE EVOLUTION OF GOD

THE EVOLUTION OF

GOD

ROBERT WRIGHT

BACK BAY BOOKS
Little, Brown and Company
New York   Boston   London

Back Bay Books / Little, Brown and Company
Hachette Book Group
237 Park Avenue, New York, NY 10017
www.hachettebookgroup.com

Originally published in hardcover by Little, Brown and Company, June 2009
First Back Bay paperback edition, May 2010

Back Bay Books is an imprint of Little, Brown and Company. The Back Bay Books name and logo are trademarks of Hachette Book Group, Inc.

Library of Congress Cataloging-in-Publication Data
Wright, Robert.
    The evolution of God / Robert Wright. — 1st ed.
        p. cm.
    Includes bibliographical references (p.) and index.
    ISBN 978-0-316-73491-2 (hc) / 978-0-316-05487-4 (int'l ed.) /
978-0-316-06744-7 (pb)
    1. God — History of doctrines.   2. Monotheism — History.
3. Religions — Relations.   I. Title.
BL473.W75 2009
200.9 — dc22   2008051303

10 9 8 7 6 5 4 3 2 1

RRD-IN

Printed in the United States of America

For John,
my odometer monitor

The partner in the dialogue with God is not the individual man but the human species as a whole.

—*Gordon Kaufman*

Contents

IV
THE TRIUMPH OF ISLAM

V
GOD GOES GLOBAL (OR DOESN'T)

THE EVOLUTION OF GOD

Introduction

I was once denounced from the pulpit of my mother's church. The year was 1994. My book *The Moral Animal* had just been published, and I'd been lucky enough to have it excerpted in *Time* magazine. The excerpt was about the various ways in which our evolved human nature complicates the project of marriage. One such complication is the natural, universally human temptation to stray, and that is the angle *Time*'s editors chose to feature on the magazine's cover. Alongside a stark image of a broken wedding band were the words "Infidelity: It may be in our genes."

The pastor of the First Baptist Church in Santa Rosa, California, saw this article as a godless defense of philandering and said so one Sunday morning. After the service, my mother went forward and told him that her son was the author of the article. I'm willing to bet that—such are the wonders of maternal love—she said it with pride.

How far I had fallen! Back around age nine, at the Immanuel Baptist Church in El Paso, Texas, I had felt the call of God and walked to the front of the church as a visiting evangelist named Homer Martinez issued the "invitation"—the call for unredeemed sinners to accept Jesus as their savior. A few weeks later I was baptized by the church's minister. Now, nearly three decades later, another Baptist minister was placing me in the general vicinity of Satan.

I doubt that, if this minister had read my *Time* piece carefully, he would have come down so hard on it. (I had actually argued that the adulterous impulse, though natural, can and should be resisted.)

On the other hand, there were people who read not just the excerpt but the whole book and concluded that I was a godless something or other. I had argued that the most ethereal, uplifting parts of human existence (love, sacrifice, our very sense of moral truth) were products of natural selection. The book seemed like a thoroughly materialist tract—materialist as in "scientific materialist," as in "Science can explain everything in material terms, so who needs a God? Especially a God who is alleged to somehow magically transcend the material universe."

I guess "materialist" is a not-very-misleading term for me. In fact, in this book I talk about the history of religion, and its future, from a materialist standpoint. I think the origin and development of religion can be explained by reference to concrete, observable things—human nature, political and economic factors, technological change, and so on.

But I don't think a "materialist" account of religion's origin, history, and future—like the one I'm giving here—precludes the validity of a religious worldview. In fact, I contend that the history of religion presented in this book, materialist though it is, actually affirms the validity of a religious worldview; not a *traditionally* religious worldview, but a worldview that is in some meaningful sense religious.

It sounds paradoxical. On the one hand, I think gods arose as illusions, and that the subsequent history of the idea of god is, in some sense, the evolution of an illusion. On the other hand: (1) the story of this evolution itself points to the existence of something you can meaningfully call divinity; and (2) the "illusion," in the course of evolving, has gotten streamlined in a way that moved it closer to plausibility. In both of these senses, the illusion has gotten less and less illusory.

Does that make sense? Probably not. I hope it will by the end of the book. For now I should just concede that the kind of god that remains plausible, after all this streamlining, is not the kind of god that most religious believers currently have in mind.

There are two other things that I hope will make a new kind of sense by the end of this book, and both are aspects of the current world situation.

One is what some people call a clash of civilizations — the tension between the Judeo-Christian West and the Muslim world, as conspicuously manifested on September 11, 2001. Ever since that day, people have been wondering how, if at all, the world's Abrahamic religions can get along with one another as globalization forces them into closer and closer contact.

Well, history is full of civilizations clashing, and for that matter, of civilizations not clashing. And the story of the role played by religious ideas — fanning the flames or dampening the flames, and often changing in the process — is instructive. I think it tells us what we can do to make the current "clash" more likely to have a happy ending.

The second aspect of the current world situation I'll address is another kind of clash — the much-discussed "clash" between science and religion. Like the first kind of clash, this one has a long and instructive history. It can be traced at least as far back as ancient Babylon, where eclipses that had long been attributed to restless and malignant supernatural beings were suddenly found to occur at predictable intervals — predictable enough to make you wonder whether restless and malignant supernatural beings were really the problem.

There have been many such unsettling (from religion's point of view) discoveries since then, but always some notion of the divine has survived the encounter with science. The notion has had to change, but that's no indictment of religion. After all, science has changed relentlessly, revising if not discarding old theories, and none of us think of that as an indictment of science. On the contrary, we think this ongoing adaptation is carrying science closer to the truth. Maybe the same thing is happening to religion. Maybe, in the end, a mercilessly scientific account of our predicament — such as the account that got me denounced from the pulpit of my mother's church — is actually compatible with a truly religious worldview, and is part of the process that refines a religious worldview, moving it closer to truth.

These two big "clash" questions can be put into one sentence: Can religions in the modern world reconcile themselves to one another, and can they reconcile themselves to science? I think their history points to affirmative answers.

What would religions look like after such an adaptation? This question is surprisingly easy to answer, at least in broad outline. First, they'll have to address the challenges to human psychological well-being that are posed by the modern world. (Otherwise they won't win acceptance.) Second, they'll have to highlight some "higher purpose"— some kind of larger point or pattern that we can use to help us orient our daily lives, recognize good and bad, and make sense of joy and suffering alike. (Otherwise they won't be religions, at least not in the sense that I mean the word "religion.")

Now for the really hard questions. *How* will religions manage these feats? (Assuming they do; and if they don't, then all of us — believers, agnostics, and atheists alike — may be in big trouble.) How will religions adapt to science and to one another? What would a religion well suited to an age of advanced science and rapid globalization look like? What kind of purpose would it point to, what kind of orientation would it provide? Is there an intellectually honest worldview that truly qualifies as religious and can, amid the chaos of the current world, provide personal guidance and comfort — and maybe even make the world less chaotic? I don't claim to have the answers, but clear clues emerge naturally in the course of telling the story of God. So here goes.

I

THE BIRTH AND GROWTH OF GODS

In summing up, then, it may be said that nearly all the great social institutions have been born in religion.

—*Emile Durkheim*

Chapter One

The Primordial Faith

The Chukchee, a people indigenous to Siberia, had their own special way of dealing with unruly winds. A Chukchee man would chant, "Western Wind, look here! Look down on my buttocks. We are going to give you some fat. Cease blowing!" The nineteenth-century European visitor who reported this ritual described it as follows: "The man pronouncing the incantation lets his breeches fall down, and bucks leeward, exposing his bare buttocks to the wind. At every word he claps his hands."[1]

By the end of the nineteenth century, European travelers had compiled many accounts of rituals in faraway and scarcely known lands. Some of these lands were inhabited by people known as savages — people whose technology didn't include writing or even agriculture. And some of their rituals seemed, like this one, strange.

Could a ritual like this be called religious? Some Europeans bridled at the thought, offended by the implied comparison between their elevated forms of worship and crude attempts to appease nature.

Maybe that's why Sir John Lubbock, a late-nineteenth-century British anthropologist, prefaced his discussion of "savage" religion with a warning. "It is impossible to discuss the subject without mentioning some things which are very repugnant to our feelings," he wrote in *The Origin of Civilization and the Primitive Condition of Man*. But he made his readers a promise. In exploring this "melancholy spectacle of gross superstitions and ferocious forms of worship," he would "endeavour to avoid, as far as possible, anything which might justly give pain to any of my readers."[2]

One pain Lubbock spared his readers was the thought that their brains might have much in common with savage brains. "The whole mental condition of a savage is so different from ours, that it is often very difficult to follow what is passing in his mind, or to understand the motives by which he is influenced." Though savages do "have a reason, such as it is, for what they do and what they believe, their reasons often are very absurd." The savage evinces "extreme mental inferiority," and his mind, "like that of the child, is easily fatigued."[3] Naturally, then, the savage's religious ideas are "not the result of deep thought."

So there was reassurance aplenty for Lubbock's readers: "Religion, as understood by the lower savage races," is not only different from civilized religion "but even opposite." Indeed, if we bestow the title "religion" on the coarse rituals and superstitious fears that observers of savage society have reported, then "we can no longer regard religion as peculiar to man." For the "baying of a dog to the moon is as much an act of worship as some ceremonies which have been so described by travellers."[4]

Maybe it shouldn't surprise us that a well-educated British Christian would so disparage elements of "primitive religion." ("Primitive religion" denotes the religion of nonliterate peoples broadly, whether hunter-gatherer or agrarian.) After all, in primitive religion there is deep reverence for raw superstition. Obscure omens often govern decisions of war and peace. And the spirits of the dead may make mischief — or may, via the mediation of a shaman, offer counsel. In short, primitive religion is full of the stuff that was famously thrust aside when the monotheism carried out of Egypt by Moses displaced the paganism of Canaan.

But, actually, that displacement wasn't so clear-cut, and the proof is in the Bible itself, albeit parts of the Bible that aren't much read by modern believers. There you'll find Israel's first king, Saul, going incognito to a medium and asking her to raise the prophet Samuel from the grave for policy input. (Samuel isn't amused: "Why have you disturbed me by bringing me up?")[5] There you'll also find raw superstition. When the prophet Elisha, preparing King Joash for battle against the Arameans, tells him to strike the ground with some arrows, he is disappointed with the resulting three strikes: "You should have struck five or six times; then you would have struck down Aram until you had made an end of it, but now you will strike down Aram only three times."[6]

Even the ultimate in Abrahamic theological refinement—monotheism itself—turns out to be a feature of the Bible that comes and goes. Though much of the scripture assumes the existence of only one God, some parts strike a different tone. The book of Genesis recalls the time when a bunch of male deities came down and had sex with attractive human females; these gods "went in to the daughters of humans, who bore children to them." (And not ordinary children: "These were the heroes that were of old, warriors of renown.")[7]

Here and elsewhere, the Hebrew Bible—the earliest scripture in the Abrahamic tradition, and in that sense the starting point for Judaism, Christianity, and Islam—holds telling remnants of its ancestry. Apparently Abrahamic monotheism grew organically out of the "primitive" by a process more evolutionary than revolutionary.

This doesn't mean there's a line of cultural descent between the "primitive" religions on the anthropological record and the "modern" religions. It's not as if three or four millennia ago, people who had been talking to the wind while pulling their pants down started talking to God while kneeling. For all we know, the cultural ancestry of Judaism, Christianity, and Islam includes no tradition of talking to the wind at all, and certainly there's no reason to think that Chukchee religion is part of that ancestry—that back in the first or second millennium BCE, Chukchee culture in Siberia somehow influenced Middle Eastern culture.

Rather, the idea is that "primitive" religion broadly, as recorded by anthropologists and other visitors, can give us some idea of the ancestral milieu of modern religions. Through the happenstance of geographic isolation, cultures such as the Chukchee escaped the technological revolution—the advent of writing—that placed other parts of the world on the historical record and pushed them toward modernity. If these "primitive" cultures don't show us the particular prehistoric religions out of which the early recorded religions emerged, they at least give us a general picture. Though monotheistic prayer didn't grow out of Chukchee rituals or beliefs, maybe the logic of monotheistic prayer did grow out of a *kind* of belief the Chukchee held, the notion that forces of nature are animated by minds or spirits that you can influence through negotiation.

Savage Logic

This, in fact, was the theory of one of John Lubbock's contemporaries, Edward Tylor, a hugely influential thinker who is sometimes called the founder of social anthropology. Tylor, an acquaintance and sometime critic of Lubbock's, believed that the primordial form of religion was "animism." Tylor's theory of animism was among scholars of his day the dominant explanation of how religion began. It "conquered the world at one blow,"[8] one early-twentieth-century anthropologist wrote.

Tylor's theory was grounded in a paradigm that pervaded anthropology in the late nineteenth century, then fell out of favor for many decades, and lately has made a comeback: cultural evolutionism. The idea is that human culture as broadly defined—art, politics, technology, religion, and so on—evolves in much the way biological species evolve: new cultural traits arise and may flourish or perish, and as a result whole institutions and belief systems form and change. A new religious ritual can appear and gain a following (if, say, it is deemed an effective wind neutralizer). New gods can be born and then grow. New ideas about gods can arise—like the idea that there's only one of them. Tylor's theory of animism aimed to explain how this idea, monotheism, had evolved out of primitive religion.

"Animism" is sometimes defined as the attribution of life to the inanimate—considering rivers and clouds and stars alive. This is part of what Tylor meant by the term, but not all. The primitive animist, in Tylor's scheme, saw living and nonliving things alike as inhabited by—animated by—a soul or spirit; rivers and clouds, birds and beasts, and people, too, had this "ghost-soul," this "vapour, film, or shadow," this "cause of life and thought in the individual it animates."[9]

Tylor's theory rested on a more flattering view of the "primitive" mind than Lubbock held. (Tylor is credited with a doctrine that became a pillar of social anthropology—the "psychic unity of mankind," the idea that people of all races are basically the same, that there is a universal human nature.) He saw animism not as bizarrely inconsistent with modern thought, but as a natural early product of the same speculative curiosity that had led to modern thought. Animism had been the "infant philosophy of mankind," assembled by "ancient savage philosophers."[10] It did what good theories are supposed to do: explain otherwise mysterious facts economically.

To begin with, the hypothesis that humans have a ghost-soul handily answers some questions that, in Tylor's view, must have occurred to early humans, such as: What is happening when you dream? Primitive societies use the notion of the human soul to solve this puzzle. In some cases the idea is that the dreamer's ghost-soul wanders during sleep, having the adventures the dreamer later recalls; decades after Tylor wrote, the anthropologist A. R. Radcliffe-Brown observed that Andaman Islanders were reluctant to awaken people, since illness might ensue if sleep was interrupted before the soul came home.[11] In other cases, the idea is that the dreamer is being visited by the souls of others. In Fiji, Tylor noted, people's souls were thought to leave their bodies "to trouble other people in their sleep."[12]

And the idea that the souls of dead people return to visit via dreams is widespread in primitive societies.[13] Thus animism handles another enigma that confronted early human beings: death itself. Death, in this scenario, is what happens when the soul checks out of the body for good.

Once early humans had conceived the idea of the soul, Tylor said, extending it beyond our species was only logical. The savage couldn't help but "recognise in beasts the very characteristics which it attributes to the human soul, namely, the phenomena of life and death, will and judgement." And plants, "partaking with animals the phenomena of life and death, health and sickness, not unnaturally have some kind of soul ascribed to them." [14]

For that matter, the idea that sticks and stones have souls is rational if viewed from the standpoint of "an uncultured tribe." After all, don't sticks and stones appear in dreams? Don't ghosts that we see while dreaming, or while delirious with fever, wear clothes or carry weapons? "How then can we charge the savage with far-fetched absurdity for taking into his philosophy and religion an opinion which rests on the very evidence of his senses?" Tylor may have had Lubbock in mind when he said of primitive peoples, "The very assertion that their actions are motiveless, and their opinions nonsense, is itself a theory, and, I hold, a profoundly false one, invented to account for all manner of things which those who did not understand them could thus easily explain." [15]

Once a broadly animistic worldview had taken shape, Tylor believed, it started to evolve. At some point, for example, the notion of each tree having a spirit gave way to the notion of trees being collectively governed by "the god of the forest." [16] This incipient polytheism then matured and eventually got streamlined into monotheism. In 1866, in an article in the *Fortnightly Review*, Tylor summed up the whole process in what may be the only one-sentence history of religion ever published — and may also be one of the longest sentences of any kind ever published:

> Upwards from the simplest theory which attributes life and personality to animal, vegetable, and mineral alike — through that which gives to stone and plant and river guardian spirits which live among them and attend to their preservation, growth, and change — up to that which sees in each department of the world the protecting and fostering care of an appropriate divinity, and at last of one Supreme Being ordering and controlling the lower hierarchy — through all these gradations of opinion we may thus see fought out, in one stage after another, the long-

waged contest between a theory of animation which accounts for each phenomenon of nature by giving it everywhere a life like our own, and a slowly-growing natural science which in one department after another substitutes for independent voluntary action the working out of systematic law.[17]

Any questions?

There have been lots of them, actually. Tylor's theory hasn't kept the stature it once held. Some complain that it makes the evolution of gods sound like an exercise in pure reason, when in fact religion has been deeply shaped by many factors, ranging from politics to economics to the human emotional infrastructure. (One difference between modern cultural evolutionism and that of Tylor's day is the modern emphasis on the various ways that "memes"—rituals, beliefs, and other basic elements of culture—spread by appealing to nonrational parts of human nature.)

Still, in one broad sense Tylor's view holds up well today. However diverse the forces that shape religion, its early impetus indeed seems to have come largely from people who, like us, were trying to make sense of the world. But they didn't have the heritage of modern science to give them a head start, so they reached prescientific conclusions. Then, as understanding of the world grew—especially as it grew via science—religion evolved in reaction. Thus, Tylor wrote, does "an unbroken line of mental connexion" unite "the savage fetish-worshiper and the civilized Christian."[18]

At this level of generality, Tylor's worldview has not just survived the scrutiny of modern scholarship, but drawn strength from it. Evolutionary psychology has shown that, bizarre as some "primitive" beliefs may sound—and bizarre as some "modern" religious beliefs may sound to atheists and agnostics—they are natural outgrowths of humanity, natural products of a brain built by natural selection to make sense of the world with a hodgepodge of tools whose collective output isn't wholly rational.

Elaboration on the modern understanding of how "primitive" religion first emerged from the human mind can be found in the appendix of this book. For now the main point is that, even if Tylor's animism-to-monotheism scenario looks deficient from a modern vantage point, there is still much in it that makes sense. In particular: to understand the early stages in the evolution of gods, and of God, we have to imagine how the world looked to people living many millennia ago, not just before science, but before writing or even agriculture; and there is no better aid to that thought experiment than immersing ourselves in the worldview of hunter-gatherer societies that have been observed by anthropologists — the worldview of "savages," as both Lubbock and Tylor would say.

Of course, it would be nice to observe *literally* prehistoric societies, the societies whose religion actually did evolve into the ancient religions on the historical record. But there can't be detailed records of beliefs that existed before writing; all that is left is the stuff archaeologists find — tools and trinkets and, here and there, a cave painting. If the vast blank left by humanity's preliterate phase is to be filled, it will have to be filled by the vast literature on observed hunter-gatherer societies.

Using hunter-gatherers as windows on the past has its limits. For example, the anthropological record contains no "pristine" hunter-gatherer cultures, cultures wholly uncorrupted by contact with more technologically advanced societies. After all, the process of observing a culture involves contact with it. Besides, many hunter-gatherer societies had been contacted by missionaries or explorers before anyone started documenting their religions.

Then again, to the extent that the religious beliefs of an indigenous culture seem "strange" — bear little resemblance to the beliefs of the cultures that have contacted it — then this contact is an unlikely explanation for them. The practice of offering bare buttocks to the wind, for example, seems unlikely to have been taught to the Chukchee by a Christian missionary from Victorian England.

When a "strange" category of belief is found in hunter-gatherer societies on various continents, then it is even less likely to be a mere import, and more likely to be a genuine product of the hunter-gatherer lifestyle. As we're about to see, there is no shortage of hunter-gatherer notions that pass these two tests: they are wide-spread and — to our eyes — strange. So with fair confidence we can reconstruct the spiritual landscape of prehistoric times, back before religion entered the historical record.

No one any longer believes, as some nineteenth-century anthropologists did, that observed hunter-gatherers are crystalline examples of religion at its moment of origin tens of thousands of years ago. But they're the best clues we'll ever have to generic religious beliefs circa 12,000 BCE, before the invention of agriculture. Cave paintings are attractive, but they don't talk.

Hunter-Gatherer Gods

The Klamath, a hunter-gatherer people in what is now Oregon, talked. And, fortunately for us, they talked to someone who understood them more clearly than visitors often understand indigenous peoples: Albert Samuel Gatschet, a pioneering linguist who in the 1870s compiled a dictionary and grammar of the Klamath language. Gatschet's writings on the Klamath capture something found in every hunter-gatherer culture: belief in supernatural beings — and always more than one of them; there is no such thing as an indigenously monotheistic hunter-gatherer society.

In fact, the anthropological record reveals at least five different *kinds* of hunter-gatherer supernatural beings, some of which are found in all hunter-gatherer societies and most of which are found in most hunter-gatherer societies. Klamath culture, with a rich theology, illustrates all five.[19]

Hunter-gatherer supernatural being Type I: elemental spirits. Parts of nature that modern scientists consider inanimate may be alive, possessing intelligence and personality and a soul. So the workings of nature can become a social drama. When the Klamath saw clouds obscuring the moon, it could mean that Muash, the south wind, was trying to kill the moon — and in fact might succeed, though the moon seems always to have gotten resurrected in the end.

Hunter-gatherer supernatural being Type II: puppeteers. Parts of nature may be controlled by beings distinct from the parts of nature themselves. By Klamath reckoning, the west wind was emitted by a flatulent dwarf woman, about thirty inches tall, who wore a buckskin dress and a basket hat (and who could be seen in the form of a rock on a nearby mountain). The Klamath sometimes asked her to blow mosquitoes away from Pelican Bay.[20]

Combining supernatural beings of types I and II into a single scenario is possible. The Klamath believed whirlwinds were driven by an internal spirit, Shukash. The nearby Modoc hunter-gatherers, while agreeing, believed that Shukash was in turn controlled by Tchitchatsa-ash, or "Big Belly," whose stomach housed bones that rattled, creating the whirlwind's eerie sound.[21] Such theological differences are found not just among different hunter-gatherer societies, but within them. Thus Leme-ish, the Klamath's thunder spirit, was sometimes spoken of as a single entity but was sometimes said to consist of five brothers who, having been banished from polite society, now made noise to scare people. (These interpretive divergences form the raw material of cultural evolution, just as biological mutations create the diverse traits that feed genetic evolution.)

Hunter-gatherer supernatural being Type III: organic spirits. Natural phenomena that even we consider alive may have supernatural powers. The coyote, for example, housed evil spirits, and, Gatschet noted, "his lugubrious voice is the presager of war, misfortune, and death."[22] One species of bird could make snow, and another made fog. Some animal spirits could help the Klamath cure disease, a collaboration facilitated by a spirit called Yayaya-ash, which would assume the form of a one-legged man and lead a medicine man to the home of these animal spirits for consultation.

Hunter-gatherer supernatural being Type IV: ancestral spirits. Hunter-gatherer societies almost always feature spirits of the deceased, and typically these spirits do at least as much bad as good. Ancestral spirits,

Gatschet wrote, were "objects of dread and abomination, feelings which are increased by a belief in their omnipresence and invisibility."[23]

Hunter-gatherer supernatural being Type V: the high god. Some hunter-gatherer societies, though by no means all, have a "high god." This isn't a god that controls the other gods. (One early-twentieth-century anthropologist wrote about the Klamath, with traces of disapproval: "there has been no attempt to marshal the spirits into an ordered pantheon.")[24] Rather, a high god is a god that is in some vague sense more important than other supernatural beings, and is often a creator god. For the Klamath this was Kmukamtch, who inhabited the sun. Kmukamtch created the world, then created the Klamath themselves (out of a purple berry), and continued to sustain them, though he had been known to rain burning pitch upon his creation in a fit of temper.[25]*

So what was the point of all these gods and/or spirits? (The line between "gods" and "spirits" is fuzzy at best. I'll use the word "gods" broadly enough to cover both.) Obviously, one thing these gods did for the Klamath is explain the otherwise mysterious workings of nature. The above inventory of supernatural beings (just the tip of the Klamath iceberg) explains why it snows, why wind blows, why clouds obscure the moon, why thunder crashes, why dreams contain dead people, and so on. Every known hunter-gatherer society has similarly explained natural dynamics in supernatural terms — or at least in terms that *we* consider supernatural; for hunter-gatherers, these invisible beings are seamlessly bound to the observed world of nature, just as, in modern science, the gravitational force is seamlessly bound to the observed, orbiting moon.

This leads us to one of the more ironic properties of hunter-gatherer religion: it doesn't exist. That is, if you asked hunter-gatherers what their religion is, they wouldn't know what you were

---

* Underlined note numbers indicate that elaboration can be found in the corresponding note at the end of this book.

talking about. The kinds of beliefs and rituals we label "religious" are so tightly interwoven into their everyday thought and action that they don't have a word for them. We may label some of their explanations of how the world works "supernatural" and others "naturalistic," but those are our categories, not theirs. To them it seems fitting to respond to illness by trying to figure out which god caused it, just as to us it seems fitting to look for the germ that caused it.[26] This fine intertwining of the — in our terms — religious and nonreligious parts of culture would continue well into recorded history. Ancient Hebrew, the language of most of the Holy Bible, had no word for religion.

With all due respect for hunter-gatherer custom (and for ancient Hebrew), I'll continue to use words like "religion" and "supernatural" — partly for easy communication with readers who use them, and partly for a deeper reason: I think the parts of hunter-gatherer life that we label "religious" are specimens of human culture that, through cultural evolution, were transmuted into modern religion.

When Bad Things Happen to Good People

Beyond a general interest in how the world works, hunter-gatherers evince a particular interest in the question of why *bad* things happen. According to the Haida Native Americans of the north Pacific Coast, earthquakes happen when an undersea deity's very large dog (whose job is to hold up the islands on which the Haida live) shakes itself.[27] If the Mbuti pygmies of Africa's Congo region find part of the forest devoid of game, that means the *keti*, forest spirits who are avid hunters themselves, have gotten there first.[28] When a !Kung Bushman of the Kalahari Desert gets sick, it is likely the work of *gauwasi* — ancestral spirits — who may be acting at the behest of a god.[29]

Of course, hunter-gatherers aren't the only people to have asked why bad things happen. The Christian tradition alone has generated roomfuls of treatises on this question. But hunter-gatherers do a better job of answering the question than many modern theologians; at least, the hunter-gatherers' answers are less bedeviled by paradox. Theologians in the Abrahamic lineage—Jewish, Christian, or Islamic—are constrained from the outset by a stiff premise: that reality is governed by an all-knowing, all-powerful, and good God. And why such a god, capable of curing cancer tomorrow, would instead watch innocent people suffer is a conundrum. Just ask Job, who after years of piety was hit by disaster. Unlike most innocent victims, Job was allowed to interrogate God himself about the seeming injustice of it all, yet in the end was forced to settle for this answer: you wouldn't understand. Numerous theologians have wrestled with this question at book length only to wind up agreeing.

In the hunter-gatherer universe, the problem of evil isn't so baffling, because the supernatural doesn't take the form of a single all-powerful being, much less a morally perfect one. Rather, the supernatural realm is populated by various beings that, as a rule, are strikingly like human beings: they're not always in a good mood, and the things that put them in a bad mood don't have to make much sense.

For example, Karei, thunder god of the Semang hunter-gatherers of Southeast Asia, would get irate if he saw people combing their hair during a storm or watching dogs mate.[30] On the Andaman Islands, the storm god Biliku could fly into a rage if someone melted beeswax or made a loud noise while cicadas were singing. The British anthropologist A. R. Radcliffe-Brown, while studying the Andaman Islanders a century ago, noticed that they did in fact melt beeswax, hoping Biliku wouldn't notice. Radcliffe-Brown puzzled at this "variance between their precepts and their actions."[31] But it's not clear that "precept" is the right word for a rule laid down by a deity that isn't a moral beacon to begin with. Radcliffe-Brown had come from a culture in which "god" meant good, but that equation is hardly universal, and among hunter-gatherers it's just about unknown.

Thus, Kmukamtch, the Klamath sun god, harbored petty resentment of his handsome adopted son, Aishish, and so spent much time and energy stealing Aishish's clothes and trying them on. (This explains why the sun is sometimes surrounded by small puffy clouds—Aishish's beaded garments.)[32] Worse still, Kmukamtch was always trying to seduce Aishish's wives. But that's nothing compared to the behavior of Gaona, the high god of the !Kung hunter-gatherers of Africa, who raped his son's wife and ate two brothers-in-law.[33]

When Bad People Go Unpunished

That hunter-gatherer gods aren't paragons of virtue helps explain an observation made by more than one anthropologist: hunter-gatherers don't generally "worship" their gods. Indeed, they often treat their gods just like you would treat a mere human—kindly on some days, less kindly on others. The Ainu, Japan's aborigines, would sometimes try to win divine favor with offerings of millet beer, but if the gods didn't reciprocate with good fortune, the Ainu would threaten to withhold future beer unless things improved.[34] !Kung medicine men have been known to punctuate a curing dance by reproaching a god named Gauwa for bringing illness: "Uncovered penis! You are bad."[35] If Gauwa (something of a bumbler) then brought the wrong medicine, a medicine man would shout, "Idiot! You have done wrong. You make me ashamed. Go away." Crude but effective: sometimes Gauwa came back with the right medicine.[36]

Even when hunter-gatherers do show ritualized respect for gods, the respect often seems more fearful than reverential, and the ritual not very formal. The Semang, faced with a violent thunderstorm and aware that it resulted from their having watched dogs mate or from some comparable infraction, would desperately try to make amends, gashing their shins, mixing the blood with water, tossing it in the relevant god's general direction, and yelling, "Stop! Stop!"[37]

Still, sometimes hunter-gatherer rituals are sufficiently solemn that you can imagine them evolving into something like a modern worship service. In the early twentieth century, when the explorer Knud Rasmussen visited some Inuit (known as Eskimo in his day), he observed the gravity with which they divined the judgments of

Takanakapsaluk, goddess of the sea. At the time of his visit, seals and other sea game were scarce. The sea goddess was known to withhold such bounty when the Inuit had violated her rules. (Understandably so, since their violations became dirt, drifted to the bottom of the sea, matted her hair, and shrouded her in suffocating filth.) So the Inuit assembled in a dark dwelling and closed their eyes while their shaman, behind a curtain, descended to the bottom of the sea and approached Takanakapsaluk. Upon learning the source of her pique, he returned to the Inuit and demanded to know which of them had committed the transgressions she cited. Confessions were forthcoming, so the prospects for seal hunting improved. The mood brightened.

In this case "precept," the word Radcliffe-Brown dubiously applied to the Andaman storm god's dictates, might be in order. The solemn air of the occasion and the tearful shame of the confessors suggest that the sea goddess's decrees were rules whose violation was thought never justified. But even here, the precepts aren't "moral" in the modern sense of the word, because they're not about behaviors that actually harm other people; the sea goddess's rules don't discourage violence, stealing, cheating, and so forth. Rather, the rules focus on breaches of ritual. (In the case Rasmussen observed, a woman had failed to throw away certain household items after having a miscarriage.) True, these violations of ritual code are *thought* to harm other people—but only because they are thought to incur supernatural wrath that falls on the violator's neighbors. In the absence of this imagined supernatural sanction, breaking the rules would be harmless and so not obviously "immoral" in the modern sense of the term. In other words, in hunter-gatherer societies, gods by and large don't help solve moral problems that would exist in their absence.

In the nineteenth century, when European scholars started seriously studying "primitive" religion, they remarked on this absence of a clear moral dimension—the dearth of references to stealing, cheating, adultery, and the like. Edward Tylor noted in 1874 that the religions of "savage" societies were "almost devoid of that ethical element which to the educated modern mind is the very mainstream of practical religion." Tylor wasn't saying that savages lack morality. He stressed that the moral standards of savages are generally "well-defined and praiseworthy." It's just that "these ethical laws stand on their own ground of tradition and public opinion," rather than on a religious foundation.[38] As the ethnographer Lorna Marshall wrote in 1962, after observing the relationship between the !Kung and the great god Gaona: "Man's wrong-doing against man is not left to Gao!na's punishment nor is it considered to be his concern. Man corrects or avenges such wrong-doings himself in his social context. Gao!na punishes people for his own reasons, which are sometimes quite obscure."[39]

This isn't to say that hunter-gatherers never use religion to discourage troublesome or destructive behavior. Some Australian aborigines used to say that the spirits are annoyed by people who are frivolous or chatter too much.[40] And when Charles Darwin, aboard HMS *Beagle*, visited Tierra del Fuego, some of the local hunter-gatherers spoke of a giant who roamed the woods and mountains, knew everything you did, and would punish such wrongdoing as murder by summoning bad weather. As the ship's captain, Robert FitzRoy, recalled one of the locals putting it, "Rain come down—snow come down—hail come down—wind blow—blow—very much blow. Very bad to kill man."[41]

But more typical[42] of hunter-gatherer societies is the observation one anthropologist made about the Klamath: "Relations to the spirits have no ethical implication."[43] Even if religion is largely about morality today, it doesn't seem to have started out that way. And certainly most hunter-gatherer societies don't deploy the ultimate moral incentive, a heaven reserved for the good and a hell to house the bad. Nor is there anything like the Hindu and Buddhist notion of karma, a moral scorecard that will determine your fate in the next life. There is always an afterlife in hunter-gatherer religion, but it is almost never a carrot or a stick. Often everyone's spirit winds up in the same eternal home. And in those societies where the land of the dead does have subdivisions, which one you wind up in often has—as some anthropologists have put it—more to do with how you died than with how you lived. Many Andaman Islanders believed that if you drowned, you wound up underwater, as a sea spirit, whereas otherwise you would become a jungle-roaming spirit.[44] Haida who died by drowning would become killer whales.[45]

The general absence of moral sanction in hunter-gatherer religion isn't too puzzling. Hunter-gatherers live—as everyone lived 12,000 years ago—in intimate, essentially transparent groups. A village may consist of thirty, forty, fifty people, so many kinds of wrongdoing are hard to conceal. If you stole a man's digging stick, where would you hide it? And what would be the point of having it if you couldn't use it? And, anyway, is it worth the risk of getting caught—incurring the wrath of its owner, his family, and closest friends, and incurring the ongoing suspicion of everyone else? The fact that you have to live with these people for the rest of your life is by itself a pretty strong incentive to treat them decently. If you want them to help you out when you need help, you'd better help them out when they need help. Hunter-gatherers aren't paragons of honesty and probity, but departures from these ideals are detected often enough that they don't become a rampant problem. Social order can be preserved without deploying the power of religion.

One reason for this is that a hunter-gatherer village is the environment we're built for, the environment natural selection "designed" the human mind for. Evolutionary psychologists tell us that human nature includes at least two basic innate mechanisms inclining us to treat people nicely. One, the product of an evolutionary dynamic known as kin selection, leads us to sacrifice for close relatives. Another, reciprocal altruism, leads us to be considerate of friends—nonkin with whom we have enduringly cooperative relationships. If you live in a hunter-gatherer village, most of the people you encounter fit into one of these two categories and so fall naturally within the compass of your decency. Yes, you will have rivals, but if they become bitter enemies, then one or the other of you may leave the group for a nearby village. And one type of relationship you definitely *won't* have in a hunter-gatherer village is an anonymous one. There are no opportunities for purse-snatching. Nor can you borrow money, hop on a bus, and head out of town.

As the anthropologist Elman Service observed in 1966, such values as love and generosity and honesty "are not preached nor buttressed by threat of religious reprisal" in these societies, "because they do not need to be." When modern societies preach these values, they are worried "mostly about morality in the larger society, outside the sphere of kindred and close friends. Primitive people do not have these worries because they do not conceive of—do not *have*—the larger society to adjust to. The ethic does not extend to strangers; they are simply enemies, not even people."[46]

That last sentence may sound extreme, and it is definitely at odds with the many flattering depictions of indigenous peoples in movies and books. But this narrow compass of moral consideration is indeed characteristic of hunter-gatherer societies. Universal love—an ideal found in many modern religions, even if it is honored mainly in the breach—is not even an ideal in the typical hunter-gatherer society.

This book is partly about how and why the moral compass has expanded, how religions came to define larger and larger groups of people as part of the circle of moral consideration. With this understanding in hand, we'll be in a better position to gauge the prospects for the circle being expanded farther—for the Abrahamic religions, in particular, to make their peace with one another, and conceive of brotherhood accordingly.

What Religion Is

You could be excused for looking at religion in hunter-gatherer societies and, like John Lubbock, concluding that it has little in common with religion as we know it. Certainly that was the reaction of more than a few Europeans of the nineteenth century. Where was the moral dimension of religion? Where was brotherly love? Where was the reverence for—not just fear of—the divine? Where was the stately ritual? Where was the quest for inner peace? And what's with this jumble of spirits and deities doing implausible things to control parts of the world that are in fact controlled by natural law?

Still, hunter-gatherer religions have at least two features that are found, in one sense or another, in all the world's great religions: they try to explain why bad things happen, and they thus offer a way to make things better. A Christian prayer on behalf of a gravely ill child may seem a more subtle instrument than the !Kung medicine man's profane confrontation of a !Kung god, but at some level the logic is the same: good and bad outcomes are under the control of a supernatural being, and the being is subject to influence. And those Christians who, in the spirit of modernism, refrain from asking God for earthly interventions are usually hoping for favorable treatment in the afterlife. Even Buddhists who don't believe in any gods (and most Buddhists do) seek through meditation or other disciplines a spiritual adjustment that renders them less susceptible to suffering.

It may seem cynical to see all religion as basically self-serving. And indeed the idea has been put pithily by a famous cynic. H. L. Mencken said of religion, "Its single function is to give man access to the powers which seem to control his destiny, and its single purpose is to induce those powers to be friendly to him.... Nothing else is essential."[47] But less cynical people have also put self-interest at the core of religion, if in loftier language. About a century ago, the psychologist William James wrote in *The Varieties of Religious Experience* that religion "consists of the belief that there is an unseen order, and that our supreme good lies in harmoniously adjusting ourselves thereto."[48]

The difference between Mencken's and James's formulations is important. In Mencken's version the object of the game is to change the behavior of the supernatural beings. James's version doesn't quite exclude this possibility, but it places more of the burden of change on us; we are to "harmoniously adjust" ourselves to the "unseen order." James seems to be making the modern assumption that the unseen order—the divine, as people say these days—is inherently good; that discrepancies between divine designs and our own aims reflect shortcomings on our part.

Of course, religion has in one sense or another always been about self-interest. Religious doctrines can't survive if they don't appeal to the psychology of the people whose brains harbor them, and self-interest is one potent source of appeal. But self-interest can assume many forms, and for that matter it can be aligned, or not aligned, with many other interests: the interest of the family, the interest of the society, the interest of the world, the interest of moral and spiritual truth. Religion almost always forms a link between self-interest and some of those other interests, but which ones it links to, and how, change over time. And over time there has been—on balance, taking the long view—a pattern in the change. Religion has gotten closer to moral and spiritual truth, and for that matter more compatible with scientific truth. Religion hasn't just evolved; it has matured. One premise of this book is that the story of religion, beginning back in the Stone Age, is to some extent a movement from Mencken to James.

Religion needs to mature more if the world is going to survive in good shape—and for that matter if religion is to hold the respect of intellectually critical people. But before we take up these questions, we'll address the question of how it has matured to date: how we got from the hunter-gatherer religions that were the norm 12,000 years ago to the monotheism that is the foundation of Judaism, Christianity, and Islam. Then we'll be in position to ponder the future of religion and to talk about how true it is or can be.

Chapter Two

The Shaman

There is in the world today a great and mysterious force that shapes the fortunes of millions of people. It is called the stock market. There are people who claim to have special insights into this force. They are called stock analysts. Most of them have often been wrong about the market's future behavior, and many of them have been wrong most of the time. In fact, it's not clear that their advice is worth anything at all. Reputable economists have argued that you're better off picking stocks randomly than seeking guidance from stock analysts; either way it's the blind leading the blind, but in one case you don't have to pay a commission.[1]

Nonetheless, stock analysis is a profitable line of work, even for some manifestly inept practitioners. Why? Because whenever people sense the presence of a puzzling and momentous force, they want to believe there is a way to comprehend it. If you can convince them that you're the key to comprehension, you can reach great stature.

This fact has deeply shaped the evolution of religion, and it seems to have done so since very near the beginning. Once there was belief in the supernatural, there was a demand for people who claimed to fathom it. And, judging by observed hunter-gatherer societies, there was a supply to meet the demand. Though most hunter-gatherer societies have almost no structure in the modern sense of the word—little if any clear-cut political leadership, little division of economic labor—they do have religious experts. So do societies that are a shade more technologically advanced: societies that, though not fully agricultural, supplement their hunting and gathering with gardening ("horticultural" societies) or herding.

The term most often applied to these religious experts is "shaman."[2] (The word comes from the language of the Tungus, a nomadic people of Siberia, and is sometimes translated as "one who knows.") This label conceals some diversity. Shamans in Eurasia and northernmost North America often go into dramatic, trance-like states, as spirits possess them and speak through them before departing. Elsewhere, including much of the Americas, the shaman is less enthralled by spirits and more inclined to just commune with them via visions or dreams and then paraphrase them.[3]

Similarly, the specific powers claimed by shamans show great variation. Some shamans in eastern North America could take a seed, pinch it between their thumb and finger, and project it with such force as to kill a person several miles away.[4] In Australia, the preferred lethal weapon was a bone, pointed at the victim after appropriate incantations.[5] Some Eskimo shamans could go to the moon, and some could turn into a bear.[6] Some Amazonian shamans could become a jaguar with help from a drug that, as described by one anthropologist, leads the shaman to lie in his hammock, "growl and pant, strike the air with claw-like fingers," convincing bystanders that "his wandering soul has turned into a bloodthirsty feline."[7] On the Andaman Islands a shaman would fight an epidemic by brandishing a burning log and instructing evil spirits to keep their distance.[8] In southern Alaska a Tlingit shaman would fight illness by putting on a special apron and mask, running circles around the patient while shaking a rattle and singing to a series of spirits (changing his mask with each new spirit), perhaps collapsing in exhaustion from time to time.[9] In Africa the !Kung San curer would dance for as long as ten hours, finally entering a trance state that converted his or her healing energy into useful vaporous form and allowed discourse with gods or spirits of the dead.[10]

What unites shamans everywhere is seeking contact with an otherwise hidden world that shapes human destiny. And they tend to focus their powers on things that are important and erratic—illness, the weather, predators, prey. A Jesuit priest who encountered the Abipon of South America in the eighteenth century summarized the professed powers of their shamans: "to inflict disease and death, to cure all disorders, to make known distant and future events; to cause rain, hail, and tempest; to call up the shades [souls] of the dead and consult them concerning hidden matters; to put on the form of a tiger; to handle every kind of serpent without danger, etc."[11] The seminal scholar of shamanism Mircea Eliade wrote, "What is fundamental and universal is the shaman's struggle against what we could call 'the powers of evil.' ... It is consoling and comforting to know that a member of the community is able to see what is hidden and invisible to the rest and to bring back direct and reliable information from the supernatural worlds."[12]

The shaman represents a crucial step in the emergence of organized religion. He (or she, sometimes) is the link between earliest religion—a fluid amalgam of beliefs about a fluid amalgam of spirits—and what religion came to be: a distinct body of belief and practice, kept in shape by an authoritative institution. The shaman is the first step toward an archbishop or an ayatollah.

This claim won't sit well with everyone. Today shamanism (sometimes cast as "neo-shamanism") has a big niche in New Age spirituality, and part of its appeal is its perceived contrast with modern religion. Shamanism, in this view, harkens back to a time before industrialization had impeded communion with nature, before church hierarchies had discouraged direct experience of the divine by making themselves official conduits to the sacred. In this view, the primordial, shamanic phase of religion was a little like the Garden of Eden before Adam and Eve ruined everything.

Certainly the annals of shamanism do include attractive themes. Some serious scholars see in the Stone Age shaman the origins of mysticism, which in modern form has brought peace of mind to many. Eliade wrote that Eskimo shamanism and Buddhist mysticism share as their goal "deliverance from the illusions of the flesh."[13] And shamanism in general, he said, is shot through with "the will to transcend the profane, individual condition" in order to recover "the very source of spiritual existence, which is at once 'truth' and 'life.' "[14]

All to the good. Still, shamans inevitably share one unfortunate characteristic with religious leaders in modern societies: being human. In the shamanistic phase of religious evolution we can see not just the sunnier side of religion, but also some of the flaws that have dogged it ever since. Religion, having come from the brains of people, is bound to bear the marks of our species, for better and worse.

How to Become a Shaman

The emergence of the shaman, of religious leadership, was a natural enough thing. Primordial religion consisted partly of people telling each other stories in an attempt to explain why good and bad things happen, to predict their happening, and if possible to intervene, thus raising the ratio of good to bad. Whenever people—hunter-gatherers, stock analysts, whatever—compete in the realm of explanation, prediction, and intervention, some of them get a reputation for success. They become leaders in their field. Through such competition did shamanhood presumably arise and sustain itself.

To judge by many observed hunter-gatherer societies, the competition was informal and ongoing, and the possession of spiritual power a matter of degree. During the all-night curing dances of the !Kung San, any man or woman was eligible to enter a trancelike state and thus summon *num*, a spiritual healing energy. But only a minority of !Kung would become known as "masters of *num*," and only the rarest of these was so gifted as to see the great god Gaona.[15] Among the Klamath, as one anthropologist put it, "some shamans have considerably more power than others, and everyone who has got power is in some degree capable of using it as a shaman does."[16] The anthropologist Robert Lowie, after studying the Crow of the North American Plains, wrote that "any tribesman might become a shaman" after going on a "vision quest" and having an apparition signifying his adoption by a particular spirit.[17]

In such societies, as Lowie wrote of the Crow, "the greater or lesser dignity" of aspiring shamans depended "on the pragmatic test of their efficacy." If their curing spells were followed by cures or their rainmaking rituals by rain, their credibility grew. Thus Crow men who, after receiving a vision, were "conspicuously fortunate in war parties would come to be regarded as favorites of some powerful being." But pity the Crow who, as Lowie recounted, felt inspired by his adoptive spirit to introduce a new effigy into the Sun Dance. When "its use was accompanied by the death of the chief dancer's wife," this inspiration was unmasked as a "pretended revelation."[18]

Competition for shamanhood has rarely been as egalitarian as among the Crow. In some societies being a famous shaman's descendant gave you a leg up, and circumstances of birth could help in other ways, too; entering the world amid a violent storm or with an odd birthmark might be a sign. In parts of Siberia, effeminate boys were good prospects, and once they were shamans some dressed as women and married a man.[19] Eerie early achievements—having a weird and prescient dream, surviving a lightning strike or a snakebite—could in some societies mark a shamanic prospect.

However they arrived at their stations, shamans everywhere, to keep their credibility high, had to muster ongoing displays of supernatural power. But how could they do that, given the seeming falseness of their supernatural beliefs?

In some realms, a high batting average is inherently likely. Among the Aranda of central Australia, one of the shaman's jobs was ensuring that solar eclipses would be temporary—nice work if you can get it.[20] And since most illnesses are, like eclipses, temporary, the average shamanic medical intervention is also likely to be vindicated. Among the Semang on the Malay Peninsula, the following shamanic procedure proved effective in exorcising the evil spirit from a sick woman: uproot two young trees, take soil from the resulting holes, rub it on her body, spit on her, then forcefully throw the trees into the jungle.[21]

Success rates are especially high in societies where shamans have the option of turning down particularly dire cases.[22] Further career protection comes via philosophical loopholes. Among the Guiana native Americans, the blame for a patient's death fell on destiny, not the shaman.[23] In Australia and many other places, a failed shamanic intervention could be attributed to the countervailing sorcery of some hostile shaman.[24] A Tlingit shaman, having failed to cure a patient, might blame it on someone he identified as a witch, who would then either confess under torture or be killed.[25]

Notwithstanding these reputation-preserving features of the shaman's practice, faith in even a reputable shaman isn't unshakable. On the Andaman Islands, Edward Horace Man observed in the nineteenth century, the death of a shaman's child was seen as a "sign that his power is waning," and he would now be under pressure to show "further proof of his supposed superiority" lest the public's awe should fade.[26]

Oddly, such declining fortunes can help sustain religious faith. The notion that a shaman's prowess waxes and wanes allows the society to witness repeated failure without questioning the overarching idea of shamanic power. It's eerily like the modern stock market: when a famous stock analyst places a series of bad bets, we say he's lost his touch and look for an analyst who hasn't, rather than question the notion that his "touch" was ever anything other than a series of lucky guesses. In modern "secular" societies, as in "primitive" religious ones, faith in expertise is sustained by the timely disposal of experts. Among the Ojibwa (also known as the Chippewa), a religious leader who failed to sustain "demonstrable rapport" with the supernatural world would simply be replaced, a scholar notes. "The leader was expendable."[27]

The Rewards of Shamanism

But it had been fun while it lasted. Shamans have often been good at converting their powers into material gain. And they've done so whether the powers were benign or malicious. Here is Man on Andamanese shamans: "It is thought that they can bring trouble, sickness, and death upon those who fail to evince their belief in them in some substantial form; they thus generally manage to obtain the best of everything, for it is considered foolhardy to deny them, and they do not scruple to ask for any article to which they may take a fancy."[28]

In some societies, the shaman's remuneration, like that of modern doctors, came on a per-service basis. In exchange for treating a patient, a shaman might receive yams (in Micronesia), sleds and harnesses (among the Eastern Eskimo), beads and coconuts (the Mentawai of Sumatra), tobacco (the Ojibwa), buckskin (the Washo of central Nevada), slaves (the Haida), or even, among some Eskimo, a sex partner—a satisfied customer's wife or daughter, on loan.[29]

Among the Nomlaki of California, if a shaman said, "These beads are pretty rough," he meant it would take more beads to send him into curing mode.[30] In other cultures the shaman could be saved from this unseemly haggling by a spirit that set the fee, leaving it to the shaman to accurately report the supernaturally regulated price. Here is an anthropologist's account of a Nootka shaman attending a seriously ill patient:

> He gave a few tentative shakes of his rattle and began to hum a spirit song, deep in his throat. It took a while to get in good voice. His humming became bolder, the clicking of his rattle sharper. By this means he called his spirit to his aid. Now the time had arrived for the immediate relative of the sick person to stand up and call his offer of payment: blankets, furs, canoes.... According to conventional belief, the shaman himself had nothing to do with accepting or refusing the offer. His spirit attended to that.... Should it be insufficient, the supernatural being would draw away, removing his aura of power. The shaman's throat weakened, his song died away to a low hum again. The patient's relative then had to increase his offer. When at length it satisfied the spirit he drew near once more, and the shaman's song welled forth.[31]

In refreshing contrast with modern medical practitioners, some shamans guaranteed their work. In western Canada, a Gitskan shaman, given blankets for his services, would return them if the patient died.[32] Among the Shasta, to the Gitskan's south, one half the fee was refundable.[33]

The Crow (who, perhaps not coincidentally, had extended contact with white culture) developed one of the more thoroughgoing spiritual marketplaces, complete with intellectual property. Those whose vision quests had been successful could sell some of their shamanic power to the less fortunate, often in the form of potent rituals and accoutrements, such as songs and styles of dress. One Crow bought a ceremonial face-painting pattern from his own mother.[34]

Even shamans who got no fees or gifts might benefit from their work. Among the Ona of Tierra del Fuego, payment for service was rare, but, as one anthropologist observed, "one abstains from anything and everything" that might put the shaman "out of sorts or irritate him."[35] Moreover, in pre-agricultural societies, as in modern societies, high social status, however intangible, can ultimately bring tangible benefits. Ojibwa shamans, one anthropologist reports, received "minimal remuneration," working for "prestige, not pay. One of the symbols of religious leadership prestige was polygyny.... Male leaders took more than one wife."[36] In his classic study *The Law of Primitive Man*, E. Adamson Hoebel observed that, among some Eskimo, "a forceful shaman of established reputation may denounce a member of his group as guilty of an act repulsive to animals or spirits, and on his own authority he may command penance.... An apparently common atonement is for the shaman to direct an allegedly erring woman to have intercourse with him (his supernatural power counteracts the effects of her sinning)."[37]

So here is the pattern: in pre-agricultural societies around the world, people have profited, in one sense or another, by cultivating a reputation for special access to the supernatural.[38] It's enough to make you wonder: Might they, in the course of establishing their bona fides, sometimes resort to deceit? Was the average shaman a fraud—or, as one anthropologist put it, a "pious fraud"?[39]

Certainly you could make a case. Anthropologists have found that shamans in several cultures used ventriloquism to help the spirits speak, sometimes learning the art by apprenticeship to a veteran.[40] Eskimo shamans, bleeding profusely after contact with a ceremonial harpoon, have wowed audiences unaware of the animal bladder full of blood beneath their clothing.[41] One of the most widespread shaman tricks is to cure illness by "sucking" a malignant object out of the patient and displaying it for all to see — sleight of hand that dots the ethnographic map from Tasmania to North America.[42]

Ojibwa shamans — known for, among other things, Houdini-like escape tricks[43] — would watch one another's performances, one anthropologist reports, with a productive combination of motives: "to learn each other's tricks and perhaps to expose a rival as fraudulent."[44] An uncovered fake would be ridiculed, even ostracized, but believers didn't take his dishonesty as tainting spiritual leaders in general, just as today the exposure of sham faith healers doesn't shake belief in the unexposed. Speaking of modern faith-healing tricks: Kwakiutl shamans used "spies" who would, like the spies employed by some modern faith healers, mingle with people, discern their ailments, and covertly relay them to the healer, infusing his diagnoses with drama.[45]

There are, in short, grounds for suspicion. Yet the very ethnographers who detect these deceptions have often judged the shaman leniently. Edward Horace Man speculated that Andaman shamans "imagine themselves gifted with superior wisdom,"[46] and Rasmussen reported that Copper Inuit shamans "consider their various tricks to be means that bring them in touch with the spirits."[47]

Altered States

Certainly shamans have had reasons to feel genuinely in touch with the supernatural world. One of these reasons, especially common in the Americas, is drugs. When a Tukanoan shaman of the Northwest Amazon went to meet the Master of Animals, and sought permission for the Tukanoa to kill their prey, his prior ingestion of hallucinogens served as a social lubricant.[48]

Another catalyst for hallucination is to go a long time without food or sleep, and such hardships are sometimes part of the shaman's initiation. When a Crow's vision quest was fruitful, success typically came after he had fasted for four days and nights while alone and half-naked, often on top of a mountain.[49] An aspiring Tlingit shaman, in southern Alaska, would for weeks eat only a kind of bark that induces vomiting, until he was "filled" with his "helping spirit" (and had found a divinely delivered otter whose tongue he could slice off).[50] Meanwhile, at the other end of the Americas, Yahgan shaman candidates were sequestered and "required to fast, to sing much, to maintain a certain posture, to go with little sleep, and to drink water through a hollow bird bone."[51]

The uplifting hardship of initiation can be heightened by violence. A Crow on a vision quest would often employ self-mutilation, cutting off one third of a finger on his left hand. In Australia, becoming a shaman could mean cutting a hole in your tongue big enough to put your little finger through — and then making sure the hole didn't close up, since closure would mean the end of shamanhood. An alternative approach was to let established shamans slice into your tongue and stick a sharp stick underneath your fingernail and use magic crystals to score your flesh for three consecutive days, drawing blood from the legs and head and abdomen. This procedure, reported the nineteenth-century ethnographer Baldwin Spencer, left the shaman-to-be "really in a low state."[52]

Also conducive to spiritual experience is the natural disposition of the kinds of people who become shamans. In some cultures shamans have struck anthropologists as psychotic, people who may indeed be hearing voices that no one else is hearing. Others have appeared deeply neurotic or, at least, seemed to possess the moody sensitivity associated with artists, including some very unhappy ones. The Chukchee used to describe someone who felt driven to the shamanistic calling as "doomed to inspiration."[53]

Indeed, in many societies the shaman's life has enough downside to discourage a pure charlatan out to make an easy buck. In addition to the aforementioned deprivation and trauma, sexual abstinence is often required. For the Jivaro of South America, a year without sex was the price for full-fledged shamanhood.[54] Among the Tlingit, a young man who sought to be a top-tier shaman might abstain for as long as four years—not to mention lying at night next to the corpse of the shaman he would replace.[55] Speaking of corpses: shamans in some societies have been killed when one of their patients dies, a hazard that could discourage practitioners who don't feel genuinely empowered.[56]

No doubt the world's shamans have run the gamut from true believer to calculating fraud. And no doubt many true beliefs have been peppered by doubt. But so it is in other spiritual traditions, too. There are deeply religious Christian ministers who urge the congregation to pray for the ill, even though they personally doubt that God uses opinion polls to decide who lives and who dies. There are ministers who have a more abstract conception of divinity than the image of God they evoke in church. And there are ministers who have wholly lost their faith but keep up appearances. For all these people, one motivation may be to fortify the faithful, and another may be to sustain their own standing as respected community leaders, with whatever perks that brings. As the anthropologist Spencer Rogers observed in his study *The Shaman*, "the limits of spiritual dedication and self-advancement have often been unclear in the history of religious denominations of the Western world."[57] Given the sometimes hazy line between conscious and unconscious motivation, the distinction may be unclear even in the mind of the religious leader in question.

Is It Real?

In any event, there is little doubt that many shamans over the years have had what felt like valid spiritual experiences. Even in technologically modern societies, people who fast or suffer trauma or spend days in solitude or ingest hallucinogens report things ranging from visions to voices to ineffable contact with ultimate reality. And sometimes the result is a life-changing conversion experience.

Granting the belief of many shamans in the validity of their transcendental experiences, was there any actual validity? Were early religious adepts making contact with something "out there"? Some would argue that the very effectiveness of shamanic techniques like fasting answers the question in the negative: if a merely physiological manipulation of the brain can bring on the experience, then it is a hallucination.

But here, perversely, modern biological science comes to the rescue of the transcendent, if in a limited way.

Evolutionary psychology, the modern Darwinian understanding of human nature, seems in some ways to deflate religion. In this chapter an emphasis on the inherently status-seeking nature of humans has lurked in the background, helping to explain why in all societies some people seek reputations as religious experts. And in the appendix of this book, evolutionary psychology is used to explain the very origins of religious belief as the residue of built-in distortions of perception and cognition; natural selection didn't design us to believe only true things, so we're susceptible to certain kinds of falsehood.

But this idea of built-in mental biases has another implication, too: our normal states of consciousness are in a sense arbitrary; they are the states that happen to have served the peculiar agenda of mundane natural selection. That is, they happen to have helped organisms (our ancestors) spread genes in a particular ecosystem on a particular planet.

There are some not-wholly-unflattering things you can say about such states of consciousness—things like "effective in Darwinian terms" and "valuable from the gene's point of view." But some properties you can't safely attribute to these states of consciousness are "conducive to deep insight into the ultimate nature of reality" and "conducive to the apprehension of moral truth." And it's at least possible that you can actually move the brain closer to one or both of these properties by manipulating it physiologically. If the biases and filters are physical to begin with, then perhaps their removal can be as well.

William James, in *The Varieties of Religious Experience*,

explored the influence on consciousness of things ranging from meditation to nitrous oxide and concluded that "our normal waking consciousness" is "but one special type of consciousness, whilst all about it, parted from it by the filmiest of screens, there lie potential forms of consciousness entirely different."[58] James's position in the book—that these alternative forms may be in some sense more truthful than ordinary consciousness—is the properly open-minded stance, and it has if anything been strengthened by evolutionary psychology.

This is not to say that any Crow was ever actually adopted by the thunder spirit, or that the !Kung San "masters of *num*" were truly perceiving the visage of a god during their trances. Then again, not everything they saw was so specifically theological. One *num* master described the experience this way: "your eyeballs clear and then you see people clearly."[59] Another said, "it makes your thoughts nothing in your head." Both of these things could well have been said by a Buddhist mystic. And both are consistent with this not outlandish metaphysical conjecture: there is such a thing as pure contemplative awareness, but our evolved mental machinery, in its normal working mode, is harnessing that awareness to specific ends, and in the process warping it.

In any event, the possible truth of some part of the *num* master's experience isn't precluded by the means of its induction. No doubt the trance state reached during hours of dancing is a result of, among other things, the rhythmic shocks delivered to the base of the brain, as many as 60,000 shocks in one dance session by the estimate of the anthropologist Melvin Konner.[60] But that doesn't steal the possibility of truth from the experience Konner himself had while dancing with the !Kung, "that 'oceanic' feeling of oneness with the world."[61] The opposite of this experience—our everyday sense of wary separation from all but a few kin and trusted friends—is a legacy of natural selection, no more and no less. It's been good at steering genes into the next generation, and thus must have in some sense faithfully reflected some features of the social landscape, but it doesn't necessarily capture the whole picture. It has been, in a sense, strategically "true," but that doesn't make it morally or metaphysically true.

The First Politicians

There is evidence that in shamanism lie the origins of formal politics. The Buryat of Asia told ethnographers that their first political leaders were shamans.[62] And the Inuit words for "shaman" and "leader" are almost identical—*angakok* and *angajkok*.[63] Further, though there have been societies with shamans but no acknowledged political leader, there have been few if any societies with a political leader but no religious experts. And in some societies the shaman and the political leader have been one and the same.[64]

Even shamans lacking explicit political power can exert great influence. They have often been counselors in matters of war and peace. If the Ona were contemplating the invasion of a neighboring people, and the shaman saw unfavorable omens, he encouraged diplomacy; if the omens were good, he urged war.[65]

In addition to thus marshaling antagonism, shamans have at times created it. The tendency is evident even *within* societies, in local competition for supernatural supremacy. Shamans from different Haida clans displayed, in the words of one anthropologist, "the keenest rivalry and hatred," to the point of trying to kill each other by sorcery.[66] And Lowie reported a duel of occult powers between two Crow shamans: Big-ox, who invoked a thunder spirit, and White-thigh, who wielded the power of a sacred rock. The exchange left White-thigh blind and Big-ox with dead relatives.[67]

Perhaps the most common way for a shaman to carry antagonism beyond the society is, having failed to cure an illness or improve the weather, to blame a shaman from a nearby people, like a modern politician who diverts attention from domestic failures by rattling the saber. Thus a Klamath shaman once explained that recent snow and sickness had been caused by a spirit atop Mount Shasta, placed there by a shaman from the Modoc people. This particular problem was solved without hand-to-hand combat. The Klamath shaman deployed a spirit that enslaved the mountaintop spirit, killing the Modoc shaman by remote control.[68] But in South America, when Jivaro shamans blamed a fatal illness on a sorcerer from a nearby village, a military raid was all but inevitable. After all, the soul of the deceased might torment his or her kin if they didn't take vengeance. The good news was that their religion would help sustain them on their mission; their combat garb symbolized affinity with Etsa, a god of hunting and fighting, and they sang sacred hymns on their way to war. Afterward they threw the skulls of their victims into a stream as an offering to the Anaconda. Having removed the skulls, they could now shrink the heads, thus imprisoning the otherwise avenging souls of their victims.[69]

The shaman's role in cultivating antipathy and violence, both within the society and beyond it, is more evidence against the romantic view of religion as fallen—having been born pure only to be corrupted later. Apparently one of religion's most infamous modern roles, fomenter of conflict between societies, was part of the story from very near the beginning.

Keeping Score

So, all told, was religion in the age of the shaman more a force for good or for ill? There are two main schools of thought on this question.

The "functionalists" see religion as serving the interests of the society as a whole. Thus the seminal French sociologist Emile Durkheim could find virtue in religion under even the most challenging conditions. Some observers, for example, have been hard pressed to explain what social good is being done by the Australian aborigines' violent mourning rituals, during which women used digging sticks to slash their heads and men with stone knives cut the muscles of their thighs so deeply that they fell down, immobilized.[70] For Durkheim this was not a problem. In *Elementary Forms of Religious Life* he wrote that weeping together not only helped the people withstand the trauma of recent death, but actually made them collectively stronger. For "every communion of mind, in whatever form it may be made, raises the social vitality. The exceptional violence of the manifestations by which the common pain is necessarily and obligatorily expressed even testifies to the fact that at this moment, the society is more alive and active than ever."[71]

Opposed to the functionalists is a group you might call the cynics, or perhaps the "Marxists"—not because they're communists, but because, like Marx, they think that social structures, including shared beliefs, tend to serve the powerful. The anthropologist Paul Radin, in his 1937 book *Primitive Religion*, depicted Eskimo shamanism as serving a single interest group: Eskimo shamans. Their "complex religious theory" and "spectacular shamanistic technique" are "designed to do two things: to keep the contact with the supernatural exclusively in the hands of the *angakok* [shaman], and to manipulate and exploit the sense of fear of the ordinary man."[72]

These two positions dominate discussion of the virtues of modern as well as primitive religion. There are people who think religion serves society broadly, providing reassurance and hope in the face of pain and uncertainty, overcoming our natural selfishness with communal cohesion. And there are people who think religion is a tool of social control, wielded by the powerful for self-aggrandizement—a tool that numbs people to their exploitation ("opiate of the masses") when it's not scaring them to death. In one view gods are good things, and in one view gods are bad things.

But isn't it possible that both sides are wrong to view the question so generically? Isn't it possible that the social function and political import of religion have changed as cultural evolution has marched on?

Actually, Marx himself allowed this possibility. In his view of cultural evolution, the hunter-gatherer phase of human history had been idyllically egalitarian; society, hence religion, got corrupted only later. (That's why I put the word "Marxist" in quotes when applying it to the generic cynical position on religion; Marx wasn't generically cynical.)

As should be clear by now, Marx's view of hunter-gatherer life was too simple. Granted, a small society that lives barely above the subsistence level is more egalitarian than a modern industrial society, which can muster massive disparities between the wealthiest and the poorest. But it's hard to claim there are no differentials of power, and no exploitation of power, in a society where shamans amass gifts by instilling irrational fear, or a society in which shamans convince women that the way to please the gods is to have sex with shamans.

Still, Marx was onto something: since social structure changes over time, and religion is at least in part a reflection of social structure, the virtues of religion may change in a patterned way as cultural evolution changes that structure. The transformation in social structure that carried religion beyond the age of shamans is the subject of the next chapter. With the invention of agriculture, the virtues of religion, and the character of gods, would start to change.

Chapter Three

Religion in the Age of Chiefdoms

When Captain James Cook visited Polynesia in the 1760s and 1770s, there were aspects of the culture that offended him. Human sacrifice, for example—"a shocking waste of the human race," he wrote in his journal. Visiting a temple on Tahiti, he counted forty-nine skulls, and since none seemed weathered, he inferred that "no great length of time had elapsed since, at least, this considerable number of unhappy wretches had been offered upon this altar of blood."[1] Cook then watched as a fiftieth corpse was offered up, its left eye removed and placed in a plaintain leaf shortly before a priest used the occasion to ask for divine aid in war with a nearby island.[2]

Later Cook would try to shake the natives' faith in this ritual by pointing out that the god in question never seemed to eat any of the sacrificed flesh. "But to all this they answered, that he came in the night, but invisibly, and fed only on the soul or immaterial part, which, according to their doctrine, remains about the place of sacrifice, until the body of the victim be entirely wasted by putrefaction." Cook could only hope that someday "this deluded people" would perceive the "horror of murdering their fellow-creatures, in order to furnish such an invisible banquet to their god."[3]

There was, however, one feature of life on some Polynesian islands that Cook approved of: social cohesion. While in Tonga he wrote, "It does not, indeed, appear that any of the most civilised nations have ever exceeded this people in the great order observed on all occasions; in ready compliance with the commands of their chiefs; and in the harmony that subsists throughout all ranks, and unites them as if they were all one man, informed with and directed by the same principle."[4]

A single principle did, in a sense, orchestrate Polynesian social harmony, and it was the same principle that inspired Polynesians to pluck eyes out of freshly created corpses: reverence for the divine. According to a Frenchman who visited Polynesia in the eighteenth century, the gods so dominated life that "there was not a single action, enterprise, or event, which was not attributed to them, submitted to their inspection, or done under their auspices."[5] This may be an exaggeration, but not by much. Whatever your reaction to life in indigenous Polynesia—whether you admire its order, bemoan its brutality, or both—the judgment rendered is largely a judgment of its religion.

The indigenous societies of the Polynesian islands, from New Zealand in the south to Hawaii in the north, from Tonga in the east to Easter Island in the west, were what anthropologists call "chiefdoms."[6] Chiefdoms are typically agricultural societies, and they are much bigger and more elaborate than the average hunter-gatherer society, usually comprising many villages and thousands of people. Leadership is in the hands of a "chief," and there may be regional chiefs beneath him.

Chiefdoms have been seen in action in the Americas and Africa as well as Polynesia, and the remains of former chiefdoms have been found by archaeologists around the world, notably in the vicinity of great ancient civilizations. The chiefdom level of social organization seems to have been a standard way station between hunter-gatherer societies and the early ancient states, such as Egypt and Shang China—bigger, urban polities that had writing. The chiefdom, the most advanced form of social organization in the world 7,000 years ago, represents the final prehistoric phase in the evolution of social organization, and the evolution of religion.

There are lots of differences among observed chiefdoms, but one thing they share is structural reliance on the supernatural. Their political and religious systems are deeply intertwined; their rulers have a special connection to the divine and put this status to political use. The Polynesian chief, one western scholar wrote, "stands to the people as a god."[7]

Shamanism, then, turns out to have been the start of something big. This early form of religious expertise, found in hunter-gatherer and horticultural societies, was at most an amorphous leadership. Though the shaman's claims to supernatural skill earned him or her social status and a kind of power over people's lives, shamanic influence rarely translated into clear-cut political clout. But as agriculture emerged and chiefdoms crystallized, political and religious leadership matured and fused, and the fusion held these newly complex societies together.

Does this mean the gods were now good? Had the amoral, sometimes immoral gods of the hunter-gatherer world been replaced by something more laudably purposeful? Had gods at last found a higher calling? These questions bring us back to the debate noted in the previous chapter, between functionalists and "Marxists": Does religion serve the people, or just the powerful?

There is no cluster of chiefdoms better positioned to shed light on this issue than those in Polynesia. By virtue of their surroundings — lots of water — they were remote from the cultural influence of more technologically advanced societies. (North American chiefdoms, in contrast, shared a continent with the Aztecs, a state-level society.) And when contact with alien cultures did come to Polynesia, much of it came via Europeans who recorded their early impressions for posterity. The observers weren't trained, modern anthropologists (who are taught not to render such value judgments as "shocking waste of the human race," even when talking about human sacrifice). But they did compile a database that, as distilled by later anthropologists, gives us a sense of what gods looked like right before they entered the historical record.

The Gods of Polynesia

Beginning more than three millennia ago, the Polynesian islands were populated by a chain of migration that issued from Southeast Asia.[8] Individual islands then carried their common cultural heritage in diverse directions. Polynesia is thus testament to the restlessness that cultural evolution shares with biological evolution, the persistent creation and selective retention of new traits. Just as Darwin noticed subtly different physiology among finches that lived on different Galápagos islands, anthropologists have been struck by the cultural variation among the Polynesian islands.

Consider the god called Tangaroa—or Tangaloa, or Ta'aroa, depending on what island you were on. He was widely considered to have played a major role in creation, but what role exactly? In some places he was credited with having lifted up the skies, in others with having dredged up the islands.[9] In Samoa it seemed that Tangaloa had created humanity, and perhaps even matter itself; he thus dwelt exaltedly in the skies, a preeminent deity.[10] In the Marquesas Islands, Tangaroa lived ignominiously under the feet of Atanua (goddess of the dawn), having lost a battle to her husband Atea (god of light).[11]

But if the various Polynesian peoples disagreed about specific gods, they agreed about gods in general. For example, everyone believed there were lots of them. In the Society Islands—the cluster anchored by Tahiti—there were gods of the sea (who used sharks to convey their pique with people) and gods of the air (who used hurricanes and tempests). There were gods of fishermen, of navigators, of netmakers, and more than a dozen gods of agriculture. There was a god of carpenters (not to be confused with the gods of house thatchers), several doctor gods (some specializing in fractures and dislocations), gods of actors and singers, and a god of "hairdressers and combers."[12]

Some anthropologists call these kinds of gods "departmental gods," and one reason there were so many of them in Polynesia is that there were so many departments. Whereas everyone in a hunter-gatherer society is a hunter and/or gatherer, the evolution of chiefdoms meant real division of labor, and gods multiplied to fill the new vocational niches.

The Polynesian gods closely supervised the economy, a fact much on the minds of their subjects. The anthropologist E. S. Craighill Handy wrote in his 1927 book *Polynesian Religion*, "All serious enterprise was regarded as consecrated activity by the Polynesians."[13]

No business was more serious than fishing. A boat, maybe a double canoe holding twenty men, would shove off and disappear from view and then return with scads of bonito and other huge fish—or would return empty, or even fail to return.[14] The stakes were high, and success meant playing by the gods' rules from the beginning.

And that meant the *very* beginning. "The building of a canoe was an affair of religion," wrote the nineteenth-century Hawaiian David Malo of his homeland's indigenous culture. When a man found a tree that seemed structurally suitable, he would tell the master canoe builder, who would sleep on the matter, lying before a shrine. If he dreamed of a naked man or woman, "covering their shame with the hand," it meant the tree was unworthy, Malo reports.[15] Attractive, well-dressed characters, in contrast, were a green light.

The night before felling the tree, artisans camped near it, prayed, and offered the gods coconuts, fish, and a pig. The next morning, in an oven built near the tree's base, they cooked the pig and—the gods now having ingested its spiritual nutrients—ate the flesh. Next they prayed to six gods and two goddesses, including deities of the forest, of the canoe, and of the ax.[16] Then they took their stone axes to the tree. After it fell, the master canoe builder donned ceremonial garb, stood over the tree near its bottom with ax in hand, yelled, "Strike with the ax and hollow it! Grant us a canoe!" and then struck the wood. He repeated those words, struck again, repeated the words, struck again, and so on, moving from the bottom of the tree to the top. Then he wreathed the tree with a flowering vine, said a prayer about cutting off its top, and cut off its top. The completion of the canoe could take many days and involved repeated appeals to gods, not to mention another round of pig, fish, and coconuts. Making just the lashings for the outrigger was a matter of "utmost solemnity," Malo wrote.[17]

Once finished, the canoe moved down the divine conveyor belt, to the supervision of new gods. The patron god of fishing, Kuula, was worshipped at small stone shrines named after him. But there were other gods of fishing—"various and numerous," Malo wrote—and each fisherman adopted "the god of his choice." The choice had consequences. The god of one fisherman, for example, had strong opinions about the color black, so no family member wore black, and all black was banished from the house.[18]

A ceremony marked the onset of the season for each kind of fishing. When it was time to catch *aku* (bonito), a nobleman ate an *aku*'s eye along with the eye of a sacrificed human. (This was good news for *aku* lovers, because it ended the period during which eating *aku* was punished by death.) The night before the season's inaugural expedition, fishermen gathered at a fishing shrine, where they would spend the night together, removed from the lure of sex with their wives, which could incur divine wrath. They brought sacrificial food, worshipped the fishing god, and before retiring for the evening did a responsive reading during which a priest said, "Save us from nightmare, from bad-luck dreams, from omens of ill."[19]

From the standpoint of a modern boatbuilder or commercial fisherman, much of the above might seem like nonessential preparation for work. And it is indeed hard to argue that removing all black from the home is, in and of itself, time well spent for the ambitious angler. Still, the combined effect of all these rituals was to cloak the business of canoe building and fishing in an air of solemnity that presumably encouraged exacting and conscientious performance.

In any event, we'll return to the question of what good was done by the religious dimension of the Polynesian economy. For now the point is just that the religious dimension was considerable.

Tapu and *Mana*

Undergirding the islands' economic life were two key religious principles, and they undergirded much of Polynesian life in general. One was *tapu*, from which comes the English word "taboo." *Tapu* referred to things set apart or forbidden. Thus, all the forbidden behaviors noted in the preceding paragraphs were *tapu:* eating *aku* before the *aku* season, wearing black if your god had forbidden it, having sex with your wife right before a key fishing expedition. These things weren't just frowned on and punished with social disapproval, the way wearing black to a regatta might be nowadays. *Tapu* violations were punished by the gods themselves, in the form of a fishless expedition, an illness, even death. *Tapu* put starch in the ritual fabric of Polynesia.

The second key concept was *mana*. Scholars disagree on what *mana* meant—in part, no doubt, because its meaning varied subtly from chiefdom to chiefdom. Some say *mana* was a magical or divine power, a kind of supernatural electricity. Others say *mana* was more mundane; it was basically just efficacy, success in getting what you want.[20] Regardless of how *mana* is defined, it was a religious thing, for *mana* was delivered to Polynesian society by the gods. It was the carrot part of the Polynesian incentive structure. Just as violations of *tapu* would bring misfortune, respect for *tapu* could shore up *mana*.

Chiefs possessed *mana* in spectacular proportions. They were conduits through which *mana* entered society and then trickled down the social scale to lesser folk. This role of divine spigot was a natural extension of the logic of shamanism: elevate your importance by claiming special access to the supernatural. (That doesn't mean the chiefs didn't themselves believe in *mana*. One senses an air of authentic desperation in the way a newly installed chief on the Solomon Islands implored the soul of his dead predecessor to "crawl to the gods for some *mana* for me." Groveling before the departed former chief, he declared, "I eat ten times your excrement.")[21]

If *mana* made the chief special, *tapu* formalized his specialness. One of the things most consistently tabooed in Polynesia was casual contact with the chief. When a Tongan chief walked around, Captain Cook noticed, people not only cleared a path for him, but sat down until he had passed. The one allowed encounter was to bow down and gingerly touch his foot.[22] On some islands, commoners couldn't even hear a chief speak; a spokesman—a "talking chief"—conveyed his pronouncements. There was no chance for familiarity to breed contempt.

As if all this weren't enough, chiefs were often descended from gods—and upon death might well become gods themselves, assuming they weren't already considered divine. On some islands the chief was also the head priest, and on islands where he wasn't, chief and priest typically worked hand in ·glove. This meant the chief could help decide what was and wasn't *tapu*—no trivial power in a society where breaches of *tapu* were intensely eschewed.

In sum, Polynesian political leaders were drenched in authority that emanated from the divine. Thus were a Tongan chief's not-infrequent harangues absorbed as Captain Cook described: "The most profound silence and attention is observed during the harangue, even to a much greater degree than is practised amongst us, on the most interesting and serious deliberations of our most respectable assemblies."[23]

This authority, and its source, are common features of chiefdoms. Among the Natchez, in present-day Mississippi, the chief was known as Brother of the Sun, an appellation bound to enhance his stature, given that the Sun was a deity without peer. Maturin Le Petit, a Jesuit missionary, observed of the Natchez in 1730, "These people blindly obey the least wish of their great Chief. They look upon him as an absolute master, not only of their property but also of their lives."[24]

After a Natchez chief's death, Le Petit reported, several of his subjects would eat enough tobacco to lose consciousness and then be ritually strangled, thus accompanying the chief to the hereafter. Burial remains on various continents suggest that this afterlife escort service was a widespread perk for chiefs. There would seem to be a general truth in Le Petit's observation of the Natchez chief: the "credulity of the people maintains him in the despotic authority which he claims."[25]

Crime and Punishment

In Polynesia the chief used his divine authority for typical chiefly endeavors: organizing feasts, organizing armies, maintaining roads and irrigation systems—and amassing the requisite resources.[26] Of course, modern politicians manage to do the same thing—spend and tax—without being thought even remotely sacred. But they have an advantage over chiefs: written laws, often resting on a hallowed constitution, and backed by courts that not only enforce compliance but lend legitimacy. Chiefs, lacking the secular sanctity these things confer, relied on the old-fashioned kind of sanctity.

In Hawaii, when it was time to collect foods for the annual *makahiki* festival, the chief (or "king," as westerners sometimes called him, so large and elaborate were the Hawaiian polities) would place all the land under *tapu*, confining everyone to their homesteads. Priests, bearing a figure of the god Lono, then joined tax collectors in touring the chiefdom, lifting the *tapu* in their wake, liberating the people district by district. If unhappy with the contribution made by a district, they would curse its people in Lono's name.[27]

Gods weren't the only coercive force. Chiefs had armed retainers who could administer beatings and enforce banishment.[28] But for any ruler, the less of that you have to do, the better. And when force must be exercised, the less mundane it seems, the better; belief that the laws being broken were gods' commands, not just chiefs' whims, may help explain why beatings, by some accounts, were absorbed without protest.[29]

Moreover, in chiefdoms there are limits on the scope of government coercion, and here arose an opportunity for religion to play a second role in ordering society. One difference between a chiefdom and a state is that a state government typically has a monopoly on the legitimate use of force: no matter what your neighbor does to you or your family—robbery, assault, even murder—you can't retaliate; the government handles punishment. But in chiefdoms, as in hunter-gatherer societies, grievances can be vented by violent retaliation. This doesn't mean these societies are lawless; the punishment for a given crime may be a matter of consensus, and may have the chief's blessing. It's just that inflicting the punishment is the job of the victims or their kin.

This sort of laissez-faire law enforcement is a shakier source of social order in chiefdoms than in hunter-gatherer societies. In a small hunter-gatherer village, you know everyone and see them often and may someday need their help. So the costs of getting on someone's bad side are high and the temptation to offend them commensurately low. In a chiefdom, containing thousands or even tens of thousands of people, some of your neighbors are more remote, hence more inviting targets of exploitation.

And there's more to exploit. Whereas in a hunter-gatherer society there is little private property, in chiefdoms families own things like fruit trees and gardens, an open invitation to theft. And as crime grows more tempting, it grows more explosive. So long as its punishment is left to the victims, the prospect of family-versus-family feuds looms. And since in chiefdoms these "families" may be big clans that amount to a small village, "feud" may be an understatement.

In this phase of cultural evolution—with personal policing having lost its charm but with government not yet taking up the slack—a supplementary force of social control was called for. Religion seems to have responded to the call. Whereas religion in hunter-gatherer societies didn't have much of a moral dimension, religion in the Polynesian chiefdoms did: it systematically discouraged antisocial behavior.

You might not notice this on casual inspection of Polynesian gods. In many ways they are reminiscent of hunter-gatherer gods, complete with a lack of consistent virtue.[30] Robert Williamson, who in the early twentieth century heroically compressed centuries of reports on central Polynesia into a few classic volumes on its religion, wrote that the Society Islands gods "ate and drank, married and indulged in sexual gratifications, and quarrelled and fought among themselves." In other words, "people imagined them to be such as they were themselves, only endowed with greater powers."[31] So the key was to give them things, such as food and respect. Prayers and sacrifices sent to gods of the air could stave off storms — or bring them on, in the event that a fleet of invaders was approaching.[32] And if you were the aggressor, and your enemy had retreated to a fortress, you could buy off the enemy's gods, placing offerings near the fort to encourage divine desertion.[33]

Similarly, anticipation of the afterlife, which today is a moral carrot or stick for so many people, retained in the Polynesian chiefdoms the heavily amoral flavor it had in hunter-gatherer societies; your life in the hereafter was shaped mainly by things other than how you treated people here. In the Society Islands, if you died at sea, your spirit would enter a shark, and if you died in battle, you would haunt the battlefield.[34] In the long run most Polynesian souls migrated to a distant place sometimes described as a dark underworld, sometimes as a faraway island. There might be a more luxurious alternative in the sky — an "abode of light and joy,"[35] as a westerner described one island's version — but if you were an ordinary Joe, living an upright life wouldn't get you there; this paradise was reserved for the ruling class and perhaps a few other elites. (In the Society Islands it was open to showpeople — singers, actors, dancers — though not for free; they had to have any babies born to them killed, or else face expulsion from the entertainers' guild that was the gateway to this paradise.)[36] In general, Handy observed, "Prestige, rites, and circumstances affecting death determine destiny in after-life."[37]

Yet if Polynesian religion lacked the moral incentives of some modern religions — a role-model god who hands out afterlife assignments according to your conduct grade — it had other moral guidance built into it.

For starters, though Polynesians didn't fret about punishment that might await them in the afterlife, there was an edifying fear of punishment that could *originate* there, via ghosts that frowned on their behavior. In a Hawaiian legend, the spirit of a dead man haunts his murderer until the murderer makes amends by building three houses, one for the dead man's kin, one for their servants, and one for the dead man's bones.[38]

Believing that anyone you mistreat might haunt you from the grave could turn you into a pretty nice person. This incentive — fear of ghosts — is also found in some hunter-gatherer or horticultural religions, but in the Polynesian chiefdoms it had acquired the added power of divine supervision: the same gods who wouldn't punish you in the next life punished you in this one. Tongan gods, for example, punished theft with shark attack. ("In consequence," the anthropologist H. Ian Hogbin observed, "thieves hesitated to swim during the season when sharks were at their worst.")[39] And these Tongan gods gave out rewards as well as punishment; *mana* was granted not just for ritual correctness but for moral goodness — eschewing theft and other antisocial acts.[40] A boost in *mana* was no mere abstraction; it meant more pigs and yams, here and now.

Still, the standard divine sanction in Polynesia was a stick, not a carrot. In Samoa, a nineteenth-century missionary reported, "calamities are traced to sins of the individual or his parents, or some other near relative." Theft, for example, might bring "ulcerous sores, dropsy, and inflammation of the abdomen."[41]

Even family life was subject to supernatural sanction. In the Society Islands, a fisherman who argued with his wife before an expedition would have bad luck. A woman who cheated on her husband while he was at sea could bring worse luck, including his drowning.[42] And on many Polynesian islands, hostility toward kin could be punished with illness.[43] In a society where extended families live together and form the basic unit of society, this alone could do wonders for social harmony.

When you add up all the little ways Polynesian religion encouraged self-restraint,[44] you wind up with a fair amount of encouragement — enough, perhaps, to compensate for the absence of a centralized legal system. And religion in chiefdoms was doing more than fill in for not-yet-invented secular laws; it was paving the way for secular laws.[45]

For example, the Polynesian chiefdoms featured land owner-ship, something generally lacking in hunter-gatherer societies. In the modern world, property markers are secular things; you may respect fenceposts or surveyors' pins, but you don't revere them. To judge by the Polynesian chiefdoms, property markers started out as something more awe-inspiring. On many islands, a family could (sometimes with a priest's help) place a taboo on its fruit trees and vegetable gardens, leaving it for the gods to prosecute thieves or trespassers via illness or death. These property taboos were adver-tised with signs made of leaves, sticks, and other handy materials. In Samoa, the signs conveniently signaled the kind of misfortune awaiting the thief. Coconut fiber molded into the shape of a shark meant shark attack; a spear stuck in the ground foretold facial neu-ralgia. (The system wasn't perfect. If Tongan natives could get some visiting westerner to remove the sign, and hence the taboo, they would happily eat fruit from a previously forbidden tree.)[46]

Samoa, unlike most Polynesian chiefdoms, had the rudiments of a jury system. If a grievance wasn't settled by retaliation, a body of locals called a *fono* would hear testimony. And here, too, law was intertwined with the supernatural. Sometimes the accused had to drink a substance that, if it caused illness or death, signified guilt.[47] And always the accused had to swear their innocence to some god. Of course, even today a defendant may swear by God to tell the truth, but in Samoa the oath was less perfunctory: fear of the god's vengeance could bring a dramatic confession.

The Dark Side of Polynesian Gods

If you compare modern life with life in a hunter-gatherer society, the differences are big. We have a complexly productive economy, featuring division of labor and capital investment and high tech-nology. We have an elaborate government, its authority resting on laws that guide enforcement and preserve legitimacy. All of this lets people interact peacefully and productively with people they know barely, if at all. And the entire system is rationalized; though it may rest partly on moral intuitions and draw on religious sentiment ("So help me God"), we justify our political, legal, and economic systems in pragmatic terms, revising them in the name of efficacy.

But apparently we didn't arrive at this rationality in a very rational way. When social structure took its first big step toward the modern world, evolving from hunter-gatherer society to agrarian chiefdom, it leaned heavily on the gods. Not all observed chiefdoms are as pervaded by religion as Polynesian ones, but compared to modern societies, chiefdoms in general are soaked in it. In chiefdoms, gods were guardians of political power, supervisors of economic performance, and supporters of social norms that let unprecedently large numbers of people live together. And this residential density — this high concentration of brains and egos — sponsored a kind of creative synergy, accelerating the rate of technological and social change, propelling society toward modern form. Whatever you think of the world you find yourself in, you have the gods of chiefdoms to thank for it.

But how thankful should the Polynesians have been? Was their social system a just one? Did religion, in upholding it, uphold the public good? Or were gods just a tool of oppression, devoutly sustained by a ruling class that wanted to keep living in the manner to which it had become accustomed?

Polynesia certainly gives some support to the latter view. Chiefs, for example, got lots of wives, as befits the quasi-divine. And the ruling class in general got lots of food. In Hawaii, precious sources of protein — pigs, chickens, fish — wound up disproportionately on elite dining tables, whereas vegetables were more widely accessible.[48] In the Society Islands, commoners couldn't enter the temple grounds, site of big sacrifices to the gods, but priests could, and they ate the part of the food the gods left behind — the physical part. Polynesian priests also profited from that hallowed shamanic service, fee-based communion with the supernatural. One of their jobs was to cure illness by divining what offense had caused it.[49] A nineteenth-century Methodist missionary described a Samoan priest entering a diagnostic trance via "preliminary yawnings and coughings," then passing through contortions and convulsions, until finally the god possessing him prescribed the restorative atonement, such as for "gifts to be given to the priest."[50]

Elites also got lavish medical care. When a Tongan commoner was sick, priests might prescribe a modest curative sacrifice: cutting off the finger joint of a relative even lower in the social hierarchy. But for a chief's illness, sometimes the only cure was to strangle a child.[51]

Equality before the law wasn't a bedrock Polynesian principle. In Tonga, murder was usually punished one way or another, but not if it was the murder of a commoner by a chief.[52] In Samoa, adultery could bring a broad range of informal punishments unless committed with a chief's wife, in which case the punishment was formal and ranged only from death by drowning to death by beating.[53] Human sacrifice seems also to have had an upper-class bias. In the Society Islands, one anthropologist noted, candidates for sacrifice fell into several categories, including prisoner of war, blasphemer, and "person obnoxious to the chief or priest."[54]

In Defense of Polynesian Gods

In the face of facts like this, what could a functionalist possibly say in defense of the claim that religion benefits society as a whole? More than you might think.

Consider human sacrifice, as appraised in the clinical terms of functionalism. Even Captain Cook, who deemed it a "waste of the human race," noted that many of the adults sacrificed were criminals. And many others were "common low fellows, who stroll about from place to place and from island to island, without having any fixed abode, or any visible way of getting an honest livelihood."[55]

Now, we might today consider death excessive punishment for many crimes, and certainly for transience and indigence. But well after Cook wrote, his native England would be locking up poor people in debtors' prison. And, in any event, the removal from society of people who take from it more than they give isn't, in cold economic terms, a "waste." It may well have made the chiefdom stronger and more efficient, and thus have been socially "functional," whatever you think of its morality. (Supernatural belief has other ways of weeding out poor performers. In various societies, including some hunter-gatherer ones, people accused of sorcery or witchcraft and punished by banishment or death tend to be notoriously uncooperative or otherwise antisocial characters.)[56] More generally, Polynesian religion seems to have kept the machine humming. Under the severe gaze of gods, canoes got made, fish got caught, pigs and yams got raised.

But wasn't there an easier way to get good workmanship—like, say, letting teams of canoe builders compete with one another to sell canoes to fishermen, and relying on the profit motive to instill craftsmanship? Ever hear of free enterprise?

These are questions asked from a modern perspective, in a society featuring things like money and efficient markets. Back when humanity made the first step toward that world, moving from small hunter-gatherer villages toward large, multivillage agrarian societies, the logic of these things wasn't so obvious. To be sure, there was barter in the Polynesian chiefdoms. But apparently things that now happen via the magic of the marketplace were needful of a boost from government and/or religion. At feasts organized by chiefs—and fueled by divinely inspired contributions from farmers and fishermen—commoners who ate delicacies from distant islands had in effect swapped their labor for desired food, something we now do with money.

Polynesian religion did things that even in many modern societies are handled by government, not by markets—building roads and irrigation systems, providing a social safety net. On many islands, chiefs used their sacred clout to extract contributions to a food storehouse that the whole society could draw on in times of scarcity, rather as a modern government collects taxes for disaster aid. And in Samoa, fishermen got the rough equivalent of unemployment insurance: at the end of a bonito fishing expedition, each canoe surrendered part of its catch to the *tautai*, the head fisherman, who used it to hold a feast for all the fishermen.[57] Since canoes with meager hauls were exempted from this tax but shared in the feast, this amounted to a redistribution from haves to have-nots. The sacred context—the fact that the *tautai* was a kind of religious leader—may have dampened the resentment of the more consistently successful fishermen.

In the functionalist view, some perks of chiefship should be viewed as payment for administrative services. After all, in modern societies, the titans of business and politics are granted wealth and/or power, and these are defended (by those who defend them, at least) as just compensation for vital social functions. Granted, the *type* of compensation given Polynesian chiefs may strike us as strange. It is with warranted pride that we can say we don't strangle children on behalf of the powerful. Still, we should probably limit our self-congratulation. In chiefdoms powerful men get many wives, whereas in modern societies they get (if they want) many mistresses. In chiefdoms the powerful could do things that if done by others would be grave offenses, whereas in modern societies the same privilege is granted less formally; the rich and powerful use pricey lawyers and key contacts to dodge justice while poorer offenders go to jail.

Moreover, even as chiefs got perks that strike us as strange, they also paid some strange prices. In Tonga, chiefs sacrificed their own children, albeit children born to lower-class women and thus not in the line of chiefly succession.[58] Less dramatic forms of noblesse oblige were also expected. As the anthropologist Marshall Sahlins observed, "even the greatest" of the Polynesian chiefs knew that "generosity was morally incumbent on them."[59]

The Saving Grace of Chiefs

Indeed, maybe we should marvel not at the chief's exploitation of his power, but at the limits of the exploitation—at the social services he performed and the sacrifices he made. You would think that someone of divine lineage, shrouded in a haze of ritual sanctity, could have gotten away with less of both. Why didn't he?

One reason is that people aren't dupes. Our brains were designed by natural selection to guard us against danger, including exploitation. They are, owing to quirks of evolutionary history, susceptible to religious ideas and feelings, but they aren't easily blinded by them. Tahitians had a phrase for chiefs who "eat the power of the government too much."[60] And avoiding this appellation was in the interests of chiefs; in Polynesia broadly, as the archaeologist Patrick Kirch noted in *The Evolution of the Polynesian Chiefdoms*, "an overly bloated chieftainship might raise the spectre of rebellion."[61] Or the specter of a bloodless coup. In Tahiti, priests and other elites would approach a persistently despotic chief and offer this guidance: "Go and eat the leg of pork seasoned with dung! Thy royalty is taken from thee, thou art put down to tread the sand, to walk like common men."[62]

Another thing that kept chiefs honest is competition with other chiefdoms. War was common in Polynesia, and among chiefdoms generally.[63] War puts a premium on social efficiency. Ruling classes that are egregiously parasitic, so thoroughly monopolizing the fruits of common labor as to leave little incentive for it, tend to wind up on the losing end, and their chiefocentric cultural templates tend to wind up in the dustbin of history. In contrast, a religion that boosts social cohesion and productivity may not only survive but prevail, spreading to weaker societies via conquest. For that matter, it may replicate peacefully. Just as people emulate successful peers, societies emulate potent societies.

This dynamic—the functionalist drift of competition among societies—offers at least speculative explanations for otherwise puzzling facts. Why would chiefs sacrifice their own children to the gods? (Because religions that called for no vivid sacrifices by elites had trouble preserving the allegiance of commoners, and thus couldn't sustain the social vigor necessary to prevail in intersocietal competition?) Why were those Society Islands showpeople, the ones destined for a paradise that commoners could only dream of, allowed to mock the chief in public performances? (Because satiric social commentary can help check a chief's self-aggrandizing tendencies before they render a society self-destructively top-heavy?)

The pattern on display in the Polynesia chiefdoms extends beyond them, to other chiefdoms and even to other kinds of societies. On the one hand, the ruling class, consisting as it does of human beings, will try, consciously or unconsciously, to steer culture, including religious belief, toward its selfish ends. But this effort will meet two countervailing forces, one internal and one external. The internal check is popular resistance to exploitation; less powerful but more numerous common folk will, consciously or unconsciously, defend their interests. This may mean rebellion, and it may just mean resisting uncongenial religious ideas. (In Tonga, elites felt sure that commoners have no afterlife; some commoners begged to differ.)[64] The external check on the ruling class's power grab is competition with alternative social systems — that is, neighboring societies.

Hence an ongoing dialectic: elites use their power to gather more power, but this self-aggrandizement will meet ongoing grassroots resistance and occasionally encounter negative feedback in the form of revolution, military defeat, or economic eclipse. Societies forged by these forces provide plenty of supporting anecdotes for both "Marxists" and functionalists, and so fully vindicate neither.

This evolutionary process doesn't pay much attention to the mythic or cosmological details of a religion. Whether you call a god Tangaloa or Tangaroa doesn't greatly affect societal efficiency, nor does your view on whether this god aided creation by raising the sky or by fishing up islands. But the kinds of behaviors your gods punish and reward does matter. Productivity and social harmony are assets in intersocietal competition, and so are favored by the endless winnowing of cultural evolution. It's no surprise that, while the biographies of gods differ greatly from one Polynesian chiefdom to the next, a product of essentially random drift, more pragmatic themes are more stable. Across Polynesia broadly, religion encouraged exacting work and discouraged theft and other antisocial acts.

Of course, by our standards, the Polynesian religions may seem far from optimally efficient. So much pointless superstition, so much emphasis on sheer ritual correctness! Wouldn't a more potent religion have reallocated time from making sacrifices to building canoes? Wouldn't it have focused more intensely on encouraging honesty, generosity, and other aids to social harmony? Wouldn't its carrots and sticks have been more potent? Sure, the threat of illness or death packs a punch. But why not throw in more ammunition — like heaven and hell?

One answer is that cultural evolution takes time. You can't expect a blind, blundering process to work magic overnight, especially during the age of chiefdoms. Back then cultural innovation didn't arise and spread in a sea of millions of electronically interlinked brains. There were just thousands of brains in a society, and communication among them depended on Stone Age technology: walking and talking. And contact *among* societies was even more arduous.

Even so, Polynesian religion developed some pretty sophisticated features. *Mana*, the very principle that rendered chiefs so powerful and helped justify their sanctity, could also usher in their demise. Just as a chief's naturally massive *mana* allowed effective governance, manifestly bad governance signified waning *mana*. So if a chief lost a few battles, he might be usurped by some noble warrior whose battlefield triumphs were thought to evince high *mana*.[65] This feedback mechanism, a way of dumping inept chiefs before their missteps reached disastrous proportions, may have been favored by cultural evolution, as chiefdoms lacking such a mechanism tended to be overrun by those possessing it.

At the same time, this doctrine also gets a boost from simple logic. If indeed chiefs favored by the gods succeed, then a chief's consistent failure suggests that he's lost the favor of the gods. Indeed, failure just about *has* to mean that, if belief in the religion is to endure the ups and downs of life. Every religion, to survive elementary logical scrutiny, has to have its explanatory loopholes. With Polynesian chiefs, as with shamans in the previous chapter, one loophole is the assumption that waning earthly powers signify a loss of the divine touch. And this loophole places a limit on how much exploitation even a divinely ordained leader can get away with.

The general principle here is that the link between the divine and the mundane works both ways. People who believe that the divine controls the earthly will sometimes be compelled, by changes at the earthly level, to revise their ideas about what's going on at the divine level. It's a kind of law of unintended symmetry, and, as we'll see in the next chapter, this law has greatly influenced the evolution of gods since the age of chiefdoms.

Science and Comfort

Although religion is shaped by intergroup tensions — elites versus commoners, society versus society — formative action also takes place at a more fine-grained level. If a religious meme doesn't find a perch in individual brains, it can't spread from brain to brain and so come to characterize a whole group in the first place. And one way for a meme to win a warm reception from a brain is to make it feel better.

Polynesian religion may sound austere (and it indeed brought Polynesians many obligations, moral and ritual, along with some performance anxiety), but at the same time, it did what religion has often done: comfort people in the face of uncertainty or doubt. In the age of chiefdoms, the doubt wasn't philosophical; it was, as in hunter-gatherer days, about material security — staying alive and healthy. A nighttime prayer in the Society Islands began,[66]

Save me! Save me!
It is evening;

It is evening of the gods.

Watch near me, O my God!

The prayer then went on to ask for protection against "sudden death" and various other things, including "the furious warrior" whose "hair is always standing on end." It ended, "Let me and my spirit live, and rest in peace this night, O my God!"

Providing this sort of comfort is a time-honored way for religious doctrine to thrive, but as cultural evolution proceeds, the things that people find comforting change. The reason is that the things making them uncomfortable in the first place change. Part of that Society Islands prayer asks for protection against "quarrels over boundary-markers," a type of quarrel that couldn't have taken place in the typical hunter-gatherer society. Religion is a feature of cultural evolution that, among other things, addresses anxieties created by cultural evolution; it helps keep social change safe from itself.

But today cultural evolution has, in addition to creating new anxieties, threatened this august instrument for addressing them. For many people, the coming of modern science has undermined the idea of gods and threatened the whole prospect of religion.

It's ironic, then, what a debt science owes to religion. Polynesians were avid students of the nighttime sky. The Tahitians, Captain Cook wrote, could predict the seasonal appearance and disappearance of stars "with more precision than will easily be believed by an European astronomer."[67] Like much of Polynesian culture, this mastery was pragmatically motivated (largely by the needs of navigation) yet couched in religion. Polynesian "navigator-priest-astronomers," as one scholar calls them, tracked heavenly bodies from observation posts on temple platforms.[68] And a key Society Islands navigational star, Ta'i-Rio-aitu, was a manifestation of Rio, who, being the god of albacore and bonito fishermen, would naturally provide such guidance.[69]

Given Polynesian beliefs about the divinity of stars and the divine control of weather, it's not surprising that some Polynesians tried to predict the weather by looking at the nighttime sky.[70] What is more surprising is that they succeeded. Cook wrote that "they can predict the weather, at least the wind, with much greater certainty than we can."[71] The apparent explanation is that both the night sky and the prevailing winds change seasonally. So there was indeed a correlation between stars and weather; the Polynesians just had the wrong explanation for the correlation. Still, this is the way scientific progress often starts: finding a correlation between two variables and positing a plausible if false explanation. In this sense, "science" dates back to preliterate times.

And the rest is history. The ancient discernment and explanation of correlation led eventually to the modern worldview that deems these early explanations so crude. Modern science, like modern economics and modern law and modern government, evolved from primordial forms that were symbiotically intertwined with religious thought. In fact, it isn't obvious that we would have any of these modern institutions had it not been for early religion, which did so much to carry human social organization and culture beyond the hunter-gatherer stage.

After the chiefdom, the next major stage in the evolution of social organization is the state-level society (or, as it is sometimes put, "civilization"). State-level societies are bigger than chiefdoms, with more elaborate, even bureaucratic, government, and they have more advanced information technology — usually a full-fledged system of writing. But in one respect they are very much like chiefdoms: religion pervades life.

This fact, as we'll see in the next chapter, is especially well documented in the two great civilizations that frame the land where the Abrahamic god would be born — Mesopotamia to the north and east, Egypt to the south and west. This framing isn't just geographic. In Egypt and Mesopotamia there would appear theological themes that, perhaps not coincidentally, would later reappear in the religion of ancient Israel, elements of divine identity that would wind up in the DNA of the Abrahamic god, Yahweh.

Also in Egypt and Mesopotamia there would appear gods that

lived on to become part of Yahweh's formative environment. Some of these gods would migrate into Israel and there attract worshippers, drawing devotion that might otherwise accrue to Yahweh, arousing his jealousy. Some would accompany and inspire Mesopotamian invaders as they entered the land of the Israelites and, in one of the most consequential acts in the history of religion, destroyed Yahweh's temple.

All of this would help shape Yahweh's character as monotheism emerged in the land of the Israelites, planting the seed of the three modern Abrahamic faiths. In ancient Mesopotamia and Egypt we begin to move from the evolution of religion writ large, and the evolution of gods generically, to the evolution of western religion, and the evolution of God.

Chapter Four

Gods of the Ancient States

In ancient Mesopotamia, where divinities first entered the historical record, they were often less than divine. A prominent god named Enki once got drunk and gave the secret powers that govern civilization to the goddess Inanna. Inanna wasn't a pillar of sober responsibility herself; though smart (she had tricked Enki into drinking excessively), she was self-indulgent, and spent much of her time having sex. A hymn from the early second millennium BCE (by which time she had acquired the name Ishtar) reports that "sixty then sixty satisfy themselves in turn upon her nakedness. Young men have tired, Ishtar will not tire."[1] For a time Inanna/Ishtar was the patron deity of prostitutes, and was also thought to help wives conceal their adultery.[2] (One Mesopotamian text imagines a woman who has been extramaritally impregnated praying to Ishtar, while looking at her husband's face, "I want to make my child to be born look like him.")[3] The great god Enlil (himself a sometime sex addict) once ordered up an epic flood, like the biblical flood that Noah would later survive; but, whereas Noah's god used the flood to punish people for wickedness, Enlil's motive was less exalted: humanity had been noisy while he was trying to sleep, so he decided to extinguish it.[4]

In short, the gods of early Mesopotamian civilization were much like their ancestors, the gods of chiefdoms and of hunter-gatherer societies: basically human—for better or worse—except with supernatural powers. So too in ancient Egypt, ancient China, and other places where, as writing appeared, social organization crossed the hazy line between chiefdoms and states: the line between "primitive" religion and "civilized" religion proved hazy, too. Gods still weren't paragons of virtue and still were noted at least as much for their cunning and ferocity as for their love and compassion. And, though mentally human, they still assumed a variety of forms, including some creepy ones. In Egypt the mummified bodies of millennia-old crocodiles have turned up in a temple honoring Sobek, a crocodile god.[5]

The most obvious difference between the "primitive" gods of prestate societies and the gods of early states was in scale and grandeur. The Polynesian gods were honored with little temple-pyramids ("marae"), the Mesopotamian gods with big temple-pyramids ("ziggurats"). The Polynesians made images of deities out of wood or stone; the Egyptians used gold and surrounded their idols with luxurious furnishings.

Some thinkers of the early Christian era, on encountering residues of religions from the early ancient states, were horrified — all those amoral animal gods, their grotesqueness only amplified by the attendant ornateness. "The god of the Egyptians," wrote Clement of Alexandria, is "a beast rolling on a purple couch."[6]

Clement lived in the late second century of the common era. By his time, the now familiar profile of western religion had appeared: belief in only one god, a fundamentally good god who focuses on the moral improvement of human beings, not the gratification of his own desires, and who cares about all people everywhere. That is: a *monotheism* that has an *ethical* core and is *universalist*.

The last two of these three elements can interact powerfully. An ethical code, by itself, isn't necessarily a great thing; even murderous racists may be nice to members of their own race, and in that sense be ethical. But if the god who commands you to treat your neighbors nicely values people of other races and nations as highly as he values your neighbors, then justifying the mistreatment of nonneighbors gets harder (in theory, at least). By Clement's time this conclusion was explicit in church doctrine, and Clement himself wrote attacks on the racism that was used to justify slavery.

So naturally Clement had high standards for divinity. It's not surprising that from his vantage point, there seemed to be two worlds—the world ushered in by the god of the Hebrews during the first millennium BCE and crystallized by Jesus Christ at the end of that millennium, and the world before, the world in which all past religions had been mired.

Still, this is a false divide. It's true that when religion enters the historical record, around the beginning of the third millennium BCE, there is no sign of monotheism, much less a monotheism focused on ethics and universal in scope. Nor would these three elements—monotheism, an ethical core, and universalism—be thoroughly combined for millennia. But it's also true that each of these elements had appeared in at least rough form, in one ancient state or another, during the third or second millennia BCE. Perhaps more important: that synergistic result of the last two elements—the extension of moral consideration to people in other lands, of other races—had started to take root. By the time the God worshipped by Clement showed up, he had been anticipated by the religions Clement disdained.

What's more, the moral progress these religions abetted turns out to be embedded in the very logic of religion as mediated by the basic direction of social evolution. Cultural evolution was all along pushing divinity, and hence humanity, toward moral enlightenment.

Gods Go on Record

The earliest written records of religion are fragmentary in various senses, starting with the literal: sometimes archaeologists rummaging around Mesopotamia find only a chunk of a clay tablet or cylinder featuring, say, a list of gods. But things could be worse. In Egypt scribes used not clay but papyrus, which is prone to perishing. So the writing left from earliest Egypt tends to be the kind of thing you'd inscribe on the walls of a tomb—which presumably doesn't capture Egyptian religion as a whole any more than modern monuments capture modern culture as a whole. In the third millennium BCE, the Egyptian sky goddess Nut is quoted as saying, "The King is my eldest son...with whom I am well pleased."[7] But we don't know how Nut felt about commoners, or how they felt about her.

In ancient China the record is similarly sketchy. The earliest durable writing, from the Shang Dynasty of the second millennium BCE, comes on cattle bones and turtle shells, in the form of questions submitted to gods. The king's engraver etched the questions on a shell or shoulder blade, the king's diviner heated the medium until it cracked, and the king interpreted the cracks. For example, when a king named Wu Ding had a toothache, his diviner made seventy cracks on five turtle shells in the course of determining whether some dead ancestor's displeasure was the root of the problem, and if so, which dead ancestor. It turns out that the culprit was Father Geng, the king's uncle—a discovery that culminated in this inscription: "[We] offer a dog to Father Geng [and] split open a sheep.... If we pray by means of these [offerings], the sick tooth will certainly be cured."[8] That's good news for the king, but it doesn't tell us how you handled a toothache in ancient China if you weren't the king.

Even in Mesopotamia, where the everyday writing medium, clay tablets, was hardy enough to await archaeological discovery, the historical record is biased. Almost nobody was literate. Script was hard to master; there was no compact phonetic alphabet, but rather hordes of complex symbols that stood for whole words or concepts. And the ruling class trained the scribes. So even here, religion as recorded in earliest history is by and large the *official* story of religion, not the complete story.

One aid in overcoming this bias is the fact that ancient states showed up at different times in different places. In the Americas, which were populated much later than the Eastern Hemisphere, farming got invented later and states evolved later. So when Europeans "discovered" America, they could witness, in the Aztecs and the Maya, the everyday lives of people whose system of writing was in the early stages of its evolution. Sadly, both for native Americans and for posterity, these Europeans were more rapacious than early European visitors to Polynesia. So the indigenous culture was quickly corrupted, and in some cases erased. In the sixteenth century one

Spanish bishop, by way of demonstrating the superiority of his religion, burned a treasure trove of Mayan texts, not to mention some Mayans.[9]

Nonetheless, we got a glimpse of everyday Mesoamerican culture. The glimpse suggests that the "undocumented" aspects of early state religions were roughly what you'd expect if you assumed that ancient states, having emerged from chiefdoms, retained many of their traits. In particular: the gods flattered and cajoled by kings in writing were respected in the street. To be sure, there was more to Mesoamerican religion than these gods — everyday omens, magical healing, and the like. Still, the "official" state religion was accepted by the masses.

The character of gods could differ from ancient state to ancient state. Ancestral spirits or deities, though found everywhere, played an especially big role in China. And some civilizations may have had more mystical or mutable gods than others (though claims that the gods of some civilizations were more like impersonal "forces" than like anthropomorphic "beings" tend not to withstand scrutiny).[10] But one thing the divine in all these lands had in common was importance. Here are some observations made by scholars about various ancient civilizations. Egypt: "The cardinal features of that culture and society were determined by the existence and power of its all-pervading religious beliefs." China: "The fate of human beings was inseparable from the extra-human world." The Maya: "Everything in the Maya world was imbued, in different degrees, with an unseen power or sacred quality." The Aztecs: "Existence revolved totally around religion. There was not a single act of public or private life which was not colored by religious sentiment." Mesopotamia: "The gods constantly intervened everywhere and participated in everything." [11]

That would explain why there were so many of them! In the second millennium BCE, when Mesopotamian scribes conducted a divine census, listing the gods in various Mesopotamian cities, they came up with nearly two thousand names.[12] The pantheon of an ancient state typically included lots of nature gods (sun, moon, storm, fertility, and so on) and gods that oversaw the ever-growing array of vocations, in particular gods for farmers, scribes, merchants, and craftsmen. Mesopotamia had gods for everything from brickmaking to brewing, and in Aztec society robbers claimed their own deity. There were also gods that defy easy categorization: the Mayan god of suicide, the Mesopotamian "Lord of Livestock Pens," the eight Egyptian deities that oversaw lungs, liver, stomach, and intestines (two gods per organ).[13]

Like the gods of prehistory, these gods expected goods and services from humans, and dished out rewards or punishment accordingly. So everywhere people made sacrifices to the gods, flattered—that is, worshipped—them, and tended to their needs in other ways. (A Mesopotamian tablet of ritual instruction begins, "When you wash the mouth of a god...")[14] Everywhere the upshot was a symbiotic relationship between people and gods, with each having something the other needed. And everywhere—as in chiefdoms—the political leaders took the lead in mediating that relationship, and indeed defining the relationship; everywhere, religion was used by the powerful to stay powerful.[15]

Hence the similarity in the way scholars describe civilizations separated by an ocean. Mayan kings were "conduits through which supernatural forces were channeled into the human realm."[16] The Egyptian king was "the sole intermediary who could serve the gods and hence maintain the flows of energy" into the world.[17]

Order and Chaos

And what would happen if the king weren't there to play this role? Chaos! According to Mesopotamian cosmology, the universe had once been on the brink of chaos, but fortunately kingship was then invented, which meant that gods who favored order could be rallied to defeat an older generation of gods who didn't.[18] In Egypt the forces of chaos posed a particular threat upon the death of a king—a doctrine that no doubt worked in favor of the heir apparent and against aspiring usurpers.[19] The Aztecs' world was, as one scholar puts it, "fragile and tenuous...inherently unstable...liable to fall out of kilter at any moment" and plunge into "emptiness and darkness."[20] Fortunately, you could head off this fate with human sacrifice, which gave the sun enough nourishment to keep fighting its way across the sky.[21] Of course, properly sacrificing hundreds of people per month isn't the kind of job you can leave to amateurs, so leaders of church and state were vital.

They worked hand in glove. First, the king would dispatch armies to conquer neighboring peoples and hence amass live bodies (a legitimate venture, since Aztecs were the chosen people of Huitzilopochtli, the god who had led them out of the wilderness).[22] The religious leaders would handle the rest, such as taking the victims to the top of the temple, ripping out their beating hearts, and rolling the corpses down the temple stairs; or (if the sacrifice was to the fire god) throwing the victims in a fire, pulling their writhing bodies out with hooks, and *then* tearing out their beating hearts.[23] The good news for the victims was that they got a nice afterlife.[24]

The church-state symbiosis didn't, at all places and all times, work so harmoniously. Priests, like the rest of us, are ambitious, and sometimes their influence reached a point where power struggles with the king broke out. Still, Herbert Spencer's nineteenth-century description of early civilization—"originally church and state are undistinguished"—is not far off the mark.[25] Politicians and priests together controlled the sacred knowledge on which their stature and influence rested.

Functionalists and "Marxists" can have their usual argument about how exploitative the church-state axis was. Marxists can note that in Egypt, Mesopotamia, China, and Mesoamerica the corpses of kings are sometimes accompanied by dozens or even hundreds of less exalted corpses; apparently servants, consorts, and other key aides were assigned to accompany the king into the hereafter.[26] Functionalists can reply that sacrifices, if less severe ones, were sometimes made by elites, too—such as the Aztec priests who fasted, never married, and periodically pierced their flesh with cactus spines.[27] Anyone who believes that religion imposed no costs on the ruling class need only contemplate the Mayan prewar ritual during which the king stuck a shard of volcanic glass through his penis and then pulled a cord through the wound.[28]

Marxists can also point suspiciously to the big economic role typically played by the church, which might have large holdings in farming, trade, or finance. In an Aztec city of two hundred thousand people, a single temple employed five thousand of them.[29] And in some Mesopotamian cities the church owned a fourth of the land. When you find a Babylonian record of someone borrowing silver from the "priestess Amat-Shamash" and committing to "pay the Sun-God's interest," you have to wonder whether the interest rate was as low as a secular market would have offered.[30]

In reply, functionalists can note that Mesopotamian temples took care of orphans, widows, the poor, and the blind.[31] And they can add that, even if the church-state industrial complex was charging high overhead, a top-heavy industrial complex is better than no industrial complex at all.

But if you want to defend ancient religion, trying to refute the Marxist position may not be your best tack. It's probably better to adopt parts of the Marxist worldview and deploy them creatively: concede that ancient religion was largely in the service of political and economic power, then look at how changes in the structure of power, over the millennia, reshaped religious doctrine. In some ways that change was for the better. In fact, this tethering of divine logic to the terrestrial logic of politics and economics helped push religion toward moral enlightenment. It is the main reason for that crucial synergy between ethics and universalism—the main reason that the circle of moral consideration has expanded over time, beyond the bounds of tribe and race. This lofty drift of the divine can be understood only by appreciating divinity's subservience to the facts on the ground.

The Moral Compass

Of course, for the moral circle to expand, it has to exist in the first place; there has to be a code encouraging people to treat their neighbors considerately. But there is always such a thing in human society. And in ancient states—more than in chiefdoms and much more than in hunter-gatherer societies—this code drew support from religion.

Mesopotamian gods laid out clear ethical guidelines, ranging from the general (try to help people, not harm them) to the specific (don't urinate or vomit in streams).[32] And, though compliance wouldn't get you to heaven, violation could get you a bit of hell on earth: illness, death, and other problems. To this end the gods deployed an elite police corps—demonic beings who were specialists in their fields. There were demons named "Fever," "Jaundice," "Cough," and "Shivers." There was a demon who caused epidemics and a female demon called "Extinguisher" who killed small children.[33] All told, it was enough to keep a person from urinating in a stream.

Egyptians and Mayans could get sick for telling a lie, among other sins.[34] Aztecs could get a skin infection for urinating on the bush that yields cocoa beans, and licentiousness could elicit penalties ranging from coughs to emaciation to a dirty liver—not to mention the death of innocent young turkeys, which would fall flat on their backs in the presence of an adulterous human.[35] And if a young Aztec man fainted while piercing his penis to honor the gods, it meant that he had failed to keep his virginity (though an alternative explanation comes to mind).[36] Meanwhile, in India, the Vedic texts of the late second millennium BCE speak of punishment, via disease and other afflictions, for such ethical lapses as stealing.[37]

Even when ancient moral guidance involved no divine policing, it could have a religious dimension. Egypt's "Instruction of Ptahhotep," a guidebook for young men of the upper classes, didn't back up its precepts with sanctions, but since its reputed author, Ptahhotep, had been posthumously deified, it carried more force than a self-help book. Further, it drew on such Egyptian metaphysical/religious concepts as *ka*, a person's spirit or soul. As in: "Do not malign anyone, Great or small, the *ka* abhors it."[38]

None of this should be surprising. Even in the Polynesian chiefdoms we saw religion starting to respond with moral sanctions to the challenge of maintaining order in a society larger and more unwieldy than a hunter-gatherer village. In ancient cities, with populations sometimes in the hundreds of thousands, the challenge had only grown. So religions that encouraged people to treat others considerately—which made for a more orderly and productive city—would have a competitive edge over religions that didn't.[39] The ancient depiction of gods as defending order against chaos, however politically convenient for elites, was also, in this sense, accurate. The gods—or, at least, belief in them—protected ancient civilizations from the forces of disarray that do in fact threaten complex social organizations.

And here, as in the Polynesian chiefdoms, the key to preserving social order was to harness self-interest. If you wanted to avoid illness, early death, and various lesser afflictions, if you wanted to avoid divinely ordained shame, if you wanted to keep your *ka* in good working order, you had to behave in ways conducive to social cohesion, which included being nice to people in your vicinity.

But what about people in other cities, other states, other societies—people with different beliefs, different skin colors? Was there any reason not to malign *them*, or not to steal their land or kill them? Why would religion encourage *expanding* the circle of moral consideration? Where would this divine inspiration come from? From the facts on the ground.

Gods as Geopolitical Lubricant

Mesopotamia at the beginning of history was a melange of city-states. Most city-states had a central temple devoted to a single, dominant god—Enlil in Nippur, Enki in Eridu.[40] Occasionally a city had two major gods, as in Uruk, where An shared top billing with Inanna, his reliably gratifying consort.[41] Each temple also had its minor gods—the major gods' relatives, advisers, and other helpers.

These cities weren't yet unified under a single regional government. But by the beginning of the third millennium, they had come into contact with one another through some combination of trade and war. As mutual awareness dawned, they faced a question that has often faced states pushed together by a shrinking world: How would they feel about one another's gods? How would they handle competing claims about religious truth?

The answer, so far as we can tell, was: quite graciously, in part because they didn't see the claims as competitive. These people were polytheists. For a polytheist there is no limit on the number of possible gods and thus no natural compulsion, upon encountering another people, to contest the existence of their gods. What's more, if you have a fruitful relationship with those people—if you trade with them, or join them in military alliance—it might be worth your while to go beyond tolerance and actually affirm your belief in their gods. And maybe they'll reciprocate.

This is what seems to have happened in early Mesopotamia: the chief gods of the different cities coalesced into a regionally accepted pantheon. Indeed, it was not just a pantheon but a clan. The gods of different cities were related to each other by blood, and as the millennium wore on, the cities came to agree on the details of the family tree.[42]

There was a rough division of labor among the gods. One city's chief god represented the sun, another represented the power in grain, another (Inanna, naturally) represented love, and so on. Since everyone in Mesopotamia needed the sun, grain, and love, this meant that, as the archaeologist W. G. Lambert put it, "Each community depended for its livelihood on most, if not all, of the deities of the country."[43]

In short, as Mesopotamian cities became enmeshed in a web of reciprocal reliance—needing one another as trade partners and sometimes as military allies—this real-world interdependence was precisely reflected at the level of the divine. And, in this act of reflection, the gods had taken a step toward universalism, expanding their domain from a single city to Mesopotamia writ large. The grain god, however provincial it had once been, now cast its blessings on Mesopotamian grain in general. Religion sometimes seems like an impediment to international harmony in a shrinking world, but apparently it doesn't have to be.

Of course, we can describe all this more cynically. Suppose you are king of a city and you want to trade with another city's king. You know that his local stature is tied to the stature of his city's chief god; as king he maintains the god's temple, which is thus a kind of showcase for him as well as for the god. What's more, the temple's priests are major economic players, and may control some of the intercity trade you'd like a piece of. So the last thing you want to do is start disrespecting that god, and the first thing you want to do is embrace it. Thus theological open-mindedness can boil down to economic self-interest. Because both parties in a trade can benefit from it—because economic interaction is "non-zero-sum"—two once-alien gods may find common ground. So too with military alliance or any other non-zero-sum game that one king wants to play with another: interfaith harmony can emerge from enlightened self-interest.

This doesn't mean such harmony is a result of conscious calculation. Self-interest can bias our beliefs in subtle ways, and there is evidence that some ancient kings genuinely believed in the foreign gods they embraced. Nor does this mean that religious sentiment was a mere "epiphenomenon"—something that reflected political and economic reality and never influenced it. Early Mesopotamia, lacking unified governance, was bound by what Lambert calls a "unity of culture,"[44] and much of the unifying force of that culture probably came from the power of religious belief. In an age when people feared gods and desperately sought their favor, an intercity pantheon of gods that divided labor among themselves must have strengthened emotional bonds among cities. Whether or not you believe that the emotional power of religion truly emanates from the divine, the power itself is real.

Early International Law

Religion's role in easing relations among polities hasn't been confined to state-level societies. Polynesians sometimes voyaged abroad for ceremonies at "international" temples.[45] But it is when social evolution reaches the state level that gods start to sponsor something worthy of the name "international law." Here is an excerpt from a second-millennium BCE peace treaty between Egypt and the Hittites:

> He who shall not observe all these words written upon this silver tablet of the land of the Hatti and of the land of Egypt, may the thousand gods of the land of the Hatti and the thousand gods of the land of Egypt destroy his house, his country, and his servants...but he who shall keep these words which are on the tablet of silver, whether he be Hittite or Egyptian, and shall not neglect them, may the thousand gods of the land of the Hatti and the thousand gods of the land of Egypt make him to be in good health and long life, as also his houses, his country and his servants.

Even earlier, in the third millennium BCE, divinity and international law were intersecting in the Mesopotamian city-states. A clay cylinder describes the laying of a boundary marker between two Mesopotamian city-states, Lagash and Umma. "Enlil, the king of all the lands and the father of all the gods, marked out a boundary for the god of Lagash and the god of Umma by his decree. The king of Kish measured it out in accordance with the word of the god of legal settlements, and erected a stone boundary marker there."[46]

Divine authority wasn't always enough. In fact, this very decree was violated by the king of Umma, who was then punished by the army of Lagash (or, as the historical record has it, by the god of Lagash *through* the army of Lagash). But often these agreements were respected because an especially potent city-state assumed the job of arbiter and, if necessary, enforcer.[47] Here, again, divinity would evolve to reflect and reinforce geopolitical logic. The elevation of a city-state to regional hegemony generally meant the elevation of its god in the regional Mesopotamian pantheon.[48] So too on a more local level: a big city's deity would outrank the deities of outlying towns in its sphere of influence. As the archaeologists C. C. Lamberg-Karlovsky and Jeremy Sabloff have written, a "theologically informed ideal" sustained a "divinely sanctioned equilibrium" among Mesopotamian communities.[49]

"Divinely sanctioned equilibrium" has a nice sound to it, but there is a nasty underside. Mesopotamia's regional equilibrium rested on the shoulders of dominant city-states, which often established their dominance the old-fashioned way: by killing lots of people. War was a big part of life in the ancient world, and in allocating blame for it, we would be remiss in not mentioning the gods. As H. W. F. Saggs has observed, "everywhere the divine will was the formal justification for war."[50] And dominance, once established, didn't just mean selflessly assuming the burden of upholding regional equilibrium; it often meant exacting tribute from lesser states.

If there is any redeeming the ancient gods for the slaughter and extortion they sponsored, it lies in the breadth of the ensuing calm. The Mesopotamian equilibrium, even if punctuated by violent shifts of power, lubricated trade and other forms of contact, thus nurturing the sinews of practical interdependence that are often the leading edge of intercultural tolerance and divine universalism.

As the third millennium BCE passed, this approach to regional order—a loose league organized around a regional hegemon—would give way to something firmer: a regional state, centrally run. Like so much geopolitical change, this would come via conquest. And like much ancient conquest, it would wind up expanding the realm of potential interdependence.

It would also demonstrate anew the adaptive malleability of the divine. Just as the gods had evolved to sustain the loose unity of southern Mesopotamian city-states in the early third millennium

BCE, they would evolve to sponsor a broader Mesopotamian unity in the late third millennium BCE. And they would do so by virtue of something that may sound surprising: in the ancient world conquerors—the great ones, at least—were less inclined to smash the idols of their vanquished foes than to worship them.

Sargon Expands the Realm

Around 2350 BCE, Sargon of Akkade became Mesopotamia's first great conqueror. In trying to subjugate southern Mesopotamia from his base in the north, he was taking on a major challenge in multiculturalism. Southern Mesopotamia was ethnically and linguistically Sumerian, whereas Sargon was a foreigner who spoke Akkadian, a Semitic tongue. (Here "Semitic" means not Jewish, but rather belonging to the language family from which both Hebrew and Arabic evolved.)

Fortunately Sargon was a theologically flexible man. Though Akkadian gods had helped him subdue the Sumerians, this didn't mean the Sumerian gods were his enemies. In the city of Nippur, he got local priests to agree with him that his victory had been the will of the eminent Sumerian god Enlil (a judgment that may have been encouraged by the display of Nippur's deposed king in a neckstock).[51] There was also reassuring news for devotees of the Sumerian sky god An: Sargon, it turned out, was An's brother-in-law![52]

And then there was Sargon's elaborate courtship of the Sumerian goddess Inanna. Though she wasn't exactly known for resisting the entreaties of men, Sargon didn't take any chances. His eloquent daughter Enheduanna—whom he'd installed as a high priestess at Ur, a religious center of Sumeria—set about writing hymns in praise of Inanna. Enheduanna pulled out all the stops: "Great queen of queens, issued from the holy womb...omniscient sage...sustenance of the multitudes...senior queen of the heavenly foundations and zenith....How supreme you are over the great gods."[53]

But not so supreme that she got to keep her name. Ishtar was an Akkadian goddess of long standing, and Sargon, in affirming the divinely sanctioned unity of his Akkadian-Sumerian empire, asserted that Ishtar and Inanna were actually the same deity.[54] So why use two names? Hereafter Inanna, while retaining her essential traits, would be known as Ishtar.[55]

The melding of religious beliefs or concepts—"syncretism"—is a common way to forge cultural unity in the wake of conquest, and often, as here, what gets melded is the gods themselves. Of course, when two cultures fuse, some of their gods may not match up. Sumerian gods with no rough Akkadian counterpart entered Akkadian culture either under their Sumerian names (Enlil, for example) or some Akkadian variation thereon (An became Anu).[56] But one way or another, most gods of the vanquished Sumerians survived, either with their identities wholly intact or via fusion with an Akkadian god. This divine durability was common amid ancient warfare. (The Aztecs, who routinized conquest, built a special temple for imported gods.)[57] One scholar has said of the waves of invasion that swept the Middle East in the second millennium BCE, "Conquered gods rarely, if ever, were ousted."[58]

So too in the first millennium. Alexander the Great, in bringing much of the known world under Greek control, would extol the gods whose land he grabbed. And Alexander's native gods would receive the same pragmatic courtesy when Greece found itself on the other side of conquest. That's why you can map the Greek pantheon onto the Roman pantheon by changing the names—Aphrodite to Venus, Zeus to Jupiter, and so on. In the polytheistic ancient world, a savvy conqueror was a theologically flexible conqueror. Once the fighting is over, and you've got an empire to run, there's no sense starting needless squabbles.

You can look at the convenient malleability of polytheism in two ways. On the one hand, it was a handy tool for ruthless imperialists—an opiate, as Marx might say, of newly subdued masses. On the other hand, it was an elixir of intercultural amity. However ruthless the conquerors, however selfish their ambitions, in the long run they drew more and more peoples, over larger and larger areas, into economic and cultural exchange.

Sargon had carried Mesopotamia closer than ever to universalism, extending the reach of Sumerian gods beyond their southern homeland and across a cultural divide. This was still nothing like the simple, streamlined, monotheistic universalism that would eventually emerge in the Abrahamic lineage: one god that governs all of humankind. But even back in Mesopotamia in the third millennium BCE, when polytheism was demonstrating its geopolitical potential, there were forces moving theology closer to monotheism.

Toward Monotheism

All along, the tendency of the divine to track the political had applied not just to politics between Mesopotamian city-states but to politics within them. And within them, the political order was vertical. Unlike hunter-gatherer societies, the city-states had clear leadership. And, as in chiefdoms, the leadership was hierarchical — but more elaborately and bureaucratically so.

As on earth, so it is in heaven. Not only did the city-states and, later, the whole region, typically have a single, head god (sometimes a god that was *called* a king); this major god had subordinate gods that plainly reflected a royal court. A Mesopotamian document from the second millennium BCE lists gods with titles such as valet, head chef, head shepherd, gardener, ambassador, vizier, grand vizier, aide-de-camp, steward, secretary, sentinel, gatekeeper, bailiff, and hairdresser.[59] And a Mesopotamian narrative has Enki — himself a subordinate of the great Enlil — appointing one god "inspector of canals" and putting another in charge of justice.[60]

In Egypt, too, the pantheon developed some semblance of hierarchy.[61] And in China of the Shang era, the god of heaven seems to have run the show, supervising the gods of wind, of rain, of rivers, mountains, and so on.[62] But nowhere was the hierarchical tendency clearer than in Mesopotamia, or as well documented. There, as the historian Jean Bottero describes it, a "simple incoherent gathering" of gods, at the dawn of civilization, had become "through centuries of evolution, mythological reflections and calculations, a true organization of supernatural power...which dominated people as the structured earthly royal authority dominated its subjects."[63]

The resulting "pyramid of powers," as Bottero calls it, was itself a kind of step toward monotheism. Enlil, during his days at the top of the pyramid, was called "the great and powerful ruler who dominates Heaven and Earth, who knows all and understands all."[64] To be sure, such passages may overstate the consensus of the day: Mesopotamian writers, like writers in some other polytheistic societies, tend to exalt whichever god they happen to be addressing, somewhat as people focus their flattery on the person they're talking to. Still, there was a theological trend afoot, a trend toward concentrated majesty, and Enlil's successor as chief of the Mesopotamian pantheon would carry it to new heights, bringing Mesopotamia closer to modern western religious thought.

The One and Only Marduk

That successor was Marduk. Marduk was a formidable figure. For example, "His heart is a kettle-drum" and "His penis is a snake" that yields sperm made of gold.[65] But these testaments appear only after Marduk has achieved greatness, and he didn't do this by himself. A key supporter was the Babylonian king Hammurabi, who entered the scene in the early second millennium, centuries after the Akkadian empire established by Sargon had come and gone, in an age when Mesopotamia was again politically fragmented.

Hammurabi is famous for producing one of the first legal codes of the ancient world. Today law is sometimes thought of as an alternative to religion—secular rules of the road, enforced by police, with no need for supernatural support. But in ancient states, domestic law, like international law, drew strength from the gods.

For starters, Hammurabi was divinely authorized to make laws. As the opening passages of his law code note, Anu and Enlil, the two senior gods in the Mesopotamian pantheon, had chosen Hammurabi as king to "bring about the rule of righteousness in the land, to destroy the wicked and the evil-doers."[66] By the end of the code, some thirty gods have been cited,[67] and in some cases they play a judicial role—as when a suspect is thrown into a river to see if the river god will seize him, thus signifying guilt (posthumously).[68] But none of these gods gets the kind of treatment Marduk gets in the code's opening passages. There Anu and Enlil declare Marduk a "great" god and assign him "dominion over earthly man."[69]

What a fortuitous development for Hammurabi himself! Marduk was god of the city of Babylon, Hammurabi's base, and Hammurabi hoped to extend Babylon's control over all of Mesopotamia.[70] It couldn't hurt for Mesopotamia's greatest gods to roll out the red carpet and extend Marduk's domain well beyond the city limits. Even so, Hammurabi didn't reach his highest aspirations; he died without ever ruling all of Mesopotamia. But in ensuing centuries Babylon did dominate Mesopotamia, and, not coincidentally, Marduk eventually became head of the Mesopotamian pantheon, displacing Enlil.[71]

Marduk's champions didn't stop at claiming his supremacy. In a major theological development, the other gods of the pantheon were demoted from being Marduk's subordinates to being mere aspects of him. Thus Adad—once known as the god of rain—was now "Marduk of rain." Nabu, the god of accounting, became "Marduk of accounting."[72] Or, to look at things from Marduk's perspective, as another text did in addressing Marduk: "Nabu, holder of the tablet stylus, is your skill."[73] And so on, down the line; Mesopotamia's major gods got swallowed up by Marduk, one by one.

Scholars disagree over how big a step toward monotheism this was, and over its main cause.[74] Some explanations are in the spirit of Edward Tylor, who believed that the shift from polytheism to monotheism was part of a natural drift toward scientific rationalism. Thus, the series of Mesopotamian god-lists that impose growing hierarchy on the pantheon were not just reflections of hierarchical government, but fruits of the human quest for intellectual order and unity of explanation. When Marduk absorbed the functions of other gods, he became a kind of grand unified theory of nature.

In some scenarios, this intellectual drift was technologically abetted. If, for example, irrigation and new storage techniques and better state planning helped insulate humanity from the whims of nature, then the idea of a bunch of willful, unpredictable nature gods might seem less plausible.[75] And, though scientific inquiry didn't exactly shift into high gear in the ancient world, it may have started taking a bit of mystery out of the universe, further eroding the intellectual need for such gods. Mesopotamians long attributed lunar eclipse to demons, and would beat drums to disperse them, but then, during the first millennium BCE, Babylonian astronomer-priests found that eclipses were precisely predictable, demonic whims notwithstanding.[76] The hallowed drum-beating ritual lived on—but then again, so do many religious customs whose rationales have collapsed. (An early Scandinavian precursor of the Christmas tree was also a demon disperser.)

In contrast to these "intellectualist" explanations of the trend toward monotheism is the sheerly political explanation: For Babylonians bent on ruling Mesopotamia forever, what better theological weapon than to reduce Marduk's would-be rivals to parts of his anatomy? Or, to put it less cynically: For Babylonians who want to suffuse all of Mesopotamia in multicultural amity and understanding, what better social cement than a single god that encompasses all gods?

Whatever the explanation for the Mesopotamians' increasingly unified conception of the divine, the trend didn't carry the day. Marduk was eventually forced into a power-sharing arrangement with another major god. Still, it had been Mesopotamia's closest approach yet to a universalist monotheism. Indeed, the logic of the monotheism and of the universalism were intertwined. If the point of Marduk's evolution toward monotheism was political—to unify an ethnically diverse region—then presumably he would cast his net wide enough to encompass these ethnicities. And he sure did. According to the Mesopotamian classic *Epic of Creation*, he had "sovereignty over the whole world." And naturally so, since "He named the four quarters of the world; mankind he created."

There are hints that he not only ruled all of humankind, but was favorably disposed toward it: "Wide is his heart, broad is his compassion." (Although—make no mistake—he would "subdue the disobedient.")[77]

True Monotheism

Meanwhile, over in Egypt, a god had come even closer than Marduk to universalistic monotheism. His story illustrates how different the roads to monotheism can be.

Marduk's bid to become the one true god had been pursued with some grace and diplomatic tact. True, other gods in the pantheon had to submit to him and even eventually—as they say in the corporate world—merge with him on unfavorable terms. But he didn't deny their prior existence or their venerable legitimacy; indeed, he drew on their legitimacy. In the *Epic of Creation*, it is they who assemble at a feast and (after some heavy drinking) anoint him their new leader, vowing that "none among the gods shall transgress thy boundary."[78] Egypt's experiment with monotheism was more abrupt and involved less bonhomie. It was the divine equivalent of a coup d'état—and not a bloodless one.

The coup was engineered in the fourteenth century BCE by an enigmatic and eccentric pharaoh known as Amenhotep IV. Whether the pharaoh was driven more by religious zeal or political plotting depends on which scholar you talk to, but few deny the relevance of the political situation he inherited upon ascending the throne, or of the theology with which that situation was intertwined.

The theology had one hallmark of an emerging monotheism: the dominance of the divine firmament by a single god, Amun. Amun had grown in power after championing a series of Egyptian military campaigns and getting credit for the ensuing victories. Vast wealth and landholdings had flowed into Amun's temples—which meant, in practical terms, that the priests of Amun, who presumably had themselves favored these wars, were now powerful, overseeing a commercial empire involving mining, manufacturing, and trade.[79]

How serious a threat this conglomerate posed to the new pharaoh's power is unknown, but certainly a young man who assumed leadership upon the premature death of his father, as Amenhotep IV did, could be excused for feeling insecure.[80] The appellations that had been given to Amun—king of the gods, prince of princes—were not something he would have found reassuring. Nor was the occasional suggestion that Amun might not just outrank other gods but absorb them, Marduk style.[81]

In subduing Amun, the new pharaoh drew obliquely on the legacy of the venerable god Re. Re had at times been associated with a simple icon—a solar disc with two arms, known as Aten, which meant "disc."[82] The sun-disc, which seems originally to have represented Re's luminous energy, had subsequently carved out a role as an independent deity, and in fact had won the favor of the young pharaoh's father, Amenhotep III.[83] Now Amenhotep IV gave Aten a promotion, elevating him from garden-variety deity to "he who decrees life"; he who "created the earth"; he who "built himself by himself"; he whose "sunbeams mean sight for all that he has created."[84]

Did this mean that Aten was even greater than Amun? You might say. The pharaoh had Amun's name erased wherever it appeared. People with names containing "Amun" had to change them. And as for the once powerful high priest of Amun, his last known feat during Amenhotep IV's reign is being dispatched to fetch stone from a quarry.[85]

Amun was hardly alone in being targeted for extinction. The word "gods" was erased from some texts and its use discontinued, for now there was one true god.[86] The former gods weren't even extended the courtesy that Marduk had offered the Mesopotamian deities he supplanted—absorption into the newly supreme being; they were just said to have "ceased," and their priesthoods were dissolved.[87] The pharaoh built a big city in Aten's honor, named it Akhetaten ("Horizon of Aten"), and moved the capital there. He renamed himself Akhenaten ("Helper of Aten"), appointed himself Aten's high priest, declared himself Aten's son, and was praised accordingly: "O beautiful child of the Sun-disc"—a sun-disc that, the king's courtiers observed, "has exalted the name of no other king."[88]

Whereas Marduk, after absorbing Mesopotamia's major gods, had kept a few deities around as spouse and servants, Aten, at the height of his power, stood alone in the divine firmament, a clear foreshadowing of the Hebrew god, Yahweh. And as for Yahweh's famous universalism: Aten had created human beings, and he took care of them—*all* of them. As the Great Hymn to Aten put it:

You set every man in his place,
You supply their needs...
Their tongues are diverse in speech,
And their characters likewise;
Their skins are distinct,
For you have distinguished the peoples.[89]

Roots of Moral Progress

But this interracial universalism wasn't wholly new, and Aten doesn't deserve the lion's share of credit. Oddly, more credit should go to his deposed rival Amun. The wars sponsored by Amun had not only made his priests rich and thus threatened the pharaoh's power, but also, as wars of conquest often do, expanded economic and cultural horizons. From conquered territories came foreign slaves as well as foreign elites, who would receive an Egyptian education before returning home to help administer colonies. The Egyptian language absorbed foreign words, the economy foreign goods, and the pantheon foreign gods, just as Egyptian gods now moved into conquered lands.[90]

The new cosmopolitanism didn't magically erase the racism and xenophobia of Egypt's insular past, but it made a dent. While some foreign gods were adopted as sons or daughters by Egyptian gods, some foreign human beings, including slaves, married into Egyptian families and saw their socioeconomic status rise. Egyptian literature, which had once depicted alien lands as alienating and foreigners as contemptible, now featured Egyptian heroes who went abroad, married foreigners, and settled down.[91]

So Akhenaten, in making Aten the one true god not only of Egyptians, but of all humankind, was just reflecting his times. In the imperial Egypt of the day, observes Egyptologist Donald Redford, cosmopolitanism was in the air. "It was this universalist sentiment that Akhenaten fell heir to and developed within the context of his monotheism."[92] Indeed, it turns out that Aten's predecessor Amun had *also* created all humankind and defined the races.[93] One hymn spoke of his concern for the well-being of "Asiatics" (which meant Mesopotamians and others east of Egypt).[94] And, in a text probably composed before Akhenaten's time, an Egyptian god is said to "protect the souls" of the four known "races" of humankind: Asiatics, Egyptians, Libyans, and blacks (Nubians, to the south).[95] All four are depicted in the land of the dead, the "underworld," where they are promised a blessed afterlife.[96]

Egypt's empire wouldn't last forever, and cosmopolitanism would wax and wane. But the drift toward intercultural connection would continue, if fitfully, for it was driven ultimately by technological evolution. The same advances in transportation and communication that had made large empires feasible would, combined with advances in manufacture, bring more and more peoples into contact with one another. To be sure, the contact would often be hostile, and that hostility would be reflected in both religious doctrines and moral attitudes. In the century after Akhenaten's reign, an Egyptian poet has a warring king saying to Amun, the very god who had once fretted over the welfare of Asiatics: "What are these Asiatics to thee, Amun? Wretches that know not God."[97]

Still, by this time in the history of the ancient Middle East, two principles had revealed themselves.

First, the basic thrust of technological evolution would make it harder and harder to ignore the existence of other peoples. This long-run pattern is reflected in the evolution of the Egyptian language, as analyzed by the Egyptologist Siegfried Morenz. A word that in the mid-third millennium BCE meant "an Egyptian"—and was used to distinguish Egyptians from suspect and perhaps subhuman inhabitants of nearby lands—had by the mid-second millennium come to mean "a human being," and was being applied even to prisoners of war destined for slavery.[98]

Second, the relationship of your gods to the gods of other peoples would often depend on your economic and political relationship to those peoples. Trade and other relationships from which both parties can benefit—non-zero-sum relationships—could lead your god to care for their welfare, and might even lead you to embrace their gods; either way, a non-zero-sum relationship would likely involve your conceding the basic humanity of these people and extending them at least some moral consideration. Of course, war and other forms of antagonism could foster a theology of intolerance and a morality of indifference, or worse. If there is any redemption for war, it lies in what sometimes followed, as a conqueror now drew diverse lands into an economic and political whole, and theology and morality expanded accordingly. On balance, through the rhythm of trade and war, the scope of non-zero-sumness grew. This boded well for the expansion of the circle of moral consideration.

So what became of Aten, who in the fourteenth century BCE was the clearest example of universalist monotheism to date? Within decades of his promotion to one-and-only god, he would fall from grace. Apparently, alienating the most powerful priests in Egypt was not a recipe for eternal life. Even if you're a god, you'll need well-placed terrestrial allies to pull off such a social revolution. With the death of Akhenaten, Aten lost his least dispensable friend.

Some people claim that Aten nonetheless changed the world forever. Sigmund Freud, in his book *Moses and Monotheism*, suggested that Moses was in Egypt during Aten's reign and then carried this idea of monotheism toward Canaan, where it would launch Judeo-Christian civilization.

As we'll see, this isn't the most plausible explanation for monotheism's emergence in ancient Israel. Indeed, it turns out that Marduk had more to do with that emergence than Aten. Many centuries after Marduk failed to carry Middle Eastern civilization over the threshold to lasting monotheism, he helped *push* Middle Eastern civilization over that threshold. He would confront and defeat, even humiliate, a god of ancient Israel, and the Israelites would respond by creating a monotheism of their own.

II

THE EMERGENCE OF ABRAHAMIC MONOTHEISM

For who in the skies can be compared to the Lord? Whom among the heavenly beings is like the Lord, a God feared in the council of the holy ones, great and terrible above all that are round about him?

—Psalm 89:6

There is no other god besides me, a righteous God and a Savior; there is no one besides me. Turn to me and be saved, all the ends of the earth! For I am God, and there is no other. By myself I have sworn, from my mouth has gone forth in righteousness a word that shall not return: "To me every knee shall bow, every tongue shall swear."

—Isaiah 45:21–3

Chapter Five

Polytheism, the Religion of Ancient Israel

The Hebrew Bible—what Christians call the Old Testament—records a memorable experience that the prophet Elijah had on Mount Sinai. God had told Elijah to stand there and wait for an encounter with the divine. Then "there was a great wind, so strong that it was splitting mountains and breaking rocks in pieces before the LORD, but the LORD was not in the wind; and after the wind an earthquake, but the LORD was not in the earthquake; and after the earthquake a fire, but the LORD was not in the fire; and after the fire a sound of sheer silence."[1] These last few words—"a sound of sheer silence"—are sometimes translated as "a still small voice." But, either way, you get the picture: the Hebrew god, Yahweh, for all the atmospherics surrounding him, was elusive.

This episode, from the first book of Kings, is often cited as a landmark in the history of religion. In "primitive" polytheism, the forces of nature may be inhabited by the gods, or loosely equated with them. But in the monotheism that was taking shape in the Middle East, there would be more distance between nature and divinity. "Unlike the pagan deities, Yahweh was not in any of the forces of nature but in a realm apart," wrote Karen Armstrong about Elijah's peak experience in her book *A History of God*.[2]

The Bible's classic pagan deity was Baal, worshipped by the much-derided Canaanites and, at times, by deluded Israelites who had strayed from devotion to Yahweh. Baal, as a fertility god, was sometimes called the Lord of Rain and Dew.[3] Yahweh, in contrast, was the Lord of nothing in particular — and of everything; he was the ultimate source of nature's power, but he didn't micromanage it; he was as much chairman of the board as chief executive.

This kind of god is often described as more modern than pagan, Baal-like gods, more compatible with a scientific worldview. After all, looking for mechanistic laws of nature wouldn't make much sense if, as the pagans of Elijah's day believed, nature was animated by the ever changing moods of various gods. There's more room for scientific principles to hold sway if there's just one god, sitting somewhere above the fray — capable of intervening on special occasions, maybe, but typically presiding over a universe of lawful regularity.

"Transcendent" is a term some scholars use to describe this god, while others prefer "remote" or "hidden."[4] In any event, this is a god that, while less conspicuous than the pagan gods, is more powerful. As the biblical scholar Yehezkel Kaufmann put it in his monumental eight-volume work *History of Israelite Religion*, "Yahweh does not live in the processes of nature; he controls them."[5]

Kaufmann, writing in the middle of the twentieth century, saw this and other distinctive traits of Yahweh as evidence that the Hebrew god had been more revolutionary than evolutionary. He rejected the idea that Israelite religion was "an organic outgrowth of the religious milieu" of the Middle East. Rather, the religion of Yahweh was "an original creation of the people of Israel. It was absolutely different from anything the pagan world ever knew."[6]

Whether Yahweh indeed took shape in such splendid isolation — and whether he took shape as early as Kaufmann and other traditionalists would have it — is an issue to which we'll return. Meanwhile, it's important to stress that, however "modern" this "transcendent" god may have been, the Yahweh of Elijah's time still didn't possess what many people would call a modern *moral* sensibility. For example, he wasn't very tolerant of alternative theological perspectives. In that episode in First Kings, God uses his "still small voice" to instruct Elijah on how to get every Baal worshipper in the vicinity killed. Then, a chapter later, after some Syrians express doubt about the Hebrew god's power, Yahweh underscores their confusion by producing 127,000 dead Syrians.[7] This god may have spoken softly, but he carried a big stick.

This is of course a common complaint about the monotheism that emerged in the Middle East—that its theology bred belligerent intolerance. Some even see this as an intrinsic property of monotheism; whereas polytheism leaves room for the validity of other peoples' gods, ardent monotheists, according to this indictment, are allergic to peaceful coexistence.

If that's true, it's momentously unfortunate. Christians and Muslims, like Jews, trace their god back to the god that, according to the Bible, revealed himself to Abraham in the second millennium BCE. These three Abrahamic religions have more than three billion adherents, a little over half of the world's population. And, though all three groups claim the same lineage for their god, they don't always see each other as *worshipping* the same god. This perception seems to have lubricated a certain amount of Yahweh-on-Yahweh violence (Crusades, jihads, and so on) that has only reinforced Abrahamic monotheism's reputation for belligerent intolerance.

So is it true? Is violence part of the character of the Abrahamic god? Is there something about this god—or something about monotheism generically—that has been conducive to slaughter through the ages? The first step in answering that question is to see how the Abrahamic god's character took shape.

You might think this is impossible. If, like me, you grew up with a Sunday school understanding of the scriptures, then you think of God as not having "taken shape" at all. He was there in the beginning, fully formed, and he then gave form to everything else. That's the story in the Bible, at least. What's more, serious scholars, including Yehezkel Kaufmann and many he influenced, have analyzed the Bible and come away with a similarly dramatic account of Yahweh's birth.[8]

But, this isn't really the story in the Bible, or at least not the whole story. If you read the Hebrew Bible carefully, it tells the story of a god in evolution, a god whose character changes radically from beginning to end.

There's a problem, however, if you want to watch this story unfold. You can't just start reading the first chapter of Genesis and plow forward, waiting for God to grow. The first chapter of Genesis was almost certainly written later than the second chapter of Genesis, by a different author.[9] The Hebrew Bible took shape slowly, over many centuries, and the order in which it was written is not the order in which it now appears. Fortunately, biblical scholarship can in some cases give us a pretty good idea of which texts followed which. This knowledge of the order of composition is a kind of "decoder" that allows us to scc a pattern in God's growth that would otherwise be hidden.

Meanwhile, archaeology has supplemented this decoder with potent interpretive tools. In the early twentieth century, a Syrian peasant plowed up remnants of an ancient Canaanite city called Ugarit. Scholars set about deciphering the Ugaritic language and combing the earth for Ugaritic texts. These texts, along with other vestiges of Canaanite culture unearthed in recent decades, have allowed the assembly of something notably absent from the Hebrew scriptures: the story from the point of view of those Baal-worshipping Canaanites.[10] And, over the past few decades, archaeology has brought another check on the story as told in the Bible. Excavations in the land of the Israelites have clarified their history, sometimes at the expense of the biblical story line.

When you put all this together—a reading of the Canaanite texts, a selective "decoding" of the biblical texts, and a new archaeological understanding of Israelite history—you get a whole new picture of the Abrahamic god. It's a picture that, on the one hand, absolves Abrahamic monotheism of some of the gravest charges against it, yet on the other hand, challenges the standard basis of monotheistic faith. It's a picture that renders the Abrahamic god in often unflattering terms, yet charts his maturation and offers hope for future growth. And certainly it's a picture very different from the one drawn in the average synagogue, church, or mosque.

God in the Flesh

For starters, though Yahweh may have wound up "in a realm apart"—a remote, even transcendent God, whose presence is felt subtly—this is not the kind of god that comes across in the earliest scriptures, fragments of the Bible that may go back as far as the closing centuries of the second millennium BCE. In fact, even in the first millennium BCE, when most if not all of Genesis took shape, God was a hands-on deity. He personally "planted" the Garden of Eden, and he "made garments of skins" for Adam and Eve "and clothed them." And he doesn't seem to have done these things while hovering ethereally above the planet. After Adam and Eve ate the forbidden fruit, according to Genesis, "they heard the sound of the LORD God walking in the garden at the time of the evening breeze, and the man and his wife hid themselves from the presence of the LORD God among the trees of the garden." Hiding may sound like a naïve strategy to deploy against the omniscient God we know today, but apparently he wasn't omniscient back then. For "the LORD God called to the man, and said to him, 'Where are you?' " [11]

In short, Yahweh is at this point remarkably like all those "primitive" gods of hunter-gatherer societies and chiefdoms: strikingly human—with supernatural power, to be sure, but not with infinite power.

It may seem strange that the God who created the whole universe would be limited in his range. But it isn't clear that the God who is "walking" through the Garden of Eden *did* create the universe. True, he created the earth and sky, and he created human beings (out of dust). But the part about creating stars and the moon and the sun and light itself—the story in the first chapter of Genesis—seems to have been added later. In the beginning, so far as we can tell, Yahweh was not yet a *cosmic* creator.

And if you go back to the poems that most scholars consider the oldest pieces of the Bible, there's no mention of God creating *anything*. He seems more interested in destroying; he is in large part a warrior god.[12] What some believe to be the oldest piece of all, Exodus 15, is an ode to Yahweh for drowning Egypt's army in the Red Sea. It begins, "I will sing to the LORD, for he has triumphed gloriously; horse and rider he has thrown into the sea... the LORD is a warrior." [13]

If Yahweh starts life as a warrior god, not a CEO, much less chairman of the board, who is running the universe? The answer seems to be that various other gods were. Back then polytheism reigned. The point here isn't just that some Israelites worshipped gods other than Yahweh; that much has long been clear to even the casual Bible reader. (Much of the Bible's plotline can be summarized as: Israelites fall for non-Yahweh gods, Yahweh punishes them, Israelites mend their ways, only to stray again from fidelity, get punished again, and so on.) The point, rather, is that even Israelites who *didn't* worship gods other than Yahweh still believed in their existence. Early affirmations of devotion to Yahweh don't single him out for being the only god, just for being the best god for the Israelites, the one you should worship. That ancient hymn to Yahweh, "man of war," asks this question: "Who is like thee, O LORD, among the gods?" [14] Indeed, the Bible sometimes mentions other gods matter-of-factly. In the book of Numbers, for example, when the Moabites are conquered, it says that their god Chemosh "has made his sons fugitives, and his daughters captives." [15]

And when the Bible doesn't note the existence of other gods, it may imply as much. The scriptures warn Israelites not to "serve other gods and bow down to them" lest "the anger of the LORD will be kindled against you." [16] Would the Bible's authors (here and elsewhere) have warned against "serving" other gods if those gods didn't even exist? And would Yahweh have declared himself "a jealous god" if there were no gods to be jealous of? Apparently God himself didn't start life as a monotheist. Even God's most famous demand for devotion—"You shall have no other gods before me," as he puts it in Exodus—hardly excludes the existence of other gods.[17]

In other words, before Israelite religion denied the existence of all gods other than Yahweh, it went through a phase of granting their existence but condemning their worship (by Israelites, at least; if the Moabites wanted to worship Chemosh, that was their business).[18] In technical terms, Israelite religion reached monotheism only after a period of "monolatry"—exclusive devotion to one god without denying the existence of others.

This much is accepted by most biblical scholars, including some who are believing Jews or Christians. But things get more controversial when you suggest that there was a long time when even "monolatry" was too strong a word for mainstream Israelite doctrine—a time when not all non-Yahweh gods were considered evil or alien; a time when Yahweh was ensconced in an Israelite pantheon, working alongside other gods.

Yet if you read the scriptures closely, you'll see hints of such a time. The Bible famously says that God "created man in his own image," but those aren't Yahweh's words. When Yahweh is actually quoted, in the previous verse, he says, "Let us make man in our image, after our likeness."[19] Then when Adam eats the forbidden fruit, Yahweh says, "Behold, the man has become like one of us, knowing good and evil." When people start building the Tower of Babel, which will reach to the heavens, and Yahweh opts for preemptive intervention, he says, "Come, let us go down, and there confuse their language, that they may not understand one another's speech."[20]

Us? Who is us? If you ask this question of some Jewish or Christian clergy, you may get such answers as "angels" or "the heavenly host, God's army." In other words, Yahweh may be accompanied by other supernatural beings, but none of them qualify as gods.[21] The Bible says otherwise. It talks more than once about a "divine council" in which God takes a seat; and the other seats don't seem to be occupied by angels. Psalm 82 says: "God has taken his place in the divine council; in the midst of the gods he holds judgment." And God himself, addressing the other council members a few verses later, says, "You are gods."[22]

The many biblical references to the existence of multiple gods are in a sense amazing. For, though the Bible was *composed* over many centuries, the earliest parts of it passed through the hands of later editors who decided which books and verses to keep and which to discard—and who seem to have had a bias against polytheism. So those hints of Israelite polytheism that remain in the Bible are probably, as the scholar Mark S. Smith suggested in his book *The Origins of Biblical Monotheism*, "only the tip of the iceberg." [23]

What did the iceberg, the full-blown polytheism of early Israel, look like? And how exactly did it melt away, leaving the monotheism that would have such impact on the world? This is a good time to turn to archaeology. Over the past century, artifacts unearthed in the Holy Land have clarified the biblical story. In fact, "clarified" is a euphemism. The story as told in the Bible has in some cases been obliterated by the facts in the ground.

Bible Stories Unearthed

The standard biblical version of early Israelite history is simple: the Israelites escape slavery in Egypt, wander in the desert, and finally arrive at the promised land, Canaan. The natives—the Canaanites—are a wicked and doomed people, on the wrong side of theology and therefore of history. The Israelites march in, conquer the city of Jericho with Yahweh's help, and then do likewise with a series of Canaanite cities. So much for these Canaanites; as the book of Joshua puts it, "Joshua defeated the whole land, the hill country and the Negeb and the lowland and the slopes, and all their kings; he left none remaining, but utterly destroyed all that breathed, as the LORD God of Israel commanded." [24] This scenario nicely fits the views of Yehezkel Kaufmann and other scholars who deny that Israelite religion evolved organically out of the local milieu. The swifter and more decisive Israel's conquest of Canaan, the less chance there was for native culture to take hold.

At first, modern archaeology seemed to support Kaufmann here. William Foxwell Albright, a contemporary of Kaufmann's who is sometimes called the founder of biblical archaeology, certainly suggested as much. In his book *From the Stone Age to Christianity*, published in 1940, he said that artifacts unearthed in the Holy Land painted a clear picture: Israelites had marched into Canaan from Egypt and "proceeded without loss of time to destroy and occupy Canaanite towns all over the country," quickly replacing indigenous paganism with a radically different Yahwism.[25]

And it was a good thing, too, in Albright's view, for otherwise Canaanite paganism would "almost inevitably have depressed Yahwistic standards to a point where recovery was impossible." Instead, "the Canaanites, with their orgiastic nature-worship, their cult of fertility in the form of serpent symbols and sensuous nudity, and their gross mythology, were replaced by Israel, with its pastoral simplicity and purity of life, its lofty monotheism, and its severe code of ethics."[26]

Albright allowed more in the way of local evolutionary influence than Kaufmann did.[27] Still, he stressed, "excavations show a most abrupt break" between the Canaanite culture first encountered by the Israelites and the culture they built in Palestine near the end of the second millennium BCE.[28]

Albright was a devout Christian and Kaufmann a devout Jew, facts that may be related to their views of Israelite history. In any event, their views now lack foundation. Recent decades of archaeological research—including painstaking excavation of various cities supposedly conquered by the Israelites—have failed to turn up the hallmarks of violent conquest. There isn't even much evidence of a slower, more peaceful influx of desert wanderers, a gradual displacement of Canaanites by Israelites. In fact, it looks more and more as if the Israelites *were* Canaanites. Biblical archaeologists disagree about a lot, but, as one of them, William G. Dever, has observed, there is now consensus on one thing: the Israelites who first settled in the highlands of Canaan "were not foreign invaders, but came mostly from somewhere within Canaanite society.... The only remaining question is *where* within Canaan."[29]

Perhaps the most intriguing theory of how the Canaanites became Israelites comes from the iconoclastic archaeologist Israel

Finkelstein, who has excavated many Holy Land sites.[30] His theory preserves the Bible's notion of an Israelite transition from nomadic herders to settled farmers, but leaves little else of the biblical story intact.

Finkelstein notes that in the twelfth century BCE, as the Bronze Age was giving way to the Iron Age, there was political and economic disruption, even collapse, across the Middle East. This would have been bad news for any nomadic Canaanite herders who were symbiotically intertwined with farmers in Canaanite villages and cities, accustomed to trading meat for grain. With the disruption of their markets, they might have been forced to give up their nomadic ways: settle down and grow their own crops even as they continued to raise livestock.

And indeed, amid this transitional chaos, Finkelstein notes, a wave of new settlements appeared on previously barren stretches of hill country in central Canaan. These settlements are oval-shaped—the shape in which Middle Eastern sheepherders have long arranged their tents, forming a courtyard that housed their animals at night. But instead of tents there are simple walled homes, and unlike nomadic herders, these people had rudimentary farming tools. They seem to be in flux, shifting from a nomadic to a sedentary life, now raising not just livestock but crops.

During this transition from the Bronze to Iron Ages, new settlements arose well beyond the land that would eventually constitute Israel, in the areas the Bible calls Moab, Ammon, and Edom. But, Finkelstein notes, there is one difference: the settlements in Israel feature no remains of pigs. One part of the Bible, at least, seems to have been accurate: the early Israelites were enjoined from eating pork. This swath of pigless villages is the earliest archaeological evidence in Canaan of a distinct group of people that can be called Israelite.

In Finkelstein's scenario, then, the biblical story is inverted. Though there was indeed social disruption in Canaan near the end of the second millennium BCE, this was the *cause* of Israel's emergence, not the result of it. And as for the business about Moses leading Hebrews out of bondage: "There was no mass Exodus from Egypt," Finkelstein writes.[31]

Finkelstein's theory hasn't won universal assent.[32] Some scholars, for example, think the early Israelites migrated to the hill country from Canaanite villages and cities, rather than just settling down on land they had long roamed as nomads. And even if most early Israelites descended from a long line of Canaanites, they may have absorbed a tribe of exiles from Egypt (a possibility that Finkelstein's basic model doesn't rule out). Still, it now seems clear that the story in the book of Joshua—sudden displacement of Canaanite culture by Israelite culture—is wrong.[33] Long after the first good evidence of a distinct Israelite people, there was ongoing contact with Canaanite culture broadly. Various data, including a lack of fortifications and weapons in those early villages, suggests the contact was often peaceful.[34] In fact, one of those early Israelite settlements illustrates the cultural continuity between Canaan and Israel that Kaufmann and Albright minimized. It features a bronze bull, exactly the kind of "Canaanite" idol that biblical devotees of Yahweh abhorred.[35]

Of course, it wouldn't come as news to Kaufmann or Albright that Israelites sometimes worshipped Canaanite idols. The Bible shows them doing that repeatedly, and paying the price. But in the biblical story, as commonly interpreted, these episodes are temporary departures from the true ancient faith, lapses from a monotheism that must have predated those earliest Israelite villages, since it had, after all, been carried toward Canaan by Moses. Indeed, both Kaufmann and Albright traced monotheism back to the time of Moses, near the end of the second millennium BCE.[36] But some biblical historians now doubt that Moses even existed, and virtually none now believe that the biblical accounts of Moses are reliable. These stories were written down centuries after the events they describe, and were edited later still, sometimes by monotheists who presumably wanted to suffuse their theology with august authority.

Who Was Yahweh Before He Was Yahweh?

From an objective standpoint, then, there is no reason to assume that the advent of Israelite monotheism took place anywhere other than Canaan, after centuries of immersion in Canaanite culture; no reason to doubt that Israelite religion is exactly the kind of organic outgrowth of the local culture that Kaufmann and Albright said it wasn't. It's even possible that Yahweh, who spends so much of the Bible fighting against those nasty Canaanite gods for the allegiance of Israelites, actually started life as a Canaanite god, not an import.

The test of this evolutionary hypothesis — or at least the first test of it — is whether it is illuminating. Does it help clear up murky parts of Yahweh's history? If we examine the Bible's scattered, cryptic clues about Yahweh's origins in light of it, do they then appear less jumbled, more coherent? The answer is yes.

Consider the "divine council" that seems at odds with the basic theology of the Bible, and yet turns up in the Bible more than once.[37] As we've seen, various ancient states, such as Egypt and China, seem to have modeled their pantheons at least partly on governmental structures. And Mesopotamia featured, more specifically, a deliberative assembly of gods — a council. Given that Mesopotamia is in the general vicinity of Canaan, it wouldn't be shocking to find some such assembly in the early Canaanite tradition.

And, indeed, that's what we find in Ugarit, the ancient city in northern Canaan whose translated texts have so illuminated the context of Israelite religion. There, at the end of the Bronze Age, on the eve of Israel's birth, is a divine council. And the god most often depicted as its chief — a god named El (pronounced *ale* or *el*) — bears a curious resemblance to Yahweh.[38] Both gods were strong yet sensitive. El was seen as a "bull," yet was also called "Kind El, the compassionate."[39] Similarly, Yahweh, even in that early appearance as a warrior god, was driven by his compassion for the Israelites — "thy steadfast love" for "the people whom thou hast redeemed."[40] Both gods appeared in dreams, became the patrons of the dreamers, and spoke often through prophets.[41] And both were paternalistic creator gods: El was "creator of creatures" and "father of humanity."[42] As Smith has put it, El was "the divine father par excellence."[43]

The literal meaning of the Ugaritic term for the Canaanite "divine council" is, not surprisingly, "Council of El." A bit more surprising is that if you peer beneath English versions of the Bible and examine the Hebrew rendering of the "divine council" on which God sits in Psalm 82, you find this phrase: *adat El*—which can be translated as "Council of El."[44] Hmmm.

And that's just the beginning. It turns out that if you peer beneath the English word "god" in some parts of the Bible, you will find not the Hebrew word for Yahweh, but rather the Hebrew word *El*. Given that the Canaanite El appears on the historical record before the Israelite god Yahweh, it is tempting to conclude that Yahweh in some way emerged from El, and may even have started life as a renamed version of El.

There is cause for at least preliminary resistance to that temptation: the Hebrew word *El* is like the English word "god"—it can refer either to deities in general ("Hermes, a god of ancient Greece") or to a particular deity (God with an uppercase *G*). The difference is that ancient Hebrew didn't use the uppercase/lowercase convention to keep things clear. So you can't infer, every time you see the Hebrew god called El, that his *name* is El.

Still, there are a few times in the Bible when the "El" applied to the Hebrew god indeed seems to be a proper noun. According to Genesis, Jacob "erected an altar and called it El-Elohe-Israel." This could be translated as "god, the god of Israel," but if you don't capitalize the first "god" it doesn't make much sense; it would be like dedicating an altar to "deity, the deity of Israel."[45] In other words, the first "god" has to be a *specific* god, and the specific god named El that we know of in that part of the world was head of the pantheon in northern Canaan. (Indeed, some English translations of Genesis render "El-Elohe-Israel" unabashedly as "El, God of Israel.")[46] If that's not a close enough link between Israelite religion and El, look at the word "Israel" itself.[47] In ancient times names were often inspired by gods, and names ending in "el" typically referred to the god El.

An especially intriguing biblical appearance of the word *El* is in the phrase *El Shaddai*, famously rendered in English as "God Almighty." As it turns out, "Almighty" is a mistranslation; though the exact meaning of *Shaddai* remains cloudy, it seems to refer to mountains, not omnipotence—but that's another story.[48] For present purposes, what's interesting is the way this name is used in the sixth chapter of Exodus, during one of Moses's conversations with God. God says, "I am Yahweh. I appeared to Abraham, to Isaac, and to Jacob as El Shaddai, but by my name Yahweh I did not make myself known to them." Even Yahweh himself says that he started life with the name El![49]

Of course, Yahweh doesn't explicitly say he started life as the *Canaanite* god El. And at the time he is speaking, the Israelites (in the Bible's telling of the story) haven't yet gotten to Canaan. But this story may have entered Israel's historical narrative much later than it is said to have happened. And if there is one lesson of modern biblical scholarship, it's that stories often say more about the era of their creation than about the era they claim to describe.

So what does Exodus 6 suggest about the era of its creation? If you were crafting a history of your god, why would you add such an odd twist, saying that he used to go by another name? Theories abound. One is this: you are trying to meld two religious traditions; you are trying to convince two groups of people—one that worships a god called Yahweh and another that worships a god called El—that they actually worship the same god.[50]

Supporters of this theory sometimes invoke a pattern in the Bible that was famously emphasized by the nineteenth-century scholar Julius Wellhausen. According to Wellhausen's "documentary hypothesis," the early phases of the biblical narrative—from creation through the time of Moses—come largely from two authors (or two groups of like-minded authors), one known as the J source and one known as the E source. The E source refers to the Hebrew god as either El or Elohim (hence the E). The J source refers to the Hebrew god as Yahweh (and is known as J because of the way Yahweh is spelled in German, the language of much pioneering biblical scholarship, including Wellhausen's).

The documentary hypothesis suggests that at some point in Israelite history there were indeed two geographically distinct traditions to reconcile, one worshipping a god named El and one worshipping a god named Yahweh.[51] Adherents of this scenario say the J author(s) lived in the south, in the part of Israel known as Judah, and the E author(s) lived to the north — which, notably, is closer to the heartland of El worship.[52]

Wellhausen's scheme doesn't enjoy the near universal esteem it had in the mid-twentieth century,[53] but there's no denying that the Bible features different vocabularies for Israel's god. And if indeed the Hebrew god was the result of a merger — perhaps between a faction whose main deity was a creator god named El and another faction that worshipped a war god named Yahweh[54] — this would be nothing new. As we've seen, the ancient world was full of politically expedient theological fusions. A common catalyst was that the two parties had a somewhat non-zero-sum relationship. Specifically: both felt they could get more from cooperation, even consolidation, than from conflict.

Certainly the Bible holds hints of once separate groups having united. It describes Israel at the end of the late second millennium BCE, before it evolved into a state-level society complete with a king, as a confederation of twelve tribes. In the Bible's earliest list of tribes, however, some of the twelve are nowhere to be found. The missing tribes are southern; apparently the tribes that constituted Israel at this early date were in northern Canaan, where worship of El would be most likely.[55] Hence, perhaps, the name Israel.

The merging of Israel's tribes may be dimly reflected in the story of the patriarchs — Abraham who begat Isaac who begat Jacob. Few scholars think this lineage is accurate, but most think it is significant. Many buy some variation on a theory put forth in 1930 by the German scholar Martin Noth: the different patriarchs had once been sacred ancestors, real or mythological, of different tribes; one tribe or group of tribes claimed Abraham as founding father, another claimed Isaac, another Jacob. Politically unifying these peoples meant weaving their founding myths into a single myth, and in the process weaving their forefathers into a single family.[56] That would explain why some presumably early accounts of the patriarchal lineage seem incomplete. In one verse in Deuteronomy, Abraham, who is identified with such southern towns as Hebron, isn't mentioned, whereas Jacob, from the north, is.[57]

This basic idea—that Israel coalesced somewhere around the land of El worship, and only adopted Yahweh later, while absorbing alien tribes from the south—gets a bit of support from ancient Egyptian inscriptions. The name "Israel" enters the historical record in 1219 BCE, on an Egyptian slab of stone known as the Merenptah Stele. The word refers to a people, not a place.[58] But these people seem to have been somewhere in Canaan, probably in the highlands of Ephraim—the northern part of what would ultimately become Israel.[59]

This stele makes no mention of Yahweh. Its only possible allusion to any god is the "el" in Israel. And centuries will pass before a text mentions both Israel and "Yhwh" (the ancient spelling of Yahweh, back before western Semitic languages were written with vowels). Intriguingly, though, there are separate Egyptian references to a "Yhw" even earlier than that first reference to Israel.[60] Here Yhw seems to be not a god, but a place. Then again, in ancient times, places and gods sometimes had the same name.[61] Moreover, the place seems to have been somewhere around Edom, in southern Canaan, as would make sense if indeed a Yahweh-worshipping people from the south eventually merged with an El-worshipping people to the north.

This piece fits into the puzzle in another way, too. The full inscription reads "Yhw [in] the land of the Shasu."[62] The Shasu were nomads who had a history of antagonism with Egypt—just what you'd expect if antagonism with Egypt was central to their chief god's biography. One ancient Egyptian relief even shows people labeled Shasu being brought in as captives by Egyptian soldiers.[63]

That earliest reference to Israel, in the Merenptah Stele, is a boast that Egypt has exterminated the Israelites. (Israel's "seed is not.")[64] This would prove a considerable underestimation of Israel's regenerative powers, and, more to the point, suggests that a merger of the Shasu and the Israelites would have made political sense. A common enemy is a great starter of friendships. (To put it more technically: the common enemy makes the friendship more non-zero-sum, since an external threat raises the mutual benefits of internal cooperation and the mutual costs of internal discord.) And this particular common enemy would of course conduce to the crafting of a shared narrative of divine deliverance from Egyptian torment.[65]

Lost in Translation

That moment in Exodus 6 is strangely abrupt: God just announces that he's changing his name from El Shaddai to Yahweh. It isn't impossible that a theological merger could happen this quickly; in ancient Mesopotamia (back in chapter 4) Sargon changed Inanna's name to Ishtar by fiat. But that was a case of radically unequal power; Sargon had just conquered Inanna's worshippers. And there's no archaeological evidence of a comparable dominance of northern Israel by southern Israel at the end of the second millennium BCE or the beginning of the first. If anything, the evidence has moved in the other direction, suggesting that biblical accounts exaggerate early southern strength—that, indeed, the southern part of Israel may have been the weaker part during the first two centuries of the first millennium.[66]

So if there was some fusion of northern and southern religion near the beginning of the first millennium BCE, you would expect it to be more gradual than a sudden displacement of El by Yahweh. You'd expect something like the convergence of Sumerian city-states back before Sargon's time, in the third millennium BCE. As these polities grew intertwined, their gods joined a collective pantheon, with the most powerful city-state's main god getting a commensurately exalted place in the pantheon. In the case of ancient Israel, this would suggest an early period of coexistence for El and Yahweh. And if indeed wandering tribes from the south joined an initially stronger northern confederation, the coexistence might be on unequal terms: Yahweh would be admitted to the pantheon of northern Canaan, but not at the top level, not on par with the great creator god El.

The Bible actually contains shards of evidence of such a time, but they're hard to find, because over the ages the Bible's editors and translators haven't exactly taken pains to highlight them. Quite the contrary. Consider this innocent-sounding verse from the thirty-second chapter of Deuteronomy as rendered in the King James Version, published in 1611:

> When the Most High divided to the nations their inheritance, when he separated the sons of Adam, he set the bounds of the people according to the number of the children of Israel.
>   For the LORD's portion *is* his people; Jacob *is* the lot of his inheritance.[67]

This verse, though a bit obscure, seems to say that God — called the "Most High" in one place and "the LORD" in another — somehow divided the world's people into groups and then took an especially proprietary interest in one group, Jacob's. But this interpretation rests on the assumption that "Most High" and "the LORD" *do* both refer to Yahweh. Do they?

The second term — "the LORD" — definitely does; this is the Bible's standard rendering of the original Hebrew *Yhwh*. But might "Most High" — *Elyon* — refer to El? It's possible; the two words appear together — *El Elyon* — more than two dozen times in the Bible. What moves this prospect from possible toward probable is the strange story behind another part of this verse: the phrase "children of Israel."

The King James edition got this phrase from the "Masoretic Text," a Hebrew edition of the Bible that took shape in the early Middle Ages, more than a millennium after Deuteronomy was written. Where the Masoretic Text—the earliest extant Hebrew Bible—got it is a mystery. The phrase isn't found in either of the two much earlier versions of the verse now available: a Hebrew version in the Dead Sea Scrolls and a Greek version in the Septuagint, a pre-Christian translation of the Hebrew Bible.

Why would some editor have invented the phrase? Was something being covered up?

Some scholars who have used the Dead Sea Scrolls and the Septuagint to reconstruct the authentic version of the verse say that "children of Israel" was stuck in as a replacement for "sons of El."[68] With that lost phrase restored, a verse that was cryptic suddenly makes sense: El—the most high god, *Elyon*—divided the world's people into ethnic groups and gave one group to each of his sons. And Yahweh, one of those sons, was given the people of Jacob. Apparently at this point in Israelite history (and there's no telling how long ago this story originated) Yahweh isn't God, but just a god—and a son of God, one among many.[69]

So how does Yahweh rise through the ranks? How does a god initially consigned to a lower level of the pantheon eventually merge with the chief god, El, and even, in a sense, supplant him? To judge by other examples of divine upward mobility in the ancient world, one likely explanation would be a shift in the relative power of northern and southern Israel, of El's heartland and Yahweh's heartland. Such an increase in southern Israel's relative power may well have been under way during the eighth century BCE—and certainly it assumed dramatic form near the end of the century, when, as we'll see in the next chapter, the north fell to Assyrian conquest. It was after this consolidation of power in the south that most of the Hebrew Bible was written, so southern scribes who were champions of Yahweh would have had a chance to augment his stature, and to downplay a northern, El-ocentric perspective.[70]

It seems like a plausible scenario: El, a powerful god from the north, admits Yahweh to the lower levels of his pantheon by way of letting Yahweh's wandering people enter a political confederation — Israel — in a junior partnership with El's people; and ultimately it's Yahweh's name, not El's, that stays attached to Israel, thanks to a reversal of fortune: Yahweh's people get more powerful, while El's people get less so, and in fact encounter catastrophe.

But, however plausible this scenario may sound, it has problems. For example, if Jacob is associated with the north, and hence presumably with El prior to an El-Yahweh fusion, then why, in that verse from Deuteronomy, is Yahweh the god of Jacob's people, even as El seems to remain separate from Yahweh, at the top of the pantheon? Wouldn't Jacob have entered Yahweh's fold only after the Yahweh-El fusion?

There may be no reconstruction of Israel's early history that gracefully accounts for all the odd evidence, including the description of Yahweh as a son of *Elyon* in the undoctored version of Deuteronomy 32 and the fusing of Yahweh and El Shaddai in Exodus 6.[71] As we'll see in chapter 8, the solution may lie in focusing on Israel's later history, long after its tribal confederation had congealed, long after it had evolved into a full-fledged state, complete with a king.

Meanwhile, whatever the truth about Yahweh's early history, there is one thing we can say with some confidence: the Bible's editors and translators have sometimes obscured it — perhaps deliberately, in an attempt to conceal evidence of early mainstream polytheism.[72]

Yahweh's Sex Life (and Other Myths)

Still, enough remains visible to complicate the task of those who claim to see large and sharp differences between the Abrahamic god and other gods in the vicinity. One oft-claimed difference, for example, is that whereas the pagan gods had sex lives, Yahweh didn't. "Israel's God," as Kaufmann put it, "has no sexual qualities or desires."[73] It's true that there's no biblical ode to Yahweh that compares with the Ugaritic boast that Baal copulated with a heifer "77 times," even "88 times," or that El's penis "extends like the sea."[74] And it seems puzzling: If Yahweh eventually merged with El, and El had a sex life, why didn't the postmerger Yahweh have one? Why, more specifically, didn't Yahweh inherit El's consort, the goddess Athirat?

Maybe he did. There are references in the Bible to a goddess named Asherah, and scholars have long believed that Asherah is just the Hebrew version of Athirat.[75] Of course, the biblical writers don't depict Asherah as God's wife—this isn't the sort of theological theme they generally championed—but rather heap disdain on her, and on the Israelites who worshipped her. However, in the late twentieth century, archaeologists discovered intriguing inscriptions, dating to around 800 BCE, at two different Middle Eastern sites. The inscriptions were blessings in the name not just of Yahweh but of "his Asherah."[76] The word "his" puts a suggestive spin on a passage in 2 Kings reporting that, near the end of the seventh century, Asherah was spending time in Yahweh's temple. A priest who didn't favor polytheism "brought out the image of Asherah from the house of the Lord, outside Jerusalem, to the Wadi Kidron, burned it at the Wadi Kidron, beat it to dust and threw the dust of it upon the graves of the common people."[77] In the next chapter we'll see what a crucial moment in the evolution of monotheism this was.

The question of Yahweh's sex life is part of a larger question that has high stakes: How mythological was Yahweh? Not "mythological" in the sense of not being true, but rather in the sense that Greek gods were mythological: Were there stories about Yahweh's dramatic dealings with other extraordinary beings? Did he fight some gods or demigods and pal around with others? Was he part of a supernatural soap opera?

Many scholars have said no. Indeed, in Kaufmann's view, the "non-mythological" nature of Yahweh "is the essence of Israelite religion" and sets Israelite religion "apart from all forms of paganism," certainly including native Canaanite religion.[78]

There is doubly bad news for those who, like Kaufmann, would hail Yahweh as a clean break from pagan myth. First, there are signs that the break wasn't so clean—that, like so much else in the history of religion, it was more evolutionary than revolutionary. Second, when you try to trace this evolution, you see that Yahweh's family tree may contain something even more scandalous than an early fusion with the Canaanite deity El. It may be that Yahweh, even while inheriting El's genes, somehow acquired genes from the most reviled of all Canaanite deities: Baal.

Baal was of course immersed deeply in myth. He did battle with Yamm, the god of the sea, and Mot, the god of death. One Ugaritic text even says that he "smote Lotan," a seven-headed "dragon."[79] Talk about mythological!

Then again, the Bible pays this tribute to Yahweh: "You broke the heads of the dragons in the waters. You crushed the heads of Leviathan."[80] And the ancient Hebrew word underlying Leviathan—Livyaton—is, so far as we can tell, just Hebrew for "Lotan"; apparently Yahweh not only slew multiheaded dragons, but slew the very multiheaded dragon that Baal slew. That same chapter of Psalms credits Yahweh with subduing the sea.[81] Or, perhaps, Sea: some translators capitalize the word, because underlying it is *yam*, the ancient Hebrew word for the sea god that Baal smote.[82] The Bible also promises, in the book of Isaiah, that Yahweh will "swallow up death forever"—and underlying "death" is the Hebrew word for Mot, the god of death with whom Baal struggled dramatically.[83]

So why do English translations of the Bible say "sea" instead of "Yamm" and "death" instead of "Mot"? Ancient Hebrew didn't have capital letters. When you see the Hebrew word *mawet* in isolation, you can't say whether it is the proper noun meaning Mot or the generic noun meaning death. So the Bible's translators can take their pick, and as a rule they've picked generic nouns. But you have to wonder about this choice. In deciding whether Yahweh was "swallowing up" Mot or merely death, for example: surely it is no coincidence that in Canaanite mythology Mot was famous for "swallowing" people at the end of their lives and delivering them to "Sheol," the afterlife underworld — or that Mot had once swallowed Yahweh's rival, Baal.[84]

Or consider the Bible's puzzling reference to Yahweh's "wrath against the rivers" and his "rage against the sea."[85] Why would Yahweh be upset with rivers and sea? How could he blame water for flowing? Wouldn't these passages make more sense if the Hebrew words for "rivers" and "sea" (*nahar* and *yam*) were translated as Nahar and Yamm, the supernatural beings with whom Baal had fought in such mythological fashion?[86] (Perhaps feeling a pang of conscience, the translators of the New Revised Standard Version obscurely acknowledge this possibility, with fine-print footnotes that say "or *against River*" and "or *against Sea*.") The case for a mythological translation only grows when you see how Yahweh himself appears in these passages. He conquers the forces of nature in a chariot ("You trampled the sea with your horses"). He brandishes a bow and intimidates the moon and the sun with "the light of your arrows" and the "gleam of your flashing spear."[87]

These last two images are generally taken to refer to lightning,[88] and here lies yet another blurring of the line between the myths of those pagan Canaanites and the religion of ancient Israel: Yahweh, in addition to fighting the very forces of nature that Baal fights against and being himself depicted in anthropomorphic terms, as mythological gods often are, is depicted as the particular *type* of mythological god that Baal was: a storm god. In Psalm 29, Yahweh is the source of thunder and lightning: "The voice of the LORD is over the waters; the God of glory thunders.... The voice of the LORD flashes forth flames of fire."[89]

In 1936, H. L. Ginsberg, a lecturer at the Jewish Theological Seminary, suggested that this poem had originally been a hymn to Baal. Ginsberg's initially eccentric theory has moved toward the mainstream as evidence for it has grown. One scholar, for instance, changed all the "Yahweh"s in the poem to "Baal"s and found that the amount of alliteration grew radically.[90]

The eminent biblical scholar Frank Moore Cross has argued that one of the keystone events of the entire Bible—the crossing of the Red Sea—has roots in Baal mythology.[91] He notes that this episode features, in a sense, the sea submitting to God's will, a faint echo of Baal's dominating Sea (Yamm) in battle. And certainly there is a mythic air about the account of the event in Exodus 15. Here the scene is nothing like the (probably later) account in Exodus 14 that is the one depicted in Cecil B. DeMille's *The Ten Commandments;* the waters don't just part majestically at Moses's request and then reunite to drown the Egyptians. Rather, God is conspicuously, anthropomorphically, involved, and his mastery over the sea commensurately vivid: "At the blast of your nostrils the waters piled up, the floods stood up in a heap."[92]

But, whatever the parallels between the Red Sea episode and the myths of Baal, there is one big difference. Whereas the Baal myths take place in a supernatural realm, the biblical story is fundamentally about *human* history. Yes, the story is crucially shaped by intervention from on high, but the real action is on the ground. As Cross puts it, Yahweh's battles, unlike the typical Baal battle, are "particularized in place and time." A "mythic pattern" has been replaced by an "epic pattern."[93] Hence the title of his influential 1973 book, *Canaanite Myth and Hebrew Epic.*

Even when Yahweh acts in plainly mythological fashion—slaying a multiheaded dragon, say—the biblical reference is fleeting; there is no lengthy plotline. "Mythic imagery is abundant in the Bible," observes Mark S. Smith, yet "myth as narrative" is nearly absent.[94] Smith's explanation for the dearth of narrative myth involves, among other things, deletion.[95] Toward the middle of the first millennium BCE, he says, mythological motifs fell out of fashion; Hebrew scriptures composed then depict God in less anthropomorphic form than before, and sometimes as formless.[96] Smith argues that during this period, when myth was frowned on, earlier texts were being edited and re-edited; maybe priests found their view of Yahweh at odds with earlier accounts of his exploits and "chose not to preserve them, thereby functionally censoring them."[97]

But why go to the trouble? Even if myth had grown unfashionable, why bother to erase memory of its previous vogue? Probably because there were great theological stakes. After all, mythological gods deal with other formidable gods and sometimes find their will thwarted; but if you're the one, all-powerful God, your will can't be thwarted! Mythology, in other words, meant polytheism. So a project to strip early mythic narrative from scripture might have been part of a larger project: reworking the scriptures to imply that from the dawn of Israelite religion Yahweh was all-powerful and worthy of exclusive devotion. (The scholar Marjo Christina Annette Korpel compared Ugaritic and biblical descriptions of the divine and found "spectacularly" similar language "where strength, honour, dignity and compassion are concerned," whereas "everything implying weakness, humiliation or desire is shunned in the Old Testament.")⁹⁸

This motivation would explain the kinds of mythological moments that *did* survive the editing. More than once, a plotline lasts just long enough to suggest that, if a basis for polytheism ever existed, it is now gone. In Psalm 82 — the aforementioned divine council scene, in which God takes his seat among other gods — the scene ends with him predicting their death; or, in one common interpretation, *sentencing* them to death for their misdeeds.⁹⁹

Similarly, Yahweh's encounter with the gods Sea and River lasts just long enough for him to casually subdue these pesky remnants of a bygone polytheism. Leaving *that* part of Baal's legacy attached to Yahweh was theologically safe. But what about Baal's setbacks, such as being "swallowed" by Mot, the god Death? Such humiliation wouldn't befit a god worthy of exclusive devotion, and indeed the scriptures, as edited, don't show Yahweh inheriting this part of Baal's identity. Instead, we see that promise in the book of Isaiah that eventually Yahweh will "swallow up" Mot "forever," a pointed assertion of Yahweh's superiority not just to Mot but to Baal.¹⁰⁰

In a sense, then, the mid-first-millennium editors who in Smith's account helped to demythologize the Bible weren't bent on extirpating myth per se. Indeed, it was only later *translators* who changed

Sea to sea and River to river and Death to death. The enemy, rather, was myth in which gods other than the star of the show were formidable. And since narrative holds interest only when its outcome is in doubt—that is, when there is more than one formidable character—the death of these motifs meant the death of true mythic narrative.

This joint demise of polytheism and mythic narrative can be glimpsed, refracted, through shards of myth that remain in the Bible. A verse in the book of Habakkuk, as commonly translated, reads, "God came from...Mount Paran" and "before him went pestilence, and plague followed close behind."[101] But the Hebrew words underlying "pestilence" and "plague" are the words for the *gods* of pestilence and plague, Deber and Resheph.[102] In the Canaanite pantheon, Deber and Resheph had been fiercely destructive,[103] but, as Smith has noted, that part of their identity doesn't make it into the Bible. Rather, they appear as unassuming members of Yahweh's retinue. And later translators, by turning the names of these gods into generic nouns, converted Pestilence and Plague from minor deities to mere aspects of Yahweh's power, and abstract aspects at that. Yahweh here seems to be repeating the strategy we saw Marduk exercise in the previous chapter, moving toward monotheism through subtle conquest, assimilating other gods into his being.

This passage from Habakkuk illustrates Smith's account of how Canaanite polytheism got streamlined into Israelite monotheism. Gods that had ranked below El in the pantheon, such as Deber and Resheph, shrank in stature and eventually disappeared altogether. With the midlevel management now gone, all that was left of the downsized pantheon was a deity at the very top—now known as Yahweh—and supernatural beings at the very bottom: the divine messengers, or angels.[104]

Cross-Fertilization

The theologian Robert Karl Gnuse presciently observed in 1997 that "a 'paradigm shift' appears to be underway," with more and more scholars acknowledging "a gradual evolution of a complex Yahwistic religion from a polytheistic past." Increasingly, "the perception of a gradual emergence of monotheism combines with an understanding that stresses Israel's intellectual continuity with the ancient world." [105]

"Intellectual continuity"—organic connection between Israelite religion and the religions preceding it—certainly holds to the pattern we've seen in the last few chapters. Gods change in character and merge with other gods and get renamed, and belief can change dramatically in the process, but you don't see whole new religions coming out of nowhere. Even the Egyptian pharaoh Akhenaten, who wasn't exactly averse to theological innovation, crafted his monotheism out of materials at hand: Aten, his one true god, had previously lived in a polytheistic context and first took shape as an offshoot of the sun god Re.

But intellectual continuity can be messy, and certainly was in the case of ancient Israel. The head of the Canaanite pantheon was El, and we saw reasons, early in this chapter, to think that Yahweh inherited much of El's character. [106] But now we've seen cause to put Yahweh in Baal's lineage as well. He is described in the language used to describe Baal, and he fights the very mythic enemies that Baal fought. (One biblical verse even seems to identify his home, Mount Zion, with Baal's home, Mount Sapan.) [107] So what's the story? How did Yahweh wind up part El and part Baal? How do we reconcile his two heritages?

The first step is to remember that gods are products of cultural evolution, not biological evolution. In biological evolution, lines of descent are neat. You get all your traits from either one parent or two, depending on whether your species reproduces clonally or sexually. Either way, once your egg cell starts to develop, your heritage is set—there is no further fiddling with your DNA. With cultural evolution, in contrast, endless cross-fertilization is possible. That's why the English language, though called "Germanic," bears a resemblance to the Romance languages. Long after Germanic tribes had settled in England, the language their descendants spoke was swapping words with the French language across the English Channel. And for that matter, the "Germanic" wellspring itself drew on several sources, famously including the Angles and the Saxons but extending to other tribes as well.

In other words: cultural evolution is fuzzy. Simple questions—such as whether Yahweh consists *more* of El or of Baal—may not have an answer, much less an answer visible through the mists of antiquity. Still, the matter is worth pursuing: How did El, the cerebral chairman of the board, ever get mixed up with Baal, the terrifying storm god who is described by one scholar as a "virile dim-bulb"?[108] And how were their identities finally reconciled in one God? However elusive the answers, seeking them is the first step toward appreciating the great contribution made by Israelite religion to the evolution of God.

One initially puzzling aspect of the situation is that Baal, throughout the Bible, is Yahweh's rival. Bitter enmity doesn't seem like a good basis for a merger. But, actually, in cultural evolution, competition can indeed spur convergence. Certainly that's true in *modern* cultural evolution. The reason operating systems made by Microsoft and Apple are so similar is that the two companies borrow (that's the polite term) features pioneered by the other when they prove popular.

So too with religions. Baal's operating system had one feature that, in an ancient agricultural society, would have been the envy of any competitor who lacked it: as the storm god, Baal brought rain.[109] Hence, perhaps, all the atmospherics in some descriptions of Yahweh—his voice as thunder, his spear as lightning; anything Baal could do, he could do better.[110] And hence descriptions of Yahweh as a god who "rides upon the clouds";[111] one of Baal's Canaanite nicknames was "rider of the clouds."

Yet however much time Yahweh spent absorbing Baal's personality, he had to finally renounce it if he was to become the god that ancient Israel is famous for having produced: all-powerful, but not conspicuously so; the governor of nature, yet transcendent. Here we return to the biblical scene cited at the beginning of this chapter,

Elijah's mountaintop encounter with a strangely elusive Yahweh in the nineteenth chapter of First Kings.

I say "strangely" elusive because only a chapter earlier, the Bible depicts a quite different Yahweh. Elijah has arranged for a public showdown between Yahweh and Baal. Yahweh devotees and Baal devotees will each prepare a bull for sacrifice and invite their god to ignite it from the heavens. Whichever god succeeds is the real god. You would think that Baal, the fearsome storm god, could toss down a lightning bolt, especially with 450 of his prophets cheering him on. But no Baal bolt is forthcoming. Yet Yahweh torches *his* sacrifice even after Elijah drenches it in water! "Then the fire of the LORD fell and consumed the burnt offering, the wood, the stones, and the dust, and even licked up the water that was in the trench."[112] Case closed: the people are convinced, the 450 Baal prophets are ignominiously slain, and Yahweh is triumphant. He has out-Baaled Baal—and, lest anyone miss the point, he finishes off the show with rain, Baal's supposed specialty.[113]

Now, with Baal vanquished, Yahweh can quit showing off, or at least cut down on it. As the biblical scholar Richard Elliott Friedman notes, this is the last time in the Hebrew Bible that God will perform a momentous miracle before a vast audience.[114] And the next chapter of First Kings will give us the new, subtle Yahweh, the god who is "not in the wind" and "not in the fire" and who speaks, if at all, in a "still small voice." Here, says Frank Moore Cross, begins a "new era" in Yahweh's "mode of self-disclosure." The "thunderous voice of Baal" has become "the imperceptible whisper" of Yahweh.[115] Yahweh, having done a good enough Baal imitation to steal the show, could now elevate his act. The El in him—the chief-executive god who speaks through prophets—has outlasted the Baal in him, only in a higher form: Yahweh will become more remote than El, and eventually transcendent.

At least, that's one interpretation. It's an open question whether this stretch of the Bible can shoulder as much symbolic weight as modern interpreters have placed on it; whether its author(s) (and later editors) meant to depict a pivotal transition from old-fashioned, hands-on, fire-hurling god to subtle, even silent, transcendent god. (Even after this transition to a "new era," as Yahweh addresses Elijah quietly or not at all, he brings fire, an earthquake, and stone-splitting wind—not hallmarks of divine reserve.)

Still, whatever this scene was meant to mean, the direction in which it points is indeed the direction in which the Bible moves. As Friedman noted in his book *The Hidden Face of God*, the Bible's depictions of a vivid, dramatically interventionist Yahweh decline in frequency as the biblical narrative unfolds. It is near the beginning of the story that Yahweh is most likely to appear to people or speak to them or do widely witnessed wonders. Near the end he is less salient; indeed there is no mention of him at all in the last book of the Hebrew Bible, Esther.[116]

Of course, the order in which the books (and chapters and verses) of the Bible appear is not the order in which they were written. But even if we look at the text in the order of its authorship, we see a trend (at least, if we use mainstream, though not unchallenged, views on the datings of the texts).[117] The early scriptures offer a hands-on, anthropomorphic god, who walks through a garden, calls out to people, makes them clothes, courteously closes up an ark before unleashing a lethal flood, and drowns Egyptians by blowing on the sea (through his nose). This god smells the "pleasing odor" of burnt sacrifices.[118] In later scriptures we see less of God in the flesh, and even start to see a god with no flesh at all. The fourth chapter of Deuteronomy, apparently a product of the mid-first millennium, stresses that even when God spoke to his people they "saw no form" (and for that reason it would be a mistake to worship idols that are made in "the form of any figure").[119]

The evolution from a hands-on, anthropomorphic deity to a less intrusive, more abstract deity is hardly smooth.[120] The latter half of the first millennium saw an upsurge in apocalyptic writing replete with mythological imagery; the book of Daniel sees God as quite fleshly. ("His clothing was white as snow, and the hair of his head like pure wool.")[121] Still, on balance, there seems to be a trend:

movement during the first millennium BCE away from an anthropomorphic polytheism toward a more abstract monotheism.

When you appraise this trend—this erratic but directional drift
from one conception of god to another—it's hard not to conclude
that the traditional story of the Abrahamic god is just wrong. Full-
fledged monotheism didn't, as Kaufmann argued, emerge early in
Israelite history "as an insight, an original intuition." [122] Early Israelite religion grew out of earlier religions, "pagan" religions, just
as they had done. And out of it, eventually, grew the more modern
god of late Israelite religion: a single, transcendent all-powerful, all-
knowing god—the god of Jews, Christians, and Muslims. It would
be a god of unprecedented influence, a god that in various centuries
would dominate peoples who were dominant in the world.

But the question remains: *Why?* What forces pushed Israel
toward monotheism? Only when we answer this question can
we answer the question raised at the outset of this chapter: What
exactly is the connection between monotheism and intolerance,
between monotheism and violence? We'll take up these questions
in the next chapter. But there is at least one thing we can already
say about monotheism and violence. A premise shared by all who
commit violence in the name of the Abrahamic god is that this god
is special—the one true god. And most of these people would say
his specialness was manifest in his mode of appearance: more than
three millennia ago, he showed up suddenly, announced his presence, and rejected the pagan polytheism of the day. If you ask them
how they know that, they're likely to say that the scriptures told
them so.

In the early twentieth century, archaeology seemed to be shor-
ing up this sort of faith. William Albright, the "father of biblical
archaeology," wrote in 1940 that we were now seeing "archaeological confirmation of the general tenor of Israelite tradition." [123] But in
the second half of the twentieth century this claim fell into doubt,
and archaeologists started asking whether it wasn't grounded more
in Albright's Christian faith than in scholarship. Increasingly, the

biblical narrative sustained damage from the facts in the ground. So today, when the faithful point to scripture as proof that their God is different from all other ancient gods—that he is the one true god—any skeptic well versed in archaeology can reply: But why would anyone place their faith in a book persistently at odds with historical reality?

In light of the past few decades of biblical scholarship, skeptics can go further. The Hebrew Bible—read carefully, and in light of ancient Canaanite writings—doesn't really tell the story the faithful have said it tells to begin with; at least, it doesn't tell that story in ultimately credible form. Alongside its monotheistic plotline lies diverse evidence casting that plotline into doubt. The story is undermined not just by the facts in the ground, but by the text itself.

Of course, a believer can choose to ignore this evidence, or can strain to accommodate it, much like early astronomers who explained the patterns of planets with increasingly baroque theories rather than just concede that the Earth revolves around the Sun. But Jews, Christians, and Muslims who are spiritually hungry and intellectually serious will have to grapple with the evidence, and somehow reconcile their beliefs with it. The next step in the grappling is to figure out when and how—and above all why—Abrahamic monotheism did in fact emerge.

Chapter Six

From Polytheism to Monolatry

You don't meet many women named Jezebel. The name fell out of fashion millennia ago and never recovered. In fact, it got so loaded with bad connotations that it is now a generic pejorative. A jezebel, according to one dictionary, is "a wicked, shameless woman."[1] It all goes back to the biblical Jezebel. She was married to Ahab, king of Israel during the ninth century BCE. She was a vigorous champion of the Canaanite god Baal, and talked King Ahab into backing Baal. This dimmed her chances of being favorably depicted in the Bible.

Jezebel was a key behind-the-scenes player in the biblical story that framed the previous chapter: Yahweh beats Baal in the showdown arranged by Elijah, and then later "appears" to Elijah—invisibly, ineffably—on Mount Sinai. It was because Jezebel had so whipped up enthusiasm for Baal that Elijah scheduled this decisive face-off between the two gods in the first place. And the rest is history: with Yahweh's biggest rival subdued, and Yahweh's identity now moving toward transcendence, Israelite religion was on the path to modern monotheism.

Or so we're told. Whether Yahweh actually did best Baal, and for that matter whether any such mountaintop showdown was even organized by Elijah, are not exactly subjects of universal agreement. The Elijah story may not have been written down until centuries after its (alleged) occurrence, and it was eventually edited by people who championed exclusive devotion to Yahweh and presumably spun the tale in that direction.[2] Still, the underlying conflict—Elijah's opposition to the pro-Baal policies of Jezebel and

Ahab—is something many biblical scholars think is rooted in fact. And this rebellion against royally sanctioned polytheism is commonly viewed as a milestone in the fitful evolution of monotheism, an evolution that would take centuries more for its culmination.

More narrowly, the incident is taken as a milestone in the evolution of *monolatry*, a way station on the road to full-fledged monotheism. Elijah wasn't necessarily claiming Baal didn't *exist* (the monotheistic position), just that he didn't deserve the respect of Israelites. Some two centuries after the time of Elijah, monolatry would be the official policy of the king of the Israelites, and the worship of gods other than Yahweh would be discouraged with zealous brutality. This chapter will address the question of how monolatry moved from the radical fringe to the center of Israelite politics—how the stage for full-fledged monotheism was set.

It would be nice to know for sure if the Elijah story is true. If it is, at least in its political essentials, then we start our search for monolatry's origins by asking what inspired Elijah to oppose Yahweh's rival Baal. If it is false, we start our search by asking what inspired later biblical writers to create the story—why they themselves had come to oppose the worship of all gods other than Yahweh, after which they read their theology back into history.

But, as it happens, those two paths lead to roughly the same place, yielding similar conclusions about what forces made Yahweh the only god of the Israelites. The best way to see this is to just pick a path and follow it. We'll begin by assuming, if only as a kind of thought experiment, that this early Bible story is true, and then move forward in the biblical narrative of Israel's unfolding theology, until we get to some episodes that are more firmly grounded in fact. Our path will eventually double back on itself, as these later episodes shed light on the authorship of the Elijah story. We'll then be in a position to explain the evolution of Israelite monolatry with some confidence.

But first let's make it clear—in case it isn't already—what philosophical bias will inform the enterprise. Attempts to explain changes in religious doctrine come in two basic varieties: the kind that stress the power of ideas and the kind that stress the power of material circumstance. Was Israel pushed toward monolatry, and ultimately toward monotheism, more by theological inspiration and reflection, or more by politics, economics, and other concrete social factors? To take the example at hand: What drove Elijah and his followers to heap disdain on Jezebel and on Baal? Was Jezebel loathed because of her association with Baal (and hence with polytheism), or was Baal loathed because of his association with Jezebel (and hence with whatever economic and political interests she represented)?

The Bible, of course, favors the first interpretation: Elijah and his followers, in the grip of divine truth, opposed the worship of Baal, and so became the enemy of anyone who favored such worship. Then again, the Bible has a natural bias in favor of the power of religious belief, the ability of ideas to shape facts on the ground. The book you're reading, in contrast, emphasizes the power of facts on the ground; it seeks to explain how the conception of God has changed in response to events on earth. So it takes seriously the possibility that, for all Elijah's religious fervor, his fight against Baal may have had mundane motivations. The theological conflict with Jezebel and her husband, Ahab, may have had as much to do with Jezebel and Ahab as with theology.

Certainly we've seen examples of mundane motivations shaping theological principles. We've seen Eskimo shamans tell sinful women that divine forgiveness depended on their having sex with an Eskimo shaman. We've seen Polynesian chiefs say that people who irritated them had to be sacrificed to the gods. We've seen Sargon of Akkadia fuse Ishtar and Inanna into a single god that served his imperial ambitions. We've seen Akhenaten, the engineer of Egyptian monotheism, kill off gods whose priests he found politically threatening. Again and again we've seen the divine, or at least ideas about the divine, reshaped by the mundane. Facts on the ground—facts about power and money and other crass things—have often been the leading edge of change, with religious belief following along.

Of course, sometimes the influence moves in the opposite

direction. Religious beliefs, especially in the short run, can shape the political and economic landscape. It's entirely possible that Elijah had deep faith in Yahweh, and this faith inspired a political movement against Ahab and Jezebel. For that matter, the influence can move in both directions at once: maybe Elijah's motivation was wholly faith-based but some of his supporters had political or economic grievances against Jezebel and King Ahab.

In short, the whole thing is messy, and focusing exclusively on any one "prime mover" is too simple. Still, I'll argue that on balance the best way to explain the centuries-long evolution from polytheism to monolatry to monotheism is via concrete social forces. At the risk of oversimplifying: politics and economics gave us the one true god of the Abrahamic faiths.

Religious people often find this claim dispiriting, as it seems to reduce belief in a higher purpose to a mirage, an illusory reflection of the mundane. By the end of this book I'll argue that the opposite is in a sense true: that seeing facts on the ground as prime movers winds up presenting a new kind of *evidence* for higher purpose. In any event, for now what I'm claiming is that to fathom why monotheism evolved in ancient Israel, we have to fathom the underlying politics and economics of ancient Israel. Only then can we see in what sense, if any, intolerance and belligerence are "built into" Abrahamic monotheism, and how firm a part of the Abrahamic god's character they are or aren't.

The Yahweh-Alone Party

So, what social forces might have helped energize opposition to the policies of Ahab and Jezebel, and hence to Baal? For starters, it helps to remember that, in ancient times, when men of royal blood married foreign women, it wasn't usually on a romantic whim. It was part of foreign policy, a way to cement relations with another nation. Jezebel was the daughter of King Ethbaal, ruler of the cities of Tyre and Sidon in Phoenicia (and in modern-day Lebanon). Her marriage to Ahab had been arranged by Ahab's father, King Omri, who no doubt realized that alliance with Phoenicia gave Israel favored access to these Mediterranean port cities. And, as usual in the ancient world, alliance with a country meant treating its gods with respect. So if, as the Bible says, Ahab built an altar for Baal[3] in Israel's capital city, Samaria, that wasn't just some concession to his zany wife. It was part of the logic of marrying Jezebel in the first place, the theological expression of the marriage's underlying political rationale.[4]

And thus had it long been. The Bible, looking back askance at the theology of King Solomon in the tenth century BCE, complains that he had hundreds of wives who "turned away his heart after other gods," inspiring official reverence for "Astarte the goddess of the Sidonians" and "Milcom the abomination of the Ammonites" and "Chemosh the abomination of Moab." But all this "evil in the sight of the LORD"[5] was presumably good foreign policy in the eyes of Solomon. An "internationalist" foreign policy—one emphasizing wide alliance and trade—entailed a certain respect for foreign gods.

By the same token, opponents of an internationalist policy might oppose the interfaith amity—the respect for, even embrace of, foreign gods—that abetted it. Maybe this is how Israel started down the path toward monolatry, via a backlash against internationalism. But why would someone oppose an internationalist foreign policy? In the case of Ahab's internationalism, various theories have been offered.

Maybe, for example, some local merchants suffered from Ahab's having let Phoenician traders come to Israel and muscle in on commerce. Certainly the structure of economics in those days made it easy for resentment of Phoenician traders to translate into resentment of Phoenician gods. As the biblical scholar Bernard Lang has noted, in ancient times, houses of worship sometimes performed "many a task of the modern bank," and there is evidence that Phoenician traders used Baal's temple as their headquarters.[6]

In this scenario, the tension between Ahab's and Elijah's constituencies boils down to political and economic self-interest. From

Ahab's perspective, alliance with Phoenicia made sense. It not only kept Mediterranean markets open to Israel via Phoenician ports, but also steered east-west commerce through Israel, creating trade routes that Ahab could profitably control. What's more, the alliance gave Israel a strong friend in the event of military conflict with one of the region's great powers. If the price for all this was tolerating Baal and letting some Phoenician traders make money, so be it. The relationship with Phoenicia was win-win, and Ahab's theology expanded accordingly. But for Israelites whose livelihood was threatened by Phoenician traders, the relationship with Phoenicia was one-way; Phoenicians won and they lost. Their theology contracted accordingly.

This resentful-merchants theory is pretty speculative. But the general principle makes sense, and we've already seen it at work in ancient Mesopotamia and elsewhere: attitudes toward a foreign god can depend on how the foreigners are perceived. If locals feel they can gain by cooperative interaction with those foreigners, they may embrace the god, or at least raise no protest when fellow citizens do. But if locals see the game as zero-sum—if they believe that their fortunes are inversely correlated with the foreigners' fortunes, that the foreigners have to lose for them to win—then their theology will probably be less inclusive. Let's call this the law of religious tolerance: people are more likely to be open to foreign gods when they see themselves playing a non-zero-sum game with foreigners—see their fortunes as positively correlated with the foreigners' fortunes, see themselves and the foreigners as, to some extent, in the same boat.

The ancient world, by linking foreign policy and theology so tightly, made this principle especially compelling, but a version of it operates in modern times, too. People who are profitably doing business with other people tend not to question their religious beliefs: live and let live.

For that matter, the basic dynamic goes beyond the question of religious tolerance to the question of tolerance in general. People naturally, without really thinking about it, judge enemies and rivals critically in various realms. If two men are pursuing the same woman, and you ask them what they think of each other's tastes — in politics, in clothes, in literature, whatever — you'll probably get some negative feedback, and it will probably be heartfelt. In contrast, people reflexively judge potential collaborators, and their beliefs, leniently. So the link between self-interest and tolerance needn't be a matter of *conscious* calculation, a fact we'll explore below. The law of religious tolerance grows organically out of human nature.

There is another theory about what inspired opposition to Ahab and Jezebel, and hence to Baal. In allying with Phoenicia, Israel was turning its back on another potent polity — Assyria, to its northeast. Indeed, Assyria's menacing power was one thing the Phoenician alliance was presumably meant to neutralize. As Lang notes, there was probably an Israelite faction that favored alliance with Assyria instead of Phoenicia. Certainly such a faction prevailed some years after Ahab's death: King Jehu, who took the throne by coup d'état, would court Assyria's favor and thus redirect Israelite foreign policy. It's probably no coincidence that, according to the Bible, Jehu would also kill every Baal worshipper in Israel, destroy Baal's temple, and replace it with a latrine.[7]

So maybe Elijah drew support from pro-Assyrian Israelites. In that event, the hatred of Baal evinced by Ahab's enemies may have been matched by their warmth toward the Assyrian god Assur — a fact that the Bible's monotheistic editors, for all we know, left on the cutting-room floor. In other words, it's quite possible that many Elijah backers were just as polytheistic as Ahab and Jezebel, and merely disagreed with them about which gods were worth worshipping. Even so, the moral of the underlying story would remain the same: people tolerate, even embrace, the theologies of foreigners to the extent that they see the possibility of mutual gain through collaboration.

Of course, if the traditional interpretation is right, and Elijah's coalition was monolatrous, devoted to the worship of Yahweh *alone,* then a pro-Assyrian faction with an affinity for Assyrian gods wouldn't fit into the coalition. And at some point in Israel-ite history, some such "Yahweh-alone" movement (as the historian Morton Smith dubbed it)[8] must have taken shape. This movement, by definition, would have rejected the worship of all gods of foreign origin. So if the preference of one ally of Israel over another entailed the active embrace of that ally's gods, then this preference wouldn't make sense as part of the Yahweh-alone movement's motivation. A skepticism about international alliance in general would be more like it.

The First Clear-Cut Monolatrist

With that in mind, let's fast-forward to a time when there is more evidence that the Yahweh-alone message *has* found voice. In the eighth century BCE, long after Jezebel was dead, the prophet Hosea appeared, and his thoughts were committed to writing, apparently during his lifetime or shortly thereafter.[9] Though his text was subject to later editing, many scholars think its core message solidified not long after his death, so that it's fair to speak of a "Hosean" theology that reflects a strand of Israelite thought somewhere around the end of the eighth century BCE.[10] Certainly many more scholars think this than think that the Elijah story is true as told. In any event, as with the Elijah story, we'll proceed for now on the assumption that the biblical record is roughly accurate: we'll see in the book of Hosea a man named Hosea whose thoughts say something about the time in which he lived.

Hosea is sometimes read as a monotheist, but there's no reason to think he was anything more than monolatrous. He never denies the existence of gods other than Yahweh, and he never says foreigners shouldn't worship them.[11] When he insists that Israelites should "know" no god but Yahweh, he doesn't mean "know" in the modern sense of "be aware of." The underlying Hebrew word meant something more like "be faithful to." It was used in treaties to express the loyalty of a vassal nation.[12]

Still, that sense of "know" does qualify Hosea as a full-fledged monolatrist. When he quotes Yahweh saying, "[Y]ou know no God but me, and besides me there is no savior,"[13] he is expressing the Yahweh-alone party line. He may also be making intellectual history, laying down a template for one of the most famous lines in the Bible. The first of the Ten Commandments—"You shall have no other gods before me" (another monolatrous verse often read as monotheistic)—probably comes from post-Hosean times.[14]

So does Hosea exhibit what the above logic suggests a monolatrist might exhibit: a certain skepticism of alliance in general? You might say. He repeatedly mentions two great powers, Assyria and Egypt, and never in a favorable light. He stresses the futility of alliance between either of these powers and "Ephraim"—the northern kingdom of Israel, where he lived. (Greater Israel is at this point divided into two states, a northern one called Ephraim or Israel and a southern one called Judah.) "Assyria shall not save us," he says, and as for negotiating with Egyptian leaders, this is just "babbling in the land of Egypt." Ephraim's leaders are "silly and without sense; they call upon Egypt, they go to Assyria."[15]

Part of Hosea's resistance to alliances seems to be grounded in their frequently demeaning terms. Because Israel is a small state wedged between great powers, "alliance" often amounts to vassalage. When the book of Hosea complains that Ephraim's leaders "make a treaty with Assyria, and oil is carried to Egypt,"[16] it is talking not about selling oil to Egypt, but about giving it to Egypt as tribute.

Still, great powers aren't the only problem.[17] Hosea, as the biblical scholar Marvin Sweeney has written, shows "hostility to foreign involvement in general."[18] Indeed, the suspicion of foreign nations is so diffuse as to verge on xenophobia. Hosea writes, "Ephraim mixes himself with the peoples. . . . Foreigners devour his strength, but he does not know it." And "Israel is swallowed up; now . . . among the nations as a useless vessel."[19] Presumably the logic of Ahab, Solomon, and other kings who had pursued an internationalist foreign policy was that immersion in the larger world could make Israel richer. Hosea takes the opposite view. He sees an increasingly poor

Israel whose poverty is only deepened by international forces. "The standing grain has no heads, it shall yield no meal; if it were to yield, foreigners would devour it."[20] If no nation can bring good to Israel, then it follows that no other nation's god should be worshipped or even respected.

Indeed, Hosea casts his religious isolationism and his political isolationism in the same metaphorical language. "You have played the whore, departing from your God," he tells the Israelites. In worshipping Canaanite gods that claim to bring rain and prosperity, Israel has "said, 'I will go after my lovers; they give me my bread and my water, my wool and my flax, my oil and my drink.'" This image of infidelity is extended to Israel's foreign policy. Ephraim's officials "have gone up to Assyria, a wild ass wandering alone; Ephraim has bargained for lovers. Though they [Israelites] bargain with the nations ... they shall soon writhe under the burden of [foreign] kings and princes."[21] In Hosea, as in the ancient world generally, theology and geopolitics are mirror images.

Justifiably Jaundiced

That advocates of the "Yahweh-alone" movement took a jaundiced view of foreign alliance is not a news flash. Scholars have long noted an anti-internationalist flavor in prophetic books that decry infidelity to Yahweh. ("Prophetic nationalism," some have called it.)[22] But that doesn't mean all these scholars buy into the view being advanced here — that political and economic forces shaped theology. A correlation between political and religious attitudes doesn't, by itself, settle the question of which caused which. It could be that Hosea's disdain of internationalism led him to be monolatrous, but it could also be that Hosea's monolatry led him to disdain internationalism. After all, internationalism tended to bring contact with foreign gods. And there may have been other reasons for monolatrists to dislike alliance. Some prophets said that reaching out for support from great powers showed a lack of faith in the ability of Yahweh alone to keep Israel safe.

So why shouldn't we take the prophets at their word, and assume that their theology shaped their view of foreign relations, rather than the other way around? In a sense, we probably should. Hosea and other prophets of his day do have the hallmarks of the true believer. According to the Bible, Hosea chose his spouse by following God's command to "take for yourself a wife of whoredom," apparently so that his marriage would be a metaphor for Israel's infidelity to Yahweh. As if this weren't fanatical enough, he named one of his sons "Not my people" to symbolize Yahweh's response to the infidelity.[23] And don't spend all your pity on Hosea's son; a child of Isaiah's went through life as "Speed spoil, hasten plunder," a walking billboard for one of Isaiah's prophecies.[24] All of this suggests that prophetic motivation could be more intense, and less mundanely rational, than you would expect if it were inspired just by geopolitical analysis.

But the question, for present purposes, isn't what motivated Hosea and other prophets to voice the monolatrous message. The question is why that message had resonance — why it caught on. Here an analogy with biological evolution is apt. Darwinian theory says that traits that spread through a population will tend to be traits that further survival and reproduction. But it doesn't say that all traits that *appear* (through, say, genetic mutation) will have that tendency, and its prediction about which traits will spread is indifferent to the question of why they first appeared. Hosea's message, you might say, was a cultural "mutation" — and no doubt other prophets were generating alternative mutations. The question of whether foreign relations shaped theology isn't so much the question of why any of these mutations arose as why some mutations spread and some didn't. Specifically: Did Hosea's message spread because people more and more believed that Israel's relationship to the world was basically zero-sum — that Israel was unlikely to profit through internationalism, through cooperation and collaboration with other countries?

Certainly Israelites could have reached that conclusion. Hosea's career began during the final years of the reign of Jeroboam II and extended for decades thereafter. As it turned out, those final years of Jeroboam's tenure were the final years of a century of stability and prosperity for the northern kingdom of Israel.[25] Shortly after the king's death in 747 BCE, Israel's foreign relations entered a quarter-century downward spiral, creating nourishment for zero-sum views of the world.

Assyria revived its earlier belligerence, marching its army westward and exacting steep tribute from weaker states, including Israel.[26] Israel sought refuge in alliance; its king joined with Damascus and some Phoenician and Philistine cities in an anti-Assyrian revolt.[27] In response, Assyria seized much of Israel's territory and razed many of its big cities, leaving only its capital city, Samaria, and some nearby hill country under Israelite control. The radically shrunken Israel for a time paid tribute to Assyria rather than vanish completely. But then, ill-advisedly counting on Egypt's support, it ended those payments. Assyria besieged Samaria and, after subduing the city in 722 BCE, deported a big chunk of its population—the "ten lost tribes of Israel."[28] This was the end of the northern kingdom of Israel. Now the sole repository of Israelite heritage was the kingdom of Judah, to the south. It's no surprise that, by the time the northern kingdom fell, Hosea's isolationist foreign policy, along with its theological correlate—an aversion to gods with foreign pedigrees—had found a large enough audience so that his message would survive and be carried to Judah, perhaps as his followers fled the Assyrian onslaught.[29]

After the fall of the northern kingdom, the foreign relations picture wasn't bright in the south, either. Judah, too, now faced Assyria's ferocity. Over the next two decades its attempts at defensive alliance, like Ephraim's earlier attempts, would fail. Judah rebelled against Assyria unsuccessfully, and two decades after Ephraim's demise, the king of Judah found himself trapped in a besieged Jerusalem like "a bird in a cage," as Assyrian annals proudly put it. Jerusalem had to give up the gold in its temple and treasury in accepting vassalage to Assyria.[30]

Judah's ensuing history would have its bright spots, and its relations with neighbors wouldn't be relentlessly zero-sum; there were times when alliance paid off. Still, over the next century it would remain in the problematic position of being a small state in a region dominated by an aggressive Mesopotamian superpower (first Assyria, and then the Chaldean, or Neo-Babylonian, Empire, which displaced Assyria). So it spent a fair amount of time either unsuccessfully resisting a superpower or accepting humiliating vassalage to one.[31] As a result, the leading contributor to respect for foreign gods—evidence of fruitful relations with foreign countries—was sometimes hard to find.

God of the Little People

Important as foreign affairs seem to have been in the emergence of monolatry, the Yahweh-alone movement may have gotten a boost from domestic politics as well. Starting in the time of Hosea, when prophets first go on record against the worship of gods other than Yahweh, class warfare is in the air. The prophet Amos, Hosea's contemporary in the northern kingdom,[32] castigates those who "trample the head of the poor into the dust of the earth, and push the afflicted out of the way," who "crush the needy, who say to their husbands, 'Bring something to drink!'"[33] Meanwhile, down in Judah, Isaiah is complaining about those "who write oppressive statutes, to turn aside the needy from justice and to rob the poor of my people of their right, that widows may be your spoil, and that you may make the orphans your prey!"[34]

Why would prophetic diatribes against the wealthy coincide with prophetic diatribes against the worship of gods other than Yahweh? Maybe because of the natural connection between resentment of Israel's upper class and opposition to the internationalism that, as we've seen, was linked to alien gods. Archaeological excavations show Hosea's era to be a time of great economic inequality among Israelites. It was also a time of expanding international trade,[35] and it could not have escaped the attention of the poor that the rich were closely tied to that trade—not just because they controlled it and profited from it, but because so many pricey imports wound up in their homes.[36]

Amos doesn't explicitly link the rich to foreign trade, but he does heap disdain on conspicuous consumption, which involved conspicuously foreign elements. He targets those who "lie on beds of ivory" (and the eighth-century ivory unearthed by archaeologists in northern Israel has Phoenician contours and is laden with Egyptian motifs).[37] Meanwhile, in the south, Isaiah is criticizing Judahites who "clasp hands with foreigners"—a reference to commercial transaction—and whose "land is filled with silver and gold."[38]

Even today, rich people like to brandish exotic imports, and even today they are resented for it. But in ancient times the link between wealth and foreign trade was stronger, because luxury items dominated long-distance trade. With transportation still arduous and costly, only goods with a high ratio of value to weight were worth trading. International trade largely connoted jewels and fabrics and spices, which in turn connoted obnoxious rich people. So the anti-internationalist impulse of the Yahweh-alone movement naturally drew strength from resentment of cosmopolitan elites.

Indeed, Zephaniah, an ardently monolatrous prophet who lived about a century after Hosea, Amos, and Isaiah, wrote that when Judgment Day comes, Yahweh will punish the ruling class and "all who dress themselves in foreign attire."[39] And there will be wailing in the business district "for all the traders have perished; all who weigh out silver are cut off."[40]

Zephaniah is a little-known figure, perhaps because the book of Zephaniah is one of the shortest books in the Bible. But he deserves attention. He is thought to have lived in the final decades of the seventh century BCE, when the Yahweh-alone movement, as we'll see, made a great leap in prominence and power. And even leaving aside when he lived, and when the book of Zephaniah was written and amended (the dating of biblical texts being the iffy thing that it is), the book is valuable as a vivid monolatrist tract, and one that is consistent with the scenario sketched out in the preceding several pages: that the Yahweh-alone movement drew strength from a wariness about international involvement and a resentment of elites who profited from that involvement.

Certainly the gods whose worship Zephaniah fiercely attacks have a foreign air about them. He warns that Yahweh will soon punish those who "bow down and swear to Yahweh, but also swear by Milcom," god of the Ammonites, who inhabited present-day Jordan. Yahweh will also punish those who "bow down on the roofs" to worship the "host of the heavens," which in this context means deified celestial bodies, perhaps of the sort that were worshipped in Assyria and by Assyrian administrators in the land of the Israelites.[41] And of course Yahweh would purge Judah of "every remnant of Baal."[42]

As with Hosea, Zephaniah's view of foreign gods correlates closely with his view of foreign nations. It is with evident pleasure that he reports Yahweh's intention to "destroy Assyria." And as for the Ammonites (along with the Moabites): their lands will become "a waste forever" as "the remnant of my people shall plunder them, and the survivors of my nation shall possess them."[43] Of course, as with Hosea, it's not immediately clear whether the influence is moving from geopolitics to theology or vice versa. A correlation between hostility toward other nations and hostility toward foreign gods doesn't mean that the former caused the latter. After all, it would make sense for a fierce monolatrist or monotheist to hope for, and even expect, the demise of nations embracing alternative gods.

But it turns out that in some cases, at least, these nations are *not* slated for punishment because of their theology alone. The anger of Yahweh, and of the prophets, sometimes stems explicitly from facts on the ground. The Ammonites and Moabites, says Zephaniah, are doomed because "they have taunted my people and made boasts against their territory."[44] Assyrians, too, seem to have been too self-assured for Zephaniah's taste. After painting a lavish picture of the devastation Yahweh will wreak on Nineveh, the Assyrian capital, Zephaniah asks, "Is this the exultant city that lived secure, that said to itself, 'I am, and there is no one else'?"[45] This sense of being treated with contempt or arrogance by the high and mighty is common in prophetic texts that stress devotion to Yahweh. Isaiah relays that Yahweh will "put an end to the pride of the arrogant, and lay low the insolence of tyrants."[46]

This sort of reaction illustrates how deeply the assessment of foreign relations — and so of foreign gods — can be shaped by such emotions as resentment and humiliation. In that sense, to talk about ancient Israelites sizing up international prospects and deeming alliance fruitful or hopeless, non-zero-sum or zero-sum, can be misleading. For in some cases the reaction is emotional; the calculation is taking place at an unconscious level.[47]

This ancient sociopolitical environment is a lot like the modern sociopolitical environment as shaped by globalization. Then as now, international trade and attendant economic advance had brought sharp social change and sharp social cleavages, delimiting affluent cosmopolitans from poorer and more insular people. Then as now, some of those in the latter category were ambivalent, at best, about foreign influence, economic and cultural, and were correspondingly resentful of the cosmopolitan elites who fed on it. And, then as now, some of those in the latter category extended their dislike of the foreign to theology, growing cold toward religious traditions that signified the alien. This dynamic has to varying degrees helped produce fundamentalist Christians, fundamentalist Jews, and fundamentalist Muslims. And apparently it helped produce the god they worship.

Two Theories

At least, that's one scenario for explaining Israel's movement toward monolatry and hence toward monotheism. Let's call it the FP scenario, since it's so intertwined with Israel's foreign policy. It sees Israel's early monolatrists as fierce nationalists, opponents of an internationalist foreign policy. More specifically, it sees them as populist nationalists, drawing support from the common man's resentment of cosmopolitan elites who profited from an internationalist foreign policy.

The FP scenario has its virtues. For one thing, it would explain why the Bible's calls for exclusive devotion to Yahweh are so often infused with a nationalist spirit, an aversion to the foreign. This spirit goes well beyond the prophetic texts cited above. The Bible's main narrative of ancient Israel's history is the so-called Deuteronomistic history, stretching from the book of Deuteronomy through the books of Joshua, Judges, First and Second Samuel, and First and Second Kings. In the Deuteronomistic history, departures from devotion to Yahweh are routinely chalked up to sinister foreign influence—to the Israelites' emulation of "the abominable practices of the nations."[48] The frequently nationalistic, sometimes even xenophobic, tone of the Bible's monolatrous passages demands an explanation, and the FP scenario provides one.

Yet the FP scenario has shortcomings, especially if it aims to be a complete, self-sufficient explanation for the evolution of monolatry in Israel. True, pure monolatry—rejecting the worship of *all* gods but Yahweh—would, in the FP scenario, result from true, pure nationalism—a rejection of alliance with *all* nations. But in real life there is no such thing as an *utterly* nationalist king, a king who sees no potential synergy in relations with any neighbor. Granted that internationalist kings were more broadly open to foreign gods than more nationalist kings, so that a nationalist foreign policy has monolatrous tendencies; still, for the FP scenario to get us all the way to monolatry, a king would need to be nationalist to an implausible degree.

Besides, even then the FP scenario wouldn't have entirely explained the evolution of monolatry. After all, monolatry presumably called for the rejection of more than just *foreign* gods. One prospect raised by the previous chapter, remember, was that Israelite monotheism evolved out of *Israelite* polytheism; there are hints of an indigenous pantheon, and the drift toward monolatry, and then toward monotheism, would have involved the extinction of every god in that pantheon except one.

Of course, some members of Israel's pantheon may have been foreign imports, but certainly not all were recent arrivals. Remember Asherah, Yahweh's presumed consort? She had been with El, longtime resident of the region and apparent source of some of Yahweh's DNA, since early times, and so was about as deeply rooted in Israelite tradition as a god could be. Yet at some point, if monolatry was to rule, she and Yahweh must get divorced, and other gods with valid Israelite pedigrees must also be shown the door; there needed to be a domestic housecleaning. For this housecleaning to succeed, it would need the support of Israel's king, and a nationalist foreign policy alone—as in the FP scenario—doesn't seem to explain why he would provide it.

Then again, foreign policy isn't the only political realm in which a king operates. There's also domestic politics. Here lies the second major explanation of how the drive toward monolatry acquired critical mass. Call it the DP scenario, for domestic politics—or, perhaps, for domestic power. Moderners think of ancient kings as autocrats who ruled with an iron fist, but in fact they usually faced rival power centers, whether in the form of other aristocrats or tribal chieftains or far-flung clan leaders or maverick priests. Israelite politics around the middle of the first millennium BCE would offer kings an opportunity to fight this centrifugal force, to draw domestic power toward the center. Seizing the opportunity would mean aligning themselves with the Yahweh-alone movement. In the DP scenario, the extinction of all gods but Yahweh would turn out to have compelling logic in the realm of power politics.

How Kings Got More Devout

The logic starts with the fact that Israelite kings had always had a special affection for Yahweh. He was, after all, the national god—the god who represented Israel on the international stage and, more to the point, gave legitimacy to the king. Indeed, the king, according to one of the Psalms, was Yahweh's son.[49] So even the most polytheistic of kings had an interest in glorifying Yahweh. Ahab, who allegedly abetted Jezebel's Baal, named his sons after Yahweh.[50]

As would lots of other powerful people. Beginning in the eighth century, as the use of writing grew, Israelites left more and more evidence of personal names—signature "seals" made of stone or bone.[51] In a pioneering study of some twelve hundred seals left over from the eighth, seventh, and early sixth centuries, the scholar Jeffrey Tigay showed that about half bore names referring to gods, and that of those, more than 80 percent referred to Yahweh.[52] For various reasons, this doesn't mean that Israel was at least 80 percent of the way to monolatry. (For example: Israelites seem not to have named people after female deities, yet archaeologists have found vast numbers of female figurines, suggesting goddess worship.)[53] But at the very least it means, as the scholar Diana V. Edelman has put it, that "a person who wanted his son to advance in the governmental bureaucracy named him after the head male deity of the pantheon, Yahweh."[54] Even before the Yahweh-alonists had triumphed, Yahweh was the divine focus of king and court, the master of state affairs. If there was any single god you could get the king to tie his fate to, it was Yahweh.

And this wasn't just because Yahweh, as the national god, gave kings the glow of divine legitimacy. There was also more concrete and fine-grained linkage between a strong Yahweh and a strong king.

In ancient Israel some of the king's most important advisers were prophets.[55] Their advice emanated from the divine. If they argued for or against launching a war, they didn't just talk about enemy troop levels; they talked about Yahweh's will, which they'd fathomed firsthand, perhaps by actually watching the divine council in action. (As one Cassandraish prophet tells Ahab, by way of establishing his bona fides, "I saw the LORD sitting on his throne...")[56] So one way for a king to keep a firm grip on policy was to decide which of Yahweh's prophets got the most airtime. And kings no doubt had a lot of say in this matter, given that Yahweh was the more-or-less official state god.[57]

Unfortunately for kings, Yahweh, though the undisputed authority on war, wasn't the only possible source of divine guidance in all policy matters. Other gods had views, as their prophets were quick to note. (There were at one point "four hundred prophets of Asherah" in the northern kingdom of Israel, the Bible reports darkly.)[58] And kings presumably had less influence over these prophets than over Yahweh's prophets.[59]

For that matter, you didn't even have to be a prophet—that is, someone with special access to a particular god—to channel supernatural advice into policy discourse. There was the usual ancient array of quasi-magical divination techniques. You could even consult the dead via a medium. This sort of necromancy might rival the influence of Yahweh's prophets; the Bible refers to spirits of the dead with the Hebrew word for god (*elohim*) that is also applied to Yahweh.[60]

In short, supernatural pluralism was an enemy of royal power. If every prophet of every god went around broadcasting divine decrees, and every clan in Israel consulted the spirit of its most revered ancestor on policy matters, the king would have trouble staying on message. To consolidate political power, he had to consolidate supernatural power; among the aims of the Yahweh-alonists was "to control the avenues of access to the divine will," notes the historian and theologian Patrick D. Miller in his book *The Religion of Ancient Israel.*[61]

As it happens, the same hostile foreign environment that stoked intolerance of foreign gods worked against Yahweh's rivals in the domestic pantheon as well. One of the most reliable laws of political science is the "rally-round-the-flag" effect. When a nation faces a crisis, whether the outbreak of war or a shocking terrorist attack, support for the nation's leader grows. In ancient times—before separation of church and state, back when a nation's ultimate political and military leader was a god—this rule presumably worked at the level of divine allegiance. And since the crises that began in the late eighth century were mainly in foreign affairs, they would have worked to Yahweh's advantage in particular.[62] From the earliest times of Israelite history, Yahweh had been the god of foreign affairs, the god who could authorize war and guide his people through it (or, instead, could counsel restraint); he was the commander-in-chief god. So Yahweh would naturally draw popular allegiance from international turmoil.[63] And because divine devotion is a finite resource, some of this attention would naturally come at the expense of other gods, including those with domestic pedigrees.

Some scholars think this dynamic alone pushed Israel well down the path toward monotheism. As the theologian Gerd Theissen has put it, "Israel lived in a state of permanent crisis," and "conditions of chronic crisis led to chronic monolatry."[64] But there was probably more at work. The reason this sort of adoration is called the rally-round-the-flag effect, remember, is that it works at the mundane as well as the divine level. In times of national crisis, the political leadership's popularity grows, and people grow willing to cede power to it. For leaders who would like to amass more power—a category that includes roughly every king who has ever lived—this is an opportunity, a magic moment to be seized.

But how to seize it? Modern politicians seize such moments by rewriting laws—giving the federal government more power of policing, of taxation, more power to override local governments or civil liberties. This sort of sheerly legalistic power grab was possible for ancient politicians, too, but richer prospects lay on another plane entirely. By weeding out the domestic pantheon, the king could render Yahweh's aggrandizement eternal and thus eternally expand the king's own power. It was the ancient equivalent of making martial law permanent.

Toward the end of the seventh century BCE, this opportunity was seized by the most important king in the theological history of Israel. He's not hard to spot. The Bible's historical narrative, after saying that king after king "did evil in the sight of the LORD,"[65] awards him that rare designation "He did what was right in the sight of the LORD."[66] His name was Josiah, and he assumed the throne around 640 BCE—about half a century after the last non-evil king, Hezekiah, had died.

Josiah was placed on the throne as a boy by a faction of "anti-Assyrian nationalists," as one scholar puts it,[67] and he pursued a heavily military foreign policy—just the kinds of things the FP scenario predicts for a monolatrist. Then again, these factors are also consistent with the DP scenario. Because foreign antagonism helps a leader centralize power, you might expect a king bent on centralizing power to foment such antagonism, as Josiah did in resisting

Assyrian dominance. Or, for that matter, even if his belligerence wasn't consciously calculated to consolidate power domestically, he might wind up going with the flow: upon sensing how strife abroad was empowering him, he might decide to sustain the trend, taking the opportunity to pare down the domestic pantheon.

Also consistent with both the FP and DP scenarios is a correlation between ideology and theology that we see in three Israelite kings who dominated the seventh century — the nationalist and monolatrous Hezekiah, an internationalist and polytheistic king named Manasseh, and the nationalist and monolatrous Josiah.[68] And since the FP and DP models aren't mutually exclusive, so much the better for both of them.

The Godfather

Each of these three kings represented a pivot point in Israel's century-long fluctuation between polytheism and monolatry, but ultimately Josiah's pivot would prove the most momentous. In retrospect, he was a kind of godfather of monotheism, even if only a monolatrist himself.[69] He set the stage for the arrival of the one true god.

Here "godfather" is meant in the innocent sense, not the Mafia sense, though when it came to tactics, Josiah wasn't averse to a little thuggery. (At least, that's the implication of the narrative in Second Kings, which scholars accord more credibility than older Bible stories, such as the Elijah episode.)[70] For starters, Josiah had priests take from Yahweh's temple and burn "all the vessels made for Baal, for Asherah" and for "all the host of heaven" (which in this context means deified celestial bodies). He removed horses used in sun worship from the entrance to the temple and "burned the chariots of the sun with fire." He wiped out shrines built for "Astarte the abomination of the Sidonians, for Chemosh the abomination of Moab, and for Milcom the abomination of the Ammonites" — and, as a kind of exclamation point, covered these sites with human bones. Josiah also banned mediums, sorcerers, household gods, idols, and miscellaneous other "abominations that were seen in the land of Judah and in Jerusalem."[71]

As had Hezekiah, King Josiah tore down "the high places"—-altars across Judah where various gods might be worshipped.[72] But the altars themselves weren't the only target. According to the Bible, Josiah "deposed" the priests linked to them, emphatically including priests who "made offerings to Baal, to the sun, the moon, the constellations." And beyond Judah, in the former northern kingdom, Josiah went further: he "slaughtered on the altars all the priests of the high places who were there, and burned human bones on them. Then he returned to Jerusalem."[73]

This was presumably a more powerful Jerusalem than the Jerusalem he had left, for all sources of divine authority outside of Jerusalem were now in disarray. Josiah had "centralized the cult," as scholars put it, and he had done so in two senses.

First and most obviously, he had transferred allegiance from various gods to Yahweh—who, conveniently, was the god who endowed Josiah with his power. Second, and more subtly, he had centralized the worship *of* Yahweh. Yahweh, after all, had been worshipped, along with other gods, at many of the "high places" Josiah had just leveled. So long as those altars had been in service, manned by local priests or prophets beyond Jerusalem's easy control, the interpretation of Yahweh's will was dangerously open-ended. Indeed, so removed were these local Yahweh cults from the Yahwists in Jerusalem, and from one another, that Yahweh sometimes splintered into different versions of himself. Archaeologists have found written references from the eighth century BCE not just to "Yahweh" but to "Yahweh of Samaria" and "Yahweh of Teman."[74] In a theocracy, this sort of divine fragmentation threatens national unity. Josiah, by confining the legitimate worship of Yahweh to the temple in Jerusalem, was asserting control over Yahweh's identity and thus over Judah's.

This may be the actual meaning of one of the most famous verses in the Bible. Jews call this verse the Sh'ma. Jesus called it the most important commandment in the Hebrew Bible,[75] and Josiah might well have agreed; it is thought to have formed part of the founding text of his religious reforms. The Sh'ma is often translated as an assertion of monotheism, or at least monolatry, as in this rendering in the New Revised Standard Version of the Bible: "Hear, O Israel: The LORD is our God, the LORD alone." But, as the editors of the NRSV acknowledge in a footnote, another possible translation is "The LORD our God is one LORD." And, since the word "LORD" is a stand-in for "Yahweh" in the original Hebrew (as is the all-uppercase LORD in most English editions of the Bible), that suggests this translation: "Hear, O Israel: Yahweh our god is one Yahweh."[76]

The point, in other words, wasn't so much that Israelites were to worship Yahweh rather than other gods (though Josiah certainly encouraged that). The point was that whichever local Yahweh they were accustomed to worshipping was merely an extension of the Yahweh in Jerusalem. So the only valid guides to his will were the Jerusalem prophets, conveniently located in the king's court. The era of local interpretive autonomy was over.

This centralization of divine and hence political power is crystallized in a biblical passage thought to reflect Josiah's agenda, when Yahweh himself declares: "Anyone who does not heed the words that the prophet shall speak in my name, I myself will hold accountable. But any prophet who speaks in the name of other gods...that prophet shall die." For good measure, if anyone—prophet or layperson—says to you, "Let us go worship other gods," you should kill that person, "even if it is your brother, your father's son, or your mother's son, or your own son or daughter, or the wife you embrace, or your most intimate friend." And should you stumble upon a town full of Israelites who worship other gods, then "you shall put the inhabitants of that town to the sword, utterly destroying it and everything in it—even putting its livestock to the sword."[77]

Notwithstanding all this firepower, Josiah wasn't completely successful. Archaeologists have found female figurines, almost certainly of a goddess and quite possibly of Asherah, in enough late-seventh-century homes to suggest that closet polytheists were legion.[78] Still, Josiah's reign marked a watershed in the movement toward monotheism. Yahweh and Yahweh alone—and, more specifically, Yahweh of Jerusalem—was now the officially sanctioned god of Israelites.

The picture of Josiah that emerges here is not flattering: a ruthless authoritarian who deprives people of their beloved gods for his own political gain. But he had his redeeming features. He didn't *just* take away the people's pantheon; he took it away and gave the people—especially lower-class people—something in return. Josiah's reforms went beyond religion, providing peasants with debt relief, protection against the seizure of their property, and what one scholar called a "rudimentary social security system."[79]

So chalk one up for the FP scenario, according to which the Yahweh-alone movement had drawn energy from both anti-internationalism and class resentment ever since the days of Hosea, Amos, and Isaiah. And, once again, this support for the FP scenario hardly rules out the DP scenario. Both dynamics may have been at work: nationalist rejection of foreign gods and downsizing the domestic pantheon to consolidate political power. And both dynamics could plausibly have drawn energy from Israel's adverse geopolitical climate. So we needn't necessarily choose between the two. Still, it would be nice to figure out whether both dynamics *did* play a big role—and, if they did, to clarify the relationship between them.

Alienating Non-Aliens

The FP scenario emphasizes the rejection of foreign gods as the pathway to monolatry. And it's certainly true that many of the gods whose worship Josiah suppressed are either explicitly or implicitly identified in the Bible as foreign. But should we really take the Bible's word about which gods were foreign? Recall from the previous chapter that some of the Bible's authors seem to exaggerate the foreignness of things they don't like. Maybe monolatrous prophets and politicians did the same. Maybe the Bible, in its unflattering characterization of gods other than Yahweh, reflects not just Josiah's theology but his rhetorical technique—labeling domestic gods as foreign to ease their expulsion from the pantheon.

The biblical scholar Baruch Halpern has argued as much. He believes that various deities who were "stigmatized as foreign" during Israel's religious reforms had in fact been Yahweh's subordinates in an Israelite pantheon.[80] Thus we see "the systematic turning of traditional xenophobic rhetoric...against the traditional religion of Israel" so that in the end Israel's religion was "alienated from itself."[81] In this view, biblical authors, in listing the worship of, say, celestial deities among "the abominable practices of the nations,"[82] were just using fear of the foreign to purge the indigenous.

This has the ring of plausibility, but one problem with evaluating it is the difficulty of figuring out which gods *were* indigenous. Scholars have tried to get to the bottom of this question for decades, with some stressing the foreign lineage of Yahweh's rivals and others positing domestic pedigrees. Both sides have been so diligent that listening to the evidence can send you into a state of high-frequency vacillation. And, actually, it's worth spending some time in that state, for in the end this irresolution tells us something important about the evolution of gods.

In favor of Halpern's argument is that, when Josiah decides to burn the accoutrements for worshipping these celestial deities, he finds them in Yahweh's own temple.[83] Apparently mainstream Israelites, including Jerusalem priests, had considered these gods a natural part of Yahweh's family, not invaders from beyond Judah's borders. On the other hand, that doesn't mean they couldn't have been fairly recent imports. Assyrian culture, which swept over the northern kingdom upon its collapse in the late eighth century and then encroached more subtly on Assyria's vassal Judah, was heavily into "astral religion," and so could have provided some of the gods the Bible has Josiah vanquishing, notably "the moon, the constellations, and all the host of heavens."[84] And maybe, by Josiah's time, these aliens had endeared themselves to Yahweh worshippers and thus become part of Yahweh's family. Indeed, archaeologists have found a Palestinian signature seal from the mid-seventh century that features an Assyrian-style lunar icon but was owned by a man named after Yahweh, one "Natan-Yahu."[85]

Then again, as the scholar Lowell Handy has noted, there are also reasons to suspect that moon worship predated Assyria's seventh-century cultural hegemony. In a Bible story that may be quite old,[86] Joshua tells the moon to stop dead in its tracks, and Yahweh uses his influence to bring about the moon's compliance.[87] Given that inanimate hunks of orbiting rock aren't the kinds of things you generally converse with, scholars have long wondered whether the Hebrew word for moon—*yareah*—in this scripture refers to a moon *god*. This suspicion grew when Ugaritic texts revealed the existence of a late-second-millennium Canaanite moon god named Yarih. And there's evidence that Yarih was a favorite deity of El,[88] whose identity, as we've seen, was primordially intertwined with Yahweh's. So Yahweh and Yareah may well have known each other for quite some time.[89] (And maybe this particular snapshot from their shared past survived the Bible's editorial process because it illustrated Yahweh's mastery over Yareah, a Kodak moment in the drift from polytheism to monotheism.)

Lots of deities on Josiah's hit list have an ancestry as murky as the moon god's, and so can be cast as either foreign or domestic. Consider the goddess Astarte (or "Ashtoreth" or "the Queen of Heaven," two biblical appellations that apparently refer to Astarte). It's true that she was worshipped in the Phoenician city of Sidon (Jezebel territory!) and thus can be aptly derided in the Bible as "the abomination of the Sidonians."[90] But it's also true that Astarte had belonged to the Ugaritic pantheon headed by El; like Yareah, she may have been in Yahweh's entourage since early days.[91] In fact, it turns out that "Astarte" is just the Canaanite name for Ishtar, the very ancient, rampantly lustful Mesopotamian goddess from chapter 4. (It should go without saying that Astarte spent some time as a consort of the famously virile Baal.)[92]

Here we've come to a big part of the problem with deciding whether gods stigmatized as foreign were in fact domestic. The family trees of gods can sprout so profusely that, though your indigenous gods bear a great resemblance to foreign gods, they do so because of common descent, not alien infection. Yes, Jezebel may have brought Baal in from Tyre. But that doesn't mean this Baal, of Phoenician extraction, was the same Baal that, as Mark Smith puts it, "belonged authentically to Israel's Canaanite heritage."[93] It just means opponents of the indigenous Baal had an easier time stigmatizing him.

Opponents such as Elijah? We've come back to the starting point of this chapter—the question of what exactly happened among Elijah, Ahab, and Jezebel, and why it happened. But now we're in a better position to answer it.

Elijah Revisited

The Elijah story comes from the first book of Kings, and hence from that seven-book stretch known as the Deuteronomistic history, so called because it tells Israelite history in a way that validates the theological, moral, and legal principles laid out in the book of Deuteronomy. And what are those principles? In a word: Josiah's. This doesn't mean that the entire Deuteronomistic history was written during Josiah's time, by Josiah's scribes. (Much of it may have been, but most scholars agree that some was written before Josiah's time and some after.) It just means, at a minimum, that the history is told from the perspective of Josianic ideology; that if Josiah's scribes *had* set out to write a masterful piece of propaganda—a history that authorized and sacralized Josiah's agenda—they would have come up with something broadly like the Deuteronomistic history.

Put yourself in their shoes. Suppose that, even as your king tried to confine devotion to Yahweh, pesky pockets of Baal devotees persisted. And suppose you were writing during times of national duress, when xenophobia had resonance—or, at least, that you were trying to marshal political support from a particularly xenophobic segment of society. Then it might help to (a) depict Baal as foreign; (b) link Baal to the conniving foreign wife of some previous king;

and (c) make it a king who had a bad reputation to begin with. The scholar William Schniedewind believes that, in early stories about Ahab, told well before Josiah's time, he was notorious, but only for seizing a citizen's vineyard. Then, long after Ahab's death, some Yahweh-alone types beefed up the indictment; Ahab, it was now said (in 1 Kings), had made an idol for the worship of the Israelite goddess Asherah. Later still, believes Schniedewind, Ahab was depicted as "an outright worshipper of Phoenician Baal"—part of a new biblical polemic that "considered any idol to be a foreign deity."[94]

In other words, the nontrivial amount of ink spilled speculating about what motivated Elijah to oppose Ahab's Baal worship may have been spilled in vain. The whole thing may be a made-up story. Near the beginning of this chapter, shortly before I spilled my share of that ink, I alluded to this possibility and said there was a sense in which it doesn't matter: assuming the Elijah story true and assuming it a piece of propaganda have some common implications.

In particular: either way, the drift toward monotheism is linked to a reaction against something foreign. If the Elijah story is true, then at least some of Elijah's support in his war against the Phoenician Baal came from anti-Phoenician elements. If the story is false, and took shape during some later monolatrous crusade, it presumably took shape because anti-Phoenician, and perhaps broadly xenophobic, rhetoric had a receptive audience. So too with the question of how accurately we can date various passages in prophetic books that speak for the Yahweh-alone movement.[95] If Hosea's two intertwined themes—monolatry and an aversion to foreign contact—were in fact amplified or even created well after Hosea's time, there must have been something in the air that made them rhetorically symbiotic. Similarly, Zephaniah's tirades against alien nations and alien gods must coexist for a reason, regardless of when they were written down. However we date these biblical texts, however much factual accuracy we attribute to them, there is no denying the air of nationalism and even xenophobia that surrounds Yahweh's movement toward the status of the one true god.

In other words, even if the FP scenario is wrong at the theological level—mistaken in its claim that monolatry drew much energy from the rejection of truly *foreign* gods—its analysis of Israel's political psychology is right. As a small nation buffeted by great powers, Israel often had to choose between war against potent enemies and a peace that many Israelites found humiliating. And the resultant hostility toward foreign powers was only intensified among commoners who resented the way cosmopolitan elites profited by befriending Israel's oppressors. This—the psychology of the FP scenario—is what was harnessed by the Yahweh-alone movement even if the DP scenario is right, and that movement was mainly about killing off indigenously Israelite gods to consolidate the king's power. Regardless of how accurate the Bible's labeling of all those "foreign" gods, the FP scenario and the DP scenario, between them, capture the psychological and political dynamics that got Israel from polytheism to monolatry.

So the law of religious tolerance—or, strictly speaking, its flip side—stands vindicated: when people see themselves as playing zero-sum games with foreigners, they will be ill disposed to embrace, or perhaps even tolerate, foreign gods and religious practices. And this law stands vindicated regardless of whether the various "foreign" gods in the Bible are really foreign.

It would still be nice to know how accurate the Bible is in its depiction of these gods. Was the Deuteronomistic history—history as told from the standpoint of King Josiah and other in the Yahweh-alone movement—a straightforward, nationalist diatribe against everything that came from beyond Israel's borders? Or was it a cunning use of xenophobia, a stigmatization of things that actually came from within Israel's borders?

It no doubt had elements of both. On the one hand, the Israelites must have absorbed some truly foreign religious elements in the not-too-distant past. The chances of a small country on Assyria's periphery in the eighth and seventh centuries BCE not hosting a single shrine to an Assyrian god are about the same as the chances of a small modern country in America's sphere of influence having no McDonald's and no Starbucks.[96] (And the chances of no Israelites resenting those shrines are roughly the chances of no one resenting the cultural intrusion of a globally hegemonic America.) On the other hand, there's no doubt that the Deuteronomistic authors used rhetorical tricks to give gods other than Yahweh the aura of the alien. Even Asherah—who had too ample an Israelite pedigree to be called foreign outright—could be given an alien taint; the Bible refers to "prophets of Asherah, who eat at Jezebel's table."[97]

Certainly, from the outset, the Deuteronomistic history maximizes the ease with which the domestic can be stigmatized as foreign. Recall, from the previous chapter, one of Israel's founding myths, from the (Deuteronomistic) book of Joshua: that Israelites had come to the promised land from the desert and promptly conquered the natives. And recall that archaeology is now showing this story not to be true. Now note a key implication of this untrue story: that just about anything indigenous to the land of Canaan is actually alien, a remnant of the "foreign" culture that had been dispelled (but alas incompletely)[98] with God's blessing.[99]

The Bible often makes this implication explicit. The denunciation of celestial deities noted above—denunciation of "the abominable practices of the nations"—is actually an abridgment. The full version is "the abominable practices of the nations that the LORD drove out before the people of Israel."[100] This formulation is invoked again and again in Deuteronomistic writings to neutralize Yahweh's rivals. In a passage that Josiah probably used to justify his reforms, Moses is said to have instructed the Israelites before they enter Canaan: "No one shall be found among you who...practices divination, or is a soothsayer, or an augur, or a sorcerer, or one who casts spells, or who consults ghosts or spirits, or who seeks oracles from the dead." And why not? Because these are the "abhorrent practices" of "these nations that you are about to dispossess." Indeed, "it is because of such abhorrent practices that the LORD your God is driving them out before you." So "when you come into the land that the LORD your God is giving you, you must not learn to imitate the abhorrent practices of those nations."[101] Apparently some Israelites *did* make the mistake of preserving indigenous religion; otherwise this text—surely written long after the Mosaic era, and quite possibly written in Josiah's day—wouldn't have been written at all.

To note the uncanny theological and political convenience of the Deuteronomistic history isn't to say that it's a product of conscious dishonesty. It probably had many authors, spanning centuries, and drew on an oral history that itself had taken shape gradually. And any anthropologist can tell you that a culture's oral history, though often based on some core truths about the past, may naturally drift toward certain biases without any one person trying consciously to steer it in that direction. One natural bias is called ethnic marking: as an ethnic group works to preserve, or initially construct, a cohesive identity, it highlights differences between itself and nearby peoples.[102] As such differences get amplified and embedded in historical myth, they can amount to a massive distortion. But that doesn't mean that any one person knowingly perpetrated the distortion.

In this sense, Israel's founding myth—Israelites roll in from Egypt and squash natives—is a natural outgrowth of Israel's founding truth: the nation of Israel emerged from within Canaan, and there it crystallized. Reclassifying indigenous Canaanite traditions as alien was part of that crystallization, part of the process by which Israel carved out an identity against the backdrop of Middle Eastern culture. As it happens, this naturally emerging myth found synergy with emerging, intertwined realities—political ones, like the Israelites' perilous international environment and a royal imperative to centralize power, and theological ones like monolatry. And the rest is history.

The Uses of Intolerance

And what of the larger question surrounding this inquiry? Did the evolution of monotheism, as monotheism's critics would claim, entail belligerent intolerance? Certainly the story so far—the evolution of monolatry—does nothing to refute that allegation. Intolerance is part and parcel of Josiah's politics. His aspirations were twofold: he wanted to make Judah a sinewy, centralized state and then use that muscle aggressively—for starters in the conquest of northern Israel (the Israel that had been lost to Assyrian aggression a century earlier), and perhaps ultimately in the conquest of lands beyond.[103] The fiercely nationalist streak in the Yahweh-alone movement served this expansionist aim well. For if nearby polytheistic peoples always threatened to corrupt Israelite religion, then Israelites should have no compunction about destroying them. As the Book of Deuteronomy puts it:

> As for the towns of these peoples that the LORD your God is giving you as an inheritance, you must not let anything that breathes remain alive. You shall annihilate them—the Hittites and the Amorites, the Canaanites and the Perizzites, the Hivites and the Jebusites—just as the LORD your God has commanded, so that they may not teach you to do all the abhorrent things that they do for their gods, and you thus sin against the LORD your God.[104]

Peoples that were farther away, and thus less likely to pollute the local culture, could be treated more leniently. If a distant city surrendered peacefully, then its inhabitants could live on as slaves, and if it resisted, you would "put all its males to the sword" but let the rest live, taking "as your booty the women, the children, livestock, and everything else in the town." [105]

Here again, the question of how many of the gods opposed by the Yahweh-alone faction were foreign and how many were domestic doesn't really matter. Either way, the fuel Josiah drew on was nationalism. Either way, once monolatry was ascendant, its nationalist energy could be wielded against foreigners or against nonconforming Israelites. And, either way, the culminating phase of the Yahweh-alone movement does nothing to dispel the notion that

Israel's drive toward monotheism was a drive toward intolerance. Slaughtering everyone in an Israelite town, slaughtering everyone in a foreign city—both are casually countenanced by the Deuteronomistic Code on grounds that the victims suffered from theological confusion.[106] Josiah's approach to religious tolerance was simple: foreign ideas about the divine are bad, and so are the people who embrace them. And this lethal intolerance is a natural expression of the Yahweh-alone movement's political logic.

In short: if exclusive devotion to Yahweh was to become something that we today would call morally laudable, Israelite religion would have to evolve further. In fact, leaving morality aside, it would have to evolve further *theologically* to earn its place in history. This wasn't monotheism, after all. Nothing in the Deuteronomistic texts, and nothing said by any prophets up to Josiah's time, expresses the clear belief that Yahweh *alone* exists—that the gods of other peoples are mere figments of their imagination. For Israel to push beyond monolatry and embrace monotheism, something more would be needed.

It turned out to be something painful. Josiah, flush with the fighting spirit of an ardent nationalist, devoted to Yahweh and confident of Yahweh's reciprocal devotion, overplayed his hand. He met disaster on the battlefield and helped usher in what would be long remembered as the greatest calamity in the history of the Israelites. Amid the ensuing trauma, the monotheistic impulse would become palpable. Through a chain of paradox that makes sense only in retrospect, the manifest failure of single-minded devotion to Yahweh would intensify that devotion, until finally it reached a whole new level, crossing the threshold from monolatry to monotheism.

Chapter Seven

———

From Monolatry to Monotheism

King Josiah of Judah may have been the most perversely successful man in the history of the world.

On the one hand, it's hard to argue with this verdict from the scholar Marvin Sweeney: "Josiah's reform was an absolute failure."[1] Josiah had wanted to unify southern and northern Israel, to restore the storied greatness of the Davidic empire and do it in the name of Yahweh, covering Israel's god in greater glory. But things went awry. Josiah was killed by the Egyptians. The circumstances of his death are hazy,[2] but it ushered in two decades of abject Israelite submission—first to Egypt and then to Babylon—followed by catastrophe. When King Zedekiah of Judah rebelled against the Babylonians, they captured him, killed his sons before his eyes, plucked out those eyes, then burned Yahweh's temple to the ground. And they completed a process they'd started years earlier, the transfer of Israel's upper classes to Babylon.[3] Now, as of 586 BCE, the Babylonian exile—the most famous trauma in the story of ancient Israel—was in full swing. No doubt the Babylonians, following theological conventions of the day, took all this to signify Yahweh's humiliation at the hands of their national god, Marduk. When, decades earlier, Josiah set out to exalt Yahweh, this is not the outcome he had in mind.

And yet, this would turn out to be the best thing that ever happened to Yahweh. Josiah's theology—worship Yahweh and Yahweh alone—would not only survive and prevail, but prevail in grander, intensified form. Jews—and then Christians and then Muslims—would come to believe that the Abrahamic god was not just the only god worth worshipping, but the only god in existence; monolatry would evolve into monotheism. As the theologian Ralph W. Klein has observed, "Israel's exilic theologians made the most of their disaster."[4]

Orchestrating a seismic theological revolution isn't the kind of thing you do overnight. But if there's one thing the exile gave Israelite intellectuals, it was time to mull the situation. They spent about a half century in Babylon before the Persians, having conquered the Babylonians and thus having inherited the Israelites, started sending exiles back to Jerusalem, where many Israelites had remained all along. In Jerusalem ideas shaped in the refiner's fire of exile would eventually carry the day.

Making Sense of Disaster

It is sometimes said that the monotheistic thesis arose as a way to "make sense of" the catastrophe that had befallen Jerusalem. This is accurate but inadequate. Yes, religions have always addressed the question of why bad things happen, and yes, that is a question Israel's exilic intellectuals had plenty of cause to ponder, and yes, this pondering led eventually to monotheism. So, there is a sense in which, as some have said, exilic theology was a solution to the "problem of evil" or the "problem of suffering." But this sense is pretty misleading. After all, the "problem of evil" doesn't arise in acute form unless you believe in a single all-powerful and good God. Only if God is omnipotent does all human suffering become something he is choosing to tolerate, and only if he is wholly benevolent does this choice become something of a puzzle. And this kind of god, infinite in power and goodness, is exactly the kind of god that, so far as we can tell, didn't exist before the exile; this is the kind of god whose emergence during the exile we're trying to *explain*. Monotheism can't be the premise of the theological reflection that created it.

Besides, describing Israel's theological revolution this way—

"making sense of" suffering, "pondering" the problem of evil—
makes the exercise sound more abstract and philosophical, and less
urgent, than such exercises were in those days. Almost certainly,
the "theological discourse" that produced monotheism began as an
orgy of political recriminations: different factions, with their different theologies, blaming each other for what had gone wrong.

The Bible recounts one exilic episode of finger pointing. A group
of Israelites, including the prophet Jeremiah, have gone to Egypt
rather than Babylon after the Babylonian conquest. There is disagreement over why things have fallen apart. Jeremiah says Yahweh
has punished Israelites because so many of them were worshipping
other gods. And if they keep it up, if they continue to "make offerings to the queen of heaven," then Yahweh will kill them all, either
by sword or by famine.[5] The queen of heaven's devotees have a different perspective. They seem to think that the root of Israel's problems is the Jeremiahs of the world—the Yahweh-alonists. They say
in unison, "We used to have plenty of food, and prospered, and saw
no misfortune. From the time we stopped making offerings to the
queen of heaven and pouring out libations to her, we have lacked
everything and have perished by the sword and by famine."[6]

And they had a point! If Jeremiah was right, and worshipping
Yahweh alone was the ticket to national greatness, how come the
nation started falling apart not long after Josiah's monolatrous
reforms? And note that the opening act in this national downfall was
the death of Josiah himself, the nation's Yahweh-alonist-in-chief.
Kind of makes you wonder about the whole premise of Yahweh-
alonism—that Yahweh was a god who could and would take care
of you so long as you confined your devotion to him.

How could Yahweh survive this potent rhetorical assault? With
a little help from his friends. In the two decades between Josiah's
death and the burning of the temple, the Yahweh-alone movement
seems to have stayed active, even if it lost the political power it
enjoyed while Josiah was king.[7] So Jeremiah was not alone: over
in Babylon there were other Israelite thinkers who had staked

their reputations on the notion of a strong, protective Yahweh. Some of the nation's finest minds would be seeking a theology that could reconcile Israel's catastrophe with the greatness of Israel's god.

Part of the solution was simple. Josiah may have done a thorough job of reforming Israel's official religion, but there was—in the ancient world as now—a difference between official religion and the actual beliefs of ordinary people. Though the Bible tells us that Josiah targeted "household gods,"[8] the abundance of goddess-like figurines found by archaeologists in Israelite households suggests that, if so, he didn't wholly succeed. So Jeremiah and other monolatrists could argue that stubborn grassroots infidelity was the sin for which Yahweh punished Israel.

And then there's the fact that Josiah's successors—the several kings who appear between his death and the exile—seem not to have shared his devotion to Yahweh. If infidelity was afoot at both the royal and the grassroots levels, no wonder Yahweh didn't spring to Israel's defense!

Of course, none of this post-Josianic backsliding would explain why Josiah himself died prematurely. But here the idea of delayed justice would prove useful. Josiah had been preceded by various polytheistic kings, notably the wicked and influential Manasseh. Manasseh's half century of theological promiscuity ended only two years before Josiah's reign began and left too big a residue of evil for even Josiah to erase. The book of Second Kings tells us that Josiah "turned to the LORD with all his heart, with all his soul, and with all his might"—but "still the LORD did not turn away from the fierceness of his great wrath, by which his anger was kindled against Judah, because of all the provocations with which Manasseh had provoked him."[9]

So far so good. These sins—epic pre-Josianic infidelity plus ongoing post-Josianic infidelity—could in theory explain why Yahweh countenanced the conquest of his people. Indeed, this became the official explanation in the Deuteronimistic history, which ends with the story of the Babylonian exile in the book of Second Kings.

Two Orders of Magnitude

Attributing geopolitical misfortune to the wrath of your national god was nothing new in Israel, or for that matter in the Middle East broadly.[10] That's how the Moabites of the ninth century BCE had explained why their national god Chemosh stood by while Israel subjugated them. As King Mesha of Moab explained in the "Mesha Stele," Israel "humbled Moab many days, for Chemosh was angry at his land."[11] Yet the Moabites didn't go on to conclude that Chemosh was the only god in existence. Nor had the Israelites been pushed to that extreme in previous attempts to explain setbacks via divine wrath. What made the Babylonian setback different? Its magnitude, in at least two senses of the word.

For starters, the Babylonian conquest was no passing dustup with some small-scale polity. It wasn't like the time when, as the Bible says, Yahweh got upset with the Israelites and "sold them into the hand of King Cushan-rishathaim of Aram-naharaim; and the Israelites served Cushan-rishathaim eight years." Nor was it like the time when Yawheh "strengthened King Eglon of Moab against Israel," forcing Israel into an eighteen-year vassalage.[12] This wasn't vassalage, but exile, and it came not at the hands of some Canaanite tribe, but at the hands of the greatest empire within Israel's realm of awareness.

This magnitude didn't push Israel's exilic thinkers inexorably toward a single, all-powerful god, but it's easy to imagine it nudging some of them in that direction. After all, any god that wields a whole empire as an instrument of reprimand must be pretty potent. This ironic logic — that the more massively your nation is menaced, the more powerful your god must be — had surfaced back in the eighth century, as the great Assyrian Empire tormented all of Israel and devastated part of it. When Isaiah quoted Yahweh nonchalantly saying, "Ah, Assyria, the rod of my anger," he was depicting no ordinary god.[13] Such a god presumably had Assyria's imperial god, the mighty Assur, in the palm of his hand.

Isaiah was writing in the relative comfort of the south—in Judah, which was beset by Assyrian might but not overwhelmed by it, as the northern kingdom of Ephraim was. In contrast, the seminal theological reaction to Babylonian subjugation came from people who had taken the brunt of a conquest, and who then pondered its implications as exiles living in a strange land. This is the second sense in which Israelite monotheism resulted from the "magnitude" of the Babylonian conquest: monotheistic theology was shaped by people who felt the ensuing trauma in massive proportion. Not only had they seen their land conquered; they had seen their land disappear—and this after witnessing the destruction of the most concrete symbol of their nationhood: the temple of their national god. They now lived among people speaking a different language, worshipping different gods. This was a crisis not just of national security but of national identity.

These two forms of magnitude—the momentousness of Israel's geopolitical defeat, and the depth of the psychological trauma—left two basic theological options on the table and rendered one of them unpalatable. First, the Israelites could just conclude that their god had lost a battle; Yahweh had done his best, only to lose to the mighty Marduk, imperial god of the Babylonians. But the thought of your national god losing has never been appealing (to Israelites, to Moabites, to people in general), and in this case it was just about unbearable. For if Yahweh had lost this battle, he had lost in an utterly humiliating way. His temple—his home—had been destroyed, and his people had been stolen. To think of your god as losing so abjectly was almost to think of your god as dead. And in those days, in that part of the world, thinking of your national god as dead meant thinking of your nationality as dead. Divine identity, national identity, and ethnic identity were essentially inseparable.

That left option two: concluding that the outcome had been Yahweh's will. But if the outcome was Yahweh's will, then he was even stronger than had been previously evident. After all, the Babylonians had conquered the mighty Assyrians. If wielding Assyria as "the rod of my anger" was testament to Yahweh's strength, what did it mean when he did the same with Assyria's conquerors? According to the book of Habakkuk, Yahweh himself directed the Israelites' attention to this question as the Babylonian onslaught unfolded. "Look at the nations, and see! Be astonished! Be astounded! For a work is being done in your days that you would not believe if you were told. For I am rousing the Chaldeans [Babylonians], that fierce and impetuous nation, who march through the breadth of the earth to seize dwellings not their own.... At kings they scoff, and of rulers they make sport."[14] Imagine how mighty you must be to make sport of *them*—to get them to unwittingly do your punishing for you! Their god Marduk must be your puppet!

Hence the irony of the emergence of Israelite monotheism. As Mark Smith has observed, "Israel stands at the bottom of its political power, and it exalts its deity inversely as ruler of the whole universe."[15] The logic may sound perverse, but it is logic nonetheless. A god who governs the actions of the greatest known empire is a god who can govern history itself.

Yet the word "logic" is misleading in its sterility. Religion has always been an interplay between thought and feeling. By exploring the emotional texture of exilic theology, we can put a finer point on its logic. And we can also answer, finally, the question of what kind of deity the Abrahamic god was at the moment he became the one true god—the moment that god became God.

The Second Coming of Isaiah

No biblical writer speaks more directly to these questions than the prophet Isaiah. This isn't the same Isaiah who wrote about Assyria's eighth-century aggression against Israel from his perch in Judah. That Isaiah, scholars now agree, is confined to the first thirty-nine chapters of the book of Isaiah. The next fifteen chapters (if not more) were written mainly during the exile, more than a century later, probably in Babylon. This other Isaiah—"Second Isaiah" or "Deutero-Isaiah"—is a shining example of exile's effect on Israelite theology. Second Isaiah calls the exile "the furnace of adversity" and is unsurpassed among biblical authors in displaying the product of that furnace.[16]

Often in the chapters of Second Isaiah, Yahweh speaks directly. He is not modest. "I am the LORD, and there is no other; besides me there is no god." "I am the LORD and besides me there is no savior." "I am the first and I am the last." "Before me no god was formed, nor shall there be any after me." "I am the LORD, who made all things, who alone stretched out the heavens, who by myself spread out the earth." "I form light and create darkness."[17] And so on. No wonder biblical scholars cite Second Isaiah as a landmark. After centuries of Yahweh-alone prophets who don't venture unambiguously beyond monolatry, monotheistic declarations finally come with clarity and force.

But there is a second theme in this text that gets at least as much attention from scholars as monotheism. If Yahweh is, as Second Isaiah says, "God of the whole earth," then the question arises as to what his stance toward the whole earth will be. And what will Israel's relation to the rest of the world be after Israel's suffering ends? The answer, as commonly rendered, is inspiring. God promises that he will "bring forth justice to the nations." He is universal not just in his power, but in his concern, and this expanded sympathy gives Israel a momentous mission. Yahweh says, in a much-quoted line, "I will give you as a light to the nations, that my salvation may reach to the end of the earth."[18]

This uplifting interpretation of Second Isaiah is popular among Christian and Jewish thinkers who acknowledge the darker side of Yahweh that, as we've seen, can be found elsewhere in the Bible. Granted, they say, Yahweh exhibits some national chauvinism and intolerance in his early history, as recounted in Joshua and Deuteronomy, but eventually he matures and we wind up with a god concerned with the welfare of all peoples. Israel, after centuries of conflict with the nations, now sets out to save them; from on high it is given the task of global enlightenment. Its worldview, you might say, pivots from zero-sum to non-zero-sum, as the world's peoples are moved from the "implacable enemies" category into the "potential converts" category.

This interpretation of Second Isaiah makes a kind of sense in light of the exile. Trauma can bring change, and often the change is commensurate with the trauma. If your car is totaled because you drove after drinking, you may vow never to drink again. If your son is killed because you drove after drinking, a whole new level of reorientation is called for: you may launch a campaign against drunk driving, and you may even decide that this campaign is your mission, your calling. Exilic thinkers in Babylon had suffered a trauma that was more like losing a son than losing a car. They needed a paradigm that could both explain their suffering and transmute it into good, a paradigm that could forge a new religious commitment with ultimately redemptive power.

And they found it—at least according to the standard interpretation of Second Isaiah: the Israelites, having suffered for their infidelity to Yahweh, would try to keep the world's other peoples from repeating their mistake. Monotheism is thus morally universalistic from its birth, and any belligerence it has shown since is an aberration, a departure from the norm and from the design.

But a candid reading of exilic texts leads to a less heartwarming conclusion—that the universalism present at monotheism's birth may not deserve the qualifier "moral." It's true that various exilic writings envision a day when all nations will, through Israel, come into contact with Israel's god. Then again, Middle Eastern history was full of nations that wanted to bring other nations into contact with their gods, and often the form of contact they had in mind was abject submission. To acknowledge the greatness of your national god was to acknowledge the greatness—the superiority—of your nation. And so it is in Second Isaiah: God is promising that the various peoples who have tormented and enslaved Israel over the centuries will eventually get their just deserts; they'll be forced to acknowledge Israel's superiority on both a political and a theological plane.

Here, for example, is what the God of Second Isaiah tells the Israelites about Egyptians, Ethiopians, and Sabeans: They "shall come over to you and be yours, they shall follow you; they shall come over in chains and bow down to you. They will make supplication to you, saying, 'God is with you alone, and there is no other; there is no god besides him.' "[19]

A few chapters later Yahweh tells the Israelites that "I will soon lift up my hand to the nations, and raise my signal to the peoples." A morally promising start, but it turns out the signal is going to instruct these peoples to serve the Israelites. And as for the rulers of these nations: "With their faces to the ground they shall bow down to you, and lick the dust of your feet. Then you will know that I am the LORD." And for good measure: "I will make your oppressors eat their own flesh, and they shall be drunk with their own blood as with wine. Then all flesh shall know that I am the LORD your Savior, and your Redeemer, the Mighty One of Jacob."[20]

In this light, the monotheism of exilic theology appears less like a radical departure from the zero-sum thinking that helped energize monolatry, and more like its apotheosis. Second Isaiah's visions of Israel's coming dominance are in the tradition of the "oracles against the nations" that appear in pre-exilic prophetic texts of a monolatrous bent. And the zero-sum pedigree of these visions may go back further than that. The biblical scholar Rainer Albertz, in his book *Israel in Exile*, argued that this whole genre descended from prophetic oracles centuries earlier that were preludes to actual war.[21]

Yet Albertz, like many other interpreters of exilic theology, tries to put the nicest face possible on all this. After appraising a series of vengeful judgments in the apparently exilic text of Ezekiel, he says they "end on a surprisingly conciliatory note: the judgment of Yahweh will bring all Israel's neighbors — except Edom — to the knowledge of Yahweh."[22]

Well, "knowledge of Yahweh" is one way of putting it; it's true that the verb "know" appears. For example, it shows up at the end of this proclamation from Ezekiel, directed by God toward the Ammonites:

> Because you have clapped your hands and stamped your feet and rejoiced with all the malice within you against the land of Israel, therefore I have stretched out my hand against you, and will hand you over as plunder to the nations. I will cut you off from the peoples and will make you perish out of the countries; I will destroy you. Then you shall know that I am the LORD.[23]

In other words: you shall "know" who's boss. And so it is with the other "surprisingly conciliatory" notes in Ezekiel. Moab shall "know that I am the LORD" after he arranges for it to be conquered by a neighbor — its punishment for thinking that Israel isn't special, that "the house of Judah is like all the other nations." And as for the Philistines and Cherethites: "I will execute great vengeance on them with wrathful punishments. Then they shall know that I am the Lord, when I lay my vengeance on them."[24]

And, Ezekiel says, Sidon (Jezebel territory) will be granted knowledge, too:

> They shall know that I am the LORD
> when I execute judgments in it,
> and manifest my holiness in it;
> for I will send pestilence into it,
> and bloodshed into its streets;
> and the dead shall fall in its midst,
> by the sword that is against it on every side.
> And they shall know that I am the LORD.[25]

The "holiness" that Yahweh here promises to "manifest" brings to mind Rudolf Otto's 1917 treatise *The Idea of the Holy.* As Otto showed, in ancient times the concept of the "holy" didn't have its modern implication of moral goodness. (Often in the Bible the

Hebrew word translated as "holy" refers to a merely ritual purity.) Indeed, Otto argued, in its primordial form, the "holy" represented what he called the "numinous"—a sublime force that inspired terror and dread; an "aweful majesty."[26]

The Ultimate Revenge

How exactly was the holy force to be delivered? Did exilic monotheists imagine Israelite armies someday conquering the world? In Ezekiel, Yahweh tells the Israelites that "the nations shall know that I am the LORD...when through you I display my holiness before their eyes."[27] Reading this verse as a military aspiration would have made sense in the ancient Middle East: a god showed his greatness through the power of his nation.

Certainly the Israelites had spent plenty of time on the receiving end of this logic. Assyria, Israel's perennial persecutor, celebrated victories by capturing or destroying foreign idols, underscoring the theological truth behind martial triumph: the inferiority of foreign gods to the great god Assur. An Assyrian inscription recording the fall of an Israelite city in the eighth century boasts, "and the gods, in which they trusted, as spoil counted."[28]

More specifically, there was precedent for the humiliated victim of imperial conquest planning and executing a grand comeback that proceeded on both a theological and geopolitical plane: the very Babylonians who had now subjugated Israel. The Assyrians had laid waste to Babylon in the early seventh century, taking the statue of Marduk from his temple. Like the Israelites a century later, the Babylonians ascribed their catastrophe to their chief god's displeasure with them. And, like the Israelites, they subsequently divined that their god's favor had shifted back in their direction.[29] Indeed, he was now bent on revenge against Assyria, and his supernatural rage and range would be exhibited geopolitically. "Marduk, great lord, looked favorably upon me," declares King Nabopolassar in a Babylonian document. "And to avenge Akkad...he selected me for dominion over the lands and the peoples of the lands, all of them, he placed in my hands."[30] Hence the Babylonians' eventual conquest of Israel — part of their god's unfolding plan of grand vengeance.

Now it was the Israelites' turn to feel vengeful. At a geopolitical level, their achievement would never — could never — match the Babylonians'.[31] Their vengeance would have to play out on a theological plane, where it would yield something of historic grandeur. Rainer Albertz refers to some anti-Babylonian exilic passages as "retribution theology,"[32] but the phrase could cover exilic theology more broadly, including the theology that gave life to monotheism.

The retributive impulse is universally human, almost certainly grounded in the genes of our species.[33] And it is deeply, often hotly, felt. But, however laden with emotion, it has an intrinsic logic, and in terms of this logic Israel's monotheism makes sense. The core of the logic is, as the Bible puts it, an eye for an eye, a tooth for a tooth; punishment is proportional to the original transgression. And what was the magnitude of the transgression that Israel's exiles had suffered? The Babylonians hadn't just conquered their land and belittled their god. They had removed them from their land and, ostensibly, *killed* their god. Whereas Assyria had stripped Jerusalem's temple of its treasures, the Babylonians had destroyed the temple itself. And a god's temple was, in the ancient Middle East, literally the god's home.[34]

The ultimate transgression calls for the ultimate punishment. An apt response when a people kills your god is to kill theirs — to define it out of existence. And if other nations' gods no longer exist, and if you've already decided (back in Josiah's time) that Yahweh is the only god in *your* nation, then you've just segued from monolatry to monotheism.

This isn't to say that monotheism followed from retributive logic as rigorously as four follows from two plus two. After all, Babylon was the only nation that had inflicted the infinite indignity of destroying Yahweh's home — and, obviously, there were a lot of non-Babylonian gods that had to disappear before monotheism could arrive. On the other hand, the exilic oracles against the nations suggest that, though the Babylonian conquest was the finest example of indignities emanating from abroad, there were so many other examples that they were starting to blur together. There is a sense of humiliation so massive that counterbalancing it would require Yahweh's elevation to unprecedented heights — which meant the demotion of the world's other gods to unprecedented depths, perilously near the subsistence level. Monotheism was, among other things, the ultimate revenge.

The Ultimate Salvation

But revenge wasn't the only motivating force in exilic theology. What about Yahweh's promise, in Second Isaiah, to bring salvation to the ends of the earth? There must be *something* to that, right?

Kind of. Calling the exilic God "universalist" is accurate in a carefully defined sense of the word. Yes, Second Isaiah sees Yahweh as the God of all peoples. But that doesn't mean God felt equally *devoted* to all peoples. The biblical scholar Harry Orlinsky, among the first to dispute the standard, sunnily internationalist interpretation of Second Isaiah and various other parts of the Bible, put it this way: "The *national* God of biblical Israel is a *universal* God, but not an *international* God" — because Israel enjoys a unique covenant with him.[35] Indeed, in Orlinsky's view, Israel would be a "light unto the nations" largely in the sense of advertising this fact. "Israel will dazzle the nations," he wrote, by "her God-given triumph and restoration; the whole world will behold this single beacon that is God's sole covenanted people. Israel will serve the world at large as the example of God's loyalty and omnipotence."[36]

This isn't to say that Yahweh had no obligations to the peoples of the world. As Orlinsky notes, murder and brutality anywhere on earth were "contrary to God's ordered universe." Ultimately, then, the imposition of his will would be good news for peace-loving people everywhere. As First Isaiah had famously dreamed, God

> shall judge between the nations,
> and shall arbitrate for many peoples;

they shall beat their swords into plowshares,
and their spears into pruning hooks;
nation shall not lift up sword against nation,
neither shall they learn war any more.[37]

So, even if no nation can expect the kind of divine devotion Israel will get, Yahweh can still sincerely say, in Second Isaiah, that, as he prepares to bring justice to the nations, "the coastlands wait for me, and for my arms they hope."[38]

Still, phase one in the plan to bring order to the world was to punish those who threatened the order—which, at the moment, was all of Israel's enemies. The exilic god was rather like a prosecutor whose ultimate goal of bringing justice to society entails the short-term goal of bringing criminals to justice. It's just that in this case criminals constituted most of the known world.

If the prosecutor's short-term goal—retributive justice—is key to understanding the evolution of monotheism, the longer-term goal of world order illuminates another major dimension of exilic theology: national salvation. Humans have various ways of coping with extended stress, and one is the anticipation of a better time. Here, as with retribution, there is often a kind of symmetry: the more intense the stress and the more hopeless the situation, the more fabulous the coming times that are anticipated. In extreme form, the result is apocalypticism—revelations of a day of salvation, often at the end of time, when long-delayed justice is finally delivered.

Apocalyptic thinking is most famously associated with early Christianity, but variants of it have surfaced in many times and places under broadly similar circumstances. Hence the Melanesian "cargo cults" of the early twentieth century. In response to European subjugation, native prophets envisioned a day of salvation when the symbols of colonial power—the docks and airstrips where goods were loaded for trade—would reverse their meaning: cargo would arrive from the gods or from sacred ancestors, ushering in a time of blessing; the political tables would turn, as whites now found themselves at the bottom of the hierarchy and life for the Melanesians got cushy.

Similarly, for ancient Israelites, Yahweh's final judgment would bring not just the joy of retribution, but the comfort of salvation—"salvation" in the mundane sense of freedom from affliction. With God having laid down his law globally, Israel wouldn't have to worry about invading armies anymore. On Judgment Day, when "the makers of idols go in confusion together," Israel would be "saved by the LORD with everlasting salvation; you shall not be put to shame or confounded to all eternity." At long last the Israelites would "come to Zion with singing; everlasting joy shall be upon their heads; they shall obtain joy and gladness, and sorrow and sighing shall flee away."[39]

No doubt this theology—a theology of monotheistic salvation—got a boost when, near the end of the sixth century, the exiles *did* return to Zion. True, they didn't do it by conquest, as some had no doubt imagined. But they did it in a way that sustained the logic behind monotheism. Persia conquered Babylonia, and Cyrus, Persia's leader, sent the Israelites home. Consider the implication: Yahweh not only controlled the empire that had conquered the Assyrian Empire; he controlled the empire that had conquered the empire that had conquered the Assyrian Empire.

As Yahweh put it in the Bible, Cyrus's "right hand I have grasped to subdue nations before him." Yahweh explained to Cyrus that he would bring him success on the battlefield, "so that you may know that it is I, the LORD, the God of Israel, who call you by your name. For the sake of my servant Jacob, and Israel my chosen, I call you by your name."[40] (Cyrus's own recollection—or at least one of his official recollections—differed. On a clay cylinder discovered in 1879, he said he had been called to conquer Babylon and lands beyond by the Babylonian god Marduk, "the great lord" whom he would now worship faithfully.)[41]

In the end, then, the logic behind monotheism was pretty simple, given the natural mind-set of Israel's exilic intellectuals. Yahweh's honor, and Israel's pride, could be salvaged only by intellectual extremes. If the Babylonian conquest *didn't* signify Yahweh's disgrace, if Yahweh *wasn't* a weakling among gods, then he must have orchestrated Israel's calamity—and orchestrating a calamity of that magnitude came close to implying the orchestration of history itself, which would leave room for little if any autonomy on the part of other gods. Besides, if Yahweh, in the course of this orchestration, were to conspicuously reclaim his dignity, the gods of Israel's oppressors would have to see their dignity, hence their power, drop near the vanishing point anyway. What's more, if Yahweh could deliver what the Israelites so wanted to count on—a coming day of salvation, a peace forever unperturbed—then his mastery of the world would have to be complete and eternal. For in the absence of such international control, as the last two centuries of the Israelites' history seemed to show, the world would keep bringing trouble to Israel.

The implication—that ultimately all gods other than Yahweh must have essentially no power—doesn't add up to monotheism per sc. You can imagine Israelite thinkers thoroughly emasculating these gods without killing them. Still, the theological logic of Israel's exile, a logic that was only natural under the circumstances, makes the appearance of the monotheistic impulse in Second Isaiah and other exilic texts unsurprising.

But Is It Monotheism?

There is a reason why I just referred to the appearance of "the monotheistic impulse" and not of "monotheism."[42] Mixed in with the monotheistic exclamations in exilic writings is the occasional phrase that sounds not so monotheistic. For example, Second Isaiah depicts Babylon's fall at Cyrus's hands by reference to Bel (another name for Marduk) and his son Nebo: "Bel bows down, Nebo stoops," and they "themselves go into captivity"[43] (which, actually, they didn't, owing to Cyrus's wise policy of embracing or at least tolerating the gods of conquered lands). For that matter, if you reread Second Isaiah's various monotheistic declarations cited above, and substitute "Yahweh" for "the LORD"—which is how the original texts read—some of them lose a bit of monotheistic luster.

Further, we know almost nothing about actual religious practice during the exile, and there is little clear evidence of monotheistic practice for centuries *after* the exile. In fact, in the book of Malachi, apparently written well after the exile, God speaks to a Jewish audience that seems skeptical of his universal jurisdiction. Just wait, he says, until he punishes the Edomites, "the people with whom the LORD is angry forever." Then "your own eyes shall see this, and you shall say, Great is the LORD beyond the borders of Israel!"[44]

Given how little is known about Jewish religion in the centuries after the first exilic glimmers of monotheistic thought, it is hard to say what closed the deal: Why did Second Isaiah's vision, among the several visions that no doubt competed for airtime during the exile, prevail and then endure? How did Israel spend centuries near polytheistic peoples and yet stay true to its monotheistic creed?

For one thing, the political psychology that had fostered monotheism reappeared at various times in the ensuing centuries. The relative autonomy that Israel seems to have enjoyed under Persian rule didn't last forever. After Alexander the Great's conquest of Palestine in 332 BCE, successive Greek-speaking rulers were in charge, and they finally got oppressive enough to trigger a revolt. The fight for independence strengthened the time-honored political impetus behind Yahweh-alonism: a nationalist resentment of gods with a foreign lineage (and, further, of Jewish elites who fraternized with hegemonic foreigners). Indeed, the climactic provocation of Jewish revolt was an attempt to put a statue of Zeus in the Jerusalem temple. And presumably the success of the revolt, which led to a period of independence from 142 BCE to 63 BCE, affirmed the theology behind the revolt.

Monotheism as a Philosophy

Greeks may have nourished Israel's monotheism at a less political, more cerebral, level as well. Long before Alexander conquered Palestine, the monotheistic hypothesis had occurred to Greek thinkers.[45] And, though Israel's reaction to Greek governance was finally one of rejection, there was in the meanwhile much mixing of Jewish and Greek culture.

Greek monotheism grew out of one of Greece's great cultural aspirations: the rational refinement of religious ideas. Some credit the Greeks with inventing theology in the strict sense of the word (though religion had always been subject to a kind of rational guidance, as when Israelite thinkers adjusted theology to their exilic predicament). Greek religious rigor foreshadowed modern attempts to reconcile religious belief with a scientific outlook, and in that sense the attraction of Greek thinkers to monotheism was natural. The more nature was seen as logical—the more its surface irregularities dissolved into regular law—the more sense it made to concentrate divinity into a single impetus that lay somewhere behind it all. In the sixth century BCE the philosopher Xenophanes (who may have been the first Greek monotheist)[46] wrote of God: "Always he remains in the same place, moving not at all; nor is it fitting for him to go to different places at different times, but without toil he shakes all things by the thought of his mind. All of him sees, all thinks, and all hears."[47]

Greeks weren't the first of Israel's imperial overlords to highlight the regularity of nature. By the time of the exile, Babylonian astronomers could predict lunar and solar eclipses. As Baruch Halpern has observed, this "notion of the predictability of the sky" could have triggered "profound theological turmoil, since the independence of the gods was suddenly called into question."[48] And, Halpern suggests, Israelite thinkers may have been digesting this early celestial science well before the exile; Babylonian astronomers were employed by the Assyrians who dominated the Israelites for much of the eighth century BCE.

In this view, the Bible's rage at those who worship the celestial deities known as the "hosts of heaven" may have had an intellectual as well as a political basis. After all, why attribute autonomy, let alone divinity, to beings that behave so mechanically? And why scan that behavior for portents? ("Thus says the LORD: Do not learn the way of the nations, or be dismayed at the signs of the heavens; for the nations are dismayed at them.")[49] More plausible to think that behind the night sky's clockwork is the one truly autonomous god (the "LORD of hosts"). As Second Isaiah says, "Lift up your eyes on high and see: Who Created these? He who brings out their host and numbers them, calling them all by name."[50]

Perhaps the most intriguing candidate for imperial influence on Israelite theology lies in Persia, Israel's ruler between the periods of Babylonian and Greek domination. The Persian religion, Zoroastrianism, is typically described as "dualistic," because it features not just a good god—a protective creator god—but a bad god with whom this good god does battle. Then again, Christianity and Judaism feature Satan, an evil and hardly impotent supernatural being, yet we still call them monotheistic. At any rate, the Zoroastrian "dualism" of Persia was closer to monotheism than was the average ancient religion.[51]

What's more, Israel's relationship with Persia featured that great lubricant of interfaith exchange: non-zero-sum logic. From the time Cyrus of Persia conquered Babylon, if not earlier, he was seen by the exiles as an ally. He then justified their faith, returning them to Jerusalem and ruling the new Israel with a long leash. Lest you doubt that this could have made the Israelites open to theological input from Cyrus: he is the only non-Israelite in the entire Bible to be called by the Hebrew word for "messiah."[52] And within a few verses of this messianic depiction of Cyrus, as the scholar Morton Smith once noted, are descriptions of Yahweh that sound like Persian descriptions of the "good" Zoroastrian god, Ahura Mazda.[53] All of this led Smith to wonder whether Persian influence on Israelite theology might have been a carefully plotted part of Persia's political strategy from early on.[54]

Conceivably. But Israel's exilic theology grows so organically out of pre-exilic, Josianic theology, and so nicely meets the psychological needs of the exiles, that it is unlikely to have been imported as a Persian novelty item. More plausible is a convergence of long-standing currents of Israelite thought with the strategic needs of

Cyrus.[55] Certainly Cyrus was in a position to favor some currents over others. He had control over which Israelites, and perhaps which Israelite texts, returned to Jerusalem to shape Israel's governance. And monotheism may have struck Cyrus as more conducive to imperial harmony than alternative theologies of the day.[56] Indeed, in the next chapter we'll see evidence that Israel's postexile theologians were guided by Cyrus's agenda.

In the end, the number of possible factors in the consolidation of Abrahamic monotheism is roughly matched by the shortage of evidence about them.[57] Humility is an apt attitude for anyone who ventures an opinion on how and why monotheism emerged and endured in ancient Israel. Still, if the biblical texts commonly considered exilic are indeed exilic, we can get a view of the forces that animated Israel's first clear monotheistic impulse and a fleeting glimpse of the character of the one true god upon his birth.

And what kind of god was he? A candid appraisal of those texts makes it hard to conclude that he was what many contemporary Abrahamic believers would like to think he was: a morally modern god, a god of universal compassion. If you had to give a simple answer to the simple question that has hovered over this whole exposition—Was the Abrahamic god a god of peace and tolerance at the moment he became ruler of the universe?—it would be no.

Of course, you'd rather *not* have to give such a simple answer. God's character at this point in history was a complex thing— no doubt there was disagreement about it even among exilic monotheists—and much of the complexity is lost in the mists of history. Still, if you look at the earliest biblical texts that plainly declare the arrival of monotheism and you ask which of their various sentiments seems to most directly motivate that declaration, the answer would seem closer to hatred than to love, closer to retribution than to compassion. To the extent that we can tell, the one true God—the God of Jews, then of Christians, and then of Muslims—was originally a god of vengeance.

Fortunately, the previous sentence has a hidden asterisk: *But it doesn't matter.* The salvation of the world in the twenty-first century may well hinge on how peaceful and tolerant Abrahamic monotheism is. But it doesn't hinge on whether these attributes were built in at monotheism's birth. That's because monotheism turns out to be, morally speaking, a very malleable thing, something that, when circumstances are auspicious, can be a fount of tolerance and compassion. As we'll see in later chapters, this fact is manifest in the subsequent history of Jews, Christians, and Muslims.

Christianity is of course the most famous illustration. The New Testament features a straightforward declaration of universal compassion and explicitly contrasts this attitude with Old Testament morality. Jesus says, "You have heard that it was said, 'You shall love your neighbor and hate your enemy.' But I say to you, Love your enemies and pray for those who persecute you."[58]

If the thesis of this book is correct, then it's wholly plausible that Jewish scripture could have produced this saying had its authors found themselves in circumstances comparable to those of the Christian authors of this passage. And indeed, as we'll see several chapters from now, a saying almost identical to this one is in fact found in the Hebrew Bible and may have inspired the version of the saying later attributed to Jesus.

The flip side of this thesis is that this generous sentiment wasn't indelibly stamped on Christian souls, any more than vengeance had been stamped on the souls of Jews. Had Christians found themselves in the position of exilic Jews, their theological response would probably have been comparable.

This isn't mere conjecture. The final book of the New Testament is Revelation. Like some exilic texts in the Hebrew Bible, Revelation is apocalyptic, looking forward to a coming day of salvation. On that day the anti-Christ would be vanquished and long-suffering Christians would get their reward. And who exactly is this anti-Christ who will get his comeuppance? He bears the emblem 666, and that turns out to be a cryptic numerical rendering of the name of Nero, the Roman emperor who so spectacularly persecuted Christians. When Christians faced oppression at the hands of Roman imperialists, they did what Jews had done when they faced oppression at the hands of Babylonian imperialists: dreamed of vengeance and enshrined the dream in theology.

As if to drive home the historical parallel, Revelation links the anti-Christ to a figure called "Babylon the great, mother of whores." Later in the book there is much rejoicing over her downfall: "Hallelujah! Salvation and glory and power to our God...he has judged the great whore who corrupted the earth with her fornication, and he has avenged on her the blood of his servants." There's more excitement on the way, only a few verses later. In comes a white horse, whose rider, called "The Word of God," is generally understood to be Jesus: "In righteousness he judges and makes war." Indeed, "He is clothed in a robe dipped in blood," and "from his mouth comes a sharp sword with which to strike down the nations, and he will rule them with a rod of iron; he will tread the wine press of the fury of the wrath of God the Almighty."[59] Second Isaiah couldn't have said it better.

What happened to the other Christian God, the one who wanted you to love your enemies? Circumstances change, and God changes with them. That dynamic—as played out within Judaism, Christianity, and Islam—is the story of much of the rest of this book.

Chapter Eight

Philo Story

In the book of Exodus, God issues this guidance to the Israelites via Moses: "You shall not revile God."[1] At least, that's the way it comes off in most modern versions of the Bible—as yet another demand for devotion to Yahweh. But in the Septuagint, the Greek translation of the Bible made during the third and second centuries BCE, the verse has a different flavor: it says you should not revile "gods."

One Jew of ancient times used this version of the verse as a window into God's soul. Philo of Alexandria, who was born near the end of the first century BCE, saw a deep streak of tolerance in Yahweh. By Philo's lights, the divine law, even while asserting the existence of only one true God, offered "support to those of different opinion by accepting and honoring those whom they have from the beginning believed to be gods."[2]

Philo didn't believe in the *existence* of other people's gods. He was a devout Jew and a fervent monotheist.[3] Still, he believed that God's law "muzzles and restrains its own disciples, not permitting them to revile these [gods] with a loose tongue, for it believes that well-spoken praise is better."[4]

What led Philo to this interpretation of Exodus 22:28? Some would answer, "Whoever translated Exodus 22:28 into Greek." In other words: Philo, fluent in Greek, read the Septuagint's injunction against reviling "gods," interpreted it straightforwardly, and the rest is history. Certainly this would be the spin placed on Philo's story by "scriptural determinists," people who think that scripture exerts overwhelming influence on the religious thought of believers, and that their social and political circumstances matter little if at all.

"Scriptural determinism" sounds like an arcane academic paradigm, but it is deployed by nonacademics in a consequential way. After the terrorist attacks of September 11, 2001, as Americans tried to fathom the forces at work, sales of several kinds of books rose. Some people bought books about Islam, some bought books about the recent history of the Middle East, and some bought translations of the Koran. And of course some bought more than one kind of book. But people who bought *only* translations of the Koran were showing signs of scriptural determinism. They seemed to think that you could understand the terrorists' motivation simply by reading their ancient scriptures—just search the Koran for passages advocating violence against infidels and, having succeeded, end the analysis, content that you'd found the essential cause of 9/11.

Some people, in the sway of scriptural determinism, have a very dark view of the future. They note that the scriptures of all three monotheistic faiths embrace the slaughter of infidels. If these scriptures have the final say in a world of nuclear and biological weapons, we'll see carnage that makes the Crusades look tame.

Fortunately, there is a different interpretation of the Philo story, one that doesn't see the Septuagint's translation of Exodus as determinative. After all, Philo didn't *have* to stop and dwell on the meaning of that verse. He didn't *have* to use it as the occasion for a sermonette about how the preservation of "peace" and "dignity" demands respect for the opinion of others.[5] Maybe there was something about his circumstances that encouraged him to seek and highlight these themes. And maybe, if he hadn't found them in Exodus, he would have found them somewhere else in the Bible.

What were the circumstances in question? What made tolerance attractive to Philo, even as some other Jews were less tolerant? For that matter, what makes tolerance attractive to some Jews, Christians, and Muslims today even as others of the same faith denounce or kill infidels? As it happens, the answers to these two questions are basically the same. The story of Philo illustrates the generic circumstances that lead people toward peaceful coexistence; it helps us add a new level of detail to the "law of religious tolerance" sketched in chapter 6.

In the process, Philo's story displays the ingredients of a god's moral growth. Gods speak through their followers, so when prevailing interpretations of a god change, the very character of the god changes. Yahweh may have been bent on punishing infidels during King Josiah's reforms, and he may have been focused on retribution at the moment monotheism was born, but whether he stayed in a bad mood would depend on what people who believed in him believed about him. Philo believed in Yahweh with all his heart and soul—believed that he was the one true god—and didn't believe he was a god of intolerance and vengeance. To the extent that this view spread, God could grow—become more morally inclusive, even more spiritually deep.

And to the extent that this view was *likely* to spread, favored by basic tendencies in human history, then maybe God's growth is in some sense "natural"—an intrinsic part of the human story, if disconcertingly fitful, prone to phases of stagnation and even regression. Philo's story suggests that this is the case. It shows why forces fostering God's moral growth have indeed often been stronger than forces favoring stagnation or regression. And it shows why, in the twenty-first century, the forces of goodness could once again win out.

You might think that illustrating—indeed, embodying—a moral directionality that's built into history would be enough accomplishment for one man. Philo's legacy goes much further. If a moral direction is indeed built into history, three questions arise: First, is this evidence of some "higher purpose," some unfolding plan that humankind is now climactically involved in? Second, is this plan in some sense divine? And, if so, could it be worked into a modern theology—a theology that didn't involve some anthropomorphic deity sitting on a throne, but instead conceived of the divine more abstractly; a theology that left room for scientific laws to hold sway on this planet? Remarkably, Philo, writing nearly two millennia before modern science would create a pressing need for such a theology, provided a rough draft of one.

But first things first. Before looking at how Philo helped give us an intellectually modern God, let's look at how he helped give us a morally modern God.

Interpretive Leeway

Vital to a god's capacity for growth is the semantic flexibility of scripture. Within limits, people can look at their holy texts and see what they want to see — see what meets their psychological, social, political needs. There are several sources of this interpretive leeway, and collectively they're momentous.

One source is sheer ambiguity. In all languages, words can have more than one meaning, so reading involves making choices. When the context of the original composition is very different from the reader's context — long ago or far away, or both — the choices made may steer the text away from the author's intent. In one episode of *The Twilight Zone,* earthlings discovered only too late that the Holy Book brought by extraterrestrial visitors, titled *To Serve Man,* was not, as initially assumed, a philanthropic manifesto; it was a cookbook.

At least these earthlings finally succeeded in divining the intended meaning; they attained warranted confidence in their revised interpretation shortly before being eaten. More commonly, certainty remains forever elusive. Exodus 22:28, the pivot point for Philo's ethics, is a case in point. In Hebrew, the word *elohim* is both singular and plural — god and gods. When *elohim* is the subject of a sentence, this ambiguity is cleared up by the form of the verb (just as, in English, the verb "creates" implies a singular subject and the verb "create" implies a plural subject). But in Exodus 22:28 *elohim* is the object of the sentence, not the subject. (You shall not revile *elohim.*) So here a translator has latitude.[6]

Did the translator in question — whoever rendered that verse in Greek for the Septuagint — use that latitude to exercise a personal bias toward interfaith tolerance? It's possible. But even without this head start, even if the translator had gone with "god," not "gods," Philo probably would have found a way to stress God's tolerant and peaceful side. For one thing, he was no amateur when it came to creative translation. (He asserted that "Jerusalem" means "vision of peace," when in fact the city was probably named after Shalem, an ancient god.)[7] For another thing, ambiguity is far from the only tool available to the creative exegete.

Another is selective retention. You can just conveniently forget certain parts of your scriptural heritage. During the Crusades, when Christians were in the mood to slaughter infidels, they were very cognizant of God's sanctioning faith-based mass murder in parts of the Bible. During the Cold War, when the United States was part of an international multifaith alliance that included Muslim and Buddhist nations, this motif was played down; whole generations of American Christians were weaned on a misleadingly sunny selection of Bible stories.

Philo, similarly, was capable of passing over the Bible's darker parts in silence. In a discourse on the idea of justice in the Hebrew Bible, he addressed the laws of war laid out in the twentieth chapter of Deuteronomy. That chapter includes the horrific verse I cited two chapters ago:

> As for the towns of these peoples that the LORD your God is giving you as an inheritance, you must not let anything that breathes remain alive. You shall annihilate them—the Hittites and the Amorites, the Canaanites and the Perizzites, the Hivites and the Jebusites—just as the LORD your God has commanded, so that they may not teach you to do all the abhorrent things that they do for their gods, and you thus sin against the LORD your God.[8]

You might think it would be impossible for Philo to reconcile this verse, which embraces the slaughter of women and children, with the just God he was bent on depicting. You might think Philo would be unable to square this verse with the doctrine of religious tolerance he had found in Exodus, since here God wants people annihilated precisely because their religion is alien. Apparently Philo thought so as well; he ignored this verse altogether. Instead he focused on a different part of Deuteronomy 20, in which God prescribes slightly milder treatment for cities that are farther away from Israel. If such a city doesn't surrender when Israel's army approaches, the Bible says, the Israelites are to just "put all its males to the sword" and, rather than kill the women, children, and livestock, "take as your booty the women, the children, livestock."[9]

Even here, Philo removes some rough edges by deploying yet another instrument of creative interpretation: loose, even misleading, paraphrasal. He stresses that Israel must "spare the women" even as it lays "the whole opposing army low in a general slaughter." That sounds a bit less brutal than killing all adult males whether or not they're in the army — which in fact is what the verse in question calls for. Moreover, Philo says this is how Israel is to punish peoples who "renounce their alliance" with Israel, when in fact it is the punishment God allots to any town that resists Israelite conquest. F. H. Colson, an early-twentieth-century British scholar who translated Philo's works into English, speculated that "the curious way in which Philo here limits this to war against those who revolt from an alliance" can "only be explained, I think, as expressing a conviction that the Law [the divine law, or Torah] could never have intended to sanction wars of conquest or aggression."[10]

Ambiguity, selective retention, and misleading paraphrasal combine to give believers great influence on the meaning of their religion. But, for raw semantic power, none of these tools rivals the deft deployment of metaphor and allegory. In a single stroke, this can obliterate a text's literal meaning and replace it with something radically different.

Thus, some twentieth-century Hindus, led by Gandhi, removed the barbaric air from the opening scene of the Bhagavad Gita, which shows the god Krishna encouraging believers to remorselessly slaughter an enemy even if it includes their kin. Actually, said Gandhi, this whole war scene was a metaphor for an *internal* war—the war against our darker side, the war to do our duty and live righteously. Similarly, some Muslims say the "struggle" signified by the word *jihad* should be thought of as an internal struggle, not a military struggle against infidels.

As for Philo: Remember that gruesome biblical scene in which a seemingly vengeful Yahweh drowns the Egyptian army in the Red Sea? Philo softens that episode by reading it as, fundamentally, a metaphysical allegory: bondage in Egypt represented a person's enslavement to the impulses of the physical body, and escape from Egypt represented liberation, passage into the realm of spiritual guidance. In this light, Egyptians gasping for their final breaths become a metaphor for the end of the soul's entrapment.[11] According to Philo, when Exodus exults, "horse and rider he has thrown into the sea…the Lord is a warrior," it is praising God for vanquishing the base appetites of the body.[12] Philo isn't saying that the story didn't happen, but he seems to be suggesting that the main takeaway lesson is about inner transformation, not outward slaughter; about escaping animal impulses, not displaying them.[13]

The dexterity exhibited by Philo has been deployed by thinkers in all of the world's great religions. That explains the big difference in moral and theological opinions held within any one faith—differences from time to time, from place to place, from person to person. So why is it that some people at some times choose peace and tolerance and other people at other times don't? Amid the Maccabean revolt that liberated Jerusalem from control of the Saleucid Empire in the second century BCE, Jews destroyed pagan shrines.[14] Now, two centuries later, in a different city, Philo was urging quite a different path. Why?

Life of Philo

Philo inhabited overlapping worlds. Ethnically and religiously he was a Jew. Politically, he lived in the Roman Empire. Intellectually and socially, his world was heavily Greek; though Alexandria was in Egypt, its upper stratum was largely Greek, a legacy of Alexander the Great's founding of the city in the fourth century BCE.[15] And then there were the Egyptians, large in number if not in per capita influence.

Philo was born into a rich and influential family. Maintaining this status meant, first of all, staying on good terms with the powers that were — Roman politicians and upper-class Greeks. For rich and powerful people to stay on good terms with other rich and powerful people isn't an intrinsically delicate task, but Philo's Jewishness complicated things. The Jews' monotheism was an occasional irritant to local polytheists, especially at times when Roman leaders, deeming themselves divine, demanded worship.[16] This is a demand that devout Jews were compelled to resist, and their resistance gave fuel to anti-Semitism among Greeks and Egyptians.

Of course, you could always renounce your Judaism. (Philo's nephew would choose this tack and rise to great power, becoming governor of Egypt.)[17] But Philo was very religious, so he had to reconcile his various worlds. He had to preserve the viability of his Jewish world — and the integrity of his Jewish faith — even amid the Greek, Roman, and Egyptian worlds.

This was not a task for the faint of heart. Imagine trying to explain to the emperor Caligula, who considered himself divine, why you would prefer that statues of him not adorn Alexandrian synagogues, let alone the Jerusalem temple. Philo tried. Alexandrian mobs had rioted against the Jews, burning some to death, after Jews refused to see their synagogues thus corrupted. Philo led a delegation to Rome to plead the Jews' case, lest official sanction of this persecution sustain it.

Philo's account of his attempt to morally enlighten a famously narcissistic man is darkly entertaining. When Caligula asks why Jews refuse to eat pork, Philo says, "Different people have different customs and the use of some things is forbidden to us as others are to our opponents." A Philo sympathizer, trying to put the point in Caligula's frame of reference, chimes in, "Yes, just as many don't eat lamb which is so easily obtainable." Caligula replies, "Quite right too, for it's not nice."[18] So much for the lamb angle.

Still, in the end Philo's delegation was successful—at least, successful enough for the Jews of Alexandria to hang on to their lives and their religion. Caligula declared in Philo's presence that, though the Jews are "foolish in refusing to believe that I have got the nature of a god," they are, at bottom, "unfortunate rather than wicked."[19]

Caligula's sanity has been much debated, but for the moment, at least, he was being rational. This grudging tolerance made sense. Whatever the theological differences between Caligula and the Jews, his relationship with them was, at bottom, non-zero-sum. They were a productive people, and they paid their taxes. Letting Alexandrians kill them all would thus have been a net economic loss, and, moreover, a disruption of social order that could prove contagious, inciting Jews and/or their enemies elsewhere in the empire. And from Philo's perspective, certainly, violence was a losing proposition. "Live and let live" was logical from both points of view, and logic—in this case, at least—won out.

The encounter with Caligula was the climax of Philo's known political career, but its non-zero-sum social backdrop had long been the context of Philo's life. The Jews' situation in Alexandria was precarious, and being allowed to practice monotheism was an achievement in itself. If they overplayed their hand and were seen as aggressively intolerant, their status would change from tolerated minority to loathed enemy. This image problem was plainly on Philo's mind when he rendered his interpretation of Exodus 22:28. In light of the tolerance expressed in this verse, he asked, how could people claim that Judaism was intent on "breaking down the customs of others"?[20]

Indeed, Philo comes about as close to expressing the non-zero-sum logic behind his doctrine of tolerance as you could expect from someone who lived nearly two millennia before the invention of game theory. Intolerance, he saw, would breed intolerance, and the result could be lose-lose. However false pagan gods may be, those who believe in them "are not peaceful toward or reconciled with those who do not gladly accept their opinion. And this is the beginning and origin of wars." And, after all, "to us the Law [the Torah] has described the source of peace as a beautiful possession."[21]

Peace, Brotherhood, and Power

To see Philo's tolerance as non-zero-sum logic incarnate, you have to see non-zero-sum logic in its true and unglamorous form. Because non-zero-sum games, unlike zero-sum games, can have "win-win" outcomes, people sometimes think of them as orgies of amiability. They can be, but they usually aren't. Almost always, within a non-zero-sum game, there is a dimension of zero-sumness—a conflict of interest. When you buy a new car, there is a range of prices that make the purchase worthwhile from your point of view (say, anything under $28,000) and a range of prices that make the sale profitable for the dealer (say, anything over $27,000). Since there is overlap of those ranges—the possibility of an outcome that improves the fortunes of both players—the game is non-zero-sum. But there is still a conflict of interest, because the closer the price is to $27,000 the better for you, and the closer it is to $28,000 the better for the dealer. Movement along the spectrum between $27,000 and $28,000 is entirely zero-sum, because it lowers the fortunes of one player exactly as it raises the fortunes of the other player. Hence bargaining, which can sometimes lead to deception, suspicion, buyer's remorse, and so on. The bargaining can also lead to the deal's falling through—a lose-lose outcome, since each player has missed out on the gain that a deal would have brought.

Philo and Caligula had a higher-stakes conflict of interest than a car buyer and a car dealer. Caligula wanted to be worshipped widely, and pockets of resistance were thus dangerous: What if pagans started emulating this Jewish stubbornness?[22] Philo, for his part, would have liked to see the end of Caligula; other emperors had been more tolerant of Jews. But, though both Caligula and the Jews might have wished the other didn't exist, trying to bring that wish to fruition had a prohibitive downside; the outcome would probably be lose-lose.

This by itself — the possibility of a lose-lose outcome — makes a game non-zero-sum. After all, an outcome that's negative for both parties doesn't add up to zero; there is a correlation of fortunes between the players, even if it's for the worse. Besides, avoiding a double loss is, in relative terms at least, a kind of double win. The decades-long nuclear standoff during the Cold War was thus non-zero-sum — not because each year of successfully avoided nuclear war brought mutual, tangible gain, but because, if the game had been played differently, it could have brought mutual, tangible loss. And here, too, the non-zero-sum dynamic brought a kind of tolerance; though East and West considered each other more or less evil, neither tried to wipe out the other.

Similarly, Philo's doctrine of tolerance didn't mean that he liked pagan gods or believed in them or even that he liked pagans. There was at least one pagan — Caligula — that he loathed, and for that matter he didn't have especially high regard for Egyptians. (In a passage that, though ambiguous, seems to apply to Egyptians broadly, he calls them "a seed bed of evil in whose souls both the venom and the temper of the native crocodiles and asps were reproduced.")[23] Still, Philo saw the folly of initiating a nuclear exchange; hence his doctrine of tolerance.

Had power been dramatically redistributed — had a Jewish rebellion against one of the more anti-Semitic Roman emperors suddenly seemed feasible — Philo might have toned down the talk about tolerance and peace. In what may have been a veiled reference to Roman rule he wrote, "Now when occasion offers it is a good thing to oppose our enemies and to destroy their power of attack, but lacking such opportunity it is safe to keep quiet, while if one wishes to get any benefit from them it is advantageous to propitiate them."[24]

Philo here illustrates an important point. The "law of religious tolerance," as laid out in chapter 6, is incomplete. It said that people are more open to foreign gods when they see themselves playing a non-zero-sum game with foreigners — see their fortunes as positively correlated with the foreigners' fortunes. Strictly speaking, the case for tolerating other people's gods doesn't *always* depend on the logic being non-zero-sum. Suppose that a Jewish uprising could have been easily overcome by Roman authorities, and that they would have benefited somehow from thus subduing the Jews, so the result would have been literally win-lose. It still would have made sense for Philo to avoid stirring up trouble, since he would be on the losing side. The amended version of the law of religious tolerance, then, is that tolerance is more likely when you see yourself as losing from intolerance, regardless of whether the dynamic seems zero-sum or non-zero-sum; but when the dynamic is seen as non-zero-sum — when both sides see themselves as losing — then *mutual* tolerance makes sense.

So, back to the original question: Why did Philo advocate tolerance, whereas Jews in Israel two centuries earlier had smashed pagan idols? Maybe just because Jews in Israel two centuries earlier thought they could get away with it. And they were right; they rebelled successfully against their imperial rulers. For all we know, Philo, put in their position, would have done the same thing.

This may sound depressing. It seems to take the "enlightenment" out of "moral enlightenment," turning "tolerance" into a tactical ploy.

But depression isn't necessarily warranted. For one thing, tactical wisdom and moral enlightenment aren't mutually exclusive. What starts as a tactical ploy, as grudging coexistence, can for various reasons evolve into a truer, more philosophical appreciation of tolerance — an appreciation, even, of the beauty of diverse belief. Having a pragmatic, selfish reason to coexist with people can be (even if it sometimes isn't) the first step toward thinking about them in a nonselfish way. And once you start down that path, there's no necessary limit. People have been known to develop — and articulate a whole philosophy of — heartfelt warmth toward humanity as a whole.[25]

Game Theory and the Bible

The non-zero-sum logic that makes tolerance tactically wise, and can sometimes lead to a morally richer tolerance, is actually a pretty common feature of life. Human existence abounds in self-serving reasons to start thinking less selfishly, and such logic crops up repeatedly in the Hebrew Bible. One way to spot it is to look for cases in which Israelites affirm the validity of a foreign god. In the book of Judges, Israel has suffered a military setback at the hands of the Ammonites and would just as soon avoid further conflict. Its military leader, Jephthah, asks the Ammonite king, "Should you not possess what your god Chemosh gives you to possess? And should we not be the ones to possess everything that our god Yahweh has conquered for our benefit?"[26] When peaceful coexistence is in your interest, foreign gods deserve respect.

At least, they deserve your *expressed* respect. In referring to the land that "your god Chemosh gives you to possess," Jephthah is tactfully refraining from making an assertion made elsewhere in the Bible: that, actually, it was Yahweh, not Chemosh, who had given the Ammonites their land. Notably, this assertion, like Jephthah's burst of interfaith tolerance, comes by way of justifying a policy of peaceful coexistence. Yahweh is advising the Israelites against stirring up trouble with the Ammonites: "Do not harass them or engage them in battle, for I will not give the land of the Ammonites to you as a possession, because I have given it to the descendants of Lot." And Lot, as a nephew of Abraham's, was family.[27]

Thus a single piece of game theoretical logic—in this case the logic of peaceful coexistence between Israel and Ammon—can have different theological manifestations, depending on the rhetorical context. When the audience is Ammonite, the upshot is respect for an Ammonite god. When the audience is Israelite, the upshot is an expanded compass of Yahweh's concern, a bit of progress toward moral universalism; the Ammonites are in a sense Yahweh's people, too, the Israelites are told. Either way, whether the drift is toward interfaith tolerance or toward universalism, there is a kind of moral progress.

The judicious extension of Yahweh's concern to the Ammonites illustrates why, as I argued in the previous chapter, the moral character of the one true God at the moment of his birth doesn't much matter in the long run. Even though one driving force behind monotheism's emergence seems to have been hostility, the God that emerged needn't *remain* hostile toward Israel's neighbors. Even if the "universalism" so often attributed to the God of the exile is partly a euphemism for far-flung retribution, this God was capable of maturing, of moving toward *moral* universalism, toward universal compassion. True, the presumably exilic writings of Ezekiel have God vowing that "Ammon shall be remembered no more among the nations."[28] But God had felt more warmly toward Ammon in the past and could feel that way again in the future.[29]

What's more, even if there is backsliding, every burst of moral growth God exhibits, once etched in scripture, can be revived later, even amplified, when circumstances are propitious. The Hebrew Bible repeatedly demands decent treatment for foreigners who migrate to Israel, and in one case goes so far as to say, "you shall love the alien as yourself, for you were aliens in the land of Egypt."[30] Philo, living in a multiethnic environment and wanting both to advertise Jewish tolerance and to welcome any willing converts to Judaism, made this verse the basis for a brief rhapsody: God wants "all members of the nation to love the incomers, not only as friends and kinsfolk but as themselves both in body and soul: in bodily matters, by acting as far as may be for their common interest; in mental by having the same griefs and joys, so that they may seem to be the separate parts of a single living being which is compacted and unified by their fellowship in it."[31]

Ruth and Jonah

The Yahweh of scripture shows repeated bursts of moral growth. The book of Ruth, near the end of the Hebrew Bible, offers up a remarkable revelation: King David had not been ethnically pure.[32] His great-grandmother Ruth was not only a foreigner, but a foreigner whose native country had given Israel much trouble over the centuries: Moab. One interpretation of David's multiethnic past—that God's love goes beyond ethnic bounds, and is available to all who worship him—is underscored by the details of Ruth's story. "Ruth the Moabite," as she is called, is accepted in Israel after declaring her allegiance to Yahweh and proving her goodness through hard work and kindness. One Israelite man, upon meeting her and learning her history, declares, "May the LORD reward you for your deeds, and may you have full reward from the LORD, the God of Israel, under whose wings you have come for refuge!"[33] Then, facilitating this process, he marries her.

How to explain the inclusive spirit of the book of Ruth? Theories differ. Some scholars think it was written after the exile and that its backdrop is interethnic marriage.[34] When the Babylonian exiles returned to Israel, they found much intermarriage between Jews and Gentiles, and arguments about its propriety erupted. In Jewish doctrine, the anti-intermarriage forces eventually prevailed, but the book of Ruth, these scholars argue, is a literary legacy of the promarriage forces; if David himself descended from a mixed marriage, the author of Ruth was saying, then surely intermarriage can't be a sin!

Other scholars give the book of Ruth an earlier origin, perhaps even going back to the time of David and Solomon. According to the Bible, Israel was then employing many foreigners as workers on royal projects and mercenaries in the army. Maybe, the argument goes, the book's theme of interethnic tolerance was meant to validate foreign intercourse of an economic sort.[35]

Note what these two theories share: non-zero-sum logic. When foreigners agree to work for Israel's elites, elites and foreigners alike see gain in the relationship. When foreigners and Israelites get married, bride and groom alike plan to gain from the relationship. In both scenarios, stories emphasizing interethnic amity—like the book of Ruth—could lubricate the non-zero-sum game in question.

And in both cases Israelites benefiting from the game might encourage the telling of such stories.

The point isn't that one of these two theories is necessarily correct. The point is just that they make sense, and that theories that make sense will tend to resemble them. If you want to explain the promulgation of themes of interethnic amity and tolerance, it helps to find people who would have profited from the promulgation, and these will generally be people who are in one sense or another playing non-zero-sum games across ethnic bounds.

Regardless of when the story of Ruth emerged and when it was first written down, the decision to include it in the Hebrew Bible came after the exile—after the monotheistic impulse emerged clearly in Second Isaiah, after Yahweh's condemnation of the Moabites had appeared in Zephaniah ("The remnant of my people shall plunder them") and in Ezekiel ("I will lay open the flank of Moab from the towns on its frontier").[36] That "Ruth the Moabite" should in the end be welcomed into the Jewish canon is a tribute to the evolutionary potential of morality.

Also encouraging is the book of Jonah, a book probably written after the exile and, like Ruth, certainly admitted to the Jewish canon then. If you ask people to name a remarkable fact about Jonah, they may note that he spent time inside a whale (or, as the Bible actually puts it, a large fish) and lived to tell about it. But that's not as remarkable as another of the book's plot twists.

As the story begins, God has told Jonah to go preach in the city of Nineveh, to reprimand the Ninevens for their evil ways. Jonah resists his calling. He tries to flee on a boat, only to get swallowed by the sea and then by the fish after a Yahweh-induced storm. God releases him but insists that he go to Nineveh and fulfill his mission. There Jonah warns the people about God's impending punishment. This gets the attention of Nineveh's king, who urgently tells his people to repent—to fast, wear sackcloth, and "turn from their evil ways and from the violence that is in their hands. Who knows? God may relent and change his mind; he may turn from his fierce anger, so that we do not perish."[37]

God indeed relents, and Jonah isn't pleased. This is just what he feared when first given his preaching assignment, he says—that Yahweh would prove in the end to be a "gracious God and merciful, slow to anger, and abounding in steadfast love."[38] Jonah's revulsion at such mercy may seem strange, but consider that Nineveh is the capital of Assyria, the empire that for so long tormented Israel.[39] In this light, if anything should seem strange it is Yahweh's compassion for the Ninevens. Certainly Jonah never fathoms it. The book ends with God trying to explain it to him: "Should I not be concerned about Nineveh, that great city, in which there are more than a hundred and twenty thousand persons who do not know their right hand from their left...?"[40]

This verse is striking not just because it is Ninevens that God is concerned about, but because of the subtlety of his concern. Though their repentance is ostensibly what won them forgiveness, God seems tolerant of the moral confusion that got them in the doghouse to begin with. When he says they "do not know their right hand from their left," he is saying, in the vernacular of the day, that they do not know good from evil.

Traditionally, this sort of ignorance—not knowing good from evil—is what had stirred God's wrath, not his compassion. This was why the Israelites had suffered so much: because they kept forgetting that worshipping gods other than Yahweh was evil, and Yahweh punished such ignorance. And this was why God had vowed to punish roughly every known nation: because they hadn't realized that it was bad to attack or insult Yahweh's people. Now suddenly Yahweh not only pities the morally obtuse, but pities them even if they're Israel's past persecutors. In the book of Ezekiel, God was proud of having made Assyria suffer "as its wickedness deserves."[41] Now, in Jonah, the suffering of Assyrians gives God no pleasure, and their wickedness he sees as lamentable confusion. This is a god capable of radical growth.

The Virtues of Empire

Capacity for growth is a good thing, but what the world really needs is a god that *does* grow. Today globalization has made the planet too small to peacefully accommodate large religions that are at odds. If the Abrahamic god—the God of Jews and the God of Christians and the God of Muslims—doesn't foster tolerance, then we're all in trouble. We need a god whose sympathies correspond to the scale of social organization, the global scale. What does the Hebrew Bible tell us about the prospects for a global god?

In ancient times, the closest thing to globalization was the formation of multinational empires. People of different ethnicities and religions were pulled together under one roof, onto a single platform of economic exchange. Life among these peoples was, like life among diverse peoples in a globalized world, non-zero-sum: there was mutual gain if they got along and collaborated, and mutual loss if they didn't. After the exile Israel found itself in this very situation; a nation that had once been independent, or had grudgingly accepted the status of vassal state, was now firmly ensconced in an empire—an empire willing to respect its religion so long as it got along with its neighbors. So the question is: Did the Abrahamic god, in the early years of monotheism, evince sensitivity to the sort of non-zero-sumness that characterizes the modern world? Did the God of Israel grow morally when moral growth was in the interest of the Israelites?

The two data points above—Ruth and Jonah—are certainly encouraging, assuming these books are indeed postexilic. Yahweh's newfound sympathy for Ninevens, in the book of Jonah, was sympathy for a people who were now part of the same empire as the Israelites. So too with the book of Ruth's inclusive attitude toward the Moabites. In parts of the Bible written before the exile, the Moabites' origins had been cast in disparaging terms; their founder, Moab, was a product of incest, born of a drunken sexual encounter between Lot and one of his daughters.[42] Now, postexile, Moabites get a more respectable place in the family tree—they are ancestors of King David himself. What a difference an empire makes!

Perhaps the best evidence for the moral growth of God after the exile comes via the biblical author (or authors) known as the Priestly source. The Priestly source (first posited as part of the Wellhausen hypothesis discussed in chapter 5) is so called because it reflects the perspective of the priestly class. Most scholars judge the Priestly source—"P" for short—to have been writing either during the exile or right after it (or, possibly, both).[43] Either way, it seems safe to say that P had the blessing of the Persian Empire's leadership. After all, the Persians, in returning Israelites to Jerusalem postexile and granting Israel some degree of self-rule, wanted Israel's ruling class to be reliably supportive of imperial aims, and would have exerted influence accordingly. So if P consists of priests who were writing shortly after the exile, these are priests who passed muster with Persia. So too if P was writing *during* the exile; had the priests who held sway in Babylon during the exile not been to Persia's liking, their writings probably wouldn't have become a formative influence in postexilic Israel. In all likelihood, P is the voice of empire, and its values are those Persia wanted to implant in the new Israel.

A look at P's worldview suggests that empire can indeed expand moral horizons. For starters, P is more inclined than earlier biblical authors to say that many nations—not just Israel—figure directly in God's plan. In pre-exilic texts, there are descriptions of God having promised Abraham that great things lay in store for his descendants: they would be many, and they would bring good things to the earth. But the only reference to an actual political entity emanating from Abraham is in the singular: "I will make of you a great nation, and I will bless you, and make your name great."[44] According to the Priestly source, God's promise to Abraham is a bit different: "you shall be the ancestor of a multitude of nations."[45]

A similar shift of emphasis comes in the story of Jacob, Abraham's grandson and the father of Israel. In a part of Genesis that seems to have been written before the exile, Jacob's destiny is spelled out in these instructions from his father, Isaac: "let peoples serve you, and nations bow down to you."[46] In P's writing, by contrast, Isaac's parting wish to Jacob is that God may bless him so that he will "become a community of peoples."[47] And, according to P, God himself reinforces this more communal vision, telling Jacob that a "nation and a community of nations" will issue from him.[48]

If the Priestly source is indeed here exhibiting the internationally inclusive impulse of empire, that could explain some other things—in particular, the curious term "El Shaddai." As we saw in chapter 5, that term is commonly rendered as God Almighty (though the "Almighty" part may be a mistranslation, and the "God" part may be misleading, since "El" could have referred either to "god" generically or the specific god named El). There we also saw Yahweh, in the book of Exodus, appear to Moses and explain that Abraham, Isaac, and Jacob hadn't known him as Yahweh but rather as "El Shaddai." In trying to make sense of this attempt to equate Yahweh with another god, we assumed that the story had entered Israelite tradition very early, perhaps reflecting the convergence of diverse tribes to form Israel: maybe, we said, Israel was formed by a merger of El worshippers and Yahweh worshippers, and this story arose to reconcile their traditions.

But it's also possible that the story took shape much later and reflects later political realities—and maybe those realities were about Israel's international environment, not its internal politics. So it's notable that this verse, Exodus 6:3, is generally attributed to the Priestly source. Is it possible that this equation of Yahweh with El Shaddai somehow served Persia's aims of imperial harmony, and hence of smooth relations between Israel and its neighbors?

Other clues suggest as much. The one other time the Bible equates Yahweh and El Shaddai also comes in a passage attributed to the Priestly source—and it comes in that very passage, described above, where P has God predicting that he will make of Abraham great "nations," not just a "nation."[49] Further, in those two passages in which a similarly communal vision is imparted to Jacob, God is again referred to as "El Shaddai" (though not explicitly identified with Yahweh).[50] So there are three separate Priestly passages where the term "El Shaddai" is linked to a communal vision of the Abrahamic lineage's future—to a community either of "nations" or of "peoples." That's a lot of passages, given that the term "El Shaddai" appears only seven times in the entire Hebrew Bible![51]

But what is the exact logical link between this particular name for God and internationally inclusive language? One possibility is that one or more of the nations that were, like Israel, part of the Persian Empire called their god El Shaddai, and P was asserting that their god and Israel's God were one and the same.[52]

Another, more interesting, possibility is that P is thinking on a larger scale, resolving a kind of tension created in Israel's psyche by the project of imperial consolidation. In Genesis, P lays out a comprehensive family tree of national patriarchs in the Middle East and thus establishes the degrees of kinship among nations. (For example, since Edom's patriarch, Esau, like Israel's patriarch, Jacob, is a son of Isaac, Israel and Edom are closely related.) This "table of nations" isn't an original composition; P is consolidating and sometimes supplementing patriarchal lineages laid down by other biblical authors. Still, as the Swiss scholar Konrad Schmid has suggested, P's assembling the material into a single family tree may be an attempt to strike a note of harmony with nearby nations.

Certainly this could make sense from a Persian point of view; since many nations on that tree were now part of the Persian Empire, the bonds of kinship within the empire were emphasized. In fact, for all we know, the same family tree was promulgated in other parts of the empire, with the same implied moral. In any event, within Israel the moral would have been clear: Israel's patriarch, Jacob, was related—however distantly in some cases—to patriarchs all across the empire.

But this is where tension arises between the imperial project and Israel's self-esteem. If assembling the family tree emphasized the previously obscure fact that Jacob was the grandson of Abraham, and if Abraham's god had traditionally been El Shaddai, then the family tree would be depicting Israel's god Yahweh as in some sense subordinate to a different god—unless, of course, it turned out that Yahweh and El Shaddai were just two different names for the same god.[53]

In this scenario P is solving the problem created by the very idea of an international family tree—keeping a given nation's god on top notwithstanding the hierarchical nature of family trees.[54] But if this was the problem facing P, equating Yahweh with the god of Abraham wouldn't by itself meet the challenge. For the tree went beyond Abraham, and suggested that some national patriarchs might outrank even him. Whereas Abraham was a tenth-generation descendant of Noah, the patriarchs of the Assyrians and the Arameans were third-generation descendants! Now, maybe such status befits two such estimable constituents of the Persian Empire, but how should an Israelite theologian, such as P, handle the implied stature of their national gods? Was the god Assur of Assyria *also* the same as Yahweh?

Maybe so. It turns out that *El Shaddai* isn't P's most common deviation from the name *Yahweh*. That title goes to the word *elohim*. And this deviation may have even broader geopolitical significance.

God with a Capital G

The word *elohim* may have entered Hebrew via Aramaic, the language of the Arameans, who lived north of Israel. This name shows up in presumably pre-exilic scriptures as well as in the Priestly source—not surprisingly, since Aramaic had been growing as a regional lingua franca since the eighth century. But by the same token—because the term *elohim* thus connoted the transcendence of national bounds—it fits especially well into P's internationalist perspective; *elohim* suggested, as one scholar has put it, a divinity that was "international and unspecific."[55]

Indeed, *Elohim* is the term used for God when P carries his governance across the entire planet. It is P who added to the Noah story the idea that the rainbow was created after the great flood as the sign of "an everlasting covenant between God and every living creature of all flesh that is on the earth"—and the word used for "God" in that passage is *Elohim*. So too it is P who, in the first book of Genesis, has "Elohim" bless the entire human species and give it custody of the earth.[56]

Konrad Schmid sees P's three different names for God— Elohim, El Shaddai, and Yahweh—corresponding to three "concentric circles." The Priestly source, he says, depicts "a circle of the world over which God stands as Elohim, an Abrahamic circle to which God relates as El Shaddai, and finally an Israelite circle inside which God can be called upon with his real and cultic name Yahweh."[57] In this view, the term *Elohim* acquires a new sense for Israelites after the exile; P has in effect changed it from a generic noun (our god, their god) into a proper noun (God).[58] In one sense, this is hardly surprising and may not have seemed new; if you're a monotheist, like P, then the generic noun for god almost *has* to be, in a sense, the same as the proper noun for God. Still, Schmid thinks this grammatical maneuver had a subtler implication that was new: P was saying that the gods of the different nations—all the elohims—are just different manifestations of the same underlying divinity: Elohim with a capital E.

Compare the kind of monotheism Schmid attributes to P with the kind found in Second Isaiah. There monotheism arises through the *exclusion* of other nations' gods. The sense is that these nations—at this point enemies of Israel—are wrong to believe in their gods, and won't see who the real God is until they have a jarring encounter with him ("I will make your oppressors eat their own flesh.... Then all flesh shall know that I am Yahweh your Savior").[59] The Priestly source, in contrast, asserts monotheism by *affirming* the existence of other nations' gods. With P, it seems, Abrahamic monotheism has been converted from a fiercely nationalistic and exclusive theology—the theology present at its creation—to a more international and inclusive one.

If so, this is yet another tribute to the malleability of God. Monotheism had emerged as a tool for elevating Israelites above their neighbors, and now it was becoming a way of putting Israel on the same platform as its neighbors. The Abrahamic god was growing.

But About Those Egyptians...

There were limits to the growth. After all, the Persian Empire didn't include the whole world. In fact, after the exile the empire had one major rival for dominance: Egypt. If indeed P is the voice of the Persian Empire around the end of exile, then you would expect its attitude toward Egypt, and Egypt's theology, to be notably lacking in charity; the postexilic God may be universal in dominion, but that doesn't mean his sympathies are evenly spread across the globe.

And, sure enough, in P's rendering Egypt seems to be on the other side of a moral divide. For starters, in that "table of nations," no nation is more distantly related to Israel than Egypt. Whereas Abraham, Israel's patriarch, is descended from Noah's son Shem, whom the Bible identifies as a Yahweh worshipper,[60] Egypt is descended from another of Noah's sons, Ham, whose religious affiliation isn't mentioned and who is emphatically of ill repute.[61]

Egypt's morally dubious status is reinforced by P's addition to the Bible's historical narrative. To be sure, the Priestly source didn't *invent* the antagonism with Egypt that pervades the book of Exodus; pre-exilic verses also convey enmity, and almost certainly some of the original tribes of Israel had a genuine history of conflict with Egypt. Still, the Priestly source deepened the Bible's demonization of Egypt.

It is P, for example, who tells us that "The Egyptians became ruthless in imposing tasks on the Israelites, and made their lives bitter with hard service." So the Israelites "groaned under their slavery, and cried out," and God heard them. And, after hearing them, God sounds, toward Egypt, the way he sounded toward just about every nation back when Second Isaiah was depicting virtually the whole world as Israel's enemy. "The Egyptians shall know that I am the LORD, when I stretch out my hand against Egypt and bring the Israelites out from among them."[62]

The Priestly source then fleshes out God's stretched-out hand: Yahweh turns Egypt's entire water supply into blood and, as if that weren't enough, has the frogs that formerly inhabited the water swarm the Egyptians. Then it's time to bring on the bugs—lice, gnats, or mosquitoes, depending on the translation. Next, Yahweh inflicts "festering boils" on the skin of all humans and animals in Egypt. Then one night he kills every firstborn human and animal in Egypt, an event that P recounts shortly before prescribing the Passover feast with which Israelites are to forever commemorate this night.[63] Here the voice of the Persian Empire is helping to ensure that enmity toward Egypt—toward an enemy of the Persian Empire—will figure centrally in Judaism's ritual calendar.

Amid the Passover narrative, the Priestly source seems to get into some theological trouble. P has Yahweh declare that "on all the gods of Egypt I will execute judgments."[64] Gods? But isn't P supposed to be a monotheist? Yes, but P may be imagining a day when there had been more than one god on earth, back before Yahweh assumed total control. And, since one of the "judgments" Yahweh may have "executed" was the death penalty, this story could serve as a milestone in the emergence of monotheism. In any event, this odd passage drives home the fact that, even if Schmid is right and the essential drift of P's theology is internationally inclusive, it isn't *universally* inclusive. Apparently if gods want to qualify for P's inclusive theology—if they want to be manifestations of Elohim—it helps for them to be attached to a nation that's within the Persian Empire.

In short, P is a voice of far-flung friendship, but not universal friendship. So the god described by P—the more or less official God of the Israelites upon their return from exile—hadn't grown as much as we might like. But could we really ask for more? After all, in the time of P, the sinews of non-zero-sumness hadn't stretched all the way around the world; Israel didn't have win-win opportunities with, say, East Asia, and there weren't even live prospects for collaboration with Egypt so long as Egypt was on Persia's enemies list. The Abrahamic god had extended his sympathies out to the frontiers of perceived non-zero-sumness, which is all we expect of a god.

But Is It God?

Or, rather, all we expect of a "god." The god I've been describing is a god in quotation marks, a god that exists in people's heads. When I said in chapter 5, for example, that Yahweh was strong yet compassionate, I just meant that his adherents *thought of him* as strong yet compassionate. There was no particular reason to believe that there was a god "out there" that matched this internal conception. Similarly, when I say God shows moral progress, what I'm really saying is that people's *conception* of God moves in a morally progressive direction.

From the standpoint of a traditional believer, of course, this isn't an inspiring thought. Indeed, all told, the worldview I'm laying out amounts to a kind of good-news/bad-news joke for traditionalist Christians, Muslims, and Jews. The bad news is that the god you thought was born perfect was in fact born imperfect. The good news is that this imperfect god isn't really a god anyway, just a figment of the human imagination. Obviously, for the traditional believer, this is all bad news.

Then again, traditional believers come into the conversation with high expectations: that an ancient theology which took shape millennia before science started revealing the nature of the world should survive modern critical reflection unscathed. These days there are people who would call themselves religiously inclined, or at least spiritually inclined, who ask for less. They are born into a scientific world that seems to offer no particular sustenance to spiritual inquiry, and they would settle for evidence that this inquiry isn't hopeless after all. They are a bit like Fyodor Pavlovich in *The Brothers Karamazov*. When told by his atheist son that there is no God and no immortality, he reflects glumly, "There's absolute nothingness, then." But then he presses on: "Perhaps there is just something? Anything is better than nothing."

Is there something? Is there anything? Is there any evidence of something? Any signs that there's more to life than the sum of its subatomic particles—some larger purpose, some deeper meaning, maybe even something that would qualify as "divine" in some sense of that word? If you approach the spiritual quest with hopes this modest—with the humble skepticism of modernity rather than the revealed certainty of the ancient world—then a rational appraisal of the situation may prove more uplifting. There may be, as Fyodor Pavlovich would put it, some evidence of something.

What might qualify as evidence of a larger purpose at work in the world? For one thing, a moral direction in history. If history naturally carries human consciousness toward moral enlightenment, however slowly and fitfully, that would be evidence that there's some point to it all. At least, it would be more evidence than the alternative—if history showed no discernible direction, or if history showed a downward direction: humanity as a whole getting more morally obtuse, more vengeful and bigoted.

Or, to put the point back into the context at hand: To the extent that "god" grows, that is evidence—maybe not massive evidence, but *some* evidence—of higher purpose. Which raises this question: If "god" indeed grows, and grows with stubborn persistence, does that mean we can start thinking about taking the quotation marks off? That is: if the human conception of god features moral growth, and if this reflects corresponding moral growth on the part of humanity itself, and if humanity's moral growth flows from basic dynamics underlying history, and if we conclude that this growth is therefore evidence of "higher purpose," does this amount to evidence of an actual god?

Let's not get ahead of ourselves. "Higher purpose" is a pretty vague term, and you can imagine it being imparted by something quite different than a god as gods are traditionally conceived.[65]

Anyway, we'll get into some of the theological implications of a morally directional history in the next chapter. Then, in subsequent chapters, we'll focus on the history itself. I'll try to show that on balance, notwithstanding bursts of backsliding, human conceptions of the divine do get morally richer—that "god" tends to grow morally because humankind is itself growing morally. And the reason, I'll argue, is that circumstances conducive to moral growth—the breadth and density of non-zero-sum dynamics—intensify as time goes by. Technological evolution (wheels, roads, cuneiform, alphabets, trains, microchips) puts more and more people in non-zero-sum relationship with more and more other people at greater and greater distances, often across ethnic, national, or religious bounds. This doesn't guarantee moral progress, but it shifts the odds in that direction, and in the long run, the odds tend to win out.

That the stubborn growth of non-zero-sumness is central to human history, built into the very engine of cultural evolution, is an argument that space doesn't permit me to make at length. (I made it in my previous book *Nonzero*.) But this growing non-zero-sumness will nonetheless be visible as this book proceeds, and God's growth continues. It will be the prime mover behind God's growth. Or maybe we should just say the "mover" behind God's growth, since the possibility persists that this growing non-zero-sumness was itself set in motion by something else—conceivably an old-fashioned god, as traditionalists might hope, and conceivably something more abstract, more philosophically modern; but in any event, something deeper.

However, before we proceed with the story of God's growth, it's worth taking a look at the ancient Abrahamic thinker who tried supremely to have it both ways: to see divinity abstractly, as a kind of logic running through history, yet to do so in a way that preserved the emotional satisfaction of traditional religion. As it happens, that thinker was Philo of Alexandria.

Chapter Nine

Logos: The Divine Algorithm

The conflict between science and religion is sometimes cast as a geographic metaphor—as a tension between Athens, ancient well-spring of secular philosophy, and Jerusalem, symbol of revealed religious truth. Many early religious thinkers ignored this tension or tried to minimize it. "What has Athens to do with Jerusalem?" asked the Christian theologian Tertullian around 200 CE. The less the better, he felt. Having received the revealed truth via Christ, "We want no curious disputation."[1]

Well, that was then. Today science is so plainly powerful that theologians can't casually dismiss secular knowledge. For most educated and thoughtful people, Athens and Jerusalem must be reconciled or Jerusalem will fall off the map.

Two millennia ago, Philo of Alexandria felt this imperative intimately. Alexandria was situated between Athens and Jerusalem—physically, not just metaphorically—and Philo was tied to both cultures. His Jewish heritage and his Greek milieu together inspired him to seek a synthesis of biblical theology and Greek philosophy. He set out to show that revealed religion could not only withstand the challenge of reason but be nourished by reason, and vice versa.

In a way, this is yet another example of non-zero-sum logic encouraging intellectual synthesis. Just as the interdependence of Mesopotamian cities in the third millennium BCE had led them to weave a pan-Sumerian pantheon, the interdependence of Jews and Greeks led Philo to fuse Jewish and Greek thought. And this wasn't just a matter of calculation, of Philo's realizing that Jews and Greeks would get along better if they saw their worldviews as compatible. Philo partook of Greek culture—theater, horse races, boxing matches—and no doubt had close friends who were Greek intellectuals.[2] The closer friends are, the stronger their need to share a common worldview. This is just human nature: our instincts for playing non-zero-sum games, for maintaining social allies, encourage intellectual convergence, just as our instincts for playing zero-sum games encourage intellectual cleavage when we define people as enemies.

And, non-zero-sumness aside, there was the problem of cognitive dissonance. Philo believed that all of Judaism and large parts of Greek philosophy were true, and so long as they seemed at odds, he couldn't rest easy.[3]

But his mission went beyond rendering them compatible. If the original revelation of ultimate truth had indeed come from Yahweh, then the deepest insights of Greek philosophy must have been prefigured in scripture. Arguing this case would demand all Philo's intellectual dexterity and would yield a creative, often allegorical, interpretation of the Bible. "He read Plato in terms of Moses, and Moses in terms of Plato, to the point that he was convinced that each had said essentially the same things," wrote the historian of religion Erwin Goodenough, whose several early-twentieth-century books on Philo helped establish his standing as one of antiquity's most important thinkers. "Indeed, he used to say that Plato had cribbed his ideas from Moses, but his biblical interpretations often read as though he thought Moses had been trained by Plato."[4]

However strained some of Philo's intellectual gymnastics, they produced something of enduring value. If people of any Abrahamic faith—Judaism, Christianity, or Islam—are looking for the most ancient Abrahamic theologian whose language lends itself to a modern sensibility, Philo may be their man. For that matter, if they are looking not for the oldest science-friendly theological language, but just for the *best* science-friendly theological language, Philo may still be their man. At the core of his sometimes ungainly body of theology is the basis of a viable modern theology.

The bridge between Athens and Jerusalem is only one of the intercultural construction projects Philo advanced. While Jesus was preaching in Galilee, Philo, over in Alexandria, was laying out a worldview with key ingredients, and specific terminology, that would show up in Christianity as it solidified over the next two centuries. Meanwhile, other parts of his writing are reminiscent of Buddhism, and for that matter of mystical traditions that would develop in Judaism, Christianity, and Islam. Here, too, Philo is anticipating the modern—anticipating a spiritual practice that needn't (though it can) involve a governing deity. But these feats are outgrowths of the mission that was dearest to Philo's heart, and with which we should begin: the reconciliation of Jewish religion and Greek philosophy.

God as Programmer

Philo's synthesis of faith and reason ranged all over the map, as he asserted the ultimate rationality of not just theology but ritual. (Apparently he was the first person to defend the Jewish rite of circumcision on grounds of personal hygiene.)[5] But from a modern standpoint, his biggest contribution may have been to confront the most obvious obstacle to rapprochement between traditional religion and a scientific sensibility: the idea of an anthropomorphic and frequently interventionist god.

In the Bible, God had occasionally been depicted as physically anthropomorphic (sitting on a throne, for example) and often as psychologically anthropomorphic (prone to jealousy, rage, and so on). This conception of gods had been falling out of favor among Greek philosophers since Xenophanes, five centuries before Philo's time, noted its arbitrariness. If horses and cattle did theology, he had asserted, "horses would draw the forms of the gods like horses, and cattle like cattle."[6] Meanwhile, a frequently interventionist god—a god that deployed plagues, storms, and bolts of fire to keep humanity on track—didn't coexist easily with a scientific worldview. That worldview wouldn't mature for nearly two millennia after Philo, but its animating spirit, and its aspiration to universal explanation, had emerged centuries earlier, by the time of Aristotle.

Philo handily dispatched the Bible's anthropomorphic depiction of God by calling it allegory.[7] And as for what God *was* like if he wasn't like a human: though Philo seems to have conceived of God as in *some* sense personal,[8] his bottom line was that "no name nor utterance nor conception of any sort is adequate."[9]

But jettisoning an anthropomorphic and often interventionist god posed a problem. It was easy enough to say that God defies human conception and is off in another realm, beyond the merely material—that he is ineffable and transcendent. But if that's the case, then what exactly is his connection to the world? How does he get credit for its everyday operation? Moreover, what is his connection to *us?* How can we get consolation, spiritual sustenance, and moral guidance from a god who has been sealed off? As Goodenough put the challenge Philo faced, "There must be an Unrelated Being who is yet somehow related."[10]

Philo answered this challenge with one word: "logos." The word was both a part of everyday Greek speech and a technical term in Greek philosophy. It was the noun form of a verb that meant "to speak" and "to count," and so naturally meant "speech" and "account" or "computation." But by the time ancient philosophers got through with it, it had come to have lots of meanings, such as "reason" and "order."[11] In his mission to reconcile a transcendent God with an active and meaningful God, Philo would draw on all these meanings, and more.

On the one hand, Philo's Logos was, as Goodenough put it, the "reasoning principle in the universe" and "Natural Law for all men and matter."[12] In that sense it was like what modern scientists would call the basic laws of physics, chemistry, and biology—the rules that keep the world operating and intact. The Logos, wrote Philo, was "such a Bond of the Universe as nothing can break."[13]

But Philo's Logos had a divine depth that mere laws of science lack. For one thing, by animating matter and men, it animated history. You might say the same about the laws of science, of course, but if those laws aren't god-given, there's no reason to expect the history they animate to lead to anything in particular. The Logos, by contrast, had in Philo's view given history a direction — in fact, a moral direction: history moved toward the good. A Logos-driven history would eventually unify humankind in political freedom; the Logos would work "to the end that the whole of our world should be as a single state, enjoying the best of constitutions, a democracy."[14]

At the same time, Philo believed the Logos had existed before humans or the earth or, for that matter, matter.[15] Prior to creating the universe, God formulated the Logos the way an architect might conceive a blueprint or the way a computer programmer might design an algorithm. Long before modern science started clashing with the six-day creation scenario in Genesis, Philo had preempted the conflict by calling those six days allegorical: they actually referred not to God's creation of the earth and animals and people, but to his creation of the Logos, the divine algorithm, which would bring earth and animals and people into existence once it was unleashed in the material world — that is, once the material world was created to serve as its medium.[16] Then God's plan could tangibly unfold. The Logos, writes the scholar David Runia, is "God's instrument both during creation and in the cosmos's providential administration."[17] As Philo himself put it, "The Logos was conceived in God's mind before all things and is manifest in connection with all things."[18]

Greek thinkers before Philo's time had talked about a *logos* that was active in human beings in two ways — within the mind (in the formation of a thought), and in speech (as the thought is sent into the physical world).[19] Philo's theology applied this dichotomy to God. First God conceived the Logos in his mind. Then, upon creating the world, he, in a sense, uttered the Logos, infusing matter with it. He spoke to the universe at its beginning, and, via the ongoing guidance of the Logos, he speaks to us now. You can choose other metaphors, and scholars have — the Logos is "the breath of God" or a "stream" emanating from God or "the face of God turned toward creation"[20] — but in any event the Logos is humankind's point of contact with the divine.

This is how the Logos reconciles the transcendence of God with a divine presence in the world. God himself is beyond the material universe, somewhat the way a video game designer is outside of the video game. Yet the video game itself—the algorithm inside the box—is an extension of the designer, a reflection of the designer's mind. Similarly, if God imbued the Logos with his spirit and his values, then to know the Logos is to sense divine intention, even to know a part of God.[21] God may be outside the physical universe, but, as Goodenough puts it, there is "an immanent presence and cooperation of divinity in the created world."[22] The job of human beings, you might say, is to in turn cooperate with the divinity, a task they'll do best if they sense this presence and the purpose it imparts.

Getting With the Program

Somewhere in the journey through Philo's complex worldview, we have to either abandon or radically amend the video game analogy (which, come to think of it, Philo never endorsed in the first place). However transcendent God is, we can get closer to actual contact with him than Pac-Man could ever have gotten to Toru Iwatani, Pac-Man's creator. Philo's various interpreters differ on how close we can get. Some say Philo believed a kind of direct contact with God was somehow possible; others talk about a union with "the divine" that falls short of communion with God himself.[23]

But, however direct the connection, the first step to making it was to try to understand God and God's will. Thus deciphering the Logos could bring enlightenment not just intellectually but spiritually. "The *logos* was meant to guide the human soul to the realm of the divine," writes the scholar Thomas Tobin. And, though perfect knowledge of a transcendent and ineffable God wasn't possible, the quest was worth the effort, because the further you got, the more God-like you could become.[24] Goodenough puts it this way: "One can do or be the superhuman because the superhuman has become in some measure a part of oneself."[25] The key was to find harmony with the Logos.

So how do you figure out what that would entail? How do you decipher the Logos in the first place? Well, if you're Jewish, you've got a head start. Philo believed that God had privileged the Jews with the initial revelation. The Logos, he said, was reflected in the Torah, the Jewish law as given to Moses. In fact, the Torah didn't just reflect the Logos—it didn't just tell you how to behave in order to harmonize yourself with the principle that governs the universe and everything in it; the rules of living laid out in the Torah were *part of* the Logos. In that sense, the Logos is a little like the Buddhist concept of dharma: it is both the truth about the way things are—about how the universe works—and the truth about the way we should live our lives given the way things are. It is the law of nature and it is the law for living in light of nature.

This double entendre is hard for some people to accept, as today we often separate description (scientific laws) from prescription (moral laws). But to many ancient thinkers the connection was intimate: if basic laws of nature were laid down by a perfect God, then we should behave in accordance with them, aid in their realization; we should help the Logos move humanity in the direction God wants humanity to move in.

And what direction *does* God want us to move in? Toward greater harmony with other people and other peoples, said Philo. The Torah as rendered by Moses was quite detailed, but Philo felt that much of its upshot could be captured simply: "This is what our most holy prophet through all his regulations especially desires to create, unanimity, neighbourliness, fellowship, reciprocity of feeling, whereby houses and cities and nations and countries and the whole human race may advance to supreme happiness."[26]

Okay, so that's a start: be nice to people, even people who aren't of your tribe. But surely there must be more to Philo's recipe for blissful union with the divine than that. Besides, how were Gentiles supposed to use this recipe? Why should they follow Philo's CliffsNotes version of the Torah, given that God hadn't revealed the Torah to them in the first place? Were they supposed to use Jews as role models?

Philo certainly approved of that approach, but it wasn't necessary. The beauty of the Logos was that you didn't have to take anybody's word for it. Indeed, look at how well Greek philosophers had done without the advantage of a Jewish upbringing. "What the disciples of the most excellent philosophy gain from its teaching, the Jews gain from their customs and laws, that is to know the highest, the most ancient Cause of all things..."[27] Anyone in the world, in Philo's day or now, can in principle figure out what it takes to achieve a kind of concord with God. It's an empirical question.

As for where exactly those not privy to special revelation should begin this inquiry: Philo isn't as concise and straightforward as would be preferred by the modern seeker of divine communion, pressed for time as he or she is. In fact, Philo is often less than straightforward. Scholars have argued at length about the meaning of his work, trying to resolve its paradoxes and flesh out its contours, interpolating when necessary to fill in blanks. (Some of his writing survives only in fragments, some not at all.)

In this case — in figuring out how the Logos can be fathomed through observation and reflection — interpolation can begin with a single crucial fact: Philo equates the Logos with wisdom, often using the terms interchangeably.[28] One moment it will be the Logos that is transporting souls to divine communion, and the next minute it will be wisdom that is doing the work, carrying them beyond the material world ("wisdom, by which alone suppliant souls can make their escape to the Uncreated").[29]

This Logos-wisdom equation may not seem to be what the spiritual seeker most needs at this point in the strenuous effort to comprehend Philo. For one thing, dragging wisdom into the picture further complicates our picture of an already multifaceted Logos. For another, the seeming implication — that the path to God lies in acting wisely — sounds disappointingly commonsensical and prosaic. But the equation of the Logos and wisdom is the key to cracking Philo's code, seeing how the Logos can serve as the path to the divine. As a bonus, this equation turns out to have a kind of spiritual poetry about it.

The Anatomy of Wisdom

The poetry is especially powerful if you approach it, as many of Philo's readers did, against the backdrop of scripture. By equating the Logos and wisdom, Philo was invoking the Jewish "wisdom literature"—such biblical books as Proverbs and ancient books that wouldn't make it into the Bible but were considered sacred at the time, such as the Wisdom of Solomon and the book of Sirach. In these works, wisdom is a lot more than street smarts. In Proverbs, "Wisdom" is depicted as a woman. "Happy are those who find wisdom," for "her income is better than silver, and her revenue better than gold." Indeed, "nothing you desire can compare with her...her ways are ways of pleasantness, and all her paths are peace. She is a tree of life to those who lay hold of her; those who hold her fast are called happy."[30] In short: a woman worth pursuing.

Some people take this as poetic personification, but in fact Wisdom had probably once been considered a goddess, possibly Yahweh's daughter.[31] Certainly in Proverbs she is depicted as in *some* sense an offspring of Yahweh's. She says, "The LORD created me at the beginning of his work, the first of his acts of long ago." And, having been born, she began functioning very much like the nascent Logos depicted by Philo, as a key intermediary in the creation of the universe. She says that when God "drew a circle on the face of the deep...when he marked out the foundations of the earth, then I was beside him, like a master worker; and I was daily his delight."[32]

This raises a question. When Philo says that wisdom is what transports us beyond the material world, he seems to be talking about a kind of insight available to humans. But when Proverbs talks about Wisdom being the creation of God that in turn created the world, it seems more like the wisdom that God brought to bear on the design of physical reality. And surely the kind of wisdom people possess is a wholly different wisdom from the kind that God possesses. Right?

Not so fast. The beauty of the Philonic worldview is the potential continuity between the two—the way ordinary human beings can, if they're diligent, partake of God's wisdom. You see this metaphorically in the two roles assigned Wisdom in Proverbs: she is both the being who helped God create the world and the being who now beckons ordinary mortals to embrace her. But let's drop the metaphor. For all the inspirational power that Wisdom (and hence the Logos) had for ancients when she was personified, even deified, treating wisdom in modern, abstract terms is the way to explain Philo's worldview to people in the modern age. For then we can understand exactly how God might have set up the world so that ordinary people, just by using their heads, can achieve a kind of communion with the divine. In other words: how God could have set up the Logos so that earnest seekers of spiritual truth could follow it back to him—or, as we would say today, him, her, or it.

The Logic of Biblical Wisdom

Proverbs and the other Jewish wisdom books are part of a larger wisdom tradition in the ancient Middle East, seen from Egypt to Mesopotamia. This literature was initially intended for upper-class boys as they approached manhood. In one sense, it is moral exhortation. The book of Proverbs announces at its outset that it aims to impart a sense of "integrity, justice, and honesty." Yet the very next verse shifts into the realm of pragmatic self-help, promising that the book will "teach shrewdness to the simple" and "prudence to the young."[33]

In the logic of the wisdom literature, there is no great gap here. You learn virtue by learning the *wisdom* of virtue, learning that virtue is in your self-interest. In Proverbs, Lady Wisdom says, "I, Wisdom, am neighbor to shrewdness, and the knowledge of prudence is at my disposal."[34] That is why you can start down the path to knowledge of the Logos even without being born a Jew, without access to the Torah. You can just watch how the world works and see what kinds of behaviors bear fruit and what kinds of behaviors lead to sorrow. The fruitful behaviors are more likely to reflect virtue, to embody wisdom, to converge on the Logos.

To be sure, Philo would advise you to heed authority, to accept the teachings in the wisdom literature. Even leaving aside the fact that this was holy scripture, reflecting God's will, it had been accumulated over the ages by some of the most astute observers of the human condition. Taking it on faith was thus a real time-saver. Still, the wisdom of the sages was in principle available firsthand, empirically, by simply watching the consequences of behavior. When Proverbs reports that "pride goes before destruction, and a haughty spirit before a fall,"[35] it is indeed *reporting* it, asserting that, as a matter of fact, proud and haughty people usually get their comeuppance. This is the way the world works.

So too when the book of Sirach, by way of questioning the value of wealth, observes: "Many a man is prevented from sinning by poverty, and when he rests he is not tempted." Meanwhile, "The rich man's sleeplessness wastes away his flesh, and his anxiety drives away sleep." These are claims of fact, as is Sirach's observation that "Jealousy and anger shorten life, and worry ages a man prematurely." Modern studies of emotions and physical health bear out this claim—and this claim, too, from Sirach: "A glad heart is good for the body."[36]

Even in the realm of the moral, the wisdom literature deals in cause and effect. Proverbs warns young men not to fall in with murderous thieves, for people who live by the sword die by it. "They lie in wait—to kill themselves! And set an ambush—for their own lives! Such is the end of all who are greedy for gain; it takes away the life of its possessors." And a man shouldn't sleep with another man's wife because he loses honor and perhaps more: "For jealousy arouses a husband's fury, and he shows no restraint when he takes revenge."[37]

These generalizations aren't absolute. Taken as a whole, the wisdom literature isn't saying that evil is always punished via social consequence, or that bad people never thrive. Indeed, the literature is peppered with laments of earthly injustice. Still, its upshot is that there are statistically valid generalizations about the consequences of behavior—that virtue is usually rewarded and wrongdoing usually punished. The wisdom literature is meant to rest largely on a *science* of human behavior, and there lies part of its modernity; it sees the social world as an extension of the natural world and both worlds as amenable to empirical study. ("The north wind produces rain, and a backbiting tongue, angry looks," says Proverbs.)[38] In searching for statistical regularity beneath the seeming chaos and complexity of life, the wisdom literature senses "an order which is at work behind the experiences," as Gerhard von Rad wrote in his classic book *Wisdom in Israel*.[39]

And where does the order come from? Here is the pivot point between the scientific and the theological. The order at work is the Logos, and it came originally from God. He set up the world so that mere self-interested learning—the study of cause and effect, and preference for happy effects—would steer people toward virtue. So when Proverbs reports that "whoever digs a pit will fall into it, and a stone will come back on the one who starts it rolling," we can think of God not as pushing people into pits and pushing stones back on people, but as the one who designed the social "gravity" that brings these effects.[40] Maybe that's why he doesn't have to spend all his time hurling thunderbolts—because here on earth, everything is under control, in accordance with the original plan, the Logos.

In this worldview, there is little difference between a scientist's faith—faith in the orderly laws that govern the world—and religious faith. As von Rad puts it, "in proverbial wisdom, there is faith in the stability of the elementary relationships between man and man, faith in the similarity of men and of their reactions, faith in the reliability of the orders which support human life and thus, implicitly or explicitly, faith in God who put these orders into operation."[41]

By the same token, coming to terms with this social order (learning that behaving badly tends to bring painful consequences) is coming to terms with God. The book of Proverbs may stress the mundane social forces that bring punishment to sinners—warning would-be adulterers to fear jealous husbands—but it also asserts that "the fear of the LORD is the beginning of knowledge."[42] Lady

Wisdom, in Proverbs, says, "My child, if you accept my words and treasure up my commandments within you . . . if you indeed cry out for insight, and raise your voice for understanding . . . then you will understand the fear of the LORD and find the knowledge of God."

This is the link between the two wisdoms, the everyday garden-variety wisdom of human beings and the Wisdom of God: God was so wise that he set up a world in which the rational pursuit of self-interest leads people to wisdom. This explains why Lady Wisdom, in Proverbs, can play her two roles. She is both God's own Wisdom — the Wisdom that went into the initial design of the world, when she was God's "master worker" as he "marked out the foundations of the earth" — and the giver of wisdom to humans. For the Wisdom of the world's initial design was that it would lead human beings toward wisdom.

And hence, in a sense, toward Wisdom — toward God's own mind. "For wisdom is a straight high road," Philo wrote. "And it is when the mind's course is guided along that road that it reaches the goal which is the recognition and knowledge of God."[43] When we navigate social reality wisely, we are following the Logos back toward its source.

And, not incidentally, this wise compliance with the Logos means adherence to virtue, which Philo personifies as a woman: "For the Logos of God, when it arrives at our earthy composition, in the case of those who are akin to virtue and turn away to her, gives help and succour, thus affording them a refuge and perfect safety, but sends upon her adversaries irreparable ruin."[44]

This, then, is a sense in which contact with the divine is possible. Attaining wisdom entails concordance with the Logos, and the Logos, God's Wisdom, is an extension of God; it is a dimension of the divine that can be accessed in the material world. Sounds fine in theory. That's the problem — it sounds so theoretical! When people think about communion with the divine, they generally envision something that will feel special, feel rapturous, feel . . . well, divine. So far all we've heard is that if you pay attention and behave virtuously, you'll in some technical sense be merging with the Logos, which is a divine emanation.

Of course, for the ancients, the personification of—or deification of—the Logos as Lady Wisdom packed an emotional punch. In Proverbs, she borders on the seductive: "Do not forsake her and she will guide you," says Proverbs. "Love her, and she will guard you."[45] (No wonder Philo at one point refers to Wisdom—or, as he put it in Greek, Sophia—as his wife.)[46] But if the key to Philo's version of religious rapture was taking such images seriously, we moderners are in trouble. Even when you call wisdom Sophia, I still can't picture it as a woman, much less as a goddess.

Fortunately, Philo's powerful sense of contact with the divine didn't wholly depend on this archaic personification. His metaphysics permitted a more modern route to Nirvana, and he sketched it out in some detail

Recipe for Nirvana

According to Philo, each human mind has a twofold relationship to the Logos.[47] First, as microcosm: the mind is to the body as the cosmic Logos is to the physical world; it is the reasoning principle that governs us, just as the cosmic Logos is the reasoning principle that governs the universe. Second, each human mind is a piece of the divine Logos, a fine-grained extension of it; the mind, Philo wrote, is "an inseparable portion of the divine and blessed soul."[48] In that sense, you don't have to try to achieve union with the divine—you're born with it.

But there's union and then there's Union. The part of the mind that is a direct extension of the Logos is the *rational* mind. And in Philo's view, the rational mind is often at war with base, animal impulses, which would, if they had their way, distort our vision and corrupt our motivation. The more your rational mind dominates your base impulses, the more plugged into the divine you are.

And if you want Union—if you want to know God as intimately

as possible—you need to make your link to the Logos as pure as possible: keep your rational mind fully in charge of the show, resisting passions and temptations. Of the path to wisdom, Philo says, "Every comrade of the flesh hates and rejects this path and seeks to corrupt it. For there are no two things so utterly opposed as knowledge and pleasure of the flesh." The great impediment to the good is "passions pricking and wounding the soul."[49]

Here Philo sounds like an earlier thinker who had seen passion as the enemy of enlightenment. Among the earliest sayings attributed to the Buddha is: "The best of virtues [is] passionlessness; the best of men he who has eyes to see." The parallel between Philonic and Buddhist thought can be carried to a finer level. In Buddhist philosophy there is a deep suspicion not just of violent passions, but of subtler distortions, ingrained in the mechanism of sensory perception itself. The Buddha expressed grave doubts about what he called "the senses' evidence," with their tendency to encourage, among other things, an undeservedly low opinion of our fellow human beings.[50] Here, similarly, is Philo's depiction of the senses—or, as he called them collectively, "sense": "Its standards of judgment," he wrote, are "spurious and corrupt and steeped in false opinion," and "equipped to ensnare and deceive and ravish truth away from its place in the heart of nature."[51] And Philo, like the Buddha, understood that part of this corruption of pure cognition came from egoistic biases; he railed especially against the corrupting role of "envy."

Philo also shared the Eastern mystic's suspicion of language, the conviction that speech, in its crudeness, is powerless to capture the true texture of reality and is therefore an impediment to apprehending the divine. He condemns speech for its "self-exaltation and self-pride," marveling at its "audacity, that it should attempt the impossible task to use shadows to point me to substances."[52]

Philo believed, like the Buddha, that the situation called for radical surgery. If you want to get closer to the divine, the path to follow, Philo wrote, was "not that way of thinking which abides in the prison of the body of its own free will, but that which released from its fetters into liberty has come forth outside the prison walls, and if we may so say, left behind its own self."[53] And it was hard to do this with anything much short of monastic solitude. For you must first separate yourself from the "body and its interminable cravings"; your soul must "rid itself, as I have said, of that neighbour of our rational element, the irrational, which like torrent in five divisions pours through the channels of all the senses and rouses the violence of the passions." The "reasoning faculty" must "sever and banish from itself that which has the appearance of being closest to it, the word of utterance." The object of the game is "that the logos or thought within the mind may be left behind by itself alone, destitute of body, destitute of sense-perception, destitute of utterance in audible speech; for when it has been thus left, it will live a life in harmony with such solitude." Only then can the logos that lies within us all give "its glad homage to the Sole Existence"[54]—that is, to God (here rendered by Philo in abstract language akin to such modern theological terms as "ultimate reality" and "the ground of being").

In short, communion with God consisted of austerely ridding your mind of all its ungodly inclinations, after which you would be left with something like pure reason and pure wisdom. Your own little logos, uncorrupted, could then enjoy a clear connection to the cosmic Logos. Your mind would be an essentially continuous extension of the mind of God. Philo wrote, "so if you wish to have God as the portion of your mind, first you yourself become a portion worthy of him."[55] Only then could you enjoy the paradox: that the triumph of reason over feeling can lead to the most profoundly good feeling—a "sober intoxication," as Philo called it.[56]

Did he speak from experience? One fragment of his writing suggests that he did, that he once achieved something like rapturous union with the divine:

There was once a time when by devoting myself to philosophy and to contemplation of the world and its parts I achieved the enjoyment of that Mind which is truly beautiful, desirable, and blessed; for I lived in constant communion with sacred utterances and teaching, in which I greedily and insatiably rejoiced. No base or worldly thoughts occurred to me, nor did I grovel for glory, wealth or bodily comfort, but I seemed ever to be borne aloft in the heights in a rapture of the soul, and to accompany sun, moon, and all heaven and the universe in their revolutions. Then, ah, then peering downwards from the ethereal heights and directing the eye of my intelligence as from a watchtower, I regarded the untold spectacle of all earthly things, and reckoned myself happy at having forcibly escaped the calamities of mortal life.[57]

Back to Reality

Alas, Philo reports, his days of rapturous contemplation came to an end when "that hater of the good, envy" suddenly "set upon" him and, through a sequence of events he leaves vague, somehow dragged him back into the world of human events.[58] Things were never the same. In the "vast sea of political cares," he wrote, "I am still tossed about and unable even so much as to rise to the surface." (Though sometimes, when "there is temporary quiet and calm in the political tumults, I become winged and skim the waves, barely flying, and am blown along by the breezes of understanding." Then he could open his eyes and be "flooded with the light of wisdom.")[59]

In a sense Philo is overplaying the tension between the life of action and the life of contemplation, between politics and enlightenment. As we've seen, he employed "the light of wisdom" in his role as a leader of Alexandria's Jewish community. He found himself in a situation where the relationship of Jews to Greeks and Romans was non-zero-sum, and responded to the situation with wisdom in the biblical sense: by rationally pursuing self-interest (the interests of the Jews), he wound up on the side of virtue (championing interfaith tolerance and mutual respect). He was thus, in his political life, doing the bidding of the Logos.

Here, in Philo's life, we are again at the nexus between Wisdom and wisdom, between the cosmic Logos, the divine plan unfolding on earth, and the logos in Philo's mind. Philo's logos, by mirroring the cosmic Logos—by stripping itself of the distortions of passions, revealing pure reason—manifests the cosmic Logos, furthering the divine plan.

Here we are also at the nexus between Logos as governing principle, as the prime mover of history, and Logos as moral principle. In response to the prompting of the former, Philo helps advance the latter—helps realize the ideals of the Torah as he understood them.

But a piece of the puzzle is still missing. How had the Logos managed to "prompt" Philo? How had it "arranged" for Philo to be in a non-zero-sum situation to begin with? The whole point of the Logos, remember, was to get rid of the need for a hands-on, interventionist God, the kind of God who could peel down, pick Philo up, and set him down in some non-zero-sum situation so that by acting wisely he could further God's plan. The Logos was supposed to be less like a personal god and more like the laws of nature or of a computer program—something that cranked on automatically, relentlessly. But how could something so rote and general give Philo his opportunity for wise action?

Philo, alas, isn't here to answer that question. But it's not hard to piece together a scenario that answers it and is consistent with his writings. Here's one such scenario, one kind of cosmic algorithm that could explain how Philo wound up in a non-zero-sum situation:

Suppose that part of the Logos, as channeled through humans, is the inquisitive, inventive part of the rational mind, the part that has given us an ever growing array of technologies, ranging from the wheel to the space shuttle, from cuneiform to the World Wide Web. (*Logos spermatikos*, a phrase used by Philo and earlier Greek philosophers, has as one of its meanings "seed-bearing reason," which yields new insights in a person.)[60] Suppose that a consequence of the resultant technological evolution is to put people into non-zero-sum situations with a greater and greater variety of other people, including, increasingly, people of different ethnicities and even people at great distances. So, repeatedly, a different part of the rational mind would be called on — a part that can respond to such situations wisely, thus advancing tolerance.

The rest, as they say, would be history. Of course, many of these encounters would result in violence and destruction. But to the extent that people responded to growing non-zero-sumness as Philo did — wisely, with enlightened self-interest — tolerance would win out more often than intolerance, respect for the rights of others would on balance advance, and humanity would thus move, if fitfully, toward moral enlightenment. And sometimes the key would be dispassionate reason, as deployed by Philo when he found common ground with adversarial figures, such as Caligula, notwithstanding his dislike of them.

I'm not suggesting that if Philo himself were asked to sum up the essence of the Logos-logos interface in 250 words, he'd recite the previous paragraph. Still, I am saying that this is one rendering of that interface that makes sense and is broadly compatible both with his worldview and with the observed drift of history. What's more, Philo probably *would* sign off on something like the above formulation. In order "that the universe may send forth a harmony like that of a masterpiece of literature," he wrote, the Logos "mediates between the opponents amid their threatenings, and reconciles them by winning ways to peace and concord."[61] Or, to put it another way: the wisdom of individual human beings, such as Philo, leads to peace and concord, thus vindicating the larger Wisdom, the divine Wisdom, by realizing its goals.

Philo understood that wisdom favors peace and concord not just because peace is preferable to war, but because peace brings the chance of mutual gain through fruitful interaction. And a primary source of this gain is the fact that different nations have different resources, and different people have different skills; they have a complementarity that can be harnessed, so long as they aren't fighting. At one point Philo describes the direction of history (a direct product of the Logos, in his worldview) in a way that puts this complementarity, this form of non-zero-sumness, at its core. Referring to "all created things"—by which he means different animal and plant species, but also different people and different peoples—he writes that God "has made none of these particular things complete in itself, so that it should have no need at all of another. Thus through the desire to obtain what it needs, it must perforce approach that which can supply its need, and this approach must be mutual and reciprocal. Thus through reciprocity and combination, even as a lyre is formed of unlike notes, God meant that they should come to fellowship and concord and form a single harmony, and that a universal give and take should govern them, and lead up to the consummation of the whole world."[62]

Two millennia after Philo wrote, we still haven't gotten to universal brotherhood. Yet, as he anticipated, history has brought moral progress and cause for real hope. And if you don't feel hopeful, just go back and read your Hebrew Bible. This may sound strange, given how sober, if not cynical, my reading of biblical scripture has been. And certainly many people react to such sober, cynical readings by *losing* hope. Some people are disappointed to find, for example, that a famous verse in Leviticus, "love your neighbor as yourself," referred only to fellow Israelites, not to people in neighboring nations. Indeed, the disappointment is evident even in the voice of Harry Orlinsky, the pioneering deflator of seemingly buoyant Bible verses who deflated this particular verse. "Alas," he says of Leviticus 19:18, "its author had no one but fellow Israelites in mind."[63] But there are two reasons why disappointment is the wrong reaction.

Reasons to Be Cheerful

First, the injunction to love all Israelites represented real moral progress at the time. Before the tribes of Israel were forged into a single polity—first a confederacy and then a nation—it is safe to say that empathy and affection rarely exceeded the bounds of individual tribes. The expansion of social organization from the tribal to the national level opened up new opportunities for non-zero-sumness, notably intertribal cooperation to fight common enemies; and the doctrine of national, as opposed to merely tribal, brotherhood evolved as a way to help realize these opportunities. In that sense Moses, in mediating God's utterance of the Torah, with its nationally cohesive effect, was in the service of the Logos. "Love your neighbor as yourself" may not have been meant globally, and so may not represent humankind's all-time moral zenith, but it still represented a moral watershed; it expanded the circle of brotherhood.

The second reason people shouldn't feel disappointed to hear that "Love your neighbor" was originally nationalist is that people *do* feel disappointed to hear that "Love your neighbor" was initially nationalist. This widespread sense of disappointment, reflecting the moral universalism of the modern world, is itself proof that there has been progress since biblical times. Harry Orlinsky's "Alas" is cause for cheer.

And the progress didn't just begin in modern times. As Orlinsky himself writes, "There can be little doubt that early in the postbiblical period, first among the Jews and later among the Christians also, Leviticus 19:18 became the biblical cornerstone of internationalism, of the concept of world brotherhood and the essential equality of all mankind."[64]

Of course, if this was really driven by the kind of Logos I've described—the wise response to inexorable technological progress—then it wouldn't be confined to Jews and Christians, since neither wisdom nor technological innovation is their exclusive possession. As the tentacles of technology bound larger and larger groups of people into an interdependent, multiethnic web, you'd expect to find comparable progress well beyond the Middle East. And you do.

The Global Logos

In the first millennium BCE, as various Hebrew scriptures stressed loving your neighbor, or treating foreigners decently, or hoped for a day when swords would be beaten into plowshares, other cultures were moving in the same direction.

In China, Confucius said the paramount virtue is *ren*—a sensitive concern for others—and summarized this law roughly as Hillel would later crystallize the Torah, saying: "Do not do to others what you would not wish for yourself."[65] Confucius also said, "Love your fellow man."[66] As with the parallel biblical injunction, in Leviticus, this love may have been confined to national scope. But a generation later the Chinese philosopher Mozi went further, explicitly advocating love of all humankind.[67] According to Mozi, the supreme Chinese god, Tian, "desires men to love each other and to benefit each other, and does not wish them to hate or to harm each other."[68] And: "There are no great states in the world, and no unimportant states. All are the city-states of Tian."[69]

Meanwhile, in India, Buddhist scripture had this to say:

Let none cajole or flout
his fellow anywhere;
let none wish others harm
in dudgeon or in hate.
Just as with her own life
a mother shields from hurt
her own, her only, child,
let all-embracing thoughts
for all that lives be thine,
an all-embracing love
for all the universe
in all its heights and depths
and breadth, unstinted love,
unmarred by hate within,
not rousing enmity.[70]

Repeatedly, these moral insights—like insights in the biblical wisdom literature—are grounded pragmatically; virtue's benefits to the virtuous are stressed.[71] The Buddha says that "the virtuous man is happy in this world." For example: forsaking hatred brings "serenity of mind."[72] Confucius says, "The wise man is attracted to benevolence (*ren*) because he finds it to his advantage." After all, "If the gentleman forsakes benevolence, in what way can he make a name for himself?"[73]

All told, the first millennium BCE brings a strikingly broad pattern: across the Eurasian landmass, from the Pacific to the Mediterranean, sages argue for expanding the circle of moral concern, for harnessing sympathy and hindering antipathy. And "sages" is indeed the word, for they speak in the spirit of the wisdom literature, in terms of enlightened self-interest: if you want peace, and if you want peace of mind, you would do well to rein in your dark side and push the envelope of benevolence.

None of this is to say that history brings simple, linear progress, that every century people grow less ethnocentric, less vindictive, more tolerant, more peace loving. Many great moral insights of the first millennium BCE were honored largely in the breach, and would be until the present day. A glance at the atrocities of the past century should make that clear. Moreover, it's not clear that our moral record will dramatically improve, that humanity will respond wisely to the vast web of interdependence that constitutes global society. All the Logos does is create situations in which ever larger circles of moral inclusion make rational sense; the rest is up to us, and often we fail. Still, there can be no doubt that, since civilization began, there has been net progress in the moral doctrines on offer. And one burst of progress came in the first millennium BCE.

Why? Why in the first millennium BCE are these insights suddenly finding fertile soil so broadly? What incarnations of the Logos are moving humanity forward?

Certainly this is a millennium of great material change.[74] Coins are invented, and appear in China, India, and the Middle East.[75] Commercial roads grow, crossing political bounds. In the course of this millennium, markets, as the historian William McNeill has noted, supplant state-controlled economies.[76] Cities get accordingly big and vibrant and, in many cases, more ethnically diverse.

All of this brings at least three things.

First, expanded economic engagement meant more non-zero-sum relationships among people of different ethnicities and even different polities. So more people had a selfish interest in the continued welfare of people who were in one sense or another unlike them. Selfishness may not have dictated loving these people, but it strengthened the logic behind not hating them.

Second, more and more people found themselves in an environment radically unlike the environment natural selection had "designed" people for. Emotions that functioned fairly well in the ancestral environment were now of dubious value. In a hunter-gatherer village, vengeful anger can help people defend their interests, but when you feel it welling up after some driver cuts you off, its main effect is to raise your risk of coronary disease. Of course, there were no cars in ancient India or China or Egypt, but, as laws and police came to replace vengeance as a guarantor of social order, anger and hatred lost some of their utility and became increasingly pointless, if not downright counterproductive, from both the individual's and the society's point of view. Even as early as the second millennium BCE, an Egyptian text of moral instruction had warned that, since "turmoil spreads like fire in hay," you should "control yourself around hot-headed people" and not "provoke them with words....If you leave them alone, the gods will answer them."[77] Loathing just wasn't what it used to be.

Third, as more people were in contact with more other people than ever, there was more interchange of ideas. And that included ideas about how to handle the first and second changes above. If dampening hatred, extending sympathy, exhibiting benevolence prove to be good self-help advice, then these ideas will spread rapidly through a dense web of minds. Notably, it is amid crowds that, according to Proverbs, Lady Wisdom does her best work. "Wisdom cries out in the street; in the squares she raises her voice. At the busiest corner she cries out; at the entrance of the city gates she speaks." As technology pushes and pulls people together, it both creates new problems and propagates the solutions, and often the result is to equate self-help with virtue. "On the heights, beside the way, at the crossroads she takes her stand.... 'O simple ones, learn prudence.... All the words of my mouth are righteous.' "[78]

The Journey

In a sense we've come full circle. We started out several chapters ago seeing Yahweh initially embedded in a polytheistic context and surrounded by mythological figures (Plague and Pestilence, for example). And this seemed like evidence of the "primitive" origins of Israelite religion. Yet in the end, one of the Bible's more obscure mythological figures — Wisdom — is a vital link to a fairly modern and even plausible theology whose broad outlines were envisioned by Philo, and whose core dynamic was *exhibited* by Philo in the way he crafted a doctrine of interfaith tolerance.

A few decades after Philo's death, the Logos made an appearance in a Greek book that would become world famous. But the role of the Logos would be obscured, because when the book was translated into other European languages, including English, "Logos" would be rendered as "Word." For example: "In the beginning was the Word." The book was the Gospel of John, the last and most mystical of the New Testament's four gospels.

In alternative translation, the book of John begins, "In the beginning was the Logos, and the Logos was with God, and the Logos was God." As the book proceeds, it becomes clear that this Logos has assumed the form of Jesus Christ: "And the Logos became flesh and lived among us, and we have seen his glory, the glory as of a father's only son, full of grace and truth."[79]

Philo, writing during Jesus's lifetime, had himself referred to the Logos as the son of God. What influence, if any, his writing had on the Gospel of John is unknown.[80] In any event, it is almost certain that the author of John, in using "Logos," had more than the word

"word" in mind. Any intellectual in the Graeco-Jewish world of the late first century CE would have encountered the use of "Logos" in philosophical or theological writing. And Philo's work was not an eccentric specimen of this sort of writing; such works as the Wisdom of Solomon also equated the Logos with wisdom, depicting a force of divine origin and enlightening effect.[81] So it made perfect sense for the Gospel of John to describe Jesus as "The true light, which enlightens everyone."[82]

Was Jesus really an incarnation of the Logos? He certainly sounds like a good candidate. According to the Bible, he preached generosity, tolerance, even universal love, and that message would seem to be doing the work of the Logos: the expansion of the circle of moral consideration.

But what if what the Bible says about Jesus isn't true? What if Jesus *didn't* really say all the compassionate things attributed to him? What if it turns out that one of the few things we can say about Jesus with much confidence is that he was quite different from the Jesus depicted in the Bible? Does that make him less an incarnation of the Logos? And should it sap our faith in the Logos? These questions will be forced on us by the next chapter.

III

THE INVENTION OF CHRISTIANITY

They stood still, looking sad. Then one of them, whose name was Cleopas, answered him, "Are you the only stranger in Jerusalem who does not know the things that have taken place there in these days?" He asked them, "What things?" They replied, "The things about Jesus of Nazareth, who was a prophet mighty in deed and word before God and all the people, and how our chief priests and leaders handed him over to be condemned to death and crucified him. But we had hoped that he was the one to set Israel free."

—Luke 24:17–21

Finally, brothers and sisters, farewell. Put things in order, listen to my appeal, agree with one another, live in peace; and the God of love and peace will be with you. Greet one another with a holy kiss.

—Paul's Second Letter to the Corinthians (13:4)

Chapter Ten

―――――――――――――

What Did Jesus Do?

Historians of religion have an ironic rule for evaluating the Bible's claims about history: the less sense a claim makes, the more likely it is to be true. That is, the less *theological* sense a claim makes, the more likely it is to be true. After all, if the Bible's authors were going to fabricate things, you'd expect them to fabricate things that coexisted easily with their religious beliefs. When you see them struggling to reconcile some ill-fitting fact with their theology, chances are that the fact is indeed fact—a truth so well known in their circles that there was no way of denying or ignoring it.

That's one reason the biblical accounts of King Josiah's zealous devotion to Yahweh, discussed in chapter 6, are credible. Given that Josiah goes on to die ignominiously, and that Israel's fortunes then spiral toward catastrophe, it would have been theologically simpler for the Bible's monotheistic editors to describe Josiah as a rampant polytheist who incurred God's enduring wrath. His opposition to polytheism is so theologically inconvenient that the best explanation for its inclusion in the Bible is its truth.

This criterion of credibility—call it the rule of theological inconvenience—is one reason biblical historians attach so much credence to the Crucifixion of Jesus. There is no written reference to Jesus being crucified until two decades after his death, but we can be pretty sure the Crucifixion happened, in part because it made so little theological sense.[1]

That may sound strange. What could make more sense to a Christian than Jesus's dying on the cross? The Crucifixion embodies one of Christianity's central themes, God's love for humanity.

As the iconic Christian verse John 3:16 puts it: "For God so loved the world that he gave his only begotten son..." And, as powerfully as these words ring now, imagine their impact in the ancient world. Throughout history, gods had been beings to whom you made sacrifices. Now here was a god that not only demanded no ritual sacrifices from you but himself made sacrifices—indeed, the ultimate sacrifice—for you.² All of humanity's sins, including yours, could be wiped off the ledger by God's self-sacrificing redemption.

And this reversal of sacrifice was only Act One of Crucifixion theology. Act Two—the Resurrection of Jesus after his execution and burial—was an equally potent symbol. It illustrated both the possibility of eternal life and the fact that anyone of any ethnicity and any social class could qualify for it; all they had to do was accept and comprehend the Resurrection of Jesus himself. In full form John 3:16 reads: "For God so loved the world that he gave his only begotten son, that whosoever believeth in him should not perish but should have everlasting life." The book of Galatians spelled out this open admissions policy: "There is no longer Jew or Greek, there is no longer slave or free, there is no longer male and female; for all of you are one in Christ Jesus."³ Universal salvation was on offer from a deeply compassionate and giving God, and it's hard to imagine a more resonant symbol of this fact than the Crucifixion of his son.

Why, then, if the Crucifixion fits into Christian theology so logically and powerfully, would scholars say that it passes the test of theological inconvenience (or, as they call it, the "criterion of dissimilarity")? Because, however theologically convenient the Crucifixion may seem now, it didn't seem that way back when it happened. For Jesus's followers the Crucifixion was, in addition to emotionally wrenching, a serious rhetorical problem.

After all, Jesus was supposed to be the Messiah.⁴ ("Messiah" is the meaning of the Greek word that became Jesus's title: Christos—or, in English, Christ.) Today Christians understand the Messiah as someone sent from on high who makes the ultimate sacrifice—his life—for humanity, bringing spiritual salvation to the world. But back in Jesus's time, losing your life wasn't part of the Messiah's job description.

The word "messiah" came from the Hebrew verb meaning "to apply oil to," to anoint. In the Hebrew Bible, Israel's kings were sometimes called Yahweh's "messiah"—God's anointed one.[5] By the end of the first millennium BCE, as Jesus's birth approached, some Jewish sects saw an "anointed one," a messiah, figuring centrally in their apocalyptic visions of a coming, final battle with God's enemies.[6] The most common expectation seems to have been that this messiah would be, like most of the Hebrew Bible's "anointed ones," a king.[7] Hence the words that, according to the Gospel of Mark, were inscribed on the cross by Jesus's persecutors: "King of the Jews." And hence their sarcasm as he died: "Let the Messiah, the King of Israel, come down from the cross now, so that we may see and believe."[8]

Being a king wasn't a strict prerequisite for being messiah. The Hebrew Bible had occasionally referred to a high priest or even a prophet as divinely anointed.[9] This diversity was reflected in apocalyptic thought around the time of Jesus. According to the Dead Sea Scrolls—left behind by a sect that settled near the Dead Sea more than a century before Jesus's birth—the climactic battle between good and evil would be fought under the leadership of two messianic figures, a priest and a prince.[10] And even if the messiah was a king, his triumph wouldn't necessarily come by military force alone. The "Psalms of Solomon," written in the decades before Jesus's birth, envisioned a messianic king who would "destroy the unlawful nations with the word of his mouth."[11]

Still, one thing that all anticipated messiahs of Jesus's era had in common was that they would aid a climactic triumph over evil by exercising leadership here on earth—which meant, for starters, not dying before the climactic triumph over evil.[12] Thus, according to prevailing logic, the death of Jesus should have been a devastating blow for any disciples who had been claiming that he was the Messiah.

Then again, according to prevailing logic, the death of King Josiah in the late seventh century, along with Judah's ensuing catastrophe, should have vindicated polytheists and spelled doom for monolatry, to say nothing of monotheism. But the Yahweh-alone movement had proved creative then, and so would the Jesus movement now.[13] Judah's Yahwists found a way to turn calamity into a symbol of God's universal power, and Jesus's followers found a way to turn calamity into a symbol of God's universal love.

How did they do it? Why did they do it? In answering these questions, it helps to appreciate that this lemons-into-lemonade theological maneuver isn't the only thing incipient Christianity has in common with incipient Judaic monotheism. In both cases, also, ensuing scriptures had a tendency to cover theologians' tracks — to recast the past in a way that obscured the actual evolution of doctrine. The Hebrew Bible's latter-day monotheistic authors and editors, in recounting Israel's history, created the illusion of an indigenous Israelite monotheism by depicting gods other than Yahweh as foreign, whether they were or not. The New Testament's authors, in recounting the life of Jesus, created the illusion that post-Crucifixion belief was basically the same as precrucifixion belief. The Christianity that evolved in the decades and centuries after Jesus's death — the Christianity that had Crucifixion as its natural core — was made to look like a straightforward extension of what Jesus himself had said and done. And in some cases that meant twisting what Jesus had actually said and done.

This isn't to say, in either case, that conscious dishonesty was rampant. As stories spread orally, from person to person to person, an overarching dishonesty can take shape without a conscious attempt to mislead. Imagine followers of the crucified Jesus trying to win converts — possessed by a conviction so powerful that they embellish the story here and there, yet a conviction so earnest that they believe their embellishments.

Anyway, for present purposes the honesty of the Bible's authors isn't what matters. Rather, the take-home lesson is that, in deciphering the Christian revolution, we have to bring to the New Testament the same perspective we brought to the "Old" Testament, the Hebrew Bible. We have to remember that biblical narratives reflect not just the times when the events recounted took place, but the times when the narrative coalesced. With this in mind we can understand how exactly the Crucifixion, an act that in theory should have thrown this would-be messiah into disgrace beyond recovery, wound up turning him into a symbol of universal love.

Certainly this took some doing. For the real Jesus—the "historical Jesus"—didn't emphasize universal love at all. At least, that's what a close and critical look at the scripture strongly suggests.

The "Historical Jesus"

Hard evidence about the "historical Jesus" is scanty. The Bible's gospel accounts of Jesus's life and words—the books of Matthew, Mark, Luke, and John—were written sometime between 65 and 100 CE, thirty-five to seventy years after his death.[14] By that time, their raw material, stories then circulating about Jesus in oral or written form, had no doubt been shaped by the psychological and rhetorical needs of his followers. (The letters of Paul—New Testament books such as Philippians and Romans—were written earlier, beginning around twenty years after Jesus's death. Unfortunately, they say almost nothing about Jesus's life and very little about his words.)

The book of Mark is generally considered the most factually reliable of the four gospels. It was written around 70 CE, roughly four decades after the Crucifixion. That's a long lag, but it offers less time for the accrual of dubious information than the roughly five decades available for Matthew and Luke or the six or seven decades for John. What's more, during Mark's composition there would have been people sixty or seventy years old who as young adults had personally witnessed the doings and sayings of Jesus and knew his biographical details—and whose recollections may have constrained the author's inventiveness. This population would shrink during the decade or more before other gospels took shape, expanding creative freedom.

Certainly as we move through the gospels in the order of their composition, we can see the accumulation of more and more dubious information. Mark doesn't give us anything like "the plain unvarnished truth," but his story is plainly less varnished than are later accounts. (The actual name and identity of the author of Mark, as with the other gospels, is unknown, but in all cases, for convenience, I'll call the authors by the names of their books.)

Consider the problem of Jesus being from a humble village, Nazareth. The Hebrew Bible had said that the Messiah would be a descendant of King David and, like David, would be born in Bethlehem.[15] Mark never addresses the question of how "Jesus of Nazareth" could have been born in Bethlehem. But by the time Matthew and Luke were written, an answer had emerged—two answers, even. Luke says Jesus's parents went to Bethlehem for a census and returned to Nazareth after his birth. In Matthew's version, Jesus's parents just seem to live in Bethlehem. How then would Jesus wind up in Nazareth? Through an elaborate side story that has the family fleeing to Egypt under duress and then, upon leaving Egypt, deeming a return to Bethlehem dangerous, and settling in "a town called Nazareth."[16] This contradiction between Luke and Matthew suggests that in this case, Mark, the earliest gospel, is the place to find the awkward truth: Jesus of Nazareth was Jesus of Nazareth.

So too with the question of Jesus's attitude toward his own death. If Jesus was the son of God, sent here to die, you would think he might accept his death with grace—not happily, perhaps, but at least with a certain dignified resignation. After all, he's known about the plan all along, and he knows, too, that he'll be resurrected in the end anyway. Yet in Mark his last words are "My God, my God, why have you forsaken me?"—as if the Crucifixion was a terrible surprise and the last act. In Luke, written a decade or two later, there is no such puzzlement, and Jesus's last words are instead the more equanimous "Father, into your hands I commend my spirit." In John his last words are simply "It is finished," and, again, there are no signs of doubt or surprise.[17] (And as for the most magnanimous of Jesus's sayings on the cross—"Father, forgive them; for they do

not know what they are doing"—this, uttered early in Luke's Crucifixion scene, seems to have been added after Luke was written.)[18]
Once again, Mark, the earliest account, has an inconvenient feature
of the Jesus story that later gospels obscure.

Still, there are at least two inconvenient truths that live on not
only in Mark but in Matthew, Luke, or both. First, when the Pharisees challenged Jesus to generate heavenly signs—"to test him,"
as Mark puts it—he failed to deliver. Second, he was rejected in
his own hometown, and here, too, he failed to perform powerfully
persuasive miracles. That these failures live on in gospels written
later than Mark may mean that, as scholars have suggested, some
of Jesus's failures became talking points for opponents of the Jesus
movement and perhaps worked their way into a unified, written critique that lived on for decades.[19]

Even here, where Mark is not alone in conceding awkward facts,
he comes across as the most candid, lacking layers of artifice that
accumulate in later accounts. In Mark, when some Pharisees ask for
a "sign from heaven," Jesus just gets in his boat and leaves in a huff
after saying, "Why does this generation ask for a sign? Truly I tell
you, no sign will be given to this generation." By the time of Matthew, the story has gotten better. Here, too, Jesus says that this generation will receive no sign, but now there's a reason: this generation
is evil. Moreover, Jesus turns the request for a sign on its head by
indicting the Pharisees for failing to read the "signs of the times."
On a second occasion in Matthew, Jesus uses such a challenge as an
occasion to cryptically predict his own death and resurrection; now
the Pharisees *have* received a sign and are too blind to see it. And by
the time of Luke—considered later than Matthew by most scholars
who don't judge them essentially contemporary—the problem has
been downgraded; the request for a sign no longer comes from the
Pharisees at all, but from mere anonymous onlookers, and is dispatched with a confidently oblique reply that includes the encoded
prediction of Jesus's death and resurrection.[20]

Especially awkward for defenders of Jesus, no doubt, was rejection in the town where he was raised. Nazareth had only about three

hundred residents. Most would have known Jesus personally, and many were probably kin. It's no surprise that the story of so jarring a rebuke would live on long enough for Mark, Matthew, and Luke to feel compelled to confront it, which they do with growing success.

In all three, Jesus dismisses the debacle with an aphorism that would wind up in *Bartlett's Familiar Quotations*. The seminal version, as relayed in Mark: "Prophets are not without honor, except in their hometown, and among their own kin, and in their own house." Thereafter, the gospel accounts differ. Mark says of Nazareth that Jesus "could do no deed of power there" and left the people in a state of "unbelief." Matthew, ingeniously adding that the latter caused the former, turns the episode into an object lesson on the importance of faith: "And he did not do many deeds of power there because of their unbelief." Luke takes another tack. First, Jesus, rather than seem unresponsive to a popular wish that he do miracles, preemptively anticipates the wish:

> "Doubtless you will quote to me this proverb, 'Doctor, cure yourself!' And you will say, 'Do here also in your hometown the things that we have heard you did at Capernaum.' " And he said, "Truly I tell you, no prophet is accepted in the prophet's hometown."

Then he cites precedent in the Hebrew Bible for prophets applying their miraculous powers abroad rather than at home: the time Elisha cured a Syrian leper even while Israelite lepers suffered. In Luke's telling it is this teaching — a sympathetic reference to Gentiles — that turns the crowd against Jesus, not his failure to perform miracles.[21]

The accretion of suspiciously convenient lore and interpretation after the writing of Mark doesn't mean that Mark itself is anywhere near being a reliable document, or that its author is guileless. Mark seems responsible for one of the most striking defensive devices in the gospels: the explanation of why Jesus, sent by God to convince people that the kingdom of God was at hand, convinced so few people.

In the fourth chapter of Mark, Jesus shares a cryptic parable with a large and presumably uncomprehending crowd. Then, later:

> When he was alone, those who were around him along with the twelve asked him about the parables. And he said to them, "To you has been given the secret of the kingdom of God, but for those outside, everything comes in parables; in order that
>
> 'they may indeed look, but not perceive,
> and may indeed listen, but not understand;
> so that they may not turn again and be forgiven.' "[22]

Odd—the one sent from heaven to spread the divine word purposely encodes the word so that most people won't get it! The oddness is only mildly diluted by the fact that this has Hebrew Bible precedence (in the story of the prophet Isaiah, to which Jesus here alludes). In all likelihood, this was an early attempt to explain why Jesus, who ostensibly came to enlighten people, had enlightened so few by the time he died—an explanation so needed that the story is preserved in Matthew and Luke.

Such is the general, asymmetrical pattern. Mark is more inclined than later gospels to concede inconvenient facts ("Why have you forsaken me?"). And when later gospels do include such facts (the Nazareth fiasco, for example), they tend to retain Markian devices that explain them away, and they sometimes throw in additional exculpatory devices not found in Mark. The later gospels shroud Jesus's life in more obfuscation, and more successful obfuscation, than Mark does. As the decades go by—70 CE, 80 CE, 90 CE—the Jesus story gets less constrained by historical memory and more impressive.

This trend culminates in John, the latest of the gospels. Here unfortunate facts that even Matthew or Luke felt compelled to concede are ignored or even inverted. There is no mention of the Nazareth fiasco, and as for Jesus's failure to perform signs for the Pharisees: time after time, in the book of John, Pharisees are convinced that Jesus can perform signs and wonders. As one of them marvels, "No one can do these signs that you do apart from the presence of God."[23]

Indeed, by the time of John there has been a general change in the tenor of Jesus's miracles. In Mark, Jesus didn't do miracles ostentatiously, and sometimes he even took pains to perform them in private. (An answer to critics who noted that few people other than Jesus's followers claimed witness to his miracles?) In John, Jesus turns miracles into spectacles. Before raising Lazarus from the dead — something Jesus does in no other gospel — he says Lazarus's illness was "for God's glory, so that the son of God may be glorified through it." Moreover, the miracles are now explicitly symbolic. When Jesus heals a blind man, he says, "I am the light of the world."[24]

A fairly immodest claim — but John's Jesus is not a modest man. In no previous gospel does Jesus equate himself with God. But in John he says, "The Father and I are one."[25] Christian legend and theology have by this point had sixty or seventy years to evolve, and they are less obedient than ever to memories of the real, human Jesus.

All of this suggests that if we are going to try to make a stab at reconstructing the "historical Jesus," even in broadest outlines, Mark, the earliest gospel, is the place to start. There, more than in any other account of Jesus's life and sayings, the number of plainly awkward and barely varnished facts suggests at least some degree of factualness.

Thy Kingdom Come

What is the Jesus of Mark like? For starters, adventurous. Early on, after being immersed in the Jordan River by John the Baptist, he spends forty days alone in the wilderness. This episode could be apocryphal, but it's a plausible prelude to a messianic career. We know from the "vision quests" of young native American men that ascetic solitude can impart a sense of purpose, sometimes catalyzed by presumably hallucinatory contact with supernatural beings. In the book of Mark, the supernatural being was Satan, whose temptations failed to divert Jesus from his mission.

That mission was twofold.

One part was to go around healing people, exorcising their demons and, occasionally, multiplying foodstuffs. Here Jesus sounds rather like other healers and exorcists who roamed Palestine at the time.[26] He also sounds like a classic shaman in a "primitive" society: after an apprenticeship that involves the blessing of an older practitioner (John the Baptist) and a fortifying phase of ascetic privation, he is empowered to cure the physically or mentally ill.[27] Did Jesus employ the sleight of hand that many real-life shamans have been known to employ? (One scholarly book on Jesus is called *Jesus the Magician*.) Or did he just have a "gift" — say, a soothing effect on people with hysterically induced illnesses — that produced enough success stories for his followers to publicize, along with some embellishment? Or were his miraculous deeds wholesale inventions of his followers, designed to outweigh the famous occasions on which he was challenged to produce "signs" and failed?

Hard to say. In any event, if Jesus had just been another wandering Palestinian wonder worker, we would never have heard of him. It is the second, nonshamanic part of Jesus's mission that would prove momentous. In Mark, his first act upon returning from the wilderness is to go to Galilee and start predicting the arrival of the "kingdom of God."

Here Jesus is picking up where Second Isaiah left off half a millennium earlier: in apocalyptic mode. Isaiah had envisioned a day when Yahweh would finally bring justice to the world, when the long-suffering faithful could rejoice, as oppressive imbalances of power were inverted. Jesus shared Isaiah's anticipation of a time when the "last shall be first and the first shall be last," as he put it. But Jesus was more specific about when this time would come: very,

very soon. The day of salvation, when good would finally triumph over evil, was near. Hence the term "gospel"—"good news." Jesus's first words in the Gospel of Mark are "The time is fulfilled, and the kingdom of God is at hand; repent, and believe in the good news."[28]

What would the coming of the kingdom be like? Some passages attributed to Jesus make it sound like a subtle spiritual thing, perhaps just a metaphor. "The kingdom of God is not coming with things that can be observed; nor will they say, 'Look, here it is!' or 'There it is!' For, in fact, the kingdom of God is among you." But this verse, from Luke, was written some fifty years after Jesus's death, perhaps to assuage growing doubts about Jesus's prediction that the kingdom of God would arrive any day now. More reliable evidence comes from Mark in the form of the prediction itself: "Truly I tell you, there are some standing here who will not taste death until they see that the kingdom of God has come in power." And they'll know it when they see it: "the sun will be darkened, and the moon will not give its light, and the stars will be falling from heaven."[29]

Drama was in order, since the blessed event was nothing less than the imposition of God's ideal state—which heretofore had existed only in heaven—on the otherwise imperfect world of human beings. As the Lord's Prayer puts it, "thy kingdom come, thy will be done, on earth as it is in heaven."

God's will was that those unworthy of citizenship would be cast out, consigned to eternal suffering. Here Jesus clearly means business: if your foot causes you to stumble while treading the path to salvation, he says, you should cut it off, and "if your eye causes you to stumble, tear it out; it is better for you to enter the kingdom of God with one eye than to have two eyes and to be thrown into hell, where...the fire is never quenched."[30]

Where Is the Love?

And what were the criteria of admission? What was Jesus's conception of righteousness? If we do our best to reconstruct the "historical Jesus," which of the moral teachings attributed to him seem to be authentically his? The answer that emerges from the earliest renderings of his message will disappoint Christians who credit Jesus with bringing the good news of God's boundless compassion.

In the book of Mark, the word "love" appears in only one passage.[31] Jesus, asked by a scribe which biblical commandment is foremost, cites two: "The first is… 'you shall love the Lord your God with all your heart, and with all your soul, and with all your mind, and with all your strength.' The second is this, 'You shall love your neighbor as yourself.'"[32] When the scribe agrees and deems these commandments "more important than all whole burnt offerings and sacrifices," Jesus says, "You are not far from the kingdom of heaven."

This is definitely a message of love. But love of what breadth? We've already seen that in the verse Jesus quotes—the Hebrew Bible's injunction to love your neighbor—the meaning of "neighbor" was probably confined to other Israelites. In other words: neighbor meant neighbor. There is no obvious reason to believe that this part of the earliest gospel, the only part of Mark where the word "love" shows up at all, was meant more expansively.

In fact, there is reason to believe otherwise. Two gospels carry the story of a woman who asks Jesus to exorcise a demon from her daughter. Unfortunately for her, she isn't from Israel. (She is "Canaanite" in one gospel, "Syrophoenician" in another.) Jesus takes this into account and replies, with one of his less flattering allegories, "It is not fair to take the children's food and throw it to the dogs." Pathetically, the woman answers, "Yet even the dogs eat the crumbs that fall from their masters' table,"[33] after which Jesus relents and tosses her some crumbs by tossing out the demons.

Defenders of Jesus might say he was just piquantly driving home the fact that Gentiles can find salvation through faith. Indeed, that is the way the story plays out in Matthew, as Jesus exclaims, "Great is your faith!" But in Mark, the earlier telling of the story, there's no mention of faith. What wins Jesus's favor, it seems, is the woman's acknowledging her inferior status by embracing her end of the master-dog metaphor; with the woman bowed before him, Jesus answers only, "For saying that, you may go—the demon has left your daughter."[34]

This Jesus doesn't sound like the ethnicity-blind Jesus in the modern Sunday school song:

> Jesus loves the little children,
> All the children of the world.
> Red and yellow, black and white,
> All are precious in His sight,
> Jesus loves the little children of the world.

Defenders of the traditional idea of a color-blind Jesus might point out that, at the end of Mark, Jesus tells his disciples, "Go into all the world and proclaim the good news to the whole creation. The one who believes and is baptized will be saved." But it turns out that this passage was added well after Mark was written.[35] Besides, bringing word of Israel's god to the world doesn't necessarily mean granting foreigners the status of Israelites. Second Isaiah had wanted the world's people to witness Yahweh's grandeur, and thus find a salvation of sorts, but the idea was that they would then bow to Zion in subservience to Israel's god and hence to Israel. In fact, when Jesus says, in Mark, "Is it not written, 'My house shall be called a house of prayer for all the nations'?" he is alluding to a passage in which Second Isaiah envisions foreigners being brought to God's house in Israel "to be his servants."[36]

In short, if we are to judge by Mark, the earliest and most reliable of the four gospels, the Jesus we know today isn't the Jesus who really existed. The real Jesus believes you should love your neighbors, but that isn't to be confused with loving all humankind. He believes you should love God, but there's no mention of God loving you. In fact, if you don't repent for your sins and heed Jesus's message, you will be denied entry into the kingdom of God. (What about the Jesus who said, "Let he who is without sin cast the first stone"?[37] That verse not only comes from the last gospel, John, but apparently was added centuries after John was written.) In Mark there is no Sermon on the Mount, no beatitudes. Jesus doesn't say, "Blessed are the meek" or "Turn the other cheek" or "Love your enemy."

The Gospel According to Q

For people who would like to think Jesus said those three things, there is a ray of hope. The hope is called "Q." The books of Matthew and Luke share many stories, and the stories fall into two categories: the kind that are found in Mark, and the kind that aren't. Most scholars infer that the authors of Matthew and Luke had access both to the book of Mark and to some other source—an actual document, presumably—that is referred to as Q. If Q existed, it must have been earlier than Matthew and Luke, and some scholars think it was much earlier, bearing at least as close a connection to the "historical Jesus" as Mark does. And Q includes the Sermon on the Mount, which features, among several striking utterances, this fairly radical one: "You have heard that it was said, 'You shall love your neighbor and hate your enemy.' But I say to you, Love your enemies and pray for those who persecute you, so that you may be children of your Father in heaven; for he makes his sun rise on the evil and on the good, and sends rain on the righteous and on the unrighteous."[38]

That definitely sounds like universal love. After all, if you love your enemies, who *don't* you love? But is it really clear that Jesus is here talking about Gentile enemies—about enemies *of* the Jews, as opposed to enemies *among* the Jews? Certainly Jesus's attitude toward Gentiles doesn't sound very charitable two verses later, when, elaborating on the need to spread your love widely, he says, "And if you greet only your brothers and sisters, what more are you doing than others? Do not even the Gentiles do the same?"[39] Citing this and other parts of Q, the scholar C. M. Tuckett has observed: "The natural language of Q seems to assume that 'gentiles' are those who are outside the sphere of salvation." The "terms of reference seem to be wholly Israel-oriented."[40] In other words, "love your enemy," like "love your neighbor," is a recipe for Israelite social cohesion, not for interethnic bonding.

Tuckett could be wrong, of course, but that may be a moot issue. In the next chapter we'll find reason to doubt that the real Jesus actually uttered the phrase "Love your enemies" anyway.

To find Jesus explicitly carrying the mandate of love beyond the bounds of Israel, we have to go to the book of Luke. After establishing that "Love your neighbor" lies at the core of the Jewish Law, Jesus is asked, "And who is my neighbor?" He replies with a story about a man from Jerusalem who is beaten and left lying by the road. Two fellow Jews, a priest and a Levite, pass him without helping, and then a man from Samaria passes by, takes pity on him, and restores him to health. (Samaria had been part of the northern kingdom of ancient Israel, but, after successive imperial conquests, Judaism didn't take root there, so Samaritans were foreigners to Judeans.) Jesus says, "Which of these three, do you think, was a neighbor to the man who fell into the hands of the robbers?" His listener says, "The one who showed him mercy." Jesus replies, "Go and do likewise."[41]

This, the Parable of the Good Samaritan, is a staple of Sunday school classes, and understandably so; it explicitly carries love across ethnic bounds. But it isn't found in either candidate for earliest gospel source—the Gospel of Mark or the posited Q. So it is an unlikely utterance of the historical Jesus, especially given its clash with things that *are* found in earlier sources, such as Jesus's calling foreigners "dogs." It clashes, too, with other sources that, if not the earliest, are at least as early as Luke. For example, in Matthew, Jesus has only this to say about Samaritans, shortly before sending his disciples out to spread the saving word: "Go nowhere among the Gentiles, and enter no town of the Samaritans, but go rather to the lost sheep of the house of Israel."[42]

The Israelocentric nature of the coming kingdom of God is echoed elsewhere in the New Testament. Ever wonder why there were twelve disciples? In both Matthew and Luke Jesus says that, once the kingdom of God has arrived, each disciple will get to rule one of the twelve tribes of a reconstituted Israel. And since they'll be seated alongside the ruler of this kingdom—presumably Jesus or some other divinely anointed figure, if not Yahweh himself—this suggests a prominent role for Israel in the scheme of things; it suggests that the "kingdom of God" is also the "kingdom of Israel."[43] Indeed, in the book of Acts the apostles ask Jesus, "Lord, is this the time when you will restore the kingdom to Israel?"[44]

This conversation, set after the Resurrection, is unlikely to have taken place. But the point is that the author of Acts (who was also the author of Luke) must have been steeped in local lore about Jesus's ministry, and he still considered this the kind of question the apostles might well have asked. Moreover, Jesus doesn't take the opportunity to correct them by waxing universalistic and saying, "This isn't about Israel." He seems to accept the premise of a coming Israelite kingdom, correcting them only on the question of timing: "It is not for you to know the times or periods that the Father has set by his own authority."[45]

What Exactly Was New?

Jesus is often called a radical, a revolutionary, but our attempt to trace the rough contours of the "historical Jesus" leaves him looking in many ways traditional.

For starters, he was above all—as Albert Schweitzer famously argued in the 1906 book *The Quest of the Historical Jesus*—an apocalyptic prophet.[46] And he was a direct heir of earlier Jewish apocalyptic prophets, notably Second Isaiah. Jesus's "kingdom of God," though rendered by Matthew as a "kingdom of Heaven," was going to be Second Isaiah's anticipated kingdom, right here on earth. And, also like Isaiah's kingdom, it would place not just Israel's God, but Israel itself, front and center. E. P. Sanders, a scholar of early Christianity, has written, "Jesus' hope for the kingdom fits into long-standing and deeply held hopes among the Jews, who continued to look for God to redeem his people and constitute a new kingdom, one in which Israel would be secure and peaceful, and one in which Gentiles would serve the God of Israel. Jesus harboured traditional thoughts about God and Israel: God has chosen all Israel, and he would someday redeem the nation."[47]

Nor was there anything new about speaking up on behalf of the poor and the weak. Biblical prophets had been doing that since at least the time of Amos and First Isaiah, more than seven centuries earlier. Exploitation of the powerless, they complained, was among the ways Israel defied Yahweh's will.

But if there was nothing new in Jesus's apocalypticism or in his progressive politics, there may have been something creative in his combination of the two. As we've seen, the apocalyptic vision—in ancient Israel and elsewhere—has typically featured a reversed polarity: someday the oppressed will rise to the top of the heap, and the oppressors will find themselves at the bottom. Usually this inversion of power plays out on an international stage: an entire people, such as Israel, finally rises above long-dominant neighboring peoples. Jesus, though, seems to have envisioned this reversal of fortunes not just *among* nations but *within* the Israelite nation as well. His famous promise that the "first will be last and the last will be first" could have summed up Second Isaiah's prediction of the geopolitical future, but Jesus seems to have applied it internally, to Israel's social future. When he said, "It is easier for a camel to go through the eye of a needle than for someone who is rich to enter the kingdom of God," he meant that, come Judgment Day, poor Israelites would rise in the nation's social hierarchy. Jesus combined the progressive politics of First Isaiah with the apocalyptic inversion that reaches such heights in Second Isaiah and justified the former in terms of the latter.[48]

This rhetorical maneuver may have been politically convenient. The downtrodden seem to have been a big part of Jesus's constituency, and they no doubt would have warmed to visions of their coming ascendancy. This message may also have won Jesus a few not-so-downtrodden followers. Every time he trots out the camel-needle metaphor, it is while trying to convince people of means to sell their possessions and join his cause.

Of course, we can't be sure that Jesus embraced the cause of the downtrodden. It is not a theme that gets a lot of play in Mark, and even in the Q source, in the Sermon on the Mount, it is ambiguous; Luke has him saying, "Blessed are the poor," while Matthew has him saying, "Blessed are the poor in spirit."[49]

Still, at least this message makes political sense; rabble-rousers often have lower-class constituencies. And at least it isn't contradicted by a lot of passages in the earliest gospel. His message of universal love, in contrast, is flatly contradicted by passages in Mark and is not a natural political winner. So how did that message enter the Christian tradition?

To answer that question we need to move beyond the "historical Jesus." We need to understand not the hills of Galilee where Jesus preached, or even the streets of Jerusalem where his ministry reached its violent climax. We need to understand the cities across the Roman Empire through which the Jesus movement spread in the following decades. That is where the Jesus Christians know today took shape, after the real Jesus died. That is where Jesus Christ—the crucified Messiah who wasn't supposed to die in the first place—was born again.

Chapter Eleven

The Apostle of Love

If indeed, as the previous chapter suggested, love wasn't a big part of Jesus's actual message, who made it a major Christian theme? Lots of people, but the seminal role was probably played by the apostle Paul.

In the modern world, Paul's views on love are best known through the famous piece of scripture read at so many weddings: "Love is patient; love is kind; love is not envious or boastful..."[1] But this passage from a letter to the Corinthians is just a small sample of Paul's work on the subject. Whereas Jesus utters the word "love" only twice in the entire Gospel of Mark, Paul uses it more than ten times in a single epistle, his letter to the Romans. Sometimes he is talking about God's love for man, sometimes about the need for man to love God, and about half the time he is talking about the need for people to love one another—the need for, as he sometimes puts it, "brotherly love."[2] Indeed, Paul is the author of the New Testament's pithy extension of brotherhood across bounds of ethnicity, class, even (notwithstanding the term "brotherhood") gender. It was his letter to the Galatians that was quoted in the previous chapter: "There is no longer Jew or Greek, there is no longer slave or free, there is no longer male and female; for all of you are one in Christ Jesus."[3]

The "apostle Paul" was not one of Jesus's twelve apostles.[4] Quite the opposite: after the Crucifixion he seems to have persecuted followers of Jesus. According to the book of Acts, he "was ravaging the church by entering house after house; dragging off both men and women, he committed them to prison."[5] But then, while on his way to treat some Syrian followers of Jesus in this fashion, he underwent his "road to Damascus" conversion. He was blinded by the light and heard the voice of Jesus. This changed his perspective. He eventually decided that Jesus had died in atonement for humanity's sins.

Paul devoted the rest of his life to spreading this message, and he was very good at it. As much as Jesus himself, some scholars say, Paul was vital to the eventual success of the religious movement that came to be called Christianity. And, *more* than Jesus, apparently, Paul was responsible for injecting that religion with the notion of interethnic brotherly love.

Why did Paul become the point man for a God whose love knows no ethnic bounds? Is it because he was naturally loving and tolerant, a man who effortlessly imbued all he met with a sense of belonging? Unlikely. Even in his correspondence, which presumably reflects a filtered version of the inner Paul, we see him declaring that followers of Jesus who disagree with him about the gospel message should be "accursed"—that is, condemned by God to eternal suffering.[6] The scholar John Gager has described Paul as a "feisty preacher-organizer, bitterly attacked and hated by other apostles within the Jesus movement."[7]

No, the origins of Paul's doctrine of interethnic love lie not in his own loving-kindess, though for all we know he mustered much of that in the course of his life. This doctrine doesn't flow naturally from his core beliefs about Jesus, either. Paul's gospel message can be broken down into four parts: Jesus was the long-awaited Messiah, the Christ; the Messiah had died as a kind of payment for the sins of humanity; humans who believed this—who acknowledged the redemption Christ had realized on their behalf—could have eternal life; but they'd better evince this faith quickly, for Judgment Day was coming.

This message may suggest a loving God, but it says nothing directly about the importance of people loving one another, much less about the importance of extending that love across ethnic bounds. So where did the doctrine that some people now think of as "Christian love" come from? It emerges from the interplay between

Paul's driving ambitions and their social environment. In the end as much credit should go to the Roman Empire as to Paul.

Lacking in Love

In the Roman Empire, the century after the Crucifixion was a time of dislocation. People streamed into cities from farms and small towns, encountered alien cultures and peoples, and often faced this flux without the support of kin. The classicist E. R. Dodds has written of the "rootless inhabitants of the great cities" in the empire: "the urbanised tribesman, the peasant come to town in search of work, the demobilised soldier, the rentier ruined by inflation, and the manumitted slave."[8]

It was somewhat like the turn of the twentieth century in the United States, when industrialization drew Americans into turbulent cities, away from their extended families. Back then, as the social scientist Robert Putnam has observed, rootless urbanites found grounding in up-and-coming social organizations, such as the Elks Club and the Rotary Club. You might expect comparable conditions in the early Roman Empire to spawn comparable organizations. Indeed, Roman cities saw a growth in voluntary associations.[9] Some were vocational guilds, some more like clubs, and some were religious cults ("cults" in the ancient sense of groups devoted to the worship of one or more gods, not in the modern sense of wacky fringe groups). But whatever their form, they often amounted to what one scholar has called fictive families for people whose real families were off in some distant village or town.[10]

The familial services offered by these groups ranged from the material, like burying the dead, to the psychological, like giving people a sense that other people cared about them. On both counts, early Christian churches met the needs of the day. As for the material: The church, Dodds wrote, provided "the essentials of social security," caring for "widows and orphans, the old, the unemployed, and the disabled; it provided a burial fund for the poor and a nursing service in time of plague."[11] As for the psychological: In Paul's writing, "brothers" is a synonym for "followers of Jesus." A church was one big family.

To some extent, then, Paul's "brotherly love" was just a product of his times. The Christian church was offering the spirit of kinship that people needed and that other organizations offered. A term commonly applied to these organizations was *thiasos*, or confraternity; the language of brotherhood wasn't, by itself, an innovation.[12] Still, early Christian writings "utilize kinship vocabulary to a degree wholly unparalleled among contemporary social organizations," one scholar has noted.[13] In that letter to the Corinthians that is featured at so many weddings, Paul used the appellation "brothers" more than twenty times.

It isn't hard to think up reasons why early Christians had a stronger-than-average sense of family. For example: they were monotheists. Whereas the pagans who formed most of the population might distribute their allegiance among several religious cults, Christians worshipped in one congregation and one congregation only. Relationships with fellow congregants were commensurately intense. But in a way this only deepens the puzzle of Paul's devotion to the theme of love. If brotherhood came so naturally to monotheistic congregations in the Roman Empire, why did Paul have to spend so much time preaching about it?

The key to understanding why Paul became the Apostle of Love and a symbol of universal brotherhood is to remember that he was far more than a committed follower of Jesus. He was a man of much ambition. That ambition seems to have been earnestly spiritual, harnessed to a message Paul considered the true path to salvation. Still, it's illuminating to compare Paul to modern entrepreneurs of more mundane motivation. He was a man who wanted to extend his brand, the Jesus brand; he wanted to set up franchises — congregations of Jesus followers — in cities across the Roman Empire. Oddly, these imperial aspirations infused Paul's preaching with an emphasis on brotherly love it might never have acquired had Paul been content to run a single mom-and-pop store.

Paul as CEO

Anyone who wanted to set up a far-flung organization in the ancient world faced two big problems: transportation technology and information technology. In those days information couldn't travel faster than the person carrying it, who in turn couldn't travel faster than the animal carrying the person. Once Paul had founded a congregation and left to found another one in a distant city, he was in another world; he couldn't return often to check on the operation, and he couldn't fire off e-mails to keep church leaders in line.

Faced with what strike us today as such glaring technological deficiencies, Paul made the most of what information technology there was: epistles. He sent letters to distant congregations in an attempt to keep them consonant with his overall mission. The results are with us today in the form of the New Testament's Pauline Epistles (or, at least, the seven, out of thirteen, that most scholars consider authentic). These letters aren't just inspiring spiritual reflections — though they are often that — but tools for solving administrative problems.

Consider that famous ode to love in 1 Corinthians. This letter was written in response to a crisis. Since his departure from Corinth, the church had been split by factionalism, and Paul faced rivals for authority. Early in the letter he laments the fact that some congregants say, "I belong to Paul," whereas others say, "I belong to Cephas."[14]

There is a second and possibly related problem. Many in the church — "enthusiasts," some scholars call them — believed themselves to have direct access to divine knowledge and to be near spiritual perfection. Some thought they needn't accept the church's guidance in moral matters. Some showed off their spiritual gifts by spontaneously speaking in tongues during worship services, something that might annoy the humbler worshippers and that, in large enough doses, could derail a service. As the scholar Gunther

Bornkamm has put it, "The mark of the 'enthusiasts' was that they disavowed responsible obligation toward the rest."[15]

In other words: they lacked brotherly love. Hence Paul's harping on that theme in 1 Corinthians and, especially, in chapter 13 (the "love chapter," which has figured in so many weddings). In light of this context, the language in that chapter makes a new kind of sense. It is in reference to disrupting worship by speaking in tongues that Paul writes, "If I speak in the tongues of mortals and of angels, but do not have love, I am a noisy gong or a clanging cymbal." And when he says that "love is not envious or boastful or arrogant," he is chastising Corinthians who deploy their spiritual gifts—whether speaking in tongues, or prophesying, or even generosity—in a competitive, showy way.

Paul didn't go so far as to ban speaking in tongues. But he did stress that speaking to your brothers in a language they can't understand isn't a loving act, whereas to speak intelligibly is to "speak to other people for their upbuilding and encouragement and consolation." Accordingly, he laid down some guidelines. As a rule, no one should speak in tongues unless there is someone present who can validly interpret, and even then the speakers should be few and orderly: "If anyone speaks in a tongue, let there be only two or at most three, and each in turn." Prophecy, on the other hand, is fine, because it is intelligible and hence can serve others. (But mightn't people use their claimed prophetic powers to question Paul's authority? Don't worry—Paul is way ahead of you: "Anyone who claims to be a prophet, or to have spiritual powers, must acknowledge that what I am writing to you is a command of the Lord. Anyone who does not recognize this is not to be recognized.")[16]

The beauty of "brotherly love" wasn't just that it produced cohesion in Christian congregations. Invoking familial feelings also allowed Paul to assert his authority at the expense of rivals. After all, wasn't it he, not they, who had founded the family of Corinthian Christians? He tells the Corinthians that he is writing "to admonish you as my beloved children.... Indeed, in Christ Jesus I became your father through the gospel. I appeal to you, then, be imitators of me."[17]

Had Paul stayed among the Corinthians, he might have kept the congregation united by the mere force of his presence, with less preaching about the need for unity—the need for all brothers to be one in "the body of Christ."[18] But because he felt compelled to move on and cultivate churches across the empire, he had to implant brotherly love as a governing value and nurture it assiduously. In the case of 1 Corinthians, chapter 13, the result was some of western civilization's most beautiful literature—if, perhaps, more beautiful out of context than in.

Love That Crosses Borders

Thus, for the ambitious preacher of early Christianity, the doctrine of brotherly love had at least two virtues. First, fraternal bonding made churches attractive places to be, providing a familial warmth that was otherwise lacking, for many, in a time of urbanization and flux. As the scholar Elaine Pagels has written, "From the beginning, what attracted outsiders who walked into a gathering of Christians...was the presence of a group joined by spiritual power into an extended family."[19] (And there is no doubt that Paul wanted his churches to project an appealing image. In 1 Corinthians he asks: If "the whole church comes together and all speak in tongues, and outsiders or unbelievers enter, will they not say that you are out of your mind?")[20] Second, the doctrine of brotherly love became a form of remote control, a tool Paul could use at a distance to induce congregational cohesion.

Strictly speaking, this emphasis on brotherhood didn't always mean an emphasis on *interethnic* brotherhood. For all we know, some of these early congregations weren't ethnically diverse—in which case cohesion within individual churches didn't need to involve bonding across ethnic bounds. So where does this connotation of Christian brotherly love come from?

Part of the answer is that transcending ethnicity was built into

Paul's conception of his divinely imparted mission. He was to be the Apostle to the Gentiles; he was to carry the saving grace of the Jewish messiah—Jesus Christ—beyond the Jewish world. Here, at the origin of Paul's aspirations, he is crossing the bridge he famously crossed in saying there is no longer "Jew or Greek," for all are now eligible for God's salvation.

In putting Jew and Greek on an equal basis, Paul was, in a sense, placing pragmatism above scriptural principle. By Paul's own account, the scriptural basis for his mission to the Gentiles lay in the prophetic writings, notably in the apocalyptic expectations of Second Isaiah, who envisioned a coming messiah and a long overdue burst of worldwide reverence for Yahweh. And, as we saw in chapter 7, these passages aren't exactly an ode to ethnic egalitarianism. The basic idea is that the Gentile nations will abjectly submit to the rule of Israel's god and hence to Israel. God promises the Israelites that after salvation arrives, Egyptians and Ethiopians alike "shall come over to you and be yours, they shall come over in chains and bow down to you. They will make supplication to you." Indeed, "every knee shall bow, every tongue shall swear." Thus, "In the LORD all the offspring of Israel shall triumph and glory."[21]

Of course, Christians like to look back and stress the less nationalistic passages of Second Isaiah—such as Yahweh's promise to bring salvation "to the end of the earth," with Israel ultimately serving a selfless role of illumination, as a "light unto the nations."[22] But these aren't the passages Paul himself emphasized. Explaining his mission to the Gentiles in a letter to the Romans, he quotes the verse about every knee bowing and every tongue swearing without mentioning anything about a light unto the nations. He declares that his job is to help "win obedience from the Gentiles." In line with past apocalyptic prophets, he seems to think that the point of the exercise is for the world to submit to Israel's messiah; Jesus, Paul says in quoting First Isaiah, is "the one who rises to rule the Gentiles."[23] And Paul seems to accept the idea that ethnic bloodlines can guarantee divine favor, even salvation, for those who wouldn't otherwise merit it; though many Jews don't see that Jesus is the

Messiah, "as regards election they are beloved, for the sake of their ancestors."[24]

But ultimately these and other theoretical dispositions mattered little compared to the facts on the ground. Any residual scriptural overtones of Jewish superiority to Gentiles that Paul may have carried into his work were diluted by a key strategic decision he made early on.

Paul's Business Model

There were other Jewish followers of Jesus who, like Paul, wanted to carry the gospel to the Gentiles. But many of them insisted that in order to qualify for Jesus's saving grace, Gentiles had to abide by the Jewish Law, the Torah, which meant following strict dietary rules and, moreover, undergoing circumcision. In the days before modern anesthesia, requiring grown men to have penis surgery in order to join a religion fell under the rubric "disincentive."

Paul grasped the importance of such barriers to entry. So far as Gentiles were concerned, he jettisoned most of the Jewish dietary code and, with special emphasis, the circumcision mandate: "For in Christ Jesus neither circumcision nor uncircumcision counts for anything; the only thing that counts is faith working through love." Paul was so intent on dropping the circumcision barrier that, when he argued with fellow Jesus followers over this issue, his sense of brotherly love sometimes deserted him. In his letter to the Galatians he expressed the wish that those who preached mandatory circumcision would "castrate themselves!"[25] (And some scholars say that "castrate" is a euphemistic rendering of a Greek passage signifying more dramatic surgery. "Cut the whole thing off!" is an alternative translation.)[26]

There is little doubt about Paul's strategic wisdom. Many religions of the day, including some of the "mystery religions," were open to people of varied ethnicities. But these movements tended to have hurdles to membership, including financial ones, such as priests who charged initiation fees.[27] Christian churches enjoyed a competitive edge by having no such financial barriers, and Paul kept the edge sharp by making sure these weren't replaced by other kinds of barriers.

This decision to leave recruiting unshackled by the Jewish Law not only mitigated the drift of Paul's letter to the Romans—the idea that his mission was to subjugate Gentiles on behalf of Israel's messiah. It also got Paul accused of "rejecting" the Torah. But this "rejection" was meant to apply to *Gentile* recruits to the Jesus movement. Indeed, Paul may have considered himself a good, Torah-abiding Jew, albeit one who, in contrast to most other Jews, was convinced that the Jewish messiah had finally arrived. (In none of his letters does Paul use the word "Christian.")[28]

Whether or not Paul thought of his identity as now severed from Judaism, he couldn't afford to sever Judaism's ties to the Jesus movement, because he needed to use the infrastructure of Jewish worship. According to the book of Acts, when he came to a city and set out to recruit people to the movement, he sometimes started his preaching at the local synagogue. Indeed, according to Acts, some of Paul's most important early recruits were Jews. So, even as practical considerations distanced Paul's variant of the Jesus movement from Jewish ritual, they encouraged ongoing contact with the Jewish world. And, even as Paul chafed at the rejection of his doctrines by some Jews within the Jesus movement (to say nothing of Jews outside it), he continued to seek rapprochement, trying to preserve a broad base.

In short, the kind of bridge Paul built to the Gentile world wound up alienating a lot of Jews, and maybe even alienating Paul from them, but it was a bridge he couldn't afford to burn. So an interethnic symbiosis persisted and colored Paul's writing. Thus did the phrase "neither Greek nor Jew" enter the scripture, with its enduring connotations of ethnic egalitarianism.

There were aspects of Paul's business model that pushed even more powerfully toward interethnic bonding. To see them, begin with the reference above to some "important early recruits" being Jews. Now leave aside the part about some of them being Jews and focus on the idea of "important" recruits—Jewish, Gentile, whatever. What kinds of people in the Roman Empire would qualify as "important" recruits? How would you recruit them? What would you ask of them? What would they get in return? Mundane, even Machiavellian, as these questions sound, answering them will show how deeply the idea of interethnic harmony was embedded in the logistics of Paul's mission, and how conducive his environment was to the success of that mission. And in this light it will be clear why he wound up preaching not just interethnic tolerance or even amity, but interethnic brotherhood, interethnic *love*.

Flying Business Class

In ancient times, as now, one prerequisite for setting up a franchising operation was finding people to run the franchises. Not just anyone would do. Though Christianity is famous for welcoming the poor and powerless into its congregations, to actually *run* the congregations Paul needed people of higher social position. For one thing, these people needed to provide a meeting place. Though historians speak of early "churches" in various cities, there were no buildings dedicated to Christian worship. Borrowed homes and meeting halls were the initial infrastructure. Judging by the book of Acts, Paul's founding of Christian congregations depended heavily on, as the scholar Wayne Meeks has put it, "the patronage of officials and well-to-do householders."[29]

The book of Acts recounts a telling episode from Paul's ministry in Philippi, a city in the Roman colony of Macedonia. Paul and his companions start speaking with women gathered at a river outside the city's gates. Acts reports that "a certain woman named Lydia, a worshiper of God [that is, a Jew] was listening to us; she was from the city of Thyatira and a dealer in purple cloth. The Lord opened her heart to listen eagerly to what was said by Paul."[30] Lydia—the first known European convert to what would later be called Christianity—began her service to the church by recruiting her "household," which almost certainly included not just her family, but servants and maybe slaves.[31] And her service didn't end there. The author of Acts writes, "When she and her household were baptized, she urged us, saying, 'If you have judged me to be faithful to the Lord, come and stay at my home.' And she prevailed upon us." Then, apparently, they prevailed upon her; Lydia's home became the meeting place of the local Christian congregation.[32]

To find people like Lydia, Paul had to move in what were, by the standards of the day, elite circles. The "purple cloth" Lydia sold was a pricey fabric, made with a rare dye. Her clientele was wealthy, and she had the resources to have traveled to Macedonia from her home in Asia Minor. She was the ancient equivalent of someone who today makes a transatlantic or transpacific flight in business class.

From Paul's point of view, the advantage of preaching to business class went beyond the fact that people who fly business class have resources. There's also the fact that people who fly, fly — that is, they're in motion. To judge by the book of Acts, many of Paul's early Christian associates were, like him, travelers.[33] As Meeks has noted, "much of the mission" of establishing and sustaining Christian congregations "was carried out by people who were traveling for other reasons."[34]

There were at least two ways that bodies in motion could be harnessed. First, in an age when there was no public postal service, they could carry letters to distant churches.[35] Second, they might even be able to found distant congregations.

Consider Aquila and Priscilla, husband and wife. According to Acts, when Paul went from Athens to Corinth and first encountered them, they had moved to Corinth from Rome. Among the things they had in common with Paul was their vocation. "Because he was of the same trade," reports Acts, "he stayed with them, and they worked together." Aquila and Priscilla then became two of his key missionaries, moving to Ephesus and founding a church in their home.[36]

The trade Paul shared with them was, depending on how you interpret a Greek word, either tentmaking or leatherworking. Either vocation would have allowed Paul to mix with the commercial class, but tentmaking was an especially opportune profession. In those days tents weren't recreational. They were what the more affluent travelers used to avoid staying in inns, which were prone to vermin and vice.[37] Tents were, in short, standard equipment for those who flew business class. Indeed, tents *were*, in a sense, business class. By making and selling tents, Paul would have been mingling with exactly the kind of people he needed to mingle with.

These people, like business-class fliers today, were cosmopolitan. They came from varying ethnicities, they dealt with people of varying ethnicities, and their financial interest thus dictated some tolerance of ethnic difference, some extension of amity across ethnic bounds. These cosmopolitan values were built into the logic of long-distance commerce in the multinational Roman Empire, just as they are built into the logic of long-distance commerce in an age of globalization. When economics draws people of different ethnicities and cultures into non-zero-sum relationships, interethnic and intercultural tolerance is likely to ensue. In that sense, a nontrivial part of Paul's work had been done for him by the tenor of the times.

Still, there's a difference between interethnic tolerance, even amity, and interethnic brotherhood. To fully explain the early Christian emphasis on brotherly love, we need to explore Paul's business model more deeply.

Fringe Benefits

When people open a local franchise of something—a McDonald's, a Pizza Hut—they do so because they expect to get something in return. What did people get in return for making their homes Christian franchises? In some cases, no doubt, it was mainly the benefit of the gospel; Lydia presumably found Paul's initial teachings gratifying, and what additional benefits she got from hosting a church—social, economic, whatever—we'll never know. But as the franchising continued and the church expanded to more and more cities, it offered new benefits to church leaders.

In particular: reliable lodging. Tents were adequate for overnight stays on the road, but when you reached the big city, nicer accommodations were desirable—especially if you planned to stay awhile and do business. Paul's letters to Christian congregations often include requests that they extend hospitality to traveling church leaders.[38] Such privileges, as one scholar writes, would increasingly be "extended to the whole household of faith, who are accepted on trust, though complete strangers." This was a revolution of sorts, since "security and hospitality when traveling had traditionally been the privilege of the powerful."[39] The Roman Empire had made distant travel easier than at any time in history, and Christianity exploited this fact. It was, among other things, the Holiday Inn of its day.

But there was at least one big difference. The proprietor of a Holiday Inn isn't inviting lodgers into his or her home. Besides, their credit card numbers are on record in the event that they should turn out to be bad apples. Ancients who hosted travelers they didn't know personally were being asked to take a bigger risk. And they were more likely to make the effort if they could believe that the lodger was no mere guest but rather a spiritual sibling, a "brother."

Once a traveler in the Roman Empire arrived in a city, there was a problem: information and orientation were vitally needed, yet the Internet didn't exist. The net to plug into was other people. But where to find people willing to provide you with valuable information, show you around town, help you make contact with other people in your profession or with possible clients? Well, how about a congregation full of "siblings"—all of whom are more likely to lend a hand if they indeed consider you as such. Paul wrote to the Romans, "I commend to you our sister Phoebe, a deacon of the church at Cenchreae, so that you may welcome her in the Lord as is fitting for the saints, and help her in whatever she may require from you."[40]

Cenchreae was a seaport near Corinth. Paul was here asking Romans to extend familial love to a Greek, and he was doing so in the process of knitting his imperial organization together. As the scholar Wayne McCready has noted, the early Christian language of familial intimacy not only "underscored the internal cohesion that distinguished the assemblies of early Christians" but also "was applied as a universal principle which transcended local and geographic references and united numerous local communities into a collective whole."[41] Paul's international church built on existing cosmopolitan values of interethnic tolerance and amity, but in offering its international networking services to people of means, it went beyond those values; a kind of interethnic love was the core value that held the system together.

It may sound cynical to explain the growth of a religion, especially a religion of *love*, in crass commercial terms, as though religions were mere networking services. But such practical functions play some role in the power of religion even today. The Mormon church, whose growth rate has been compared to that of early Christianity,[42] is a smooth conduit of commercial contact. And in the ancient world, religious bonds played a much bigger role in commerce. Indeed, ancient Greek and Roman associations that were essentially vocational—associations of shippers or of artisans or whatever—seem to have never been wholly secular. As the scholar S. G. Wilson has written, "an element of religious devotion" was "a ubiquitous feature of ancient associations, as indeed of ancient life in general."[43] The trust in transaction on which business depends—a trust that today often rests on elaborate laws and their reliable enforcement—rested in ancient times partly on laws but largely on faith in the integrity of individual people. And religious fellowship was one of the great foundations of such faith.

Empire as Opportunity

This chapter's pragmatic rendering of Paul's emphasis on love is somewhat speculative. We don't know enough about the early church to explain its growth with complete confidence. What we can say with much confidence, though, is that Paul's accomplishment was some combination of opportune conditions and effective exploitation of them.

The Roman Empire was, among other things, a huge commercial opportunity. By linking once remote cities via solid roads, and bringing them under a uniform legal code, it opened up new vistas for the ambitious merchant, and in Paul's day merchants were starting to get the picture. This is what made Paul's mammoth ambitions for the church conceivable—not just the vastness of the Roman platform, but the fact that it had already created commercial currents he could harness. Paul saw an unprecedented entrepreneurial opportunity: the possibility of building a religious organization of imperial proportions.

Yet there must have been something challenging about his goal, because, though the Roman Empire had existed for nearly a century, no one else had achieved it. Yes, other religions flourished, especially Greek and Roman mystery religions, but they seem to have lacked centralized leadership and uniform doctrine. Dionysian cults spread from city to city (as you would expect of a religion that involved drinking large amounts of wine) but, as one scholar has observed, "once established, local cults remained largely autonomous and could take quite divergent forms from one city to another."[44] Apparently there were challenges facing anyone who aimed to found congregations in various cities and keep them on the same page.

We'll never know for sure what Paul's secret was, but some of the best candidates are the ones I've stressed. First, he used the information technology of the day—hand-carried letters—with unusual adroitness to keep distant congregations intact. This meant hammering home the theme of familial love. Second, he extended this sense of brotherhood beyond local congregations and particular ethnicities. This lubricated the provision of hospitality for traveling church leaders and, as time wore on, for Christians more broadly. In this and other ways, brotherly love helped keep the church unified—or at least more unified than other multicity religions, and unified enough to stay strong over the long haul.

A general principle here is that in a multiethnic polity like the Roman Empire, anyone who wants to start a vast organization should be ethnically inclusive, lest valuable resources go unused and potential recruits go unrecruited. The synagogues scattered across the Roman Empire were one example of a valuable resource. The Christian church in Rome was another example. Paul hadn't founded the church in Rome, and there presumably were doctrinal differences between these Latin Christians and the Christians in Greece and Asia Minor whom Paul had cultivated. Had Paul chosen to, he could have harped on these differences to the point of schism. But he wanted to use the resources of the Roman church as he prepared for missions to Spain and elsewhere, and that may help explain the warmth of his letter to the Romans: "To all God's beloved in Rome....I thank my God through Jesus Christ for all of you....I remember you always in my prayers....I am longing to see you."[45] Pretty intimate, given that almost all of them were people he'd never met! Yet this was a simple application of the early Christian formula for success.

How Universal Is Universal?

It may sound implausible that a doctrine of true, pure, boundless love could emerge from the strategic imperatives of entrepreneurship, even when the enterprise is a religion. And, actually, it *is* implausible. What emerged with early Christianity isn't really, strictly speaking, a god of *universal* love. The core appeal of the early church, remember, was that "brotherly love" was a form of familial love. And familial love is by definition discerning — it is directed inwardly, not outwardly; toward kin, not toward everyone.

This is the kind of love Paul usually preaches — love directed first and foremost toward other Christians. "Love one another with mutual affection," he tells the Romans. "Through love become slaves to one another," he instructs members of the Galatian congregation. He reminds the Thessalonians that they "have been taught by God to love one another; and indeed you do love all the brothers [followers of Jesus] throughout Macedonia. But we urge you, beloved, to do so more and more."[46]

This isn't to say that Paul's preachings offer no foundation for truly universal love. He often exhorts Christians to extend generosity and hospitality to the unconverted, and he occasionally goes further. He tells the Thessalonians, "And may the Lord make you increase and abound in love for one another and for all." Still, he isn't in the habit of putting Christians and non-Christians on *quite* the same plane. He tells the Galatians: "Let us work for the good of all, and especially for those of the family of faith."[47]

Paul is treading a fine line—occasionally exhorting a kind of "love" for non-Christians yet suggesting that it be a less powerful motivator for generosity than the "brotherly love" he relentlessly champions among Christians. This may sound paradoxical, but treading this line was a key to Christianity's early success.

On the one hand, Christianity made a name for itself by extending generosity to non-Christians. Some of those it befriended joined the church, others no doubt spoke highly of it thereafter, and various observers were impressed by the church's sympathy for the unfortunate.

Yet Christianity couldn't extend generosity to non-Christians infinitely. After all, it was an organization that wanted to grow, and central among its enticements was that joining it brought the benefits of an extended family, including material assistance in times of need. If anyone could get these things forever without joining, how many people would join? Besides, how can a small group of people afford to give endlessly to all who call if many of these recipients will never contribute anything in return? The key to Christianity's growth was to be nice to outsiders, but not endlessly nice—unless, of course, they became insiders, after which they were expected to give and not just get.

This discerning nature of Christian love is reflected more than a century after Paul in the words of the Christian theologian

Tertullian: "What marks us in the eyes of our enemies is our loving-kindness: 'Only look,' they say, 'look how they love one another!' "[48] One another, not everyone.

This discernment is also reflected in a famous utterance of Jesus in the book of Matthew. Jesus is telling his followers that they should treat even the lowliest as if they were Jesus himself, so that on Judgment Day he can say to them: "For I was hungry and you gave me food, I was thirsty and you gave me something to drink, I was a stranger and you welcomed me, I was naked and you gave me clothing, I was sick and you took care of me, I was in prison and you visited me." This seeming call for boundless compassion is followed by a rarely noted qualifier. After Jesus's followers ask in puzzlement, "When was it that we saw you sick or in prison and visited you?" Jesus answers: "Truly I tell you, just as you did it to one of these who are members of my family [sometimes translated as "these my brothers"], you did it to me."[49] Brothers? Family? In common early-Christian usage, that would have meant other Christians.

Of course, if Paul is the one who pioneered that usage, then maybe terms like "brothers" had a different, more truly universal, connotation back when Jesus spoke. But the book of Matthew wasn't written until after Paul's time, so its language should be interpreted in that light. And in that light, this passage is so consistent with Paul's instrumental use of the idea of brotherly love as to suggest that maybe these weren't the words of Jesus but rather were put in his mouth to justify a strategy that, by the time Matthew was written, had proved its value. (They don't appear in the earliest gospel, Mark, or in the possibly early, hypothetically reconstructed Q source—only in Matthew.)

Though membership in one of Paul's churches allowed you to enjoy brotherly love, it didn't guarantee that privilege for life. Once a brother, you would be monitored, and extreme self-indulgence could lead to expulsion. The same letter to the Corinthians that bears Paul's famous ode to love contains this passage: "I am writing to you not to associate with anyone who bears the name of brother who is sexually immoral or greedy, or is an idolater, reviler, drunkard, or robber. Do not even eat with such a one.... Drive out the wicked person from among you."[50] Paul's church had generous criteria for joining the brotherhood but strict grounds for expulsion.

This membership policy helps explain how Christianity could afford to accept members from all social classes, including the indigent. So long as they didn't exploit generosity and succumb to vice, they could be rendered productive. Indeed, Christian churches seem to have been tools of social mobility, giving education to aspiring students. A second-century Christian remarked, "Not only do the rich among us pursue our philosophy, but the poor enjoy instruction for free.... We admit all who desire to hear."[51]

It was a solid formula: reach out to all, and hang on to the honest and earnest. But an implication of this formula was to keep "universal love" from being truly "universal." Love was extended beyond the brotherhood of Christians tentatively and conditionally; the fullest form of love would be denied to those who didn't join the brotherhood and to those who joined but didn't keep earning their membership. The result was to make the early church organically cohesive. As Paul put it, "we, who are many, are one body in Christ, and individually we are members one of another."[52]

The meaning of the Hebrew Bible's injunction to love your neighbor as yourself had always depended on the definition of "neighbor." Paul did change that definition, but he didn't give it infinite compass. A "neighbor" wasn't just *any* "Jew or Greek." As Peter Brown has written of the Roman Empire in the third century, "The teaching of the church defined for the Christian who was *not* his neighbor: the neighbor of the Christian was *not* necessarily his kinsman, *not* his fellow dweller in a *quartier*, *not* his compatriot or his fellow townsman; his neighbor was his fellow Christian."[53]

Brothers, Yes, but Enemies?

There is one kind of Christian love that doesn't fit into this formula, and so can't be explained in terms of intracongregational or intercongregational bonding. In two of the gospels Jesus says, "Love your enemies."[54] What is the practical logic behind *that* kind of love? And if there is a practical logic behind it, why isn't the logic sensed by Paul, who never utters these words?

Actually, though Paul doesn't say "Love your enemies," he comes pretty close. So close, in fact, as to suggest that he *did* sense the logic behind it—that, in fact, he may be the one who injected the idea into Christian literature. Only later, perhaps, was it attributed to Jesus, if in fuller and richer form.

The "Love your enemy" injunction, as we've seen, appears in both Matthew and Luke. In the Matthew version, Jesus says, "I say to you, Love your enemies and pray for those who persecute you." In the letter to the Romans, written more than a decade before Matthew or Luke was written, Paul says, "Bless those who persecute you; bless and do not curse them." And if Paul doesn't quite say to *love* your enemies, he does add "if your enemies are hungry, feed them; if they are thirsty, give them something to drink." Paul also says, in that same passage, "Do not repay anyone evil for evil...never avenge yourselves." Similarly, Jesus, just before advising people to love their enemies, says, "Do not resist an evildoer. But if anyone strikes you on the right cheek, turn the other also."[55]

Of course, it's not surprising that Paul would favor the same cluster of ideas as Jesus, given that he's something of a Jesus aficionado. But if Paul is repeating the words of Jesus, why doesn't he buttress their authority by saying so? He is, after all, talking to a bunch of Jesus worshippers. And why doesn't he repeat the pithiest and most dramatic version of Jesus's sayings on this subject: "Love your enemy"?

It's possible that Paul just isn't very conversant with the sayings of Jesus—but not probable. After all, by Paul's account he had spent two weeks in Jerusalem lodging with the apostle Peter, and he also met Jesus's brother, James.[56] For that matter, he spent pretty much all of his time in the circles where Jesus's words circulated. Surely he would have caught wind of one of the most striking things Jesus ever said—if, that is, Jesus actually said it.

The same question arises with the doctrine of brotherly love. By the time the book of John quotes Jesus telling his followers, "I give you a new commandment, that you love one another," this actually *wasn't* a new commandment;[57] Paul had started issuing that injunction to Jesus's followers decades earlier. Similarly, before the other three gospels depicted Jesus telling people to fulfill the Jewish Law by loving your neighbor as yourself, Paul had told the Galatians that "the whole law is summed up in a single commandment, 'You shall love your neighbor as yourself.' " And here, too, he makes no mention of Jesus having said much the same thing.[58]

We've seen the pragmatic value of brotherly love and so seen how Paul could have happened on this precept without inspiration from Jesus. But what about "Love your enemy"? If Jesus didn't really say that, then where on earth did Paul get the idea?

Maybe from facts on the ground — facts that gave Paul reason to see the wisdom of passive perseverance in the face of enmity. Paul was part of a religious minority that was widely resented and that, if it didn't demonstrate restraint amid provocation, could be persecuted to the point of extinction.[59] In that sense his situation was quite like that of Philo, another adherent of a suspect faith in the Roman Empire of the first century. Philo, as we've seen, adapted by urging fellow Jews not to antagonize the pagan majority — and by working to find a doctrine of interfaith tolerance in the Jewish scripture.

Certainly Paul seems to have known that an onslaught of kindness can frustrate the enemy by denying him what he most wants: a rationale for hatred, a pretext for attack. After urging Christians to give food and drink to their enemies, he adds, "for by doing this you will heap burning coals on their heads."[60]

Actually, Paul wasn't the first to figure out that befriending an enemy can be a potent counterattack. His "burning coals" line comes from Proverbs, where it is preceded by this advice: "If your enemies are hungry, give them bread to eat; and if they are thirsty, give them water to drink."[61] Paul, in injecting the doctrine of kindness toward enemies into Christianity, wasn't just being wise; he was being wise with the guidance of the Hebrew wisdom literature.

The Growth of God (Cont'd.)

We last encountered the wisdom literature in a theological context. In Philo's theology—and, I suggested in chapter 9, in a plausible modern theology—the accumulation of human wisdom is a manifestation of divine purpose. The direction of history, as set by basic dynamics of cultural evolution, pragmatically pushes people toward useful doctrines that, wondrously enough, contain elements of moral truth. As people find themselves in more and more non-zero-sum situations with more and more people at greater geographic and cultural remove, the intelligent pursuit of self-interest dictates acknowledging the interests, hence the humanity, of a growing number of other human beings.

Or, to put this bit of theology in its most ambitious form, as phrased in chapter 7: Maybe the growth of "God" signifies the existence of God. That is: if history naturally pushes people toward moral improvement, toward moral truth, and their God, as they conceive their God, grows accordingly, becoming morally richer, then maybe this growth is evidence of some higher purpose, and maybe—conceivably—the source of that purpose is worthy of the name divinity.

The main line of the growth of "God" traced in this chapter has been the evolution of a doctrine of interethnic love. On close examination, it has turned out to be both less original than it may at first seem and less impressive—less truly universal. Still, it's not nothing. The idea that all people, regardless of race or nationality, are equal candidates for God's love (so long as they don't squander the opportunity!) is a form of ethnic egalitarianism. And ethnic egalitarianism is probably closer to moral truth than the alternatives.

So, for theological purposes, it would be nice to know: Was this morally progressive doctrine indeed a highly likely outcome of the historical process? Or was it a fluke, a product of one man's eccentric interpretation of another man's eccentric prophetic career? If the former—if it is a natural outgrowth of history—then it is more likely that this "growth of God" signifies the existence of God, or at least the existence of something you might call divine, however unlike ancient conceptions of God.

These are questions I've been trying to illuminate by treating Paul one-dimensionally — as just another savvy and ambitious man who happened to be in the religion business. To the extent that any such man was likely to have wound up preaching interethnic tolerance, even love, then these doctrines can be seen as outgrowths of the social, political, and economic context of the day. And to the extent that this context is in turn an expression of history's natural drift toward expanded social organization, these doctrines can be seen as an expression of history itself.

Tentatively, we can say that this seems to be the case. As social organization expanded, as Roman roads crossed the bounds of more and more nations, economic interests drew people into a cosmopolitan, multiethnic world, and the "God of Love" evolved in reflection of that fact. If Paul's organizational aspirations were indeed to be realized on the scale of the Roman Empire, then the empire's ethnic diversity would have to be accommodated by the values of his organization.

But questions remain. For example: *Were* Paul's organizational aspirations likely to be realized on the scale of the Roman Empire? Or could Paul's version of Christianity easily have fallen by the wayside amid the tough competition among religions in that empire? And, if Pauline Christianity had indeed perished as some other religion prevailed, what properties would the winning religion have possessed? Such questions help us answer the bigger question of whether the doctrine of transethnic brotherly love was "in the cards" — likely, all along, to flourish. We'll never settle the question definitively; there are too many imponderables. But the next chapter will bring us closer to an answer.

Chapter Twelve

Survival of the Fittest Christianity

It didn't take Christians long to start annoying people. As early as 64 CE, before all the books of the New Testament had been written, the emperor Nero was having followers of Jesus smeared with pitch, put on crosses, and set on fire.[1] Ever the thrifty persecutor, Nero (according to the Roman historian Tacitus) used the flaming bodies "to serve as lights when daylight failed."[2] The emperor's immediate aim was to make Christians scapegoats, to blame them for a devastating fire that some people were blaming on him. But there was a less ephemeral source of tension between Christians and Roman rulers. Like Jews, Christians didn't fit the Roman model of religion.

The Roman government let people worship whatever gods they chose so long as they also paid homage to the official gods of the empire. Christians refused to worship state gods, and they couldn't honestly grant legitimacy to the various other gods people worshipped, either. In fact, they actively challenged that legitimacy, because Christians weren't just monotheists; they were monotheists prone to proselytizing.

The proselytizing outweighed the persecution, and Christianity grew until, in 312, it crossed its famous threshold: Emperor Constantine, inspired by a vision, decided to fight a crucial battle under the symbol of the cross. The ensuing victory elevated Jesus in his esteem and helped usher in an era of official tolerance for Christianity.[3] By the end of the fourth century, Christianity was the official religion of the empire, and pagan religions were banned.

Constantine's conversion is a touchstone in the debate over the roles of chance and necessity in history. Some see it as a tribute to contingency: without Constantine's change of heart, Christianity might never have displaced paganism as the religion of Europe, and all of history might have been different. Others say Christianity, though far from a majority religion, had already achieved critical mass and would have prevailed in any event.

Suppose Christianity's triumph within the Roman Empire was indeed Constantine-dependent—as, for all we know, it was. And suppose Constantine had lost that battle, or hadn't happened to fight it under the cross, and Christianity had fallen by the wayside. Then what would have become of the idea of interethnic brotherly love, an idea that by then had grown so closely associated with Christianity?

It's a theologically important question. In chapter 9, while appraising Philo's ancient yet in some ways modern theology, we came across the idea of the Logos—a divine driver of unfolding cosmic purpose that, in the process, serves as a kind of engine of moral growth. If Paul's doctrine of interethnic amity might have perished but for a single military victory, then how powerful could that engine really be? If the Logos is real, shouldn't moral enlightenment be driven by something ultimately stronger than the vagaries of history? But what evidence is there of such power? Why should we think that, regardless of Constantine's fate, interethnic amity had a good chance of carrying the day in the Roman Empire's battle among religious values?

An Open Platform

For one thing, because the creation of the Roman Empire had made interethnic amity a more valuable commodity than it was before. We saw glimpses of this in the previous chapter, in dissecting Paul's strategy for building an international church. To get a clearer sense for the value added by empire, let's take a look at the Greek island of Delos in the second century BCE, the century before the Roman Empire was born.

One god worshipped on that island was Heracles-Melkart (a

fusion of the Tyrian god Melkart and the divine Greek figure Heracles, aka Hercules). Heracles-Melkart had a big following among merchants and shippers hailing from the city of Tyre. Indeed, the official name of the "religious" organization devoted to his worship was the Heraclesiastai of Tyre Merchants and Shippers.[4]

Merchants and shippers who belonged to this cult made sacrifices to Heracles-Melkart in hopes of winning his favor. But it wasn't really Heracles-Melkart who did the favors. Belonging to his cult meant picking up useful business information from other merchants and shippers, and building fruitful bonds with them; the cult was, from a vocational point of view, both a database and a network of useful contacts. If you were a merchant or shipper from Tyre on the island of Delos, you would naturally join the cult, because membership was valuable.

Crucially important, for purposes of this analysis, is that your joining would make membership even more valuable, because by joining you slightly enlarged the stock of data and the number of potentially useful contacts. In general, *the more members of the cult, the more valuable membership was.*

This phenomenon is known by economists as "positive network externalities"—the more units of something there are, the more valuable each unit is. Of course, economists don't generally apply the idea to religion. They apply it to things like software. The classic example is Microsoft Windows. Once millions of copies of Windows were in use, lots of software was being made for Windows, so Windows was more valuable to own than it would have been if only thousands of copies were in use. Every time someone "joined" the network by buying a computer with Windows, they increased the value of membership by increasing the incentive to create software for the Windows platform.

The idea of network externalities can be applied to most things that in some sense constitute a network, and religions certainly do. Whenever positive network externalities exist, a common principle obtains: to fully exploit the externalities, organizations should avoid arbitrary barriers to membership. Which brings us back to Delos.

Years after the worshippers of Heracles-Melkart built a temple to him on Delos, another group built a temple to the sea god Poseidon on Delos. These men hailed from the city of Berytos — Beirut — and were called the Poseidoniastai of Berytos Merchants, Shippers, and Warehousemen.[5] Same vocational composition as the Tyrian Heraclesiastai (give or take some Warehousemen), but they wound up at a different temple worshipping a different god.

Mightn't it have benefited the two groups to merge? Double the resources, double the database? And wouldn't that have made business travel easier, since you could then travel among Delos, Tyre, and Beirut with guaranteed hospitality? In other words: wouldn't membership in the merged religion have been more valuable, more attractive, than membership in either of the religions alone, thanks to the logic of network externalities?

Of course, merging groups from Tyre and Beirut was hard, because there was a big cultural divide between those cities. Still, it was an *arbitrary* divide; in strictly commercial terms, members of the two groups could have profited (on balance) from friendly interaction with one another. In other words, these two cults, by letting culture divide them, were leaving potential synergy untapped, network externalities unrealized. In theory, this failure would leave them vulnerable to competition from a religion that was open to people from Tyre and Beirut alike.

Maybe this sort of failure wasn't very consequential back in the second century BCE. Maybe merchants from Tyre and merchants from Beirut moved in largely separate commercial worlds, so there wasn't much potential synergy among them anyway. But later, as Rome subjugated nation after nation, that would change. With the "Pax Romana" — the Roman Peace — of the first two centuries CE, a huge arena of commerce opened up, with lots of potential for business among people of different cities, different nations, different ethnicities. An inclusive group could harness the expansive energy of network externalities better than ethnically or nationally specific groups.

Suppose, for example, that there were two sects within a religion called Christianity. Suppose that in both cases members profited from their contacts with other members of the sect. But suppose that one sect welcomed people of all nationalities and the other one made it hard for people of most nationalities to join. Wouldn't the former have more potential network externalities? Wouldn't it be likely to grow faster than the latter? And, as its size exceeded that of its rival by a growing margin, wouldn't its competitive advantage get only bigger, thanks to the logic of network externalities? In other words, wouldn't the Christianity of Paul do better than a hypothetical alternative Christianity whose doctrines didn't foster interethnic bonding?

Actually, this is no mere thought experiment. There were several sects within early Christianity — several versions of the Jesus movement that in principle could have won the intramural competition and become "mainstream" Christianity, as Paul's version finally did. And at least one of them fit the description of this hypothetical alternative.

Jews for Jesus

Remember the followers of Jesus whom Paul wished would "castrate themselves" because their insistence on circumcision would discourage non-Jews from joining the Jesus movement? It's unlikely that they did so literally, and apparently they didn't do so metaphorically, either; their spiritual heirs were still around two centuries later.[6] Fourth-century documents refer to a group called the Ebionites, who insisted that Jesus worshippers be thoroughly Jewish. Gentiles were eligible for salvation, but only after conversion to Judaism, which meant abiding by the letter of the Jewish Law in ritual matters, ranging from kosher dining to circumcision.

As Bart Ehrman noted in his book *Lost Christianities*, the Ebionites' conception of Jesus was probably closer to Jesus's own view of himself than was the picture that eventually prevailed within Christianity. Jesus was no god, said the Ebionites, just a messiah. And though he, like some past Israelite kings, was a son of God, he'd been born like any other human, to a biologically impregnated woman. (In fact, said the Ebionites, Jesus was God's *adopted* son, chosen for his exemplary conduct.)

Here the Ebionites were being more faithful to Hebrew scripture than the Christians of today. When the Gospel of Matthew asserts virgin birth, it alludes to the book of Isaiah's prophecy that "the virgin shall conceive and bear a son, and they shall name him Emmanuel."[7] But in fact the Hebrew word in Isaiah that had been translated as "virgin" in the Septuagint just means "young woman."

Still, in the competition among memes, truth isn't the only thing that matters. And the Ebionites, by making it hard for a Gentile to join the Jesus movement, hobbled their version of the movement.[8] Ebionite doctrine suppressed network externalities, whereas Paul's version of Christianity seems almost designed to maximize those externalities. And Paul's version won.

The Runner-Up

The version of Christianity that seems to have finished second in the struggle for the title of mainstream Christianity shared these network-externality-maximizing properties. This was a monolatrous kind of Christianity known as Marcionism. Its founder, Marcion, believed that the Hebrew Bible reflected one god—a wrathful creator god—and that Jesus had revealed another god: a loving god who offered escape from the earthly cesspool devised by the creator god. And Marcion embraced Paul's doctrine of interethnic "brotherly love."

Indeed, Marcion—who, two centuries before the New Testament started to coalesce, became the first person to collect early Christian writings into an official canon—included many of Paul's letters, as well as one of the four gospels, Luke.[9] (Lest the god of salvation be conflated with the creator god, Marcion edited Luke; now Jesus referred to God not as "Lord of Heaven and Earth" but as "Lord of Heaven.")[10]

Marcion's embrace of Paul didn't keep his church from being

a rival to what scholars would later call the Pauline church—that is, the version of Christianity that eventually became mainstream and assembled the New Testament as its canon. Indeed, the rivalry got intense as Marcionite Christianity proved robust. One second-century Pauline Christian noted with alarm that Marcion was spreading his version of the gospel to "many people of every nation." As late as the fifth century, Christian bishops warned travelers to avoid entering a Marcionite church by accident.[11] Maybe a bitter battle for dominance of Christianity shouldn't surprise us, given that both sides wielded a doctrine as powerful as brotherly love.

There's one feature of Marcionite Christianity that might seem strategically suboptimal: Marcion, unlike Paul, burned all bridges to Judaism. By rejecting the Hebrew Bible and excising Jewish themes from his canon, he made it impossible to do what Paul seems to have done: draw on the infrastructure of Judaism for logistical support and recruits. But by the time Marcion showed up, the "Pauline" church had effectively burned those bridges, too. At the end of the first century Christianity was no longer thought of as a species of Judaism, and blatant anti-Semitism would soon surface within the church.

This emerging tension between Christians and Jews follows the now familiar pattern: tolerance and amity often thrive when the game is seen as non-zero-sum but are less robust when it is seen as zero-sum. In the Roman Empire, anyone who refused to worship the state gods needed a special exemption, and the best hope for getting one lay in a deep historical heritage—showing that your religious tradition long predated the Roman Empire. Both Christians and Jews could point to the Hebrew scriptures as evidence of their deep roots, but whether both could do so successfully was another question. After all, could there really be more than one rightful heir to the Hebrew tradition?

So Christians, in pressing their claim for an exemption, had to undermine the Jewish claim to legitimacy. They argued that Jews had forsaken their own god by killing his son. That, explained the church father Justin in the second century, is why Jewish males are circumcised—a divinely mandated sign of their guilt. (And as for why the circumcision ritual predated the killing by more than a millennium: God is prescient, Justin noted.)[12]

This is the same Justin who in other contexts hailed Christianity's transcendence of ethnic bounds: "We who...refused to live with people of another tribe because of their different customs, now live intimately with them."[13] But apparently this tolerance depended on the tribe and the context. When Corinthians and Romans swap favors under the rubric of their common faith and share a stake in the success of that faith, the game is non-zero-sum. But two tribes competing for a single prize, the title of rightful heir to the Hebrew tradition—that's another matter.

Was Jesus Really Necessary?

The mass appeal of Marcionite Christianity suggests that if the faith we now know as Christianity—Pauline Christianity—had fallen by the wayside in the second or third century, another version of Christianity probably would have prevailed. Specifically: a version featuring the doctrine of interethnic amity, the doctrine that realized the network externalities offered by the open platform of the Roman Empire. But what if there had been no Jesus—then there couldn't have been any versions of Christianity to sponsor that doctrine, right? Well, there might not have been anything called Christianity. But even if Jesus had never been born, or had died in obscurity, some other vehicle for the meme of transethnic amity might well have surfaced.

There were plenty of vehicles around. Ever hear of Apollonius of Tyana? Like Jesus, he lived in the first century CE. According to stories later told by his devotees, he traveled with his disciples from town to town doing miracles: curing the lame and the blind, casting out demons. These powers emanated from his special access to the divine—he was the son of God, some said—as did his gift of prophecy. He preached that people should worry less about material comforts and more about the fates of their souls, and he espoused an ethic of sharing. He was persecuted by the Romans, and upon death he ascended to heaven. This imparted a nice symmetry to his life, since his birth had been miraculous in the first place; before he was born, his divinity had been proclaimed to his mother by a heavenly figure.[14]

Sound familiar?

But, you might protest, Apollonius of Tyana didn't posit a doctrine of interethnic love! Well, as we've seen, Jesus probably didn't, either. The doctrine was developed by Paul, a religious entrepreneur who used it as the cement in his far-flung enterprise.

And what if Paul had never been born? Well, then Paul wouldn't have been the Bill Gates of his day, the person who saw an open platform and launched an enterprise that dominated it. But someone probably would have. When a big new platform emerges — whether via the invention of the microcomputer or the founding of the Roman Empire — somebody usually figures out a way to exploit it.

Or, to put the point in more technical language: when the emergence of a new platform creates potential positive network externalities, someone will probably find a way to realize them at the expense of the competition. *Some* microcomputer operating system would have flourished big-time once microcomputers became affordable, regardless of whether Bill Gates had been born.

The parallels between Apollonius and Jesus may be no coincidence. By the time stories about Apollonius were collected in a book, the Christian gospels had appeared, and his followers — whether by conscious or unconscious embellishment — may have steered his profile toward Jesus's. But that's the point: convergence of this sort was natural. Ancient religious proselytizers were working in a competitive environment. They were trying to get people's attention and hold it, tell a story that could occupy a special place in their spiritual lives. For a religion to thrive, it had to offer at least as much as the competition. So religions naturally evolved in the direction of successful rivals, just as rival softwares are forced by the market to adopt one another's best features.

Hence the irony that convergence of form is often a product of intense rivalry. Jesus devotees belittled Apollonius, just as Apollonius devotees belittled Jesus — and just as Apple devotees and

Microsoft devotees belittle one another, even while the two operating systems absorb one another's innovative features.[15]

In the end, it's the features that are close to inevitable, not the particular companies or religions. Even if neither Bill Gates nor Steve Jobs had been born, any operating system that became dominant would have been amenable to features like word processing and e-mail. Even if Paul hadn't been born, any religion that came to dominate the Roman Empire would have been conducive to interethnic amity. For only that kind of religion could harness network externalities to outpace rivals.

Constantine's Conversion

That kind of religion might also prove attractive to an emperor. If you were ruling a multiethnic empire, wouldn't you favor ethnic harmony? Mightn't you even consider promoting a religion that encouraged it? Maybe Constantine's conversion to Christianity wasn't such a fluke after all. The empire's days of conquest and expansion were over. Now the challenge was consolidation, keeping the whole thing together. (The battle that occasioned Constantine's conversion was part of a civil war.) Maybe Constantine just knew a good social cement when he saw one.[16]

It wouldn't be the first time an emperor had a useful religious conversion. Ashoka, an Indian emperor of the third century BCE, was to Buddhism what Constantine was to Christianity. After violently subjugating the Kalinga, he decided that they and his people were actually brothers. He had this epiphany after converting to Buddhism, which had started as a maverick, grassroots movement but now, with Ashoka's support, would take hold across the Indian Empire. Since we don't have any Buddhist texts reliably dated before Ashoka's time, we don't know for sure that the Buddha himself actually espoused universal love and harmony. But Ashoka engraved his own interpretations of Buddhism in rocks, pillars, and caves, and some have survived, such as "Concord alone is commendable."[17] For an emperor, that's an understandable sentiment.

If you doubt that imperialism tends to foster interethnic amity, just look at the Roman Empire *before* the Christian church gained critical mass. Even then, without the help of Paul, the Roman state was working toward ethnic harmony; it championed tolerance toward diverse gods of diverse ethnicities. In that sense, Christianity was just reinventing the wheel. Before Christianity showed up, the empire sponsored doctrines conducive to ethnic harmony: everyone pays homage to state gods but beyond that is free to worship whatever gods they choose. After Christianity became the official creed, the empire sponsored doctrines conducive to ethnic harmony; it espoused brotherly love among Christians and strongly encouraged everyone to be a Christian.

To be sure, back before Christianity was the official creed, Rome showed bursts of intolerance toward those who didn't buy into its system of tolerance—Christians and Jews. Then again, there was intolerance after Christianity gained the upper hand—intolerance of non-Christians.

So, in moral terms, it isn't clear that Paul's mission culminated in progress. Before Christianity the imperial formula for interethnic tolerance was doing pretty well, and after Christianity the imperial formula for interethnic tolerance was doing pretty well. And in both cases the few who dissented from the formula risked persecution.

So what was the point of the whole exercise? Well, you'd have to ask Paul. And what was the point of *this* exercise—analyzing how and why Paul's version of Christianity prevailed over other versions of it, and indeed over other versions of religion?

The Point of the Exercise

The point was twofold: to show that some doctrine of interethnic amity was likely to prevail within the Roman empire all along, because that doctrine extracts more value from an imperial platform than other doctrines; and to show how utterly adaptable a given god can be in service of this logic.

Yahweh had begun life with a decided ethnic bias, in favor of the Israelites. And even when, during the Babylonian exile, he decided that worldwide, hence transethnic, allegiance lay in his future, he deemed the proper stance of non-Israelites to be one of abject submission—not just the submission you'd expect from any worshippers of an almighty god, but a submission more abject than that of Yahweh's Israelite worshippers. Indeed, it was ultimately a submission *to* Yahweh's Israelite worshippers; when the monotheistic impulse first clearly showed itself in the Abrahamic tradition, in Second Isaiah, it was in the service of an ethnic hierarchy.

Even so, Yahweh soon mellowed. Once Israel was a member in good standing of the Persian Empire, the case for interethnic amity grew. As we've seen, of the major authorial sources in the Hebrew Bible, the Priestly source—"P"—seems to be the most internationally inclusive; at least, P takes a relatively benign view of nationalities within the Persian Empire. And the best explanation is that P reflects the values promulgated by the Persian leadership after the exile. Here, even before Emperor Ashoka would illustrate the point, Cyrus the Great showed that empire could be a morally benign force.

Half a millennium after the return from exile, in the Christian lineage of the Abrahamic family, God underwent another change. P's God had been a national god—the God of Israel. (At least, under the name *Yahweh*, P's God had been national, though as we've seen, P's language can be read to mean that other nations' gods, with their various names, were manifestations of the one true God.) In contrast, the God of Jesus—or at least the God of Paul—was explicitly transnational.

Still, it is misleading to say, as some Christians have, that Christianity replaced the "particularist" god of the Jews with a god of "universal love." For one thing, the "particularist" god of the Jews hadn't found ethnicity per se an insuperable barrier. Long before Paul—even long before P—the Hebrew Bible had enjoined the just and compassionate treatment of immigrants. For another thing, as we've already seen, Paul's "brotherly love" wasn't truly "universal." It focused more heavily on fellow Christians than on outsiders.

Indeed, the Christian God of supposedly infinite love condemned nonbelievers to an afterlife of suffering. And, since the suffering lasted forever, God can't say it was "for their own good," the way loving parents can honestly describe the educational punishment of their children.

In other words, Christianity replaced one kind of particularism with another. The new particularism was based not on ethnicity but on belief. If you were outside the circle of proper belief, Christians didn't really love you — at least, they didn't love you the way they loved other Christians. And God didn't love you either; or if he *did* love you, he had a funny way of showing it! Even the people who had introduced this God to the world, the Jews, didn't qualify for salvation under Christian doctrine as it coalesced after Paul.

The Return of the Logos

So there was moral progress yet to be made. Still, God had proven his flexibility once again. He had shown that when different groups, including different ethnic groups, play non-zero-sum games, he can adapt, growing along the moral dimension to facilitate the playing of the games. Given that technological evolution had evinced a tendency to expand the realm of non-zero-sumness, this augured well for the future. Maybe this realm would continue to grow and God would continue to grow with it.

Of course, "God" belongs in quotation marks, because what's growing is people's image of God, not God himself — who, for all we know, may not exist. Still, as suggested in chapter 8, this growth of "God" could be evidence of, if not God with a capital G, higher purpose in some sense of the term. Specifically, as suggested in chapter 9, Philo's notion of the Logos might be a useful way to think of this divine purpose.

Elements of Philo's theology figured in Gnosticism, a version of ancient Christianity that, like Ebionitism and Marcionitism, fell by the wayside as Paul's brand of Christianity grew. One theme commonly attributed to Gnosticism is that self-knowledge is the path to salvation, an idea that, as we've seen, Philo was big on.[18] Also like Philo, the Gnostics spoke of God in terms of both wisdom and the Logos.[19] They saw Jesus as a manifestation of the Logos, of a book "written in the thought and the mind of the Father," as the Gnostic Gospel of Truth put it. Jesus "put on that book; he was nailed to a tree; he published the edict of the Father on the cross."[20]

This is a little reminiscent of the Gospel of John's declaration that the word, the Logos, "became flesh and lived among us, and we have seen his glory, the glory as of a father's only son, full of grace and truth."[21] (John is sometimes said to be the one gospel with Gnostic themes.)

Viewing Jesus as the Logos has a certain logic to it. The Logos expands humanity's circle of moral concern. To the extent that Jesus is furthering this cause, he is indeed, in a sense, the "Word" made flesh, a physical incarnation of the Logos. And certainly the Jesus in the Gospel of John is a big advocate of expansive moral concern — of brotherly love. "I give you a new commandment, that you love one another."[22]

In Mark, the earliest gospel, Jesus had said to love "your neighbor," a reference to the Hebrew scripture that almost certainly meant, in context, love your fellow Israelite. But in John, the last gospel, Jesus, like Paul, is carrying love beyond nationality. True, Jesus also, like Paul, is confining the most intense love to fellow followers of Jesus. He adds, in John, "By this everyone will know that you are my disciples, if you have love for one another."[23] Still, by the time the Gospel of John was written, near the end of the first century, the Christian church was broadly multinational, so even if this love wasn't universal, it was quite multiethnic, and so a step toward universalism. The message of Jesus is the Logos in action at that point in time, and in that sense it's not far-fetched to call Jesus an incarnation of the Logos.

Of course, there's the problem that the real Jesus, the "historical Jesus," probably *didn't* say these things. But if we can't equate the Logos with the "historical Jesus," can we at least equate the Logos with the "imagined Jesus" — the Jesus Christians have in mind when they worship, the Jesus who *did* say those morally progressive things?

It may sound paradoxical to say that a Jesus who exists only in imagination is the Logos, or anything else, made flesh. But when Christians revere Christ *as they conceive him*, they may—according to the theology of the Logos—be revering something authentically divine. For it is the Logos that shaped their conception of him, that infused this conception with a notion of brotherly love that crosses ethnic bounds; it was the expansion of social organization, and the attendant non-zero-sum intertwining of ethnicities—the Logos at work—that led Paul to emphasize interethnic amity and led subsequent Christians to put this message into Jesus's mouth. When Christians conjure up their image of Jesus, putting flesh around the message of love, the word—the Logos—is in a sense being made flesh.

There is a parallel with an ancient doctrine linked to the Gnostics and long deemed heretical: docetism. According to docetism, Jesus wasn't *really* made of flesh and blood. He was pure spirit, and the flesh-and-blood part was a phantasm, a kind of illusion. (In one ancient docetic account of the Crucifixion, Jesus is laughing on the cross; lacking a body, he feels no pain.) But in this docetic scenario there is an authenticity to the Christian reverence for Jesus as he appeared, because this appearance, though an illusion, was an illusion sponsored by God and hence a true manifestation of the divine. So too in a theology of the Logos: to revere Jesus *as Christians conceive him* is, on the one hand, to revere a construct of the imagination, but, on the other, to revere a manifestation of the divine. It could be that the Jesus Christians know is both an illusion and a true face of God.

And maybe, for that matter, worshipping a divinely sponsored illusion is about as close as people can get to seeing the face of God. Human beings are organic machines that are built by natural selection to deal with other organic machines. They can visualize other organic beings, understand other organic beings, and bestow love and gratitude on other organic beings. Understanding the divine, visualizing the divine, loving the divine—that would be a tall order for a mere human being.

Chapter Thirteen

How Jesus Became Savior

For many Christians, the word "Jesus" is virtually synonymous with the word "savior." God sent his son so that, as the New Testament puts it, "all flesh shall see the salvation of God."[1]

In a sense, actually, God's salvation had long been visible. The Israelites were saved from the Egyptians by Yahweh. ("God, their Savior, who had done great things in Egypt," as the Hebrew Bible has it.) They were later saved from various other tormentors, sometimes by a human being sent for that purpose. ("The LORD gave Israel a savior, so that they escaped from the hand of the Arameans.") And even as Yahweh subjected them to the wrath of the Babylonians—his subtle reminder that salvation is not unconditional—he was preparing Cyrus of Persia to carry divine salvation to the Israelites yet again. Thus the prophet Jeremiah could call Yahweh the "hope of Israel, its savior in time of trouble."[2]

But none of this is what Christians mean by "salvation." When they call Christ the savior, they're not talking about the salvation of the society or even the physical salvation of the individual, but rather the salvation of the individual's soul upon death. The heart of the Christian message is that God sent his son to lay out the path to eternal life.

Jesus is, in this view, a heavenly being who controls access to heaven. He "is seated on the right hand of the Father" and will "judge the living and the dead," as it is put in the Nicene Creed, a foundational document of ancient Christianity and to this day a common denominator of Roman Catholic, Eastern Orthodox, and most Protestant churches.

This Christian notion of salvation was a watershed in the evolution of the Abrahamic god—or, at least, in the non-Jewish lineage of that evolution. In both its Christian and Muslim forms, it would prove influential in ways both fortunate and unfortunate. Believing that heaven awaits you shortly after death makes death a less harrowing prospect. And this, in turn, can make dying in a holy war a more attractive prospect, a fact that has shaped history and even today shapes headlines.

After Jesus's death, there was good news and bad news for anyone who would set out to carry the Christian message of salvation across the Roman Empire. Both kinds of news are embodied in little figurines that archaeologists have found in the northern regions of the empire. There, scattered across burial sites, are bronze renditions of a god named Osiris.[3] Exploiting trade routes, this god had traveled all the way to Gaul—what is now France—from his native Egypt.

Osiris, who had been a major god in Egypt for millennia, bore a striking resemblance to the Jesus described in the Nicene Creed. He inhabited the afterworld, and there he judged the recently deceased, granting eternal life to those who believed in him and lived by his code. Hence the good news for Christian evangelists: Osiris's penetration of the Roman Empire suggested a widespread thirst for a divine figure of this sort, a sizable niche that a figure like Jesus might fill. And hence the bad news: at least some of the demand for this kind of divinity had already been met. As Christians carried the gospel across the Roman Empire, they would face competition from a god that already embodied some of the emotional appeal we associate with Christianity.

The earliest of these evangelists faced a second kind of bad news as they preached the gospel in the Roman Empire. Not only was there already some crowding in the market for a blissful afterlife via spiritual salvation; Jesus himself, it turns out, didn't initially fit into this market niche very well. This will strike some people, including Christians, as strange. Doesn't the Nicene Creed describe a Jesus tailor-made for that niche? Yes, but the Nicene Creed was written centuries after Jesus died. The common picture of Jesus it reflects—Jesus as heavenly arbiter of immortality—would have seemed strange to followers of Jesus during his lifetime. So would its corollary: that the righteous ascend to heaven in the afterlife.

Eternal life of a certain kind may well have been part of Jesus's original message. But it may not have been, and in any event the details of the story—the part about heaven, for example—changed consequentially in the decades after the Crucifixion. The way the now official story took shape is a case study in how God evolves to fill the psychological needs of his followers and also the survival needs of himself.

How Heaven Became Heaven

The idea of followers of Jesus getting to join him in heaven upon dying probably didn't take shape until about a half century after he died. To be sure, his followers believed from early on that the faithful would be admitted to the "kingdom of heaven," as the New Testament calls it. But "kingdom of heaven" is just Matthew's term for what Mark had called the "kingdom of God"—and, as we've seen, the kingdom of God was going to be on earth. In Matthew, Jesus says, "Just as the weeds are collected and burned up with fire, so will it be at the end of the age." Angels will come down and scour the land for "all causes of sin and all evildoers, and they will throw them into the furnace of fire, where there will be weeping and gnashing of teeth. Then the righteous will shine like the sun in the kingdom of their Father."[4]

Note the dynamic: angels come to earth from heaven and weed out the bad people, after which the good people remain on the new, improved earth. There's nothing about the souls of dead people ascending to heaven.

In fact, there's nothing about *dead* people at all. Jesus, convinced that the kingdom of God was "at hand," didn't spend much time describing the afterlife; he spoke as if the day of reckoning was going to arrive any moment, before his listeners had a chance to die, and told people how to prepare. Judgment Day was about the living, not the dead.

But just out of curiosity: What *was* going to become of dead people? Would they be resurrected and enter God's kingdom? And what was existence like for them in the meanwhile? In the years after the Crucifixion, such questions would grow salient as Jesus's followers saw friends and family, people with whom they'd expected to enter the kingdom, die. In a letter Paul wrote to Christians in the Macedonian city of Thessalonica — probably the earliest document in the New Testament — he confronts the unease: "We do not want you to be uninformed, brothers and sisters, about those who have died, so that you may not grieve as others do who have no hope."[5] Those who stand in God's good graces, Paul assured his fellow believers, can look forward to an afterlife even if they die before Judgment Day.

This probably reflects Jesus's own view. The idea that the dead would be resurrected at the culmination of history is found in the Jewish apocalypticism that Jesus inherited (including the book of Daniel), and Jesus affirms the idea in the earliest gospel.[6] Besides, Paul's credentials as a witness to Jesus's teachings are good, as such credentials go. Paul was alive when Jesus died and was attuned to the doctrines of Jesus's followers — first as one of their persecutors and then as one of their brethren.[7] In that sense, this passage from First Thessalonians, written some two decades before the book of Mark, is the earliest written evidence we have of Jesus's view of the afterlife.

In any event, Paul's view of the afterlife is the earliest documented Christian view, and it is notable for two things. First, though Jesus, being the son of God, went to heaven shortly after dying, ordinary Christians don't follow that path. They have to wait for Jesus to return before things get blissful; "the dead in Christ will rise" only when "the Lord himself, with a cry of command, with the archangel's call and with the sound of God's trumpet, will descend from heaven."[8] Second, even then, heaven isn't where the dead are going; rather, they will live out eternity on earth — the much improved earth of the kingdom of God.

The "Rapture" Myth

But what about "the Rapture"—the idea of many Christians today that Christ will come down and escort both living and dead Christians up to heaven? This idea rests on a dubious interpretation of Paul's letter to the Thessalonians, in which he describes how, upon Christ's arrival, first the resurrected dead and then the still-living will rise into the sky: "the Lord...will descend from heaven, and the dead in Christ will rise first. Then we who are alive, who are left, will be caught up in the clouds together with them to meet the Lord in the air; and so we will be with the Lord forever." A fact rarely noted by evangelical Christians—including readers of the Left Behind series of apocalyptic novels—is that this passage leaves open the question of what happens after earthlings and Jesus "meet" in midair. Will they all go to heaven together (the "Rapture" interpretation) or come back to earth together?[9] If anything, the fact that the earthlings "meet the Lord" rather than the other way around suggests the latter—that it's the humans who are playing host, welcoming Christ to terra firma.

This suggestion is confirmed elsewhere in Paul's writing. We learn from a letter to the Corinthians that the returning Messiah, after raising the dead, will have some mundane business left on his agenda: wiping out the world's many unsavory politicians. Paul, again reassuring Christians about the fate of the dead, writes: "All will be made alive in Christ. But each in his own order: Christ the first fruits [that is, after Crucifixion he became the first to return from the dead], then at his coming those who belong to Christ. Then comes the end, when he hands over the kingdom to God the Father, after he has destroyed every ruler and every authority and power. For he must reign until he has put all his enemies under his feet."[10]

The final enemy to die, says Paul, will be death itself. ("Where, O death, is your sting?" he asks in a phrase destined for immortality.)[11] But even then, once Christians are thus rendered immortal, they apparently spend eternity on earth. After Jesus "hands over" the kingdom to God, there's no mention of it being relocated.

The "Rapture" scenario actually rests on a double confusion. There is confusion about how Paul envisioned Jesus's return unfolding, and Paul is himself confused about how Jesus envisioned the return. In fact, he is confused to think that Jesus envisioned his return to earth at all.

In the gospels, Jesus doesn't *say* he'll return. He does refer to the future coming of a "Son of Man"—a term already applied, in the Hebrew Bible, to a figure who will descend from the skies at the climax of history; and the authors of the New Testament seem to have taken this as a reference to Jesus himself.[12] And plausibly so, since Jesus at one point predicts that the Son of Man will be killed and then arise three days later. Yet Jesus never explicitly equates himself with the Son of Man. And in some cases he seems to be referring to someone other than himself. ("Those who are ashamed of me and of my words in this adulterous and sinful generation, of them the Son of Man will also be ashamed when he comes in the glory of his Father with the holy angels.")[13]

How to account for this odd pattern of usage? One scenario does a pretty good job. Jesus, like any good Jewish apocalyptic preacher of the time, affirmed apocalyptic scenarios in the Hebrew Bible, notably the one about the coming of the "Son of Man." Then, after he died, his followers, stunned by the Crucifixion and trying to make sense of it, speculated that Jesus's references to the Son of Man had been veiled references to himself. It would have been an appealing theory: since Jesus predicted the future descent from heaven of the Son of Man, that must mean Jesus wasn't really dead after all![14]

Once the disciples agreed that Jesus had meant this term self-referentially, they would have been empowered not only to give new interpretations to his actual utterances about the Son of Man; they could also invent—or hazily if earnestly half imagine—whole new "Son of Man" utterances. If a disciple claimed that Jesus had once told him that the Son of Man was destined to be killed and resurrected, how could anyone convincingly doubt it? Of course, if the disciple claimed Jesus had said, "I will be crucified," doubt would have abounded. His peers would have asked, "Why didn't you tell us this back while he was still alive?" But if the disciple could insist he hadn't understood the true meaning of the remark at the time—because Jesus used the code phrase "Son of Man" instead of the word "I"—then his report would be invincible.

All of this would explain one of the most dramatic scenes in the New Testament, a scene that is otherwise puzzling. Several days after Jesus is killed, Jesus's mother and Mary Magdalene have found Jesus's tomb empty and are "perplexed." Two mysterious men appear, and

> the men said to them, "Why do you look for the living among the dead? Remember how he told you, while he was still in Galilee, that the Son of Man must be handed over to sinners, and be crucified, and on the third day rise again." Then they remembered his words, and returning from the tomb, they told all this to the eleven and to all the rest.[15]

Then they remembered his words? If Jesus's followers had known during his lifetime that "Son of Man" referred to him, and if he had indeed told them that the Son of Man would be crucified and resurrected after three days, it's unlikely that this prediction would have eluded their consciousness during the Crucifixion itself!

How could a gospel author write so incoherent a scene? Maybe it wasn't incoherent at the time it was written. If the idea that Jesus was the Son of Man arose only after the Crucifixion—and indeed was at that time famous for having arisen only after the Crucifixion—then the scene would have made perfect sense: the two Marys were having a major epiphany. Yes, they had heard that he might be the Messiah, the man who would save Israel, but they'd never dreamed he could be something even greater: the Son of Man—the figure Jesus himself had so often glorified.

The image of Jesus as the "Son of Man," seated serenely in

heaven, ready to welcome the souls of good Christians, may have been crucial in the eventual triumph of Christianity. This image gave it an edge over the religions that didn't offer hopes of a pleasant afterlife and kept it competitive with the many religions that did. It also inspired Christians to die on behalf of their faith. In the book of Acts, when Stephen is about to be martyred, he faces death with equanimity: "He gazed into heaven and saw the glory of God and Jesus standing at the right hand of God. 'Look,' he said, 'I see the heavens opened and the Son of Man standing at the right hand of God!' "[16] The postmortem identification of Jesus with the Son of Man was a key evolutionary adaptation.

Actually, a second adaptation was necessary before Stephen could have that vision. Half of his reassuring imagery—the Son of Man residing in heaven—took root shortly after the Crucifixion, but, as we've just seen, the part about faithful Christians eventually joining him in heaven didn't. Nor did the idea, which Stephen apparently shared, that the reunion with Jesus would come shortly after death. Indeed, Paul's silence on the question of the state of dead people prior to the coming resurrection suggests that his answer was the traditional answer in the Hebrew Bible: they spend their time in *sheol*, a murky underworld.[17]

Heaven Can Wait

It is more than a decade after Paul's ministry before Christian literature clearly refers to immediate reward for the good in the afterlife. In Luke, written around 80 or 90 CE, we're told that the God-fearing criminal hanging on the cross next to Christ will find himself in "paradise" alongside Christ that very day.[18] We're also told a story about the afterlives of a rich man and a poor man. The rich man, who died without repenting his sins, goes to a part of the underworld where, he observes, "I am in agony in these flames." The poor man has better luck. He finds himself in the company of Abraham—perhaps, as some have argued, in heaven, but at the very least in a more hospitable part of the underworld: someplace where "he is comforted."[19]

Some scholars argue that this idea of immediate reward for the Christian dead goes back to Jesus himself—who, after all, is the one who in Luke makes these two references to the afterlife.[20] Yet neither reference is found in the earliest gospel, Mark, or in the earlier-than-Luke Q source. The mid-twentieth-century scholar S. G. F. Brandon was almost certainly right to see this idea as developing after Paul and well after Jesus. It is, he noted, a pivotal idea, a departure from "the essentially eschatological figure who was about to intervene catastrophically in the cosmic process, and gather to their eternal reward his Elect." Toward the end of the first millennium CE, "Christ now began to be imagined as dwelling in heaven as the mediator between God and men."[21]

What caused the shift? For one thing, as the decades rolled by and the kingdom of God failed to materialize, there was growing concern among Jesus's followers over the state of the not-yet-resurrected dead. Paul's reassurance that believers' recently departed family and friends would join "the rest of us" in the kingdom had worked for a while. But by the time of Luke, more than a decade after Paul's death, that expectation was no longer operative. Now the attentive Christian was concerned not just about whether dead friends and relatives would eventually be resurrected but about what death would feel like *until* resurrection, since it increasingly looked as if the Christian in question would join his or her friends and relatives in that state before Christ returned. (It's probably no coincidence that Luke, the first New Testament author to hint at the modern Christian heaven, is also the first New Testament author to downsize hopes of a coming kingdom of God. The kingdom, Luke says, "is not coming with things that can be observed...the kingdom of God is within you.")[22]

This was another crucial pivot. Now the payoff from salvation wouldn't be expected within a person's lifetime, but it could come right after death—the next best thing. Had Christian doctrine not made this turn, it would have lost credibility as the kingdom of God failed to show up on earth—as generations and generations of Christians were seen to have died without getting their reward. But now, with the kingdom of God relocated from earth to heaven, generations of Christians had presumably gotten their reward, and you could, too, if you accepted Christ as your savior.

Foreign Competition

Why is it Luke, not the roughly contemporary Matthew, who makes this pivot? Maybe because Luke is the most "Gentile" of the synoptic gospels. Whereas Matthew often seems to be trying to convert devout Jews to the Jesus movement, stressing its compatibility with traditional Judaism, Luke is focused on winning "pagan" converts. And if he is going to compete with pagan religions, he'd better make sure that Christianity can match their most popular features. Which brings us back to Osiris, gateway to a blissful afterlife.[23]

It brings us back to lots of other gods, too, because Osiris was hardly the only god in ancient Rome who held this sort of appeal. Though the official gods of the Roman state offered no blissful afterlife, the empire had been besieged by foreign cults that, by filling this void, had won followings.[24] These religions of salvation came under a variety of brands. There were gods not just from Egypt but from Persia and Greece. Persian cults talked of souls migrating through the planetary spheres to paradise, and Greek cults offered bliss in Hades, the underworld that had once offered only a humdrum existence for the average soul but now featured lush subdivisions.[25]

Am I saying that Luke stole his afterlife scenario from a competing religion? Not with great confidence, no. But if you wanted to indict him on this charge, you would not be wholly lacking in evidence.

Certainly that story in Luke about the rich man and the poor man in Hades has Osirian overtones. At the time Luke was writing, a written copy of an Egyptian story about the afterlife was circulating in the Roman Empire. It was about a rich man and a poor man who died and went to the underworld. Both were judged at the court of Osiris. The rich man's bad deeds outweighed his good, and so he was consigned to one of the less desirable stations. (Specifically, the story explains: the "pivot of the door" to the underworld was "planted in his right eye and rotating on this eye whenever the door is closed or opened." Understandably, his "mouth was open in great lamentation.") In contrast, the poor man, whose good deeds outweighed his bad, got to spend eternity in the company of the "venerable souls," near the seat of Osiris.[26] Plus, he got the rich man's clothes—"raiment of royal linen." (The rich man in Luke's story wore "purple and fine linen.") The moral of the story: "He who is good upon earth they are good to him in Amenti (the underworld), while he that is evil they are evil to him."[27]

Luke's story about the rich man and the poor man seems to have no precedent in earlier Jewish or Christian tradition.[28] So there is indeed a chance that Luke heard or read the Egyptian story and adapted it for Christian use. But we'll probably never know, and anyway, that isn't the point. The point is that whether or not Luke borrowed this particular story from Egypt's heritage, this *theme*—immediate reward in the afterlife—must have come from somewhere, and the likely source is one of the religions with which Christianity competed in the Roman Empire.[29]

Of these religions, Egyptian religion is the leading candidate. And it came in more than one variety. In addition to Osiris himself, there was a mutant Osiris named Serapis. Centuries earlier, after the conquests of Alexander, Greek imperialists who wanted to bond with their Egyptian subjects had fused Osiris and the Greek god Apis. They called the hybrid Oserapis, later shortened to Serapis. Now, in the Roman Empire, Serapis was worshipped alongside Isis—who, in Egyptian religion, was both the sister and wife of Osiris. By the time Paul wrote his canonical letters to Christians in Rome, Corinth, and Thessalonica, those cities already had cults devoted to Isis, Serapis, or both.[30] If Christianity was to compete successfully, as it did, it would have to meet the psychological needs these cults met.

Born Again

These needs aren't confined to the question of the afterlife. Though the basic meaning of spiritual salvation in Christianity is the saving of the soul from damnation, the term has broader resonance. For many Christians, salvation has been not just a heavenly expectation, but an earthly experience: a dramatic sense of release. What the release is "from" may vary—maybe just from fear of damnation upon physical death, but maybe from something else; maybe from some enslaving influence, such as alcohol, maybe from free-floating anxiety or guilt. And the release can be dramatic. Many evangelical Christians are firmly affixed to faith at the moment they feel "born again," perhaps while walking to the front of a congregation to accept Christ as their savior or during the subsequent ritual of baptism.

It's probably no coincidence that religions with which Christianity competed during its formative years also featured moments of transformative release. In the second century CE the Greek writer Lucius Apuleius described an initiation ritual in the Isis cult as a "voluntary death and a salvation obtained through prayer," a way of being "reborn to a course of new salvation."[31]

Apuleius's account, though fictional, seems to draw on his own experience as a devotee of both Isis and Osiris, and it provides plenty of detail about the born-again experience. Here the initiate recounts his attempt to utter a prayer after a multiday ritual designed to culminate in a sense of contact with Isis:

> I began so greatly to weep and sigh that my words were interrupted, and as devouring my prayer, I began to say in this sort: O holy and blessed dame, the perpetual comfort of humankind, who by thy bounty and grace nourishest all the world, and bearest a great affection to the adversities of the miserable, as a loving mother thou takest no rest.... Thou art she that puttest away all storms and dangers from man's life by thy right hand, whereby likewise thou restrainest the fatal dispositions,

appeasest the great tempests of fortune and keepest back the course of the stars...thou givest light to the Sunne, thou governest the world, thou treadest down the power of hell.[32]

Note how many things the Isis initiate is being released from: the threat of hell, all kinds of "storms and dangers" of life, and, indeed, the very root of misfortune; back then astrology was for some a grim determinism, and a religion could prosper by promising to liberate people from the fate that their stars foretold. Hence the initiate's gratitude to Isis who "keepest back the course of the stars."

There has probably never been a religion that was saving people from only one thing. And certainly in the ancient world most religions, like the Isis cult, addressed various threats to physical and mental well-being.

Original Sin

Among the things religions can save people from is a burdensome sense of their moral imperfection—the sense of sin. Apparently sin was integral to the salvation message of early Christianity. Paul put the theme front and center. "All, both Jews and Greeks, are under the power of sin, as it is written: 'There is no one who is righteous, not even one.'"[33]

Certainly not Paul. "I am of the flesh, sold into slavery under sin. I do not understand my own actions. For I do not do what I want, but I do the very thing I hate.... But in fact it is no longer I that do it, but sin that dwells within me. For I know that nothing good dwells within me, that is, in my flesh. I can will what is right, but I cannot do it. For I do not do the good I want, but the evil I do not want is what I do."[34]

Scholars differ over whether this is Paul's self-appraisal or whether he is speaking generically about the human condition. Either way, this passage must have been consistent with his personal experience.

Indeed, seeing how Jesus could solve his problems with sin may have been Paul's defining intellectual epiphany—the thing that turned him into a zealous organizer of the early church. Suddenly, in Paul's mind, it all made sense. One man, Adam, had brought sin, and hence death, into the human race through his weakness, and now one man, Jesus, had through his strength, and through his death, offered release from sin and death. And it was all a sign of love. God, to whom humans had long made sacrifices, so loved humanity that now he sacrificed his son. Thus did a story with an unhappy ending—the story of a supposed Messiah who'd wound up crucified—become a compelling message of salvation and eternal life.

But if you're going to start a religion that becomes the most powerful recruiting machine in the history of the world, an appealing message is only half the battle. The message has to not just attract people, but get them to behave in ways that sustain the religious organization and spread it. For example: it would help if sin is defined so that the avoidance of it sustains the cohesion and growth of the church.

This is something Paul did masterfully. Look at the list of sins he enjoins the Galatians to avoid: "Now the works of the flesh are obvious: fornication, impurity, licentiousness, idolatry, sorcery, enmities, strife, jealousy, anger, quarrels, dissensions, factions, envy, drunkenness, carousing, and things like these." Only two of these—idolatry and sorcery—are about theology. The rest are about workaday social cohesion. The last two—drunkenness and carousing—make people unreliable and unproductive members of the community. The first three—sexual excess—could rend the congregation with jealousy and threaten the marriages of congregants. The middle seven—enmities, strife, jealousy, anger, quarrels, dissensions, factions, envy—are explicitly divisive; they are lapses from the brotherly love that was central to Paul's strategy.

And how strongly did Paul urge the Galatians to avoid these sins? After listing them he says, "I am warning you, as I warned you before: those who do such things will not inherit the kingdom of God."[35]

That's a powerful formula: if you don't live the kind of righteous life that helps keep the church robust, then you won't get to live forever in God's coming kingdom on earth. After the amendment seen in Luke — you won't get to live forever in God's *existing* kingdom in *heaven* — this formula would become if anything more powerful.

You might call this a "morally contingent afterlife," because it makes a blissful afterlife contingent on your moral fiber — a fiber that, in turn, gives sinew to the church itself. Christianity would harness this incentive to carry the God of Israel well beyond Israel, into the religious marketplace of the Roman Empire, where he would thrive. The morally contingent afterlife was a major threshold in the history of religion.

Yet Christianity was nowhere near being the first to cross that threshold. Once again, we come back to Osiris. That Egyptian story about the bad rich man whose soul is condemned in the court of Osiris has a very long lineage. The code of Osiris — the formula for a happy afterlife — was spelled out more than a millennium earlier in chapter 125 of the "Egyptian Book of the Dead." This "book" is actually an amalgam of writings used to help secure a happy afterlife, and the writings span millennia. But with chapter 125, which shows up in the second millennium BCE, we see a clear example of a morally contingent afterlife. This chapter tells the deceased exactly what to say when arguing for his soul's salvation before a court of gods overseen by Osiris. For example:

> I have brought about no evil.
> I did not rise in the morning and expect more than was due to me.
> I have not brought my name forward to be praised.
> I have not oppressed servants.
> I have not scorned any god.
> I have not defrauded the poor of their property.
> I have not done what the gods abominate.
> I have not caused harm to be done to a servant by his master.
> I have not caused pain.
> I have caused no man to hunger.

I have made no one weep.

I have not killed.

I have not given the order to kill.

I have not inflicted pain on anyone.

I have not stolen the drink left for the gods in the temples.

I have not stolen the cakes left for the gods in the temples.

I have not stolen the cakes left for the dead in the temples...

I have not diminished the bushel when I've sold it.

I have not added to or stolen land.

I have not encroached on the land of others.

I have not added weights to the scales to cheat buyers.

I have not misread the scales to cheat buyers.

I have not stolen milk from the mouths of children...

I am pure.

I am pure.

I am pure.

I am pure.

Here, long before the birth of Christ (and for that matter long before the birth of Abrahamic monotheism), is Judgment Day in a fairly Christian sense of the term.[36] There is a reward for moral behavior—eternal happiness—and maybe a second, more immediate reward: release from the sense of immorality itself—the sense of sin, the sense of impurity. One funeral spell found inscribed on a coffin was intended to liberate the soul of an Egyptian who had been trapped in "incrimination, impurity and wrongdoing" while on earth.[37]

Civilization and Its Discontents

Why all the interest in moral purity? When did it become a big human concern? Certainly the annals of anthropology aren't loaded with reports of hunter-gatherers lamenting their moral impurity.[38] In their societies the list of regrets about earthly existence features things more along the lines of hunger. Is there something about the advent of agriculture, and the attendant growth in social complexity, that made people feel deficient even when they had enough food? A couple of possible culprits spring to mind.

One is religion itself. As we've seen, once social complexity moves beyond the hunter-gatherer level, theft and other forms of antisocial behavior grow more feasible, and religion starts to discourage them. The result could be burdensome. Those Polynesian gods who afflicted thieves with shark attacks are the kind of thing that could weigh on the mind of someone who has once or twice strayed from virtue and is in the mood for a swim.

More generally, if gods punish with earthly afflictions a variety of moral transgressions, some of which a person is bound to occasionally commit, then everyday misfortunes become haunting reminders of moral imperfection. In India in the late second millennium BCE, a hymn to the sky god Varuna, who upheld the moral order, features this line: "O Varuna, what was the terrible crime for which you wish to destroy your friend who praises you? Proclaim it to me so that I may hasten to prostrate myself before you and be free from sin."[39] And here is a prayer from ancient Mesopotamia: "May my guilt be distant, 3,600 leagues away, May the river receive it from me and take it down to its depths.... My iniquities are many: I know not what I did.... I have continually committed iniquities, known and unknown."[40]

Varieties of Sin

Paul himself, the man who put salvation from sin at the center of Christianity, attributed the burden of sin at least partly to religion. A well-educated Pharisee, Paul felt the demands of the Jewish Law. "If it had not been for the law, I would not have known sin. I would not have known what it is to covet if the law had not said, 'You shall not covet.' "[41]

The burdensome strictures placed on behavior by religions in ancient times came in at least two varieties. First, there were the kind we've been talking about, the kind that are moral in the mainstream sense of the term: rules that keep people from harming their neighbors via theft, assault, dishonesty, and various other weakeners of the social fabric. Second—and sometimes intertwined with the first—were rules discouraging behaviors that were bad for the sinners themselves.

The second kind of sin, like the first, was partly a product of social organization's evolution beyond the hunter-gatherer level. Once people get much past subsistence, there are whole new opportunities for self-destructive behavior. As civilization advanced, alcohol was mass-produced, and money could be squandered in new games invented for that purpose. That Indian hymn to the sky god Varuna depicts a sinner who has isolated the cause of his sin: "Wine, anger, dice, or carelessness led me astray."

And, leaving aside alcohol, gambling, and other famously addictive products of progress, there were human emotions that, however valuable they'd been back in the environment natural selection designed us for, were increasingly problematic. Note the mention of "anger" in that Indian hymn—an emotion that, as we saw in chapter 9, is less useful in a state-level society than in a hunter-gatherer village.

Even an impulse as innocent as hunger could, for the more affluent and sedentary ancient citizens, lead to trouble. And this, too, is something the average hunter-gatherer didn't have to worry about. It's yet another case of a functional impulse becoming potentially dysfunctional once removed from the environment it was designed for. Natural selection designed us to get "addicted" to food, but that was in the days when scarcity kept addiction from getting out of hand.

Maybe it shouldn't surprise us that Buddhism, with all its early austerity, was founded by a man who, as a member of the ruling class, could presumably indulge his appetites fully. In any event, the very possibility of overindulging appetites, a possibility that grew as civilization advanced, suggests that some behaviors came to be considered sins not just because they were bad for society, but because they were bad for individuals. Religion has long been partly about self-help.

A Flawed Society

By some accounts, the thirst for salvation in the ancient world was grounded partly in a sense that earthly existence itself was impure. By the first millennium BCE, according to the sociologist Robert Bellah, there was "an extremely negative evaluation of man and society and the exaltation of another realm of reality as alone true and infinitely valuable."[42]

It's certainly true that the long movement from the simplicity of hunter-gatherer society to the complexity of urban civilization had given people new reasons to view social experience dimly. It's easy to see this in the modern world: just go to a cocktail party. Rapid-fire interactions with a number of people you know less than intimately can lead to a discomfiting postgame analysis and lasting anxieties. Did I offend her? Was he being purposely rude? Was she lying to me? Will he now ridicule me behind my back? These questions are hard to resolve when you may not see the person in question again for weeks, months, or ever.

There weren't many cocktail parties in the ancient world, but things were moving in that direction, drifting away from the small social universe of the hunter-gatherer and toward a world with more social contacts and hence more uncertain ones. Here is a plaint from second-millennium Mesopotamia:

> The wrongdoer hoodwinks me:
> I lay hold of the handle of the sickle for him.
> My friend speaks to me words not reliable,
> my companion imputes falseness to words I truthfully speak,
> the wrongdoer says shaming things to me,
> but you, my god, do not answer them back.[43]

It's kind of ironic. You'd think the whole point of civilization — of the evolution of agrarian states in Egypt, Mesopotamia, China,

India, and elsewhere—was to reduce threats to physical and psychic well-being. And on some fronts civilization did just that. Presumably you were less likely to be attacked by a wild beast in ancient Sumer or Memphis than in a hunter-gatherer village; and, with irrigated agriculture, your day-to-day sustenance became less iffy. Still, even as civilization defused old sources of insecurity, it seems to have created new ones, and the new ones, if less physically perilous, may in some cases have been more unsettling.

Father Figures

Maybe these insecurities, together with the new sense of sin, help explain why, as civilization wore on, people more and more seem to have wanted gods with parental qualities—protective, consoling, and, if demanding, at least able to forgive. In the second millennium BCE, a Mesopotamian prayer refers to a moon god as "merciful and forgiving father." Granted, the same prayer calls him a "strong bull, with terrible horns" whose "divinity is full of fear."[44] According to the scholar Thorkild Jacobsen, Mesopotamian conceptions of god are in this millennium moving toward that of the "stern but loving father," with the gods' terrible awe increasingly "in tension with underlying love."[45]

Egypt, too, saw the evolution of a loving, parental god. Osiris himself, notes the scholar J. Gwyn Griffiths, had been a god of "fear and terror" before assuming friendlier form.[46] And in the second millennium BCE the great Egyptian god Amun is showing a compassionate side, to judge by this encomium: "My heart longs to see you, joy of my heart, Amun, champion of the poor! You are the father of the motherless, the husband of the widow."[47]

Christians worship a loving father God, and many of them think this god is distinctively Christian: whereas the God of the Old Testament features an austere, even vengeful, father, the God of the New Testament—the God revealed by Christianity—is a kind and forgiving father. This view is too simple, and not only because a god who is kind and merciful shows up repeatedly in the Hebrew Bible, but because such gods had shown up long before the Hebrew Bible was written.

And, as we've just seen, so too with a lot of other main ingredients of Christianity — the born-again experience, Judgment Day, a morally contingent afterlife: nothing really new here.

It shouldn't surprise us that early Christianity was a mildly novel recombination of spiritual elements already in the zeitgeist. Any religion that grew as fast as Christianity did must have been meeting common human needs, and it's unlikely that common human needs would have gone unmet by all earlier religions.

Linkage

Another thing a successful religion has to do is meet its own needs — remain a vibrant and cohesive social movement. As Paul understood when he labeled disruptive behavior sin, his church, first and foremost, had to stay intact.

The word Romans used for "intact" was *salvus*. Something that was *salvus* was whole, in good working order. The expression *salvus sis* meant "May you be in good health." *Salvus* is the word from which "salvation" comes. God, in moving from Israel into the wider world — the Roman Empire — continued to pursue the goal he had pursued in ancient Israel: provide salvation — keep the social system safe from forces of destruction and disintegration.

There were differences between the way this job description played out in ancient Israel and in Rome. With early Christianity, the social system in question was a nongovernmental organization; it was just a church — not, as with Israel, a church-based state. Still, in both cases, for the religion to remain enduringly viable, it had to keep the system intact; it had to provide salvation at the social level. Paul's formula for preserving the church's cohesion — deeming divisive behavior damning sin — could be described as a way of linking individual salvation to social salvation.

If you define individual salvation broadly enough—as the saving of the individual or the soul from all kinds of afflictions—then this linkage has fueled successful religions in many times and places. The Polynesian religion that punished theft with shark attack made individual salvation contingent on behaviors conducive to social salvation. So did the Mesopotamian religion whose gods sent suffering to people who imperiled the health of others by urinating in drinking water. So did Moses when he laid out the Ten Commandments, then told the Israelites that God wanted to instill in them the fear of his wrath "so that you do not sin."[48] (Eventually the contours of the fear would be spelled out: if you sin, and then fail to atone for your sins via repentance and good works during the High Holy Days, your chances of dying during the next year go up.)

Certainly the Osirian religion of Egypt linked individual and social salvation—and, by defining individual salvation to include a blissful afterlife, strengthened the linkage. This improved formula, once adopted by followers of Jesus, would help Christianity dominate the Roman Empire.[49] It would later, as we're about to see, help drive the expansion of Islam. There's no denying its effectiveness in making some of the world's dominant religions dominant religions.

But its modern-day effectiveness is a more complex question. When Christianity reigned in Rome, and, later, when Islam was at the height of its geopolitical influence, the scope of these religions roughly coincided with the scope of whole civilizations. The bounds of the Roman Empire were the bounds of an economically and politically integrated expanse, as were the bounds of the Islamic Empire. Yes, both empires did business with people beyond their borders, but the world's polities hadn't become nearly the dense collective web they would eventually become; there was no global civilization. Today's world, in contrast, is so interconnected and interdependent that Christianity and Islam, like it or not, inhabit a single social system—the planet.

So when Christians, in pursuing Christian salvation, and Muslims, in pursuing Muslim salvation, help keep their religions intact, they're not necessarily keeping the social system they inhabit intact. Indeed, they sometimes seem to be doing the opposite. Before addressing this problem, we'll see how the Islamic doctrine of salvation took shape and what shape it took.

IV

THE TRIUMPH OF ISLAM

There is no other god besides me.

—Isaiah 45:21

No apostle have we sent before thee to whom we did not reveal that "Verily there is no God beside me."

—The Koran 21:25

Chapter Fourteen

The Koran

Learned westerners have said some unkind things about the Koran. The historian Edward Gibbon called it an "endless incoherent rhapsody" that "seldom excites a sentiment or an idea." Thomas Carlyle said it was "as toilsome reading as I ever undertook; a wearisome, confused jumble." Even Huston Smith, a scholar known for his dogged sympathy toward the world's religions, allowed that "no one has ever curled up on a rainy weekend to read the Koran."[1]

And these observations were made decades ago, before Islamic radicalism burgeoned, provoking a search for its roots. Since then, some have opined that those roots lie in the Koran—that what coherence the book has is pernicious, encouraging intolerance, even belligerence, toward people other than Muslims.

There is no denying that the Koran is unlike the religious text westerners are most familiar with, the Bible. For one thing, it is more monotonous. The Bible is a cornucopia of genres: the cosmic mythology of Genesis, the legal and ritual code of Leviticus, a multibook national history of ancient Israel, the plaints and alarms of the prophets, the pithy self-help and deep reflection of the wisdom literature, the poetry of Psalms, the gospel profiles of Jesus, the mystical theology of John, the early church history in Acts, the apocalyptic visions of Revelation and Daniel, and so on. The Bible came from dozens of different authors working over a millennium, if not more. The Koran came from (or through, Muslims would say) one man in the course of two decades.[2]

Suppose the Bible had been composed by only one of its authors. Suppose it was all the work of the prophet Hosea, a man possessed by a sense of how badly his people had strayed from the right and the true, a man intent on warning of the dire consequences that would ensue. What kind of book would the Bible be then? A book like the Koran. Or, at least, about a third of the Koran; Muhammad didn't spend *all* his time in apocalyptic prophet mode, as we'll see.

Or suppose the whole Bible had been written by Jesus. Not the Jesus of the Bible — not the Jesus who took shape in the century after the Crucifixion as the gospel adapted to its competitive environment. Rather, the Jesus who, so far as we can tell, was the real Jesus: a fire-and-brimstone apocalyptic preacher who warned his people that Judgment Day was coming and that many of them were a long way from meriting favorable judgment. Even more than a book by Hosea, this book would have the flavor of the Koran. Jesus and Muhammad probably had a lot in common.

Indeed, at times Muhammad may have been more like Jesus than Jesus — that is, more like the Jesus of story than was the Jesus of history. Jesus is reputed to have said, "Turn the other cheek" and to have preached the story of the good Samaritan as a parable of interethnic harmony. But, as we've seen, he probably didn't do either of these things. Neither did Muhammad, but he does seem to have said some fairly pacific things, and to have urged religious tolerance: "To you your religion, and to me my religion." On the other hand Muhammad also said some less pacific, less tolerant things. Such as: "When ye encounter the infidels, strike off their heads till ye have made a great slaughter among them."[3]

If you read the Koran from start to finish, these shifts in tone, from tolerance and forbearance to intolerance and belligerence and back, will seem abrupt and hard to fathom. One solution is to read the Koran in a different way. Like the Bible, the Koran isn't organized in the order of its composition. Just as tracing the development of Israelite theology meant keeping this fact in mind — remembering that the second chapter of Genesis was written long before the first, for example — understanding the evolution of Muhammad's thought requires reordering the Koran.

The Koran consists of "suras" — chapters — that reflect oral proclamations by Muhammad. They are arranged, roughly speaking, from longest to shortest. Yet Muhammad's earliest proclamations tended to be short and his later ones long, so if you want to read the Koran in chronological order, you're better off reading it backward than forward.

Better still is to read it neither backward nor forward, but somewhere in between—in the actual order of its composition. While there's no way to reconstruct that order exactly, most scholars agree on roughly where the different suras fit into Muhammad's life.[4] To read the Koran in light of this consensus—moving from earliest suras to latest ones—is to watch Muhammad's career, and Islam's birth, unfold. This is the key to seeing how the Koran, like the Bible, came to encompass wild fluctuations of moral tone.

Understanding the conditions that gave rise to the Koran's tolerance and intolerance, forbearance and belligerence, doesn't reconcile these themes. But it is a step toward understanding how later Muslims tried to reconcile them, and how Muslims today are influenced by them.

According to Muslim tradition, the revelation of the Koran to Muhammad began when he was forty, around the year 609. He was in the habit of retreating to a mountain for contemplation. One night, he had a vision. A glorious being appeared and conveyed a message from Allah along with the instruction to share it. ("Recite!" is the opening command of the sura that according to Muslim tradition is Muhammad's first revelation.)[5] Like the biblical Jesus, and like shamans over the ages, Muhammad emerged from seclusion with a mission. In the final two decades of his life he would again and again receive these divine revelations, and he would share them with others—first with a small band of devotees, later with a larger audience.

The Koran describes the glorious being—the angel Gabriel, apparently—coming within "two bows' length" of Muhammad, after which Gabriel "revealed unto His slave that which He revealed." At this moment, the Koran tells us, Muhammad's "heart lied not (in seeing) what it saw."[6] Maybe not, but this is not a question we are in a position to address. A question we *should* address before proceeding further is: Does the Koran lie in reporting what Muhammad said? Whatever the inspiration for Muhammad's subsequent utterances, is the Koran a reliable guide to them?

The Koran has a better claim to that status than the gospels have of being a reliable record of Jesus's sayings. Parts of it may have been written down during Muhammad's life, perhaps under his supervision.[7] Almost certainly some of it was being written down shortly after his death, and many scholars believe it was essentially complete within twenty years of his death.[8] Of course, twenty years is plenty of time for distortion—even wholesale fabrication—to set in. Still, two factors make a fair degree of fidelity plausible.

First, beginning in Muhammad's day, Koranic verses seem to have been ritually recited in Muslim communities. Second, the Koran is particularly amenable to retention via recitation; in the original Arabic, much of it rhymes, at least loosely, and is rhythmic.

The contours of the Koran also suggest authenticity. By the time of his death, Muhammad had gone from being a monotheistic prophet, preaching in the largely polytheistic city of Mecca, to being the head of an Islamic state with expansionist tendencies. And in the years after his death, the Islamic state expanded rapidly. If the Koran were mainly a post-Muhammad concoction, you would expect it to mainly reflect the needs of the rulers of such a state.[9] Yet, as we'll see, most of the Koran consists of the kinds of things you would say not if you were a powerful political leader, but if you were a freelance prophet frozen out of the local power structure. And the smaller fraction of the Koran that seems keyed to the needs of an expanding Islamic state would, for the most part, make sense as the sayings of Muhammad himself in the final years of his career, when he had segued from prophet to statesman.

Still, no serious scholar believes that the Koran is wholly reliable as a guide to what Muhammad actually said.[10] Indeed, ancient sources outside the Islamic tradition raise the possibility that on one key theme—Muhammad's attitude toward Jews during the final years of his life — the Koran may have been amended, or at least creatively interpreted, after his death.

We'll look at this question two chapters from now, when it becomes relevant. But first let's stress the sense in which it doesn't matter. As we'll see, even if one phase in the Koran's shifting attitude toward Jews reflects post-Muhammad amendment, the pattern we've seen in this book so far will stand: tolerance and belligerence, even when conveyed by the lofty language of scripture, are ultimately obedient to the facts on the ground.

Mecca

In the case of Muhammad, the ground was in Arabia. He lived in the town of Mecca. "Mecca" is today a generic noun — "mecca" — denoting "a center of activity sought as a goal by people sharing a common interest." [11] The reason is that Mecca is the destination of Muslim pilgrims every year. But Mecca was something of a mecca even before there were Muslims. In Muhammad's time, it was a trading center, a transit point for goods heading to or from Yemen to the south, Syria to the north, and, perhaps, the Persian Empire to the northeast. [12]

Meccan trade was dominated by a tribe called Kuraysh. Muhammad was born into the Kuraysh, and so wouldn't seem like a person destined to make waves. If your team is already winning, why change the rules?

But the more you know about Muhammad's early life, the more natural it seems that he wound up unsettling things. He wasn't born into a powerful clan within the Kuraysh tribe, and his place within his clan was insecure. He was an orphan. His father died either before or not long after his birth, and his mother died when he was six. His new guardian, a grandfather, died only two years later, and Muhammad passed into the care of an uncle.

As a young man, Muhammad married a wealthy woman some fifteen years older, a previously married businesswoman who had been impressed by his commercial savvy. But even then, the system didn't work to his advantage. His wife's surviving offspring were all females, and in Arabia a man's stature seems to have depended partly on the number of sons he had.[13] In fact, daughters were sometimes buried alive at birth so that the mother could focus on the important business of producing male offspring. No wonder Muhammad decried this tradition, envisioning in one sura a "girl who hath been buried alive" asking "for what crime she was put to death."[14]

Linking the values in the Koran to Muhammad's personal situation isn't just speculation. The Koran itself makes the link. In one sura God, speaking about himself in the third person, says to Muhammad, "Did He not find thee an orphan, and shelter thee?... Did He not find thee needy, and suffice thee? As for the orphan, do not oppress him, and as for the beggar, scold him not." Muhammad did as told. He enjoined his followers to live compassionately and to "enjoin compassion on others." He said that Allah would smile on "the freeing of a slave, or giving food upon a day of hunger to an orphan near of kin or a needy man in misery." He conveyed Allah's critique of the Meccan ethos: "You honor not the orphan, and you urge not the feeding of the needy, and you devour the inheritance greedily, and you love wealth with an ardent love."[15]

This isn't the only part of Muhammad's message that was bound to disturb the status quo. Muhammad was a monotheist, and many of the Meccans were polytheists. They believed in deities named Al-'Uzza, Manat, and Al-Lat—as well as a creator god named Allah. In Muhammad's view, they were mostly wrong.

From the standpoint of high-status Meccan polytheists, if there was one thing worse than someone who denounced the wealthy and preached monotheism, it was someone who did the two synergistically. That was Muhammad. Like Jesus, he was intensely apocalyptic in a left-wing way; he believed that Judgment Day would bring a radical inversion of fortunes. Jesus had said that no rich man would enter the kingdom of heaven. The Koran says that "Whoso chooseth the harvest field of this life" will indeed prosper; "but no portion shall there be for him in the life to come."[16]

Such parallels between the Bible and the Koran shouldn't surprise us. Muhammad's basic claim was that he was a prophet sent by the god who had first revealed himself to Abraham and later had spoken through Moses and Jesus. (One slightly ambiguous Koranic verse seems to say that he is the last in this lineage—the "seal of the prophets.") The Koran is full of stories from the Bible and allusions to the Bible, including a monotheistic declaration that seems to come right out of Isaiah: "There is no God beside me."[17]

In light of Muhammad's conviction that he spoke for the Abrahamic god, I'll depart from current convention and refer to Allah as "God." Of course, many Christians and Jews wouldn't agree that their God is the God worshipped by Muslims. Then again, many Jews wouldn't agree that their God is the God worshipped by Christians, since (for one thing) their God never assumed human form. In calling both the Jewish and Christian gods "God," we defer to the claim of Christians that their God is the same God who spoke through Moses. It only makes sense to extend that deference to Muhammad's claim that the God who spoke through him is the same God who had spoken through Moses and Jesus. Besides, if we look closely at how Muhammad turned Allah into the one true god of the Arabs, we'll see that Allah's Judeo-Christian lineage is, if anything, stronger than is commonly appreciated.

Making Contact with the God of Abraham

How and when did Muhammad decide that the Abrahamic god was the one and only God? According to one early oral Muslim tradition, Muhammad's wife had a wise old cousin who was a Christian. When Muhammad had his initial revelation, it was so disorienting—Was he going crazy? Was he demon-possessed?—that he sought guidance from his wife, and she consulted this cousin.[18]

If indeed Muhammad fleshed out an initially vague religious experience with the help of a Christian, that could explain why he concluded that his mission was to spread a monotheist message, and, more specifically, the message of the Abrahamic god;

especially if, as that early Islamic tradition has it, the Christian in question had long believed that God would send a prophet to the Arabs—and declared upon hearing of Muhammad's experience, "Verily Muhammad is the Prophet of this people."[19] This is the kind of pronouncement that could help a seeker with messianic leanings but no clear mission fill in the blanks.

Even aside from the Christian cousin-in-law, Muhammad had chances to learn about the Judeo-Christian God. There may have been pockets of Christians and Jews in the Meccan vicinity, and there was a sizable Christian community in Yemen, one of Mecca's two main trade partners. And the other big trade partner, Syria, was part of the Byzantine Empire and hence heavily Christian.[20] Muhammad is said to have traveled to Syria as a boy with his uncle on trade trips.

He would probably have carried an open attitude toward Syrian religion. Mecca was a polytheistic society that, in classic ancient fashion, was tolerant of the gods of trade partners. In fact, Mecca's famous shrine the Ka'ba—today the destination of the hajj, the annual Islamic pilgrimage—was in pre-Islamic times surrounded by idols of gods favored by various tribes and clans, and this pluralism seems to have lubricated commerce. According to one early Muslim source, a Christian had been allowed to paint an image of Jesus and the Virgin Mary on an inner wall of the Ka'ba[21]—the sort of formalized respect for the beliefs of trade partners that would have been unexceptional in an ancient polytheistic city.

In this case the respect probably went beyond the formal. The Byzantine Empire was more cosmopolitan, more technologically advanced, than Arabian society, and the culture of a powerful neighbor often holds a special fascination to a less developed people. So long as that power isn't viewed as an enemy, the fascination can be alluring.

This leads to one way of looking at Muhammad—as a man who had the ingenuity to fill a wide-open spiritual niche. He took a foreign god that was already making inroads in Arabia and became that god's official Arab-language spokesman. To put it in modern commercial terms, it's as if no one before Muhammad had thought to secure Arabic translation rights to the Bible, even though demand for such a book was taking shape.

The Koran itself comes close to saying as much: "Before this, was the Book of Moses.... And this Book [the Koran] confirms (it) in the Arabic tongue."[22]

However, there's a crucial difference between this line and the Muhammad-as-translator analogy. In the translator scenario, Judeo-Christian theology is transmitted to Muhammad by contact with Jews and Christians and/or their scriptures. In the Koran's scenario, Judeo-Christian theology was transmitted to the Jews and Christians by God and then to Muhammad by God. When God, in the Koran, tells Muhammad that he has "made it an Arabic Koran that ye may understand: And it is a transcript of the archetypal Book,"[23] the archetypal Book isn't the Bible. Rather, the archetypal book is the word of God — the Logos, as some ancient Christians and Jews would have put it — of which the Bible is equally a "transcript." Muhammad didn't get the Word *via* Moses. Rather, like Moses, he had a direct line to God.

So Islam, by its own account, isn't *descended* from other Abrahamic religions, even though it is rooted firmly in the Abrahamic lineage. Yes, Islamic tradition may highlight Muhammad's contact with a Christian relative, but the idea isn't that the relative was an invaluable tutor in Christianity; more important was his role in helping Muhammad see which god was already doing the tutoring.

This distinction would have been crucial to Muhammad. The way to attract a devoted following in those days was to have special access to the supernatural. Just having access to a cousin-in-law conversant in biblical scripture wouldn't be very impressive. Indeed, that Muhammad's "revelations" were in fact coming from human sources is an allegation Muhammad's enemies made in trying to blunt his appeal. As the Koran describes the charge, Muhammad's message was dismissed as "tales of the ancients that he [Muhammad] hath put in writing! And they were dictated to him morn and even." At one point the Koran even addresses a specific accusation about who was doing the dictating. "They say, 'Surely a certain person teacheth him.' But the tongue of him at whom they hint is foreign, while this Koran is in the plain Arabic."[24] Case closed.

Was Muhammad a Christian?

Whatever the position of the Koran on the matter, the guiding assumption of *this* book is that people get their ideas about gods from mundane sources—from other people, from scriptures, or from their own creative synthesis of such input. Presumably Muhammad got theological ideas from other people, including Jesus, just as Jesus got ideas from earlier apocalyptic Jews, and just as one of those Jews, Second Isaiah, had taken strands of existing thought about Yahweh, mingled them with circumstance, and become the Bible's first unambiguously monotheistic prophet.

This basically secular view of religious inspiration is of course shared by many books, including most western books about Islam. Ultimately, they either state or imply, the explanation for Islam's origins lies in mundane facts of history; Muhammad's inspiration was less exalted than Muslim tradition would have it. But there is a sense in which even these secular accounts typically defer to the Muslim insistence that Islam isn't really a *descendant* of Judaism and Christianity.

This deference lies in their account of Allah's origins. They depict Allah's evolution as initially independent of the evolution of the Judeo-Christian God and then credit Muhammad with uniting the two lineages. In Mecca before the time of Muhammad, they say, there was an indigenously Arabian god called Allah. And, as Karen Armstrong puts it in her book *Islam*, by Muhammad's time some Arabs "had come to believe that the High God of their pantheon, al-Lah (whose name simply meant 'the god'), was the deity worshipped by the Jews and the Christians."[25] But it took Muhammad, and the Koran, to complete the merger, convincing Arabs that the god they'd long worshipped was in fact the god of Abraham.

This story has a nice ring to it, and the fusion of two previously distinct gods has plenty of precedent in the ancient world. But in this case the story may well be wrong, all the way down to the detail about the Arabic word Allah meaning "the god."

To be sure, a god called Allah shows up in ancient Arabic poetry that, so far as we can tell, is pre-Islamic. But there's no good reason to think he had deep roots in Arabian religious history. So why shouldn't we assume that Allah was just the Judeo-Christian God—maybe accepted into the Meccan pantheon some time earlier to cement relations with Christian trading partners from Syria, or maybe brought to Arabia by Christian or Jewish migrants earlier still?[26] Why shouldn't we assume that Allah and God were one and the same from the very beginning?

In the Koran, Muhammad's most common complaint about the theology of Meccan infidels is that they "join gods with God [Allah]"—that is, believe in a pantheon of gods that includes Allah. There doesn't seem to be any disagreement over Allah's identity. Though Muhammad clearly believes that Allah is the same god as the God of Christians and Jews, he doesn't spend any time arguing the point. Indeed, he seems to assume that everyone in his audience already ascribes to Allah a key trait of the Judeo-Christian God—being creator of the universe.[27]

To be sure, the average Meccan doesn't seem to accept other features of Judeo-Christian belief. Such as: monotheism, or the apocalyptic idea that Allah will judge all humans at the end of time and condemn infidels to hellfire. But this is what you'd expect if, say, a foreign god had been accepted for pragmatic economic or political purposes: most Meccans wouldn't become enamored of him, worshipping him in all aspects. And certainly they wouldn't buy those aspects they would find unsettling. (For example, the idea that the gods you've long worshipped don't exist, or that worshipping them will get you broiled at the end of time.) But all signs point to their having accepted his existence. This explains the rhetorical thrust of the Koran—not to convince Meccans to believe that Allah exists or that he is the creator God, but to convince them that he is the only God worthy of devotion, indeed the only God in existence.

If Allah was indeed the Judeo-Christian God all along, that would solve at least one riddle. Marshall Hodgson, a highly respected mid-twentieth-century scholar of Islam, observed in his magisterial work *The Venture of Islam* that, before Muhammad came along, Allah "had no special cult"—no community of Arabs who worshipped him with special devotion. Then, a paragraph later, he reports in parentheses something that strikes him as curious: for some reason, "Christian Arabs made pilgrimage to the Ka'ba, honoring Allah there as God the Creator."[28] Maybe the explanation is simple: Christian Arabs *were* Allah's cult, and had been from the day Allah first showed up at the Ka'ba under Christian sponsorship. (To this day, Christian Arabs refer to God as Allah.)

Does this mean Muhammad started his prophetic career as a Christian? As we'll see, to even put the question that way is to oversimplify the social landscape he faced. But certainly Muhammad didn't wind up accepting the theology of Christianity as now understood. And certainly, though he hoped his message would appeal to Christians, he also hoped it would appeal to Jews.

Of all the reasons to believe that the Arabian god Allah had always been the Judeo-Christian God, imported from Syria, the most powerful is phonetic. The word Syrian Christians used for God is, depending on context, either *allaha* or *allah*.[29] How likely is it that Syrians and Arabs had come to believe in two different gods who happened to have essentially the same name and to both be creator gods? That would be hard to believe even if Arabia and Syria were separated by an ocean; that they were nearby trading partners makes it only harder.

To be sure, scholars who embrace the independent-evolution scenario have an explanation for the phonetic likeness of the Arabian god Allah and the Christian God of Syria. In Arabic, the generic word for god—for any deity—was *ilah*, and the phrase for "the god" was *al-ilah*. Through contraction, they say, this phrase could have been compressed to *allah*.[30] If this is indeed what happened, then the resemblance between the Arabic *allah* and the Syriac *allaha* has an explanation that doesn't involve direct transmission from Syriac to Arabic. After all, Syriac and Arabic are, like ancient Hebrew, Semitic tongues. So if you could precisely trace the history of the Syriac word *allaha* back a millennium or so, and you could do the same with the Arabic word *ilah*, the two lineages might well converge somewhere in the trunk of the Semitic-language family tree. Specifically, they might converge in the vicinity of a word that is enough like *ilah* and *allaha* in sound and meaning to suggest close kinship with them: *Elohim*, Hebrew for God (and for god—lowercase—as well). Thus the phonetic resemblance between the Syriac word for God and the Arabic word for god could be the legacy of a common, distant ancestor, rather than signifying that the former gave birth to the latter.

The problem with this scenario lies in the next step: the idea that the name *Allah* arose as a contraction of "the god" (*al-ilah*) to refer to a god who was pre-Islamic and non-Judeo-Christian—in other words, a god that dwelt among polytheists. How likely is it that Arabs would have been referring to a particular god simply as "the god" before they had come to believe that he was in fact "*the* god"—before they had accepted that there was such a thing as the one and only god? A more plausible sequence of linguistic evolution is the more straightforward one: the Arabic *Allah* is descended from the Syriac *allaha*, and *allaha*'s lineage, in turn, leads back to close kinship with *Elohim*. The names change—a little—but the God remains the same.[31]

God's Phonetic Footprints

Another Semitic language was Aramaic, the language spoken by Jesus and a language ancestral to the Syriac language of Muhammad's time. Together these four languages—Hebrew, Aramaic, Syriac, Arabic—trace some crucial stages in the evolution of God. The Hebrew *Elohim* had, by the middle of the first millennium BCE, come to signify the one and only God, a god who, to the Israelites, was the arbiter of national salvation. This God as rendered in Aramaic—*elaha*—was a god who, Jesus (or at least his followers) would emphasize, could bring *individual* salvation, judging souls at the end of time. By Muhammad's day, some Christians had made individual salvation more ornate and more compelling, elaborating vividly on what paradise and hell would be like; the Syriac name for God, *allaha*, or *allah*, probably embodied this vividness for Syrian believers.[32]

If so, these connotations would have carried over into the Arabic name for God, *Allah*. In any event, the word carried these connotations after Muhammad got through with it, and put flesh on the Judeo-Christian God that Meccan pagans had previously accepted only in skeletal form. Allah, Muhammad informed the Arabs, was not a god to be casually accepted in the service of commercial diplomacy. If you believed in him at all, you believed in a god that was omnipotent and omniscient, a god that was fair but stern, a god that would eventually judge everyone on their merits. At the end of time, said Muhammad, "every soul shall know what it hath produced."[33]

The theology Muhammad preached to the Arabs was a natural extension of the economic logic of the day: Mecca had accepted Syria as a vital trading partner, and in keeping with pragmatic polytheistic custom it accepted the Syrian God. Muhammad just brought Meccans in touch with some distinctive properties of this god—such as an aversion to coexistence with other gods.

However logical an outgrowth of Mecca's economy Muhammad's message was, it threatened to upset that economy. The Ka'ba was a sanctuary of regional significance, drawing nearby devotees of various gods. (By some accounts it was surrounded by 360 idols.)[34] This was good for Meccan commerce, notably during an annual pilgrimage, when fighting was forbidden and trade flourished.[35] The Ka'ba was thus one key to what regional solidarity there was in Arabia, and the Meccans profited from holding the key. Now Muhammad seemed to be saying that the whole system must be swept away, beginning with the Ka'ba's idols, the magnetic force that helped make the town the core of regional commerce.

So even if Muhammad's God hadn't focused his ire on the

wealthy, the Meccan ruling class probably wouldn't have warmed to Muhammad's message. The essence of the Prophet's mission—-monotheism—rendered ongoing resistance all but inevitable.

The Koran's fluctuations between tolerance and belligerence reflect changing strategies for dealing with that resistance. This may sound like a crass way to look at scripture, but in a sense this view is shared by Muslim scholars themselves; the Islamic intellectual tradition has long recognized a correlation between the Koran's content and its context. In that sense this inquiry is true to Islamic belief.

But there's a difference. Muslims see God as having tailored the Koran's different verses to the varying circumstances Muhammad would encounter. My assumption, in contrast, is that Muhammad himself was doing the tailoring—even if often unconsciously, and even if convinced that God was doing it. So when I depict the Koran as a strategic guide whose changing tone reflects changes in strategic context, I'll depict Muhammad, not God, as the strategist and as the author of the Koran. As we'll see in the next chapter, few books have documented the rejection of their authors with such painful candor as the Koran.

Chapter Fifteen

Mecca

Muhammad had a lot in common with Moses. Both men were out-raged by injustice—Moses by how Egyptians treated Hebrews, Muhammad by how rich Arabs treated poor Arabs. Both men raised their voices in protest. Both met resistance from the powers that be. Both decided to relocate. Muhammad, after ten years as a routinely shunned street prophet in Mecca, moved to the nearby town of Medina—the promised land—where Islam finally flourished.

Even before his exodus, Muhammad saw the parallels between himself and Moses as biblical affirmation of his mission. "Hath the story of Moses reached thee?" he asked an audience in Mecca. He often told that story, in which the Hebrew followers of Moses fare better than the Egyptian doubters of Moses, notably in their respective attempts to cross the Red Sea. Lest any Meccans miss the point, he added: "Verily, herein is a lesson for him who hath the fear of God."[1]

Muhammad also seems to have sensed parallels between himself and Jesus. In the Koran he has a young Jesus saying, "I am the servant of God; He hath given me the Book, and He hath made me a prophet."[2] But the parallels between the two men go beyond their missions, extending to their political circumstances and the receptions they got. The gospel allusion to Jesus's hostile reception in Nazareth—"No prophet is accepted in the prophet's hometown"—certainly applies to Muhammad's years in Mecca.

It's no great surprise that Muhammad didn't stress this parallel. For one thing, he doesn't seem to have had access to the written gospels. (Muslim tradition has him as illiterate, and in any event his version of the Jesus story sometimes departs from the biblical version.) Besides, Jesus's rejection, as we've seen, is a theme the gospels play down—more and more so as time goes on; by the time the Gospel of John is written, more than half a century after the Crucifixion and centuries before Muhammad's revelation, Jesus is wowing the masses by raising the dead.

The Koran, in contrast, never tries to hide the uncomfortable truth about its central figure. Here is a prophet who repeatedly fails to win over people who matter. Throughout the Meccan years—that is, for most of the Koran—the story of Muhammad is a story of rejection.

With this rejection begins the path to comprehending the Koran's moral vacillation. At one point Muhammad is urging Muslims to kill infidels and at another moment he is a beacon of religious tolerance. The two Muhammads seem irreconcilable at first, but they are just one man, adapting to circumstance.

Judgment Day

As we've seen, one of the more plausible parts of the gospel story has Jesus declaring, upon emerging from the wilderness, "The Kingdom of God is at hand." Judgment Day was near; it was time for sinners to repent and affirm their belief in the one true god. From early in Muhammad's ministry, this seems to have been his message, too. The apocalypse was coming, and when it came everyone would be accountable for their actions. Muhammad sketched this culmination of history in glorious detail:

When the Heaven shall cleave asunder,
And when the stars shall disperse,
And when the seas shall be commingled,
And when the graves shall be turned upside down,
Each soul shall recognise its earliest and its latest actions.

O man! what hath misled thee against thy generous Lord,
Who hath created thee and moulded thee and shaped thee
aright?
In the form which pleased Him hath He fashioned thee.
Even so; but ye treat the Judgment as a lie.[3]

That last line is far from the only Koranic verse reflecting the rejection of Muhammad's message. Time and again in the Meccan suras, Muhammad is dismissed out of hand—as a "sorcerer," as an "impostor." Like Jesus, he is accused of being controlled by demonic forces, possessed by "djinn." (And, unlike Jesus, he is accused of being a "poet." Sounds flattering, but this explanation for the beauty of his Arabic verse was pejorative compared to his own explanation—that the Koran emanated from God and was conveyed via his chosen intermediary.)

According to one sura, the Meccans treated Muhammad's ministry as a joke. "The sinners indeed laugh the faithful to scorn: And when they pass by them they wink at one another, And when they return to their own people, they return jesting."

Another sura describes the reaction of an influential Meccan to Muhammad's preaching: "Then looked he around him, Then frowned and scowled, Then turned his back and swelled with disdain."[4]

Sometimes the doubters got disruptive: "The unbelievers say, 'Hearken not to this Koran, but keep up a talking, that ye may overpower the voice of the reader.' "[5] According to Islamic tradition, Meccan elites were so intent on shutting Muhammad up that they punished his clan not just with an economic boycott but with a *marriage* boycott.[6]

All of this left Muhammad with a challenge: How do you keep intact a minority religious movement that faces harassment sanctioned by the most powerful people in the city? Fortunately for Muhammad, this wasn't the first time the Abrahamic god had encountered such a problem. The elements of a solution were already in place.

Some of them came courtesy of a Christian who lived four centuries earlier. Irenaeus, bishop of Lyons near the end of the second century CE, faced circumstances even more dire than Muhammad's. Christians were a minority in Lyons, and they were being not just persecuted, but sometimes killed. How to keep the faithful on board when staying on board made life so harsh? In part, by painting a lavish picture of rewards in the afterlife. According to Irenaeus, the hereafter would feature lots of grain, delicacies galore, and highly fertile women. Plus: no work, and bodies that never tired anyway.[7] It wasn't clear what people would do with all this recreational time, but certainly there would be no shortage of wine to drink. "Vines shall grow, each having ten thousand branches, and in each branch ten thousand twigs, and in each true twig ten thousand shoots, and in each one of the shoots ten thousand clusters, and on every one of the clusters ten thousand grapes, and every grape when pressed will give five and twenty metretes of wine."[8]

The paradise sketched by Irenaeus would be denounced by Christian theologians of an ascetic bent, but not by Muhammad. Like Irenaeus, he faced a steep motivational challenge, and like Irenaeus, he met it by offering his followers ample long-term compensation. After resurrection, these people of the desert could live amid "tall trees clad with fruit, and in extended shade, and by flowing waters." There would be "couches with linings of brocade" on which you could lie while food was "within easy reach." There would be "damsels with retiring glances" whom no man "had touched before." Somehow these dark-eyed beauties would remain "ever virgins, dear to their spouses." And they would never age — something they had in common with their husbands.[9]

This was half of the incentive structure. The other half was the alternative — the place you would wind up if you *weren't* one of Muhammad's followers. While the faithful were in paradise wearing "silken robes" and "silver bracelets," the infidels would sport "chains and collars" amid "flaming fire." If they asked for relief, they would be given "water like molten copper, that shall scald their faces."[10]

The Koran's recurring theme of reward and punishment wasn't

just another carrot-and-stick device. The specter of hell—the stick—was frightening, to be sure, but it was more than an instrument of fear. It also appealed to the sense of retributive justice; it assured the Prophet's followers that the Meccans who now mocked them would someday get their comeuppance. Remember that man who "swelled with disdain" upon seeing the Prophet preach? God "will surely cast him into Hell-fire." And remember the Meccans who tried to disrupt Koranic recitations? "The Fire! it shall be their eternal abode." [11]

The social standing of Muhammad's followers must have made these images all the more gratifying. When you're not rich and your enemy is, his impending demise acquires a special glow. "He thinketh surely that his wealth shall be with him for ever. Nay! For verily he shall be flung into the Crushing Fire." Don't worry, said Muhammad to his followers: "Let them feast and enjoy themselves, and let hope beguile them: but they shall know the truth at last. Many a time will the infidels wish that they had been Muslims." [12]

This is classic apocalyptic rhetoric. Muhammad is imagining a day when the lowly will be exalted and the powerful humbled, when the last shall be first and the first shall be last. Like Second Isaiah imagining the future suffering of Israel's enemies, like the author of Revelation envisioning the demise of a repressive Roman emperor, Muhammad is sure of the coming misfortune of his tormentors. The Koran's retributive vision is no more vividly violent than that of Second Isaiah or of Revelation, but the Koran offers much more of it, pound for pound, than the Bible as a whole.

And that's not surprising, given that most of the Koran was uttered while Muhammad was in Mecca, trying to hold together a besieged band of followers. Their cohesion depended on believing that the derision they endured would reverse its polarity someday, when the faithful, in paradise at last, "reclining on bridal couches," would "laugh the infidels to scorn." [13]

No doubt the thought of divine justice was gratifying to Muhammad himself. After all, he was the one being called a liar, an impostor—charges that seem often to have been on his mind when he spelled out the fate of infidels on Judgment Day. "Woe on that day to those who charged with imposture!" And "Taste ye the torment of the fire, which ye treated as a lie." And "This is the day of decision which ye gainsaid as an untruth." [14] And so on.

During the Meccan years, these images of divine retribution were as close to payback as Muslims got. The Prophet's few and lowly followers were in no position to exact retribution themselves. When critics mounted a show of force, Muhammad couldn't respond in real time; the end of time would have to do. "Let him summon his associates," says Muhammad about one critic; for our part, we "will summon the guards of Hell." The strength Muhammad asked of his followers lay in resolve, not aggression. "Nay! obey him not; but adore, and draw nigh to God." [15]

This is the moral irony of the Koran. On the one hand, it is vengeful; people who read it after hearing only whitewashed summaries are often surprised at the recurring air of retribution. Yet most of the retributive passages don't *encourage* retribution; almost always, it is God, not any Muslim, who is to punish the infidels. And during the Meccan years — most of the Koran — Muslims are encouraged to *resist* the impulse of vengeance. When you encounter infidels, says one sura, "Turn thou then from them, and say, 'Peace.'" Let God handle the rest: "In the end they shall know their folly." Another Meccan sura suggests how to handle a confrontation with a confirmed infidel. Just say: "I shall never worship that which ye worship, Neither will ye worship that which I worship. To you be your religion; to me my religion." [16]

This message of restraint is driven home not just by Muhammad to Muslims but by God to Muhammad. God assures his prophet that he knows full well "what the infidels say: and thou art not to compel them." Just "warn . . . by the Koran those who fear my menace," leaving those who don't fear it to their deserved fate. After all: "thou art a warner only: Thou hast no authority over them." [17]

This theme is constant through Muhammad's days in Mecca. In what is considered one of the earliest Meccan suras, God says to Muhammad: "Endure what they say with patience, and depart from them with a decorous departure."[18] And, in what is often called the last of the Meccan suras, God says: "Thy work is preaching only"; leave it for God to "take account." And here's something from the middle: "And the servants of the God of Mercy are they who walk upon the Earth softly; and when the ignorant address them, they reply, 'Peace!' "[19]

The principle at work here is familiar. The interpretation of God's will is obedient to facts on the ground and how they're perceived. The live-and-let-live philosophy flourishes when there seems nothing to be gained by fighting. That had been Paul's situation. Christians were a minority, hopelessly outgunned by polytheistic Romans, so no wonder he told his followers, "Bless those who persecute you" and "Do not repay anyone evil for evil." And no wonder Muhammad, in roughly the same situation, said, "Turn away evil by what is better, and lo! he between whom and thyself was enmity, shall be as though he were a warm friend."[20]

And likewise, as we've seen, in the Hebrew Bible. The Israelites, after suffering a setback at the hands of the Ammonites, waxed theologically tolerant in making a peace overture to their next-door neighbors: "Should you not possess what your god Chemosh gives you to possess? And should we not be the ones to possess everything that our god Yahweh has conquered for our benefit?" When, on the other hand, fighting seemed to offer easy gains, religious tolerance faded. Thus are the Israelites told in the book of Deuteronomy to "annihilate" the Hittites, Amorites, Canaanites, Perizzites, and so on, "so that they may not teach you to do all the abhorrent things that they do for their gods, and you thus sin against the LORD your God."[21]

After moving to Medina and mobilizing its resources, Muhammad would, like the Israelites of Deuteronomy, find war a more auspicious prospect. And, as we'll see, God's views on fighting infidels would change accordingly, as they did in the Bible. But so long as Muhammad remained in Mecca, fighting was unappealing and religious tolerance expansive. Indeed, at moments when collaboration with the pagans seemed attractive, Muhammad's tolerance grew so large that he was willing to give up monotheism itself. This, at least, is the apparent upshot of the "satanic verses."

The Satanic Verses

What Muslims call the satanic verses aren't in the Koran. At least, they aren't anymore. According to Muslim tradition, they were uttered by the Prophet and thus entered scripture, but were expunged when he realized they had been inspired by Satan.

The verses involve three goddesses — Al-Lat, Al-'Uzza, and Manat — who had a big following in Arabia and whom some pagans considered daughters of Allah. Acknowledging their existence and power would have made it easier for Muhammad to do business with their adherents, and some of their adherents were influential. A nearby town where some Meccan elites owned property featured a shrine to Al-Lat.[22]

Apparently Muhammad succumbed to the temptation. In the now expunged utterance, he said of the three goddesses that they are "exalted," adding: "And truly their intercession may be expected."

This concession seems to have proved in one sense or another ill advised. Maybe the pagans rebuffed Muhammad's overture, and maybe his followers rebelled at his apostasy. (According to Muslim tradition, pagans applauded the initiative but then Muhammad got negative feedback from the angel Gabriel.) In any event, the sura was amended. Today it calls these goddesses not "exalted" but "mere names," and there's no mention of them having the power to intercede in anything.[23]

The idea of Muhammad turning suddenly polytheistic doesn't fit easily into Muslim tradition, and it is precisely this "theological inconvenience" — the label we put on comparable Christian and Jewish anomalies in chapter 10 — that gives the story credibility. As the seminal twentieth-century scholar of Islam Montgomery Watt put it, the story is "so strange that it must be true in essentials."[24]

And certainly the *moral* of the story makes sense: when people see the prospect of non-zero-sum interaction across religious bounds, tolerance grows. Hopes of fruitful alliance tempted Muhammad to forsake monotheism.

Even in Meccan suras that didn't get expunged, there are signs of Muhammad trying to build interfaith coalitions. He seems, for starters, to be reaching out to Jews. The evidence for this doesn't lie in his extensive reference to Jewish scripture. (It is natural that he'd cite the Judeo-Christian Bible as authority for his otherwise radical pronouncements, given its connection to the august and cosmopolitan Byzantine Empire.) Rather, the evidence lies in the fact that while in Mecca he says nothing bad about the Jews and says some flattering things about their ancestors. God, in his "prescience," chose "the children of Israel...above all peoples."[25]

And in a sura normally dated late in the Meccan period, Muhammad seems eager to reach an accommodation with both Jews and Christians. The sura explains how to relate to recipients of "earlier revelations."[26] Muslims are not to argue with them "unless in the mildest manner" (though if the Christian or Jew in question has behaved "injuriously toward you" no such reserve is in order). Instead, they should emphasize common ground: "We believe in what hath been sent down to us and hath been sent down to you. Our God and your God is one."[27]

In short, Muhammad was a savvy politician, eager to build coalitions, mindful of muting differences that would impede that project. Some Muslims might reject this use of the word "politician," along with its implication that Islamic scripture can be seen as mere rhetoric. And some critics of Islam might welcome the word as support for the claim that Muhammad's "revelation" was just an elaborate ploy, part of the Prophet's scheme to amass power.

Both of these reactions are modern reactions. They come from a world in which the realms of religion and politics are often clearly distinct. In earlier times, as we've seen again and again, religion and politics were flip sides of the same coin. No doubt Muhammad's special access to God's word gave him mundane authority in the eyes of believers. No doubt the same was true of Jesus and of Moses. But that doesn't mean that any of these men considered their link to the divine less than genuine. Whatever you think about the reality of divine inspiration, human nature permits people to believe they are under its influence. More to the point: people can believe they are under the influence of divine guidance that, as it happens, is politically savvy in light of their own perception of the facts on the ground. We are political animals, and natural selection gave us political gyroscopes that can work in strange and wondrous ways.

After moving to Medina, Muhammad would make the connection between religion and politics clear. "Obey God and obey the Apostle" is a phrase that occurs several times in Medinan suras and never in Meccan suras.[28] While in Mecca, Muhammad doesn't yet have the clout to make such demands — at least, not explicitly; Meccan suras often say things like "Fear God and obey me," but these words are put in the mouths of biblical figures with whom Muhammad is implicitly comparing himself.[29] His followers were free, of course, to draw their own conclusions.

So too with suggestions that infidels might get punished not just in the hereafter but in the here and now. Meccan suras note how often in the Bible people who don't believe in God wind up dying en masse — a hint, perhaps, that, notwithstanding the great Koranic emphasis on the unpleasantness of hell, a taste of divine retribution might conceivably show up *before* Judgment Day. Yet the Muhammad of Mecca never makes this threat explicit or encourages his followers to realize it. He has no army; the mission would have been suicidal.

The Muhammad of Mecca, in short, is like Jesus. He never acquires the formal political power of Moses, much less of Israel's King Josiah, who ruled a mature state and whose scriptural legacy is the sanctioning of genocide against infidels. And the Muhammad of Medina certainly never acquires the power of an Emperor Constantine. By some accounts, Constantine had nails he believed to have come from Jesus's cross melted down and made into a bit for his warhorse. Whether or not this story is true, it captures a truth: Constantine, perhaps forgetting the part about turning the other cheek, had used the cross partly as an icon of large-scale violence.

We'll never know what Jesus would have been like had his

mission succeeded politically before he could be crucified. We'll never know what Moses would have been like had he wound up with a potent army at his disposal. In Muhammad's case, we know. After a decade of preaching in Mecca, he and a band of followers went to Medina (then called Yathrib). Muhammad was about to acquire real power, and things were about to change.

Chapter Sixteen

Medina

When Muhammad and other Muslims from Mecca first rode their camels into Medina, men and women lined the route crying "Come is the Prophet of God! Come is the Prophet of God!"[1] At least that's the story that entered Islamic tradition in the centuries after Muhammad's death. Its spirit lives on in popular western accounts of Islam's birth. In this telling, the tribal chiefs of Medina, fed up with mutual strife, ask Muhammad to come quell the infighting, vowing to abide by his arbitration.[2] He shows up, is warmly welcomed, and calmly assumes his ordained role of leadership.

But that story about Muhammad's welcome in Medina is no more reliable than the stories about Jesus in the gospels, also written well after the fact. The Koran itself, a more immediate witness to events, paints a different picture.

Consider that simple refrain first uttered in one of the earliest Medinan suras: "Obey God then and obey the apostle." Apparently people couldn't be counted on to obey Muhammad without the occasional reminder. And maybe not even then; the next line in this sura is a disclaimer: "but if ye turn away, our apostle is not to blame, for he is only charged with plain preaching."[3]

Indeed, suras from Medina suggest that there, as in Mecca, Muhammad was still nurturing a movement, trying to win converts. In one early Medinan sura, God gives Muhammad recruiting instructions, employing the same formula used by Paul to recruit Christians half a millennium earlier: "*Say:* If ye love God, then follow me: God will love you, and forgive your sins, for God is Forgiving, Merciful." And there is the flip side of the incentive structure: "*Say:* Obey God and the Apostle; but if ye turn away, then verily, God loveth not the unbelievers."[4]

If the standard account of Muhammad's entry into Medina is too simple, what is the real story? It's almost certainly true, as early Islamic tradition holds, that while in Mecca he had cultivated a group of supporters in Medina. When he and his Meccan coterie settled in Medina they had a base of support and more security than they'd known before. You might even say, as some scholars have put it, that Muhammad had created a new Medinan "tribe" — a tribe based on common belief, not common ancestry, but still a tribe, a tribe that would now grow to dominate the city and then the region.[5]

To be sure, Islam wouldn't replace existing tribes; it was a tribe you could join even while preserving your kin-based ties. Still, the Medinan suras suggest that Muhammad was asking for a commitment that could strain traditional lines of devotion. "O ye who believe! Verily, in your wives and your children ye have an enemy: wherefore beware of them."[6]

This line is quite like an utterance attributed to Jesus in the gospels: "I have come to set a man against his father, and a daughter against her mother, and a daughter-in-law against her mother-in-law; and one's foes will be members of one's own household. Whoever loves father or mother more than me is not worthy of me; and whoever loves son or daughter more than me is not worthy of me; and whoever does not take up the cross and follow me is not worthy of me."[7]

However jarring these passages from the Koran and the gospels, both make sense. If Muhammad's movement in Medina was to succeed, and if the Jesus movement in the Roman Empire was to succeed, they had to inspire a devotion that transcended existing allegiance. Both religions were engaged in re-engineering, creating a new kind of social organization. And if you want to make an omelet, you have to break some eggs.

In fact, the births of all three Abrahamic religions were exercises in large-scale social engineering. With ancient Israel, once-autonomous tribes drew together, first into a confederacy and then into a state. The birth of Christianity saw a second kind of social consolidation, not of tribes but of whole ethnicities. There was "no longer Jew or Greek"—or Roman or Egyptian—for all believers were "one in Christ Jesus." The Roman Empire within which Christianity spread was a multinational empire, and Christianity became a multinational religion.

With the birth of Islam both of these thresholds—the conglomeration of tribes and of national ethnicities—would be crossed in short order. When Muhammad made the *hijra*, the migration from Mecca to Medina, there was no centralized governance of the tribes in Medina, much less in the Arabian Peninsula writ large. By the time he died in 632, tribes in Medina, Mecca, and much of surrounding Arabia acknowledged his authority. Five years later, Islamic rule would encompass not just the Arabs, but Syrians—people whom we now consider Arabs but who didn't speak the Arabic language before they came into Islam's fold. And, as Muslim armies were taking Syria from the Byzantine Empire, they were also taking Iraq from the Persian Empire. Next came Egypt and Palestine;[8] within a decade of the Prophet's death, both had passed from Byzantine to Islamic hands, and the conquest of Iran, heart of the Persian Empire, had begun.[9] In the quarter century after Muhammad migrated from Mecca to Medina, possessing less power than the mayor of a small town, an Islamic state formed and became a multinational empire.

This expansion is all the more amazing when you look at the unpromising social fabric that awaited Muhammad upon his arrival in Medina. The town's Arab tribes, in addition to being heavily polytheist, had a history of feuding. There was a further complication that apparently hadn't existed in Mecca: whole tribes of Jews. And there seem to have been an appreciable number of Christians.[10] A religious and ethnic landscape this diverse wasn't naturally amenable to centralized political control. Mobilizing and unifying these constituencies was a job of nearly superhuman proportions.

And Muhammad didn't succeed at it. To judge by the Koran, his political domination of Medina, then Mecca, then lands beyond, proceeded without many Jews and Christians buying into the project. In fact, that may be putting it mildly. According to Islamic scripture and oral tradition, and to the western histories based on these sources, Muhammad's relations with Christians and Jews grew hostile and, in some cases, violent.

What was the source of the hostility? Some of Muhammad's Koranic utterances suggest that theology was the problem: both Christians and Jews fell short of the pure monotheism of Islam, said Muhammad, and so were disturbingly reminiscent of polytheists. They "imitate what the unbelievers of old used to say. God's curse be on them: how they are deluded away from the Truth!" [11]

The idea that theological differences were the prime mover of intra-Abrahamic conflict has natural appeal today, when dogmatic certainty pervades tensions among Muslims, Christians, and Jews. But the truth is more complicated. A close look at the Koran suggests that the issues Muhammad had with Christians and Jews weren't only, or even mainly, theological. What's more, as we'll see, the depth of the tensions, including the intensity of Muhammad's famous "break with the Jews," may have been exaggerated in Islamic tradition and in history books. In any event, to think of Muhammad as clinging to a rigid creed is to misunderstand who he was and how he built Islam into a force that has been with the world ever since.

Building the Base

In one sense, the difference between Muhammad in Mecca and Muhammad in Medina is the difference between a prophet and a politician. In Medina, Muhammad started building an actual government, and the Medinan suras reflect that. They are on balance more legalistic than the Meccan suras, less poetic, less—well, inspired. Still, even as Muhammad became a politician, he remained a prophet. In an age when political authority depended on divine authority, building a government was always in some measure a religious enterprise—and all the more so when the head of the church and the head of the state were the same man. Allegiance to Muhammad and allegiance to his God would have to grow in synergy.

The way to win allegiance to a god in the ancient world was to demonstrate his or her power. It could be the power to bring life-giving rain, or cure disease, or just improve the quality of life. No doubt this last power gave Islam some of its appeal. Its moral stringency[12] could help order a life and order a society, and its concern for the downtrodden must have helped, at the very least, the downtrodden. Still, during the crucial Medinan phase of Islam's evolution, when a religious movement became a system of governance, God's claim to authority seems to have rested largely on battlefield success.

It all started when Muhammad decided to stage a raid on a trade caravan run by Meccans. Raiding wasn't exceptional behavior in Arabia back then. Some tribes made a living by asserting control over stretches of turf and charging traders for safe passage—and one index of "control" was your ability to stage raids on caravans that didn't pay up. Though Islam would eventually deem highway robbery illegal, it's not clear that before Islam there was even an Arabic word for "robbery," and some scholars believe robbery wasn't a crime in the Arabia of Muhammad's day.[13]

Still, Muhammad did feel a need to justify the raid. And, having been persecuted by the Meccan establishment for ten years and finally forced to seek a home elsewhere, he didn't have to get wildly creative. God says in the Koran, "Leave is given to those who fight because they were wronged...who were expelled from their habitations without right, except that they say 'Our Lord is God.' "[14]

The raid wasn't a great triumph, but Muhammad inflicted enough damage to elevate his authority within Medina. And the raid started a series of skirmishes that eventually raised his stature further: the Meccans, fed up with the caravan-raiding, launched a major assault on Medina that Muhammad fended off. As his following in Medina grew, and with it his armed might, he felt he could approach Mecca and demand the right to worship at its shrine, the Ka'ba. The result was a treaty that lasted less than two years before Muhammad, claiming the Meccans had violated it, had his big moment. He amassed a force so overwhelming that he took Mecca with little resistance and little violence. The prophet who, like Jesus, had been without honor in his own town was suddenly running the place. The Ka'ba, once a place to worship Muhammad's God among others, was now a place to worship Muhammad's God, period.

Now the Islamic project had real momentum. Muhammad had more military might than ever and controlled a large swath of trade. Nearby tribes increasingly recognized the logic of subordinate alliance with him. By the time Muhammad died in 632, his "supertribe," as some have called it, covered most of Arabia, and he had started challenging the Byzantine Empire's control of Syria. The decade since he entered Medina had been a productive one—at least, from the point of view of the Prophet's followers.

Muhammad the Ecumenicist

But what about the nonfollowers? Why is it that Muhammad's relations with Medina's Jews and Christians seem not to have worked out?

It's hard to reconstruct the story with confidence, but one thing seems clear: it wasn't a simple case of Muhammad demanding conversion to Islam and being rebuffed. For a time, at least, his goal seems to have been to unite the Abrahamic religions but not to merge them. In an apparently authentic document known as the Constitution of Medina, Muhammad is deemed the arbiter of disputes in Medina—hence, in effect, its leader—but the separateness of the Jewish religion is acknowledged. Similarly, the revelation that justified that initial attack on the Meccan caravan cast it as an act of preemptive defense on behalf of the distinct Abrahamic faiths. "For if God had not enabled people to defend themselves against one another, monasteries and churches and synagogues and mosques—in which God's name is abundantly extolled—would surely have been destroyed."[15]

For purposes of municipal government, it was best that all

Medinans see Muhammad not just as a defender of their right to worship, but as a man with genuine divine authority. So he wanted to show Christians and Jews that they could grant the validity of his pronouncements without abandoning their own traditions. He explained that God had "sent down the Torah and the Gospel aforetime, as guidance to the people," and now had sent down the Koran "confirming what was before it." And he encouraged Jews and Christians to focus on the Abrahamic common denominator: "O followers of earlier revelation! Come unto that tenet which we and you hold in common: that we shall worship none but God, and that we shall not ascribe divinity to aught beside Him."[16]

Of course, the larger the zone of agreement among the Abrahamic faiths, the more completely Christians and Jews could acknowledge Muhammad's authority. The more common rituals the faiths could share, and the more theological differences they could iron out, the more cohesive a polity Medina could be.

Here Muhammad was willing to bear some of the burden of adaptation. Once in Medina, he decided that his followers should have an annual twenty-four-hour fast, just as Jews did on Yom Kippur. He even called it Yom Kippur—at least, he used the term some Arabian Jews were then using for Yom Kippur.[17] And the Jewish ban on eating pork was mirrored in a Muslim ban on eating pork, probably first enunciated in Medina.[18] Muhammad also declared that his followers should pray facing Jerusalem. Indeed, so thoroughly did Muhammad intermingle Islamic and Jewish ritual that half a century after his death, a Byzantine Christian would describe Muhammad as a "guide" who had instructed Arabs in the Torah.[19]

But reaching out to Christians was more complicated. Muhammad had staked out the basic Muslim position on Jesus back in Mecca. He had lauded Jesus as a great prophet but had refused to say he was the son of God. Yes, he said, Jesus was sent as a sign from God; and yes, he was of virgin birth. But "It beseemeth not God to beget a son."[20]

This position may have had an essentially logical basis. Among the Arab polytheists Muhammad denounced in the course of his monotheistic mission were those who accepted the existence of Muhammad's God, Allah, but insisted that Allah had daughters. No, Muhammad said, there was only one God—no daughter gods allowed (except during the overture to polytheists that, as we've seen, seems to have created the subsequently erased "satanic verses"). Well, if God couldn't have daughters, how could he have a son? One Meccan sura suggests that this is a rejoinder Muhammad himself had received from pagan skeptics in a rare moment when he was treating Jesus with the sort of reverence reserved for divinity. "They said, 'Are our gods or is he the better?' They put this forth...only in the spirit of dispute. Yea, they are a contentious people."[21]

This may have been a theological turning point for Muhammad: he went as far as he could toward embracing Jesus's divinity and then realized he was painting himself into a corner, undermining the monotheistic thrust of his message.

That raises a question: Why would Muhammad bother praising Jesus at all if he was going to deny his divinity and thus alienate all true Christians?

Here the phrase "true Christians" misleads. As we've seen, ancient Christianity was a motlier thing than the seamless version of it that was later read back into history. Remember the Ebionites, the "Jewish" Christians who considered Jesus the *adopted* son of God—a messiah but a human one? We don't know what happened to them after their existence was noted in fourth-century texts, but their influence certainly could have drifted toward Arabia. J. M. Rodwell, a nineteenth-century British translator of the Koran, deemed it "quite clear that Muhammad borrowed...from the doctrines of the Ebionites."[22] If Ebionite doctrines were indeed floating around Arabia, some Ebionites—or people rather like them—probably were, too.[23] And Muhammad could have hoped to win them over by revering a merely human Jesus.

And the Ebionites weren't the only source of Christian diversity. Because Arabia had commercial contact not just with Byzantine Syria to the north but with the Persian Empire to the east, there were "Nestorian" Christians, who believed Christ, though divine, had a more human side than Roman or Greek Christians allowed. Persia also featured Manichaeans, who considered Jesus a prophet but not divine. And then there were the more orthodox Christians, from Syria. All told, it was a smorgasbord of "Christian" belief.[24]

For that matter, Arabian Jews in Muhammad's day may have been anywhere along the spectrum from evangelically apocalyptic to sedately conservative.[25] Mecca in the seventh century was kind of like the world today, a place where diverse cultures were coming together, and the time was ripe for creative synthesis. The tendency to analyze the Koran by dividing Muhammad's audience into "Christians," "Jews," and "pagans" understates both the cultural complexity of the time and the subtlety of the political challenge Muhammad faced.

All of this could explain the otherwise mysterious fact that in Medina, Muhammad continues to seek the allegiance of Christians while denouncing "Christian" theology more clearly than in Mecca. Here, for the first time, he rejects the doctrine of the Trinity by name. "Say not, 'Three,' " he advises followers of Jesus.[26]

Yet even in this sura, while denying Jesus the status of God, Muhammad emphasizes how special he was, calling him Messiah and nodding toward the assertion in the Gospel of John that Jesus was an incarnation of the divine Logos, the "Word." "People of the Book," he says, "the Messiah, Jesus son of Mary, was only the Messenger of God, and His Word that He committed to Mary, and a Spirit from Him." Muhammad also lauded Christian values; God, according to the Koran, gave Jesus the gospel and "put into the hearts of those who followed him kindness and compassion."[27]

Even if Muhammad could have sold Christians on this formula, he would still have faced a problem. He was calling Jesus the Messiah, and Jews were of the view that the Messiah hadn't shown up yet. If Muhammad's aspiration was indeed, as it sometimes seems, to build a common religious platform for Christians and Jews and then call that platform Islam, his work was cut out for him.

And, to further complicate things, there was the awkward

question of the exact relationship of Christians and Jews to Muhammad. Yes, Muhammad was willing to have Muslims eschew pork, to pray toward Jerusalem, even to have a holy day called Yom Kippur. Yes, he was willing to accept the virgin birth of Jesus, to call Jesus the Word and the Messiah. But, at the end of the day, he wanted Jews and Christians to accept his religion — to accept that their own scriptures, however sacred, had been a prelude to the Koran; that their own prophets, however great, had been preludes to himself. Any merger of religions he may have envisioned wasn't a merger of equals.

The Abrahamic Inversion

The terms of the merger can be seen in the question of Abraham. Muhammad accepted the biblical claim that God had nominally revealed himself to Abraham as the one true god. And he accepted the biblical claim that the Israelites had descended from Abraham. This would seem to place the Israelites, hence Judaism, at the root of the Abrahamic family tree. But Muhammad told the Abraham story in a way that invited a different interpretation, one that put Islam, and indeed Arabs, at the center of things.

Hidden within the biblical story of Abraham, there had always been a commentary on the relative status of Israelites and Arabs. The nomadic Bedouin tribes that inhabited the part of Arabia near Israel were known as Ishmaelites, because they were thought to be descendants of Ishmael. So the Bible's depiction of Ishmael is, implicitly, a depiction of Ishmaelites, of Arabs as they were known to the ancient Israelites.

And how is Ishmael viewed through Israelite eyes? The good news for Ishmael is that he was an offspring of Abraham's. The bad news is that he was the child of Abraham's slave Hagar. He thus ranked below Abraham's son Isaac, who was born of Abraham's wife Sarah and from whom the Israelites descended.

As if this didn't bode sufficiently ill for the social status of Arabs, consider the circumstances of Ishmael's birth. According to

Genesis, Sarah drives the pregnant Hagar into the desert to bear her child alone. And later Sarah abandons her child in the desert. An angel prophesies his fate in a way that doesn't bespeak a favorable Israelite view of Arabs: "He will be a wild ass of a man, his fist against all, and everyone's fist against him."[28]

Naturally, Muhammad was inclined to cast Ishmael, father of the Arabs, in a more flattering light. And here he didn't have to break radically new ground. For there was a second biblical view of Ishmael, a more flattering view, subtly woven into the Hebrew Bible alongside the first one. It was put there by P — the "Priestly source," the author (or authors) who, as we've seen, seems to have reflected the aims of the Persian Empire at the end of the Babylonian exile. Judging by P's depiction of Ishmael, Cyrus the Great must have wanted his Israelite subjects to live in peace with their Arab neighbors, on terms of mutual respect. (This would make sense. His great enemy in that area was Egypt, and the last thing he needed was for the Bedouins of Arabia to ally with their Egyptian neighbors against his empire.)

The difference between the Bible's pre-exilic view of Ishmael and its postexilic view as presented by P is so stark that the biblical narrative, read closely, borders on the incoherent. In a pre-exilic verse Sarah, unable to bear children, encourages Abraham to take the Egyptian Hagar as a convenient concubine. "Go in to my slave-girl; it may be that I shall obtain children by her." But in the subsequent verse, written after the exile by P, Hagar is no mere concubine; she is Abraham's "wife," and the polygamous marriage has Sarah's blessing. And, whereas the pre-exilic verse has Hagar giving birth alone in the desert, a Priestly verse suggests that Abraham is present, for it is Abraham who names the newborn child Ishmael.[29]

And as for the pre-exilic angelic prophecy that Ishmael will be a "wild ass of a man" — according to the Priestly source, God himself has higher hopes. Abraham asks God to look after Ishmael and God replies: "I will bless him and make him fruitful and exceedingly numerous; he shall be the father of twelve princes, and I will make him a great nation."[30]

Even in the eyes of P, Arabs don't quite rank up there with Israelites. Immediately after shedding kind words on Ishmael, God says, "But my covenant I will establish with Isaac, whom Sarah shall bear to you at this season next year." So it is Isaac, progenitor of the Israelites, not Ishmael, father of the Arabs, who mediates the contract with God. Still, if the Arabs aren't quite Israelites, they're close. The one thing this covenant demands is that Abraham's offspring—God's people—should be circumcised if they're males. And Ishmael, according to the Priestly source, gets circumcised—on the same day as Abraham, no less.[31]

By depicting Ishmael as Abraham's beloved son, P had given Muhammad a theme he could amplify. In Muhammad's account Abraham and Ishmael somehow wind up in Mecca together, where they build and purify the Ka'ba so that the God of Abraham can be worshipped there. What's more, this was part of a "covenant" God had made with Ishmael and Abraham.[32]

Talk about a grand unifying narrative! By making Abraham co-builder of the Ka'ba, Muhammad had taken the most ancient sacred figure in Jewish and Christian tradition and linked him to the most sacred shrine for Arab polytheists. Just about every religious tradition represented in Muhammad's vicinity could find a touchstone in the religion he was creating. It was an ingenious way to try to bring all the peoples in the area under a single roof.

Still, they were all being asked to sacrifice a part of their heritage in order to stay there. Yes, polytheists could keep their shrine, but they'd have to let go of all their gods except one. Yes, Christians and Jews could stay in the Abrahamic lineage, but they'd have to concede that they had strayed from the pure Abrahamic tradition as laid down in the days of Isaac and Ishmael. The Koran describes the appropriate response to people who "say, 'Be Jews or Christians and you shall be guided' ": "Say thou: 'Nay, rather the creed of Abraham, a man of pure faith.' "[33]

And what is the name for this "pure faith"? The Koran has Abraham saying, "O my sons, God has chosen this as the faith for you. Do not die except as those who have submitted to God." And the word that means "submitted" is the same word from which "Islam" and "Muslim" are derived. Indeed, some translators have this verse as: Do not die "except in the faith of Islam" or "except as Muslims." So, too, with this Koranic verse: "Abraham was not a Jew, nor yet a Christian; but he was an upright man who had surrendered (to God)." Some translators have this as "Abraham was not a Jew nor a Christian but he was upright, a Muslim."[34]

Top Down or Bottom Up?

In light of all this, the Koran's intermittent hostility toward Jews and Christians isn't shocking. Muhammad was asking them to accept major amendments: the promotion of Ishmael relative to Isaac, the demotion of Jesus relative to God. No wonder they balked. And if Muhammad was possessed by the conviction that his divinely ordained mission was to bring all Medinans into a common understanding of their relationship to God, no wonder he took their rebuff as grounds for enmity.

At least, that's the way things look if you view religious belief as the prime mover: the logical incompatibility of beliefs leads to the social and political incompatibility of the believers. But what if you see the causality moving in the other direction, see facts on the ground as the prime mover? Consider this Koranic characterization of Christians and Jews, presumably uttered after Muhammad's ecumenical mission had begun to falter: "O Believers! take not the Jews or Christians as friends. They are but one another's friends."[35] Muhammad is recommending enmity, or at least a chilly reserve, as the proper attitude toward Christians and Jews, but the reason he gives isn't that they are theologically confused. The problem, rather, is that they aren't being friendly: they're not people you can do business with. Indeed, the implication is that if Christians and Jews were friendlier to Muslims, friendship toward them would be in order, notwithstanding their failure to convert to Islam.

And why weren't the Christians and Jews being friendly? If belief is the prime mover, the answer is easy: Muslims were asking Christians and Jews to embrace a religion they didn't want to embrace. But remember: the religion Muhammad wanted them to embrace was a reflection of the power structure he wanted them to accept. He wanted to be their political leader, and for them to signify allegiance by granting that he was the designated spokesman for the one true god. Maybe their resistance to this package deal lay less in its theological dimension than in its political dimension. Maybe they just sized him up and decided they didn't trust his leadership in day-to-day affairs, or that his political goals weren't theirs.

Consider the famous "break with the Jews." According to Islamic tradition, Muhammad successively expelled Medina's three Jewish tribes (and with the third tribe "expelled" is a euphemism; he executed their adult males). The circumstances are hazy, but in all three cases the most plausible explanations have to do with facts on the ground, facts that point to underlying political tensions.

The first tribe, the Kaynuka, were craftsmen and traders, and so, as the scholar Fred Donner has argued, would have favored good relations with Mecca—a position at odds with Muhammad's growing belligerence toward Mecca.[36] The second tribe, the an-Nadir, seem to have challenged Muhammad's leadership of Medina after he suffered a military defeat in his war against Mecca.[37] The third tribe, the Qurayzah, were suspected of secretly negotiating to help the Meccans during a battle that, alas for the Qurayzah, Muhammad finally won. In no case was religion per se the likely problem.

The point here is just that incompatibility of Islam with Judaism and Christianity at the levels of theology and ritual may not have been an intellectual inevitability. Muhammad's ecumenical project might conceivably have succeeded had its political implications— especially including acceptance of Muhammad's leadership—been to the liking of more Christians and Jews.

We'll probably never know for sure, and one reason is that we'll never know exactly what Muhammad's ecumenical project initially was. I've assembled the project's elements—the ritual and theology Muhammad embraced, his version of the story of Abraham—from the Medinan suras as a whole. But the Medinan suras accumulated over a decade, and we don't have a clear enough idea of their exact order to say which elements coalesced when. We don't really know, for example, whether his story of Abraham was one he tried to sell Christians and Jews, or whether it emerged only after he'd given up on converting them, and needed to reassure Muslims of their Abrahamic primacy.

For that matter, we don't even know that converting Christians and Jews was ever high on his list of priorities. If indeed, as the Constitution of Medina suggests, Muhammad initially aimed to lead a diverse community and accept the religious autonomy of Jewish tribes, maybe failure in that endeavor kept him from seriously pursuing the more ambitious goal of intra-Abrahamic fusion.

Still, there is, in one Medinan sura, evidence of such a grand ambition thwarted. God seems to tell Muhammad to give up on unifying people at the level of ritual: "To every people have we appointed observances which they observe. Therefore, let them not dispute this matter with thee, but bid them to thy Lord, for thou art on the right way."[38] So long as Muhammad was directing people to the one true god, that was enough—or, at least, all he could reasonably hope for.

Did the "Break with the Jews" Really Happen?

There is one more thing we don't know, and it is something that is virtually never called into question: whether Muhammad's "break with the Jews" really happened—or, if it happened, whether it was as dramatic as it is said to have been.

The standard story is that (a) the Jews resist Muhammad's theological message, noting contradictions between their Bible and his teachings; (b) Muhammad essentially gives up on Jewish conversion, and signals this turn in a stark change of ritual: Medina's Muslims had been praying toward Jerusalem, but henceforth they'll face Mecca; (c) one by one, he expels the Jewish tribes from Medina, with the final "expulsion" so bloody that it's closer to annihilation.

But much of this story rests on Islamic oral tradition that developed after Muhammad's death; the Koran's references to such events are much vaguer. The key Koranic verse—linked by oral tradition to the final, violent confrontation—refers to some "People of the Book" who aided the enemy; and, as a result "some you [Muhammad] slew, some you made captive. And He [God] bequeathed upon you their lands."[39]

This passage could indeed, as widely assumed, refer to a specific incident involving Jews, but it could also refer to Christians, since the term "People of the Book" encompassed both. In any event, Islamic tradition is famously creative in associating cryptic Koranic verses with particular historical events. Sometimes a single Koranic verse is confidently ascribed by several different Muslim thinkers to several different sets of circumstances.[40] Is the standard interpretation of this passage an example of such creativity?

A good reason to suspect so would be if there were influential Muslims in the decades after Muhammad died who would have benefited from the idea that the Prophet was at war with the Jews. There may be one such Muslim: Umar ibn al-Khattab, who became the leader of the Islamic state in 634, two years after the Prophet's death.

In 638, Umar conquered Jerusalem. In the history books this is depicted straightforwardly: the Muslims take Jerusalem from the Christian Byzantine Empire and claim it for their faith, and several decades later they build their mosque—the Dome of the Rock—atop the ruins of the Jewish temple that the Romans had destroyed half a millennium earlier. But that story, too, rests partly on the oral tradition, and so shouldn't be taken at face value. There are ancient documents, written by people outside the Islamic tradition, that tell a different story.

The oldest document to give a coherent account of early Islam is an Armenian chronicle from the 660s attributed to the Bishop Sebeos. It calls Muhammad an "Ishmaelite" merchant and preacher who knew the story of Moses and presented himself to Jews "as though at God's command." And, in this account, the Jews were convinced. Jews and Arabs "all united under the authority of a single man." Muhammad then urged them to regain their common homeland, the promised land. "Go and take possession of your country which God gave to your father Abraham, and none will be able to resist you in the struggle, for God is with you."

This document has its flaws as a historical narrative. It takes biblical stories about Ishmaelite lineage and fuses them imaginatively into a streamlined account of early Islamic history. Still, the fact remains that it was written no more than three decades after Umar wrested Jerusalem from the Greek Christians of the Byzantine Empire, and it depicts Jews and Muslim Arabs as a united military front. "These are the tribes of Ishmael. . . . All that remained of the peoples of the children of Israel came to join them, and they constituted a mighty army. Then they sent an embassy to the emperor of the Greeks, saying: 'God has given this land as a heritage to our father Abraham and his posterity after him; we are the children of Abraham; you have held our country long enough; give it up peacefully, and we will not invade your territory; otherwise we will retake with interest what you have taken.' "⁴¹

It's a disorienting prospect: contrary to Islamic tradition, and the western histories built on it, the conquest of Jerusalem was the work not of a Muslim army but of a Jewish-Muslim alliance. Strange as it sounds, though, there are other reasons to take this scenario seriously. In particular, it would help make sense of a puzzling feature of an earlier document, a Greek work from the 630s that refers to a "prophet who has appeared among the Saracens." ("Saracen" was a Greek word for Arabs and, later, Muslims.) The prophet claims that "he has the keys to paradise"—sounds like Muhammad so far—but also proclaims "the advent of the anointed one who is to come." Why would Muhammad, or any other Islamic leader, be buying into the Jewish idea that the Messiah was yet to come? Maybe because he was in fact closely allied with the Jews, long after his supposed "break with the Jews."

These discrepancies between the standard Islamic account and the earliest written non-Islamic sources were emphasized in the 1977 book *Hagarism*, written by two young scholars of Islam, Patricia Crone and Michael Cook. Their thesis was radical: Islam had actually begun as a movement that included apocalyptic Jews, and only long after the conquest of Jerusalem did it carve out a religious identity wholly distinct from Judaism. In this scenario, the Koran was in fact compiled in the eighth century, not the seventh — an attempt to claim deep roots for a new Abrahamic faith; an attempt, that is, to depict a new religion as old.

This thesis got a chilly reception from scholars and didn't catch on. But you don't have to buy the entire argument of Crone and Cook to see that the data they pointed to demand an explanation: Why does the earliest Byzantine document that clearly refers to Muhammad depict his people as allied with the Jews, united in their quest to retake Jerusalem? Maybe because that's the truth? And maybe after the conquest, when there finally was an actual "break with the Jews," Muhammad's successor Umar sought to justify it by ascribing to Muhammad a fiercer antagonism toward Jews than he actually held?

Certainly the conquest of Jerusalem by a combined force of Jews and Muslims would have provided a natural occasion for a falling-out. The Jews would have expected to resurrect the temple that was destroyed by the Romans half a millennium earlier. If the Muslims preferred to build a mosque on the temple's ruins, the dispute could have grown heated. And indeed, that Armenian document from the 660s depicts an argument between Jews and Arabs over the temple site, with the Jews rebuilding a temple but then being chased away by Arabs.[42] If the standard history were true — an army of Muslims, long divorced from the Jews, marching in and taking Jerusalem — it's hard to imagine any Jews in Jerusalem even bothering to start an argument they were so sure to lose.

Even if Islamic tradition, and standard western histories, have assigned too early a date to a "break with the Jews" that in fact happened after Muhammad's death, it's unlikely that the whole idea of tension between Muhammad and the Medinan Jews is made up. There are too many Koranic verses reflecting such tension, and indeed tension with Christians, and they make too much sense. Given Muhammad's ambitions, his ten years in Medina would have featured, at a minimum, ups and downs with Christians and Jews.

Even so, it's worth remembering that the Koran hadn't congealed into a standard text when Umar took office. Indeed, well after his career — and half a century after Muhammad's death — Islamic coins were being produced with Koranic inscriptions that diverge at least slightly from what has become the canonical text.[43] So there would have been time for Umar and other influential Muslims to, at the very least, be selective about which of the divergent Koranic verses made the final cut. And presumably any attendant thematic reshaping of the Koran would have tended to meet the needs of the people who controlled the shaping.[44]

Distortion as the Norm

Whatever the truth about the "break with the Jews," the source of our uncertainty about it is worth bearing in mind. Namely: Muhammad's immediate successors had an interest in distorting his message. This doesn't mean they fabricated parts of the Koran out of whole cloth (though they may have). But the manifestly divergent early traditions in the exact wording of Koranic verses would have offered chances to amend the book's meaning by choosing which traditions to draw on. And widening this latitude was the fact that the earliest written versions (like the earliest written Hebrew scriptures) lacked vowels; the words aided recitation but weren't definitive. No doubt later clerics, in choosing which vowel to put in the blank, occasionally found themselves with real semantic leeway. And, further, long after vowels were supplied, there remained obscurities and ambiguities to be worked out.

It's conceivable that no great distortion of the Koran set in after Muhammad's death. But if indeed the truth about his times evaded corruption, that would make Islam unique among the Abrahamic faiths. As we've seen, the official Jewish story reads back into history an earlier monotheism than is plausible. The ancient Israelites, notwithstanding the Bible's protestations, were finely intertwined with those polytheistic Canaanites—to the point of being, well, polytheistic Canaanites.

And, notwithstanding the claims of the Christian gospel, the "historical Jesus" was in all likelihood an apocalyptic Jew of the sort you'd expect to find wandering around the villages of Palestine in his time, waiting for the day when Israel would take its place of greatness among the nations. The cosmopolitan morals attributed to him—ethnic inclusion, interethnic love—were read back into his message by the cosmopolitans who later founded Christianity. And some post-Jesus Christians, perhaps like post-Muhammad Muslims, played up a kind of "break with the Jews"; they exaggerated Jewish responsibility for the Crucifixion.

In short, religions that reach great stature have a tendency to rewrite their history in the process. They cast themselves as distinctive from the get-go, rather than as growing organically out of their milieu. They find an epoch-marking figure—a Moses, a Jesus, a Muhammad—and turn him into an epoch-making figure. They depict his message as contrasting sharply with a backdrop that, in fact, his message was infused with.

To be sure, Muhammad, more clearly than Moses or Jesus, was a man who, in his own time, made a difference. He founded a government, and from this base he waged war and peace in a way that launched an empire. But here, too, in his pronouncements about war and peace, his message would be shaped and reshaped by posterity. Even today, some Muslims like to emphasize his belligerence—they wage holy war and say they do so in the finest tradition of the Prophet—while other Muslims insist that Islam is a religion of peace, in the finest tradition of the Prophet.

This argument, the argument about the doctrine of jihad, may ultimately do more to shape relations between Muslims and other Abrahamic faiths than the many and diverse references to those faiths in the Koran. This argument is the subject of the next chapter.

Chapter Seventeen

Jihad

In the mid-twentieth century, many American and European parents worried about the younger generation — the loud music, the raucous parties, the disrespect for authority. Meanwhile, in Egypt, a middle-aged man named Sayyid Qutb was complaining not about the younger generation but about his own. And the problem wasn't rambunctiousness but reserve.

In a book called *Milestones,* written in the 1950s and early 1960s, he complained about "the sorry state of the present Muslim generation" and cited, as exhibit A, the prevailing interpretation of the doctrine of jihad. Most Muslim jurists insisted that holy war was justified only when a Muslim nation had been attacked. Such thinkers, said Qutb, misunderstood the Koran. They had "laid down their spiritual and rational arms in defeat. They say, 'Islam has prescribed only defensive war!' and think that they have done some good for their religion by depriving it of its method, which is to abolish all injustice from the earth, to bring people to the worship of God alone, and to bring them out of servitude to others into the servants of the Lord."[1]

Among the unjust things that should be abolished, Qutb believed, were insufficiently fundamentalist regimes in Muslim countries. One example, the Egyptian government, had Qutb executed in 1966. But his ideas lived on and influenced, among others, Osama bin Laden.

After bin Laden's tactical triumph on September 11, 2001, an argument broke out in the West. Some, including President George Bush, said Islam is "a religion of peace" that had been "hijacked" by bin Laden and other radicals. In this view, modern-day jihadists don't understand the Koran and don't understand Islam; the prevailing Muslim interpretation that so perturbed Qutb is the true interpretation, faithful to the Prophet's words.

Other westerners—especially on the right—said Islam is a religion of violence, and in that regard reflects its scripture. There are lots of things they fault radical Muslims for, but misinterpreting the Koran isn't one of them.

Who is right? Is Islam a religion of peace? Of war? In one sense, the answer is the same as it would be for any other Abrahamic religion. That is: the answer is reminiscent of Certs commercials circa 1971, in which two people argued about whether Certs is a candy mint or a breath mint until they were interrupted by an authoritative voice that said, "Stop! You're both right!" Religions, as should be clear by now, have their good moments and their bad moments, their good scriptures and their bad scriptures. The ratio of good to bad scriptures varies among the Abrahamic faiths, but in all religions it's possible for benign interpretation of scripture to flourish. (Witness the "sorry state of the present Muslim generation"—the generation that as of the mid-twentieth century considered jihad a doctrine of defensive war.) In short: to ask "Is Religion X a religion of peace?" is to ask a silly question.

Still, there are less silly questions you can ask. *Is* the doctrine of jihad rooted firmly in the Koran? *Would* Muhammad approve of what the jihadists are doing? Or, to put that last question in Muslim terms: Would God—who Muslims believe inspired Muhammad to say what he says in the Koran—approve of what the jihadists are doing? Granted that the answers Muslims give to these questions will vary over time, which answers are true?

Muhammad on a Wartime Footing

The word *jihad* means "striving" or "struggle," and could apply to anything from violent struggles, like wars, to quiet struggles, like the struggle within your soul to do right. In the wake of 9/11, some people argued that this internal struggle was the true meaning of the term. Others insisted that jihad refers to violent struggle against infidels.

Who is right? You won't find the answer in the Koran. Though the verb form of *jihad—jahada—*appears often in the Koran, *jihad* per se—the noun—appears only four times, typically in the phrase "striving in the way of God."[2] And depending on which of those four verses you pick, you could make the case that jihad is either about an internal struggle toward spiritual discipline or about war; there is no "doctrine" of jihad in the Koran.[3] It was in the decades and centuries after Muhammad's death that Muslim thinkers turned jihad into a legal concept, and they've been arguing about its exact meaning ever since.

To be sure, the Koran is relevant. It is one of the two main sources these arguments cite (the other being the hadith, sayings of the Prophet as recalled in the oral tradition). But Muslim thinkers searching the Koran for the meaning of jihad go well beyond those four inconclusive appearances of the noun *jihad.* They look at the dozens of uses of the verb form of *jihad,* in particular those (maybe half) that occur in a military context.[4] And they look at the larger number of references to military fighting that use another verb.[5]

There are plenty of these martial verses in the Medinan suras, because during the Medinan years Muhammad did a lot of fighting. There are calls for Medinans to join God's battle, and guarantees that those who die in battle will find a place in paradise. There are exhortations to strike terror in the hearts of infidels, to slaughter them, to cut off their heads. These verses leave no doubt that at times Muhammad felt he had God's license to kill people who hadn't converted to Islam.

The question is how restricted the license was. When God tells Muhammad to go kill infidels is he saying that killing infidels is always good? Or is God more like an American officer before the Normandy invasion exhorting his troops to go kill Germans—not because killing Germans is always a good thing, and not because killing all Germans is a good thing even at the moment, but rather because, so long as a war is on, killing the enemy is the job at hand?

Right-wing Web sites devoted to showing the "truth about Islam" array searing verses that seem to show the Koran offering a nearly unlimited license to kill. (A few years after 9/11, a list of "the Koran's 111 Jihad verses" was posted on the conservative Web site freerepublic.com.)[6] But the closer you look at the context of these verses, the more limited the license seems.

The passage most often quoted is the fifth verse of the ninth sura, long known to Muslims as the "Sword verse." It was cited by Osama bin Laden in a famous manifesto issued in 1996, and on first reading it does seem to say that bin Laden would be justified in hunting down any non-Muslim on the planet.[7] The verse is often translated colloquially — particularly on these right-wing Web sites — as "kill the infidels wherever you find them."

This common translation is wrong. The verse doesn't actually mention "infidels" but rather refers to "those who join other gods with God" — which is to say, polytheists. So, bin Laden notwithstanding, the "Sword verse" isn't the strongest imaginable basis for attacking Christians and Jews.[8]

Still, even if the Sword verse wasn't aimed at Christians and Jews, it is undeniably bloody: "And when the sacred months are passed, kill those who join other gods with God wherever ye shall find them; and seize them, besiege them, and lay wait for them with every kind of ambush." It seems that a polytheist's only escape from this fate is to convert to Islam, "observe prayer, and pay the obligatory alms."

But the next verse, rarely quoted by either jihadists or right-wing Web sites, suggests that conversion isn't actually necessary: "If any one of those who join gods with God ask an asylum of thee, grant him an asylum, that he may hear the Word of God, and then let him reach his place of safety." After all, polytheists are "people devoid of knowledge."[9]

And the following verse suggests that whole tribes of polytheists can be spared if they're not a military threat. If those "who add gods to God" made "a league [with the Muslims] at the sacred temple," then "so long as they are true to you, be ye true to them; for God loveth those who fear Him." For that matter, the verse immediately *before* the Sword verse also takes some of the edge off it, exempting from attack "those polytheists with whom ye are in league, and who shall have afterwards in no way failed you, nor aided anyone against you." [10]

In short, "kill the polytheists wherever you find them" doesn't mean "kill the polytheists wherever you find them." It means "kill the polytheists who aren't on your side in this particular war." [11]

Presumably, particular wars were the typical context for the Koran's martial verses—in which case Muhammad's exhortations to kill infidels en masse were short-term motivational devices. Indeed, sometimes the violence is explicitly confined to the war's duration: "When ye encounter the infidels, strike off their heads till ye have made a great slaughter among them, and of the rest make fast the fetters. And afterwards let there either be free dismissals or ransomings, till the war hath laid down its burdens." [12]

Of course, if you quote the first half of that verse and not the second half—as both jihadists and some western commentators might be tempted to do—this sounds like a death sentence for unbelievers everywhere and forever. The Koran contains a number of such eminently misquotable lines. Repeatedly Muhammad makes a declaration that, in unalloyed form, sounds purely belligerent—and then proceeds to provide the alloy. Thus: "And think not that the infidels shall escape Us! . . . Make ready then against them what force ye can, and strong squadrons whereby ye may strike terror into the enemy of God and your enemy." Then, about thirty words later: "And if they lean to peace, lean thou also to it; and put thy trust in God." [13]

If the Koran were a manual for all-out jihad, it would deem unbelief by itself sufficient cause for attack. It doesn't. Here is a verse thought to be from the late Medinan period: "God doth not forbid you to deal with kindness and fairness toward those who have not made war upon you on account of your religion, or driven you forth from your homes: for God loveth those who act with fairness. Only doth God forbid you to make friends of those who, on account of your religion, have warred against you, and have driven you forth from your homes, and have aided those who drove you forth."[14]

Besides, even when enmity is in order, it needn't be forever: "God will, perhaps, establish good will between yourselves and those of them whom ye take to be your enemies: God is Powerful: and God is Gracious."[15]

Realpolitik

Modern-day critics of Muhammad who carefully skip parts of the Koran in amassing their lists of "jihad verses" are right about one thing: Muhammad pursued an expansionist foreign policy, and war was a key instrument. But to successfully pursue such a policy — and he was certainly successful — you have to take a nuanced approach to warfare. You can't use it gratuitously, when its costs exceed its benefits. And you can't reject potentially helpful allies just because they don't share your religion — especially when your turf is surrounded by people who don't share your religion. Muhammad may have been aggressive, and may even have been ruthlessly aggressive, but no one who accomplishes what he accomplished could be mindlessly aggressive. So he couldn't have enunciated a policy that literally meant you should fight everyone in your vicinity who doesn't share your religion. Indeed, if the standard versions of Muslim history are correct, he was forging alliances with non-Muslim Arabian tribes until the day he died.[16]

Once you see Muhammad in this light — as a political leader who deftly launched an empire — the parts of the Koran that bear on war make perfect sense. They are just Imperialism 101. Like the Byzantine and Persian Empires that the Islamic Empire would largely displace, Muhammad used a combination of war and diplomacy to expand his turf. All-out jihad — attack the infidels wherever you find them — wouldn't have made sense for an incipient military power, and that is why you don't find it in the Koran.

You do find something like it in the decades after Muhammad's death. Now a true *doctrine* of jihad takes shape: Muslims, it is said, have a duty to engage in ongoing struggle—military when necessary—to expand Islam's bounds. In the strong version of the doctrine, which crystallized more than a century after Muhammad's death, the world is divided between the "House of Islam" and the "House of War."[17] The House of War is the part of the world still laboring under unbelief even though Islamic doctrine has reached it. It is called the House of War because the duty of Islam's leader is to fight there.

The extremity of this doctrine is in one sense puzzling. After all, Islam was still, in these post-Muhammad decades, an expansionist power. Why wouldn't it preserve the realpolitikal nuance we see in Muhammad's time, as reflected in the Koran itself? Maybe there were times during the rapid growth of the Islamic Empire when conquest of the world—at least, of the known world—seemed within reach.[18]

In any event, why post-Muhammad thinkers opted for a full-throated version of jihad is only part of the puzzle. Another part is how they justified it. As we've just seen, even the more belligerent parts of the Koran, found among the Medinan suras, don't form a solid basis for such a doctrine.[19] And many verses seem to contradict a full-throated version of jihad—most of them Meccan ("To you be your religion; to me my religion") but some of them Medinan ("Let there be no compulsion in religion").[20]

The Invention of Jihad

So how did the creators of the doctrine of jihad do it? If the Koran is indeed God's word, and doesn't itself articulate any such doctrine, how did later Muslim thinkers manage to sell the idea that jihad had God's blessing? Largely through two intellectual maneuvers.

First was a crucial decision by Islamic jurists about how to resolve internal contradictions in the Koran. They decided that the more recently Muhammad had uttered a Koranic verse, the more likely it was to reflect the enduring will of God.[21] This skewed interpretation toward belligerence, since the earlier suras, revealed in Mecca, tended to be more tolerant.

Second, the architects of the jihad doctrine didn't confine themselves to the Koran. They drew on the hadith, the oral tradition of Muhammad's sayings. And here they had a smorgasbord to choose from, because there was no shortage of claims about things Muhammad had supposedly said.

For example, if you asked Muhammad to start listing Islam's basic values, what would he say? Option A, from a part of the hadith relayed by a man named Abdullah ibn 'Amr: "A person asked God's Apostle, 'What (sort of) deeds in or (what qualities of) Islam are good?' He replied, 'To feed (the poor) and greet those whom you know and those whom you don't know.'" Option B, from a part of the hadith that comes from a man named Abu Hurayra: "Allah's Apostle was asked, 'What is the best deed?' He replied, 'To believe in God and His Apostle (Muhammad).' The questioner then asked, 'What is the next (in goodness)?' He replied, 'To participate in jihad in God's Cause.'"[22]

For the aspiring jihadist, B is the preferred choice.

Of course, it's possible that Muhammad, in two different moods, said these two different things in response to essentially the same question. But there's no reason to think so. The hadith spent much more time in sheerly oral transmission before being written down than the Koran did.[23] This long phase of fluidity was open season for people who wanted to give their pet causes the Prophet's validation. This doesn't mean they were consciously dishonest. It just means that memory is a funny thing—as is the process by which people decide whose memories have the ring of truth.

Here, for example, is a jihadist utterance attributed to Muhammad that may not have been written down until more than a century after he died: "I was ordered to fight all men until they say 'There is no god but Allah.'"[24] If God indeed gave this order to Muhammad, that would pretty much settle the question of whether jihad is a divine doctrine, because the injunction to fight "all men" is plainly universal. But it's curious that Muhammad would say God ordered him to do this when the Koran itself—the real-time record of things God ordered Muhammad to say and do—has no trace of any such order. It is, after all, a pretty important order.

The Koranless Jihad

It's in one sense surprising that jihad, a doctrine taken seriously by Muslim thinkers over the years, has no solid grounding in what they consider the most reliable record of Muhammad's, and God's, utterances. In another sense, it's par for the course. The consistent moral of the story of the Abrahamic religions is that any given book of scripture can be put to a wide variety of uses.

But if the bad news is how malleable scripture is, that's also the good news. Yes, when you see your interests opposed to those of another group, you can find scriptural validation of animosity. But when your interests seem to lie in cooperation with another group, you may find your God counseling restraint.

This second edge of the sword was illustrated by Muhammad's successors as the Islamic Empire grew and some of its borders stabilized. By the early 800s, only a few decades after Muslim thinkers had divided the world between a "House of Islam" and a "House of War," a seminal Islamic jurist had declared that there was actually a third house: the "House of Truce or Treaty."[25] And by the late 800s, another Islamic thinker had labeled war in the name of Islam the "lesser jihad" and said, "the greater jihad is the struggle against the self."[26] As we've seen, this idea of two kinds of jihad is consistent with the different uses of the term in the Koran. But on what basis would anyone say which was greater and which was lesser? The hadith to the rescue! By one account, Muhammad had himself told Muslims returning from war, "You have returned from the lesser jihad to the greater jihad." This account was late to surface, but better late than never.

An especially important doctrine was *fard kifaya*—the idea

that jihad, though a duty, was a communal duty, not an individual duty.[27] So if war seemed inappropriate in your part of the empire, you could live a peaceful yet devout life, secure in the knowledge that somewhere, some Muslim was fighting on behalf of Islam.

But all such moderating influences were hostages to fortune. They might dominate when cooperation with neighbors, or at least peaceful coexistence, seemed auspicious, but things could always change. When Muslims were being attacked, the definition of jihad changed from *fard kifaya* to *fard aynl*—a duty incumbent on each Muslim. When Christian crusaders reached Syria, for example, a treatise published in Damascus announced the shift to *fard aynl.*[28] As ever, swings between the non-zero-sum and the zero-sum could change the mood of a religion.

The Price of Tolerance

The malleability of the doctrine of jihad was as evident within Islam's borders as along them. Though making all the world the "House of Islam" would seem to imply turning everyone you subjugate into a Muslim, that goal, if it was ever part of jihad, didn't stay that way for long. The more unbelievers you subjugate, the clearer it becomes that their ongoing antagonism won't be an asset, and the less attractive is the prospect of incurring their wrath by coercing them into conversion. Once you've got an empire to run, the less friction within it, the better.

Here again, useful guidance could be found in scripture so long as you looked hard enough. The Koranic verse that comes closest to calling for jihad on a global scale also has a crucial loophole. It begins, "Make war upon such of those to whom the Scriptures have been given as believe not in God, or in the last day, and who forbid not that which God and His Apostle have forbidden," but then ends, "until they pay tribute out of hand, and they be humbled."[29] In the end, money would substitute for theological fidelity.

There was nothing new about this. Ancient empires expanded as far as was feasible and demanded tribute of their vassal states.

That, after all, was half the point of being an empire. The Roman Empire had done it, and so had the two empires that Islam was now taking land from—the Persian Empire and the eastern heir of the Roman Empire, the Byzantine Empire. So subjects of the emerging Islamic Empire shouldn't have found the taxes imposed on them disorienting.

In fact, some Christians preferred the new Muslim overlords to the old Christian ones. The Byzantine Empire had fought heretical Christian sects, whereas to the Muslims, a Christian was a Christian; so long as they paid their taxes, heretics could worship as they wished. It was win-win: formerly suppressed Christians got their freedom for a price they considered a bargain, and Muslim rulers got peace within their empire and, to boot, a steady source of revenue. In fact, around 700, Muslim rulers *banned* conversion to Islam lest revenue fall.[30]

It was a deft maneuver that Muhammad's successors pulled off: declare war on a people because of their religion and then, shortly after the conquest, feel tolerance welling up. Fortunately, Islamic rulers had the ambiguity of the Koran to back them up. They cited the Koranic injunction against "compulsion in religion"—a passage that, perhaps, had receded to the margins of their awareness during the conquest itself, back when more pungent verses sprang to mind.[31]

And then there was the ever flexible hadith. When ruling over unbelievers, Muslims recalled that Muhammad had said, "If they convert to Islam it is well; if not, they remain (in their previous religion); indeed Islam is wide."[32] This from the same man who supposedly had said, "I was ordered to fight all men until they say 'There is no god but God.'"

Sometimes there was no contradiction between these statements. Subjects who were Jewish did, in fact, believe that there was no god but God even though they hadn't converted to Islam. So too with Christians (even if their monotheism was a bit suspect in light of Jesus's divinity). Conquest of the largely Christian lands of Syria and Egypt, then, entailed little doctrinal amendment. "People of the Book," it was said, were allowed to keep their religion.

But what about the conquest of Persian lands? Here tolerance of the native faith, Zoroastrianism, took creativity. After all, Zoroastrians didn't have scriptures devoted to the Abrahamic god—and so weren't in any clear sense "People of the Book." But, hey, the Zoroastrians did have a book of scripture—the Avesta—so they were in *some* sense People of the Book, or at least, People of *a* Book. Conclusion: they could be tolerated, too![33] And later, as Muslim conquests spread deep into Asia, it turned out that there was a way to extend this basic idea—taxes in exchange for toleration—to Buddhists and Hindus.[34] And Muslim rulers in Africa decided that there, too, polytheists could be tolerated.

In the end, the basic modus operandi of the Islamic Empire was the basic m.o. for ancient empires: conquer and then tax. And an easily collected tax requires empire-wide pax, whether it be Pax Romana or Pax Islamica.

Over the centuries, Islamic tolerance of Christians and Jews (like Christian tolerance of Muslims and Jews) would fluctuate. As voluntary conversion to Islam set in—sometimes with the goal of escaping the tax, sometimes with the goal of easing career advancement—the population of Christians dwindled to a point where Muslims found it less crucial to stay on good terms with them. This change in attitude presumably heightened the incentive to convert to Islam. Jews, more averse to conversion, stayed intact and sometimes faced persecution. But on balance, as the scholar Claude Cahen has observed, Islam showed more tolerance toward Jews over the centuries than did Christian Europe.[35]

Meanwhile, the reinterpretation of jihad went on and on, swinging between truculence and reserve as circumstances warranted. By the early twentieth century, many mainstream Muslim thinkers had stripped the doctrine of its offensive connotations: Islamic "holy war" was justified only in self-defense.[36] This convergence with western views on just war is, of course, what led Sayyid Qutb to complain in the mid-twentieth century about "the sorry state of the present Muslim generation." Qutb's complaint foreshadowed a resurgence of militant interpretations of jihad. And here we are.

Muhammad and bin Laden

Now back to our earlier questions: Is the doctrine of jihad rooted firmly in the Koran? Would Muhammad approve of what the jihadists are doing? Would the God of the Koran approve?

The answer to the second question is "almost certainly not." There is no hint anywhere—not in the Koran, not in the hadith—that Muhammad would countenance the killing of women or children, a favorite practice of modern-day jihadists.

The answer to the first question—and to the third—is also negative. The *doctrine* of jihad, the doctrine that modern-day jihadists cite, came into being after Muhammad's death, and the Koran provides no firm foundation for it. Indeed, that the authors of the doctrine relied so heavily on sayings attributed to the Prophet—and that these attributions often showed up a suspiciously long time after he lived—is itself testament to how hard it would be to ground jihad in the Koran.

But there's a larger question: Does the doctrine of jihad really matter much anyway? Though Osama bin Laden was an indirect heir of Sayyid Qutb, and though bin Laden emphasizes the "Sword verse," which when read in isolation seems to justify offensive jihad, he doesn't, in the end, deploy that doctrine. Bin Laden's exhortations to fight America, as in his 1996 manifesto, involve a ritual recitation of America's crimes against Islam; there is always some provocation other than merely being unbelievers.[37] He always manages to cast the jihad in question as in some sense an act of defense.

And so it goes. When people feel like fighting, they are pretty good at coming up with reasons why the fighting is justified—reasons why God is on their side. A doctrine of offensive jihad might in theory save a person the time of formulating specific provocations, but in fact that time is going to be spent anyway. Human psychology is such that it's vanishingly rare for attack to precede grievance, regardless of how much creativity the grievance's creation requires.

None of this is to say that scripture doesn't matter. If you are recruiting suicide bombers, it matters that the Koran says martyrs who die in holy war go to heaven, and that it paints heavenly delights with such brio. (And it mattered that Christian soldiers of the Crusades could imagine heavenly streets paved with gold as they marched to war.)

Other parts of the Koran matter, too. Presumably if you spend much time reciting verses that embrace the torment of your enemies, you are more likely to embrace their torment, and perhaps even do the tormenting yourself. And certainly the Koran features many such verses.

To be sure, in the Koran as a whole, the "jihad verses" are a small fraction of the verses that embrace the torment of Islam's enemies. Most of those verses aren't about Muslims punishing infidels in the here and now, but rather about God punishing infidels in the afterlife.

Still, is it possible that these visions of divine retribution in the afterlife wind up encouraging human retribution in the real world? Are madrassahs in which young men chant the Koran, and indeed memorize the whole book, inciting violence out of proportion to the belligerence encouraged in the book itself? Yes, that's possible. (So we can be thankful that many of these young men in places like Pakistan and Afghanistan don't speak Arabic and so don't understand verses they're memorizing phonetically.)

Scripture matters enough that, if we could magically replace the Koran with a book of our choosing, or could magically replace the Bible with a book of our choosing, we could probably make Muslims, Jews, and Christians better people. But we don't have that option. So we're lucky that scripture isn't as important in shaping behavior as the circumstances on the ground, circumstances that shape the interpretation of scripture. Circumstances can be stubborn, but at least they're not fixed in print.

———————————

Chapter Eighteen

Muhammad

Who was Muhammad? It depends on when you look at him. We've already seen his resemblance, at various times in his career, to earlier figures in the Abrahamic tradition, notably Moses and Jesus. There are other biblical characters we could add to the list. Indeed, it's possible to depict Muhammad's whole career as a kind of rotation among Abrahamic predecessors.

It was in Mecca that Muhammad had much in common with Jesus. He led a small band of devotees, warning that Judgment Day was coming. The message fell on deaf ears, after which he started to sound a bit like Second Isaiah. Second Isaiah, while enduring the humiliation of exile, had dreamed of a day when the nations that had oppressed his people would bow to a restored Israel and to its God. Now Muhammad envisioned his present persecutors getting their comeuppance as his faith in the one true god was grandly vindicated. In glorious detail, he imagined Judgment Day, again and again.

Next he spent some time as a kind of Moses, leading his harassed followers toward the promised land, the town of Medina. In Medina he came to resemble the apostle Paul. Paul had tried to convince extant Abrahamics—the Jews—that his brand of the Abrahamic faith was essentially the same as theirs, even if it had a few new twists. Muhammad made much the same case to the Abrahamics of his day, a group that, thanks to Paul's only mixed success, now included both Jews and Christians. Muhammad had little if any more success than Paul; most of his followers, it would seem, came from the ranks of pagans.

But there is a big difference between Muhammad and Paul. Paul was working wholly outside formal political power, and had no real choice about that. His fledgling church had to settle for being a non-governmental organization. Muhammad, in contrast, could aspire to run a municipal government, and he succeeded, securing control of Medina.

Now the Pauline side of Muhammad fell away, and he started to resemble King Josiah, the man who put the ancient Israelites on the path toward monotheism in the course of gathering power. For Muhammad, as for Josiah, the exclusive devotion to God that he demanded was intertwined with—was almost identical with—the political obedience he sought. And, like Josiah, Muhammad wanted to expand the scope of obedience, via conquest if necessary.

So that's Muhammad: a one-man recapitulation of some great moments in Abrahamic history, not exactly in chronological order. If a primary thesis of this book is correct—if the tone of scripture is set by the circumstance of its creation—then you would expect Muhammad's checkered past to leave a scriptural legacy that defies easy generalization. If the last several chapters show nothing else, they show that.

But generalize we must. The parallels between Muhammad's circumstances and circumstances of biblical authorship raise a question that people tend to raise anyway: How does the tenor of Islamic scripture compare with the tenor of Jewish and Christian scripture? Actually, that's the polite way of putting it. What many of these people want to know is: Which scripture is, you know, best? Which is on the highest moral plane? That this is a question we can't easily answer doesn't mean it's a question we shouldn't tackle. Religions aren't reducible to a checklist of moral qualities, but comparing them across such a checklist has its illuminating aspects.

Brotherly Love, and Hate

The Koran lauds those who "master their anger, and forgive others! God loveth the doers of good." Such values had been in the Abrahamic tradition since the Hebrew Bible was written. In fact, such values are a feature of pretty much all traditions. Tensions between people must be subdued for any society, or any religion, to cohere, and the punishment for lack of coherence is often extinction. (If the people themselves don't perish, the culture may.) After all, there is often a competing group poised to profit from disarray. The Koran is fairly explicit about the logic: "The infidels lend one another mutual help. Unless ye do the same, there will be discord in the land and great corruption."[1]

This ultimately pragmatic nature of intrasocial bonding can drain seemingly high-minded scriptures of their idealism. As we've seen, scholars doubt that the Hebrew Bible's "Love thy neighbor as thyself" was meant to extend beyond the borders of ancient Israel. Some of the Koran's odes to brotherly love are sufficiently candid to need no such scholarly deflating. "Only the faithful are brethren," says one sura attributed to the late Medinan period. Another from the same period says that Muhammad's comrades are "vehement against the infidels but full of tenderness among themselves."[2]

This is a long way from the "Love your enemies" passage attributed to Jesus. Then again, as we've seen, Jesus probably never said this anyway. And the person who probably did inject the idea into the Christian scripture—Paul—was a mere proselytizer who couldn't afford to antagonize his movement's powerful enemies. He was, in short, like the Muhammad of the early Medinan years, or the Muhammad of Mecca, the Muhammad who said to "turn away evil by what is better" and to greet antagonists by saying, "Peace."[3]

A Jewish analogue of Paul, and of the Meccan Muhammad, was Philo of Alexandria. Seeing that an interfaith war would doom Jews in the Roman Empire, Philo found messages of tolerance in his scripture and creatively downplayed parts of Deuteronomy in which God tells the Israelites to slaughter infidels.

Those verses are associated with King Josiah. Not coincidentally, Josiah's circumstances match the circumstances of Muhammad when Muhammad was producing his most belligerent sayings. Both men were political rulers who wanted to expand their turf. Their moral compasses made the necessary adjustments.

To be sure, Josiah's moral compass seems to have been more thoroughly skewed by his ambitions than Muhammad's. The prescription in Deuteronomy for neighboring infidel cities is all-out genocide—kill all men, women, and children, not to mention livestock. There is nothing in the Koran that compares with this, arguably the moral low point of the entire body of Abrahamic scripture.

Still, if Muhammad never countenanced the killing of women or children, he did countenance a lot of killing. At least, he expressed approval of it quite a few times. In sheer numbers, such expressions in the Koran may not exceed those in the Bible. (Deuteronomy alone celebrates the utter "destruction" and "dispossession" of infidel cities again and again, and the book of Joshua also takes a festive attitude toward urban mayhem.) But the Koran is a shorter book than the Bible; pound for pound, it no doubt features more exhortations to violence.

So if you ask which book is "worse" in terms of belligerence, you might say that *qualitatively* the Hebrew Bible (and hence the Christian Bible) takes the trophy—thanks to that unrivaled embrace of genocide in Deuteronomy—but that *quantitatively* the winner is the Koran, at least in terms of the frequency of belligerent passages, if not in absolute numbers. And if, on top of the verses espousing violence in the terrestrial world, you add verses gleefully envisioning the suffering of infidels in the afterlife, the Koran wins the quantitative competition more decisively. (As we've seen, the Christian notion of hell, a notion Muhammad inherited, hadn't fully crystallized by the time the gospels were written.)

Salvation

Both the Koran and the Bible have their saving graces. In their warmer moments, they envision the salvation of neighboring peoples—indeed, the salvation of the whole world.

To be sure, salvation is sometimes a polite term for what they have in mind. As we've seen, Second Isaiah imagined salvation coming to the nations in the form of abject submission to Yahweh and Israel, a submission prefaced by violent retribution for past offenses. Similarly, when Muhammad is in Second Isaiah mode — a powerless, humiliated prophet in Mecca — the global salvation he imagines carries a punitive edge. Someday, God will "raise up a witness out of every nation: then shall the infidels have no permission to make excuses, and they shall find no favor."[4] A sense of persecution can take some of the charity out of Christian salvation, too. We're seen that the book of Revelation, written amid Roman oppression, envisions an apocalypse in which the savior carries "a sharp sword with which to strike down the nations, and he will rule them with a rod of iron."[5]

There are sunnier versions of salvation. According to Second Isaiah, Israel will be a "light unto the nations." Jesus's disciples will go teach the "good news" to all peoples. And Muhammad's conception of paradise is definitely good news.

If, that is, you qualify for admission. But more people qualify than you might imagine. The Koran says more than once that not just Muslims but Jews and Christians are eligible for salvation so long as they believe in God and in Judgment Day and live a life worthy of favorable judgment.[6]

This inclusiveness may reflect Muhammad's frustration at the Jewish and Christian claims to exclusive possession of salvific truth. He marveled: "The Jews assert, 'The Christians have no valid ground for their beliefs,' while the Christians assert, 'The Jews have no valid ground for their beliefs' — and both quote the divine writ!" He reminded them that they "are but a part of the men whom He hath created! He will pardon whom He pleaseth, and chastise whom He pleaseth."[7]

Muhammad doesn't go so far as to embrace *universal* salvation. To be saved you do have to accept that the Abrahamic god is the one and only God. Still, in deeming all Abrahamics eligible for salvation he is opening the gates to salvation wider than Christians were opening them. And at one point he seems to open them wider still; he lists Zoroastrians along with Christians, Jews, and Muslims, and says that God — who "guideth whom He pleaseth" — will be their judge on the day of resurrection.[8]

There is a funny thing about this Koranic mention of the Zoroastrians: it's the only one. By and large the Koran offers no evidence that Muhammad had contact with Zoroastrians—except for this one verse in which they appear out of nowhere and are suddenly deemed eligible for paradise. It's enough to make you wonder whether this verse wasn't added, or at least amended, after Muhammad's death, when the conquest of Persian lands brought many Zoroastrians under Islamic governance.[2] As we've seen, this conquest inspired a doctrinal amendment under which Zoroastrians were lumped in with "People of the Book"—a designation that made it easier for them to be amiable imperial subjects and ample sources of tax revenue.

There's another reason to suspect that this verse is a product of the post-Muhammad era. It grants salvation not only to Zoroastrians, but to "Sabeans." To judge by the beliefs of their modern day heirs (sometimes called Mandeans), the Sabeans, like the Zoroastrians, would have been hard to fit into the Abrahamic fold; they revered John the Baptist but considered Jesus, Abraham, and Moses false prophets. And (again, to judge by their modern heirs), they would have had another thing in common with Zoroastrians: their residential epicenter was to the east of Muhammad's turf, in modern-day Iraq and Iran, lands conquered not by Muhammad but by his successors.[10]

Whether the verse is from Muhammad's time or after it, it seems to represent the peak of a growing salvific inclusiveness. There are many verses in the Koran suggesting that Jews and Christians are eligible for salvation. Three of those verses add Sabeans to the list, and, of the three, this one verse adds Zoroastrians as well. (And actually, this verse can be read—fairly straightforwardly, even—as including polytheists in the pool of eligibility, but some scholars dispute this interpretation.)[11]

It's possible that all three verses carrying salvation beyond the Abrahamic compass were indeed uttered by Muhammad. Maybe near the end of his career he found small pockets of Sabeans and Zoroastrians within the ambit of his conquest, or maybe he found himself in alliance with towns populated by these non-Abrahamics. But, regardless of whether these verses come from Muhammad's time or later, the best explanation for them is an expanded scope of non-zero-sumness. Whether by allying with non-Abrahamics or governing them, Islamic leadership seems to have acquired an incentive to stay on cooperative terms with them.

This is reminiscent of the growing inclusiveness we saw in the Hebrew Bible. Before the exile, Israel had frequently been on antagonistic terms with neighbors, as reflected in both exilic and pre-exilic scriptures. Around the end of exile, with Israel now part of the Persian Empire, the "Priestly source," apparently speaking in harmony with Persian leadership, struck a more accommodating tone. In Hebrew scripture as in Islamic scripture, imperial conquest had eventually translated into tolerance—at least within the empire.

The same is true, in a sense, of Christianity. In the Roman Empire Christian salvation was conceived more narrowly than Islamic salvation was described in those several Koranic verses; it wasn't generally granted to those outside the faith.[12] Still, at its birth Christianity had been innovatively inclusive in carrying the Abrahamic scriptures beyond ethnic bounds. And the reason for this openness was that the founders of Christianity were operating within a multiethnic empire. Trying to build a big religious organization put them in a non-zero-sum relationship with potential recruits, and potential recruits were an ethnic smorgasbord.

Time and again, empire has brought once antagonistic ethnicities into peaceful coexistence, and time and again religion has reached out to further that cause. This is cause for hope, since, as we've noted, the multinational milieu of a new empire is the closest ancient analogue of globalization. To be sure, the inchoate global platform of today lacks something ancient empires had—unified leadership. And to be sure, globalization so far has done as much to divide Abrahamic religions as to unite them. Still, the ancient imperial experience shows that if these religions never manage to see eye to eye, it won't be because they lack adaptive capacity.

The inclusive spirit of empire is captured in a sura typically dated to the late Medina period—and, for all we know, in fact dating from later—when God tells humankind that he has "made you into nations and tribes, so that you might come to know one another." [13] Compare this to the Bible's story of the Tower of Babel, written well before the exile. Here God's plan is for the world's nations to always have trouble getting to know one another.

Of course, if the *existence* of empire conduces to harmony, the *expansion* of empire—the process of actually conquering new lands—heightens intolerance of nearby faiths and peoples. This, as we've seen, explains the pliability of the jihad doctrine: amid expansion its intolerant edge took the lead, but when the time came to govern conquered lands, its soft side surfaced.

This also explains why the New Testament has fewer belligerent verses than either the Koran or the Hebrew Bible. During the formative years of Christian scripture, Christianity wasn't the official religion of an expanding power. Doctrines of holy war would surface when needed—as during the Crusades—but the gospels and epistles took shape too early to reflect them.

We could go on all day trying to decide which of the Abrahamic religions is "best" or "worst." But we'd find no uncontested winner. What we'd find is that all three fluctuate between best and worst according to the same dynamic: scripture ranges from tolerant to belligerent, and the reason lies in the facts on the ground, in the perceived non-zero-sumness, or lack thereof, among human beings.

And Muhammad, more than any other figure in the Abrahamic tradition, embodies this dynamic, illustrates it across its entire range. At times he is the belligerent Josiah, at times the embittered Second Isaiah, at times the defensively inclusive Philo or Paul, at times the confidently inclusive Priestly source—or the confidently inclusive Jesus of the gospels (even if the historical Jesus was more like an earlier Muhammad, the inspired but ignored prophet of Mecca). This one man embodies the moral history of the Abrahamic faith, with all its twists and turns. This isn't always something to be proud of, but it's quite a feat. It's also illustration of what gives that history its structure: the exquisite responsiveness of human moral equipment to facts on the ground.

The Modernity of Muhammad

Of course, the moral dimension isn't the only dimension along which religions are compared. A common complaint about the Koran is that it lacks the sweep and depth of the Holy Bible. There isn't, for example, the sometimes profound reflection on human existence found in Proverbs, Job, and other examples of the "wisdom literature." There aren't the arcane philosophical allusions — notably John's riffing on the Logos — found in the New Testament.

Then again, the Hebrew Bible and the New Testament are repositories of an intellectual heritage that went well beyond the Hebrew and Christian worlds. Composed by legions of urban elites, they captured ideas of great civilizations, from Mesopotamia to Egypt to Christianity's Hellenistic milieu. The Koran took shape in two desert towns on the margin of empires, uttered by a man who was more a doer than a thinker and was probably illiterate.

It's ironic, then, that in important senses the Koran was a more modern work than the Bible, and Muhammad a more modern figure than Moses or Jesus.

For one thing, Muhammad, in contrast to the key figures in the Hebrew Bible and the New Testament, has no special powers. He can't turn a rod into a snake or water into wine. Yes, later Muslims would depict him as a miracle worker, and they would claim that an opaque Koranic verse or two (most famously one about "splitting the moon") demonstrates such powers. But the Koranic Muhammad, unlike the biblical Jesus and Moses, doesn't depend on miracle-working for proof of proximity to God.

The contrast is especially clear when both Muhammad and Jesus face skeptics who ask: if you really have a special link to God, prove it by producing wondrous "signs." Muhammad doesn't respond by trying to do anything supernatural.[14] He doesn't raise people from the dead or feed a big crowd on a tight budget. Of course, the historical Jesus—as opposed to the biblical Jesus—probably didn't do those things, either. But Jesus may well have engaged in faith healing and exorcism; certainly these would have been normal for a wandering Palestinian preacher circa 30 CE. In any event, the historical Jesus probably *was* asked to show signs. And even when, in the earliest gospel, we see him fail to deliver, his explanation rests on the premise that he *could* produce signs if his audience deserved them. ("Truly I tell you, no sign will be given to this generation.")[15]

Here lies the second sense in which the Koran is paradoxically modern—in its style of theological argumentation. The style is set by the way Muhammad handles the challenge to show "signs." He defines the word "signs" in a way that gives him an empirical riposte, shifting attention from supernatural wonders to the wonders of nature.[16] If you want signs of God's greatness, he says, just examine the everyday evidence. Look at the world. Note how it seems to have been built for the benefit of humans. Doesn't a god who would create such a world deserve devotion?

God "hath sent down rain from Heaven, and by it we bring forth the kinds of various herbs: 'Eat ye, and feed your cattle.' Of a truth in this are signs unto men endued with understanding." And: "Among fruits ye have the palm and the vine, from which ye get wine and healthful nutriment: in this, verily, are signs for those who reflect." And, of course, the ecosystem includes the human species itself: "And one of His signs it is, that He hath created wives for you of your own species, that ye may dwell with them, and hath put love and tenderness between you. Herein truly are signs for those who reflect." And consider the splendor of the whole human species: "Among His signs are . . . your variety of tongues and colour. Herein truly are signs for all men."[17]

This amassing of evidence of God's goodness and grandeur makes the Koran come much closer than the Bible to fitting the description Darwin gave to his book *The Origin of Species:* "one long argument." That's not the only thing the two books have in common. Both arguments purport to explain the exquisitely fine fit between humans and their natural surroundings. Muhammad notes how conducive the ecosystem is to human flourishing and explains it via God's design of the ecosystem. Darwin notes the same close match between humans and their ecosystem and posits a different explanation: humans were shaped to fit their ecosystem—not the other way around.

The "signs" Muhammad saw weren't confined to the organic. Note how nicely God had adapted the inanimate world to human needs: "He causeth the dawn to appear, and hath ordained the night for rest, and the sun and the moon for computing time! The ordinance of the Mighty, the Wise! And it is He who hath ordained the stars for you that ye may be guided thereby in the darknesses of the land and of the sea! Clear have we made our signs to men of knowledge."[18]

Here again, a modern thinker would invoke evolution: both the biological evolution that adapted our sleep patterns to cycles of the sun, and the cultural evolution by which humans came to quantify time with sundials and calendars, turning the sun and moon into tools for "computing time." Muhammad, in contrast, sees God as the ultimate explanation of all such synchronous goodness, and the Koran dwells on this goodness at length. The Koran is in no small part a book about gratitude: look around you; count your blessings. The pre-Islamic meaning of one of several Arabic words that the Koran uses to denote "unbelievers" seems to have been "those who are ungrateful."[19]

In defining a blessing, Muhammad could be creative. Thunder and lightning are scary, and sometimes lightning is fatal. But are these really bad things? Thunder brings "awe of Him." Lightning brings "fear and hope," and has the added virtue of occasionally eliminating people who spend too much time arguing about theology and not enough time buying into it: "He sendeth His bolts and smiteth with them whom He will while they are wrangling about God!"[20]

From a modern vantage point, it is natural to read Muhammad's litany of "signs" and think that the "argument" he's making is for the existence of God. It's not. The *existence* of God wasn't something he needed to argue for. His skeptics came in several varieties, but atheists weren't among them. Indeed, his skeptics accepted not just the existence of one or more gods, but the existence of Allah, who had earned his way into the pantheon of Meccan polytheists. Further, Meccans seem to have agreed that Allah was a creator god. The question was how much of a worshipper's devotion should go to that creator god. If Muhammad could argue that the creation—Allah's handiwork—showed Allah to be a god of tremendous power and goodness, then the answer would be: a whole lot of the devotion, like all of it. Allah was God.

The modern world is said to suffer from "disenchantment." As science explains more of the workings of nature, there seems less mystery, and so less room for a god that accounts for the otherwise mysterious. But in Muhammad's scheme, nature's obedience to laws is tribute to the god who designed them so adeptly that he could then remove himself from the the day-to-day drudgery of running a universe: "It is God who hath reared the Heavens without pillars thou canst behold; then mounted His throne, and imposed laws on the sun and moon: each travelleth to its appointed goal. He ordereth all things. He maketh His signs clear." And: "He created the sun and the moon and the stars, subjected to laws by His behest: Is not all creation and its empire His?" And if nature exactingly complies with God's laws, what is the point of worshipping nature deities? "Bend not in adoration to the sun or the moon, but bend in adoration before God who created them both."[21]

All told, it sounds like an effective rhetorical strategy: Take something Meccans already agree on—Allah is the creator god—and leverage this consensus logically, leading people to conclude that Muhammad's entire theology is on target.

That Was Then . . .

Today, of course, it doesn't work that easily. Today the argument isn't over *which* gods exist but over whether any god exists; or even whether anything you could call a higher purpose exists. Still, if Muhammad's argument doesn't work today, the *kind* of argument he made is, more than ever, the kind of argument that has to be made if people are to be persuaded: an argument that evidence of divine purpose—the signs—are embedded in the natural world; an empirical argument.

The conventional wisdom is that such arguments are either intrinsically illegitimate or unfailingly ineffectual. In fact, there's a standard historical anecdote that is trotted out to show how hopeless they are. The funny thing is that this anecdote, when closely examined, shows something quite different.

The anecdote is the story of the "blind watchmaker." It involves William Paley, a British theologian who wrote a book called *Natural Theology* in 1802, a few years before Darwin was born. In it he tried to use living creatures as evidence for the existence of a designer. If you're walking across a field and you find a pocket watch, Paley said, you know immediately that it's in a different category from the rocks lying around it. Unlike them, it is manifestly a product of design, featuring a complex functionality that doesn't just happen by accident. Well, he continued, organisms are like pocket watches: they're too complexly functional to just happen by accident. So organisms must have a designer—namely, God.

Thanks to Darwin, we now know that Paley was wrong. We can explain the complex functionality of organisms without positing a god. The explanation is natural selection.

Darwinians who are atheists have been known to celebrate the failure of Paley's explanation. They love to note how futile this attempt to empirically argue for the existence of God turned out to be. What they tend not to emphasize is that Paley was half right. The complex functionality of an organism *does* demand a special kind of explanation. It seems pretty clear that hearts are in some sense here *in order to* pump blood, that digestive systems are here *in order to* digest food, that brains are here *in order to* (among other things) help organisms find food to digest. Rocks, in contrast, don't seem to be here in order to do anything. The kinds of forces that created a rock just don't seem likely to be the kinds of forces that would create an organism. It takes a special kind of force to do that—a force like natural selection.

Indeed, so special is natural selection that lots of biologists are willing to talk about it *designing* organisms. (Or, actually, *"designing"* organisms; they tend to put the word in quotes, lest you think they mean a conscious, foresightful designer.) Even the famously atheist Darwinian philosopher Daniel Dennett uses that kind of terminology; he says this process of "design" imbues organisms with "goals" and "purposes." For example: organisms are "designed" ultimately to maximize genetic proliferation, and are thus "designed" to pursue goals subordinate to that ultimate goal, such as finding mates, ingesting nutrients, and pumping blood.

The take-home lesson is simple. It is indeed legitimate to do what Paley did: inspect a physical system for evidence that it was imbued with goals, with purpose, by some higher-order creative process. If the evidence strongly suggests such a thing, that doesn't mean the imbuer was a designer in the sense of a conscious being; in the case Paley focused on, it turned out not to be. Still, the point is that you can look at a system and argue empirically about whether it has, in *some* sense, a "higher" purpose. There are hallmarks of purpose, and some physical systems have them.

Well, the entire process of life on Earth, the entire evolving ecosystem—from the birth of bacteria through the advent of human beings through the advent of cultural evolution, through the human history driven by that evolution—is a physical system. So in principle we could ask the same question about it that we asked about organisms; it could turn out that there is strong evidence of imbued purpose, as Paley and Dennett agree there is in organisms. In other words, maybe natural selection is an algorithm that is in some sense *designed* to get life to a point where it can *do something*—fulfill its goal, its purpose.

And, actually, when you think about it, some of the evidence you might point to as the hallmark of purpose in organisms has analogues in the evolving ecosystem.

Here is some of the evidence in the case of the organism. A single fertilized egg cell replicates itself, and the offspring cells in turn replicate themselves, and so on. Eventually the resulting lineages of cells start evincing distinctive specialties; there are muscle cells that beget muscle cells, brain cells that beget brain cells. If Paley were around today to watch videos of this process, he would say, Wow!—look at how exquisitely directional this process is; the system grows in size and in functional differentiation until it becomes this large, complex, functionally integrated system: muscles, brains, lungs, and so on; this directional movement toward complex functional integration is evidence of design![22] And, in some sense of the word "design," he would be right.

Now here is a somewhat parallel description of the history of the ecosystem on this planet. First, a few billion years ago, a single primitive cell divides. The resulting offspring cells in turn replicate themselves, and eventually different lineages of cells (that is, different species) emerge. Some of these lineages eventually become multicellular (jellyfish, birds) and evince distinctive specialties (floating, flying). One lineage—let's call it *Homo sapiens*—is particularly good at thinking. It launches a whole new process of evolution, called cultural evolution, that spawns wheels and legal codes and microchips and so on. Humans use the fruits of cultural evolution to organize themselves on a larger and larger scale. As this social organization reaches the global level and features a richer and richer division of economic labor, the whole thing starts to resemble a giant organism. There's even a kind of planetary nervous system, made of fiber optics and other stuff, connecting the various human brains into big megabrains that try to solve problems. (And some of the problems are global—how to head off global warming and global epidemics, for example.)

Meanwhile, as the human species is becoming a global brain, gradually assuming conscious stewardship of the planet, other species—also descended from that single primitive cell that lived billions of years ago—perform other planetary functions. Trees are lungs, for example, generating oxygen.

In other words, if you watched evolution on this planet unfold from a distance (and on fast-forward), you would find it strikingly like watching the maturation of an organism: there would be directional movement toward functional integration. So why can't the part of Paley's argument that can be *validly* applied to an organism's maturation — the idea that it suggests a designer of *some* sort — be applied to the whole system of life on Earth?

This is just a question, not a rigorous argument. To argue seriously that the system of life on Earth, the evolving ecosystem, is a product of design, or at least "design," and thus in some sense imbued with higher purpose, or at least "higher" purpose, would take a whole book. This is not that book.

And even if you had successfully made that book-length argument, questions would remain. Was the purpose imbued by some conscious being or just by some unconscious process? And, in either event, is the purpose in some sense good? Good enough, at least, so that even if you couldn't specify the exact nature of the designer, you would be tempted to characterize the purpose itself as, perhaps, *divine?*

This question, too, could encompass an entire book — and this book isn't that book, either. Still, this book has shed light on a question that would certainly arise in the course of that book: Does human history by its nature move toward something you could call morally good?

That's a question we'll treat more fully in the next chapter. But you can no doubt guess some of the territory we'll cross in treating it. It will have something to do with the forces conducive to amity and tolerance as opposed to the forces conducive to belligerence and intolerance. It will have to do with the effect of changing circumstance on human moral consciousness.

As we've seen, those forces are evident in all the Abrahamic scriptures if you look closely enough. But in no other Abrahamic scripture are they as evident as in the Koran. No other scripture so deeply cuts across the full spectrum of dynamics, from intensely zero-sum to intensely non-zero-sum, or so sharply expresses the attendant moral tenor. In no other scripture do you so quickly move from "To you be your religion; to me my religion" to "Kill the polytheists wherever you find them" to "There is no compulsion in religion," and back again. All of the Abrahamic scriptures attest to the correlation between circumstance and moral consciousness, but none so richly as the Koran. In that sense, at least, the Koran is unrivaled as a revelation.

V

GOD GOES GLOBAL (OR DOESN'T)

They have neither knowledge nor understanding,
they walk around in darkness;
all the foundations of the earth are shaken.

—Psalms 82:5

Chapter Nineteen

The Moral Imagination

Things may look bad, but salvation is possible so long as you understand what it requires. This is the message of the Abrahamic prophets. Muhammad said it, Jesus said it, and both Isaiahs — among other Israelite prophets — said it.

They didn't all mean the same thing by "salvation." Muhammad was talking about the salvation of your soul in the hereafter. Both Isaiahs were talking about the salvation of the social system — Israel (or, in some passages, the whole world). As for Jesus: the Jesus Christians remember was, like Muhammad, focused on personal salvation, though the real Jesus may have been, like the Isaiahs, more concerned with social salvation.

But even religions that emphasize personal salvation are ultimately concerned with social salvation. For Muslims and Christians the path to personal salvation involves adherence to a moral code that keeps their social systems robust. As we've seen, successful religions have always tended to salvation at the social level, encouraging behaviors that bring order.

As we've also seen, pre-Abrahamic religions of the Middle East were especially explicit about this goal. Civilization was constantly threatened by the forces of chaos, and obeying the gods, or at least the good gods, was the way to keep chaos at bay.

Today the social system, an incipiently global social system, is again threatened by chaos. But now religion seems to be the problem, not the solution. Tensions among Jews, Christians, and Muslims — or at least among some Jews, Christians, and Muslims — imperil the world's order. And the tensions are heightened by the scriptures of

these religions—or at least by the scriptures as they're being interpreted by the people who are heightening the tensions. Three great
religions of salvation have helped put the world in need of salvation.

Can we now say what the Abrahamic prophets said—that,
though things look bad, salvation is possible so long as we understand what it requires? And if so, what does it require?

Conveniently, clues are provided by the three Abrahamic religions. (It's the least they can do, given their role in creating the
question.) Their scriptures are, beneath the surface, maps of the
landscape of religious tolerance and intolerance, maps that amount
to a kind of code for the salvation of the world. The core of the code
should by now be clear. When people see themselves in a zero-sum
relationship with other people—see their fortunes as inversely
correlated with the fortunes of other people, see the dynamic as
win-lose—they tend to find a scriptural basis for intolerance or belligerence (though, as we've seen, if they feel hopelessly outgunned,
sure to wind up on the losing side of any conflict, they may keep
their hostility suppressed for the time being). When they see the
relationship as non-zero-sum—see their fortunes as positively correlated, see the potential for a win-win outcome—they're more
likely to find the tolerant and understanding side of their scriptures.

So the salvation of the world would seem straightforward: heed
the lessons embedded in the Abrahamic scriptures; arrange things,
wherever possible, so that people of different Abrahamic faiths find
themselves in non-zero-sum relationships.

The good news is that some of these arrangements have already
been made. The world is full of non-zero-sum relationships, many
of which cross the chasms that supposedly separate humankind.
The bad news is that the mere existence of non-zero-sumness isn't
enough. After all, I've never said people summon tolerance in
response to non-zero-sum dynamics. I've said people summon tolerance in response to *seeing* the dynamics as non-zero-sum. And
even this is putting it too simply. Depending on the exact circumstances, responding wisely to non-zero-sum opportunities can call
for more than just seeing the non-zero-sumness. Sometimes it calls

for a kind of "sight" that goes deeper. It can call for an apprehension not just of the pragmatic truth about human interaction, but of a kind of moral truth. And moral truth is sometimes elusive.

Non-Zero-Sumness Today

But first, back to the good news. Globalization, for all its dislocations, entails lots of non-zero-sumness. You buy a new car, and you're playing one of the most complex non-zero-sum games in the history of humanity: you pay a tiny fraction of the wages of thousands of workers on various continents, and they, in turn, make you a car. A popular term for this is interdependence — they depend on you for money, you depend on them for a car — and interdependence is just another name for non-zero-sumness. Because the fortunes of two players in a non-zero-sum game are correlated, the welfare of each of them depends partly on the situation of the other.

You could look at other parts of the economy — consumer electronics, clothing, food — and find similarly far-flung chains of interdependence. And they all add up to a larger kind of interdependence. Economic downturn, or upturn, in one part of the world can be contagious. So nations broadly have a shared interest in keeping the global economy humming; they're playing a non-zero-sum game. This is just the natural culmination of the expansion of social organization. Villages merged to form chiefdoms, tribes merged to form states, states merged into empires. These mergers created vaster webs of non-zero-sumness, and often, as we've seen, religion reacted adaptively, helping to keep the webs intact.

Encouragingly, in the modern world this non-zero-sumness often does translate into an expansion of concord and tolerance, in keeping with the pattern seen in Abrahamic scripture. France and Germany, which spent much of the modern era in enmity, today have a high degree of economic entanglement, and the chances of their going to war are commensurately low.

American attitudes toward the Japanese are an especially clear case of globalization expanding the circle of concord. In the 1940s,

Americans saw Japan as an enemy, and their regard for individual Japanese was accordingly low. One comic-book cover had Superman encouraging readers to "slap a Jap" by buying war bonds. The accompanying caricature, with racial traits exaggerated, suggested that the Japanese were almost a separate species. And that was the attitude implied by the final weeks of World War II, after atomic bombs fell on Hiroshima and Nagasaki. America evinced virtually no moral anguish over the tens of thousands of innocent children who had perished, to say nothing of some presumably innocent adults.

After the war, things moved toward the non-zero-sum. By the 1970s, Americans and Japanese were allies in the fight against communism, and, as a bonus, Japanese were building solid cars for American consumers. Now the average American didn't even call Japanese "Japs," much less suggest slapping them.

Backtracking can always happen. In the late 1980s, the Cold War ended, so Japan seemed a less crucial U.S. ally. Meanwhile, the Japanese economy started to seem like a peril to American jobs. In 1989, the same year the Berlin Wall fell—and the half-century policy of "containing" communism was vindicated—the *Atlantic Monthly* ran a cover story titled "Containing Japan." The World War II motif of the sly, insidious Japanese even started to make a comeback, notably in the bestselling 1992 novel *Rising Sun* by Michael Crichton.

But the Japanese economy proved not to be the juggernaut of paranoid fantasy, and besides, Japanese companies had the political wisdom to locate some of their auto manufacturing plants in the United States. That meant they were playing a non-zero-sum game not just with American consumers, but with American workers. *Rising Sun* turned out not to be a harbinger. On balance, between the end of World War II and the end of the twentieth century, relations between the United States and Japan moved decisively toward the non-zero-sum, and on balance the international vibes got warmer: Japanese just seemed like better people to Americans than they had seemed decades earlier. Which is to say: they seemed like people.

This is the way moral evolution happens—in ancient Israel, in the Rome of early Christianity, in Muhammad's Arabia, in the modern world: a people's culture adapts to salient shifts in game-theoretical dynamics by changing its evaluation of the moral status of the people it is playing the game with. If the culture is a religious one, this adaptation will involve changes in the way scriptures are interpreted and in the choice of which scriptures to highlight. It happened in ancient times, and it happens now.

In that sense it's good news that, on balance, the United States–Japan story reflects the way of the world in the age of globalization: more and more people getting intertwined in non-zero-sum relations. Even some of the bad-news stories may be good news. Transnational environmental problems, ranging from overfishing the seas to global warming, are in themselves unfortunate, but at least these negative-sum prospects give humanity an interest in cooperating to head them off.

So maybe the world's peoples will move into a proper frame of mind for doing that. Maybe they'll overcome prejudice that impedes communication, muster tolerance for diversity of culture and belief; maybe they'll warm up to each other. That, after all, is the pattern we've seen in scripture: the prospect of successfully playing a non-zero-sum game breeds decency. So in theory everything should work out fine!

Messy Reality

In theory. But in fact various things can keep non-zero-sum potential from translating into the feelings that will realize that potential.

First is the problem of recognizing that you're in a non-zero-sum game. How many car buyers are aware of how many workers in how many countries helped build their car?

Second is the problem of trust. Palestinians and Israelis are playing a non-zero-sum game, because neither is going to expel the other from the area; given the inevitability of coexistence, lasting peace would be good for both sides and lasting war bad for both. And many people on both sides see this correlation of fortunes, at least in the abstract. But it's still hard to reach a deal because each side suspects that the other would violate it.

These two barriers to non-zero-sum solution—recognition, trust—may sound formidable, but in a sense neither is really the big problem. The big problem is something that compounds the problems of recognition and trust and also brings whole new problems to the table. The big problem is the human mind, as designed by natural selection.

Indeed, the human mind is such a big problem, and such a convoluted one, that it's hard to state the problem in the abstract. Better to illustrate it by example. One example lies along the borderline that has gotten so much attention since September 11, 2001: relations between Muslims on the one hand and Christians and Jews on the other—or, as it is sometimes oversimplified, between the "Muslim world" and the "West." (For reasons we'll come to, I'll look at this example from the vantage point of the "West," asking what westerners could do to ameliorate the situation—although, of course, ameliorative efforts are welcome, and required, from the other side as well.)

You might not guess it to read the headlines, but by and large this relationship is non-zero-sum. To be sure, the relationship between *some* Muslims and the West is zero-sum. Terrorist leaders have aims that are at odds with the welfare of westerners. The West's goal is to hurt their cause, to deprive them of new recruits and of political support. But if we take a broader view—look not at terrorists and their supporters but at Muslims in general, look not at radical Islam but at Islam—the "Muslim world" and the "West" are playing a non-zero-sum game; their fortunes are positively correlated. And the reason is that what's good for Muslims broadly is bad for radical Muslims. If Muslims get less happy with their place in the world, more resentful of their treatment by the West, support for radical Islam will grow, so things will get worse for the West. If, on the other hand, more and more Muslims feel respected by the West and feel they benefit from involvement with it, that will cut support for radical Islam, and westerners will be more secure from terrorism.

This isn't an especially arcane piece of logic. The basic idea is that terrorist leaders are the enemy and they thrive on the discontent of Muslims — and if what makes your enemy happy is the discontent of Muslims broadly, then you should favor their contentment. Obviously. Indeed this view has become conventional wisdom: if the West can win the "hearts and minds" of Muslims, it will have "drained the swamp" in which terrorists thrive. In that sense, there is widespread recognition in the West of the non-zero-sum dynamic.

But this recognition hasn't always led to sympathetic overtures from westerners toward Muslims. The influential evangelist Franklin Graham declared that Muslims don't worship the same god as Christians and Jews and that Islam is a "very evil and wicked religion." That's no way to treat people you're in a non-zero-sum relationship with! And Graham is not alone. Lots of evangelical Christians and other westerners view Muslims with suspicion, and view relations between the West and the Muslim world as a "clash of civilizations." And many Muslims view the West in similarly win-lose terms.

So what's going on here? Where's the part of human nature that was on display in ancient times — the part that senses whether you're in the same boat as another group of people and, if you are, fosters sympathy for or at least tolerance of them?

It's in there somewhere, but it's misfiring. And one big reason is that our mental equipment for dealing with game-theoretical dynamics was designed for a hunter-gatherer environment, not for the modern world. That's why dealing with current events wisely requires strenuous mental effort — effort that ultimately, as it happens, could bring moral progress.

Processing the Clash of Civilizations

If you are a Christian or Jew in, say, the United States, and you're trying to come to terms with the "Muslim world," much if not most of your input is electronic. You may not encounter many Muslims in real life, but you see them on TV. So your feelings toward Muslims in general depend largely on which Muslims wind up on TV.

For starters, there's Osama bin Laden. His interests are sharply opposed to America's interests, so if American minds are working as designed, they should sense this zero-sumness and react with antipathy and moral revulsion. And that is indeed the standard reaction.

And what about bin Laden's foot soldiers—the people who actually commit the acts of terrorism? If anything, the western relationship with them is even more unalterably zero-sum than with bin Laden. Bin Laden, after all, is at some level a rational actor. He seems to want to stay alive and hold on to prominence, and sometimes goals like that lead people toward compromise. Some terrorist foot soldiers don't even seem to want to stay alive. So certainly when westerners look at terrorists and view them with antipathy and intolerance, the mental equipment is working as designed: westerners are sensing a stubborn zero-sum dynamic and reacting aptly.

Of course, terrorists and their leaders are a pretty small subset of Muslims. If you're going to develop an attitude toward the "Muslim world," it would be nice to have more data points. What other Muslims show up on TV? Well, there were the thousands of Muslims protesting in sometimes violent fashion the publication of cartoons of Muhammad. And every once in a while you see a clip of Iranian Muslims burning the American flag.

Here, too, the images evoke reactions of antipathy, and here, too, this reaction would seem to make sense. Surely burning a country's flag suggests that you see your relationship to it as antagonistic, as zero-sum—and that you're unlikely to warm up to it anytime soon. And people so fervent as to get riled up over a cartoon don't look like plausible negotiating partners, either. In mustering antipathy toward these seemingly confirmed foes, the mind is working as designed.

But is it working well? Is antipathy toward Muslims who seem opposed to western values, if not the West itself, really in the interest of westerners? Maybe not, for two reasons.

The first is fairly obvious. You could call it the Franklin Graham reason. Antipathy toward radical Muslims you see on TV could lead you to retaliate rhetorically in a broad-brush way and say things offensive to all Muslims. You might, for example, call Islam a "very evil and wicked religion." This may alienate Muslims who aren't yet cartoon protesters or flag burners but would be more likely to burn a flag post-alienation.

There's a second reason why antipathy toward flag burners and cartoon protesters may make for bad strategy, and it's less obvious.

If one of this book's main premises is correct—if scriptural interpretation is obedient to facts on the ground—then flag burners and cartoon protesters who are acting under the influence of radical religious ideas came under that influence for a reason. Somewhere in the past are facts that account for their interpretation of their faith. And even if that interpretation has become basically unshakable—even if every flag burner and cartoon protester is beyond changing—there would still be virtue in finding out what those facts are. After all, keeping more moderate Muslims from joining the ranks of the exercised would be nice, and knowing what circumstances made the exercised Muslims exercised might aid that task. By the same token, it would be nice to understand why suicide bombers become suicide bombers—not so we could help them become moderates (good luck!), but so we could keep moderates from becoming them.

And here is the problem with feeling antipathy toward those cartoon protesters, flag burners, and even suicide bombers. It isn't that pouring lots of sympathy on them would help things. (In some ways it could hurt.) It's that, because of the way the human mind is built, antipathy can impede comprehension. Hating protesters, flag burners, and even terrorists makes it harder to understand them well enough to keep others from joining their ranks.

Moral Imagination

The way hatred blocks comprehension is by cramping our "moral imagination," our capacity to put ourselves in the shoes of another person. This cramping isn't unnatural. Indeed, the tendency of the moral imagination to shrink in the presence of enemies is built into our brains by natural selection. It's part of the machinery that leads us to grant tolerance and understanding to people we see in non-zero-sum terms and deny it to those we consign to the zero-sum category. We're naturally pretty good at putting ourselves in the shoes of close relatives and good friends (people who tend to have non-zero-sum links with us), and naturally bad at putting ourselves in the shoes of rivals and enemies (where zero-sumness is more common). We can't understand these people from the inside.

So what do things look like from the inside? Consider a case where an interior view is available—the case of a good friend. Your friend tells you about an arrogant prima donna at work who drives her nuts, and you are reminded of an arrogant prima donna in high school—the football star, the valedictorian—who drove you nuts. With a friend this process can be automatic: you scour your memory for shared points of reference and so vicariously feel her grievance. It's part of the deal that sustains your symbiotic relationship: you validate her gripes, she validates yours. You work toward a common perspective.

This is the work you aren't inclined to do with rivals and enemies. They complain about some arrogant prima donna, and you just can't relate. (Why are they such whiners?) And that's of course especially true when they say—as a rival or enemy might—that you are an arrogant prima donna. Then you *certainly* aren't struck by the parallels with that prima donna in your high school.

So too on the geopolitical stage: if you are a patriotic American, and people who are burning an American flag say America is arrogant, that prima donna probably won't spring to mind.

This doesn't mean you're at a loss to explain their behavior, or totally blind to their interior lives. When you see people burning flags and they look enraged, you can, even while hating them, correctly surmise that somewhere within them lies rage. You may also grant that flag burners perceive America as arrogant. But you don't *relate* to this perception, so you can still characterize them in unflattering terms. You say they are driven by "resentment" of American power and "envy" of American success. And, since envy and resentment aren't noble motivations, the moral coloration of the situation suggests it's the flag burners who are to blame. And because America isn't to blame, you resist the idea that it should change its behavior.

At this point in the discussion, if not sooner, an ominous question is often asked: Wait a minute—are you saying America is an arrogant prima donna? Are you saying that America, not the flag burner, is to blame for the burning of the flags? The question has even more bite if you're talking about terrorists: Are you saying America was to blame for 9/11? After all, that's what it would seem like if you really got inside the mind of a terrorist.

The short answer is no. But it's a "no" with an asterisk, a "no" in need of elaboration—and, since the elaboration is a bit arcane, I've relegated it to an online appendix.[1] It's recommended reading, because if you buy the argument it may radically alter your view of the world. But for now the point is just that the ability to *intimately* comprehend someone's motivation—to share their experience virtually, and know it from the inside—depends on a moral imagination that naturally contracts in the case of people we consider rivals or enemies.

In other words, we have trouble achieving comprehension without achieving sympathy. And this puts us in a fix because, as we've seen, some people it is in our profound interest to comprehend—-terrorists, for example—are people we're understandably reluctant to sympathize with. Enmity's natural impediment to understanding is, in a way, public enemy number one.

It's easy to explain the origins of this impediment in a conjectural way. Our brains evolved in a world of hunter-gatherer societies. In that world, morally charged disputes had Darwinian consequence. If you were in a bitter and public argument with a rival over who had wronged whom, the audience's verdict could affect your social status and your access to resources, both of which could affect your chances of getting genes into the next generation. So the ability to argue persuasively that your rival had no valid grounds for grievance would have been favored by natural selection, as would tendencies abetting this ability—such as a tendency to *believe* that your rival had no valid grounds for grievance, a belief that could infuse your argument with conviction. And nothing would so threaten this belief as the ability to look at things from a rival's point of view.

In dealing with allies, on the other hand, a more expansive moral imagination makes sense. Since their fortunes are tied to yours—since you're in a non-zero-sum relationship—lending your support to their cause can be self-serving (and besides, it's part of the implicit deal through which they support your cause). So on some occasions, at least, we're pretty good at seeing the perspective of friends or relatives. It helps us argue for their interests—which, after all, overlap with our interests—and helps us bond with them by voicing sympathy for their plight.

In short, the moral imagination, like other parts of the human mind, is designed to steer us through the successful playing of games—to realize the gains of non-zero-sum games when those gains are to be had, and to get the better of the other party in zero-sum games. Indeed, the moral imagination is one of the main drivers of the pattern we've seen throughout the book: the tendency to find tolerance in one's religion when the people in question are people you can do business with and to find intolerance or even belligerence when you perceive the relationship to be instead zero-sum.

And now we see one curious residue of this machinery: *our "understanding" of the motivations of others tends to come with a prepackaged moral judgment.* Either we understand their motivation internally, even intimately—relate to them, extend moral imagination to them, and judge their grievances leniently—or we understand their motivation externally and in terms that imply the illegitimacy of their grievances. Pure understanding, uncolored by judgment, is hard to come by.

It might be nice if we could sever this link between comprehension and judgment, if we could understand people's behavior in more clinical terms—just see things from their point of view without attaching a verdict to their grievances. That might more closely approach the perspective of God and might also, to boot, allow us to better pursue our interests. We could coolly see when we're in a non-zero-sum relationship with someone, coolly appraise their perspective, and coolly decide to make those changes in our own behavior that could realize non-zero-sumness. But those of us who fail to attain Buddhahood will spend much of our lives locked into a more human perspective: we extend moral imagination to people to the extent that we see win-win possibilities with them.

Given this fact, the least we can do is ask that the machinery work as designed: that when we are in a non-zero-sum relationship with someone we *do* extend moral imagination to them. That would better serve the interests of both parties and would steer us toward a truer understanding of the other—toward an understanding of what their world looks like from the inside.

And this is what often fails to happen. The bulk of westerners and the bulk of Muslims are in a deeply non-zero-sum relationship, yet by and large aren't very good at extending moral imagination to one another.

So a machine that was designed to serve our interests is misfiring. The moral imagination was built to help us discriminate between people we can do business with and people we can't do business with—to expand or contract, respectively. When Americans fail to extend moral imagination to Muslims, this is their unconscious mind's way of saying, "We judge these people to be not worth dealing with." Yet most of them are worth dealing with.

We've already seen one reason for this malfunction. Technology is warping our perception of the other player in this non-zero-sum game. The other player is a vast population of Muslims who, though perhaps not enamored of the West, don't spend their time burning flags and killing westerners. But what we see on TV — and what we may conflate with this other player — is a subset of Muslims who truly, and perhaps irreversibly, hate the West. We accurately perceive the stubborn hostility of the latter and our moral imagination contracts accordingly, but in the process it excludes the former.

The Boat

There is one other feature of the modern environment that can mislead a mental guidance system designed for a hunter-gatherer environment. In the ancestral environment — the environment our brains were built for — you weren't stuck in the same boat with your enemies. If conflict between two factions within a hunter-gatherer band got too intense, they might just split up and go their separate ways. And if the conflict was between two bands, one band might achieve lasting victory — either wipe out the other band or drive it over the horizon.

Today things are more complicated. For starters, you can't drive terrorists "over the horizon" without sending them to another planet; they can damage western interests from almost anywhere. Further, though you could in principle kill them all, in practice it's impossible to do that without creating more of them. So many of them are embedded in civilian populations that a frontal assault would kill innocents — and the ensuing publicity would be good news for terrorist recruiters. For that matter to even find all the terorrists (a prerequisite for killing them), you'd have to do such heavy-handed surveillance as to again generate animosity that played into the hands of recruiters.

This complex strategic environment isn't just different from our ancestral environment — it's different from the mid-twentieth-century strategic environment. Back then, when enemies came in the form of nation-states, total victory was possible. Witness World War II — unconditional surrender by both Germany and Japan. The postwar world was pretty simple, too. You could be safe so long as every nation-state was either an ally or a cowed enemy, so long as every foreign leader either liked you or feared you.

Then things changed. Increasingly, as the end of the twentieth century approached, national security depended not just on how the leaders of nation-states felt about you, but on how ordinary people felt about you. Large swaths of grassroots hatred could produce small but consequential numbers of terrorists. And the reason wasn't just that historical circumstances happened to produce a movement known as radical Islam. The problem was deep and structural, originating in a confluence of technical trends.

First, the evolution of munitions technology — from plastic explosives to nuclear weapons and biological weapons — made it easier for a small group of highly motivated terrorists to kill lots of people. Second, information technology and other technologies made it easier for people to get hold of the recipes and ingredients for those munitions. Information technology also made it easier for interest groups to form — for people of like mind to find one another and, having organized, recruit others. When these interest groups are model airplane enthusiasts, this is not a problem, but when they're airplane hijackers, it is.

It is because of these three developments that amorphous, far-flung, grassroots hatred can easily coalesce and then morph into massive violence. This "growing lethality of hatred" is an enduring, structurally driven trend. We might as well get used to it.

And its upshot takes us back to our starting point: if grassroots hatred is indeed public enemy number one, then the West is definitely playing a non-zero-sum game with the great bulk of the world's Muslims. Things will be better for the West if things are better for the world's Muslims — if they're content with their place in the modern world and well disposed toward the West, and so don't exude the discontent that nourishes terrorism.

Reducing discontent in any population is a nontrivial engineering feat, and doing it in a group as large and diverse as the world's Muslims is especially challenging. But it may be that some of the blanks could be filled in by exercising moral imagination — by westerners doing the uncomfortable work of putting themselves in the shoes of people who don't especially like them and so starting to fathom the sources of the dislike. It's always possible to analyze people's psychology from the outside, but if you want a fine-grained appreciation for what things will needlessly antagonize them and what things will win their trust and respect, there's no substitute for being on the inside, actually relating their experience to experiences of your own.

What's more, this use of moral imagination will predispose westerners to actually act on the data once they've gathered it. They'll be more inclined to feel that addressing the grievances in question is the right thing to do — an intuition that won't be unerringly correct, but will often be a healthy counterbalance to a more common, more adversarial, impulse.

Of course, this sense of rightness will bring resistance: Does it mean that the victims of terrorism are to blame? Does it mean that the terrorists aren't to blame? The fact that the technical answer to these questions is no won't defuse them. Neither will exhortations to forget about the blame question and just focus on cool strategic calculation — just recognize when addressing grievances has a bigger payoff than ignoring them and when ignoring them is on balance cost-effective.

No, the best way to counter the visceral aversion to extending the moral imagination is through the viscera: fight fire with fire. Remember that what our true enemies — the terrorists themselves — dearly want is for most Muslims to harbor hatred and simmering grievance. So if addressing some of the enemy's grievances means addressing grievances of Muslims in general, that may be the best revenge against the enemies. The basic idea is vaguely reminiscent of the wisdom spread by the apostle Paul and derived from the Hebrew wisdom literature: "If your enemies are hungry, give them bread to eat." For by doing so you "will heap coals of fire on their heads."[2]

Asymmetrical Sermons

This has been an asymmetrical sermon in at least two senses. First, I've focused on "perceived American arrogance" as if it were the sole cause of terrorism. But that was just a rhetorical convenience. There are many such causes, involving many behaviors by many nations, and this is just one example.

Second, I've asked how westerners can employ their moral imaginations to appreciate the perspective of Muslims. Why didn't I ask how Muslims can exercise their moral imaginations to appreciate the perspective of westerners — which, after all, would be a development of comparable value?

For one thing, because there probably aren't many people in Indonesia or Saudi Arabia reading this book. The Muslim world, like the West, could use some sermonizing, but the most effective sermons will come from within.

Besides, making westerners better at seeing the perspective of Muslims is just a roundabout way of making Muslims better at seeing the perspective of westerners. The idea is to figure out what things make lots of Muslims view relations with the West as zero-sum, decide which of those things can be changed at acceptable cost, and thus make those relations more conspicuously non-zero-sum. The more conspicuously non-zero-sum the relationship, the better Muslims will be at seeing the western perspective; the more expansive their own moral imaginations will become.

Moral Progress, Then and Now

This chapter marks the first appearance in this book of the term "moral imagination." But, actually, moral imagination is what much of the book has been about. The expansion and contraction of the moral imagination lies behind the pattern that has pervaded the history of religion: when a religious group senses an auspicious non-zero-sum relationship with another group, it is more likely to create tolerant scriptures or to find tolerance in existing scriptures; and when it senses no prospect of a win-win outcome, it is more likely to summon intolerance and belligerence. Humans have innate equipment for spotting people they can do business with and doing business with them, and the moral imagination is a major part of that equipment. When it opens up to a people, religious attitudes can change accordingly. That's what we've seen again and again.

So how is it that the moral imagination, which right now is so badly malfunctioning, worked so well during Abrahamic history, reliably expanding to exploit non-zero-sum opportunities? Actually, it didn't. Though I've emphasized the successes, there have been miscalculations aplenty, leading to lose-lose outcomes. (How many Christians and Muslims died fighting over Jerusalem during the Crusades, and what lasting profit came to either faith? And how many religions that we've never heard of went extinct out of a failure to skillfully play non-zero-sum games?)

What's more, many of the successes haven't resulted from the moral imagination working on autopilot. Ever since social organization evolved from hunter-gatherer societies to chiefdoms, the moral imagination has been working in an environment that it wasn't designed for—so you would expect that it has often, as today, needed some coaxing to do its job well. And indeed, among the more commendable achievements of religion has been to sometimes step in and provide just that.

This coaxing goes back to the religion of chiefdoms—to the age when religion first acquired a distinct moral dimension—and it was well under way by the time Abrahamic history comes into clear view. Consider Israel's formative stages. If you are going to build a confederacy of tribes, you need people to extend their moral imagination farther than instincts built for a hunter-gatherer milieu might dictate. Hence the Ten Commandments, and the idea that you should "love" your Israelite neighbor. An essential property of love is to be able to share in the perspective of the beloved. Similarly, if you are the apostle Paul, and you're going to build a vast multinational religious organization within the Roman Empire, you need to stress that brotherly love should extend across ethnic bounds. And if you are building Islam, an intertribal religious organization that will then become an expanding imperial government, you have to emphasize both of those things, extending affinity beyond the bounds of tribes and of ethnicities.

These thresholds in the history of the Abrahamic faiths—and in the evolution of God—have consisted of expanding the moral imagination, carrying it to a place it doesn't go unabetted. This expansion is religion at its best. Religion at its worst is... well, there are too many examples these days to bother elaborating.

Has the best outweighed the worst? Certainly there has been a kind of net moral progress in human history, if only in the sense that moral imagination today routinely extends farther than the circumference of a hunter-gatherer village. And certainly religion has played a role in this progress. Even when the Abrahamic religions are defensive and inward-looking, you see Muslims identifying with Muslims half a world away, and Christians and Jews doing the same. In all cases, that's a bigger moral compass than existed anywhere on this planet 20,000 years ago, when all religions were "savage" religions. Moreover, within all three of those faiths you see some people working to extend the moral imagination beyond the bounds of their particular religion.

Obviously there's room for more progress. In fact, there's an urgent need for it. Maybe it's not too much to say that the salvation of the planet—the coherence and robustness of an emerging global social organization—depends on this progress. That's what happens when the zone of non-zero-sumness reaches planetary breadth; once everybody is in the same boat, either they learn how to get along or very bad things happen. If the Abrahamic religions don't respond to this ultimatum adaptively, if they don't expand their moral imaginations, there is a chance of chaos on an unprecedented scale. The precursors of these religions—the ancient religions of Mesopotamia and Egypt—had it right when they depicted the triumph of chaos as the failure of the religious enterprise.

But Is It Truth?

At the outset of this chapter I said that successfully playing the great non-zero-sum games of our time would require a closer approximation of moral truth. In what sense would the expansion of the moral imagination—the thing that, I contend, is a prerequisite for this success—bring us closer to moral truth? Two senses, one a bit cold and clinical, perhaps even cynical sounding, and one more warm and fuzzy.

First, the expansion of moral imagination can bring it into closer alignment with its original Darwinian purpose. The moral imagination was "designed" by natural selection to help us exploit non-zero-sum opportunities, to help us cement fruitfully peaceful relations when they're available, to help us find people we can do business with and do business with them. If it is going to do that today, it has to grow. It has to grow in the western world, and it has to grow in the Muslim world.

Of course, these opportunities are exploited for the sake of self-interest, and it may sound ironic to say that we move closer to moral truth by doing a better job of serving our own interests. But in this case—and here we start drifting toward the warm and fuzzy—the pursuit of self-interest has some by-products that are moral in a more traditional sense.

To begin with, the exploitation of these non-zero-sum opportunities—notably the one between the western and Muslim worlds—would serve the interests of both parties, and human welfare would grow in the aggregate. (That's the magical thing about non-zero-sumness; it translates rational selfishness into the welfare of others.) Making humankind on balance better off may not intrinsically involve moral truth, but it does constitute a kind of moral progress. Moreover, in this case it *does* involve a kind of moral truth. For its prerequisite, the expansion of the moral imagination, forces us to see the interior of more and more other people for what the interior of other people is—namely, remarkably like our own interior. Like our own interior, it is deeply colored by the emotions and passions that are our Darwinian legacy; like our own interior it in turn colors the world with self-serving moral judgment; like our own interior it possesses intrinsic value.

To say that other people are people, too, may sound like an unremarkable insight. But it is one that is often ignored, and one that is in some sense unnatural. After all, any organism created by natural selection is, by default, under the illusion that it is special. We all base our daily lives on this premise — that our welfare is more important than the welfare of pretty much anyone else, with the possible exception of close kin. Indeed, the premise is that our welfare is *much* more important than the welfare of others. We work hard so we can afford dessert while other people don't have dinner. We see our own resentments as bona fide grievances and we see the grievances of others as mere resentments. And we are all like this — all of us walking around under the impression that we're special. Obviously, we can't all be right in any objective sense. The truth must be otherwise. The extension of moral imagination brings us closer to that truth.

So, in the end, the salvation of the global social system entails moral progress not just in the sense of human welfare; there has to be, as a prerequisite for that growth, a closer encounter by individual human beings with moral truth. And this is an inevitable outcome of human history. It isn't inevitable that we'll prevail — that our species will get close enough to moral truth to attain salvation. But it was an inevitable outcome of history's stubborn drive toward growing non-zero-sumness that we would at least face this predicament: either move closer to moral truth or descend into chaos.

I said in the previous chapter that this book isn't the place to mount a full-fledged argument that human history has some larger purpose. But certainly one fact that would figure in such an argument is this: history has driven us closer and closer to moral truth, and now our moving still closer to moral truth is the only path to salvation — "salvation" in the original Abrahamic sense of the term: salvation of the social structure.

For Abrahamics of the Christian and Muslim variety, especially, the question of salvation doesn't end with this Hebrew Bible sense of the term. They may ask: Does the growth of moral imagination conduce to salvation in the sense of individual salvation? Will it save my soul? That is a question for them to answer as their doctrines continue to evolve. But we can say this much: traditionally, religions that have failed to align individual salvation with social salvation have not, in the end, fared well. And, like it or not, the social system to be saved is now a global one. Any religion whose prerequisites for individual salvation don't conduce to the salvation of the whole world is a religion whose time has passed.

Even if time does pass them by, all Abrahamic religions will always be able to say this much: their prophets were right. Things may look bad, but salvation is possible so long as you understand what it requires. Still, it will be a shame if they don't manage to illustrate the point.

Chapter Twenty

Well, Aren't We Special?

Among the things Muslims, Christians, and Jews have had in common over the years is a tendency to exaggerate their past specialness.

Hebrew scripture depicts the Israelites as theological revolutionaries: they marched into Canaan backed by the one true god and vanquished the ignorant polytheists. In truth, as we've seen, Israelite religion emerged from the Canaanite milieu and was itself polytheistic; monotheism didn't prevail in Israel until after the Babylonian exile of the sixth century BCE.

Christians think of Jesus as a man who brought the Jews a radically new message of personal salvation and was determined to carry it to the peoples of the world. But Jesus was himself a Jew, preaching to other Jews, and his essential message was probably a familiar one—a message of national salvation, a message about the coming restoration of Israel to greatness. His agenda probably didn't include transethnic outreach or its moral corollary, a brotherly love that knows no national bounds. That doctrine entered Christianity in the decades after his death—a reflection not of his true teachings, but of the cosmopolitan, multiethnic milieu of the Roman Empire. His teachings were then reshaped accordingly, and the resulting distortion became the gospel.

Muslims think of Muhammad as a man who carried two revolutionary messages: he told Arab polytheists that there was only one god, Allah, and he explained to Christians and Jews that their God and Allah were the same god. But the chances are that when Muhammad arrived on the scene Allah was already known to be the

God of Christians and Jews, a fact that helps explain why so much Christian and Jewish belief and ritual survive in Islam. And as for the question of whether Allah was the only god—here Muhammad was equivocal. In deference to the political power of Arab polytheists, he seems to have at one point granted the existence of other gods, only later settling back into permanent monotheism; and even then he was careful to preserve such originally polytheistic customs as the annual pilgrimage to Mecca. Islam was born not with a starkly new and firm character, but as a fluid compromise among Judaism, Christianity, and Arab paganism.

So if neither Moses nor Jesus nor Muhammad arrived on the scene with breathtaking news, and if indeed the origin of all three Abrahamic faiths can be viewed as a kind of cultural synthesis, an organic recombination of preexisting elements, what becomes of the claim that they are religions of revelation?

Scripture as Revelation

Certainly things are looking bad for the traditional claim that they're religions of *special* revelation. But there is still a sense, if a less dramatic one, in which the Abrahamic scriptures can be validly viewed as revelation.

For starters, these scriptures reveal the arrow of moral development built into human history. This revelation is cryptic, because moral progress has been fitful, with lots of backsliding—and, to compound matters, the scriptures aren't arranged in chronological order. So messages of tolerance and belligerence, of love and hate, are mixed in seemingly random fashion. But seen in context they fall into a pattern: when people face win-win situations and think they can work together, they are open to one another's worldviews, not to mention one another's continued existence. So as technological evolution expands the realm of non-zero-sumness—one thing it has stubbornly done throughout history and shows every sign of continuing to do—there is incentive to acknowledge and respect the humanity of an ever widening circle of humans.

Of course, this kind of scriptural "revelation"—the revealing of a pattern in history—wouldn't by itself make most Jews, Christians, and Muslims beam with pride. After all, the most secular historical documents could be revelations in this sense. Scriptures are supposed to emanate from a divine source, from the revealer. And they're supposed to confirm not just some vague claim about a moral pattern in history, but specific theological claims—in this case claims about whether it's Christians or Muslims or Jews who have the details right about God and his will.

Still, there's one way this less dramatic kind of revelation could be welcome ammunition for Abrahamics who find themselves in a theological debate—namely, if the debate finds them all on the same side. If you step back from the differences they have with one another and with other religions, you'll see a bigger divide in modern thought. It's between people who think there is in some sense a divine source of meaning, a higher purpose in this universe, and people who think there isn't.

On one side are people like Steven Weinberg, the Nobel Prize–winning physicist who famously wrote, "The more the universe seems comprehensible, the more it also seems pointless." In his view, there is no transcendent source of meaning or moral orientation. "It's not a moral order out there," he once said. "It's something we impose." [1]

But what the Abrahamic scriptures illustrate, however obscurely, is that there *is* a moral order out there—and it's imposed on us. Built-in features of history, emanating from the basic logic of cultural evolution, give humankind a choice between progressing morally and paying a price for failing to. Hence the pattern, over the millennia, of people placing larger and larger numbers of other people within their circle of moral consideration. And hence the bursts of suffering for failing to. And hence the current, culminating moment in that pattern, a moment when the only way to avoid great and possibly catastrophic harm is to expand that moral circle across the whole planet. The march of history challenges people to expand their range of sympathy and understanding, to enlarge their moral imaginations, to share the perspective of people ever farther away. Time has drawn us toward the commonsensical-sounding yet elusive moral truth that people everywhere are people, just like us.

To say that this signifies a moral order doesn't mean order will prevail; it doesn't mean that we'll embrace this truth, pass the test, and usher in an age of tranquillity. Enough people may resist the truth so that, instead, chaos ensues. The moral order lies in the fact that this price will indeed be paid if moral truth doesn't dawn widely. The moral order is the coherence of the relationship between social order and moral truth.

The fact that there's a moral order out there doesn't mean there's a God. On the other hand, it's evidence in favor of the God hypothesis and evidence against Weinberg's worldview. In the great divide of current thought—between those, including the Abrahamics, who see a higher purpose, a transcendent source of meaning, and those, like Weinberg, who don't—the manifest existence of a moral order comes down clearly on one side.

What's more, though believing in this moral order doesn't make you a believer in God, it may make you, in some sense, religious. In the first chapter, when we were looking for a definition of religion broad enough to encompass the many things that have been called religion, we settled on a formulation by William James. Religious belief, he said, "consists of the belief that there is an unseen order, and that our supreme good lies in harmoniously adjusting ourselves thereto." Presumably one thing that would qualify as "our supreme good," in James's view, is clearly perceiving, and abiding by, moral truth. And if the unseen order is a moral one, then harmoniously adjusting yourself to it entails as much.

Of course, you could interpret James's "supreme good" in more practical terms. Our supreme good, you could say, is our survival and health, our flourishing. But even under this interpretation, the moral order revealed in the Abrahamic scriptures complies with James's formulation. After all, the way history draws people toward moral truth is by rewarding them for moving toward it and punishing them for resisting. As technological evolution brings larger and larger swaths of people within shouting distance, they either muster the tolerance and mutual respect to do business with one another or fail to flourish. The moral order offers us the prospect of social health—salvation in the Hebrew Bible's sense of the term—but only if we abide by its logic; only if we "harmoniously adjust ourselves" to the "unseen order."

We saw in the last chapter that the Abrahamic prophets were right at least in the sense of believing that salvation is possible so long as you know what it requires. Now we can say they were right in a deeper sense—in believing that salvation requires closer alignment with the moral axis of the universe.

Of course, they didn't put it like that. They didn't use phrases like "the moral axis of the universe." They just said salvation required aligning yourself with God's will. Then again, they believed that God's will *was* the moral axis of the universe. In that sense, even if we assume that all their specific ideas about God were wrong—even if we assume that they were wrong to think there *is* a God—they were closer to the truth about the essence of things than Steven Weinberg is. Either there is a moral order or there isn't. They said there is, he said there isn't. They seem to have been right.

The Growth of God So Far

In chapter 8, when I talked about the "growth" of the Abrahamic god, it wasn't because I feel confident that this god, or any god, exists (a question I'm unqualified to answer). It was because the god of the Abrahamic scriptures—real or not—does have a tendency to grow morally. This growth, though at times cryptic and superficially haphazard, is the "revelation" of the moral order underlying history: as the scope of social organization grows, God tends to eventually catch up, drawing a larger expanse of humanity under his protection, or at least a larger expanse of humanity under his toleration.

So when the tribes of Israel coalesced into a single polity, Yahweh expanded to encompass them all, reflecting a kind of moral advance—mutual acceptance among those tribes, the acceptance that allowed the Israelite nation to form. And after the exile, when Israel gained a secure place in the multinational Persian Empire, the fierce nationalism of an earlier Israel abated. Now Hebrew scriptures emphasized kinship with other nations of the empire and downplayed past enmities.

The Christian God, like the God of Israel, drew moral nourishment from the multinational nature of empire, in this case the Roman Empire. Salvation was granted to all believers without regard for nationality. Vestiges of a narrower god—the god reflected in Jesus's calling a woman a "dog" because she wasn't from Israel—were left behind.

Islam's formation, in a sense, telescoped a millennium or so of God's Judeo-Christian history. First, Allah transcended tribal distinctions, as he had done under the name Yahweh in ancient Israel. Then Islam, toward the end of its formative period, acquired the multinational perspective of empire, admitting, like Christianity (and like modern Judaism), people of all nations to the community of belief. But Islam went further than the Christianity of the Roman Empire; in places its scripture granted the possibility of salvation to people outside the fold—to Christians and Jews and even to Zoroastrians, who fell within the realm of empire upon Islam's conquest of Persia.

Of course, this progressive-sounding list of theological milestones was selected with a bias. I could just as easily have listed the downsides of imperial affiliation—the doctrine of jihad, a product of early imperial Islam, or the Christian doctrine of holy war, both of which smoothed slaughter during the Crusades. Throughout human history, as zones of non-zero-sumness have expanded, and with them the extent of polities and religions, amity within the zones has often been matched by enmity between them. The movement toward moral truth, though regionally significant, has been globally modest, at best.

Now we've reached a stage in history where the movement toward moral truth has to become globally momentous. Technology has made the planet too small, too finely interdependent, for enmity between large blocs to be in their enduring interest. The negative-sum side of the world's non-zero-sumness is too explosively big to be compatible with social salvation. In particular: in any envisioned "clash of civilizations" between Islam and the West, neither side can realistically hope for conquest.

So if the God of the Abrahamic faiths is to keep doing what he has often managed to do before—evolve in a way that fosters positive-sum outcomes of non-zero-sum games—he has some growing to do. His character has to develop in a way that permits, for starters, Muslims, Christians, and Jews to get along as global-ization keeps pushing them closer together.

If the modern world offers cause for pessimism on this front, at least cause for optimism can be found in the ancient world. As we saw in chapter 8, the closest thing in that world to globalization were periods of incipient empire, when nations were thrown together in new combinations and new avenues of contact were opened. And, as we've just seen, the God of all three faiths passed the imperial test in the ancient world; when put in the multinational context of empire, he summoned enough broad-mindedness to facilitate the playing of non-zero-sum games. God's character may not seem to be growing at the moment, but he has it in him.

Of course, God's character is a product of the way Muslims, Christians, and Jews think of him. So to say the Abrahamic god must grow means they must start thinking of him in a slightly dif-ferent way—as a god who is less inclined to play favorites among them. In other words, they need to start thinking of themselves as a bit less special.

For starters, they could think of the different Abrahamic faiths as having been involved, all along, in the same undertaking. And it's true: all three faiths have been struggling to make sense of the world in ultimate terms, in terms of the meaning of it all and the point of it all. And this struggle has in a sense succeeded: the strug-gle itself has evinced a pattern that strongly suggests there *is* a point to it all—a higher purpose, a transcendent moral order. What's more, this evidence corroborates a conclusion their prophets had all reached in their own ways—that salvation is possible if we know what it requires, and that what it requires is closer alignment with the moral order of the universe. The Abrahamic religions should pat themselves on the back, or better yet, pat each other on the back.

This may sound like advice, but it isn't meant that way. If there's one thing this book shows, it's that advising religious people on what stance to take toward other religions will, by itself, get you nowhere. The facts on the ground have to be conducive to reconciliation for reconciliation to happen. But we can see forces at work that could have this effect, and we know that such forces can work in fairly short order.

Only four decades ago, the difference between Catholic and Protestant was no small thing in many parts of America. "Intermarriage" was a term applied to Catholic-Protestant weddings, and such weddings weren't widely welcomed. Today "intramarriage" better captures the aura of such weddings. The reasons—that is, the sources of non-zero-sumness—are many, including an economy that has brought Protestants and Catholics into everyday workplace interdependence, and a sense that secularism threatens their common beliefs and values. Maybe comparable forces can move the world's Abrahamic faiths closer together. Certainly the religious sensibility writ large is under assault, and they have a common interest in meeting that challenge.

How to Be Humble: Lesson Number Two

Another way to make the Abrahamic religions feel less special would be to point out that, in trying to make sense of the world in ultimate terms, they haven't been alone. Non-Abrahamic religions have been involved in the same task, and some of them have arguably done a better job.

Consider this idea that social salvation—averting chaos—requires closer adherence to moral truth. This is in a sense the ultimate validation of the enterprise in which Judaism, Christianity, and Islam have been involved. It's an idea, I've argued, that the basic direction of history bears out, and it's an idea expressed in all three faiths. Yet in none of these faiths has it found so central and so explicit an expression as it found long before any of them was born, in the religion of ancient Egypt.

In chapter 13 we saw that a morally contingent afterlife, an idea famously central to Christianity, was anticipated in Egypt well before the time of Jesus: at the court of the god Osiris, the moral record of the deceased was judged and the fate of the deceased thus determined. But we didn't get into the symbolic richness of the adjudicatory process. When the deceased made their professions of moral purity, their veracity was checked by placing their heart on a scale and balancing it against a feather that represented Maat, the goddess of truth. (This was a tense moment. Standing nearby was Ammut the devourer, a hideous goddess who would eat the deceased if the heart was found corrupt.)[2] Then the question would be settled: Was it true, as they claimed, that they had respected the property and persons of their fellow Egyptians, even including servants and the poor?

But the feather on that Judgment Day scale was more than a symbol of Maat, the goddess of truth, and thus more than a gauge of truthfulness. For Maat herself embodied *maat*—a kind of metaphysical substance composed of truth, order, and cosmic harmony.[3] One job of the pharaoh was to present *maat* to the gods and thus sustain the world's precarious order. Egyptian writings taught people how to "live in *maat*"—live a moral life—and thus give the pharaoh a hand. So when Egyptians, mindful of their coming day of reckoning, cultivated *maat,* they were struggling not just against personal mortality but against social dissolution. And Osiris—sometimes called "the lord of *maat*"—precisely symbolized this dual struggle.[4] For he (in this and so many other respects like Jesus) was a god who had been raised from the dead, and Seth, the god who had killed Osiris in the first place, the god over whom Osiris triumphed through resurrection, was the god of chaos.

It may well be that this plotline—whose basics were laid down several millennia ago—has never been surpassed as a mythic assessment of our situation: either we strive toward moral truth, which centrally entails respect for the other, or we dissolve into chaos.

For that matter, no religion has since surpassed ancient Egyptian religion in the strength of its incentive to encourage this striving: only if you strive do you get to spend eternity in bliss. As we've seen, pretty much all religions link social salvation to some sort of individual salvation, but eternal bliss has to rank near the top of the heap of individual salvations in terms of motivating power. Christians and Muslims matched this power, but they didn't surpass it.

These days this incentive isn't available to everyone. Lots of people don't believe in an afterlife—an increasing number perhaps, and certainly an increasing number of well-educated people. Lots of people don't think of themselves as pursuing personal salvation in any other sense, either. Which raises a question: in the modern age, how do you employ the time-tested formula for strengthening the social fabric—forging a link between individual salvation and social salvation? If many people don't seek salvation in the first place, how do you make closer adherence to moral truth a prerequisite for it?

Fortunately, it turns out that everyone does seek salvation. The word "salvation," remember, comes from a Latin word meaning to stay intact, to remain whole, to be in good health. And everyone, atheist, agnostic, and believer alike, is trying to stay in good mental health, to keep their psyche or spirit (or whatever they call it) intact, to keep body and soul together. They're trying, you might say, to avert chaos at the individual level.

So the basic challenge of linking individual salvation to social salvation can be stated in equally symmetrical yet more secular language: the challenge is to link the avoidance of individual chaos to the avoidance of social chaos. Or: link the pursuit of psychic intactness to social intactness. Or: link the pursuit of personal integrity to social integrity. Or: link the pursuit of psychic harmony to social harmony.

Or whatever. The exact language depends on the context: devout

Abrahamics will use different language from New Age "seekers," from agnostic neo-Buddhists, from secular humanists, and so on. Some people will take heart from the idea that to seek a personal salvation linked to social salvation is to align yourself with a cosmic purpose manifest in history, and some won't (either because they don't agree that the purpose is manifest or because they don't care). But however you describe the linkage, whatever the nature of the incentive structure, the linkage will have to be made in a fair percentage of human beings around the world for it to work. Social salvation may or may not be at hand, depending on the extent to which individual people, in working out their own salvations, expand their moral imaginations and hence expand the circle of moral consideration.

The Future of God

At the risk of seeming to harp on the nonspecialness of the Abrahamic faiths: this expansion of the moral circle is another area in which non-Abrahamic religions have sometimes outperformed the Abrahamics.

Consider Buddhism under the influence of the Indian emperor Ashoka of the third century BCE, whom we briefly encountered in chapter 12. Ashoka's conversion to Buddhism, like Constantine's later conversion to Christianity, assured his new religion a solid place on an imperial platform. And Buddhism's emphasis on brotherly love and charity, rather like comparable Christian emphases in ancient Rome, was presumably good for the empire's transethnic solidarity. Yet, like the early Islamic caliphates—and unlike Constantine—Ashoka insisted on respecting other religions in the empire; he never demanded conversion.

In short, Ashoka combined the best of the Abrahamic tradition's two imperial religions. And then he did them one better. Whereas Christianity and Islam were both enlisted in imperial holy war, Ashoka renounced conquest, horrified by the event that had preceded and triggered his conversion to Buddhism—his own bloody conquest of a neighboring region. "The most important conquest," he announced, is "moral conquest." Thus "the sound of war drums" would be replaced by the "call to Dharma," to the path of moral truth.[5]

What if the Abrahamic religions really did relax their sense of specialness — with respect to one another and even, eventually, with respect to non-Abrahamic faiths? No doubt it would feel to many Christians, Jews, and Muslims like an injury to their faith. Yet it would amount to a kind of vindication. At the core of each faith is the conviction that there is a moral order, and for the Abrahamic conception of God to grow in this fashion would be yet more evidence that such an order exists. For Jews, Christians, or Muslims to cling to claims of special validity could make their faiths seem, and perhaps be, less valid. As Ashoka put it in a different context: "If a man extols his own faith and disparages another because of devotion to his own and because he wants to glorify it, he seriously injures his own faith."[6]

Is it crazy to imagine a day when the Abrahamic faiths renounce not only their specific claims to specialness, but even the claim to specialness of the whole Abrahamic enterprise? Are such radical changes in God's character imaginable? Changes this radical have already happened, again and again. Another transformation would be nothing new.

There is a proven theological formula for dissolving the special-ness of different faiths. It's most famously associated with Hindus, who seem to have used it as a way to unite different regions that emphasized the worship of different Hindu gods. The idea is that all gods, with their different names, are manifestations of a single "Godhead." As an ancient Vedic text put it: "They call it Indra, Mitra, Varuna, and Agni, and also heavenly, beautiful Garutman. The real is one, though sages name it variously..."[7]

This idea may also be reflected, if obscurely, in Abrahamic scripture. As we saw in chapter 8, the Hebrew Bible often refers to God as "Elohim" — a term that seems to have entered Hebrew via a lingua franca that was used well beyond Israel's borders. As we also saw, some scholars think this word, with its international aura, was in some cases used as a way of suggesting that the gods of the region, including the god Israel called Yahweh, were all the same god.

If so, this would help make sense of something that has long been puzzling: the last two letters of *Elohim* give it the form of a plural noun. Indeed, the Bible sometimes uses it that way, as in referring to the "gods" of another nation.[8] But when applied to the God of Israel, this superficially plural noun behaves as if singular. Maybe this grammatical anomaly, like the word's international pedigree, was a way of driving home the idea that the various gods in Israel's vicinity — various elohim — were different faces of the one Godhead.

As it happens, the word *Elohim* looks a lot like early names for God in the Christian and Islamic traditions: *Elaha* in the Aramaic that Jesus would have spoken, and *Allah* in the Arabic of Muhammad.[9] This is probably no coincidence but rather, as suggested in chapter 14, a result of common linguistic ancestry; *Elaha* and *Allah* share some of *Elohim*'s DNA. In that sense, glimmers of the notion of the Godhead are visible in ancient names for divinity in all three Abrahamic faiths. Maybe these three faiths can together use that notion to find harmony with non-Abrahamic faiths, should they ever evince an enduring ability to get along with one another. But first things first.

By the Way, What Is God?

In this book I've used the word "god" in two senses. First, there are the gods that have populated human history—rain gods, war gods, creator gods, all-purpose gods (such as the Abrahamic god), and so on. These gods exist in people's heads and, presumably, nowhere else.

But occasionally I've suggested that there might be a kind of god that is real. This prospect was raised by the manifest existence of a moral order—that is, by the stubborn, if erratic, expansion of humankind's moral imagination over the millennia, and the fact that the ongoing maintenance of social order depends on the further expansion of the moral imagination, on movement toward moral truth. The existence of a moral order, I've said, makes it reasonable to suspect that humankind in some sense has a "higher purpose." And maybe the source of this higher purpose, the source of the moral order, is something that qualifies for the label "god" in at least some sense of that word.

The previous sentence is hardly a fervent expression of religious faith; in fact, it's essentially agnostic. Even so, I don't recommend uttering it at, say, an Ivy League faculty gathering unless you want people to look at you as if you'd started speaking in tongues. In modern intellectual circles, speculating seriously about God's existence isn't a path to widespread esteem.

Indeed, the first decade of the twenty-first century made godtalk an even graver breach of highbrow etiquette than it had been at the end of the twentieth. In the wake of the attacks of September 11, 2001, antireligious attitude was central to a slew of influential cultural products (books by Sam Harris, Christopher Hitchens, Daniel Dennett, and Richard Dawkins, a film by Bill Maher, a one-woman act by Julia Sweeney). In the space of only a few years, the more-or-less official stance of intellectuals toward believers moved from polite silence to open dismissal if not ridicule.

So is there any hope for the believer who would like to be considered cool — or, more realistically, not too uncool? Maybe. After all, the version of God being ridiculed by the cool people is the traditional, anthropomorphic god: some superhuman being with a mind remarkably like our minds except way, way bigger (indeed, a god that, in the standard rendering, is omniscient, omnipotent, and, as a bonus, infinitely good!). And this isn't the only kind of god that could exist.

Of course, we can't rule out the possibility that some superhuman version of a human lies above and beyond the universe. Philosophers seriously discuss the possibility that the universe is some kind of simulation, and in one version of that scenario our creator is a computer programmer from a very advanced extraterrestrial — or, rather, extrauniversal — civilization. (And certainly if the human predicament is the creation of an adolescent hacker, that would explain a lot!) But we have no reason to assume as much, and there is precedent in theology for using the word "god" in a nonanthropomorphic way. For example, the twentieth-century Christian theologian Paul Tillich described God as "the ground of being."

As critics of Tillich have pointed out, "the ground of being" sounds a bit vague, maybe too vague to qualify as a god. In fact, it sounds a lot like the "ultimate reality" invoked by some mystics who consider themselves atheists. What good does a "god" this abstract do for traditional believers, who envision a superhuman, anthropomorphic god — a "personal" god that they can talk to and thank and love and apologize to? In what sense could their belief be vindicated by the existence of a god so abstract that, really, "god" may not be the right word for it? ("Divinity," maybe?)

Vindication lies in the eyes of the beholder. But one plausible ground for vindication would be if it turned out that a personal god, as commonly conceived, is a reasonable approximation of the more abstract god, given the constraints on human conception.

Suppose, for example, that we accept as our abstract conception of God "the source of the moral order." (Tillich's equally abstract "ground of being" is something I'm not qualified to articulate, much less defend. I brought it up only as an example of theological abstraction.) Could it be that thinking of this source, and relating to this source, as if it were a personal god is actually an appropriate way for human beings to apprehend that source, even if more appropriate ways might be available to beings less limited in their apprehension?

This sounds fishy, I know. It sounds like a strained, even desperate, intellectual maneuver, a last-ditch attempt to rescue a prescientific conception of God from the onslaught of modern science. But, oddly, an argument that it's not comes from modern science; physicists commonly do something that is in some ways analogous to believing in a personal god.

The Ultimate Reality of Science

It's a bedrock idea of modern physics that, even if you define "ultimate reality" as the ultimate *scientific* reality—the most fundamental truths of physics—ultimate reality isn't something you can clearly conceive.

Think of an electron, a little particle that spins around another little particle. Wrong! True, physicists sometimes find it useful to think of electrons as particles, but sometimes it's more useful to think of them as waves. Conceiving of them as either is incomplete, yet conceiving of them as both is...well, inconceivable. (Try it!) And electrons are just the tip of the iceberg. In general, the quantum world—the world of subatomic reality—behaves in ways that don't make sense to minds like ours. Various aspects of quantum physics evince the property that the late physicist Heinz Pagels called quantum weirdness.[1]

The bad news for the religiously inclined, then, is that maybe they should abandon hope of figuring out what God is. (If we can't conceive of an electron accurately, what are our chances of getting God right?) The good news is that the hopelessness of figuring out exactly what something is doesn't mean it doesn't exist. Apparently some things are just inconceivable—and yet are things nonetheless.

At least, *some* physicists believe electrons are things. The fact that nobody's actually *seen* an electron, and that trying to imagine one ties our minds in knots, has led some physicists and philosophers of science to wonder whether it's even accurate to say that electrons *do* exist. You could say that with electrons, as with God, there are believers and there are skeptics.[2]

The believers believe there's *something out there*—some "thing" in some sense of the word "thing"—that corresponds to the word "electron"; and that, though the best we can do is conceive of this "thing" imperfectly, even misleadingly, conceiving of it that way makes more sense than not conceiving of it at all. They believe in electrons while professing their inability to really "know" what an electron is. You might say they believe in electrons even while lacking proof that electrons per se exist.

Many of these physicists, while holding that imperfectly conceiving subatomic reality is a valid form of knowledge, wouldn't approve if you tried to perform a similar maneuver in a theological context. If you said you believe in God, even while acknowledging that you have no clear idea what God is—and that you can't even really prove God per se exists—they would say your belief has no foundation.

Yet what exactly is the difference between the logic of their belief in electrons and the logic of a belief in God? They perceive patterns in the physical world—such as the behavior of electricity—and posit a source of these patterns and call that source the "electron." A believer in God perceives patterns in the moral world (or, at least, moral patterns in the physical world) and posits a source of these patterns and calls the source "God." "God" is that unknown thing that is the source of the moral order, the reason there is a moral dimension to life on Earth and a moral direction to time on Earth; "God" is responsible for the fact that life is sentient, capable of good and bad feelings, and hence morally significant; "God" is responsible for the evolutionary system that placed highly sentient life on a trajectory toward the good, or at least toward tests that offered the opportunity and incentive to realize the good; in the process "God" gave each of us a moral axis around which to organize our lives, should we choose to. Being human, we will always conceive of the source of this moral order in misleadingly crude ways, but then again you could say the same thing about conceiving electrons. So you'll do with the source of the moral order what physicists do with a subatomic source of the physical order, such as an electron—try to think about it the best you can, and fail. This, at least, is one modern, scientifically informed argument that could be deployed by the believer in God.

The Atheist Strikes Back

There are plausible rejoinders that an atheist scientist who believes in electrons could make, because there are places where the analogy between God and an electron breaks down. In particular, the scientist could say, "But something like an electron is *necessary* to explain patterns we see in the physical world. In contrast, something like God isn't *necessary* to explain the moral order of the universe."

It's a good point. This book's account of the moral direction of history has been a *materialist* account. We've explained the expansion of the moral imagination as an outgrowth of expanding social organization, which is itself an outgrowth of technological evolution, which itself grows naturally out of the human brain, which itself grew naturally out of the primordial ooze via biological evolution. There's no mystical force that has to enter the system to explain this, and there's no need to look for one.

Indeed, when the religious believer talks about the "source" of the moral order, the scientist could reply that the source of the moral order is... *the electron*—or, strictly speaking, other subatomic particles that are more fundamental than the electron. After all, the primordial ooze ultimately consisted of subatomic particles; if the expansion of the moral imagination can be explained in materialist terms, then its deepest explanation is the deepest explanation for the material world in general—the grand unified theory that physicists have been looking for. So why start talking about God?

The believer has a reply, and it takes us back to chapter 18. There we saw something that modern biologists and the nineteenth-century Christian theologian William Paley agree on: the existence of animals—compared to, say, the existence of rocks—demands a special kind of explanation. And the reason isn't that the creation of an animal can't be explained in material terms; indeed, with growing success scientists understand how an animal's intricately integrated functionality (organs of digestion, of perception, and so on) grows from a fertilized egg via explicable physical processes. Rather, the idea is that this emphatically material process—the emergence of integrated functionality via biological maturation—-seems like the kind of physical system that wouldn't "just happen"; it must be the result of a creative process that imbues things with functionality—either a designer (such as a god, as Rev. Paley argued) or a "designer" (such as natural selection, as Darwin later argued).

Turns out it was the latter—a "designing" *process,* not a designing god. But, however big a setback that fact is for Rev. Paley's religious beliefs, there is a moral to this story that modern believers will want to emphasize: biologists agree that a strictly physical system or process—whose workings can be wholly explained in material terms—can have such extraordinary characteristics that it is fair to posit some special creative force as its source and ask about the nature of that force. Darwin inquired into the creative force behind plants and animals, and his answer was evolution. Surely the believer is entitled to ask the same question about evolution: Where did the amazing algorithm of natural selection come from?

Such a believer, by the way, would *not* here be making an argument for "intelligent design," the idea that natural selection isn't adequate to account for human evolution. On the contrary, the idea here is that natural selection is such a powerful mechanism that its origin demands a special explanation; that evolution by natural selection has patterns and properties every bit as extraordinary as an animal's maturation toward functional integration.

We spelled out some of those patterns in chapter 18: as natural selection ground along, creating more and more intelligent forms of life, it eventually created a form of life so intelligent as to give birth to a second creative process, cultural evolution; and as cultural (especially technological) evolution proceeded, the human species exhibited larger and larger expanses of social organization, and eventually this expanse approached global proportions; and in the process there appeared a *moral order,* linkage between the growth of social organization and progress toward moral truth. This moral order, to the believer, is among the grounds for suspecting that the system of evolution by natural selection itself demands a special creative explanation.

This suspicion may be wrong, but the argument behind it is intelligible and legitimate—parallel in structure to the argument that, before Darwin, provided motivation to search for the theory of natural selection. And if the believer, having concluded that the moral order suggests the existence of some as-yet-unknown source of creativity that set natural selection in motion, decides to call that source "God," well, that's the believer's business. After all, physicists got to choose the word "electron."

Of course, you could ask why the believer is entitled to suspect a creative source as exotic-sounding as a "god," when the creative source of organic life turned out to be a mere mechanical process known as natural selection. To which the believer might reply that a physical system exhibiting *moral* order demands a more exotic explanation than a physical system exhibiting only a more mundane form of order.

Even if the atheist scientist found this argument persuasive, the believer would still have some work to do. For there's a formidable argument the scientist could make against the whole idea of comparing the conjectured existence of God to the conjectured existence of the electron. It's a very pragmatic argument. Namely: Granted, we believe in the existence of the electron even though our attempts thus far to conceive of it have been imperfect at best. Still, there's a sense in which our imperfect conceptions of the electron have *worked*. We manipulate physical reality on the assumption that electrons exist as we imperfectly conceive them and—voilà—we get the personal computer. However crude our conceptions of the sources of material order, these conceptions have brought *material progress*.

The Believer Replies

To which the believer can reply: Well, thinking about the source of the universe's moral order crudely has on balance brought *moral progress*. Our conception of God has "grown"—that is, the moral compass of the gods we believe in has grown, and our moral imagination has thereby grown—as we've moved from hunter-gatherer societies to the brink of a unified global civilization; and, if we make it over that final threshold, we'll have gotten closer still to moral truth in the bargain. So to quit thinking about God now would be to abandon a path that has been successful on its own terms—not a path of scientific inquiry that has brought scientific progress, but a path of moral inquiry that has brought moral progress.[3]

The atheist scientist probably wouldn't buy this argument, and the resistance might assume roughly this form: Even if it's true that the idea of God helped get us to our present stage of moral evolution, can't we jettison this idea—this *illusion*—and go it alone from here? Can't we pursue moral truth for the sake of moral truth? Do you really *need* God in order to sustain moral progress the way physicists *need* the electron in order to sustain scientific progress?

It depends on who "you" is. Some people can lead morally exemplary lives without the idea of God. Others need God—and not necessarily because they can lead a virtuous life only if they fear hell and long for heaven; often it's because they can most readily lead a virtuous life if they think of moral truth as having some living embodiment. They need to feel that if they're bad they'll be disappointing some *one* and if they're good they'll be pleasing some *one* — and this one is the one whom, above all others, it is good to please and bad to disappoint.

This is hardly a surprising need. After all, the human moral equipment evolved in the context of human society, as a tool for navigating a social landscape; our moral sentiments are naturally activated *with respect to other beings;* we are "designed" by natural selection to be good out of obligation to others, for fear of the disapproval of others, in pursuit of the esteem of others. And for many people, carrying these human relations to the superhuman level works well. They are better people, and often happier people, thinking of a God who is aware of their daily struggle and offers solace or affirmation or reprimand; they can best stay aligned with the moral axis of the universe by thanking God, asking God to help them stay righteous, seeking forgiveness from God for their lapses. It's nice that some people can be paragons of virtue without this kind of help, but in a way it's surprising; the natural human condition is to ground your moral life in the existence of other beings, and the more ubiquitous the beings, the firmer the ground.

In other words: given the constraints on human nature, believers in God are interacting with the moral order as productively as possible by conceiving its source in a particular way, however imperfect that way is. Isn't that kind of like physicists who interact with the physical order as productively as possible by conceiving of its subatomic sources in a particular way, however imperfect that way is?

Indeed, you might even describe both forms of interaction as a kind of communication. The scientist manipulates reality in ways that implicitly say, "I think the subatomic world has a certain structure," and then reality speaks back, providing positive or negative feedback. The scientific process — the evolution of scientific ideas — is a long dialogue with nature. As we've seen, the evolution of God, and the attendant evolution of our moral imagination, could be described as a long dialogue with nature, too; our species, in the course of its history, has gotten feedback that has amounted to a moral education, feedback that has steered it toward moral truth. It is the profound directionality of this evolution that leads believers to suspect that the source of this feedback is somehow deeper than nature per se.

The average atheist scientist, if forced to read up to this point, would probably still be resisting the parallel between physicist and theist, insisting that there's a difference between conceiving imperfectly of an electron that in fact *exists* and conceiving imperfectly of a God that *doesn't exist.*

But this is a bit too simple. As noted above, some physicists think that electrons really *don't* exist. Yes, they say, there must be *some* source of the patterns we attribute to electrons, and yes, it makes sense to think of that source as electrons, because thinking that is productive — but in fact the source of the patterns is so unlike an electron that electrons per se can't be said to exist. (According to string theory, the patterns we attribute to particles are actually the "vibrations" emitted by stringlike entities. And even if string theory turns out to be empirically fruitful — which it hasn't been yet — why should we doubt that someday we'll learn that the image of vibrating strings is as misleading as string theorists say the image of a particle is?) In this view, the electron isn't just imperfectly conceived; it's an illusion, albeit a useful one.

Maybe the most defensible view — of electrons and of God — is to place them somewhere between illusion and imperfect conception. Yes, there is a source of the patterns we attribute to the electron, and the electron as conceived is a useful enough proxy for that source that we shouldn't denigrate it by calling it an "illusion"; still, our image of an electron is very, very different from what this source would look like were the human cognitive apparatus capable of apprehending it adroitly. So too with God: yes, there is a source of the moral order, and many people have a conception of God that is a useful proxy for that source; still that conception is very, very different from what the source of the moral order would look like were human cognition able to grasp it.

This gets us back to square one. Some people question whether there *is* a moral order. Like Steven Weinberg (in chapter 20), they might say that there is no moral order "out there" independent of moral laws we assert. But it's important to understand that this is where a lot of the disagreement lies: Is there a transcendent moral order or is there not? If there is, then people who take electrons seriously would seem hard pressed to deny the legitimacy of trying to conceive the source of that order; especially if you stress to them that the source of the moral order isn't necessarily inconsistent with a scientific worldview — it needn't be some kind of gratuitously interventionist anthropomorphic God or some mystical "force" that trumps the laws of the universe; maybe the laws of the universe, even when operating with normal regularity, are subordinate to the purpose, because they were designed with the purpose in mind. (Or, perhaps, "designed" with the purpose "in mind." After all, the "designer" could be some meta-natural-selection process. For all we know, universes evolve by a kind of cosmic natural selection, and universes that spawn life that evolves toward a belief in moral truth and closer adherence to it do a better job of replicating themselves than universes that lack this sort of moral order and teleological drift.)[4] Whatever we posit as the source of the moral order — anthropomorphic God who spawned natural selection or mechanistic selective process that spawned natural selection or something in between — the point is that if you believe the moral order exists, then the believer's attempt to conceive of its source, and relate to its source, would seem a legitimate exercise even by the standards of science regardless of how crude the conception of that source, regardless of how circuitous the means of relating to it.

And, anyway, maybe feeling that you're in contact with a personal god *isn't* such a circuitous way to relate to the source of the moral order. I suggested a couple of pages ago that when people feel the presence of a humanlike god, they're drawing on parts of the moral infrastructure built into them by natural selection — a sense of obligation to other people, guilt over letting people down, gratitude for gifts bestowed, and so on. And these things are in turn grounded in more basic components of the evolved moral infrastructure, including the very sense that there is such a thing as right and wrong. All these elements of human nature—all these ingredients of the sense of contact with a personal and sometimes judgmental God—are the product of non-zero-sum logic as realized via evolution; they are natural selection's way of steering us toward fruitful relationships; they embody natural selection's "recognition" that by cooperating with people (some people, at least) we can serve our own interests. And this non-zero-sum dynamic, remember, is central to the "Logos," the underlying logic of life that Philo of Alexandria, for one, considered a direct extension of God. So you might say that the evolution of the human moral equipment by natural selection was the Logos at work during a particular phase of organic aggregation; it was what allowed our distant ancestors to work together in small groups, and it set the stage for them to work together in much larger groups, including, eventually, transcontinental ones.

If you accept this argument—if you buy into this particular theology of the Logos—then feeling the presence of a personal god has a kind of ironic validity. On the one hand, you're imagining things; the divine being you sense "out there" is actually something inside you. On the other hand, this something inside you is an expression of forces "out there"; it's an incarnation of a non-zero-sum logic that predates and transcends individual people, a kind of logic that—in this theology of the Logos, at least—can be called divine. The feeling of contact with a transcendent divinity is in that sense solid.

Of course, there are lots of believers—most, in fact—who won't be on board for this whole exercise anyway. They don't want to just hear that *some* conception of a god might be defensible, or that a personal god is defensible as some sort of approximation of the truth. They would like to hear that, yes, their specific conception of God is right on target. Well, if that's what they would like to hear, this is not the book for them. (Maybe the Bible, or the Koran?) The best we can do within the intellectual framework of this book is posit the existence of God in a very abstract sense and defend belief in a more personal god in pragmatic terms — as being true in the sense that some other bedrock beliefs, including some scientific ones, are true.

Is God Love?

There are people who have it both ways — who harbor a fairly abstract conception of God, yet get some of the psychological perks of believing in a more personal god. One key to their success is their choice of abstraction. Perhaps the most commonly successful abstraction is love: God is love.

Is it true? Is God love? Like all characterizations of God, this one presumes more insight than I feel in possession of. But there's certainly something to the idea that love is connected to, indeed emanates from, the kind of God whose existence is being surmised here.

The connection comes via love's connection to the moral order of which that God is the source. That moral order has revealed itself via ever widening circles of non-zero-sumness that draw people toward the moral truth that mutual respect is warranted. As we saw in chapter 19, it is the moral imagination whose growth often paves the way for that truth, and it does so through the extension of a kind of sympathy, a subjective identification with the situation of the other. And as sympathy intensifies it approaches love. Love, you might say, is the apotheosis of the moral imagination; it can foster the most intimate identification with the other, the most intense appreciation of the moral worth of the other.

Sometimes love, in the course of leading to this moral truth, fosters more mundane truths. Suppose you are a parent and you (a) watch someone else's toddler misbehave, and then (b) watch your own toddler do the same. Your predicted reactions, respectively, are: (a) "What a brat!" and (b) "That's what happens when she skips her nap." Now (b) is often a correct explanation, whereas (a) — the "brat" reaction — isn't even an explanation. So in this case love leads toward truth. So too when a parent sees her child show off and concludes that the grandstanding is grounded in insecurity. That's an often valid explanation — unlike, say, "My neighbor's kid is such a show-off" — and brings insight into human nature to boot. Granted, love can warp our perception, too — happens every day. (For an extreme illustration, Google "Texas Cheerleader Mom.") Still, love at its best brings a truer apprehension of the other, an empathetic understanding that converges on the moral truth of respect, even reverence, for the other.

What's more, this empathetic understanding, the foundation of the moral imagination, might never have gotten off the ground had love not emerged on this planet. Long before history, and long before human beings, animals felt something like love for kin. And it's a pretty good bet that when animals first felt love is when they were first able to in any sense identify with the subjective interior of another animal. To put this point in physiological language: love probably sponsored the first "mirror neurons," a likely biological basis of the moral imagination and thus an essential element in the moral order's infrastructure.

There's an even deeper association between love and the moral order. The expanding moral compass sponsored by the moral order, as we've seen, is a manifestation of non-zero-sumness, of the fact that cultural (and in particular technological) evolution leads more and more people to play non-zero-sum games at greater and greater distances. And natural selection's invention of love, it turns out, was itself a manifestation of non-zero-sumness. Love was invented because, from the point of view of genetic proliferation — the point of view from which natural selection works — close kin are playing a non-zero-sum game; they share so many genes that they have a common Darwinian "interest" in getting each other's genes into subsequent generations.

Of course, the organisms aren't aware of this "interest." Even in our species — smart, as species go — the Darwinian logic isn't conscious logic; we don't go around thinking, "By loving my daugher I'll be more inclined to keep her alive and healthy until reproductive age, so through my love my genes will be playing a non-zero-sum game with the copies of them that reside in her." Indeed, the whole Darwinian point of love is to be a proxy for this logic; love gets us to behave *as if* we understood the logic; the invention of love, in some animal many millions of years ago, was nature's way of getting dim-witted organisms to seek a win-win outcome (win-win from a gene's-eye view), notwithstanding their inability to do so out of conscious strategy. And at that point the seeds of sympathy — love's corollary, and a key ingredient of the moral imagination — were planted.

Then, having been spawned by this biological non-zero-sumness, sympathy could be harnessed by a later wave of non-zero-sumness, a wave driven by cultural, and specifically technological, evolution. As interdependence, and hence social structure, grew beyond the bounds of family — and then beyond the bounds of hunter-gatherer band, of chiefdom, of state — the way was paved by extensions of sympathy. This sympathy didn't have to involve its initial sponsor, love; you don't have to love someone to trade with them or even to consider them compatriots. But there has to be enough moral imagination, enough sympathetic consideration, to keep them out of the cognitive category of enemy; you have to consider them, in some sense, one of you.

And, just as we've seen that love can foster truth within the family, this movement of sympathy beyond the family has also advanced the cause of truth. Because the fact is that other people *are* one of you. For better or worse, they are driven by the same kinds of feelings and hopes and delusions that drive you. When you keep people in the category of enemy you do so by, among other feats, willful blindness to this commonality.

It's pretty remarkable: natural selection's invention of love — in some anonymous animal many millions of years ago — was a prerequisite for the moral imagination whose expansion, here and now, could help keep the world on track; a prerequisite for our apprehension of the truth that the planet's salvation depends on: the objective truth of seeing things from the point of view of someone else, and the moral truth of considering someone else's welfare important.

Though we can no more conceive of God than we can conceive of an electron, believers can ascribe properties to God, somewhat as physicists ascribe properties to electrons. One of the more plausible such properties is love. And maybe, in this light, the argument for God is strengthened by love's organic association with truth — by the fact, indeed, that at times these two properties almost blend into one. You might say that love and truth are the two primary manifestations of divinity in which we can partake, and that by partaking in them we become truer manifestations of the divine. Then again, you might not say that. The point is just that you wouldn't have to be crazy to say it.

Appendix

How Human Nature Gave
Birth to Religion

When something appears in every known society, as religion does, the question of whether it is "in the genes" naturally arises. Did religion confer such benefits on our distant ancestors that genes favoring it spread by natural selection? There are scientists who believe the answer is yes—enough of them, in fact, to give rise to headlines like this one, in a Canadian newspaper: "Search continues for 'God gene.'"[1]

Expect to see that headline again, for the search is unlikely to reach a successful conclusion. And that isn't just because, obviously, no *single* gene could undergird something as complex as religion. Things don't look good even for the more nuanced version of the "God gene" idea—that a whole bunch of genes were preserved by natural selection because they inclined people toward religion.

Oddly, this verdict—that religion isn't in any straightforward sense "in the genes"—emerges from evolutionary psychology, a field that has been known to emphasize genetic influences on thought and emotion. Though some evolutionary psychologists think religion is a direct product of natural selection,[2] many—and probably most—don't.

This doesn't mean religion isn't in any sense "natural," and it doesn't mean religion isn't in some sense "in the genes." Everything people do is in *some* sense in the genes. (Try doing something without using any genes.) What's more, we can trace religion to specific parts of human nature that are emphatically in the genes. It's just that those parts of human nature seem to have evolved for some reason other than to sustain religion.[3]

The American psychologist William James, in his 1902 classic *The Varieties of Religious Experience,* captured the basic idea without referring to evolution: "There is religious fear, religious love, religious awe, religious joy, and so forth. But religious love is only man's natural emotion of love directed to a religious object; religious fear is only the ordinary fear of commerce, so to speak, the common quaking of the human breast, in so far as the notion of divine retribution may arouse it; religious awe is the same organic thrill which we feel in a forest at twilight, or in a mountain gorge; only this time it comes over us at the thought of our supernatural relations."[4]

If you want to put James's basic point in the language of evolutionary biology, you have to drag in the concept of an "adaptation." An adaptation is a trait whose underlying genes spread through the gene pool *by virtue of* their giving rise to that trait. Love, for example, seems to be an adaptation. Love of offspring, by inspiring nurturance of those offspring, can help genes get into future generations; as a result, genes underlying parental love seem to have spread *by virtue of* their conduciveness to love. You can similarly make arguments that awe and joy and fear—the other sentiments James cites—were, in themselves, adaptations. (Fearing a big aggressive animal, or a big aggressive human being, could save your skin and thus save the genes underlying the fear.) But that doesn't mean *religion* is an adaptation, even though religion may involve love, awe, joy, and fear and thus involve the genes underlying these things.

To shift back into less technical terminology: you might say that we were "designed" by natural selection to feel love and awe and joy and fear. (So long as you understand that "designed" is a metaphor; natural selection isn't like a human designer who consciously envisions the end product and then realizes it, but is rather a blind, dumb process of trial and error.) But to say that these emotions are a product of "design" isn't to say that when they're activated by religion they're working as "designed."

Similarly, humans were "designed" by natural selection to be able to run and were also "designed" to feel competitive spirit, but that doesn't mean they were "designed" to participate in track meets. Religion, like track, doesn't seem to be an "adaptation." Both seem to be what the paleontologist Stephen Jay Gould called a "spandrel"—a phenomenon supported by genes that had become part of the species by doing something other than supporting that phenomenon. A spandrel is an incidental by-product of the organic "design" process, whereas an adaptation is a direct product. Religion seems to be a spandrel.

And yet, you might say, religion does have the hallmarks of design. It is a complex, integrated system that seems to serve specific functions. For example, religions almost always handle some key "rites of passage"—getting married, getting buried, and so on whose ritualized handling is probably good for the society. How do you explain the coherence and functionality of religion without appealing to a designer—or, at least, a "designer"?

You don't. But biological evolution isn't the only great "designer" at work on this planet. There is also cultural evolution: the selective transmission of "memes"—beliefs, habits, rituals, songs, technologies, theories, and so forth—from person to person. And one criterion that shapes cultural evolution is social utility; memes that are conducive to smooth functioning at the group level often have an advantage over memes that aren't. Cultural evolution is what gave us modern corporations, modern government, and modern religion.

For that matter, it gave us nonmodern religion. Whenever we look at a "primitive" religion, we are looking at a religion that has been evolving culturally for a long time. Though observed hunter-gatherer religions give clues about what the average religion was like 12,000 years ago, before the invention of agriculture, none of them much resembles religion in its literally *primitive* phase, the time (whenever that was) when religious beliefs and practices emerged. Rather, what are called "primitive" religions are bodies of belief and practice that have been evolving—culturally—over tens or even hundreds of millennia. Generation after generation, human minds have been accepting some beliefs, rejecting others, shaping and reshaping religion along the way.

So to explain the existence of "primitive" religion—or for that matter any other kind of religion—we have to first understand what kinds of beliefs and practices the human mind is amenable to. What kinds of information does the mind naturally filter out, and what kinds naturally penetrate it? Before religion appeared and started evolving by cultural evolution, how had genetic evolution shaped the environment in which it would evolve—that is, the human brain?

To put the question another way: What kinds of beliefs was the human mind "designed" by natural selection to harbor? For starters, not true ones.

At least, not true ones per se. To the extent that accurate perception and comprehension of the world helped humanity's ancestors get genes into the next generation, then of course mental accuracy would be favored by natural selection. And usually mental accuracy *is* good for the survival and transmission of the genes. That's why we have excellent equipment for depth perception, for picking up human voices against background noise, and so on. Still, in situations where accurate perception and judgment impede survival and reproduction, you would expect natural selection to militate against accuracy.

Truth and Consequences

In 1974, San Francisco newspaper heiress Patty Hearst was kidnapped by a radical group called the Symbionese Liberation Army, whose goals included "death to the fascist insect that preys upon the life of the people." After being kept in a closet for a while, she came to identify with her new peer group. Before long, she was enthusiastically helping them generate income, at one point brandishing a machine gun during a bank robbery. When left alone, with an opportunity to escape, she didn't take it.

She later described the experience: "I had virtually no free will until I was separated from them for about two weeks. And then it suddenly, you know, slowly began to dawn that they just weren't there anymore. I could actually think my own thoughts." Hearst didn't just accept her captors' "subjective" beliefs, such as ideology; she bought into their views about how the physical world works. One of her captors "didn't want me thinking about rescue because he thought that brain waves could be read or that, you know, they'd get a psychic in to find me. And I was even afraid of that."

Hearst's condition of coerced credulity is called the Stockholm syndrome, after a kidnapping in Sweden. But the term "syndrome" may be misleading in its suggestion of abnormality. Hearst's response to her circumstances was probably an example of human nature functioning properly; we seem to be "designed" by natural selection to be brainwashed.

Some people find this prospect a shocking affront to human autonomy, but they tend not to be evolutionary psychologists. In Darwinian terms, it makes sense that our species could contain genes encouraging blind credulity in at least some situations. If you are surrounded by a small group of people on whom your survival depends, rejecting the beliefs that are most important to them will not help you live long enough to get your genes into the next generation.

Confinement with a small group of people may sound so rare that natural selection would have little chance to take account of it, but it is in a sense the natural human condition. Humans evolved in small groups—twenty, forty, sixty people—from which emigration was often not a viable option. Survival depended on social support: sharing food, sticking together during fights, and so on. To alienate your peers by stubbornly contesting their heartfelt beliefs would have lowered your chances of genetic proliferation.

Maybe that explains why you don't have to lock somebody in a closet to get a bit of the Stockholm syndrome. Religious cults just offer aimless teenagers a free bus ride to a free meal, and after the recruits have been surrounded by believers for a few days, they tend to warm up to the beliefs. And there doesn't have to be some powerful authority figure pushing the beliefs. In one famous social psychology experiment, subjects opined that two lines of manifestly different lengths were the same length, once a few of their "peers" (who were in fact confederates) voiced that opinion.

Given this conformist bias in human nature, it's not surprising that people born into "primitive" religions—or any other religions—accept an elaborate belief system that outside observers find highly dubious. But the question remains: How did the elaborate belief system ever come to exist? Granted that people are inclined to accept their community's official edifice of belief and ritual (especially if no alternatives are on offer). But how did the edifice come to exist in the first place? How did religion get built from the ground up?

God Bites Man

To answer this question we have to view cultural evolution at a fine-grained level. We have to think about individual units of culture—beliefs and practices, in this case—and how they spread. The biologist Richard Dawkins coined the term "meme" for units of culture, in part because it sounds a bit like "gene," and he wanted to stress some parallels between cultural and biological evolution. For example: just as genes are transmitted from body to body, down the generations, memes are transmitted from mind to mind. And just as newly minted genes "compete" for a place in the gene pool, newly minted memes "compete" for the finite space in the world's supply of human brains. In this constant struggle of meme against meme, what kinds of memes will have a "selective advantage"?

Newspapers are a good place to look for clues. Newspaper editors work hard to figure out what kinds of information people want, and to fill that demand. They are accomplished meme engineers, and thus students of human nature. One thing you'll notice about newspapers is that they have a bias toward good things and bad things. The headlines "Stock market rises by 5 percent" and "Stock market drops by 5 percent" will get better play than the headline "Stock market does nothing in particular." Here religions, and certainly "primitive" religions, are like newspapers. In every hunter-gatherer society, religion is devoted largely to explaining why bad things happen and why good things happen—illness, recovery; famine, abundance; and so on.

There is also devotion to raising the ratio of good to bad. The Andaman Islanders, convinced that whistling at night attracts bad spirits whereas singing repels them, do more singing in the dark than whistling in the dark.[5] People naturally try to exert control over their environment, and believing that they have such control naturally makes them feel good. So people's minds are open to ideas that promise to give them such control. This doesn't mean people uncritically embrace every such idea that comes their way. But it does mean that these ideas get their attention—and for a meme, that's the first step toward acceptance. While the Andaman Island meme asserting that thunderstorms are divine punishment for melting beeswax was hardly guaranteed a place in the society's religion, it had a big head start over memes saying, "Thunderstorms just happen—there's nothing you can do about it."

Another thing you'll notice in newspapers is that the strange and novel wins out over the ordinary and expected. Tuberculosis and the West Nile virus are both bad news, and in terms of the number of people killed, tuberculosis is the worse of the two. Yet the headline "Outbreak of deadly new virus puzzles experts" easily crowds out "Usual number of people expected to die of tuberculosis this year" (except, perhaps, in the humor magazine *The Onion,* which earns its laughs by violating this pattern). As journalism sages famously put it: "Dog bites man" is not a story; "Man bites dog" is a story.[6]

It makes sense that human brains would naturally seize on strange, surprising things, since the predictable things have already been absorbed into the expectations that guide them through the world; news of the strange and surprising may signal that some amendment of our expectations is warranted. But one property of strange, surprising claims is that they're often untrue. So if they get preferred access to our brains, that gives falsehood a kind of advantage — if a fleeting advantage — over truth. In the days after the terrorist attacks of September 11, 2001, one widely circulated story was that a man at the top of one of the twin towers had survived by sliding down the rubble as it formed. It was a story so incredible that it virtually compelled you to click the "forward" icon on your e-mail — and a story so incredible that it wasn't true. It was an example of the famous dictum that a lie can get halfway around the world before the truth has a chance to get its boots on.

Of course, in the long run, the truth often does get its boots on, and people often welcome it upon its arrival. Indeed, if the attraction to surprising news weren't balanced by an attraction to claims that survive subsequent scrutiny, the average human ancestor wouldn't have lived long enough to become a human ancestor. Imagine a local sage, 200,000 years ago, saying that eating a certain berry will let you live forever. Now imagine that the first two people who follow his advice drop dead. Genes that counseled continued faith in advice thus besieged by countervailing evidence would not long remain a part of the species, whereas genes that inclined the brain to take account of such evidence might. This natural human respect for evidence is the reason convincing someone that one plus one equals three, or that water flows uphill, takes real work.

But some kinds of beliefs are harder to test than those two. And hard-to-test beliefs could do well in the process of cultural evolution that gave birth to religion. Indeed, hunter-gatherer religious belief — like religious belief generally — consists largely of claims that resist falsification. The Haida, a people indigenous to the northwest coast of North America, when caught in a storm while out at sea, would try to appease the relevant authorities (killer whale deities) by pouring a cup of fresh water into the sea or putting some tobacco or deer tallow on the end of a paddle.[7] Many people no doubt returned from sea to report that these measures had kept them from drowning. No one, presumably, ever reported that they had taken these measures but drowned anyway.

To be sure, some religious beliefs can be put to a clearer test.

If the Andaman Islanders were right, and melting beeswax was a leading cause of thunderstorms, then a melting moratorium should cut down on thunderstorms. But how can you be sure that, in the days preceding a thunderstorm, no one in your village melted a smidgen of wax — or engaged in some other thunder-inducing activity, such as making a loud noise while the cicadas were singing?

Such loopholes are found in modern religions, too. If you pray for someone to recover from illness, and they don't, then prayer would seem to have lost credibility. But religions usually have ways of explaining such failure. Maybe you or the sick person had done something horribly wrong, and this is God's punishment. Or maybe God just works in mysterious ways.

So far, then, we would expect the following kinds of memes to be survivors in the dog-eat-dog world of cultural evolution: claims that (a) are somewhat strange, surprising, counterintuitive; (b) illuminate sources of fortune and misfortune; (c) give people a sense that they can influence these sources; (d) are by their nature hard to test decisively. In this light, the birth of religion doesn't seem so mysterious.

But doesn't our attraction to strangeness have its limits? It's one thing to believe that a man could survive a slide down a crumpling skyscraper through a series of lucky breaks. It's quite another to believe, with the Inuit (in chapter 1), that a sudden shortage of game is the work of a pouty female deity who lives at the bottom of the sea. In other words, "Man bites dog," however unlikely, seems more plausible than "God bites man."

Lord of the Chimps

But, actually, the idea of a personal god or spirit who peevishly withholds food, or maliciously hurls lightning, gets a boost from the evolved human brain. People reared in modern scientific societies may consider it only natural to ponder some feature of the world — the weather, say — and try to come up with a mechanistic explanation couched in the abstract language of natural law. But evolutionary psychology suggests that a much more *natural* way to explain *anything* is to attribute it to a humanlike agent. This is the way we're "designed" by natural selection to explain things. Our brain's capacity to think about causality—to ask why something happened and come up with theories that help us predict what will happen in the future—evolved in a specific context: other brains. When our distant ancestors first asked "Why," they weren't asking about the behavior of water or weather or illness; they were asking about the behavior of their peers.

That's a somewhat speculative (and, yes, hard-to-test!) claim. We have no way of observing our prehuman ancestors one or two or three million years ago, when the capacity to think explicitly about causality was evolving by natural selection. But there are ways to shed light on the process.

For starters, we can observe our nearest nonhuman relatives, chimpanzees. We didn't evolve *from* chimps, but chimps and humans do share a common ancestor in the not-too-distant past (4 to 7 million years ago). And chimps are probably a lot more like that common ancestor than humans are. Chimps aren't examples of our ancestors circa 5 million BCE but they're close enough to be illuminating.

As the primatologist Frans de Waal has shown, chimpanzee society shows some clear parallels with human society. One of them is in the title of his book *Chimpanzee Politics*. Groups of chimps form coalitions—alliances—and the most powerful alliance gets preferred access to resources (notably a resource that in Darwinian terms is important: sex partners). Natural selection has equipped chimps with emotional and cognitive tools for playing this political game. One such tool is anticipation of a given chimp's future behavior based on past behavior. De Waal writes of a reigning alpha male, Yeroen, who faced growing hostility from a former ally named Luit: "He already sensed that Luit's attitude was changing and he knew that his position was threatened."[8]

One could argue about whether Yeroen was actually pondering the situation in as clear and conscious a way as de Waal suggests. But even if chimps aren't quite up to explicit inference, they do seem close. If you imagine their politics getting more complex (more like, say, human politics), and them getting smarter (more like humans), you're imagining an organism evolving toward conscious thought about causality. And the causal agents about which these organisms will think are other such organisms, because the arena of causality is the social arena. In this realm, when a bad thing happens (like a challenge for Yeroen's alpha spot) or a good thing happens (like an ally coming to Yeroen's aid), it is another organism that is making the bad or good thing happen.

To be sure, other kinds of bad and good things happen to chimps: droughts, banana bonanzas, and so on. But there's no reason to think chimps are anywhere near consciously puzzling over those things — trying to anticipate droughts the way they try to anticipate the behavior of their neighbors. And there's no reason to think that our prehuman ancestors were, either. The best guess is that when natural selection built the mental machinery for predictively pondering causality, the causal agents in question were peers — fellow prehumans. (Is he going to punch me? Is she going to betray me?) Moreover, when our ancestors first started *talking* about causality, they were probably talking about peers. (Why did you punch me? Do you know why she betrayed me?)

I'm not just talking about a habit. I'm not saying our ancestors were *used to* pondering questions of "Why?" by thinking about human beings. I'm suggesting that the human mind is built to do that — was "designed" by natural selection to do it.

So it's no surprise that when people first started expanding their curiosity, started talking about why bad and good things emanate from beyond the social universe, they came up with the kinds of answers that had made sense within their social universe. To answer a "why" question — such as "Why did the thunderstorm come just as that baby was being born?" — with anything *other* than a human-like creature would have been kind of strange.

More than one hundred years ago Edward Tylor wrote that "spirits are simply personified causes,"[9] but he probably didn't appreciate, back then, how deeply natural personification is. Indeed, to talk about "personifying" causes is in a sense to get the story backward. Better to say that the modern scientific notion of a "cause" is a depersonified human being—or a depersonified god.

Even in modern science, the depersonification process may not be complete. Some philosophers believe that to chop the world up into "causes" and "effects" is to impose a falsely binary scheme on what is in fact a seamless reality. It may be that our "modern" way of thinking about causality still carries the vestiges of our primitive brains, still falsely reflects a social arena of causality, in which "causes" are distinct agents.

Spirits with Legs

The idea that gods and spirits got their start as a supernatural version of people encounters one obvious objection: In hunter-gatherer societies, aren't some supernatural beings thought of as animals, not humans? And aren't some supernatural beings—especially the ones anthropologists call "spirits"—too vague a life form to qualify as either human or animal? Why should we, along with Tylor, talk of *personified* causes when Tylor's own terminology—*animated* causes—would fit better?

For starters, however unlike a human a "spirit" may sound, when anthropologists ask people to draw pictures of spirits, the pictures usually look more or less like humans: two arms, two legs, a head.[10] Similarly, a great god of the ancient Chinese was called Tian, or "heaven," which sounds quite unlike a person—yet the earliest written symbol for that god is a stick figure: two arms, two legs, a head.[11]

Even when a supernatural being looks like an animal—as those snowmaking birds of the Klamath (chapter 1) presumably did—it doesn't act like an animal.[12] It may have wings or fur or scales, and it may lack various parts of a normal human being, but it won't lack the part that explains why human beings do the things they do. As the anthropologist Pascal Boyer has observed, "the only feature of humans that is always projected onto supernatural beings is the mind."[13]

Boyer believes that the genetic architecture of human cognition helps explain why people conceive of gods as they do. The mind, he says, comes with built-in assumptions about reality. People naturally divide the world into a few basic "ontological categories"—such as plants, animals, human beings—and attribute certain properties to beings that fall into a certain category. In other words, we have a mental "template" that helps us think about plants, and a different template for people, and so on. We assume that if we walk up and whack a person, the person won't like it and may retaliate, whereas whacking a plant is less hazardous. In Boyer's view, when people think about a god or spirit, their brains are invoking the template for human beings, but in amended form, with a few of the template's normal properties changed. Thus, the Abrahamic God is a lot like a person—capable of love, anger, disappointment, jealousy—except that he knows everything and can do anything.

To some people, this last part—omniscience and omnipotence—strains credulity. In a modern scientific culture, that's no surprise. But Boyer's work suggests that such scarcely credible features would have been an asset to a god meme that was just getting off the ground tens of thousands of years ago. His experiments show that things with starkly counterintuitive features—things with properties that aren't part of their template—are especially memorable. If you tell someone about a table "that felt sad when people left the room," they are more likely to remember it months later than if you tell them about a normal table, one with the unshakable stoicism generically associated with furniture.[14] Presumably they are more likely to tell people about it as well. So memes that depict gods as unlike anything you've ever seen would have a kind of advantage over more "plausible" memes.

So long as the strangeness of these gods didn't get excessive, that is. Boyer says that the meme most conducive to spreading would be one that is strange but easy to think about: it might have one or two basic "ontological violations," such as omniscience and omnipotence, but these violations wouldn't be so numerous, or so quirky, that imagining the behavior of such a deity was unwieldy.

In fact, even traits like omniscience and omnipotence seem to press against the limits of imagination. When two psychologists quizzed people about the properties of a supreme being, the answers were overwhelmingly "theologically correct"—omniscience, ubiquity, and so on. But then these same people were led to think more concretely, to imagine God actually exerting influence in specific situations. Suddenly they conjured up a more human deity. They thought of God as occupying a single point in space and being unable to do two things at once, and, in the words of one of the psychologists, "needing to see and hear in order to complete otherwise fallible knowledge." [15]

This points to a problem for modern theology: as divinity is defined more abstractly to fit more comfortably into a scientific worldview, God becomes harder for people to relate to. In the mid-twentieth century, when Paul Tillich defined God as "the ground of being," some fellow theologians approved, but he was also met with dismay, incomprehension, and the occasional charge of atheism. Still, he could rightly have replied that his critics suffered from innately narrow vision; being humans, they labored under the handicap of minds designed to fathom the social universe, not the universe writ large.

Dealing with the Supernatural

According to the book of Genesis, "God created man in his own image." [16] According to Aristotle, "men create the gods after their own image." [17] As should be clear by now, Aristotle seems to have been onto something, especially when it comes to the *minds* of gods. So, in theory, some of the more basic features of the human mind should be fairly standard equipment in gods, especially the gods of "primitive" religions.

That seems to be the case, and one of these features deserves special consideration: the part of the human mind shaped by the evolutionary dynamic known as "reciprocal altruism." In light of this dynamic, much about the origin of religion, and for that matter much about contemporary religion, makes a new kind of sense.

Thanks to reciprocal altruism, people are "designed" to settle into mutually beneficial relationships with other people, people whom they can count on for things ranging from food to valuable gossip to social support, and who in turn can count on them. We enter these alliances almost without thinking about it, because our genetically based emotions draw us in. We feel gratitude for a favor received, along with a sense of obligation, which may lead us to return the favor. We feel growing trust of and affection for people who prove reliable reciprocators (aka "friends"), which keeps us entwined in beneficial relationships. This is what feelings like gratitude and trust are *for*—the reason they're part of human nature.

But of course, not everyone merits our trust. Some people accept our gifts of food and never reciprocate, or try to steal our mates, or exhibit disrespect in some other fashion. And if we let people thus take advantage of us day after day, the losses add up. In the environment of our evolution, these losses could have made the difference between surviving and not surviving, between prolifically procreating and barely procreating. So natural selection gave us emotions that lead us to punish the untrustworthy—people who violate our expectations of exchange, people who seem to lack the respect that a mutually beneficial relationship demands. They fill us with outrage, with moral indignation, and that outrage—working as "designed"—impels us to punish them in one way or another, whether by actually harming them or just by withholding future altruism. That will teach them! (Perhaps more important, it will also teach anyone else who is watching, and in the ancestral hunter-gatherer environment, pretty much everyone in your social universe was watching.)

This is the social context in which the human mind evolved: a world full of neighbors who, to varying degrees, are watching you for signs of betrayal or disrespect or dishonesty—and who, should they see strong evidence of such things, will punish you. In such a social universe, when misfortune comes your way, when someone hits you or ridicules you or suddenly gives you the cold shoulder, there's a good chance it's because they feel you've violated the rules of exchange. Maybe you've failed to do them some favor they think they were due, or maybe you've shown them disrespect by doing something that annoys them.

Surely it is no coincidence that this generic explanation of why misfortune might emanate from a human being is also the generic explanation of why misfortune emanates from gods. In hunter-gatherer religions — and lots of other religions — when bad things happen, the root cause is almost always that people in one sense or another fail to respect the gods. They either fail to give gods their due (fail, say, to make adequate sacrifices to ancestral spirits), or they do things that annoy gods (like, say, making a noise while cicadas are singing). And the way to make amends to the aggrieved gods is exactly the way you'd make amends to aggrieved people: either give them something (hence ritual sacrifice), or correct future behavior so that it doesn't annoy them (quit making noises while cicadas are singing).[18]

In this light, bizarre superstitions seem less bizarre. The Ainu, the indigenous hunter-gatherers of Japan, scrupulously refrained from spitting into fires.[19] Strange! But if you accept their premise that hearth fires come courtesy of the fire goddess, the rest follows. You don't do things that insult people who give you gifts, because if you do they'll get in a snit and stop giving. And one thing that might well be taken as an insult is to spit on the gift.

Boyer believes that much of religion can be explained this way — a result of our attributing to supernatural causal agents the very human emotions that evolved to regulate reciprocal altruism; like our fellow human beings, gods are bent on enforcing their deals with us. This doesn't mean that the grievances of gods are always just. *Evil* deities, Boyer says, are "enforcers of unfair deals."[20] But it's only natural that there should be such unfair gods; there are, after all, unfair people. (And people who can get away with being unfair — that is, can get more than they give — tend to be powerful, like gods.)

Two and a half millennia ago the Greek poet Xenophanes speculated that if horses had gods, these gods would be horses. Could be, but we'll never know, and in any event that's not quite the point being made here. It isn't that any imaginable intelligent species, in trying to explain mysterious things, would attribute them to beings like itself. It's that the history of the human species—notably including the evolution of the human brain in a context of reciprocal altruism, of social exchange—pointed it in that direction.[21] A law of the social jungle in which the human brain evolved is this: when bad things happen to you, it often means someone is mad at you, maybe because you've done something to offend them; making amends is often a good way to make the bad things stop happening. If you substitute "some god or spirit" for "someone," you have a law that is found in every known hunter-gatherer religion.

Back into Time

That religious ideas naturally appeal to the human mind doesn't, by itself, explain how religion got off the ground. Granted that religious "memes" have a "selective advantage" in cultural evolution, how exactly would a given meme—a particular religious belief—first take shape and gain momentum? We'll never know for sure, but human nature makes it easy to sketch a plausible scenario.

First, people like to command attention, and one way to do that is to place yourself at the center of dramatic events. In Mark Twain's *The Adventures of Tom Sawyer,* Tom Sawyer runs away with his friends Huckleberry Finn and Joe to play pirates on the Mississippi River, and the townspeople conclude that the boys have drowned. Twain describes their friends gathering and

> talking in reverent tones of how Tom did so-and-so, the last time they saw him, and how Joe said this and that small trifle (pregnant with awful prophecy, as they could easily see now!)—and each speaker pointed out the exact spot where the lost lads stood at the time, and then added something like "and I was a-standing just so—just as I am now, and as if you was him—I was as close as that—and he smiled, just this way—and

then something seemed to go all over me, like — awful, you know — and I never thought what it meant, of course, but I can see now!"

Then there was a dispute about who saw the dead boys last in life, and many claimed that dismal distinction, and offered evidences, more or less tampered with by the witness; and when it was ultimately decided who *did* see the departed last, and exchanged the last words with them, the lucky parties took upon themselves a sort of sacred importance, and were gaped at and envied by all the rest.[22]

There is no reason to think that this incentive to claim special witness to high drama was any less powerful among hunter-gatherers circa 30,000 BCE than among midwestern Americans circa 1900 CE. Imagine that you are one of those hunter-gatherers and you walk past a place where someone died mysteriously, and you hear leaves rustle eerily. That's a story that will get people's attention, and you can heighten the attention by stressing how exquisitely timed the rustling was. And, by the way, didn't you catch sight of a shadowy — almost ethereal — creature out of the corner of your eye?

The anthropologist Stewart Guthrie has suggested that hunter-gatherers would be encouraged to make just such false sightings by standard human mental equipment — something called a "hyperactive agent-detection device."[23] Because the costs of failing to detect a predator lurking in the woods are much higher than the costs of detecting one that isn't there, natural selection, he plausibly argues, may have biased our brains toward "false positives": you hear a rustling, your mind flashes the vivid hypothesis of some generic animal that's doing the rustling, and you turn toward it expectantly. Did you actually see something? Kind of.

In any event, if upon recounting your eerie encounter you get caught up in the spirit of the story and *say* you saw an ethereal being, then you may convince not just your audience, but yourself. One notable finding of modern psychology is how systematically misleading memory is. People often remember events wrongly from the get-go, and even when they don't, their memory can later be steered toward falsehood. In particular, the act of reporting false details can cement them firmly in mind. You don't just recount what you remember; you remember what you recount.[24] (Football star O. J. Simpson's former agent was sure Simpson had killed his ex-wife and also sure that Simpson believed he didn't.)[25] This built-in fallibility makes sense from a Darwinian standpoint, allowing people to bend the truth self-servingly with an air of great and growing conviction. And, clearly, bent truths of a religious sort could be self-serving. If you were a close friend or relative of the deceased, then the idea that his powerful spirit is afoot may incline people to treat you nicely, lest they invite his wrath.

Another gem from social psychology: publicly espousing something not only helps convince you of its truth; it shapes your future perception, inclining you to see evidence supporting it but not evidence against it.[26] So if you speculate that the strange, shadowy creature was the disgruntled spirit of the deceased, you'll likely find corroboration. You may notice that one of his enemies fell ill only a week after your sighting, while forgetting that one of his friends fell ill a few days earlier.

If you're a person of high status, all of this will carry particular weight, as such people are accorded unusual (and often undue) credibility. If, in a hunter-gatherer band of thirty people, someone widely esteemed claims to have seen something strange—and has a theory about what it was—twenty people may be convinced right off the bat. Then the aforementioned tendency of people to conform to peer opinion could quickly yield unanimity.[27]

The number of mental tendencies involved in the creation and nourishment of religious falsehoods shouldn't surprise us. After all, the mind was built by a process that is, strictly speaking, indifferent to truth. Natural selection favors traits that are good at getting their bearer's genes into the next generation, period. If saying something false, or believing something false, often furthered that goal during human evolution, then the human mind will naturally encourage some kinds of falsity. This systematic muddle isn't an exclusive property of the "primitive" mind, as John Lubbock (chapter 1) suggested; all of the above delusory tendencies have been documented in people living in modern societies—many of them students at fine universities!

So why are people in modern societies so often aghast at "primitive" religion, so unable to comprehend how "primitive" belief got started? In part, it is the classic human failure of objectivity—an inability to see that your own beliefs may seem as strange to others as theirs seem to you. (An African Pygmy once responded to a missionary's description of heaven by asking, "How do you know? Have you died and been there?") And in part it is a failure of imagination. Imagine that you are living in a small encampment surrounded by jungle or woodland or desert, entirely untouched by science and modern technology. Within the encampment, the social universe operates by largely intelligible laws; people don't generally, say, fly into a rage and assault their neighbors without a cause of some sort or another. But from outside this universe come mighty and momentous forces—storms, droughts, deadly animals, fatal illness. You are viscerally interested in explaining and controlling these things; you readily absorb and repeat any news or conjecture bearing on this goal. And, above all, you are only human. The rest is history.

Thinking and Feeling

This view of religion's origins—the view from modern psychology—is in some ways just an updated version of Edward Tylor's view: people first conceived of gods and spirits to explain the unexplained. Indeed, Tylor even seemed to vaguely anticipate the modern focus on reciprocal altruism: "Spiritual beings are held to affect or control the events of the material world, and man's life here and hereafter; and it being considered that they hold intercourse with men, and receive pleasure or displeasure from human actions, the belief in their existence leads naturally, and it might almost be said inevitably, sooner or later to active reverence and propitiation."[28]

Still, there is a difference of emphasis. When Tylor says belief in gods "leads naturally" to their propitiation, he seems to mean that this progression was *logically* natural — that extended reflection led eventually to the conclusion that giving gods respect and foodstuffs would satisfy them. An evolutionary psychologist, in contrast, might stress how viscerally natural this propitiation is; it *feels* like the right thing to do. Tylor's oft-ridiculed reference to "ancient savage philosophers" (see chapter 1) does indeed connote more in the way of cool, detached reflection than was probably operative — and than is operative generally in human beings. Some features of the mind that undergird religious belief are "cognitive" traits that guide our "intellectual" lives but are also shot through with feeling.

Varieties of Religious Experience

In addition to our mental machinery for thinking consciously about causality — the machinery shaped by the evolution of reciprocal altruism — there are other innate tools for taking causality into account, and some of them operate almost entirely at the level of feeling.

For example, back when our ancestors didn't know that disease travels by microscopic organism, natural selection seems to have filled this knowledge gap, installing in our lineage an aversion to disease-carrying things. That is the conclusion the psychologist Paul Rozin reached by studying disgust.[29] It's no coincidence, he believes, that things which fill people everywhere with disgust — rotting corpses, excrement, putrid meat — are hazardous to our health.

However unsophisticated a feeling disgust may seem like, it actually entails a kind of metaphysics: a sense that some things are deeply impure and emit an invisible aura of badness, creating a dread zone. Pascal Boyer has suggested that disgust — our "contagion inference system" — may thus energize notions of ritual pollution that figure in many religions.[30] (Recall the sin that so peeved the sea goddess in chapter 1: failing to throw out items contaminated by proximity to a miscarriage.)

There is another feature of the human mind that may be involved in religious experience and that, like the "contagion inference system," is a way of taking account of causality without thinking consciously about it. In fact, it entered our lineage so long before consciously rational thought that it exists in all mammals. It is called "associative learning."

If a dog burns itself on rocks that surround a dying campfire, it will thereafter avoid such rocks. What is going on in the dog's mind is hard to say, but it probably isn't extended reflection on the causal link between fires and hot rocks, or between hot rocks and singed fur. Presumably the dog has just acquired something like a fear of those rocks, a fear that leads it to behave *as if* it understood the connection between rocks around dying campfires and singed fur. I once tried to walk a golden retriever past an intersection where, weeks earlier, she had been hit by a car. As we approached the intersection, she walked more and more slowly and warily until finally she came to a halt and started desperately resisting attempts to move her farther. It was as if, in her mind, the intersection was giving off a kind of spooky aura, and the closer she got to it, the stronger the aura felt.

Vestiges of this kind of crude learning mechanism in the human brain may incline people to see objects or places as inhabited by evil, a perception that figures in various religions. Hence, perhaps, the sense of dread that has been associated by some anthropologists with primitive religious experience.

And what of the sense of awe that has also been identified with religious experience — most famously by the German theologian Rudolf Otto (who saw primordial religious awe as often intermingled with dread)? Was awe originally "designed" by natural selection for some nonreligious purpose? Certainly feelings of that general type sometimes overtake people confronted by other people who are overwhelmingly powerful. They crouch abjectly, beg desperately for mercy. (In the Persian Gulf War of 1991, after weeks of American bombing, Iraqi soldiers were so shaken that they knelt and kissed the hands of the first Americans they saw even when those Americans were journalists.) On the one hand, this is a pragmatic move — the smartest thing to do under the circumstances. But it seems fueled at least as much by instinctive emotion as by conscious strategy. Indeed, chimpanzees do roughly the same thing. Faced with a formidable foe, they either confront it with a "threat display" or, if it's *too* formidable, crouch in submission.

There's no telling what chimps feel in these instances, but in the case of humans there have been reports of something like awe. That this feeling is naturally directed toward other living beings would seem to lubricate theological interpretations of nature; if a severe thunderstorm summons the same emotion as an ill-tempered and potent foe, it's not much of a stretch to imagine an ill-tempered foe behind the thunderstorm.

Even chimpanzees may at times make a dim version of this conceptual leap. The primatologist Jane Goodall has observed chimps reacting to a rainstorm or a waterfall by making a threat display. She speculates that the "awe and wonder" that "underlie most religions" may be grounded in "such primeval, uncomprehending surges of emotion."[31]

None of this is meant to deny the possibility of valid religious experience. The prospect that some states of consciousness move us closer to what mystics call "ultimate reality" — or even toward something worthy of the name "divine" — is hardly excluded by a scientific worldview. But defenders of religion would be ill advised to stake its validity on the claim, as Otto suggested in *The Idea of the Holy,* that at the dawn of religious history lies some mystical or revelatory experience that defies naturalistic explanation. Because the more we learn about the labyrinthine and sometimes irrational character of human nature, the easier it is to explain the origin of religion without invoking such a thing. Religion arose out of a hodgepodge of genetically based mental mechanisms designed by natural selection for thoroughly mundane purposes.

At times Otto himself seemed to doubt that religious experience could defy scientific explanation. In *The Idea of the Holy,* after discussing such things as spirit worship, ancestor worship, and primitive magic, he wrote,

> Different as these things are, they are all haunted by a common—and that a numinous—element, which is easily identifiable. They did not, perhaps, take their origin out of this common numinous element directly; they may have all exhibited a preliminary stage at which they were merely "natural" products of the naive, rudimentary fancies of primitive times. But these things acquire a strand of a quite special kind, which alone gives them their character as forming the vestibule of religion, brings them first to clear and explicit form, and furnishes them with the prodigious power over the minds of men which history universally proves them to possess.

Otto's exact meaning is debatable, but the general drift is intriguing: that elements of early religion, though themselves of mundane origin, could through subsequent cultural evolution come to acquire a deeply, validly spiritual character. This idea isn't implausible. But how far humanity has traveled along the path of spiritual evolution is another question altogether.

A Note on Translations

Since I don't speak Hebrew, Greek, or Arabic (to say nothing of earlier versions of these languages), I had to rely on English translations of the Abrahamic scriptures. This involved making some choices.

In the case of the Hebrew Bible (aka the Old Testament) and the New Testament, my choice was simple: I went with the New Revised Standard Version of the Bible (NRSV). This translation is the product of many accomplished scholars, who resolved disagreements systematically. (A vote was taken on whether to interpret the Ten Commandments as banning killing per se or only murder.) Translation-by-committee may have flaws, but it seemed to me that the virtues outweigh them. I also saw virtue in using translations of the Hebrew Bible and the New Testament that had common standards for annotation. Further, the version of the NRSV I most often consulted—the New Oxford Annotated Bible—added a deeper level of uniform annotation, including cross-referencing that linked verses in the Hebrew Bible to related verses in the New Testament. In a few cases I use alternative translations in the text or add supplementary translations in the endnotes. In such cases the source of the translation is stated in the endnote. (RSV stands for Revised Standard Version; KJV stands for King James Version.)

With the Koran the choice was harder. No English translation of the Koran carries an institutional pedigree like that of the NRSV or has seen a comparable degree of adoption by English-speaking scholars. So I wound up consulting a number of translations of every Koranic passage I quote in the book.

My translation of first resort was a nineteenth-century work by J. M. Rodwell. The reason is almost embarrassingly expedient: there is a free audio version of the Rodwell translation, and my acquaintance with the Koran began by listening to it as I took nightly walks. In fact, that's the form in which I assimilated the entire text—listening to the MP3 files on my Treo 650, and using the Treo to take notes on passages that seemed to bear further exploration. Fortunately, the Rodwell translation is a respected work, and, as a nineteenth-century translation, it also employs a form of English with a classical sound that befits august scripture. And, so far as I could tell, Rodwell had no particular agenda.

Before citing any Koranic passage, I always checked with other translations, in particular that of Arthur J. Arberry. The Arberry translation is known as one of the least "interpretive" translations; faced with vague or ambiguous wording, Arberry tends to leave the obscurity intact. So he provided a good baseline: if a verse as translated by Rodwell or anyone else was inconsistent with Arberry's translation—or just much *clearer* than Arberry's translation—I viewed it with some suspicion and consulted multiple other translations to see if there was anything approaching a consensus. I hope I managed to resist the temptation posed by consulting a great diversity of translations—the temptation to "cherry pick" the translation that best suits the analytical needs of the moment. In any event, whenever I quoted a passage in the text whose meaning seemed seriously in dispute, I tried to address the issue in the endnotes.

Unless otherwise noted, Koranic passages have been translated by Rodwell. The other translations I used—which in the endnotes are labeled with the last name of the translator—are those by Muhammad Asad, Muhammad M. Pickthall, Abdullah Yusuf Ali, the aforementioned Arthur Arberry, and George Sale (whose translation, though nearly three centuries old, remains highly regarded).

One downside of using multiple translations is a certain linguistic incongruity. Some of the Koranic passages use archaic English terms like "ye" and some don't. But I thought the lack of consistency was a reasonable price to pay. And it's a useful reminder—and far from the only one in this book—that scripture is, for practical purposes, malleable.

Acknowledgments

I owe a debt to two great institutions of higher learning: Princeton University and the University of Pennsylvania. At Penn, through the good offices of Dean Sam Preston, I was allowed to teach two courses that informed this book: a graduate seminar called "Religion and Human Nature" (which, as it happens, was scheduled to commence on September 11, 2001), and an undergraduate lecture course called "The Evolution of Religion." There's no education like teaching a course for the first time, and I thank my students for enduring my learning.

At Princeton I was privileged to be a Laurence S. Rockefeller Visiting Fellow at the Center for Human Values in 2004–2005. This gave me the time and resources to focus single-mindedly on this project, and weekly seminars, led by Steve Macedo, were valuable—especially the one devoted to critiquing ideas central to this book. Two years later at Princeton, I benefited from co-teaching a graduate seminar with Peter Singer on the biological basis of moral intuition.

The Center for Human Values also brought me two bona fide godsends—graduate students who became invaluable research assistants: Kevin Osterloh, whose fluency in Hebrew and conversancy in the Hebrew Bible helped guide me through largely unfamiliar terrain; and Mairaj Syed, whose fluency in Arabic and conversancy in Islamic scripture had exactly analogous value. Plus, both of them are great human beings.

In Princeton I also encountered several scholars who did me the service of reading and critiquing chapters in draft: John Gager and Michael Cook at the university; and Patrick Miller and Shane Berg at Princeton Theological Seminary. Also reading chapters in draft were Mark S. Smith, Marvin Sweeney, and Michael J. Murray. George Hatke and Konrad Schmid gave close attention to particularly tricky chapter fragments. Early drafts of early chapters were read by my friends John Judis and Gary Krist. Their lukewarm reactions led me to scrap or compress most of that material. (I'm still bitter.)

A number of scholars helped ease my submersion into the literature in their fields by submitting to interrogation, usually by phone: Joseph Blenkinsopp, William G. Dever, Richard Elliott Friedman, Baruch Halpern, Lowell K. Handy, Martha Himmelfarb, Ralph W. Klein, Elaine Pagels, Iain Provan, William Schniedewind, Jeffrey Tigay, Norman Yoffee, and the aforementioned Gager, Cook, Smith, and Miller. Plus, no doubt, some people I've forgotten to mention. And special thanks to Carl Andrew Seaquist, my teaching assistant at Penn, for helping to orient me in religious studies at the outset of this project.

Of course, the usual disclaimer applies: this book's shortcomings are the fault of the author, not the advisers.

My agent, Rafe Sagalyn, once again helped guide me through the publishing landscape and led me to a wonderfully supportive and astute editor, Geoff Shandler of Little, Brown. Chris Jerome was a scrupulous copyeditor, and Peggy Freudenthal was a patient shepherd.

Thanks also to all the folks at the New America Foundation, where I received generous support via the Bernard Schwartz fellows program while writing this book.

Now back to Princeton: The office environment at the Center for Human Values was warmed by the presence of Jan Logan, Erum Syed, Kim Girman, and John Hibbs. And thanks, for performing the aforementioned critique of ideas in this book, go to some of my fellow fellows: Justin D'Arms, Stephen Gardiner, Daniel Jacobson, Rachana Kamtekar, Susan Lape, and Rob Reich, who were joined in that task by faculty members Peter Singer and Dale Jamieson. (Dale gave me what may turn out to have been the best advice: Abandon the project.)

At Bloggingheads.tv, a staff of highly trained professionals allowed me to pretend to run a video Web site while actually writing a book. Thanks to Greg Dingle, Brenda Talbot, Sang Ngo, Sian Gibby, Aryeh Cohen-Wade, David Killoren, Milton Lawson, and the original BhTV staffer, Brian Degenhart. And thanks to Bob and Margie Rosencrans, whose belief in the idea of Bloggingheads has done so much to sustain it.

Steve Kruse said substantively valuable things on bike rides, and John McPhee valuably kept asking me when I was going to finish the damn book. Comparable but more tactful inquiries issued from Merrell Noden, Jim Sturm, Matt Feuer, Michael Lapp, Gideon Rosen, and Mickey Kaus. (Actually, Mickey's inquiries weren't so tactful, come to think of it.)

The three women in my life—Lisa, Eleanor, and Margaret—generously tolerated the occasional fits of despair that this project (along with life in general) occasioned, and provided excellent dinnertime conversation on a nightly basis. Thank God for them.

And for Frazier.

Notes

Front Matter

Epigraph: Kaufman (1972), p. 166.

Part I

Epigraph: Bella, ed. (1973), p. 191.

Chapter One **The Primordial Faith**

1. Bogoraz-Tan (1904–09).
2. Lubbock (1892), p. 205.
3. Ibid., pp. 7–9.
4. Ibid., pp. 206–18.
5. 1 Samuel 28:15.
6. 2 Kings 13:19.
7. Genesis 6:1–4.
8. Marett (1936), p. 163.
9. Tylor (1871), p. 387.
10. Ibid., pp. 431, 387.
11. Radcliffe-Brown (1922), p. 167.
12. Tylor (1871), p. 400.
13. See, e.g., Tylor (1871), p. 400, or Murdock (1934), p. 183.
14. Tylor (1871), pp. 423, 428.
15. Ibid., pp. 430–2; Tylor (1866), p. 86.
16. Tylor (1874), p. 243.
17. Tylor (1866), pp. 82–3.
18. Tylor (1871), p. 453.
19. Unless otherwise noted, all of this chapter's material about the Klamath come from Gatschet (1890), pp. lxxviii–civ. For background on Gatschet and the Klamath, see http://www.uoregon.edu/~delancey/klamath.html#KM.
20. Spier (1930), pp. 104–5.
21. The names of Klamath gods and spirits have been stripped of arcane phonetic markings that accompanied them in Gatschet's original text.
22. Gatschet (1890), p. ciii.
23. Ibid., p. xcvi.
24. Spier (1930), p. 93.
25. There is a long-standing argument among anthropologists about how many hunter-

gatherer "high gods" are truly indigenous and how many grew out of early contact with Christian missionaries and other monotheists. Again: the less "strange" a religious concept, the more plausible a western import it is. For a good analytical summary of the issue by an author who considers many high gods to have been imports, see Barnes (2000), pp. 60–2. Marett (1936), p. 170, deems at least some high gods probably indigenous. For a close examination of a single case where a high god seems to be a Christian import, see Vecsey (1983), pp. 80–2.

26. See, e.g., Smart (1969) on this point.
27. Murdock (1934), p. 255.
28. Turnbull (1965), p. 248.
29. Marshall (1962), pp. 244–5.
30. Murdock (1934), pp. 103–4.
31. Radcliffe-Brown (1922), p. 153.
32. Gatschet (1890), p. lxxxiv.
33. Marshall (1962), p. 229.
34. Murdock (1934), p. 185.
35. Marshall (1962), p. 250.
36. Ibid., p. 239.
37. Murdock (1934), p. 104.
38. Tylor (1874), vol. II, p. 360.
39. Marshall (1962), p. 245.
40. Spencer (1927), p. 424.
41. Cooper (1917), p. 146. The Fuegian native Americans had for some time lived in the vicinity of Christian missionaries, and this may explain their unusual (for hunter-gatherers) belief in an omniscient, moralistic deity.
42. In the 1960s the scholar Guy Swanson (1964) did an elaborate study of religion in fifty societies randomly selected from a larger database. Of those fifty, ten were hunter-gatherer societies. In only one of those ten societies was the quality of a person's fate in the afterlife influenced by whether he or she had helped or harmed people during life. And in only three of the ten did the religion include any other supernatural sanctions for this sort of behavior (such as illness). Given the number of hunter-gatherer societies that, before being studied, had lived in some proximity to societies that *did* feature such links between morality and religion, these numbers are notably low.

   Rasmussen (1932), pp. 31–4, reported one group of Eskimo who believed that "they who know how to feel pity go up to a bright land after death, whereas those who are not good to the lonely and orphaned go to a dark land where there is no food or drink." But he attributed this belief to an earlier visit by a British missionary: "For a punishment after death is quite un-Eskimo."
43. Spier (1930), p. 93.
44. Radcliffe-Brown (1922), p. 168.
45. Murdock (1934), p. 253.
46. Service (1966), p. 72.
47. Quoted in Howells (1962), p. 19; Howells notes the similarity between Mencken's characterization of religion and William James's.
48. James (1982), p. 53.

Chapter Two   The Shaman

1. See Burton Malkiel's *A Random Walk Down Wall Street*.
2. Whether that label *should* be applied to them is a question that can start arguments

among anthropologists. A few purists have held that it shouldn't be applied much beyond the indigenous cultures of northern Eurasia. Others say that actually, there's enough continuity between the native religious cultures of Eurasia and the Americas to warrant extending the term "shaman" across the Bering Strait. Others are willing to expand shaman territory farther still, so long as we stick with one key criterion: a true shaman derives his or her power from direct inspiration—visions, voices, bodily possession, and the like. (See, e.g., Norbeck [1961], p. 103.) Still others say: Look, in virtually all pre-agricultural societies, there are people who are thought to have special access to forces of a sort that we moderners would call supernatural—spiritual or magical or occult or whatever. We need a label for these people; why don't we just use "shaman" for convenience? That is the position taken here. "Medicine men," "witch doctors," "sorcerers"—they're all shamans in this book. (Note: In the text, generalizations about shamans are in the present tense, but specific ethnographic examples are in the past tense, reflecting the fact that, as indigenous cultures change or disappear, few of the examples are still operative.)

3. Rogers (1982), pp. 6–7; Lowie (1952), p. 336.
4. Rogers (1982), p. 11.
5. Spencer (1927), pp. 401–2. Among some Australian peoples, such as the Arunta, this power was not confined to the shaman. See Spencer (1927), p. 397. See also Rivers (1924).
6. Rasmussen (1927), p. 28.
7. Reichel-Dolmatoff (1987), p. 10.
8. Man (1932), p. 29.
9. Emmons (1991), pp. 383–4.
10. Katz (1976), p. 287.
11. Quoted in Bourke (1892), p. 459.
12. Eliade (1964), p. 509.
13. Ibid., p. 64.
14. Ibid.
15. See Marshall (1962), pp. 237–40; Katz (1976), p. 285, estimates that half of males and one-third of adult women can achieve the transcendent state of !kia, though it's not clear that all of them can use the state to heal.
16. Spier (1930), p. 107. See Radcliffe-Brown (1922), p. 176, and Vecsey (1983), p. 161, for comparable observations about the Andaman Islanders and the Ojibwa, respectively.
17. Lowie (1952), p. 14.
18. Ibid., pp. 14–15.
19. Norbeck (1961), p. 105.
20. Murdock (1934), p. 43.
21. Ibid., p. 101.
22. See, e.g., Spier (1930), p. 124, and Emmons (1991), p. 383.
23. Rogers (1982), p. 33.
24. Spencer (1927), p. 402.
25. Emmons (1991), p. 370.
26. Man (1932), p. 29.
27. Vecsey (1983), p. 165.
28. Man (1932), pp. 28–9.
29. All these examples come from Rogers (1982), pp. 5, 22, 28–9.
30. Ibid., p. 31.
31. Quoted in Service (1978), pp. 236–7.
32. Rogers (1982), p. 30.

33. Ibid.
34. Lowie (1952), pp. 16–17.
35. Gusinde (1931), p. 1041.
36. Vecsey (1983).
37. Hoebel (1983), p. 73.
38. There are reported exceptions. Lowie (1952), p. 335, notes that Siberian shamans are often not of high social rank. But the exceptions seem rare.
39. Rogers (1982), p. 8.
40. See Norbeck (1961), pp. 111–12; Rogers (1982), pp. 7, 20.
41. See Norbeck (1961), p. 112.
42. See, e.g., Murdock (1934), p. 12; Service (1978), p. 237; Spencer (1927), p. 398.
43. Norbeck (1961), p. 112.
44. Vecsey (1983), p. 163.
45. Benedict (1959), p. 213.
46. Man (1932), pp. 29–30.
47. Rasmussen (1932), p. 30.
48. Reichel-Dolmatoff (1987), p. 8.
49. Lowie (1952), pp. 3–7.
50. Emmons (1991), p. 375.
51. Cooper (1946), p. 104.
52. Spencer (1927), pp. 392–6.
53. Norbeck (1961), p. 110. Radin (1937), pp. 105–7, sees the shaman as often fitting the profile of the "thinker-artist...a man neurotically susceptible to all inward stirrings, physical and mental.... The very intensity of his inward life spurred him on and aided him in the attainment of his goal."
54. Rogers (1982), p. 24.
55. Emmons (1991), p. 373.
56. Lowie (1952), p. 335.
57. Rogers (1982), p. 8.
58. James (1982), p. 388.
59. Katz (1976), pp. 287, 291.
60. Konner (1990), p. 25.
61. Ibid.
62. See Eliade (1964), p. 181, footnote.
63. *Encyclopedia Britannica*.
64. See Norbeck (1961), p. 115.
65. Gusinde (1931), p. 1045. See Emmons (1991), p. 370, re: the somewhat similar role of the Tlingit shaman, at the other end of the Americas.
66. Murdock (1934), p. 258.
67. Lowie (1952), p. 18.
68. Spier (1930), p. 120.
69. Kelekna (1998), pp. 165–6.
70. See Spencer and Gillen (1904).
71. Durkheim (1965), p. 448.
72. Radin (1937), p. 52.

Chapter Three Religion in the Age of Chiefdoms

1. Cook (1852), p. 176.
2. Ibid., p. 172; plantain leaf: Handy (1927), p. 192.
3. Cook (1852), p. 176.

4. Ibid., p. 155.
5. Williamson (1937), p. 23.
6. For a fuller discussion of chiefdoms, including arguments over the validity of the chiefdom as a distinct analytical category, see Wright (2000), chapter 7.
7. Quoted in Kirch (1989), p. 166.
8. Ibid., p. 12.
9. Williamson (1937), pp. 45, 49. The attribution of properties to Tangaroa is complicated by the addition of suffixes to his name—e.g., "Tangaroa-of-the-skies," "Tangaroa-the-infinite," etc. There is disagreement (see Williamson, pp. 38–40) over whether these were alternative descriptions of the same god.
10. Williamson (1937), p. 38.
11. Ibid., p. 46. Williamson notes but casts doubt on suggestions by Handy (1927) that Tangaroa occupied an important position in the Marquesas. In any event—see Williamson (1937), p. 44—there were various islands in which Tangaroa was but one god among many, with no especially exalted position.
12. Williamson (1937), pp. 18–19, 88–93.
13. Handy (1927), p. 282.
14. Williamson (1937), p. 244.
15. Malo (1903), p. 168.
16. Ibid., pp. 169, 175–6.
17. Ibid., pp. 170–5.
18. Ibid., pp. 274, 278–9.
19. Ibid., pp. 199, 275–6.
20. For a review, see Firth (1940).
21. Ibid., p. 491. Firth spells the word *manu,* in keeping with local pronunciation.
22. Cook (1852), Vol. II, p. 156.
23. Ibid., pp. 155–6.
24. Thwaites (1900), pp. 127, 131.
25. Ibid., p. 127.
26. Van Bakel (1991), p. 272.
27. Hogbin (1934), p. 266.
28. See Claessen (1991), pp. 304, 314, 316.
29. Ibid., p. 316.
30. Williamson (1937), p. 19: In the Society Islands there was apparently a god not just of fornication but of adultery. Here is an excerpt (Williamson [1937], p. 104) from a prayer uttered in the Hervey Islands before a nighttime burglary:

> Oh house, thou art doomed by our God!
> Cause all things to sleep.
> Let profound sleep overspread this dwelling.
> Owner of the house, sleep on!
> Threshold of this house, sleep on!
> Ye tiny insects inhabiting this house, sleep on!

31. Williamson (1937), pp. 9, 22.
32. Ibid., p. 92.
33. Handy (1927), p. 185.
34. Williamson (1937), p. 275.
35. Quoted in Handy (1927), p. 78.
36. Williamson (1937), pp. 268–9; Handy (1927), p. 78.

37. Handy (1940), p. 311. Handy adds, "Ethical considerations are secondary and indirect factors." One classic virtue that might stand you in good eternal stead was bravery. On several Polynesian islands, wrote Handy (1927, p. 78), heroic but dead warriors would go to the "upper regions of the sky world," there to "dwell in everlasting happiness, clothed in fragrant flowers, dancing, and enjoying the full gratification of all their desires."

38. Handy (1927), p. 67.

39. Hogbin (1934), p. 262.

40. Ibid., p. 261.

41. Turner (1861), pp. 313, 345.

42. Williamson (1937), p. 251. Adultery was also punished by the gods in Tonga—see Hogbin (1934), p. 261—and Samoa—see Turner (1831), p. 313.

43. This sanction was in some places enforced by dead ancestors, not gods. See, e.g., Handy (1940), p. 319.

44. In the Polynesian chiefdoms, religion, if not centrally concerned with moral issues, did address them. Williamson wrote that on Tonga, "human crimes, such as lying, theft, adultery, and murder, were not considered by the higher gods, because of their more elevated natures." But he added that these crimes "were left to the inferior gods to deal with" (Williamson [1937], p. 16). Even this degree of divine attention to morality was a big advance compared with that in a typical hunter-gatherer society. Handy is more explicit than Williamson in recognizing the moral dimension of Polynesian religion: e.g., Handy (1940), p. 319: "Social ethics is the very core of the old institutionalized Polynesian cult. Malice, evil thought, and evil speech toward relatives is one of the commonest causes of sickness, and hence appears the interesting phenomenon of confession as prerequisite to healing. A second source of trouble is disrespect for customary law as exemplified in *tapu: tapu*-breakers are summarily afflicted by spirits and gods with illness or accident in retribution for their misdemeanours."

45. None of this is to suggest that modern law *originated* in religion. (The view that law originated in religion is sometimes attributed to the nineteenth-century social theorist Sir Henry Maine, but this attribution may be as oversimplified as the view itself. See Hoebel [1983], chapter 10, on both points.) Indeed, in hunter-gatherer societies you often see a kind of law practiced with little if any help from the supernatural: crimes such as murder are wrong, so retaliation is right, and that is that—no supernatural enforcement necessary. Rather, the suggestion is that, as society evolved beyond the hunter-gatherer phase, and this grassroots enforcement became less practical, so that something closer to modern law was needed, religion stepped in and provided crucial authority during the transition.

46. Williamson (1937), pp. 134–6; Hogbin (1934), p. 264. On p. 253, Williamson observes that in the Society Islands, a family established claim to its land by building a small-scale temple, or *marae*, on it.

47. Hogbin (1934), p. 274. The *fono* existed in other chiefdoms, but typically as an administrative body. Samoa was unusual in using it for judicial purposes.

48. Van Bakel (1991), p. 268.

49. Hogbin (1934), p. 269.

50. Quoted in ibid., p. 263.

51. Ibid., p. 262.

52. Ibid., pp. 277–8.

53. Ibid., pp. 273–4.

54. Williamson (1937), p. 122.

55. Cook (1852), p. 175.

56. See, e.g., Hoebel (1983), p. 272.

57. Williamson (1937), pp. 302–3.

58. Williamson (1937), p. 128.
59. Sahlins (1963), p. 297.
60. Ibid., pp. 297–8.
61. Kirch (1989), p. 167.
62. Williamson (1937), p. 258.
63. See Wright (2000), chapters 5, 7.
64. Dale (1996), p. 303.
65. Kirch (1989), pp. 68, 196–7.
66. Williamson (1937), p. 103.
67. Quoted in Makemson (1941), p. 19.
68. Lewis (1974), pp. 135, 137.
69. Williamson (1937), p. 249.
70. See Lewis (1974), pp. 140, 144; Makemson (1941), p. 19. In a predictive scenario mentioned by Makemson, the belief is that the winds approaching the islands first pass by the Milky Way and affect its tilt; in this case, then, the causal explanation of the observed correlation between the position of stars and the prevailing winds is more "modern"—that is, less supernatural—than other Polynesian theories explaining such correlations, which saw celestial deities controlling the winds (as on Ongton Java—see Williamson [1933], p. 153).
71. Quoted in Makemson (1941), p. 19.

Chapter Four   Gods of the Ancient States

1. Bottero (2001), pp. 66–7.
2. Jacobsen, pp. 139–40. See Bottero (2001), p. 122, re: Mesopotamian priestesses who practiced prostitution.
3. Saggs (1978), p. 173.
4. Bottero (2001), pp. 66–7.
5. Pinch (2002), p. 126.
6. Quoted in Le Page Renouf (1884), p. 2.
7. Faulkner (1969), p. 1.
8. Keightley (1998), pp. 804–7.
9. http://www.mnsu.edu/emuseum/information/biography/abcde/delanda_deigo.html.
10. For example, Sharer (1996), p. 160, voices an opinion shared by other scholars in saying that "it would be a mistake to assume they [Mayan gods] had distinct or anthropomorphic (human-like) qualities like the gods of ancient Greece or Rome." Yet he also says the gods enjoy music (p. 166) and, most important, expect to be nourished by humans via sacrifice and get angry if the humans neglect this duty (p. 164). Sharer says (personal communication) that Mayan gods were less anthropomorphic than Greek gods in the sense of being more mutable. Similarly Boone (1994), pp. 104–6, says that thinking of Aztec gods as gods is misleading; the Nahuatl word *teotl,* translated by the Spanish as "god," actually means "a sacred and impersonal force" (p. 105). The "Aztec gods were not divine humans, like Greek and Roman gods" (p. 105). But she later says "Aztec deities were this concentrated energy, manifest in anthropomorphic form as gods and goddesses" (p. 106). Indeed, "the legends and the ancient stories speak of the Aztec deities as supernatural actors on a mythic stage." But she insists this "way of humanizing the supernatural" was just "an effective narrative device" used by Aztec elders to "explain the cosmos in human terms that can readily be understood." As I understand Boone, she is saying that the vast majority of Aztecs thought of their gods as anthropomorphic, but it would be a mistake for us to think of them that way—which means, presumably, that it

was a mistake for the Aztecs to think of them that way. But if the Aztecs aren't the final authority on the nature of Aztec gods, who is? It's possible that late-twentieth-century scholars of Mesoamerica are particularly eager to see in the religions they study a more modernist, New Agey spirituality than the stodgy scholars who earlier shaped the interpretation of Egyptian and Mesopotamian religion. Or perhaps they've been influenced by the contention of Rudolf Otto (1977) that apprehension of the "numinous" precedes — chronologically and in some sense metaphysically — the perception of individual gods. One scholar, Thorkild Jacobsen (1976), explicitly brought this view to the study of Mesopotamian religion, and a number of scholars now judge that this view imposed an unfortunate bias on his interpretation (Norman Yoffee, personal communication). I don't doubt Boone's contention that Aztec laypeople had a more literal, less metaphysical conception of gods than some Aztec intellectuals. Bray (1991), pp. 155–8, suggests as much, if in a different sense. (He says some intellectuals saw many different Aztec gods as manifestations of a single underlying god.) But I'm suggesting that, if there is a single "correct" way to think of the gods of any civilization — and Boone's writing suggests she thinks there is — then it is the way the great bulk of people in that civilization thought of them. Hornung (1996), p. 105, says that over time Egyptian gods increasingly assume human, as opposed to animal, form, and endorses the phrases "anthropomorphization of power" and "from dynamism to personalism" to describe this trend. But the fact that Egyptian gods were in earlier times more likely to assume animal *form* doesn't mean they weren't psychologically anthropomorphic. Moreover, in asserting this trend, Hornung has to minimize (pp. 101–3) inconvenient evidence, such as the fact that clay and ivory figures in human form are found in prehistoric Egypt, and the fact that several Egyptian deities are found in human form at the very beginning of the historical record.

11. Egypt: Morenz (1973), p. 6; China: Poo (1998), p. 28; the Maya: Sharer (1996), p. 153; the Aztecs: Mexican archaeologist Alfonso Caso, quoted in Bray (1991), p. 152; Mesopotamia: Bottero (2001), p. 92.

12. Bottero (2001), p. 45. In some cases different names may have referred to the same god, and in any event, there was no one who worshipped all gods on the list. Saggs (1989), p. 277, refers to a contemporary census that listed 3,600 names, and Bottero, p. 45, mentions a 3,300-name list.

13. Egyptian scribes, craftsmen: Shafer et al., eds. (1991), p. 54; Mesopotamian scribes: Saggs (1989), p. 277; on Mesopotamian craft gods in general see Lambert (1975), p. 196; Aztec traders: Bray (1991), pp. 147–8; Aztec merchants (and several craft gods), Boone (1994), p. 109; Mayan merchants: Foster (2002), pp. 168–9 and Sharer (1996), p. 162; Mayan scribes: Sharer (1996), p. 161; brewers and bricklayers: Saggs (1989), p. 277; weavers, painters, goldsmiths: Boone (1994), p. 114; robbers: Bray (1991), p. 162; Mayan suicide god: Sharer (1996), p. 162; Lord of Livestock Pens: Bottero (2001), p. 47; Egyptian gods of lungs, liver, etc.: Shafer et al., eds. (1991), p. 49.

14. Walker and Dick (2001), p. 53. The ritual, described in intricate detail in this tablet from the early first millennium BCE, seems to have involved washing the mouth of a statue of a god (p. 16). How directly the people associated the statue with the god itself is unclear, but there is evidence that in ancient Mesopotamia the association could be quite direct — that gods were in some cases thought to inhabit the statues of them. See Bottero (2001), p. 65.

15. See Trigger (1993), pp. 98–102: rulers in Egypt, Mesopotamia, China, and Mesoamerica have claimed at least some kind of descent from gods.

16. Foster (2002), p. 178.

17. Trigger (1993), p. 102.

18. Ibid., p. 91.
19. Ibid. On the threat of chaos in Egypt, see Baines (1991), pp. 124–5.
20. Boone (1994), p. 117.
21. Bray (1991), p. 172; Boone (1994), p. 117.
22. Huitzilopochtli: Bray (1991), pp. 18, 172.
23. Vaillant (1950), pp. 195–7; Bray (1991), pp. 171–5.
24. Ortiz de Montellano (1990), p. 49.
25. Quoted in White (1959), pp. 303–4.
26. Trigger (1993), pp. 97–8.
27. Bray (1991), pp. 177–8.
28. Michael D. Lemonick, "Secrets of the Maya," *Time*, Aug. 9, 1993.
29. Bray (1991), p. 176.
30. See Wright (2000), p. 99.
31. Lamberg-Karlovsky and Sabloff (1995), p. 174.
32. Bottero (2000), p. 58; see also Saggs (1978), pp. 116–17.
33. Bottero (2000), pp. 58–9.
34. Mayans: Lopez Austin (1988), p. 270; Egyptians: Traunecker, p. 98.
35. Ortiz de Montellano (1990), pp. 62–3, 141, 150–2.
36. Lopez Austin (1988), pp 295, 337.
37. O'Flaherty (1981), pp. 213–4, espec. footnote 5; see also Flood (1996), p. 47.
38. Lichtheim (1975), p. 65.
39. A possible illustration of this dynamic is the conquest in China toward the end of the second millennium BCE of the Shang (whose chief god, Shang-ti, shows no clear moral disposition so far as we can tell; see Elvin [1986], p. 327), by the Chou (whose chief god, Tian, has moral concerns—see Elvin [1986], p. 327—that will eventually come to outweigh his concern for sheerly ritual propriety [p. 328]).
40. Bottero (2001), p. 53.
41. Ibid.; Lambert (1975), p. 193.
42. Lambert (1975), pp. 191–3. See also Bottero (2001), pp. 48–54, on the rationalization of the pantheon during the third millennium BCE.
43. Lambert (1975), p. 192.
44. Ibid.
45. Williamson (1937), p. 252.
46. Watson (1992), p. 26.
47. See Saggs (1989), p. 37.
48. Watson (1992), p. 27.
49. Lamberg-Karlovsky and Sabloff (1995), p. 176.
50. Saggs (1989), p. 185.
51. Ibid., p. 41.
52. Hallo and van Dijk (1968), pp. 7–8.
53. Ibid., pp. 1–9, 23, 29.
54. Ibid., pp. 9–10.
55. Saggs (1978), pp. 184–5.
56. Bottero (2001), p. 46.
57. Bray (1991), p. 155.
58. Dietrich (1974), p. 27.
59. Bottero (2001), p. 51.
60. Jacobsen, p. 85. The narrative is known as "Enki and World Order."
61. Silverman (1991), p. 32.

62. Not all scholars accept this view, but it is widely held. See Poo (1998), p. 23, and Gernet (1985), p. 49. More scholars would accept it as applied to post–Shang China. In Mesoamerica the pantheons seem relatively amorphous, but these states are in an earlier stage of social evolution than first- or second-millennium-BCE Mesopotamia or Egypt, or post–Shang China.

63. Bottero (2001), p. 52.

64. Ibid., pp. 52, 97.

65. Ibid., p. 66.

66. Code of Hammurabi, L. W. King translation.

67. Bottero (2001), p. 54.

68. Saggs (1978), p. 157.

69. Code of Hammurabi, L. W. King translation.

70. Lambert (1975), pp. 193–4. Bottero (2001), p. 54, seems to suggest that Marduk was in Hammurabi's code being elevated to the position of Babylon's municipal god, but the code's text doesn't indicate as much, and Lambert (p. 193) says Marduk was "always" city god of Babylon.

71. Bottero (2001), pp. 55–6.

72. Lambert (1975), pp. 197–8. Bottero (2001), p. 57, puts the equations in the form "Marduk is Nurta, the god of agriculture."

73. Bottero (2001), p. 57.

74. Ibid., p. 58, minimizes the monotheistic drift, while Lambert (1975), p. 198, emphasizes it.

75. See Lambert (1975), p. 199.

76. Saggs (1978), p. 184.

77. *Epic of Creation*, L. W. King translation; see also Bottero (2001), p. 56.

78. L. W. King translation.

79. Reeves (2001), pp. 44–5; Redford (1984), pp. 158–63.

80. See Reeves (2001), p. 111; Redford (1984), p. 165. There may have been a short period of co-regency prior to his father's death.

81. Redford (1984) p. 162. Redford cites an inscription that "every god is in him." Amun had already merged with the once supreme sun god Re and—though the two sometimes shared top billing as Amun-Re—Amun seemed to be the senior partner. See Redford (1984), pp. 162–3, 171; see also Hornung (1999), pp. 91–2.

82. Reeves (2001), p. 49.

83. David (2002), p. 215. See also Reeves (2001), pp. 49–50; Redford (1984), pp. 171–2.

84. Redford (1984), pp. 175–7.

85. Ibid., pp. 175–6, 179.

86. Ibid., p. 176.

87. Redford (1992), p. 381; David (2002), p. 218.

88. Ibid., pp. 166, 178–180.

89. David (2002), p. 226.

90. See Redford (1992), pp. 226–33. This theological cross-pollination, though politically convenient for an imperial ruler, wasn't necessarily disingenuous. Akhenaten's own father, toward the end of his reign, sent off to Mesopotamia for a statue of Ishtar of Nineveh to help cure his illness. See Redford (1992), p. 231, and Morenz (1973), p. 240.

91. See Redford (1992), pp. 230, 233.

92. Ibid., p. 231.

93. Ibid., p. 230; David (2002), pp. 227–8.

94. Wente and Baines (1989), p. 158. This concern is attributed to Amun-Re, Amun's name during a period when he had merged with Re.

95. Morenz (1973), p. 51.
96. Hornung (1996), p. 167. The earliest copy of this text, the Book of Gates, appears shortly after Akhenaten's reign, but a number of scholars think it was written earlier.
97. Morenz (1973), p. 52.
98. Ibid., pp. 47–9.

Chapter Five   Polytheism, the Religion of Ancient Israel

1. 1 Kings 19:11–12, RSV. Mount Sinai is also known as Horeb, Mount of God, which is the term used in this passage.
2. Armstrong (1994), p. 27. She is commenting on the translation found in *The Jerusalem Bible,* in which the phrase is rendered not as "a sound of sheer silence" (NRSV) or "a still small voice" (RSV) but as "the sound of a gentle breeze."
3. Baal wasn't *just* a fertility god; see Albertz (1994), p. 172.
4. On Yahweh's "hiddenness" see Friedman (1997), espec. pp. 77–80.
5. Kaufmann (1972), p. 70.
6. Ibid., p. 2. Kaufmann's view wasn't, strictly speaking, anti-evolutionary. He believed that there had been an evolutionary progression from pagan religion to monotheism (p. 7). But he believed that the monotheistic phase had arrived abruptly, rather than as a continuous outgrowth of earlier religion. It had come to the Hebrews "as an insight, an original intuition" (p. 60).
7. 1 Kings 19:15–18; 20:29–30.
8. See Gnuse (1997), p. 66, on how widely held and influential, especially between 1940 and 1970, was the idea of an early (i.e., Mosaic) and abrupt emergence of monotheism.
9. See, e.g., Friedman (2003).
10. Some scholars frown on referring to Ugaritic literature as "Canaanite," but, e.g., Pitard (2002), pp. 251–2, argues in favor of such a designation, citing cultural continuity between the city of Ugarit and Canaanite lands to the south. Of course, Ugaritic literature isn't precisely representative of the culture of the "Canaanites" described in the Bible, but it seems fair to view it as broadly reflective of their milieu.
11. Genesis 2:8; 3:21; 3:8; 3:9.
12. Niehr (1995), p. 52, asserts that Yahweh was initially a weather god, like Baal. And, similarly, Day (2000), p. 14, emphasizes Yahweh's association with storms in apparently early fragments of the Bible, such as Judges 5:4–5. The weather-god thesis can't be ruled out, but it's notable that even the passage cited by Day emphasizes Yahweh's violent storm-making power (as opposed to, say, merely associating him with rain and hence fertility): "Lord…when you marched…the earth trembled, and the heavens poured, the clouds indeed poured water, The mountains quaked before the Lord…" For examples of the divine warrior theme in early Hebrew scriptures, see Cross (1973), chapter 5. Cross writes (p. 157) that hymns depicting "the march of the Divine Warrior to battle, convulsing nature by his wrath…include all of Israel's oldest hymns." Freedman (1987), p. 319, lists five poems that are likely among the oldest—Genesis 49; Exodus 15; Numbers 23–4; Deuteronomy 33; Judges 5—and says these fall into two categories: odes to military victory and "tribal blessings."
13. Exodus 15:1–3.
14. Exodus 15:11.
15. Numbers 21:29. See Kaufmann (1972), p. 9. On another verse indicating monolatry but not monotheism—Deuteronomy 4:19—see Nikiprowetzky (1975), p. 77.
16. Joshua 23:16. See Judges 3:7–12 for comparable language.
17. Exodus 20:3.

18. See, e.g., Judges 11:24, discussed in chapter 8.
19. Genesis 1:26–7. This use of the first-person plural by God is typically attributed to the P source, unlike Genesis 3:22 and 11:7, which are typically attributed to the J source. (See chapter 7 for elaboration on the P source, and see this chapter, below, for elaboration on the J source.) Since P's writings are generally monotheistic, this has puzzled scholars. (See Garr [2003], pp. 17–21.) Some believe it an inadvertent preservation of an earlier usage in P's source material, while others believe it is purposefully preserved to make a theological point. (See Garr [2003], e.g., p. 202.) In either of these scenarios, though, the fact that this language was part of P's heritage indicates that at some time polytheism had been part of the Israelites' tradition, even if P's use of the language doesn't indicate polytheism on P's part.
20. Genesis 3:22; 11:7.
21. Actually, "host of heaven," a term whose meaning seems to have evolved during biblical times, does seem to have referred to celestial deities in some cases. See Niehr (1999).
22. Psalms 82:1, 6. Some read this passage as a mythic account of a time in the distant past when God took control of the world of the gods. (At one point he says, "You are gods...nevertheless, you shall die like mortals, and fall like any prince," which can be interpreted as him giving them a death sentence or at least noting their mortality, presumably in contrast to his immortality.) In this view, the passage, far from being evidence of Israelite acknowledgment of the existence of many gods, could have been written by monotheists who were explaining how, long ago, a single God came to be ruler of heaven and earth. Working against this interpretation, perhaps, is that the account isn't written in the past tense. On the divine council's Canaanite and Israelite origins, see Smith (2002a), pp. 37, 143–4.
23. Smith (2001), p. 157.
24. Joshua 10:40.
25. Albright (1957), p. 278. For a sympathetic critique of Albright that nonetheless notes the error of such Albrightian declarations, see Schloen (2002).
26. Albright (1957), p. 281.
27. See, e.g., Nikiprowetzky (1975), p. 75.
28. Albright (1957), p. 285.
29. Dever (2003), pp. 153, 167. For a recent argument that important aspects of the Joshua narrative remain consistent with archaeological evidence, see Rainey (2001). An early and influential version of the theory of Israel's indigenously Canaanite origin was G. E. Mendenhall's mid-twentieth-century suggestion that the Israelites had initially been Canaanite peasants who revolted against their urban overlords. See Halpern (1983), chapter 3, for a good summary.
30. Finkelstein and Silberman (2002), pp. 105–22.
31. Ibid., p. 118.
32. For reviews of the issue, see Callaway (1999) and Dever (2003).
33. Another part of the Bible, the first chapter of Judges, may be closer to the truth; in contrast to the claims in Joshua, this chapter speaks of the survival of numerous Canaanite cities after the Israelites' arrival. See Callaway (1999), p. 56.
34. Finkelstein and Silberman (2002), pp. 109–10.
35. Ibid., p. 109. See Day (2000), pp. 34–39, for evidence that the golden calves which, according to the Bible, were established by King Jeroboam I "reflect ancient Yahwistic symbolism deriving from the god El."
36. On Kaufmann, Albright, and other scholars who have traced monotheism back to the

Sinai wanderings, see Smith (2001), p. 149. See Halpern (1987), pp. 77–83, for a sympathetic discussion of Kaufmann's view.

37. See Smith (2001), pp. 47–53, and Smith (2002a), pp. 37–8, for examples of the divine council in the Bible.

38. On resemblances between Yahweh and El, see, e.g., Cross (1973), p. 72; Smith (2002a), pp. 39–42; Day (2000a), pp. 13–41; Pitard (2002), pp. 258–9.

39. Smith (2002a), p. 39.

40. Exodus 15:13.

41. Smith (2002a), p. 39; prophets: Oden, lecture 4.

42. Smith (2001), p. 137; Pitard (2002), p. 256.

43. Smith (2001), p. 160.

44. See Cross (1973), pp. 44–5: "there can be no doubt that the origin of the designation *'adat 'El* is in Canaanite myth."

45. Genesis 33:20. See Albertz (1994), vol. 1, p. 76. The NRSV editors, in a footnote, render the translated phrase as "God, the God of Israel," but their capitalizing the second "god"—which surely seems to be a generic noun—is dubious. For a discussion of some biblical scriptures in which "El" seems to refer to the Canaanite god El, see Day (2000), pp. 24–6.

46. Friedman (2003), p. 87, translates it this way.

47. See, e.g., Day (2000), p. 16; Theissen (1984), p. 52.

48. On the meaing of "Shaddai," see, e.g., Cross (1973), pp. 52–60.

49. See Day (2000), p. 33, for tentative evidence that Shaddai "derives from an epithet of El." According to de Moor (1990), p. 228, Exodus contains other equations of Yahweh and El. E.g., Exodus 34:14—translated in the NRSV as "...the LORD [i.e. Yahweh], whose name is Jealous, is a jealous God"—de Moor renders as "...Yahweh the jealous one is his name—He is El the jealous one."

50. See, e.g., McCarter Jr. (1999), pp. 20–2.

51. Some have argued that Yahweh and El were originally identical, as opposed to being previously distinct gods that were fused. See chapter 1 of Day (2000).

52. Theissen (1985), pp. 54–5, writes that during the divided monarchy the northern kingdom was "much more exposed to the influence of the great Canaanite coastal states than Judah." But he argues that Judah, too, encountered Canaanite culture, notably in Jerusalem (where, he says, El Elyon was worshipped) and handled the encounter gracefully: "El and Yahweh were identified with each other, the symbol of the peaceful course of the social integration between Israelites and Canaanites in the Southern Kingdom."

53. For a review of the issue, see Collins (2009), chapter 2.

54. Theissen (1985), pp. 53–4, champions this scenario.

55. Judges 5:14–18; see McCarter Jr. (1999), pp. 13–17.

56. On Noth, see, e.g., McCarter Jr. (1999), pp. 12–15, and Finkelstein and Silberman (2002), pp. 43–5.

57. Jacob but not Abraham mentioned: This assumes the common interpretation of the phrase "a wandering Aramean" in Deuteronomy 26:6 as a reference to Jacob, and also assumes the (again, fairly common) dating of this verse as early relative to verses that do mention Abraham. See, e.g., Oden (1996), lecture 1.

58. See text of Merenptah Stele in Pritchard (1958).

59. See Redford (1992), p. 275. (During Israel's "divided monarchy" of the early first millennium BCE, the northern kingdom would be called Ephraim as well as Israel.)

60. Cross (1973), pp. 61–2, says the southern Palestinian lists featuring the name are from the fourteenth and thirteenth century BCE. See also Redford (1992), p. 273; Dever (2003),

pp. 150–1; Rainey (2001), pp. 68–75. Both Redford and Rainey seem to assume that the Shasu, rather than merging with a preexisting Israelite people, are precursors of the Israelites. In other words, in between the reference to the "land of the Shasu" in the general vicinity of Edom, and the subsequent (late-thirteenth-century) reference to Israel, the Shasu migrate northward and come to be known as Israelites. Yet Rainey also notes that during the time of Merenptah, when the first reference to a people called Israel appears, we also find the relief in which people labeled Shasu have been captured by Egypt (an image whose resonance with the biblical story of Egyptian bondage is clear). This would seem to raise a question: If the Rainey-Redford assumption that the Shasu *became* the Israelites is correct, why would two roughly contemporaneous Egyptian inscriptions refer to them as Shasu in one case and Israel in another?

61. See Redford (1992), p. 273, footnote 71.
62. Ibid., p. 272.
63. Rainey (2001), pp. 73–4.
64. See Rainey (2001) for a defense of this standard translation against the claim that the reference is to crops ("grain").
65. Among the evidence that doesn't fit neatly into the theory of a southern Yahweh, worshipped by Shasu freed from Egyptian dominance, merging with a northern El, is this passage in the book of Numbers: "El who freed them from Egypt has horns like a wild ox"—a description of El reminiscent of the Ugaritic description of him as "bull El." See Smith (2002b), p. 21. Another group of people who appear in Egyptian inscriptions and are sometimes posited as early constituents of Israel are the Apiru. For a time it was thought that the term *Apiru* had evolved into the word *Hebrew,* but that view has been cast into doubt. Moreover, the idea of the Apiru as an ethnic group has given way to the idea that *Apiru* was a socioeconomic designation, perhaps referring to transient, socially marginal peoples sometimes drawn to crime. See Finkelstein and Silberman (2002), pp. 102–3; Dever (2003), p. 74.
66. See Finkelstein (1999) and Finkelstein and Silberman (2002). Finkelstein (1999), p. 40, appraises the archaeological evidence and concludes that the northern kingdom reached "full-blown statehood no later than the first half of the 9th century BCE," whereas in the tenth and ninth centuries, Jerusalem, the supposed capital of a mighty Davidic kingdom to the south, seems to have been "a small, poor, unassuming highland stronghold, not very different from other hill country mounts." For recent evidence challenging Finkelstein's view, see Ethan Bronner, "Find of Ancient City Could Alter Notions of Biblical David," *New York Times,* Oct. 29, 2008.
67. Deuteronomy 32:8–9.
68. Smith (2001), p. 143; Halpern (1987), p. 107, footnote 1. Some scholars—e.g., Lowell K. Handy (personal communication)—think this reconstruction is overly creative. Handy doesn't deny that the phrase "children of Israel" in the Masoretic and King James texts is mistaken; he just finds reconstructing the original phrase problematic.
69. In the New Revised Standard Version of the Bible some of this verse's original meaning has been restored:

> When the Most High apportioned the nations,
> when he divided humankind, he fixed the boundaries of the peoples according
>   to the number of the gods;
> the LORD's own portion was his people, Jacob his allotted share.

But even here, though a trace of polytheism is visible in the word "gods," there is no clue that "Most High" and "the LORD" may be different gods. Indeed, the translator, by gratuitously adding "own" after "LORD's," accents the probably mistaken impression that they're one and the same. See Coogan, ed. (2001), p. 301, footnote.

70. Finkelstein and Silberman (2002), e.g., pp. 43–7, stress the role of a strong Judah in the late eighth and seventh centuries in shaping the countours of the story told in the Bible. For a good treatment of the question of when various parts of the Bible were written, see Schniedewind (2004).

71. Certainly there's no shortage of theories about the early relationship between Yahweh and El. Among the more interesting is the suggestion in Cross (1973), pp. 71–2, that *Yahweh* derives from what was originally an epithet for El, an epithet meaning "He who creates the heavenly armies" — where "creates" would have been the word *yahwi*. Cross seems to be arguing that over time this particular description of El gave rise to a specific cult, distinct from other El cults and concentrated in the south; eventually the name of the cult's god was shortened to the part of the epithet that had originally meant "creates," by which time the severing of this god's identity from El's identity was complete. Subsequently this god became El's rival, "ultimately ousting El from his place in the divine council." Even if Cross is right about the origins of the word *Yahweh*, much of the scenario I sketch could still apply: e.g., the shift of power from north to south as an explanation for the ascendancy of a southern god. The essential disagreement would be on how there came to be a southern god named Yahweh, rival to the northern El, in the first place. So too with a scenario put forth by de Moor (1990), p. 244, in which Yahweh "was not a foreign God who merged with El in Canaan, as is commonly assumed, but he was a manifestation of El from the very beginning. Only when it became necessary to differentiate between the strong El, whose exclusive position was put into ever sharper relief to refute the arguments of the Baalists, and the weak El, who was on the brink of succumbing to Baal, YHWH-El split off from the old head of the pantheon. Even his very name 'Let El Be' was appropriate under the circumstances." For a scenario that involves a merger of Yahweh and El but doesn't involve a north-south power shift, see Albertz (1994), pp. 76–9.

72. Another example of apparently intentional obfuscation: Day (2000), p. 145, notes that in the Masoretic text, references to the "Queen of Heaven" have been systematically altered via a slight but semantically consequential phonetic change, "and it is widely agreed that this was an apologetic alteration to avoid the suggestion that the people of Judah worshipped the Queen of Heaven."

73. Kaufmann (1972), pp. 60–1.

74. Smith (2001), pp. 84, 175.

75. Day (2000), p. 47.

76. See Ackerman (2003), pp. 455–9; Smith (2002a), chapter 3; Day (2000), chapter 2; Gnuse (1997), pp. 69–71; Blenkinsopp (1996), p. 58; Horn (1999), p. 158. There is disagreement over whether biblical and archaeological instances of the word *asherah* refer to the *goddess* Asherah or merely a cultic object — possibly a wooden pole or a stylized tree. But surely any such cultic object would have *represented* Asherah, so (assuming it didn't lose this representative meaning over time, as a few scholars have argued) its use would signify the worship of Asherah (and indeed, it might well be *equated* with Asherah, as Ackerman notes). In any event, Smith (2001), pp. 73–4, says biblical scholars have "generally embraced" the view that the archaeological references to Yahweh and "his Asherah" attest to belief in a goddess, and not just a cult object, though opinion is not unanimous. Day (2000) argues that most appearances of *asherah* refer to a cult object but some to a goddess, and, in any event, believes there was Israelite worship of the goddess Asherah.

77. 2 Kings 23:6, NRSV.

78. Kaufmann (1972), p. 60. Kaufmann conceded that the Bible features the "occasional

mythological fragment," such as a battle between Yahweh and a primeval monster, but said this is mere "poetical allusion." And as for such images as the wind being God's breath: the Bible "never crosses, the threshold of paganism. For these are no more than poetic figures." And in any event such Canaanite mythological motifs were "acquired, in all likelihood, before the rise of Israelite religion," a religion that quickly demythologized them. See Kaufmann (1972), pp. 60–70.

79. Cross (1973), p. 119.
80. Psalms 74:13–14.
81. Psalms 74:13. NRSV says God "divided" the sea, but another translation has it as "smashed." See Smith (2001), p. 36.
82. The Hebrew word is *yam.* Another adversary common to Baal and the biblical God is Tannin ("Dragon"). All told, Psalm 74:12–17, in which Yahweh overcomes Yam, Tannin, and Leviathan, seems to have a clear kinship to the Ugaritic tradition. See Pitard (2002), pp. 261–2.
83. Isaiah 25:8. The Hebrew word that could have meant either death or Mot is *mawet.* See Smith (2001), p. 36. For the time being, according to Hosea 13:4, Yahweh still has to pay a ransom to Mot if he wants to save people from death. The footnote to the verse in Coogan, ed. (2001), notes that "Death" probably refers to Mot here.
84. Day (2000), pp. 185–6.
85. Habakkuk 3:8. See Cross (1973), p. 140.
86. See Cross (1973), p. 140.
87. Habakkuk 3:9–11, 15.
88. See footnote to this verse in Coogan, ed. (2001).
89. Psalms 29:3–7.
90. See Fitzgerald (1974); Cross (1973), pp. 151–5; Day (2000), pp. 97–8; Day argues that Psalm 29 is derived from the Baal tradition in a looser sense than Ginsberg's argument suggests.
91. Cross (1973), chapter 6.
92. Exodus 15:8. The probably later account of the crossing, Exodus 14:20–27, may be a compilation of passages written at different times by different authors. See Friedman (2003), pp. 143–4.
93. Cross (1973), p. 163.
94. Smith (2001), p. 174.
95. Among the other factors Smith cites (see his *Memoirs of God*) are the dynamics of oral transmission and their influence on cultural memory and cultural "amnesia."
96. E.g., Deuteronomy 4:12; see Smith (2001), p. 176.
97. Smith (2001), p. 177. See also Keel and Uehlinger (1998), p. 317.
98. Korpel (1990), p. 625.
99. As Mark S. Smith has noted, in this verse, as in Deuteronomy 32:8, above, the phrase "Most High" (or *Elyon,* a traditional name for El) makes the meaning less straightforward than standard interpretations would have it. In other words, Yahweh may not here be the *head* of the divine council. The assumption that he is would seem to facilitate the common interpretation that he is sentencing the gods to death rather than just predicting their death.
100. Isaiah 25:8; see Smith (2001), p. 36.
101. Habakkuk 3:5; see Smith (2001), p. 149. Coogan (1987), pp. 119–20, and others have argued that biblical references to a female "wisdom" are not mere personifications but references to a goddess, possibly a goddess that was one of God's consorts. For more about Wisdom, see chapter 9 of this book. See also Lang (1999).
102. See Smith (2001), p. 149.
103. See Xella (1999) and del Olmo Lete (1999). Deber in the Ugaritic texts is a "god of

destruction." Resheph in the Ugaritic texts is the lord of battle and diseases. Olmo Lete says this verse in Habakkuk "follows the ancient Mesopotamian tradition in which 'plague' and 'pestilence' are present in the entourage of the great god Marduk"; in Psalm 91:6 "it is Yahweh who liberates his faithful from the fear of this nocturnal demon Deber." Biblical references to Resheph as a god or demon seem to include Job 5:7 and possibly other verses; see Day (2000), pp. 197–208.

104. Day (2000), pp. 232–3, posits a somewhat different scenario: "The seventy sons of God, originally denoting the gods of the pantheon under El, with whom Yahweh became identified, now became demoted to the status of angels, the seventy guardian angels of the nations attested in *1 Enoch.*"

105. Gnuse (1997), pp. 12, 14, 62–3. See Gnuse pp. 66–7 on the popularity, between 1940 and 1970, of the thesis of an early monotheistic revolution.

106. It is sometimes asserted that by the early first millennium BCE, Baal had unseated El at the top of the Canaanite pantheon, but Handy (1994), pp. 70–2, casts doubt on this view.

107. See, e.g., Parker, ed. (1997), p. 86. The relevant passage is Psalms 48:1–3, where various scholars see the text as equating Yahweh's home Mount Zion with Mount Sapan. See Day, pp. 107–16, for an extensive analysis.

108. Handy (1996), p. 34.

109. On the appeal of Baal's rainmaking powers, see, e.g., Day (2000), p. 70. As Day notes (pp. 1–2), among the evidence of Baal's appeal in ancient Israel is that some Israelites mentioned in the Bible were named after Baal, possibly including Eshbaal, the son of Israel's first king, Saul.

110. But see Halpern (1987), p. 88, for a view that de-emphasizes the evolutionary significance of the application of Baalesque storm-theophany language to Yahweh on grounds that this "accretion of language" is in keeping with the character Yahweh had already established, especially as a war god.

111. "rides upon the clouds" is the NRSV rendering of Psalms 68:4. An alternative translation (see NRSV footnote to that verse) is "rides through the deserts." See Day (1992), p. 548, and Cross (1973), p. 157.

112. 1 Kings 18:38. Many scholars interpret "fire" as a reference to lightning.

113. See Day (2000), pp. 76–7.

114. Friedman (1997), pp. 21–2.

115. Cross (1973), p. 194.

116. Friedman (1997), pp. 87–95, plausibly conjectures that the Bible's authors were more inclined to see God conspicuously involved in human affairs when writing about the distant past than when writing about the recent past. (Esther is not the last book in the Old Testament, because Christians rearranged the Hebrew Bible.)

117. Korpel (1990), pp. 621–4, notes that many biblical passages considered archaic describe God with "most unusual imagery" not found in more recently written parts of the Bible — including much anthropomorphic and otherwise mythic language that is found also in Ugaritic descriptions of the divine. All told, "the Ugaritic literature shares at least half of its metaphors for the divine with the Old Testament." See list of biblical metaphors for God, pp. 622–4.

118. Genesis 8:21. On the demise of anthropomorphism over time, see Smith (2001), p. 176.

119. Deuteronomy 4:12–15. Campbell and O'Brien (2000) judge this passage to have been written after the time of King Josiah.

120. See Smith (2002a), p. 145, and Smith (2001), pp. 87–90, 175–7.

121. Daniel 7:9, NRSV.

122. Kaufmann (1972), p. 60.

123. Albright (1957), p. 14.

Chapter Six From Polytheism to Monolatry

1. *Random House Dictionary,* second unabridged edition.
2. On the unreliability of the biblical story of Jezebel and Elijah, see, e.g., Lang (1983), p. 26, Horn (1999), p. 141, Halpern (1987), p. 92. Albertz (2003), p. 279, judges "many portions" of the Elijah narrative "post-Deuteronomistic," which would mean more than two centuries after the events. Schniedewind (1993) argues that the specific attribution of Baal worship to Ahab was inserted in the story no earlier than the exile—again, more than two centuries after Ahab lived. For an earlier dating, see Campbell and O'Brien (2000).
3. According to 1 Kings 16:32, Ahab "erected an altar for Baal in the house of Baal, which he built in Samaria." Niehr (1995), p. 56, argues that this passage obscures an earlier and in his view more plausible tradition according to which Ahab had built an altar for Baal in the temple of Yahweh.
4. Tigay (1986), p. 39, among others, sees Ahab's tolerance of polytheism as motivated by the same policy considerations that motivated his marriage to Jezebel.
5. 1 Kings 11:4–8.
6. Lang (1983), p. 27. Lang speculates that Baal's priests attracted worshippers who otherwise would have patronized Yahweh's priests, and this "financial loss for Yahweh's priesthood" made Yahweh's priests "ill-disposed toward Baal." See II Maccabees 3:1–12, written centuries after Ahab's time, for an example of Yahweh's temple serving as a bank.
7. 2 Kings 10:18–27. And see Lang (1983), p. 28.
8. Smith (1987).
9. This is the mainstream view. See, e.g., Blenkinsopp (1996), p. 88, who suggests that the sayings "may have been transcribed in some cases shortly after they were delivered." Morton Smith (1987), p. 30, seems to dissent, suggesting that "the collection of their [Amos's and Hosea's] prophecies probably took place a generation later"—though this doesn't preclude the individual prophecies having been written down earlier.
10. The dating of the various parts of Hosea, like most issues in biblical scholarship, is not a subject of universal agreement. Many scholars see amendments to Hosea in the time of Josiah or later, and some would say these amendments are quite significant theologically. For an assessment consistent with the view I adopt, see, e.g., Sweeney (2001), pp. 270–1, and Sweeney (2000), vol. 1, pp. 4–6. For an assessment that illustrates the complexity of dating this text, see Albertz (2003), pp. 230–7.
11. See Smith (2001), p. 163.
12. See footnote in Coogan, ed. (2001), for Hosea 5:4. Seow (1992), p. 296, says the verb refers to "intimate knowledge as of partners in a covenant or marriage."
13. Hosea 13:4.
14. Exodus 20:3 and Deuteronomy 5:7. Friedman (2003) attributes Deuteronomy's version of the Ten Commandments to the Deuteronomistic historian (and specifically to the "first" such historian) and more tentatively (p. 153) identifies the Exodus version as an "independent document" that was "inserted here by the Redactor." Collins (1992), p. 384, notes that some scholars have argued that "the first commandment was unthinkable before Hosea." Collins also notes (p. 385) that the first commandment "technically enjoins monolatry..."
15. Hosea 14:3; 7:16; 7:11; footnote to 7:16 in Coogan, ed. (2001), notes that "babbling" refers to negotiations in Egypt. See also Hosea 5:13 (and, relatedly, Blenkinsopp [1996], p. 84).
16. Hosea 12:1. Re: tribute: see footnote to this verse in Coogan, ed. (2001). Some—see, e.g., Albertz (2003), pp. 231–4—would argue that this verse was inserted well after Hosea's

time. All other verses from Hosea that I cite in this chapter emerge from Albertz's analysis with their traditional earlier dating intact.

17. Hosea seems to disapprove of a recent treaty with Syria. See Blenkinsopp (1996), p. 87; Albertz (1994), vol. I, p. 169; and Meeks, ed. (1993), footnotes to Hosea 5:11 and 8:9.

18. Sweeney (2000), vol. 1, p. 62. See also Albertz (1994), pp. 169–70, on the various counterproductive foreign entanglements to which Hosea alludes.

19. Hosea 7:8–9; 8:8.

20. Hosea 8:7. Albertz (1994), vol. 1, p. 169, sees this verse as a reference to Israel's being drained by payments required by vassalage.

21. Hosea 9:1; 2:5; 8:9–10. Footnote to 8:9–10 in Coogan, ed. (2001) notes that the "burden of kings and princes" refers to foreign subjugation.

22. Lang (1983), p. 15, attributed to, e.g., Nikiprowetzky (1975) the view that "prophetic nationalism…is the cradle of monotheism."

23. Hosea 1:2; 9.

24. Isaiah 8:3. The prophecy was about Assyria's coming conquest of Israel; see Blenkinsopp (1996), p. 101.

25. Coogan, ed. (2001), p. 1278.

26. Horn (1999), pp. 165–6; Blenkinsopp (1996), p. 67.

27. Finkelstein and Silberman (2002), pp. 214–5; Horn (1999), pp. 168–9.

28. Finkelstein and Silberman (2002), pp. 217–20; Horn (1999), pp. 171–2; Blenkinsopp (1996), p. 68.

29. Some think Hosea himself may have fled to Judah.

30. Horn (1999), p. 180–4; Blenkinsopp (1996), pp. 68–70.

31. Of course, one person's "humiliating" vassalage is another person's relatively advantageous vassalage. Indeed, the acceptance of vassalage meant that Israel's king judged it preferable to rebellion, and if the economic relations entailed by vassalage were fruitful enough, you could even say the vassalage was positive-sum from the point of view of both Israel and the hegemon in question. At any rate, vassalage probably brought, for at least some Israelites, the acceptance of foreign gods, whereas rebellion was often accompanied by their official rejection. (See Cogan [1974], p. 95: "Although Assyria made no formal demands for cultural uniformity among its subjects…Judah was faced with the problem of assimilation of foreign norms, on a national scale, for the first time in its history…Judahites succumbed to the lure of new gods.") As Joseph Blenkinsopp (1996, p. 69) writes of Judah after the fall of Ephraim: "Vassalage would have strengthened syncretic tendencies. On the other hand, the frequent attempts at political emancipation were invariably associated with movements of religious repristination and reform." Certainly, as I discuss below, the Bible describes the theology of Judah's eighth-century kings as broadly consistent with this model: the rebellious Hezekiah and Josiah are monolatrous, whereas Manasseh, who accepts vassalage to Assyria, is condemned as polytheistic.

32. Amos is thought to have been born in the southern kingdom of Judah but to have prophesied for an audience in the northern kingdom. Amos spends less time on theology than Hosea, and many scholars say his explicit theological utterances don't warrant the label "monolatry." But Morton Smith (1987), p. 31, argues that the very preservation of Amos's text suggests it was approved by Yahweh-alonists, and, as he notes, later monolatrist prophets (such as Zephaniah, discussed below) employ Amos's themes. In any event, Amos does (5:26) criticize the worship of Sakkuth and Kaiwan, deities of possibly Assyrian lineage (see Coogan, ed. [2001], footnote p. 1311; van der Toorn et al., eds. [1999], pp. 478, 722; and Cogan [1974], p. 104). And he nowhere validates the worship of any god other than Yahweh. By the way, to say that, e.g., Amos or Isaiah deploy anti-elite

rhetoric isn't to say that they themselves were not elites, but rather that their constituency included non-elites.

33. Amos 2:7, 4:1.

34. Isaiah 10:2. Some scholars think this chapter of Isaiah, though placed amid chapters generally attributed to Isaiah himself, was added well after Isaiah lived.

35. Economic inequality and expanding trade: Blenkinsopp (1996), pp. 71, 81.

36. Schniedewind (1999), pp. 55–8, discusses the role of urbanization and social stratification in creating resentment of cosmopolitan elites in both the north, as reflected in Amos and Hosea, and the south.

37. Amos 6:4; Horn (1999), p. 161; Finkelstein and Silberman (2002), pp. 212–3.

38. Isaiah 2:6–7. See footnote in Coogan, ed. (2001).

39. Zephaniah 1:8. See Sweeney (2001), p. 197, for an alternative interpretation.

40. Zephaniah 1:11. See Blenkinsopp (1996), p. 114.

41. Zephaniah 1:4–5. On the meaning of the "host of heavens," see footnote to 1:5 in Meeks, ed. (1993); van der Toorn et al., eds. (1999), pp. 428–9. On the likely Assyrian lineage of astral deities, see Blenkinsopp (1996), p. 114. See Keel and Uehlinger (1998), pp. 288, 294, for archaeological evidence that Assyrian administrators in Palestine were worshipping such heavenly deities as stars and the moon in the eighth and seventh centuries BCE. Keel and Uehlinger see a growth in astral worship in Israel beginning around the end of the eighth century, a trend they attribute (p. 294) to Assyrian and Aramean influence.

42. Zephaniah 1:4. The interpretation of these passages from Zephaniah is problematic. First, there is the question of whether "every remnant of Baal" is meant to *include* the host of heaven, as asserted by Halpern (1987), p. 94, or is a freestanding phrase. My interpretation follows Blenkinsopp (1996), p. 114, who summarizes Zephaniah's message thus: "the political elite is indicted for engaging in the worship of Baal, Assyrian-type cults of sun, moon, and stars, and the Ammonite deity Milcom..." Blenkinsopp also notes (p. 114) that the apostate elites "have adopted foreign customs and dress and profess an enlightened skepticism about the traditional religion." Related to the question of whether these gods were (or were perceived as) foreign is the question of when these passages from Zephaniah were written. Some scholars believe much of Zephaniah is exilic or even later. See Albertz (2003), pp. 217–21, for a discussion. Albertz himself suspects that the book's pre-exilic core is 1:7–2:4 (which includes the denunciation of foreign-friendly elites but not the rejection of the worship of specific gods). Still, even if denunciation of, e.g., astral deities was added during the sixth century, Albertz (p. 217) still believes that they refer "primarily to the alien cults that had invaded Judah in the seventh century, during the long period of Assyrian occupation." It should be noted that this sort of fine-grained dating of individual verses has fallen out of favor among some scholars who consider it a hopeless task and/or believe there was less fine-grained redaction of biblical texts than this methodology presupposes.

43. Zephaniah 2:9–13.

44. Zephaniah 2:8. This passage illustrates the difficulty of linking specific indictments of nations to specific historical grievances. Sweeney (2001), p. 195, notes that during the ninth century BCE, Moab and Ammon had occupied land that the Israelites considered theirs—land that Assyria took over in the eighth century, and that thus would have been vulnerable to Moab and Ammon upon Assyria's withdrawal around Zephaniah's era. Other scholars, Sweeney notes, see this passage as an exilic addition to Zephaniah and link it to a Babylonian invasion of Moab. Meanwhile, Albertz (2003), p. 185, attributes a comparable, and presumably exilic, judgment against Moab, Ammon, and Edom in

Jeremiah to the participation of these nations in an anti-Babylonian conspiracy. (Jeremiah favored vassalage to Babylon.) And others — see Provan et al. (2003), p. 284 — note evidence that Edom, another of Jeremiah's indictees, took advantage of the exile to seize Judean territory.

45. Zephaniah 2:15.

46. Isaiah 13:11. And see Isaiah 2:11–17.

47. Emotions such as resentment were built into the human mind by evolution, and the context was a small social universe that featured zero-sum and non-zero-sum dynamics. In some cases these emotions seem to be "designed" — by natural selection — to react adaptively to those dynamics. Resentment of someone's arrogance, for example, may be the unconscious mind's way of saying that this person would be too demanding an alliance partner for alliance to be worthwhile. (According to evolutionary psychology, the mind is designed to take into account imbalances in status or power in deciding how "giving" to be in a friendship or in a coalition.)

   This doesn't mean that human emotions are always reliable guides to the non-zero-sum opportunities in one's environment. When you take emotions that were built for a hunter-gatherer village and apply them in a radically different environment, they may malfunction. Then again, malfunctions can happen when you try to consciously and rationally size up the prospects for non-zero-sum interaction; you may wrongly conclude that conflict is better than alliance and eschew the other nation's gods to disastrous effect. In both cases — whether the decision is emotionally or rationally mediated — what matters is your *perception*. If you perceive the situation as zero-sum, you'll probably be less tolerant of a foreign theology (unless you see yourself as hopelessly outgunned: see chapter 8). In general on these issues, see chapter 19.

48. 2 Kings 21:2–3.

49. Psalms 2:7, which seems to be part of a coronation ritual: "You are my son; today I have begotten you." See also, e.g., 2 Samuel 7:14.

50. Smith (2002a), p. 72; Day (2000), p. 71.

51. Tigay (1986), p. 10.

52. This is a conservative estimate. Of the 669 names with a divine element, 557 were Yahweh-derived. But of the 112 other names, 77 were based on the divine element *el* — which could refer to the Canaanite god El but could also be the generic name for a god and so could actually refer to Yahweh. See Tigay (1986), pp. 11–12.

53. See Day (2000), pp. 227–8, who notes that figurines of a goddess he takes to be Asherah were present in "vast numbers" in eighth- and seventh-century-BCE Judah — to say nothing of the references to Yahweh "and his Asherah" discussed in the previous chapter.

54. Edelman, ed. (1996), p. 19.

55. See Miller (2000), pp. 178–84, on the diversity of roles prophets could play in ancient Israel.

56. 1 Kings 22:19.

57. The Ahab instance just cited — from 1 Kings 22 — is a good example of royal discretion. King Ahab, after hearing four hundred of Yahweh's prophets recommend war, solicits (with the encouragement of the king of Judah, his ally) another opinion, from a Yahweh prophet known for his pessimism.

58. 1 Kings 18:19, and see Miller (2000), p. 184. For a good analysis of the allocation of power among prophets, priests, and kings, see Miller's chapter 5.

59. Patrick D. Miller, personal communication. This isn't to say Yahwistic prophets never criticized or contradicted a king. (David's prophet Nathan, e.g., indicted David for his illicit romance with Bathsheba.) It's just to say that kings probably had more influence

over pronouncements emanating from Yahweh's prophets than over pronouncements by, e.g., Asherah's or Baal's prophets.

60. 1 Samuel 28:13–15. NRSV here translates *elohim* as "divine being." See also Isaiah 8:19 and the discussion in Day (2000), p. 218.

61. Miller (2000), p. 54. He's referring specifically to "Yahwism's denunciation of traditional means of divination." But he agrees (personal communication) that a king would probably have had more influence over Yahweh prophets than over the prophets of other gods. On religious centralization as a means to political centralization, see also, e.g., Finkelstein and Silberman (2002), p. 249.

62. Morton Smith considered monolatry a pre-exilic expression of nationalism of the sort found in time of national crisis. See Gnuse (1997) on Smith. Halpern (1987), p. 101, notes a correlation between military crisis, xenophobia, and calls for devotion to Yahweh.

63. Some have argued that this sort of "temporary monolatry"—lavishing devotion on the god whose expertise was most needed at the time (which in other circumstances might be, e.g., a rain god)—was seen repeatedly in the ancient Middle East. See van Selms (1973).

64. Theissen (1984), pp. 56–7.

65. If you start reading 2 Kings at the beginning of chapter 13, you'll see this phrase repeatedly and will also see that, until the arrival of Hezekiah, the evil kings outnumber the good kings by a ratio of around 3 to 1.

66. 2 Kings 22:2.

67. Halpern (1987), p. 97.

68. Hezekiah and Manasseh, though father and son, seem to have followed different theologies. Hezekiah, says the Bible, did "what was right in the sight of the LORD"—lavished devotion on Yahweh and discouraged the worship of other gods (2 Kings 18:3). Manasseh, in contrast, "erected altars for Baal" and worshipped various other gods, thus doing "what was evil in the sight of the LORD" (2 Kings 21:2–3).

As for their ideologies: Hezekiah, as the scholar Joseph Blenkinsopp puts it, pursued an "expansive nationalism," attacking "Edomites to the south and Philistines to the west." (Blenkinsopp [1996], p. 107.) He also rejected (as had the emphatically monolatrous Hosea) a subservient alliance with Assyria, opting instead for a doomed rebellion that left Judah besieged and isolated. (In the Bible, Hezekiah is shown heroically resisting complete conquest at the hands of the Assyrians, but various scholars—e.g. Halpern [1987], p. 97—have argued that this is spin control, putting the best face on a largely bad outcome.)

In contrast, the polytheistic Manasseh, as one archaeologist has put it, was "intent on integrating Judah into the Assyrian world economy," and so accepted vassalage to Assyria (Finkelstein and Silberman [1999], p. 267). Horn (1994), p. 184, argues that Manasseh's religious policies weren't tailored to his rapprochement with Assyria, since Assyria didn't demand worship of Assyrian gods as a condition of vassalage. On the other hand, as Blenkinsopp (1996), p. 68, notes, vassalage did mean signing a treaty accepting the "yoke of Assur," Assyria's imperial god. And, even if the Israelites' worship of Ashur wasn't demanded by Assyria, banning it might have ruffled relations with Assyria.

And recent archaeology suggests that Manasseh's pursuit of non-zero-sum gains paid off; there are signs of expanded trade, as Manasseh's policies bring economic recovery to a Judah desolated under Hezekiah's rule (see Finkelstein and Silberman [2002], pp. 267–8). In short, Israel's foreign policy during this crucial century seems to bear out the general prediction that people are more open to foreign religious practices if they see themselves benefiting from collaborative interaction with the foreigners.

The fit between theory and evidence shouldn't be overstated. Hezekiah wasn't totally isolationist—and in fact allied with Egypt in his rebellion against Assyria. Still, on balance, Manasseh seems to have been more internationalist in spirit and policy than Hezekiah.

69. Some have doubted that the religious reforms attributed to Josiah actually took place during his reign. For references, and a defense of the view that they did, see Day (2000), pp. 227–32.

70. Relative credibility of 2 Kings on Josiah vs. on Elijah: the two main reasons for this view are (1) The events happened nearer in time to the crystallization of the text in the case of Josiah than in the case of Elijah and Ahab; (2) From the theological perspective of the Deuteronomist, Josiah's reforms are narratively inconvenient in light of Josiah's death and his ultimate political failure; that a theologically right-minded king should meet such a fate seems more like a stubborn fact that the Deuteronomist had to reckon with than a convenient fiction.

71. 2 Kings 23:4, 11, 13–14, 24.

72. 2 Kings 23:8. Whether, as has been claimed, there is archaeological evidence of this destruction is a subject of disagreement. See Finkelstein and Silberman (2002), pp. 250, 288.

73. 2 Kings 23:5, 20.

74. McCarter (1987), p. 139.

75. Deuteronomy 6:4 and Mark 12:29.

76. Similar to the NRSV's alternative translation is the version that is perhaps the most common rendering in American Judaism—"Hear, O Israel: The LORD is our God, the LORD is one." And—with "Yahweh" substituted for "LORD"—this is semantically equivalent to one plausible English translation of the Masoretic Text, the oldest extant Hebrew edition of the Bible: "Hear, O Israel, Yahweh our god, Yahweh [is] one god" (Kevin Osterloh, personal communication). McCarter (1987), p. 142, rejects this interpretation of Deuteronomy 6:4, arguing that (for reasons that are unclear to me) Deuteronomy 6:5 is inconsistent with it. McCarter also says there is no evidence that the *purpose* of Josiah's cult centralization was to end the veneration of local Yahwehs, even if that was a consequence. Still, McCarter notes that the different local versions of Yahweh "must have been thought of and worshipped quite differently" (p. 141) and observes that, in an analogous ancient Assyrian case—that of Ishtar of Nineveh and Ishtar of Arbela—the inclusion of both deities on a single list of deities indicates that they were "thought of as semi-independent." Albertz (1994), vol. I, p. 206, sees this verse as having two meanings—the one I stress as well as a monolatrous one; that is: (a) Yahweh is only one god, and (b) Yahweh is the only god for Israel.

77. Deuteronomy 13:6–9; 18:19–20; 13:15. Deuteronomy 18:19–20 also gives the death sentence to a prophet "who presumes to speak in my name a word that I have not commanded the prophet to speak." It doesn't say that the king is in charge of deciding which Yahweh prophets falsely presume to speak in his name. Rather, it says that those prophets who relay a prediction of Yahweh's that turns out to be inaccurate are the ones who qualify for the death penalty. But presumably the king's court, being responsible for judicial matters, could exploit interpretive leeway.

78. Finkelstein and Silberman (2002), p. 288, and see Ackerman (2003), p. 463.

79. Social security: Blenkinsopp (1996), p. 161. See pp. 159–62 on the reforms in general. Among the reforms was insistence (Deuteronomy 17:17) that a king "must not acquire many wives"; though the rationale is theological—wives can "turn away" the king's heart from Yahweh—the effect of any systematic discouraging of polygamy would be

egalitarian in the sense that polygamy leaves fewer wives available for poorer and lower-status men.

80. Halpern (1987), p. 94. Halpern's interpretation, unlike mine, sees this harnessing of xenophobia to stigmatize domestic gods beginning at least as early as Hosea (p. 96), but this argument depends on reading Hosea's denunciation of foreign alliances, and his parallel denunciation of (often unnamed, notes Halpern) gods, as a subtle rhetorical device designed to stigmatize domestic gods as foreign without saying as much. My interpretation, suggested earlier in this chapter, is rather that this parallelism indicates the xenophobic *motivation* for Hosea's rejection of *foreign* gods in favor of monolatry (a motivation Hosea may or may not have been aware of). I suspect that if Hosea wanted to harness xenophobia, he would have stigmatized the gods as foreign more overtly. In any event, clear examples of the explicit use of xenophobic rhetoric to stigmatize gods that are plausibly part of a domestic pantheon seem to begin well after Hosea's time (assuming mainstream dating of texts). And even Halpern agrees (p. 97) that it is well after Hosea's time that this process is most conspicuous: "It is, as is commonly observed, at Josiah's reform that the clearest stigmatization of traditional practice as alien takes place." For an interpretation of Hosea that is in some ways similar to Halpern's, see Albertz (1994), vol. I, pp. 172–4.

81. Halpern (1987), pp. 94, 96. Halpern also notes (p. 93) that gods subordinate to Yahweh could be in a sense domestic and foreign at once. Using the term "baal" in its generic sense ("lord") he writes that " 'baal'-worship and vassalship or even alliances could very well be equated, the subsidiary deity being at the same time the god of a foreign people."

82. 2 Kings 21:2–3.

83. 2 Kings 23:4 has "all the vessels made for Baal, for Asherah, and for all the host of heaven" being removed from the temple. And 2 Kings 23:11 mentions horses used for sun worship located at the entrance to the temple (though, among those who stress foreign influence on Israelite religion—e.g., Keel and Uehlinger [1998]—solar worship is often attributed less to Assyrian dominance than to earlier Egyptian dominance).

84. 2 Kings 23:5. Lohfink (1987), p. 468, contends that, though the deities being denounced in this part of the Bible (2 Kings 23:4–14) are often given "Canaanite names," it nonetheless "appears clear that Josiah's cult reform consisted in great measure of the destruction of Assyrian cults," and may have reflected a "national independence move away from Assyria." Also arguing that much of the religious practice attacked by Josiah was Assyrian—the residue of Assyrian influence as Assyrian power receded—is Albertz (1994), vol. I, e.g., pp. 198, 207, 210–11.

85. See Schmidt (1999). The seal is from Gezer. For an archaeologically based argument that Israel's astral religion derived significantly from Assyrian influence, see Keel and Uehlinger (1998), e.g., pp. 294–5, 367–9.

86. Campbell and O'Brien (2000), who are fairly mainstream in their dating of texts, consider this passage pre-Josianic, and the passage itself asserts that this story comes from an earlier text called "the Book of Jashar," an extra-biblical source alluded to elsewhere in the Bible as well.

87. Joshua 10:12. See Handy (1996), pp. 39–40, and Schmidt (1999). In the verse it is Joshua who is quoted as instructing the moon and sun to stop, but he does so in Yahweh's presence, and the idea is clearly that in some sense Yahweh conveys the command to the moon with his divine authority added.

88. Smith (2001), p. 61. See also p. 63 re: the role of astral deities in El worship and in Yahweh worship.

89. Day (2000), p. 164, notes that the case for an indigenous moon god is further strength-ened by the fact that when the Bible denounces the worship of a moon god, it doesn't use the proper name (e.g., Sin or Sahar) of nearby foreign moon gods, but rather the Hebrew word for "moon." See Day (2000), chapter 6, in general for the argument that celestial deities whose worship in Judah is often attributed to Assyrian or Aramean or other for-eign influence may have been more locally "Canaanite" in origin.

90. 2 Kings 23:13. Re: the Sidonian Astarte, see Day (2000), p. 129. The view that Astarte, Ashtoreth, and the Queen of Heaven are one and the same is a common view among scholars but not unanimous. See Ackerman (1992), chapter 1; Ackerman (2003), p. 461; Wyatt (1999).

91. Though the Bible blames Solomon for importing Astarte via a Sidonian wife, it elsewhere reports Astarte worship long before Solomon's time. See Judges 2:11–13. On Astarte's role in Ugaritic religion, see Day (2000), p. 131, and Smith (2001), pp. 47, 74–5. According to Stern (2003), p. 309, Astarte was the chief female deity of many Canaanite nations.

92. Day (2000), p. 131.

93. Smith (2001), p. 190. And see pp. 65–79, including Smith's judgment on p. 75: "From the cumulative evidence it appears that on the whole Baal was an accepted Israel-ite god…There is no evidence that prior to the ninth century Baal was considered a major threat to the cult of Yahweh." See Day (2000), pp. 73–77, who, arguing by his own account against the majority view, says Jezebel's Baal was Baal-Shamem, "the same Baal who had been worshipped by the Canaanite population of Israel and syncretistic Israelites" (p. 76), and was not Melqart or "Baal of Tyre"—though Baal-Shamem, in Day's view, was "the most important Tyrian god at this period" (p. 75).

94. Schniedewind (1993).

95. On the issue of whether Amos, Hosea, and "first" Isaiah were substantially edited from a Josianic standpoint, roughly a century after Amos, Hosea, and Isaiah are thought to have lived, see Sweeney (2001), p. 17 and after. As for the book of Zephaniah, the bulk of which is now thought by some scholars—see Sweeney (2001), p. 16—to have been authored decades after Zephaniah lived: Sweeney (2001), chapter 11, defends the tradi-tional view that Zephaniah is substantially rooted in the Josianic era.

96. For a discussion of the ongoing debate about how much influence Assyria's imperial dominance had on Israelite religion, see Day (2000), pp. 231–2, and Holloway (2002).

97. 1 Kings 18:19.

98. For Canaanite peoples whom Joshua didn't wholly extinguish, see Joshua 13.

99. As the Deuteronomistic history progresses, its political and theological convenience persists. Though biblical writers depicted the tenth-century kingdom of David as a vast and potent state—a full-fledged "civilization," in the archaeologist's sense of the word—some archaeologists now doubt this picture. For starters, during this period of the "united monarchy," the northern and southern parts of Israel may in fact not have been united; David and his successor Solomon may have ruled only Judah. And, though the Israelite "kingdom" to Judah's north may have deserved that label, there's little archaeological evidence that Judah itself had achieved the state level of organization. Maybe, as one anthropologist suggests, the great "kings" David and Solomon were "little more than hill country chieftains" (Finkelstein and Silberman [2002], p. 190). Niehr (1996), p. 53, agrees that prior to the eighth century there was "a modest Judahite chief-dom" and suggests that it was "politically and economically dependent on Tyre." Indeed, Judah may not have become a full-fledged state until the seventh century BCE—the era of Hezekiah and Josiah, when evidence of extensive literacy shows up.

    If this revisionist view is right, then the triumph of the Yahweh-alone movement may have coincided symbiotically with the maturation of the state of Judah: The Yahweh-alonists heightened the Israelite nationalism that geopolitical adversity had stoked, and harnessed it to produce an advanced state with centralized rule.

But if the revisionist view is right, where did the prerevisionist view—i.e., the Bible's version—come from? What would biblical writers, trolling Israel's oral traditions for attractive motifs, have found so tempting about the idea of a golden age when Israel was a vast kingdom spanning north and south? For one thing (see Finkelstein and Silberman [2002]), this story would have validated Josiah's plan to redraw Judah's borders. Perhaps, with Assyrian power now receding, the time seemed right to annex the northern kingdom of Israel by force; and if this political union could be cast as a *re*union, a return to God's original game plan, that could help pacify the northerners—who, after all, might not be initally enthusiastic about the takeover. Indeed, northern resistance would explain why Josiah's treatment of unorthodox priests differed by region: southern ones were forced into early retirement, northern ones were killed. (This expansionist aim further blurs the line between purging domestic gods and expelling foreign gods. The northern kingdom, under Assyrian control since the late eighth century, was presumably richer in Assyrian gods than the south.)

100. 2 Kings 21:2–3.
101. Deuteronomy 18:9–13.
102. "Ethnic marking" is most commonly noted in the evolution of language, as an ethnic group develops a dialect distinct from neighboring groups'.
103. See Sweeney (2001), p. 19.
104. Deuteronomy 20:16–18. Some have argued that this genocide was to be employed in nearby cities only in the event that these peoples refused to be subjugated peacefully. The text doesn't say this explicitly; it directly connects this sort of conditionality only to the case of distant cities. But the wording does leave open the possibility that this conditionality was meant to apply to the case of nearby cities as well. However, working against this interpretation is the Bible's justification for the genocide: the people are to be wiped out because, being nearby, they might teach their religion to the Israelites if left alive. Presumably this prospect would have been just as abhorrent, and so just as fiercely discouraged, in the event that the nearby cities offered peaceful submission. But in the end the ambiguity in this passage seems beyond resolving.
105. Deuteronomy 20:13–14.
106. Strictly speaking, the Deuteronomistic Code isn't intolerant of foreign religions per se. The slaughter of whole cities full of foreigners is justified not on grounds that their worship of their own gods is bad in itself, but on grounds that this worship could infect Israelite religion. But as a practical matter, this distinction made little difference.

Chapter Seven From Monolatry to Monotheism

1. Sweeney (2001), p. 317.
2. 2 Kings 23:29 reports the death with police-blotter economy: "When Pharaoh Neco met him at Megiddo, he killed him." 2 Chronicles 35 offers more detail, depicting Josiah as ill-advisedly picking a fight with an Egyptian army that meant him no harm (and even, uncharacteristically, ignoring prophetic advice emanating ultimately from "the mouth of God"). But, since Chronicles was written later than Kings, many scholars attach more doubt to its accuracy.
3. See 2 Kings, chapter 25, for the Bible's version of these events, which seem to withstand historical scrutiny.
4. Klein (1979), p. 7.

5. Jeremiah 44:25–7.
6. Jeremiah 44:17–18. See Albertz (1994), vol. II, p. 377.
7. See, e.g., Albertz (2003), p. 135. 2 Kings 24 identifies all four kings who succeeded Josiah as "evil," presumably meaning they tolerated polytheism, but Albertz argues that the Yahweh-alone movement stayed intact.
8. Household gods ("teraphim" in the Bible): 2 Kings 23:24.
9. 2 Kings 23:25–6.
10. That Israelites had previously explained geopolitical misfortune via Yahweh's wrath assumes that at least some of the various verses explaining pre-exilic setbacks that way (e.g., Isaiah 9:11–12, Isaiah 10:5, Amos 5:26, Judges 3:8, Judges 3:12) are themselves pre-exilic. But even if they aren't, it is likely that this common explanatory maneuver was used. See Blenkinsopp (1996), p. 105.
11. Pritchard, ed. (1958), p. 209.
12. Judges 3:8, 12.
13. Isaiah 10:5.
14. Habakkuk 1:5–6, 10.
15. Smith (2001), p. 165.
16. Isaiah 48:10. On Second Isaiah as the earliest unambiguous monotheist, see, e.g., Niki-prowetzky (1975), p. 82.
17. Isaiah 45:5; 43:11; 44:6; 43:10; 44:24; 45:7.
18. Isaiah 54:5; 42:1; 49:6.
19. Isaiah 45:14.
20. Isaiah 49:22–3; 49:26.
21. Albertz (2003), p. 188.
22. Ibid., p. 187. (Albertz thinks some parts of Ezekiel may be postexilic.)
23. Ezekiel 25:6–7.
24. Ezekiel 25:11; 25:8; 25:17.
25. Ezekiel 28:22–3.
26. Otto (1977).
27. Ezekiel 36:23.
28. Niehr (1995), p. 57. This from Sargon II's Nimrud-prism.
29. Gerardi (1986), p. 32.
30. Ibid., p. 35. And see Albertz (2003), p. 51. King Nabopolassar isn't mentioned by name, but there is little doubt that he is doing the talking.
31. There presumably were differing expectations as to whether Israel would do the requisite conquering of the world itself or whether, as Second Isaiah implies, the conquering would be done on its behalf by the mighty Persian Empire that displaced Babylon as hegemon during the exile. See Isaiah 44:28, 45:1.
32. Albertz (2003), p. 196.
33. See Wright (1994).
34. Postexilic Jews would argue that Yahweh had never actually *lived* in the temple that was destroyed; he had just placed his "name" there. And, indeed, they could point to apparently pre-exilic Bible verses that seemed to say as much. But Schniedewind (2003) has argued that in the vernacular of early Israel, saying that your "name" resided somewhere was just a way of saying that you owned it; this locution permitted creative postexilic thinkers to claim ancient sanction for a "name theology" that was in fact a clever adaptation to the destruction of the temple.
35. Orlinsky (1974), p. 88.
36. See ibid., p. 105.
37. Isaiah 2:4.

38. Isaiah 51:4–5.
39. Isaiah 45:16–17; 51:11.
40. Isaiah 45:1; 45:1–4.
41. Pritchard, ed. (1958), pp. 206–8.
42. Marvin Sweeney, personal communication.
43. Isaiah 46:1–2. Of course, this could be a kind of sardonic understatement.
44. Malachi 1:4–5.
45. See Frede (1999) for the argument that Plato and Aristotle, among others, were monotheists in the sense that later Christians were.
46. This designation depends on the interpretation of this phrase (whose full context doesn't survive): "One god, greatest among gods and men." Kirk et al. (1983), p. 169, consider it doubtful that Xenophanes would have recognized "other, minor deities as being in any way related to the 'one god,' except as dim human projections of it." Aristotle, at any rate, called Xenophanes (see p. 171) "the first...to postulate a unity."
47. Kirk et al. (1983), pp. 169–70.
48. Halpern (2003), pp. 324–5. Halpern suggests that correspondences between Greek religious philosophy and postexilic religious thought in Israel may have been due not just to the former's influence on the latter—i.e., Hellenization—but to parallel Greek and Israelite reactions, going back centuries, to notions of scientific regularity that emerged from Babylonian astronomy and reached the Greeks and the Israelites independently. Halpern lays out fascinating if speculative ideas about how such scientific understanding may have found its way into the Bible in cryptically metaphorical form.
49. Jeremiah 10:2.
50. Isaiah 40:26.
51. But it's not certain whether Zoroastrian dualism had emerged from an earlier Persian polytheism by the time Israel fell under Persian rule.
52. Isaiah 45:1. Cyrus is called "anointed," the Hebrew word underlying "messiah."
53. Almost all the posited parallels are in Isaiah 44:24–45:15. See Smith (1963), p. 420.
54. As Smith (1963) noted, Second Isaiah's account of how Yahweh summoned Cyrus parallels a Persian account, found on the aforementioned clay cylinder, of how the Babylonian god Marduk summoned Cyrus. Yahweh, according to Isaiah 45:1, appointed Cyrus "to subdue nations before him and strip kings of their robes." Marduk, says the cylinder seal, deemed that Cyrus become "ruler of all the world" and that "princes and governors bowed to him" (Pritchard, ed. [1958], pp. 206–7). Smith speculated that both messages were crafted ultimately by Cyrus—one for Bablyonian consumption, and one for the consumption of Israelites. In both cases, he suggested, the message was spread by Persian agents who infiltrated the Babylonian Empire and prepared the ground for Cyrus's invasion by cultivating support among the empire's many malcontented subjects. In this view, Second Isaiah, correctly sensing that Cyrus could deliver the exiles to Zion, became a willing propagandist.
55. Smith himself leaves room for this possibility, noting that Second Isaiah's openness to Persian input would be explained by "the apologetic needs of the Yahwist community in Babylonia, and in the development of devotional rhetoric within the Israelite tradition" (p. 421).
56. Halpern (personal communication).
57. Yet another candidate for influence on the evolution of Israelite monotheism is Assyrian religion, which was, argues Parpola (2000), p. 165, "essentially monotheistic."
58. Matthew 5:43–4.
59. Revelation 17:5; 19:1–2; 11–15.

Chapter Eight   Philo Story

1. Exodus 22:28.
2. Philo (1929), supp. II, pp. 40–1.
3. Runia (1990), p. 12.
4. Philo (1929), supp. II, pp. 40–1.
5. Ibid., p. 41.
6. On balance, the context of this verse seems to favor translating *elohim* in the singular. Still, the translator's choice was not technically determined.
7. Philo (1929), vol. 5, p. 555; Freedman, ed. (1992), vol. 3, p. 751.
8. Deuteronomy 20:16–18.
9. Deuteronomy 20:13–14.
10. Philo (1929), vol. 8, p. 145, footnote.
11. Goodenough (1986), p. 151.
12. Goodenough (1935), p. 207.
13. Goodenough (1986), p. 47. Philo wrote a whole book on allegory. He dismissed the literal truth of some scripture, but sometimes defended literalism (see p. 48).
14. Goldenberg (1998), p. 69.
15. Schenck (2005), p. 11.
16. As Goodenough (1986), p. 53, notes, monotheism was also threatening to Roman leaders because syncretism—fusing or otherwise reconciling elements of the diverse religious traditions represented within Rome's borders—was part of the strategy for imperial cohesion.
17. Goodenough (1986), p. 3.
18. Philo (1929), vol. 10, p. 181. Philo reports that some bystanders laughed at this remark, and some have interpreted it as jocular, a slyly ironic comment on the hypocrisy of intolerance. This may be giving Caligula too much credit.
19. Philo (1929), vol. 10, p. 183. See Goodenough (1938), p. 1.
20. Philo (1929), supp. II, p. 40. See Goldenberg (1998), p. 68.
21. Philo (1929), supp. II, p. 41.
22. Presumably to preempt such contagion, the Romans later formalized a narrow basis for Jewish exemption from state religious rituals: the Jews had an ancient tradition of monotheism not shared by other groups.
23. Philo (1929), vol. 10, p. 85. The entire sentence's structure leaves open the technical possibility that he was just referring to anti-Semitic Egyptians, but the substance of the indictment—that these people had inherited characteristics of wildlife native to Egypt—suggests that the indictment would apply to all Egyptians.
24. Quoted in Goodenough (1986), pp. 56–7; Goodenough's plausible interpretation of this passage: "If Philo had been able to destroy the Roman power he would gladly have done so." For an analysis that finds Philo's attitude toward Rome less hateful than Goodenough's see Collins (2000), pp. 133–4.
25. See Singer (1981) for an account of humankind's moral progress that emphasizes the role of philosophical reflection.
26. Judges 11:24 (the NRSV reads "the LORD our God," but the original Hebrew would have been not "lord" but YHWH). This verse seems to have gotten muddied at some point in scriptural history; Chemosh is elsewhere in the Bible, and for that matter in other ancient sources, called the god of the Moabites, not the Ammonites. And since he seems to be the Moabites' national god, he is unlikely to double as the national god of another people. See footnote to the verse in Coogan, ed. (2001).

27. Deuteronomy 2:19. Notably, a damning detail about the Ammonites' lineage isn't mentioned in this verse: though they are descendants of Abraham's nephew Lot, they issued from an incestuous relationship between Lot and one of his daughters. The same is true of the Moabites, and in the case of both peoples this story of illicit lineage presumably arose as an explanation of their frequently contentious relationship with Israel—that is, as a manifestation of frequently zero-sum dynamics. But it wouldn't make sense for Yahweh to stress this product of zero-sum dynamics—the illegitimacy of Ammon's heritage—when the object of the game is to nudge Israelites toward the non-zero-sum behavior of peaceful coexistence.

28. Ezekiel 25:10. The meaning seems to be not that all Ammonites will be annihilated, but rather that Ammon will be conquered by another nation and never regain its national identity.

29. This assumes that at least one of the two references to Ammon I've cited were pre-exilic, which most scholars would judge to be the case.

30. Leviticus 19:34.

31. Philo (1929), vol. 8, pp. 225–6.

32. The book of Ruth appears among the early, "historical" books of the Christian Old Testament but appears near the end of the Hebrew Bible.

33. Ruth 2:12.

34. See Hubbard (1988), pp. 35–6. This view was once dominant but has lost ground over the years. See Nielsen (1997), pp. 28–9.

35. See Hubbard (1988), pp. 45–6.

36. Zephaniah 2:9; Ezekiel 25:9.

37. Jonah 3:8–9.

38. Jonah 4:2.

39. This antagonistic relationship with Israel would have been part of the context of the *historical* setting of the story, which refers to a prophet Jonah who according to 2 Kings lived in the mid-eighth century; see Bickerman (1967), p. 15. And it would have been part of the Israelites' historical memory whenever the book of Jonah was written.

40. Jonah 4:11. On the book of Jonah's illustration of the theme of God's universal compassion, see, e.g., Limburg (1993), pp. 34–5. On doubts about and/or qualifications of this traditional interpretation of Jonah, see Sasson (1990), pp. 24–6, 324–5; Bickerman (1967), pp. 25–8.

41. Ezekiel 31:11.

42. Genesis 19:30–38, traditionally attributed to the J source.

43. For an evenhanded summary of the evidence on the dating of P, see Collins (2004), pp. 173–8.

44. Genesis 12:2. God *does* promise in presumably pre-exilic texts that the other nations and peoples of the world will be blessed *through* Abraham, but he doesn't talk about Abraham *becoming* or *begetting* multiple nations except in the Priestly version of the covenant.

45. Genesis 17:4.

46. Genesis 27:29.

47. Genesis 28:3, Friedman (2003) translation. The NRSV has it as "a company of peoples," but the modern, corporate connotation of the word "company" seems inappropriate.

48. Genesis 35:11, Friedman (2003) translation. The NRSV has "company of nations." (God repeats the phrase in his guidance to Jacob in the Priestly verse Genesis 48:4.)

49. Genesis 17:1.

50. Genesis 35:11; 48:3.

51. Of the seven "El Shaddai" references in the Hebrew Bible (Genesis 17:1, 28:3, 35:11, 43:14, 48:3; Exodus 6:3; Ezekiel 10:5), only two are not identified in Friedman (2003) as Priestly. (In general, I use Friedman's scheme in this chapter in identifying verses as authored by P.) One is from Ezekiel, which is generally dated to sometime around the exile, and one is from the source identified as E, or "the Elohist," which was once confidently dated to well before the exile but whose very validity as a coherent source has come under some attack, along with J's. It should be said that all of Wellhausen's sources have fallen into some doubt lately. But P has on balance held up better than J and E as a distinctive and coherent voice. At the same time, there has also been a trend toward dating the sources later and later. So, even if P's authorial identity has grown somewhat fuzzier in recent decades, it's also the case that the minority of scholars who have held to a pre-exilic date for P have seen support for their view, if anything, fade. The first of those trends tends to hurt my analysis of P in this chapter and the second tends to help it.

52. Another possibility is that P is melding not two different contemporary names for God but rather two different historical memories: maybe a neighboring member of the Persian Empire (such as Edom) that also considered itself descended from Abraham had long believed that Abraham called his god El Shaddai—in which case P's equation of El Shaddai and Yahweh is designed to make it easier for Israel and a neighbor to see themselves as siblings.

53. This tension is not only a plausible explanation of the famously puzzling Exodus 6:3, but also may shed a kind of oblique light on that other passage we puzzled over in chapter 5: the undoctored version of the thirty-second chapter of Deuteronomy, which depicts Yahweh as a son of the god "Elyon" and says that Elyon's various sons were the gods of the world's various peoples.

  As we've seen, "Elyon"—"most high"—may refer to "El Elyon," and so refer to El himself, the god known to have once been head of a pantheon in the vicinity of Canaan. And it's possible that "El Shaddai" originally referred to that same god—that these were two different names for El, with "Elyon" and "Shaddai" being two adjectives (just as you might refer to God as both "Almighty God" and "Gracious God"). If so, then the pantheon being depicted in the undoctored version of Deuteronomy 32 is a kind of theological rendering of the patriarchal lineage asserted by P and other biblical authors. If Yahweh is the God of Jacob, and Jacob is a descendant of Abraham, then the picture painted in Deuteronomy 32 follows: Yahweh is a descendant of Abraham's god El, and so occupies a lower level of the pantheon than El.

  In this scenario, whoever doctored Deuteronomy 32 was just doing, at a much later date, what P had done in Exodus 6:3: ending the subordination of Israel's god to another god by asserting the equivalence of the two gods. The only difference is the method of operation. The doctorer of Deuteronomy was working centuries after P, by which time the equivalence of Yahweh and all the Els—Shaddai, Elyon, whatever—was taken for granted. So all that was necessary was to change the line that depicted Yahweh as a descendant of Elyon; with that change made, the equivalence of Elyon and Yahweh would be assumed.

54. Indeed, P further reinforces Israel's specialness by stressing that God's covenant with Abraham doesn't transfer to all of Abraham's offspring (which would include, e.g., Esau, patriarch of Edom), but rather is passed down only through the specific lineage that leads to Jacob. Genesis 17:21, which is generally attributed to P, establishes that the covenant passes from Abraham to Isaac, not Isaac's brother Ishmael. And Genesis 28:1–6, also attributed to P, emphasizes that God's blessing to Abraham passes from Isaac to Jacob, not to Isaac's son Esau.

55. Rose (1992), vol. 4, p. 1006.
56. Genesis 9:16; 1:26–8.
57. Schmid (2009).
58. Schmid credits this idea to Albert de Pury.
59. Isaiah 49:26.
60. Genesis 9:26. In Genesis 10:9, Cush, grandson of Noah, is identified with Yahweh, but nothing is said about Yahweh and Cush's brother Egypt.
61. See Genesis 9:20–6. In Ham's lineage you'll also find the reviled Canaanites whom Israel had purportedly conquered. Meanwhile, in Shem's lineage, alongside Israel, are lots of nations in the Persian Empire. And, specifically: if we accept Friedman's (2003) delineation of biblical sources in Genesis 10, P has surgically shoehorned the Assyrians ("Assur") and Arameans ("Aram") into Shem's lineage.
62. Exodus 1:13–14; 2:23; 7:5.
63. Exodus 7:19, 8:1–2; 8:16–17; 9:9; 12:12–20.
64. Exodus 12:12.
65. To say that a system has a purpose that originated at a "higher" level needn't imply the existence of a god or of immaterial forces. For example, some biologists and philosophers are comfortable saying that animals are purposive systems—after all, animals have such goals as eating and, ultimately, reproducing—and in this case what imparted the purpose is natural selection, a wholly material system. In general—in this book and elsewhere—when I've suggested that the unfolding of life on this planet, from primordial bacterium to World Wide Web, has the hallmarks of a larger or "higher" purpose, I'm remaining agnostic as to the source of the purpose. The source could be something godlike—a very intelligent being—but it could also be something quite different; for example, a very large-scale process of natural selection. (For all we know, universes evolve by a kind of cosmic natural selection; universes that spawn life that evolves toward a belief in moral truth and closer adherence to it do a better job of replicating themselves than universes that lack this sort of moral order and teleological drift.) For related scenarios, see Gardner (2003).

Chapter Nine   Logos: The Divine Algorithm

1. See Runia (1990), who begins an illuminating discussion of Philo's socioeconomic context by relating Philo's situation in Alexandria to Tertullian's famous question.
2. See Borgen (1992).
3. This theological mission also grew out of Philo's great moral mission—to convince the world that Yahweh was a god of tolerance and peace. Philo bought into the exilic idea that someday all nations would come to "know" Yahweh, and that Jews would crucially advance this enlightenment. But he didn't think, as some exilic prophets had suggested and as some Jews of his day hoped, that such enlightenment would be imposed militarily. (See Borgen [1992], p. 336.) Rather, Philo would pick up on the more upbeat prophetic imagery: work on making Israel a "light unto the nations"—help Jews lead pagans to the truth of Yahweh via example and reason, not force of arms. See Winston (1985), pp. 54–7, on Philo's attempt to "depoliticize" Jewish messianism and his corresponding de-emphasis of the Messiah's military might notwithstanding his "intensely nationalistic inclinations." Philo does at one point envision a messianic figure someday subduing "great and populous nations," but as Collins (2000) argues (pp. 134–6), the conquest envisioned here isn't of all Gentiles, and indeed the envisioned battle lines are not ultimately ethnic; "Philo is interested in the spiritual triumph of virtue rather than in the physical victory of a messianic king," Collins writes (p. 135), and it remains an open question whether he expects "a visible triumph of Judaism" (p. 136).

4. Goodenough (1986), p. 10.
5. Ibid., p. 41.
6. Kirk et al. (1983), p. 169.
7. See, e.g., Philo (1894), p. 61.
8. See Runia (1990), p. 11, and Tobin (1992), p. 351.
9. Philo (1929), vol. 5, p. 331.
10. Goodenough (1986), p. 101. For a dissent from the common view that Philo's Logos doctrine served primarily to bridge the chasm between a transcendent, unknowable god and the material world, see Winston (1985), p. 49, though his dissent is nuanced, more a qualification than a wholesale rejection.
11. See Runia (1999), Tobin (1992), Goodenough (1986).
12. Goodenough (1986), p. 108.
13. Philo (1929), vol. 3, p. 217, and see Winston (1985), p. 17.
14. Philo (1929), vol. 3, p. 97.
15. See Runia (1999) and Goodenough (1986), p. 36.
16. Strictly speaking, according to Winston (1985), p. 24, Philo thought the construction of the entire Logos had taken place on day one.
17. Runia (1990), p. 9.
18. See Goodenough (1986), p. 100.
19. See Winston (1985), p. 17, and Goodenough (1986), p. 103.
20. Goodenough (1986), pp. 37, 100; Winston (1985), p. 50.
21. See, e.g., Philo [1929], vol. 2, p. 427.
22. Goodenough (1986), p. 37.
23. See, e.g., Winston (1985) and Runia (1990), p. 11.
24. See Tobin (1992), p. 351, and Runia (1990), p. 11.
25. Goodenough (1986), pp. 25–6.
26. Philo (1929), vol. 8, p. 235.
27. Ibid., p. 65.
28. Before Philo's time there was a Jewish tradition of associating God's logos with wisdom. See Runia (1999). Both the Wisdom of Solomon (also known as the Book of Wisdom) and the Wisdom of Ben Sira (also known as Sirach) make this equation. The former was almost certainly written before Philo's career, though only shortly before it, by an Alexandrian Jew, and the latter was probably written in Jerusalem more than a century before Philo. On Philo's interchangeable use of wisdom and the Logos, see Winston (1985), p. 20.
29. Philo (1929), vol. 3, p. 91.
30. Proverbs 3:13–18.
31. See Lang (1999).
32. Proverbs 8:22; 8:27–31.
33. Proverbs 1:3 as translated in von Rad (1972), p. 13; Proverbs 1:4.
34. Proverbs 8:12, as translated in von Rad (1972), p. 12.
35. Proverbs 16:18.
36. See von Rad (1972), pp. 125–7.
37. Proverbs 1:18–19; 6:34.
38. Proverbs 25:23.
39. von Rad (1972), p. 124. And see Murphy (1992), pp. 922–3.
40. Proverbs 26:27. See Koch (1955), p. 64. Koch was among the first to note the mechanical nature of the reward-punishment system outlined in Proverbs; he argues that even when Yahweh is depicted as involved in punishment, he is in most cases merely overseeing the workings of the mechanical system.
41. von Rad (1972), pp. 62–3.

42. Proverbs 1:7.
43. Philo (1929), vol. 3, pp. 82–3.
44. Philo (1929), vol. 5, p. 343.
45. Proverbs 4:6.
46. Winston (1985), p. 16.
47. See Tobin (1992); Runia (1990), pp. 65–7.
48. See Winston (1985), p. 29.
49. Philo (1929), vol. 3, pp. 82–3; vol 5, p. 343. And see Philo (1929), vol. 8, p. 417: "His own Word [Logos], from whom as its archetype the human mind was created."
50. Burtt, ed. (1982), p. 37.
51. Philo (1929), vol. 4, pp. 317–9.
52. Ibid.
53. Ibid.
54. Philo (1929), vol. 5, pp. 59–60.
55. See Runia (1988), p. 57. Runia argues that the final "him" refers to Moses, but the consensus view has been that it refers to God. F. H. Colson, in Philo (1929), vol. 5, p. 157, translates "mind" as "heart."
56. Philo (1929), vol. 1, p. 57. And see Winston (1985).
57. See Goodenough (1986), p. 5.
58. Philo (1929), vol. 7, p. 477.
59. See Goodenough (1986), p. 6.
60. Sandmel (1979), p. 97.
61. Philo (1929), vol. 3, p. 217.
62. Philo (1929), vol. 2, pp. 73–5.
63. Orlinsky (1974), p. 83.
64. Ibid.
65. Elvin (1986), p. 333. And see D. C. Lau's introduction to Confucius (1979), pp. 14–16. Note that ren and jen are different renderings of the same word.
66. Analects XII:22 — Confucius (1979), p. 116.
67. Elvin (1986), pp. 334–5.
68. Ibid., p. 334.
69. Ibid., p. 335.
70. Burtt, ed. (1982), p. 47 (from the Sutta-Nipata).
71. This pragmatism extends to the social level, as virtue's contribution to that time-honored religious goal, social order, is made explicit. Among the problems with hate, as noted in the Buddhist passage above, is its "rousing [of] enmity," a destabilizing effect spelled out in another passage attributed to the Buddha: "If I should deprive you of your life, then your partisans would deprive me of my life; my partisans again would deprive those of life. Thus by hatred, hatred would not be appeased" [Burtt, ed. (1982), p. 42 (from the Maha-Vagga)]. Mo Ti, defending the imperative of universal love, implicitly noted the non-zero-sum benefits of peace when he asserted that no war had demonstrably benefited humankind [Elvin (1986), pp. 334–5]. See Armstrong (2006), pp. 270–2, for elaboration on the pragmatic nature of Mo's moral system. And Confucius's entire values system, including his emphasis on benevolence, is based squarely on the imperative of maintaining social order.
72. Burtt, ed. (1982), pp. 53–4 (from the Dhammapada, chapter 1).
73. Analects, IV:2, IV:5 — Confucius (1979), p. 72. But Confucius seems disdainful (see XII:20) of putting up a façade of benevolence merely for the sake of reputational effects.
74. Armstrong (2006) notes the role of social change, including urbanization, in the development of morally progressive thought during this period. See also Eisenstadt, ed. (1986).

75. See Hodgson (1977), vol. 1, p. 111.
76. McNeill (1990), p. 13, and see McNeill (1980), p. 34.
77. Instruction of Amenemope: see http://pages.stern.nyu.edu/~wstarbuc/distrust.html.
78. Proverbs 1:20–1; 8: 2, 5, 8.
79. John 1:1; 1:14.
80. "son of God": See, e.g., Goodenough (1986), p. 102; Tobin (1992), pp. 350–1. On Philo's various names for the Logos (from "shadow of god" to "chief of angels") see Winston (1985), p. 16.
81. For an extended comparison of John and the Jewish wisdom literature, see Tobin (1992).
82. John 1:9; 1:4–5.

Part III

Epigraph: "Set Israel free" is the alternative translation provided by the NRSV for "redeem Israel."

Chapter Ten What Did Jesus Do?

1. E.g., Galatians 3:1 mentions the Crucifixion and is typically dated to the early sixth decade CE.
2. By many accounts, sacrifice to God was waning in Judaism more broadly around the time opposition to sacrifice was solidifying within the Jesus movement. Some trace the trend to the destruction of the second temple by the Romans in the early eighth decade CE.
3. Galatians 3:28.
4. There is disagreement over whether the "historical Jesus" considered himself the Messiah and whether his disciples did. (In the earliest gospel, Peter opines that Jesus is the Messiah [Mark 8:29], and Jesus, though noncommittal at that point, says shortly before his death that he is the Messiah [Mark 14:62].) My guess is that both he and some of his followers at least actively entertained the possibility that he was the Messiah in some sense of the word. On the related question of whether he considered himself the "Son of Man," see chapter 13.
5. E.g., 1 Samuel 12:3, 5. The NRSV has "anointed [one]" in this and comparable passages, but the underlying Hebrew word would have sounded roughly like "messiah." See de Jonge (1992), p. 779.
6. For an excellent synthesis of recent literature on the meaning of "messiah" in and before Jesus's era, see Dunn (2003), chapter 15, esp. pp. 617–22, 660–4. See also de Jonge (1992).
7. This is the expectation in, e.g., the Psalms of Solomon (esp. Psalm 18), composed some decades before Jesus's birth. See de Jonge (1992), p. 783.
8. Mark 15:32.
9. See de Jonge (1992), pp. 778–9.
10. See de Jonge (1992), pp. 782–3.
11. Dunn (2003), p. 619, and see Horsley (1993), pp. 22–3.
12. One exception to this view is found in the work of Israel Knohl, who contends that the Hebrew inscription on a tablet from the late first century BCE speaks of a messiahlike figure who is instructed by the Angel Gabriel to return to life in three days. His reconstructed line reads, "By three days, live, I Gabriel command you, prince of princes, the dung of the rocky crevices" (see Knohl [2008], appendix). But other scholars consider some of these words—notably the one he reads as "live"—to be illegible, and Knohl concedes that his intepretation, which would support his earlier contentions about anticipations of a suffering messiah before Jesus's time, is in some places conjectural.
13. Halpern and Vanderhooft (1991), p. 66, hint at this comparison.

14. On the basic relationship among the four gospels, I adopt the view of most, though not all, scholars: Mark was written first, based on oral and/or written sources, probably shortly after 70 CE, though possibly as early as the mid-60s—that is, around four decades after Jesus's death. Luke and Matthew were written around 80 or 90 CE by authors who had access either to the text of Mark or to a body of information closely corresponding to it. John was written last—but before 100 CE—by an author who may well not have had access to the earlier gospels, but rather may have been dependent on oral and other written sources. For discussions see Meier (1991), pp. 43–5; Sanders (1995), pp. 58–63; Ehrman (2004), p. 49.

15. See John 7:42, Micah 5:2–5.

16. Matthew 2:23. John (1:46–9) solves the Nazareth problem in yet another way.

17. Mark 15:34; Luke 23:46; John 19:30. Matthew (27:46) features Mark's version: Why have you forsaken me? (This is consistent with the belief by many scholars that Matthew was written before Luke, hence closer to the time of Mark.)

18. Luke 23:34. See footnote in NRSV.

19. See Smith (1978), pp. 141–2.

20. Mark 8:12; Matthew 16:3, 12:40; Luke 11:16–41.

21. Mark 6:4–5; Matthew 13:58 (and see Smith [1978], pp. 140–1); Luke 4:23–4. And see footnote to Luke 4:28 in Coogan, ed. (2001).

22. Mark 4:10–12. This refers to the sixth chapter of Isaiah, where God instructs Isaiah to prophesy to deaf ears. Schweitzer (2001), pp. 322–3, explains Jesus's calculated obscurity in terms of a doctrine of predestination.

23. John 3:2, 9:16, 11:47.

24. Mark 5:37 (= Luke 8:51); John 11:4; 9:5. And see Ehrman (2004), pp. 160–1.

25. John 10:30.

26. See Ehrman (1999), p. 199.

27. See Smith (1978), e.g., p. 143.

28. Mark 1:15.

29. Luke 17:20–1 (an alternative translation of "among" is "within"); Mark 9:1 (the NRSV says "with power," but its editors offer the alternative translation "in power"); Mark 13:24–5.

30. Mark 9:47–8.

31. Mark 12:30–3. The word "loved" appears in Mark 10:21: "Jesus, looking at him, loved him and said..."

32. Mark 12:29–31.

33. Matthew 15:27.

34. Matthew 15:28; Mark 7:29.

35. See Achtemeier (1992), vol. 4, p. 546, footnotes for Mark 16:15–16 in NRSV, Meeks, ed. (1993), and Coogan, ed. (2001). These verses are missing from the earliest manuscripts of Mark. A common speculation is that they were added in the early second century.

36. Isaiah 56:6; Jesus (in Mark 11:17) is quoting Isaiah 56:7. The other Markian reference to preaching to the nations—Mark 13:10—might be interpreted in similar light and, anyway, sounds suspiciously like a post-Jesus creation designed to explain why the kingdom of God is taking so long to show up ("And the good news must first be proclaimed to all nations"). Meeks, ed. (1993), p. 1944, notes that Mark 13:10 echoes Isaiah 49:6 and 52:10.

37. Common rendering of John 8:7.

38. Matthew 5:43–5.

39. Matthew 5:47. Luke's parallel verse says "sinners" instead of "Gentiles," but Tuckett (1992) notes that this is generally considered an amendment of the original.
40. Tuckett (1992), p. 570.
41. Luke 10:25–37. Luke 4:24–7 also carries a message of interethnic compassion.
42. Matthew 10:5.
43. Matthew 19:28; Luke 22:30. See discussion in chapter 13 of the meaning of "Son of Man." This is the term used in Matthew 19:28 to describe the ruler of the coming kingdom, though in Luke 22:30 Jesus explicitly refers to "my kingdom."
44. Acts 1:6.
45. Acts 1:7.
46. Schweitzer's basic view is cogently corroborated by Bart Ehrman (See, e.g., Ehrman [1999] and Ehrman [2004]), whose interpretation guided my own.
47. Sanders (1995), p. 193.
48. Mark 10:31; Mark 10:15 (and see Luke 18:25 and Matthew 19:24). There are apocalyptic themes in First Isaiah—see especially chapters 2, 4—but they aren't nearly as vivid as in Second Isaiah, nor do they so prominently feature the motif of a reversal of fortunes. Also, First Isaiah does make a kind of connection between progressive politics and apocalyptic thinking, but it's different from the kind of connection I'm here attributing to Jesus. Isaiah says—see chapter 2—that Israel will have to correct its domestic injustice before it can be granted salvation and exalted among the nations.
49. Matthew 5:3.

Chapter Eleven   The Apostle of Love

1. 1 Corinthians 13:4.
2. This is the emphasis in Romans 12:9, 12:10, 13:8, 13:9, 13:10. The phrase "brotherly love" is in 12:10 of the King James Version. (The NRSV has neutralized the gender.) As for Paul's letters in general: even if we confine ourselves to the seven Pauline letters that most scholars consider authentic, sixty verses contain the word "love" or some variation on it, according to an electronic search I conducted. The number for the four gospels is sixty-five, but most of those verses are not sayings attributed to Jesus.
3. Galatians 3:28.
4. See Bornkamm (1971), pp. 74–5.
5. Acts 8:3.
6. Galatians 1:8–9.
7. Gager (2000), p. 4.
8. Dodds (1990), p. 137.
9. Hellerman (2001), p. 4.
10. Kloppenborg and Wilson, eds. (1996), p. 13.
11. Dodds (1990), p. 137.
12. Malherbe (1983), p. 88.
13. Hellerman (2001), p. 22. And see Meeks (2003), p. 86.
14. 1 Corinthians 1:12. (This actually *wasn't* his first letter to the congregation he had founded in Corinth, but it's the first one that is preserved. See Bornkamm (1971), p. 70, and 1 Corinthians 5:9.)
15. Bornkamm (1971), p. 73. See also pp. 71–2 and Fee (1987), p. 573.
16. 1 Corinthians 14:3 (and see Fee [1987], pp. 569–74, especially p. 573); 14:27, 37–8.
17. 1 Corinthians 4:14–16.
18. 1 Corinthians 12:27.

19. Pagels (2003), p. 6.
20. 1 Corinthians 14:23.
21. Isaiah 45:14, 22–3, 25.
22. Isaiah 49:6.
23. Romans 14:10; 15:18 (and see Sanders [1991], pp. 2–4); 15:12.
24. Romans 11:28. Paul's ideas about the relationship between Jews and Gentiles are complex and sometimes contradictory. This vision of Gentile submission to Israel's messiah is not his only utterance on the subject, and scholars argue about what exactly his views were—if, indeed, he had coherent and stable views. See Gager (2000).
25. Galatians 5:6, 12.
26. Sanders (1991), p. 62.
27. Pagels (2003), p. 6, contrasts early Christianity with the cult of Asclepius, god of healing, whose priests charged for consultation.
28. Gager (2000) makes this point. The view of Paul as fundamentally Jewish has gained scholarly adherents as a result of the pioneering work of Gager and, earlier, Krister Stendahl.
29. Meeks (2003), p. 28. And see Mahlerbe (1983), pp. 97–8.
30. Acts 16:14.
31. See MacMullen (1984), p. 106, and Meeks (2003), p. 30.
32. Freedman, ed. (1992), vol. 4, pp. 422–3. And see Acts 16:40.
33. See Malherbe (1983), p. 95, esp. footnote 9.
34. Meeks (2003), p. 17.
35. See Gager (2000), p. 78.
36. Acts 18:2–3. And see Freedman, ed. (1992), vol. 5, pp. 467–8.
37. See Sanders (1991), p. 13, and Malherbe (1983), p. 95.
38. See Meeks (2003), p. 109, and Malherbe (1983), p. 97.
39. E. A. Judge, quoted in Meeks (2003), p. 109. And see Meeks (2003), p. 17.
40. Romans 16:1–2.
41. McCready (1996), p. 63.
42. See Stark (1997).
43. Kloppenborg and Wilson, eds. (1996), p. 7.
44. Ibid., p. 3.
45. Romans 1:7–11.
46. Romans 12:10; Galatians 5:13; 1 Thessalonians 4:9–10.
47. 1 Thessalonians 3:12; Galatians 6:10.
48. See Stark (1997), pp. 87, 10.
49. Matthew 25:35–6, 39–40.
50. Corinthians 5:11–13.
51. Hellerman (2001). I've changed "gratuitously," an ambiguous element in the translation, to "for free."
52. Romans 12:5.
53. Brown (1993), p. 77.
54. Luke 6:27, Matthew 5:37.
55. Matthew 5:44; Romans 12:14–20; Matthew 5:39.
56. Galatians 1:18–19.
57. John 13:34. Here love is confined to fellow believers; see Freedman, ed. (1992), vol. 4, p. 390.
58. Galatians 5:14–5. And see Ehrman (1999), p. 79. Paul says the whole Jewish Law is summed up in this imperative of neighborly love, whereas Jesus says it ranks as one of

the two most important imperatives in the Jewish Law, along with loving God. See Mark 12:28–34, Luke 10:25–8, Matthew 22:39–40.
59. See Corinthians 4:12 for a reference by Paul to his own experience of persecution.
60. Romans 12:20.
61. Proverbs 25:21.

Chapter Twelve   Survival of the Fittest Christianity

1. Latourette (1975), p. 85; Ehrman (1999), p. 58.
2. See Sanders (1991), p. 21.
3. Latourette (1975), pp. 91–2.
4. McLean (1996), p. 191.
5. Ibid., p. 196.
6. See Ehrman (2003a), p. 100.
7. Matthew 1:23. The NRSV, unlike the King James Version, renders Isaiah 7:14 as "young woman."
8. See Ehrman (2003a), p. 110.
9. Latourette (1975), p. 127. Freedman, ed. (1992), vol. 1, pp. 855–6, notes that only in the fourth century are there clear attempts to make lists of authoritative Christian texts; not until the end of that century, in the 390s, do we find church councils endorsing a list of the twenty-seven books now in the New Testament.
10. Clabeaux (1992), in Freedman, ed. (1992), vol. 4, p. 517.
11. See Ehrman (2003a), pp. 108–9.
12. Dialogue of Justin with Trypho, Chapter XVI.
13. See Pagels (2003), p. 13.
14. Ferguson (2003), pp. 384–6; Burkett (2002), pp. 86, 543; Ehrman (2004), pp. 19–21.
15. See Ehrman (2004), pp. 20–1; Burkett (2002), p. 529.
16. Certainly Constantine later showed that he saw the virtue of keeping the Christian church unified. See Burkett (2002), pp. 407–8.
17. Nikam and McKeon, eds. (1959), p. 52.
18. See Pagels (1989).
19. "While his [God's] wisdom meditates on the Logos, and since his teaching expresses it, his knowledge has been revealed." Robert M. Grant translation of the Gospel of Truth: http://www.gnosis.org/naghamm/got.html.
20. See Ehrman (2003b), p. 47.
21. John 1:1, 1:14.
22. John 13:34.
23. John 13:35.

Chapter Thirteen   How Jesus Became Savior

1. Luke 3:6.
2. Psalms 106:21; 2 Kings 13:5; Jeremiah 14:8.
3. Turcan (1996), pp. 99–103.
4. Matthew 13:40–3.
5. 1 Thessalonians 4:13. Re: age of 1 Thessalonians: see Freedman, ed. (1992), vol. 6, p. 516.
6. See Daniel 12:2–3; Isaiah 26:19; Mark 12:18–27; Matthew 22:23–33; Luke 20:27–40. And see Brandon (1967), p. 100.
7. On some issues there seems to have been a split between Paul and some Jesus followers

in Jerusalem, and the latter may have hewed more closely to Jesus's own views, but (see, e.g., Brandon [1967], p. 99) in general the Jerusalem contingent's tendency would have been to emphasize traditional Jewish apocalypticism more heavily than Paul, and in this case the belief Paul implicitly ascribes to Jesus is wholly consistent with that tradition.

8. 1 Thessalonians 4:16.

9. Sanders (1991), p. 37, is among the scholars who entertain a back-to-earth scenario.

10. 1 Corinthians 15:22–5.

11. 1 Corinthians 15:55.

12. Daniel 7:13 envisions "one like a son of man" descending from heaven. Sometimes, as in the NRSV, "son of man" is translated as "human being." The Aramaic term for "son of man" was used to refer to "a man"—and, sometimes, a man who was taken to represent humankind. See Dunn (2003), p. 726.

13. Mark 8:31, 38.

14. My argument about the "Son of Man" is made at greater length at www.evolutionofgod .net/sonofman.

15. Luke 24:6–9.

16. Acts 7:55–6. Stephen goes on to say, right before dying, "Lord Jesus, receive my spirit."

17. Certainly this is, overwhelmingly, the most common view in the Hebrew Bible. Whether there are any clear exceptions to it is controversial: e.g., Psalm 49:15, "But God will ransom my soul from the power of Sheol, for he will receive me." If the "ransom" is taken to occur shortly after death, and God's "receiving" the soul is taken to mean its ascent to heaven, then this would be an exception. (There are undoubtedly affirmations of eventual *resurrection* in the Hebrew Bible, but they tend to be associated, as they seem to have been in Jesus's mind, with apocalyptic expectations: e.g., Isaiah 26:19, Daniel 12:2–3.) And see McDannell and Lang (2001), p. 14.

As for Paul's view on the afterlife: See McDannell and Lang (2001), p. 33. Two verses in Paul's letters—Philippians 1:23 and 2 Corinthians 5:8—do state or at least suggest that after death a person is "with Christ" or "at home with the Lord." But the more explicit of these, in Philippians, refers only to Paul, and could reflect the belief that he, as the great apostle, would get special dispensation. Moreover, both verses were written later than the passage in First Thessalonians cited above, which clearly states Paul's expectation that union with Christ doesn't come until after the return of Christ from heaven. And there are other Pauline verses, e.g., Romans 2:14–16, with which they also seem incompatible. They could represent an evolution in his views, owing either to his continued contact with the Gentile "market" for religious beliefs or to a growing sense that he himself would die before the coming of Christ.

18. Luke 23:43. (Paradise needn't refer to heaven, and of course this particular human being may here be singled out for special treatment, rather than representing saved human beings writ large.)

19. Luke 16:24–5. For the view that he is in heaven, see McDannell and Lang (2001), pp. 26–9.

20. See McDannell and Lang (2001), chapter 1.

21. Brandon (1967), p. 109.

22. Luke 17:20–1. (An alternative translation of "within you" is "among you.")

23. Even aside from the role of Osiris on Judgment Day, his life story bore a certain resemblance to Jesus's story. As described by Plutarch in the decades after Jesus's death, Osiris had appeared on earth in human form, was brutally killed and then resurrected. This isn't to say, as some have argued, that the whole story of Jesus—Crucifixion and all—is modeled on Osiris. Indeed, if you examine Plutarch's account of Osiris in fuller form,

without boiling it down to Christian parallels, there are elements emphatically not reminiscent of the life of Jesus. For example: when Osiris died, his corpse was cut up and buried piecemeal all over Egypt; he regained life only after his body parts were retrieved and reassembled by his sister/wife Isis—who, incidentally, never succeeded in locating his penis and so fitted him with a prosthetic device that worked well enough for her to conceive a child by him. See Gabriel (2002) and Brandon (1970).

24. Ogilvie (1969), p. 2.

25. See Ferguson (2003), pp. 249, 295. Plutarch, who lived in Luke's time, observed that many people "think that some sort of initiations and purifications will help: once purified, they believe, they will go on playing and dancing in Hades in places full of brightness, pure air and light." See Hellerman (2001), p. 3.

26. See Brandon (1967), p. 44, and Scott-Moncrieff (1913), p. 48.

27. Bell (1953), pp. 13–14.

28. Brandon (1967), p. 111.

29. The story of the martyrdom of the seven sons in Second Maccabees, a Jewish text written about a century before the birth of Christ, does suggest that the mother anticipates that her sons, upon death, will join Abraham in the afterlife as a result of their righteous self-sacrifice. But the way Paul wrestles with the question of the recently deceased in his epistles suggests that, during the early years of the Jesus movement, immediate reward in the afterlife wasn't the standard expectation.

30. Hegedus (1998), pp. 163, 167. And see Stark (1997), p. 199. Comparing cities to which the Isis cult and Christianity are known to have spread, Stark finds a .67 correlation.

31. Hegedus (1998), p. 163, footnote 8.

32. Apuleius, *The Golden Ass,* chapter 48 (William Adlington translation).

33. Romans 3:9–10.

34. Romans 7:14–9.

35. Galatians 5:19–21.

36. Osirian salvation didn't necessarily require the deceased to be telling the whole truth and nothing but the truth. By some readings, Chapter 125 is a bit of a sales pitch—a claim of purity by people less than pure, and perhaps, as well, a ritual of forgiveness, rather like confession for a Catholic, except without the confessing; or maybe more like baptism, which, especially in the early years of Christianity, was considered not just symbolic, but a genuine cleansing, the removal of past sin from the body. (The title of Chapter 125 is: "So that he may be separated from every sin which he hath done" [Morenz (1973), p. 132.) Brandon (1970) compares baptism's role in Christian salvation with the role of Osirian ritual in Egyptian salvation, though he emphasizes the earlier Osirian rituals of the pyramid texts, rituals that were more "magical" than moral. In any event, Chapter 125 reflects a religion that has made moral behavior, not just animal sacrifices and other rituals, central to the quest for eternal life.

37. Morenz (1973), p. 132, and see p. 122.

38. There is, of course, concern with *ritual* purity in hunter-gatherer societies, as with the story of the Eskimo sea goddess in chapter 1.

39. Rig-Veda 7.86. The words "sin" and "crime" don't necessarily denote moral, as opposed to ritual, transgressions. But Varuna did punish moral transgressions. See O'Flaherty (1981), p. 213; Smart (1969), p. 64; and Flood (1996), p. 47.

40. Bottero (2001), p. 189.

41. Romans 7:7.

42. Bellah (1969), p. 68.

43. Jacobsen (1976), p. 153.

44. Bottero (2001), p. 32. The second-millennium dating is tentative, but there are more confidently dated second-millennium references to Mesopotamian gods as "father" or "mother."
45. Jacobsen (1976), p. 226. Re: parental god names in Mesopotamia, see Jacobsen (1976), pp. 158–9, 225–6, 236–7.
46. Griffiths (1980), p. 216.
47. Assmann (2001), p. 223.
48. Exodus 20:20.
49. Some have blamed the empire's collapse on Christianity, but in any event the social system Christian doctrine was devoted to—the international Christian church—stayed intact.

Chapter Fourteen   The Koran

1. Smith (1991), p. 233.
2. More precisely: twenty-three years, according to early Islamic sources and current mainstream reckoning.
3. Koran 109:6 (Arberry); 47:4.
4. On the merits of different ordering schemes, see Robinson (2003), pp. 76–97.
5. Koran 96:1. A minority of translators, e.g., Pickthall, render this "Read."
6. Koran 53:9–11 (Pickthall). See Watt (1964), p. 15.
7. Welch (2003).
8. See Cook (1983), p. 67. For a recent survey of debates surrounding the Koran's historical origin, see Donner (2008).
9. Peters (1991), pp. 288–9, makes a related point: that the Koran seems not to have been redacted in the "afterglow" of military triumphs after Muhammad's death.
10. See Donner (2008), Watt (1964), p. 17, Cook (1983), p. 74.
11. *Merriam-Webster's Collegiate Dictionary*, 10th edition.
12. Some scholars now think traditional accounts overstate Mecca's significance as a trade center—both the magnitude of trade and the extent to which the trade featured exotic items, like spices, as opposed to mundane items, such as leather goods. The seminal work (and in some ways a particularly extreme view) is Patricia Crone (1987), *Meccan Trade and the Rise of Islam,* Princeton University Press.
13. The exact reason for the emphasis on sons is not entirely clear. One possibility would apply only to relatively affluent Arabs, which Muhammad would presumably have been after his marriage: in a polygamous society, sons born to the upper classes can attract multiple wives, and so produce more grandchildren than daughters. Another possibility is speculatively suggested by Watt (1964), pp. 152–3: sons would inherit the administration of property from their mother's brothers and so would bring wealth and prestige into the immediate family.
14. Koran 81:8–9 (Sale).
15. Koran 93:6–11 (Arberry); 90:16; 90:13–6 (Arberry); 89:18–21 (Arberry).
16. Koran 42:20.
17. Koran 21:25.
18. Lings (1983), pp. 16, 29, 44.
19. Ibid., pp. 16, 44; Watt (1964), p. 22.
20. Indeed some Arab tribes in modern Syria, Iraq, and Jordan had converted to Christianity. See Hoyland (2001), pp. 146–50.
21. Lings (1983), p. 17.
22. Koran 46:12 (Yusuf Ali). See also Koran 26:192–8.

23. Koran 43:2–4. "The archetypal Book" is literally "Mother of the Book," as in the Yusuf Ali translation.
24. Koran 77:6; 16:105.
25. Armstrong (2002), p. 3.
26. According to MacDonald (2003), some Arab philologists have argued that Allah is a loan word from Syriac, as I argue here.
27. Among the Koranic verses that state or imply that Arabs consider Allah the creator god: 29:61, 31:25, 39:38, 43:9. That the Koran never complains about a failure to believe in Allah, but rather about "those who join gods with God," was pointed out to me by Michael Cook.
28. Hodgson (1977), vol. 1, pp. 155–6. Armstrong (2002), p. 11, is struck in the same way by the same point.
29. The word is sometimes rendered *alaha*.
30. MacDonald (2003).
31. This scenario, in which the Arabic god Allah is from the beginning the Judeo-Christian god, is necessarily conjectural (as is the more conventional scenario of Allah's independent origins). The most salient evidence against it is a quirk of usage involving "Allah." Namely, when the word *Allah* is preceded in certain contexts by words ending in vowels, the initial *A* is dropped. (Thus, when *Allah* is preceded by the Arabic word for "he"—*huwa*—in the sentence "He is God," the result is spoken as "huwallahu," not "huwa allahu.") This sort of elision is unusual in an Arabic noun, yet it is standard practice to in comparable circumstances drop an article *preceding* an Arabic noun. So this quirky convention is consistent with the theory that the "Al" in Allah initially *was* an article, as in the scenario I'm arguing against—the scenario in which *Allah* began as *al-ilah,* or "the god." Of course, it's possible this unusual property was somehow acquired by the noun *Allah* in reflection of the unique status of God's name in Arabic culture. Still, it tends to work against the theory I'm advancing.
32. None of this is meant to imply that Syriac is a direct descendant of the Aramaic of Jesus's day. But the two languages do share a common origin in the Aramaic spoken in the early part of the first millennium BCE. The relationship of the Aramaic of Jesus's day to the Syriac of Muhammad's day might be compared to that between an uncle and a nephew.
33. Koran 81:14.
34. "Ka'ba" in Bearman, et al., eds. (2003).
35. Lapidus (2002), p. 14; "Hadjdj" in Bearman, et al., eds. (2003).

Chapter Fifteen Mecca

1. Koran 79:26.
2. Koran 19:30.
3. Koran 82:1–9. Muhammad's sense of the *nearness* of the apocalypse seems to have been most intense in passages generally dated to the middle Meccan period, e.g., 21:1, 53:57, 54:1.
4. Koran 15:6, 34:8; 37:36–7, 21:5; 83:29–31; 74:21–3.
5. Koran 41:26.
6. Lings (1983), pp. 88–92; some, e.g., Watt (1964), p. 77, doubt the severity of the boycott.
7. McDannell and Lang (2001), p. 52.
8. Irenaeus, *Against Heresies*, 5:33.
9. Koran 56:29–31; 55:54; 55:56; 56:36–7.
10. Koran 76:4; 18:29.
11. Koran 74:26; 41:28.

12. Koran 104:4; 15:3.
13. Koran 83:34–5.
14. Koran 77:24; 32:20; 37:21.
15. Koran 96:19.
16. Koran 43:89; 109:4–6.
17. Koran 50:45; 88:21–2.
18. Koran 73:10. Rodwell places this third. Blachere, another authority, places it thirty-fourth, which would make it about one-third of the way, chronologically, through the Meccan era.
19. Koran 13:40; 25:63.
20. Koran 41:34.
21. Judges 11:24; Deuteronomy 20:16–18.
22. Watt (1964), pp. 58, 61.
23. Koran 53:23.
24. Watt (1964), p. 61.
25. Koran 44:32.
26. Koran 26:46. Translation by Mairaj Syed (personal communication).
27. Koran 26:46 (Sale). Rodwell believes this refers to Jews only, not Christians and Jews. And (see Rodwell translation, footnote 12) Theodor Noldeke dates the verse to Medina and offers a translation that makes the verse less diplomatic. But the verse is more commonly dated to Mecca, and the translation I've provided reflects the common interpretation.
28. At least, it never appears in Meccan suras so long as you consider Sura 64, Mutual Deceit, Medinan, as Rodwell does but some scholars don't. See Rodwell's footnote 1 to that sura.
29. See such suras as The Poets, Ornaments of Gold, Family of Imran.

Chapter Sixteen Medina

1. Lings (1983), p. 123.
2. This simple version of the story is conveyed by, e.g., Armstrong (2002), pp. 13–14. Specialists in Islam—e.g., Watt (1964), pp. 95–6—have long recognized in the Koran signs that in the early parts of the Medinan period, Muhammad fell far short of complete authority. However, Watt speculatively accepts the idea that Muhammad was from the beginning recognized by other clans as a valid arbitrator.
3. Ibid. Some scholars consider this sura late Meccan.
4. Koran 3:31–32.
5. Watt (1964), pp. 95–6, compares Muhammad to a clan leader. Buhl (2003) compares Muhammad to a tribal leader.
6. Koran 64:14.
7. Matthew 10:35–8.
8. Syria, Egypt, Palestine: These terms carry their modern geographic meanings; in Muhammad's time, Syria would have encompassed much or all of Palestine.
9. Lapidus (2002), pp. 32–3; Kennedy (1986), pp. 59–72.
10. This surmise isn't corroborated by the Islamic oral tradition. But it's hard to come up with an alternative explanation of the number of Medinan verses in the Koran that address Christian issues and, in particular, either seem concerned with finding common ground with Christians or imply a failure to have done so.
11. Koran 9:30, Yusuf Ali translation. Muhammad is here referring to the Christian belief that Jesus was the son of God and a Jewish belief that Ezra was the son of God. It's unclear where Muhammad got the idea that Jews consider Ezra a son of God. See Rodwell and Sale footnotes to this verse.

12. Compared to other religions, Islam wasn't necessarily stringent in terms of ritual. Muhammad made a point of having more relaxed dietary rules than, e.g., Judaism. But Islam's sanctions against socially disruptive vices—e.g., drinking, gambling, adultery—were severe.

13. Schacht (1982), p. 9. The Arabic word for robbery seems to have been imported from another language. But it's possible that this importation predated Muhammad's era, in which case robbery may well have been a crime before the coming of Islam.

14. Koran 22:39–40 (Arberry). See also Koran 2:217.

15. Koran 22:40 (Asad). Some, e.g., Arberry and Rodwell, use "oratories" where Asad uses "synagogues." Among other translators who use "synagogues" are Yusuf Ali and Sale. Asad—see his footnote to this verse—argues that here, in what may be Islam's earliest version of a just-war doctrine, religious freedom is given lofty status.

16. Koran 3:3 (Arberry); 3:64 (Asad).

17. See Buhl (2003) and Watt (1964), p. 114.

18. Koran 2:173 (Yusuf Ali). Of the two other suras prohibiting pork consumption, one (Sura 5) is routinely considered Medinan, and the other (Sura 6) is often classified as Meccan, but as very late Meccan—frequently listed, indeed, as the very last Meccan sura. It seems likely that this part of the sura, at least, was actually an early Medinan utterance.

19. Berkey (2003), pp. 74–5. Praying toward Jerusalem would have pleased not just Jews, but some Arabian Christians who were already in that habit. See Buhl (2003).

20. Koran 19:35.

21. Koran 43:57–8. My interpretation is guided by footnote 15 in Rodwell's translation. Most translators don't agree with Rodwell that the Koran has Muhammad offering Jesus as "an instance of divine power"—just that he was holding Jesus up as an example of some sort. But some subsequent parts of the sura, including those quoted above, seem best explained by Rodwell's interpretation. Sale, e.g., offers a different interpretation.

22. Preface to Rodwell's translation of the Koran. (Koran 5:14 alludes to infighting among Christians over doctrinal issues.)

23. It may be relevant that the word for "Christians" in the Koran is a word that actually means "Nazarenes," a term that had sometimes been applied to such "Jewish Christians" as the Ebionites. But there is also reason to believe that the word—which even today is the word used by Arab Muslims to refer to Christians—had a similarly broad reference to Christians in general in Muhammad's day. See Fiey (2003) on this and diversity of Christian belief in general.

24. One Koranic verse—4:157—seems to subscribe to the docetic "heresy" that the Crucifixion of Jesus was an illusion.

25. See Crone and Cook (1977). The book's provocative thesis, that Muhammad's initial followers included apocalyptic Jews, seems to be no longer advanced by the book's authors, but the fact that it can't be definitively dismissed is a reminder of how little we know for sure about the array of religious belief Muhammad faced.

26. Koran 4:171 (Arberry).

27. Koran 4:171 (Arberry); 57:27.

28. Genesis 16:12.

29. Genesis 16:2–3, 15–16, and see Knauf (1992).

30. Genesis 17:20.

31. Genesis 17:21, 25–6.

32. Koran 2:125 (Arberry).

33. Koran 2:135 (Arberry).

34. Koran 2:132 (Arberry); 3:67 (Pickthall); 3:67 (Shakir).

35. Koran 5:51. At other times Muhammad seems to have sensed a difference in the

receptivity of Christians and Jews (5:82): "Thou wilt surely find that, of all people, the most hostile to those who believe [in this divine writ] are the Jews as well as those who are bent on ascribing divinity to aught beside God; and thou wilt surely find that, of all people, they who say, 'Behold, we are Christians' come closest to feeling affection for those who believe [in this divine writ]." In a sura usually dated to the late Meccan period, Muhammad had seen no grounds for enmity toward either Christians or Jews (29:46): "And do not argue with the followers of earlier revelation otherwise than in a most kindly manner—unless it be such of them as are bent on evildoing and say: 'We believe in that which has been bestowed from on high upon us, as well as that which has been bestowed upon you: or our God and your God is one and the same, and it is unto Him that We [all] surrender ourselves.'"

36. See Donner (1979), p. 232. Moreover, because of their central role in Medinan commerce (see Kennedy [1986], p. 36)—they lived astride the town's marketplace and made their living there—the Kaynuka would have been tempting targets for Muhammad; if you are trying to start a theocratic state, you would like its commercial base to be in the hands of believers, not because of the content of their beliefs per se, but because those beliefs signified allegiance to your political leadership.

37. See Stillman (1979), pp. 13–14.

38. Koran 22:67. See also 5:48–9, considered by many the final Medinan sura.

39. Koran 33:26–7 (Arberry). Another verse (59:2) refers to "unbelievers among the people of the Book" being exiled but makes no reference to killing.

40. See, e.g., Peters (1994), p. 156.

41. Crone and Cook (1977), pp. 6–7.

42. Thomson (1999), p. 102. (The wording is unclear, but Sebeos seems to say that what is now known as the al-Aksa Mosque was actually built by the Jews.) And see Crone and Cook (1977), p. 10.

43. Cook (1983), p. 74. As Cook notes, the differences are trivial. Still, they suggest some degree of ongoing fluidity.

44. An example of Koranic verses that seem to reflect a "break with the Jews," and show signs of not being pristine, is the account of the "changing of the kiblah"—the decision to quit praying toward Jerusalem and start praying toward Mecca. The verses don't mention Mecca or Jerusalem, but they do refer to a change in the direction of prayer and note that the direction now diverges from the preferred Christian and Jewish direction of prayer—which would seem to indeed indicate a turning away from Jerusalem (2:142–50). Yet half a century ago, the esteemed scholar of Islam Montgomery Watt noted that these verses, though arrayed consecutively, as if uttered by Muhammad all at once, "give the impression of having been revealed at different times" (Watt [1964], p. 113). Also, Crone and Cook (1977) point to evidence, both architectural and literary, suggesting that decades after Muhammad's death Muslims were facing somewhere well to the north of Mecca when they prayed. But Cook (personal communication) is now inclined to suspect that this evidence is essentially "noise."

Chapter Seventeen Jihad

1. *Milestones,* chapter 4.

2. Watt (1974).

3. The four passages are 9:24, 22:78, 25:52, and 60:1. In no case is the jihad reference by itself explicitly military (See Bonner [2006], p. 22), but in 9:24 the context seems military. In 25:52 the injunction is to strive, or struggle, against "those who deny the truth," but the context makes a military interpretation unlikely. In 60:1 friendship with unbelievers is dis-

couraged but there is no allusion to violence. In 22:78, the emphasis is on serving as a "witness" to God's truth; Muslims are urged to "strive hard in God's cause with all the striving [jihad] that is due to Him," then reminded that they are "those who have surrendered themselves to God"; the passage culminates with the injunction to "be constant in prayer, and render the purifying dues, and hold fast unto God." That the doctrine of military jihad can't be coherently grounded in the Koran is made by Bonner (2006); see, e.g., p. 20.

4. Bonner (2006), p. 22, says that of forty-one Koranic uses of words deriving from the root *jhd,* only ten refer "clearly and unambiguously to the conduct of war." Peters (1987), p. 89, may be including less explicit references to war when he says that "about two thirds" of the uses "denote warfare."

5. Other, and less ambiguous, verbs are *qaatala,* which means fighting, and *qatala,* which means killing. The ambiguity of *jahada* can be seen by comparing these four translations of 66:9. Yusuf Ali: "O Prophet! Strive hard against the Unbelievers and the Hypocrites, and be firm against them." Pickthall: "O Prophet! Strive against the disbelievers and the hypocrites, and be stern with them." Shakir: "O Prophet! strive hard against the unbelievers and the hypocrites, and be hard against them." Rodwell: "O Prophet! make war on the infidels and hypocrites, and deal rigorously with them."

6. http://www.freerepublic.com/focus/f-news/1128382/posts.

7. http://www.pbs.org/newshour/terrorism/international/fatwa_1996.html.

8. Though Muhammad sometimes accused Christians, and occasionally Jews, of having polytheistic tendencies, this term is used by the Koran to refer to non-Abrahamics.

9. Koran 9:6. The most common interpretation of this verse is, as Sale put it in a footnote to his translation of the Koran, "That is, you shall give him a safe-conduct, that he may return home again securely, in case he shall not think fit to embrace Mohammedism."

10. Koran 9:7, 4. Strictly speaking, 9:4 is exempting these polytheists from the permission God grants in 9:3 to dissolve treaties with polytheists. But keeping the treaties of these exempted polytheists from dissolution would clearly exclude them from the group of polytheists who are to be killed.

11. And, for that matter, the verb translated as "kill" could be translated as "fight" or "combat," though there's no doubt that Muhammad went into combat willing to kill. A similar example is 4:89–90. Here infidels who leave their people to convert but then turn back are to be slain "wherever ye find them" — with the exception of "those who shall seek an asylum among your allies, and those who come over to you — their hearts forbidding them to make war on you... if they depart from you, and make not war against you and offer you peace, then God alloweth you no occasion against them."

12. Koran 47:4.

13. Koran 8:59–61.

14. Koran 60:8–9. Another Koranic verse, 2:190, is often cited as an outright ban on warring with infidels who haven't attacked first. And that's certainly what it says as commonly translated — e.g., "And fight for the cause of God against those who fight against you: but commit not the injustice of attacking them first: God loveth not such injustice." But some scholars argue that the part that's translated "attacking them first" should be translated as "transgressing," and could just mean, for example, that women and children are not to be killed in the course of the war (Michael Cook, personal communication).

15. Koran 60:7.

16. See, e.g., Watt (1956), pp. 362–5.

17. Watt (1974), p. 152; Goldziher (1981), p. 102. See Bonner (2006), p. 92, footnote 11, re: the dating of this doctrine.

18. Mairaj Syed, personal communication.

19. Even leaving aside the fact that the Koran never makes war against infidels an explicitly universal principle, there is the fact that the verses most commonly characterized as jihadist, when read in context, tend to provide reasons to suspect that the intended meaning isn't universal. Sometimes there is explicit circumscription in time or place. For example, 9:123, often cited as a jihadist verse, says to "fight the unbelievers *who are near to you*" (Arberry, emphasis added). Sometimes there are hints that the recommended fighting may be in response to specific provocation. Thus, 9:29— "Fight those who believe not in God and the Last Day"—follows a verse suggesting that maybe this fighting is to be directed toward infidels who have the nerve to approach the Holy Mosque. Some verses said to be jihadist in spirit are just too vague to warrant clear categorization. The oft-cited 8:39 says to fight unbelievers until "there is no persecution and the religion is God's entirely"(Arberry). The previous verse says unbelievers should be forgiven if they "desist" but not if they "persist" (Yusuf Ali). Some translators (e.g., Yusuf Ali) think this means that to be forgiven they must desist from unbelief, and other translators (e.g., Pickthall) think it means they must desist from persecuting Muslims. The first interpretation renders the verse much more jihadist in spirit than the second interpretation. Other times the problem isn't vagueness but ambiguity. Thus, 48:16 envisions a day when Muslims will "be called against a folk of mighty prowess, to fight them until they surrender" (Pickthall); and the occasional translator (e.g., Rodwell), playing on the fact that "Islam" means "surrender," translates this as until they "profess Islam." But that's a minority translation, and in any event this refers to a specific, if unspecified, battle, not to a crusade that should encompass the world. (This passage was interpreted by Muhammad's successors as specifically envisioning conquest of the Byzantine and Persian worlds. See Goldziher [1981], p. 28.) Finally, there is the interpretive problem posed by the fact that in the days of theocracy, to fight against the state was to in some sense fight against the God. Thus, the oft-cited 8:12–13 recommends this treatment for infidels: "Strike off their heads then, and strike off from them every finger-tip." Then the Koran adds: "This, because they have opposed God and his apostle" (Rodwell). Does that mean they've opposed God by not believing in him—which is also, by definition, to oppose his prophet? Or does it just mean they've opposed Muhammad on the battlefield—which would have been equated with opposing Muhammad's God? These passages (9:29, 8:39, 48:16, 8:12–13), along with passages I've addressed in the text, are the passages that, so far as I can tell, are those most commonly cited by critics of Islam who want to argue that the doctrine of jihad can be found in the Koran. And note that, even if each of these verses, read in context, didn't provide specific reason to doubt that the exhortation to violence against unbelievers was meant universally, there would be no reason to assume that the verse *was* meant universally, rather than as a specific exhortation made at a particular time with reference to a particular enemy.

20. Koran 109:4–6; 2:25.

21. Bonner (2006), p. 26.

22. *Sahih Bukhari*, vol. 1, book 2, no. 25–7, http://www.usc.edu/schools/college/crcc/engagement/resources/texts/muslim/hadith/bukhari/002.sbt.html.

23. This is the dominant view among scholars. There have been alternative views—such as John Wansbrough's contention that the hadith took shape before the Koran—but they haven't won wide acceptance.

24. Karsh (2006), p. 4. Attributed to Muhammad ibn Umar al-Waqidi, who died in the early ninth century.

25. Bonner (2006), p. 92.

26. Watt (1974).

27. Berkey (2003), p. 200.
28. Ibid.
29. Koran 9:29.
30. Watt (1974).
31. Goldziher (1981), p. 33; Karabell (2007), p. 31.
32. Goldziher (1981), p. 33, footnote 4.
33. Cahen (2003).
34. Watt (1974).
35. Cahen (2003).
36. See Peters (1987), pp. 90–1. E.g., in the Middle East around the turn of the twentieth century, Muhammad Abduh and Muhammad Rashid Rida influentially promulgated doctrines of defensive jihad (though these interpretations left room for fighting colonial rulers for liberation). And, in India, Sayyid Ahmad Khan promulgated an even more limited doctrine of jihad, one that didn't warrant rebellion against British colonial rule since Britain was allowing the practice of Islam in India.
37. Bin Laden did cite the presence of infidel armies (i.e., American troops) in Saudi Arabia as a grievance, but here the alleged transgression is being in Saudi Arabia, not just being infidels.

Chapter Eighteen   Muhammad

1. Koran 3:134; 8:73.
2. Koran 48:29.
3. Koran 41:34; 25:63.
4. Koran 16:84.
5. Revelation 19:15.
6. E.g., Koran 2:62: "Verily, they who believe (Muslims), and they who follow the Jewish religion, and the Christians, and the Sabeites — whoever of these believeth in God and the last day, and doeth that which is right, shall have their reward with their Lord: fear shall not come upon them, neither shall they be grieved." And 5:69: "Verily, they who believe, and the Jews, and the Sabeites, and the Christians — whoever of them believeth in God and in the last day, and doth what is right, on them shall come no fear, neither shall they be put to grief." The verse most commonly cited by theologically conservative Muslims to prove that only Muslims are eligible for salvation is 3:85: "Whoso desireth any other religion than Islam, that religion shall never be accepted from him, and in the next world he shall be among the lost." Reconciliation of these seemingly contradictory verses may lie in the fact that the word translated as "Islam" meant, literally, "submission" (to God), and in some Koranic passages may be meant as a generic noun, encompassing all who submit to the one true god — though, to be sure, the word "religion" in this passage seems to reduce the plausibility of that interpretation in this case. Of course, it's also possible that trying to reconcile these verses is just a mistake; they were uttered at different times, under different circumstances. See also 2:112: "Whosoever submits his will to God, being a good-doer, his wage is with his Lord, and no fear shall be on them, neither shall they sorrow."
7. Koran 2:113 (Asad); 5:18.
8. Koran 22:16–17.
9. The Muslim tradition does include an anecdote that explains why Muhammad might opine on the salvific status of Zoroastrians, involving a query he receives from a governor whose area of governance includes Zoroastrians. On the other hand, if the Koranic

verse in question was inserted after Muhammad's death out of political convenience, inserting the supporting anecdote into the tradition would be a natural accompaniment.

10. The Sabeans are offered salvation two other times, both times clustered with Jews, Christians, and Muslims: 2:62 and 5:69. One possibility is that these verses arose after conquest of Iraq, and Zoroastrians were added to the list after conquest of Iran.

11. Koran 22:16–17. Here is the passage (Rodwell), with "Sabeans" substituted for Rodwell's "Sabeites": "Thus send we down the Koran with its clear signs (verses): and because God guideth whom He pleaseth. As to those who believe, and the Jews, and the Sabeans and the Christians, and the Magians, and those who join other gods with God, of a truth, God shall decide between them on the day of resurrection: for God is witness of all things." In theory, this formulation, with God deciding "between" these groups, leaves room for God to exclude whole groups, letting Muslims alone make the cut. But that interpretation seems strained, because in at least two other verses — 2:62 and 5:69 — Jews, Christians, and Sabeans are explicitly deemed eligible for salvation (and Sabeans aren't mentioned in any other context anywhere in the Koran). And in another verse (2:112) the formulation of God deciding "between" groups is applied to Christians and Jews in a context that also clearly leaves open the prospect of salvation for them. So all signs point to this verse including Zoroastrians ("Magians") in the salvific fold — or, at least, including them in the population *eligible* for salvation, with salvation itself depending on the beliefs and behavior of the individual Zoroastrian. In this light it would seem that polytheists — "those who join other gods with God" — are also included in the eligible pool. And some — e.g., Yusuf Ali, footnote 2788, p. 854 — have argued as much. Others — see, e.g., the Asad translation — say God will distinguish between the polytheists, on the one hand, and all the other (more or less) monotheistic peoples mentioned, on the other.

12. Some early Christian thinkers did believe salvation extended beyond Christians. In the third century CE, Origen of Alexandria embraced the doctrine of universal salvation. And at one point (Romans 26:28) Paul writes as if Jews will be saved regardless of their views on Jesus, owing to their venerable ancestry. Still, as a rule early Christians thought of the circle of salvation as excluding Jews, to say nothing of other non-Christians.

13. Koran 49:13 (Asad).

14. To be sure, later Islamic tradition attributed miracles to Muhammad, and sometimes this attribution was grounded interpretively in the Koran. Thus the tradition that Muhammad split the moon was linked to this verse: "The hour hath approached and the MOON hath been cleft: But whenever they see a miracle they turn aside and say, This is well-devised magic" (54:1). But the Koran never unambiguously attributes miracles to Muhammad, as the gospels do to Jesus.

15. Mark 8:12.

16. See Phipps (1996), p. 40, and Smith (1991), p. 227, though neither explicitly notes the contrast with Jesus.

17. Koran 20:53–4; 16:67; 30:21, 22.

18. Koran 6:96–7.

19. Mairaj Syed, personal communication.

20. Koran 13:12–13.

21. Koran 13:2; 7:54; 41:37.

22. Darwinian philosopher and atheist Daniel Dennett has agreed that this sort of directionality is indeed among the evidence of design in the case of organisms. See www.meaningoflife.tv/video.php?topic=direvol&speaker=dennett and www.nonzero.org/dennexcerpt.htm.

Chapter Nineteen   The Moral Imagination

1. See www.evolutionofgod.net/blame.
2. Proverbs 25:21–2.

Chapter Twenty   Well, Aren't We Special?

1. Weinberg (1979); videotaped exchange between Weinberg and John Polkinghorne on counterbalance.org.
2. Silverman (1991), pp. 48–9; Hornung (1999), p. 102.
3. See Hornung (1996), pp. 213–15; Teter (2002), p. 189; Silverman (1991), pp. 34, 48; Pinch (2002), pp. 159–60.
4. Griffiths (1980), p. 177.
5. Nikam and McKeon, eds. (1959), pp. 29, 31.
6. Ibid., p. 52.
7. Rig-Veda I, 169; see Smart (1969), p. 67.
8. Exodus 12:12.
9. The exact historical relationship among the words *elohim, elaha,* and *allah* is unclear, and I don't mean to suggest that there's a tidy lineage—that, for example, the Aramaic *elaha* and the Arabic *allah* both descended from the Hebrew *elohim.* Indeed, as noted in chapter 8, it's more likely that the word *elohim* entered Hebrew via Aramaic, albeit an earlier version of Aramaic than Jesus would have spoken. (See Rose [1992].) My point is just that, even if the kinship among these words is oblique and/or collateral—maybe more like a relationship between cousins than between parent and offspring—there is some kinship; the phonetic similarities among the three words are almost certainly not a coincidence. See chapter 14 for my argument that *allah* derives from the Christian world for god in Syriac, a close relative of Aramaic. As noted in that chapter, my argument is unorthodox; more commonly it's asserted that *allah* derives from the Arabic generic noun for god, *ilah.* But even if this latter account is correct, there is still a likely kinship between *allah* and *elohim,* for *ilah* is itself thought to be related to *elohim.* In general, when languages are as closely related as Hebrew, Arabic, and Aramaic—all of which are Semitic—phonetic resemblances often turn out to be a reflection of common descent.

Afterword   By the Way, What Is God?

1. Some scientists and philosophers argue that we can strip quantum mechanics of its seeming contradictions, but their attempts to do so often entail scenarios even weirder than the contradictions. For example: it isn't that a particle exists in more than one place, but rather that it exists nowhere at all—nowhere in particular, you might say—until it is measured or observed. Huh? And then there's the famous "many worlds" interpretation, under which there's a version of you reading this book right now and lots of versions of you not reading it. And so on: every attempt to escape from the inconceivable aspects of quantum physics produces either inconceivable conjectures or scarcely credible conjectures. For a classic popular introduction to quantum paradoxes, see Heinz Pagels's 1982 book *The Cosmic Code.* Though I'm not sure whether he coined the term "quantum weirdness," he seems to have been the first to expound on it at length under that label.
2. The comparison between belief in God and belief in electrons is drawn, and put to

somewhat different use, in J. J. C. Smart's essay "The Existence of God." See Timothy A. Robinson, ed. (2003), *God*, Hackett Publishing.

3. This "pragmatic" argument for the legitimacy of the concept of God is much in the spirit of arguments made by William James, notably in his essay "The Will to Believe."

4. For related scenarios, see Gardner (2003), and citations therein of Lee Smolin's work.

Appendix How Human Nature Gave Birth to Religion

1. *National Post,* April 14, 2003.

2. Most evolutionary psychologists who consider religion a direct product of natural selection (an "adaptation," in the terminology developed later in this appendix, as opposed to a "spandrel") subscribe to a "group-selectionist" explanation. Group-selectionist logic is illustrated by a scientist quoted in the aforementioned Canadian newspaper article: "Survival of our species has demanded a capacity to work together, to form societies. A willingness to live, and if necessary die, for a belief is a powerful selective advantage. I think there is a genetic propensity for us to believe." As this quote suggests, in group-selection scenarios, "god genes" needn't earn their keep by directly helping the particular individual possessing them. Indeed, in this case the possessor would "if necessary die" out of religious belief; but such sacrifices would help the larger group, and so genes in this group would on balance do better than genes in alternative groups lacking religion.

The plausibility of "group-selectionist" explanations is controversial. Pretty much all Darwinians agree that group selection is possible under some circumstances. But many evolutionary psychologists ("individual selectionists") believe that, in human evolution, these circumstances rarely applied; so natural selection rarely favored traits that cause individuals to make big sacrifices for the "good of the group" in the sense of the larger society, beyond the family. (These individual selectionists generally refer to a genetic predisposition to sacrifice for family members as resulting from "kin selection," and distinguish kin selection from group selection, whereas group selection advocates often label this same dynamic a form of group selection. Terminological squabbles aside, no evolutionary psychologists dispute that sacrifices for kin have been favored by natural selection.) The scientist quoted in the Canadian newspaper article is an atypical group selectionist, because most group selectionists don't believe natural selection often works for the "survival of the species."

Perhaps the best-known account of religion by a group selectionist is David Sloan Wilson's book *Darwin's Cathedral.* The book doesn't lay out a rigorous or detailed account of how religious impulses would evolve by group selection, but Wilson is certainly a group selectionist, and the aspects of religion he emphasizes are the aspects group selectionists tend to emphasize — aspects that facilitate the efficient functioning of large social groups. What Wilson doesn't make clear is why those group-level adaptations couldn't be explained via cultural evolution (and in some cases, no doubt, he would acknowledge that cultural evolution played a role).

3. See, e.g., Barrett (2000), p. 29.

4. James (1982), p. 27.

5. Radcliffe-Brown (1922), p. 139.

6. See Boyer (2001), chapter 2, for a more precise rendering of the *kind* of strangeness that, according to his data, makes a religious concept attractive to the human mind.

7. Murdock (1934), p. 256.

8. de Waal (1982), p. 98.

9. Quoted in Swanson (1964), p. 13.

10. Robert Carneiro (personal communication).

11. Creel (1970), pp. 496, 501–3.
12. See Guthrie (1993), chapter 7.
13. Boyer (2001), p. 144.
14. Ibid., p. 80.
15. Barrett and Keil (1996).
16. Genesis 1:27, RSV.
17. See Evans-Pritchard (1965), p. 49.
18. On the naturalness of religious sacrifice, see Boyer (2001), pp. 241–2.
19. Murdock (1934), p. 184.
20. Boyer (2001), p. 200.
21. If my emphasis on reciprocal altruism and social exchange sounds like the result of evolutionary psychologists imposing their Darwinian angle on the study of religion, it's worth noting that they aren't the only ones who see the centrality of social exchange to religious thought. See Stark and Finke (2000). These authors have spent decades studying religion in many guises. And, though they evince no awareness of the theory of reciprocal altruism, they see exchange as being the basic fulcrum of interaction between people and gods. See, e.g., p. 91. For an extended defense of the idea that gods are fundamentally anthropomorphic, see Guthrie (1980) and Guthrie (1993)—though Guthrie's argument, like that of Stark and Finke, is not informed by evolutionary psychology.
22. Chapter 17.
23. See Boyer (2001), pp. 145, 195, 301, and Barrett (2000), p. 31.
24. See Roediger (1996), p. 86.
25. "On the Record with Greta Van Susteren," Fox News Channel, June 17, 2004.
26. See Boyer (2001), p. 301.
27. Ibid., p. 300.
28. Tylor (1871), pp. 385–6.
29. See Boyer (2001), pp. 119–20.
30. Ibid.
31. See Guthrie (1980).

Bibliography

Achtemeier, Paul J. 1992. "Mark, Gospel of." In Freedman, ed. (1992).

Ackerman, Susan. 1992. *Under Every Green Tree: Popular Religion in Sixth-Century Judah.* Scholars Press.

———. 2003. "At Home with the Goddess." In Dever and Gitin, eds. (2003).

Ackroyd, Peter R. 1968. *Exile and Restoration.* SCM Press.

Albertz, Rainer. 1994. *A History of Israelite Religion in the Old Testament Period,* trans. John Bowden. 2 vols. Westminster/John Knox Press.

———. 2003. *Israel in Exile,* trans. David Green. Society of Biblical Literature. Brill Academic Publishers.

Albright, William Foxwell. 1957. *From the Stone Age to Christianity.* Doubleday Anchor.

Armstrong, Karen. 1994. *A History of God.* Ballantine Books.

———. 2002. *Islam.* Modern Library.

Aslan, Reza. 2005. *No God but God.* Random House.

Assmann, Jan. 2001. *The Search for God in Ancient Egypt,* trans. David Lorton. Cornell University Press.

Atran, Scott. 2002. *In Gods We Trust.* Oxford University Press.

Baines, John. 1987. "Practical Religion and Piety." *Journal of Egyptian Archaeology* 73:79–98.

———. 1991. "Society, Morality, and Religious Practice." In Shafer, ed. (1991).

Barnes, Michael Horace. 2000. *Stages of Thought: The Co-evolution of Religious Thought and Science.* Oxford University Press.

Barrett, J., and F. Keil. 1996. "Conceptualizing a Non-natural Entity: Anthropomorphism in God Concepts." *Cognitive Psychology* 31:219–47.

Barrett, Justin L. 2000. "Exploring the Natural Foundations of Religion." *Trends in Cognitive Science* 4 (1)29–34.

Basham, A. L. 1989. *The Origins and Development of Classical Hinduism.* Beacon Press.

Bearman, P. J. et al., eds. 2003. *The Encyclopedia of Islam.* New edition, 12 vol.; WebCD edition. Brill Academic Publishers.

Bell, H. Idris. 1953. *Cults and Creeds in Graeco-Roman Egypt.* Liverpool University Press.

Bellah, Robert. 1969. "Religious Evolution." In Norman Birnbaum and Gertrud Lenzer, eds. (1969), *Sociology and Religion.* Prentice-Hall.

———, ed. 1973. *Emile Durkheim on Morality and Society: Selected Writings.* University of Chicago Press.

Benedict, Ruth. 1959. *Patterns of Culture.* Houghton Mifflin/Sentry.

Berkey, Jonathan P. 2003. *The Formation of Islam.* Cambridge University Press.

Bickerman, Elias. 1967. *Four Strange Books of the Bible.* Schocken.

Blenkinsopp, Joseph. 1996. *A History of Prophecy in Israel.* Westminster/John Knox Press.

Bogoraz-Tan, Vladimir Germanovich. 1904–09. *The Chukchee*. 3 vol. E. J. Brill, Ltd.; G. E. Stechert and Co.

Bonner, Michael. 2006. *Jihad in Islamic History*. Princeton University Press.

Boone, Elizabeth. 1994. *The Aztec World*. Smithsonian Books.

Borgen, Peder. 1992. "Philo of Alexandria," in Freedman, ed. (1992).

Bornkamm, Gunther. 1971. *Paul*. Harper and Row.

Bottero, Jean. 2000. "Religion and Reasoning in Mesopotamia." In Jean Bottero, Clarisse Herrenschmidt, and Jean-Pierre Vernant, *Ancestor of the West*. University of Chicago Press.

———. 2001. *Religion in Ancient Mesopotamia*, trans. Teres Lavender. University of Chicago Press.

Botterweck, G. Johannes, and Helmer Ringgren, eds. 1974. *Theological Dictionary of the Old Testament*, trans. John T. Willis. Eerdmans.

Bourke, John Gregory. 1892. *The Medicine-men of the Apache*. Bureau of American Ethnology.

Boyer, Pascal. 2001. *Religion Explained*. Basic Books.

Brandon, S. G. F. 1967. *The Judgment of the Dead*. Scribner's.

———. 1970. "Redemption in Ancient Egypt and Early Christianity." In R. J. Zwi Weblowsky and C. Jouco Bleeker, eds., *Types of Redemption* (1970). E. J. Brill.

Bray, Warwick. 1991. *Everyday Life of the Aztecs*. Peter Bedrick Books.

Brown, Peter. 1993. *The Making of Late Antiquity*. Harvard University Press.

Buhl, F. 2003. "Muhammad" [revised by A. T. Welch]. In Bearman et al., eds. (2003).

Burke, Trevor J. 2003. "Paul's Role as 'Father' to His Corinthian 'Children' in Socio-Historical Context." In Trevor J. Burke and J. Keith Elliott, eds. (2003), *Paul and the Corinthians*. E. J. Brill.

Burkett, Delbert. 2002. *An Introduction to the New Testament and the Origins of Christianity*. Cambridge University Press.

Burtt, E. A., ed. 1982. *The Teachings of the Compassionate Buddha*. Mentor Books.

Byrne, Peter. 1989. *Natural Religion and the Nature of Religion*. Routledge.

Cahen, Claude. 2003. "Dhimma." In Bearman et al., eds. (2003).

Callaway, Joseph A. 1999. "The Settlement of Canaan." In Shanks, ed. (1999).

Campbell, Antony F., and Mark A. O'Brien. 2000. *Unfolding the Deuteronomistic History*. Fortress Press.

Clabeaux, John J. 1992. "Marcion." In Freedman, ed. (1992).

Claessen, Henri J.M. 1991. "State and Economy in Polynesia." In Henri J.M. Claessen and Pieter van de Velde, eds., *Early State Economics*. Transaction Publishers.

Cogan, Morton. 1974. *Imperialism and Religion: Assyria, Judah and Israel in the Eighth and Seventh Centuries, B.C.E.* Scholars Press.

Collins, John J. 2000. *Between Athens and Jerusalem*. 2d ed. Eerdmans.

———. (2004). *Introduction to the Hebrew Bible*. Fortress Press.

Collins, Raymond F. 1992. "Ten Commandments." In Freedman, ed. (1992).

Confucius. 1979. *The Analects,* trans. D. C. Lau. Penguin Books.

Coogan, Michael D. 1987. "Canaanite Origins and Lineage: Reflections on the Religion of Ancient Israel." In Miller, Jr. et al., eds. (1987).

———, ed. 2001. *The New Oxford Annotated Bible*. 3d ed. Oxford University Press.

Cook, James. 1852. *The Voyages of Captain James Cook Round the World*. Vol. 2. John Tallis and Co.

Cook, Michael. 1983. *Muhammad*. Oxford University Press.

———. 2000. *The Koran: A Very Short Introduction*. Oxford University Press.

Cooper, John M. 1917. *Analytical and Critical Bibliography of the Tribes of Tierra del Fuego and Adjacent Territory*. U.S. Government Printing Office.

———. 1946. *The Yahgan*. U.S. Government Printing Office.

Creel, Herrlee G. 1970. *The Origins of Statecraft in China*. Vol. 1. University of Chicago Press.

Crone, Patricia, and Michael Cook. 1977. *Hagarism*. Cambridge University Press.

Cross, Frank Moore. 1973. *Canaanite Myth and Hebrew Epic*. Harvard University Press.

Dale, Paul W. 1996. *The Tonga Book*. Minerva Press.

David, Rosalie. 2002. *Religion and Magic in Ancient Egypt*. Penguin.

Davidson, Robert F. 1947. *Rudolf Otto's Interpretation of Religion*. Princeton University Press.

Day, John. 1992. "Baal." In Freedman, ed. (1992).

———. 2000. *Yahweh and the Gods and Goddesses of Canaan*. Sheffield Academic Press.

de Jonge, Marinus. 1992. "Messiah." In Freedman, ed. (1992).

del Olmo Lete, G. 1999. "Deber." In van der Toorn et al., eds. (1999).

de Moor, Johannes C. 1990. *The Rise of Yahwism*. Leuven University Press.

Dever, William G. 2003. *Who Were the Early Israelites and Where Did They Come From?* William B. Eerdmans.

Dever, William G., and Seymour Gitin, eds. 2003. *Symbiosis, Symbolism, and the Power of the Past*. Eisenbrauns.

de Waal, Frans. 1982. *Chimpanzee Politics*. Johns Hopkins University Press.

de Waal Malefijt, Annemarie. 1968. *Religion and Culture: An Introduction to Anthropology of Religion*. Macmillan.

Dietrich, B. C. 1974. *The Origins of Greek Religion*. Walter de Gruyter.

Dodds, E. R. 1990. *Pagan and Christian in an Age of Anxiety*. Cambridge University Press.

Donner, Fred M. 1979. "Muhammad's Consolidation in Arabia up to the Conquest of Mecca." *Muslim World* 69:229–47.

———. 1986. "The Formation of the Islamic State." *Journal of the American Oriental Society* 106(2):283–96.

———. 2001. "Review of G. R. Hawting's *The Idea of Idolatry and the Emergence of Islam*." *Journal of the American Oriental Society* 121(2):336–8.

———. 2008. "The Qur'ān in Recent Scholarship: Challenges and Desiderata." In Reynolds, ed. (2008).

Dozeman, Tom, and Konrad Schmid, eds. 2006. *A Farewell to the Yahwist?* Society of Biblical Literature.

Duling, Dennis C. 1992. "Kingdom of God, Kingdom of Heaven." In Freedman, ed. (1992).

Dunn, James D. G. 2003. *Jesus Remembered: Christianity in the Making*. Vol. 1. William B. Eerdmans.

Durkheim, Emile. 1965. *The Elementary Forms of the Religious Life*, trans. Joseph Ward Swain. Free Press.

Dutcher-Walls, Patricia. 1991. "The Social Location of the Deuteronomists: A Sociological Study of Factional Politics in Late Pre-Exhilic Judah." *Journal for the Study of the Old Testament* 52:77–94.

Edelman, Diana Vikander, ed. 1996. *The Triumph of Elohim: From Yahwisms to Judaisms*. William B. Eerdmans.

Ehrman, Bart D. 1999. *Jesus*. Oxford University Press.

———. 2003a. *Lost Christianities*. Oxford University Press.

———. 2004. *The New Testament*. 3rd ed. Oxford University Press.

———, ed. 2003b. *Lost Scriptures*. Oxford University Press.

Eisenstadt, S. N., ed. 1986. *The Origins and Diversity of Axial Age Civilizations*. State University of New York Press.

Eliade, Mircea. 1964. *Shamanism*, trans. Willard R. Trask. Princeton University Press.

Elvin, Mark. 1986. "Was There a Transcendental Breakthrough in China?" In Eisenstadt, ed. (1986).

Emmons, George Thornton. 1991. *The Tlingit Indians*. University of Washington Press; American Museum of Natural History.

Evans-Pritchard, E. E. 1965. *Theories of Primitive Religion*. Clarendon Press.

Faulkner, R. O. 1969. *The Ancient Egyptian Pyramid Texts*. Oxford University Press.

Fee, Gordon D. 1987. *The First Epistle to the Corinthians*. William B. Eerdmans.

Feiler, Bruce. 2002. *Abraham*. Morrow.

———. 2005. *Where God Was Born*. HarperCollins.

Ferguson, Everett. 2003. *Backgrounds of Early Christianity*. William B. Eerdmans.

Fiensy, David A. 2002. "What Would You Do for a Living?" In Anthony J. Blasi et al., eds. (2002), *Handbook of Early Christianity*. Altamira Press.

Fiey, J. M. 2003. "Nasara." In Bearman et al., eds. (2003).

Finkelstein, Israel. 1999. "State Formation in Israel and Judah." *Near Eastern Archaeology* 62:1.

Finkelstein, Israel, and Neil Asher Silberman. 2002. *The Bible Unearthed*. Simon and Schuster/Touchstone.

Firth, Raymond. 1940. "The Analysis of *Mana*: An Empirical Approach." *Journal of the Polynesian Society* 49:483–510.

Fitzgerald, Aloysius. 1974. "A Note on Psalm 29." *Bulletin of the American Schools of Oriental Research* 215.

Flood, Gavin. 1996. *An Introduction to Hinduism*. Cambridge University Press.

Foster, Lynn V. 2002. *Handbook to Life in the Ancient Maya World*. Facts on File.

Frede, Michael. 1999. "Monotheism and Pagan Philosophy in Later Antiquity." In Polymnia Athanassiadi and Michael Frede (1999), *Pagan Monotheism in Late Antiquity*. Oxford University Press.

Freedman, David Noel. 1987. " 'Who Is Like Thee Among the Gods?' The Religion of Early Israel." In Miller, Jr. et al., eds. (1987).

———, ed. 1992. *The Anchor Bible Dictionary*. 6 vols. Doubleday.

Freud, Sigmund. 1953. *The Future of an Illusion*, trans. W. D. Robson-Scott. Liveright.

Friedman, Richard Elliott. 1997. *The Hidden Face of God*. HarperCollins.

———. 2003. *The Bible with Sources Revealed*. HarperSanFrancisco.

Gabriel, Richard A. 2002. *Gods of Our Fathers: The Memory of Egypt in Judaism and Christianity*. Greenwood Press.

Gager, John. 1975. *Kingdom and Community: The Social World of Early Christianity*. Prentice-Hall.

———. 2000. *Reinventing Paul*. Oxford University Press.

Gardner, James. 2003. *Biocosm*. Inner Ocean Publishing.

Garr, W. Randall. 2003. *In His Own Image and Likeness: Humanity, Divinity, and Monotheism*. Brill Academic Publishers.

Gatschet, Albert Samuel. 1890. *The Klamath Indians of Southwestern Oregon*. U.S. Government Printing Office.

Gerardi, Pamela. 1986. "Declaring War in Mesopotamia." *Archiv fur Orientforschung* 33: 30–38.

Gnuse, Robert Karl. 1997. *No Other Gods: Emergent Monotheism in Israel*. Sheffield Academic Press.

Goedicke, Hans. 1975. "Unity and Diversity in the Oldest Religion of Ancient Egypt." In Goedicke and Roberts, eds. (1975).

Goedicke, Hans, and J. J. M. Roberts, eds. 1975. *Unity and Diversity*. Johns Hopkins University Press.

Goldenberg, Robert. 1998. *The Nations That Know Thee Not: Ancient Jewish Attitudes toward Other Religions*. New York University Press.

Goldziher, Ignaz. 1981. *Introduction to Islamic Theology and Law*. Princeton University Press.

Goode, William J. 1951. *Religion Among the Primitives*. Free Press.

Goodenough, Erwin R. 1935. *By Light, Light*. Yale University Press.

———. 1938. *Politics of Philo Judaeus*. Yale University Press.

———. 1986. *An Introduction to Philo Judaeus*. 2nd ed. University Press of America.

Griffiths, J. Gwyn. 1980. *The Origins of Osiris and His Cult*. E. J. Brill.

———. 2002. "Osiris." In Redford, ed. (2002).

Grosby, Steven. 1991. "Religion and nationality in antiquity." *European Journal of Sociology* 32:229–65.

Gusinde, Martin. 1931. *The Fireland Indians*. Vol. 1. *The Selk'nam: On the Life and Thought of a Hunting People of the Great Island of Tierra del Fuego*. Mödling bei Wien: Verlag der Internationalen Zeitschrift.

Guthrie, Stewart E. 1980. "A Cognitive Theory of Religion." *Current Anthropology* 21 (2):181–204.

———. 1995. *Faces in the Clouds: A New Theory of Religion*. Oxford University Press.

Hallo, William W., and J. J. A. van Dijk. 1968. *The Exaltation of Inanna*. Yale University Press.

Halpern, Baruch. 1983. *The Emergence of Israel in Canaan*. Scholars Press.

———. 1987. " 'Brisker Pipes than Poetry': The Development of Israelite Monotheism." In Jacob Neusner et al. (1987), *Judaic Perspectives on Ancient Israel*. Fortress Press.

———. 2003. "Late Israelite Astronomies and the Early Greeks." In Dever and Gitin, eds. (2003).

Halpern, Baruch, and David S. Vanderhooft. 1991. "The Editions of Kings in the 7th–6th Centuries B.C.E." *Hebrew Union College Annual* 62.

Handy, E. S. Craighill. 1927. "Polynesian Religion." *Bernice C. Bishop Museum Bulletin* 34.

———. 1940. "Perspectives in Polynesian Religion." *Journal of the Polynesian Society* 49:309–30.

Handy, Lowell K. 1994. *Among the Host of Heaven: The Syro-Palestinian Pantheon as Bureaucracy*. Eisenbrauns.

———. 1996. "The Appearance of Pantheon in Judah." In Edelman, ed. (1996).

Harland, Philip A. 2002. "Connections with Elites in the World of the Early Christians." In Anthony J. Blasi et al., eds. (2002), *Handbook of Early Christianity*. Altamira Press.

———. 2003. *Associations, Synagogues, and Congregations*. Fortress Press.

Hayden, Brian. 1993. *Archaeology: The Science of Once and Future Things*. W. H. Freeman.

Hegedus, Tim. 1998. "The Urban Expansion of the Isis Cult: A Quantitative Approach." *Studies in Religion* 27:161–78.

Hellerman, Joseph H. 2001. *The Ancient Church as Family*. Fortress Press.

Henricks, Robert G. 1994. *The Religions of China*. Audiotape lectures. The Teaching Company.

Ho, Ping-ti. 1975. *The Cradle of the East*. University of Chicago Press.

Hodgson, Marshall G. S. 1977. *The Venture of Islam*. 2 vol. University of Chicago Press.

Hoebel, E. Adamson. 1983. *The Law of Primitive Man*. Atheneum.

Hogbin, H. Ian. 1934. *Law and Order in Polynesia*. Harcourt Brace.

Holloway, Steven W. 2002. *Assur Is King! Assur Is King!: Religion in the Exercise of Power in the Neo-Assyrian Empire*. Brill Academic Publishers.

Horn, Siegfried H. 1999. "The Divided Monarchy: The Kingdoms of Judah and Israel." In Shanks, ed. (1999).

Hornung, Erik. 1996. *Conceptions of God in Ancient Egypt: The One and the Many*, trans. John Baines. Cornell University Press.

———. 1999. *Akhenaten and the Religion of Light*, trans. David Lorton. Cornell University Press.

Horsley, Richard. 1993. "Palestinian Jewish Groups and Their Messiahs in Late Second Temple Times." In Wim Beuken et al., eds. (1993), *Messianism Through History*. Orbis Books.

Horsley, Richard, and Neil Asher Silberman. 2002. *The Message and the Kingdom*. Fortress Press.

Horton, Robin. 1960. "A Definition of Religion, and Its Uses." *Journal of the Royal Anthropological Institute of Great Britain and Ireland* 90 (2):201–26.

———. 1967. "African Traditional Thought and Western Science." *Africa* 37:50–71.

———. 1982. "Tradition and Modernity Revisited." In Martin Hollis and Steven Lukes (1982), *Rationality and Relativism*. Basil Blackwell.

Howells, William. 1962. *The Heathens: Primitive Man and His Religions*. Sheffield Publishing.

Hoyland, Robert. 2001. *Arabia and the Arabs*. Routledge.

Hubbard, Robert L. 1988. *The Book of Ruth*. William B. Eerdmans.

Jacobsen, Thorkild. 1976. *The Treasures of Darkness: A History of Mesopotamian Religion*. Yale University Press.

James, E. O. 1961. *Comparative Religion*. Methuen.

James, William. 1982. *The Varieties of Religious Experience*. Penguin.

Jenness, Diamond. 1959. *The People of the Twilight*. University of Chicago Press.

Karabell, Zachary. 2007. *Peace Be upon You: Fourteen Centuries of Muslim, Christian, and Jewish Coexistence in the Middle East*. Knopf.

Karsh, Efraim. 2006. *Islamic Imperialism: A History*. Yale University Press.

Katz, Richard. 1976. "Education for Transcendence: !Kia-Healing with the Kalahari !Kung." In Richard B. Lee and Irven DeVore, eds. (1976), *Kalahari Hunter-Gatherers*. Harvard University Press.

Kaufman, Gordon D. 1972. "Revelation and Cultural History." In Gordon D. Kaufman (1972), *God the Problem*. Harvard University Press.

Kaufmann, Yehezkel. 1972. *The Religion of Israel: From Its Beginnings to the Babylonian Exile*. Abridged trans. by Moshe Greenberg of the first 7 vol. of the 8-vol. *History of Israelite Religion from Its Beginnings to the End of the Second Temple*. Schocken Books.

Keel, Othmar, and Christoph Uehlinger. 1998. *Gods, Goddesses, and Images of God in Ancient Israel*, trans. Thomas H. Trapp. Fortress Press.

Keightley, David N. 1978. *Sources of Shang History: The Oracle-Bone Inscriptions of Bronze Age China*. University of California Press.

———. 1998. "Shamanism, Death, and the Ancestors: Religious Mediation in Neolithic and Shang China (ca. 5000–1000 B.C.)." *Asiatische Studien* 52:763–831.

Kelekna, Pita. 1998. "War and Theocracy." In Elsa M. Redmond (1998), *Chiefdoms and Chieftaincy in the Americas*. University Press of Florida.

Kennedy, Hugh. 1986. *The Prophet and the Age of the Caliphates*. Longman.

King, Philip J. 1988. *Amos, Hosea, Micah—An Archaeological Commentary*. Westminster Press.

Kirch, Patrick Vinton. 1989. *The Evolution of the Polynesian Chiefdoms.* Cambridge University Press.

Kirk, G. S., J. E. Raven, and M. Schofield. 1983. *The Presocratic Philosophers.* Cambridge University Press.

Klassen, William. 1992. "Love: New Testament and Early Jewish Literature." In Freedman, ed. (1992).

Klein, Ralph W. 1979. *Israel in Exile.* Fortress Press.

———. 1988. *Ezekiel: The Prophet and His Message.* University of South Carolina Press.

Kloppenborg, John S., and Stephen G. Wilson, eds. 1996. *Voluntary Associations in the Graeco-Roman World.* Routledge.

Knauf, Ernst Axel. 1992. "Ishmaelites." In Freedman, ed. (1992).

Knohl, Israel. 2008. " 'By Three Days, Live': Messiahs, Ressurrection, and Ascent to Heaven in *Hazon Gabrie.*" *Journal of Religion* 88:147–58.

Koch, Klaus. 1955. "Is There a Doctrine of Retribution in the Old Testament?" In James L. Crenshaw, ed. (1983), *Theodicy in the Old Testament.* Fortress Press.

Konner, Melvin. 1990. *Why the Reckless Survive.* Viking.

———. 2003. *Unsettled: An Anthropology of the Jews.* Viking.

Korpel, Marjo Christina Annette. 1990. *A Rift in the Clouds: Ugaritic and Hebrew Descriptions of the Divine.* Munster.

Kramer, Samuel Noah. 1952. *Enmerkar and the Lord of Aratta.* University Museum, University of Pennsylvania.

Lamberg-Karlovsky, C. C., and Jeremy Sabloff. 1995. *Ancient Civilizations: The Near East and Mesoamerica.* Waveland Press.

Lambert, W. G. 1975. "The Historical Development of the Mesopotamian Pantheon." In Goedicke and Roberts, eds. (1975).

Lang, Bernhard. 1983. *Monotheism and the Prophetic Minority.* Almond Press.

———. 1999. "Wisdom." In van der Toorn et al., eds. (1999).

Lapidus, Ira M. 2002. *A History of Islamic Societies.* 2d ed. Cambridge University Press.

Latourette, Kenneth Scott. 1975. *A History of Christianity.* Vol. I. *Beginnings to 1500.* HarperCollins.

Le Page Renouf, Peter. 1884. *Lectures on the Origin and Growth of Religion.* Williams and Norgate.

Lewis, D. 1974. "Voyaging Stars: Aspects of Polynesian and Micronesian Astronomy." *Philosophical Transactions of the Royal Society of London* A, 276:133–48.

Lichtheim, Miriam, ed. 1975. *Ancient Egyptian Literature.* Vol. 1. University of California Press.

Limburg, James. 1993. *Jonah: A Commentary.* Westminster/John Knox Press.

Lings, Martin. 1983. *Muhammad: His Life Based on the Earliest Sources.* Inner Traditions International.

Lohfink, Norbert. 1987. "The Cult Reform of Josiah of Judah: 2 Kings 22–23 as a Source for the History of Israelite Religion," trans. Christopher R. Seitz. In Miller, Jr. et al., eds. (1987).

Lopez Austin, Alfredo. 1988. *The Human Body and Ideology: Concepts of the Ancient Nahuas,* trans. Thelma Ortiz de Montellano and Bernard Ortiz de Montellano. University of Utah Press.

Lowie, Robert. 1952. *Primitive Religion.* Grosset & Dunlap.

Lubbock, John. 1892. *The Origin of Civilization and the Primitive Condition of Man.* 5th ed. Appleton.

MacDonald, D. B. 2003. "Ilah." In P. J. Bearman et al., eds.

MacMullen, Ramsay. 1984. *Christianizing the Roman Empire (AD 100–400)*. Yale University Press.

Maddox, John Lee. 1923. *The Medicine Man*. Macmillan.

Makemson, Maude Worcester. 1941. *The Morning Star Rises: An Account of Polynesian Astronomy*. Yale University Press.

Malherbe, Abraham J. 1983. *Social Aspects of Early Christianity*. Fortress Press.

Malo, David. 1903. *Hawaiian Antiquities,* trans. N. B. Emerson. Hawaiian Gazette Co.

Man, Edward Horace. 1932. *On the Aboriginal Inhabitants of the Andaman Islands*. Royal Anthropological Institute of Great Britain and Ireland.

Mann, Michael. 1986. *The Sources of Social Power*. Cambridge University Press.

Marett, R. R. 1909. *The Threshold of Religion*. Methuen (from facsimile edition published 1997 by Routledge/Thoemmes Press).

———. 1936. *Tylor*. John Wiley and Sons.

Marshall, Lorna. 1962. "!Kung Bushman Religious Beliefs." *Africa* 32:221–51.

McCarter, Kyle P. Jr. 1987. "Aspects of the Religion of the Israelite Monarchy: Biblical and Epigraphic Data." In Miller et al. (1987).

———. 1999. "The Patriarchal Age: Abraham, Isaac and Jacob." In Shanks, ed. (1999).

McCready, Wayne O. 1996. "Ekklesia and Voluntary Associations." In Kloppenborg and Wilson, eds. (1996).

McDannell, Colleen, and Bernhard Lang. 2001. *Heaven: A History*. 2d ed. Yale University Press.

McLean, B. Hudson. 1996. "The Place of Cult in Voluntary Associations and Christian Churches on Delos." In Kloppenborg and Wilson, eds. (1996).

McNeill, William. 1980. *The Human Condition*. Princeton University Press.

———. 1990. "The Rise of the West after Twenty-five Years." *Journal of World History* 1:1–21.

McNutt, Paula M. 1999. *Reconstructing the Society of Ancient Israel*. Westminster/John Knox Press.

Meeks, Wayne A. 2003. *The First Urban Christians*. Yale University Press.

———. ed. 1993. *The HarperCollins Study Bible*. HarperCollins.

Meier, John P. 1991. *A Marginal Jew: Rethinking the Historical Jesus*. Vol. 1. Doubleday.

Miles, Jack. 1995. *God: A Biography*. Knopf.

Miller, Patrick D. 2000. *The Religion of Ancient Israel*. Westminster/John Knox Press.

Miller, Patrick, Jr. et al., eds. 1987. *Ancient Israelite Religion*. Fortress Press.

Morenz, Ziegfried. 1973. *Egyptian Religion,* trans. Ann E. Keep. Cornell University Press.

Murdock, George Peter. 1934. *Our Primitive Contemporaries*. Macmillan.

Murphy, Cullen. 1998. *The Word According to Eve*. Houghton Mifflin.

Murphy, Roland E. 1992. "Wisdom in the Old Testament." In Freedman, ed. (1992).

Nickelsburg, G. W. E. 1992. "Son of Man." In Freedman, ed. (1992).

Niehr, Herbert. 1995. "The Rise of YHWH in Judahite and Israelite Religion." In Diana Vikander Edelman, ed. (1995), *The Triumph of Elohim*. William B. Eerdmans.

———. 1999. "The Host of Heaven." In van der Toorn et al., eds. (1999).

Nielsen, Kirsten. 1997. *Ruth: A Commentary*. Westminster/John Knox Press.

Nikam, N. A., and Richard McKeon, eds. 1959. *The Edicts of Asoka*. University of Chicago Press.

Nikiprowetzky, V. 1975. "Ethical Monotheism." *Daedalus* 104:69–89.

Norbeck, Edward. 1961. *Religion in Primitive Society*. Harper & Brothers.

Oden, Robert. 1996. *The Old Testament: An Introduction*. Audio lectures. The Teaching Company.

O'Flaherty, Wendy Doniger, trans. 1981. *The Rig Veda: An Anthology.* Penguin.

Ogilvie, R. M. 1969. *The Romans and Their Gods in the Age of Augustus.* Norton.

Olyan, Saul M. 1988. *Asherah and the Cult of Yahweh in Israel.* Society of Biblical Literature.

Orlinsky, Harry Meyer. 1974. *Essays in Biblical Culture and Bible Translation.* Ktav.

Ortiz de Montellano, Bernard R. 1990. *Aztec Medicine, Health, and Nutrition.* Rutgers University Press.

Otto, Rudolf. 1977. *The Idea of the Holy,* trans. John W. Harvey. Oxford University Press.

Oxtoby, Willard G. 1973. "Reflections on the Idea of Salvation." In Eric J. Sharpe and John R. Hinnells, eds., *Man and His Salvation.* Manchester University Press.

Pagels, Elaine. 1989. *The Gnostic Gospels.* Vintage.

————. 2003. *Beyond Belief.* Random House.

Pardee, D. 1999. "Eloah." In van der Toorn et al., eds. (1999).

Parker, Simon B., ed. 1997. *Ugaritic Narrative Poetry.* Society of Biblical Literature.

Parpola, Simo. 2000. "Monotheism in Ancient Assyria." In Barbara Nevling Porter, ed. (2000), *One God or Many?* Casco Bay Assyriological Institute.

Peters, F. E. 1991. "The Quest of the Historical Muhammad." *International Journal of Middle East Studies* 23:291–315.

————. 1994. *A Reader on Classical Islam.* Princeton University Press.

Peters, Rudolph. 1987. "Jihad." In Mircea Eliade, ed. (1987), *The Encyclopedia of Religion.* Vol. 8, 88–91.

Philo of Alexandria. 1929. *Works.* 10 vol., 2 suppl. Heinemann; Putnam.

Philo. 1894. *The Works of Philo Judaeus.* Vol. 1, trans. C. D. Yonge. George Bell and Sons.

Phipps, William E. 1996. *Muhammad and Jesus.* Continuum.

Pinch, Geraldine. 2002. *Handbook of Egyptian Mythology.* ABC-CLIO.

Pinker, Steven. 1997. *How the Mind Works.* Norton.

Pitard, Wayne T. 2002. "Voices from the Dust: The Tablets from Ugarit and the Bible." In Mark W. Chavalas and K. Lawson Younger, Jr., eds. (2002), *Mesopotamia and the Bible.* Sheffield Academic Press.

Poo, Mu-chou. 1998. *In Search of Personal Welfare: A View of Ancient Chinese Religion.* State University of New York Press.

Pritchard, James B., ed. 1958. *The Ancient Near East.* Vol. 1. Princeton University Press.

Provan, Iain, V. Philips Long, and Tremper Longman III. 2003. *A Biblical History of Israel.* Westminster/John Knox Press.

Quirke, Stephen. 1992. *Ancient Egyptian Religion.* British Museum Press.

Rad, Gerhard von. 1972. *Wisdom in Israel.* Trinity Press International.

Radcliffe-Brown, A. R. 1922. *The Andaman Islanders.* Cambridge University Press.

Radin, Paul. 1937. *Primitive Religion.* Viking.

Rainey, Anson F. 2001. "Israel in Merenptah's Inscription and Reliefs." *Israel Exploration Journal* 51:57–75.

Rasmussen, Knud. 1932. *Intellectual Culture of the Copper Eskimos.* Gyldendal.

Redford, Donald B. 1984. *Akhenaten: The Heretic King.* Princeton University Press.

————. 1992. *Egypt, Canaan, and Israel in Ancient Times.* Princeton University Press.

————, ed. 2002. *The Ancient Gods Speak: A Guide to Egyptian Religion.* Oxford University Press.

Reeves, C.N. 2001. *Akhenaten: Egypt's False Prophet.* Thames and Hudson.

Reichel-Dolmatoff, Gerardo. 1987. *Shamanism and Art of the Eastern Tukanoan Indians: Colombian Northwest Amazon.* E. J. Brill.

Reynolds, Gabriel Said, ed. 2008. *The Qurān in Its Historical Context.* Routledge.

Ridley, Matt. 1996. *The Origins of Virtue.* Penguin.

Rivers, W. H. R. 1924. *Medicine, Magic, and Religion*. Kegan Paul, Trench, Trubner and Co.

Roberts, J. J. M. 1975. "Divine Freedom and Cultic Manipulation in Israel and Mesopotamia." In Goedicke and Roberts, eds. (1975).

Robinson, Neal. 2003. *Discovering the Qur'an*. Georgetown University Press.

Roediger, H. L. 1996. "Memory Illusions." *Journal of Memory and Language* 35:76–100.

Roediger, H. L., J. D. Jacoby, and K. B. McDermott. 1996. "Misinformation Effects in Recall: Creating False Memories through Repeated Retrieval." *Journal of Memory and Language* 35:300–18.

Rogers, Spencer L. 1982. *The Shaman: His Symbols and His Healing Power*. Charles C. Thomas.

Rose, Martin. 1992. "Names of God in the Old Testament." In Freedman, ed. (1992).

Runia, David T. 1988. "God and Man in Philo of Alexandria." In David T. Runia (1990), *Exegesis and Philosophy*. Variorum.

———. 1990. "Philo, Alexandrian and Jew." In David T. Runia (1990), *Exegesis and Philosophy*. Variorum.

———. 1999. "Logos." In van der Toorn et al., eds. (1999).

Saggs, H. W. F. 1978. *The Encounter with the Divine in Mesopotamia and Israel*. Athlone Press, University of London.

———. 1989. *Civilization Before Greece and Rome*. Yale University Press.

Sahlins, Marshall. 1963. "Poor Man, Rich Man, Big-man, Chief: Political Types in Melanesia and Polynesia." *Comparative Studies in Society and History* 5:285–303.

Sanders, E. P. 1991. *Paul*. Oxford University Press.

———. 1995. *The Historical Figure of Jesus*. Penguin.

Sandmel, Samuel. 1979. *Philo of Alexandria*. Oxford University Press.

Sasson, Jack M. 1990. *Jonah*. Anchor Bible/Doubleday.

Schacht, Joseph. 1982. *An Introduction to Islamic Law*. Oxford University Press.

Schenck, Kenneth. 2005. *A Brief Guide to Philo*. Westminster/John Knox Press.

Schloen, J. David. 2002. "W. F. Albright and the Origins of Israel." *Near Eastern Archaeology* 65:56–62.

Schlogl, Hermann A. 2002. "Aten." In Redford, ed. (2002).

Schmid, Konrad. 2009. "Judean Identity and Ecumenicity: The Political Theology of the Priestly Document." In Gary Knoppers, Oded Lipshits, and Manfred Oeming (eds.), *The Judeans in the Achaemenid Age*. Eisenbrauns.

Schmidt, B. B. 1999. "Moon." In van der Toorn et al., eds. (1999).

Schniedewind, William M. 2003. "The Evolution of Name Theology." In M. Patrick Graham et al., eds., *The Chronicler as Theologian*. Continuum.

———. 1993. "History and Interpretation: The Religion of Ahab and Manasseh in the Book of Kings." *Catholic Biblical Quarterly* 55:4.

———. 2004. *How the Bible Became a Book*. Cambridge University Press.

———. 1999. *Society and the Promise to David*. Oxford University Press.

Scholem, Gershom. 1971. *The Messianic Idea in Judaism*. Schocken Books.

Schweitzer, Albert. 2001. *The Quest of the Historical Jesus*, trans. W. Montgomery et al. Fortress Press.

Scott, R. B. Y. 1978. *The Relevance of the Prophets*. Macmillan.

Scott-Moncrieff, Philip David. 1913. *Paganism and Christianity in Egypt*. Cambridge University Press.

Seow, C. L. 1992. "Hosea." In Freedman, ed. (1992).

Service, Elman R. 1966. *The Hunters*. Prentice-Hall.

———. *Profiles in Ethnology*. HarperCollins.

Shafer, Byron E., ed. 1991. *Religion in Ancient Egypt.* Cornell University Press.

Shanks, Hershel, ed. 1999. *Ancient Israel: From Abraham to the Roman Destruction of the Temple.* Prentice-Hall.

Sharer, Robert J. 1996. *Daily Life in Maya Civilization.* Greenwood Press.

Silverman, David P. 1991. "Divinity and Deities in Ancient Egypt." In Shafer, ed. (1991).

Singer, Peter. 1981. *The Expanding Circle.* Farrar, Straus and Giroux.

Smart, Ninian. 1969. *The Religious Experience of Mankind.* Scribner's.

Smith, Huston. 1991. *The World's Religions.* HarperCollins.

Smith, Mark S. 2001. *The Origins of Biblical Monotheism.* Oxford University Press.

———. 2002a. *The Early History of God: Yahweh and the Other Deities in Ancient Israel.* William B. Eerdmans.

———. 2002b. "Ugaritic Studies and Israelite Religion: A Retrospective View." *Near Eastern Archaeology* 65:1.

———. 2004. *The Memoirs of God: History, Memory, and the Experience of the Divine in Ancient Israel.* Fortress Press.

Smith, Morton. 1963. "Isaiah and the Persians." *Journal of the American Oriental Society* 83:415–421.

———. 1978. *Jesus the Magician.* Harper and Row.

———. 1987. *Palestinian Parties and Politics that Shaped the Old Testament.* SCM Press.

Spencer, Baldwin. 1927. *The Arunta: A Study of a Stone Age People.* Macmillan.

Spencer, Baldwin, and F. J. Gillen. 1904. *The Northern Tribes of Central Australia.* Macmillan.

Sperber, Dan. 1982. "Apparently Irrational Beliefs." In Martin Hollis and Steven Lukes, eds., *Rationality and Relativism.* Basil Blackwell.

Spier, Leslie. 1930. *Klamath Ethnography.* University of California Press.

Stark, Rodney. 1997. *The Rise of Christianity.* HarperCollins.

Stark, Rodney, and Roger Finke. 2000. *Acts of Faith: Explaining the Human Side of Religion.* University of California Press.

Stern, Ephraim. 2003. "The Phoenician Source of Palestinian Cults at the End of the Iron Age." In Dever and Gitin, eds. (2003).

Stillman, Norman. 1979. *The Jews of Arab Lands.* Jewish Publication Society of America.

Swanson, Guy E. 1964. *The Birth of the Gods.* University of Michigan Press.

Sweeney, Marvin A. 2000. *The Twelve Prophets.* 2 vols. The Liturgical Press.

———. 2001. *King Josiah of Judah.* Oxford University Press.

Teter, Emily. 2002. "Maat." In Redford, ed. (2002).

Theissen, Gerd. 1985. *Biblical Faith: An Evolutionary Approach,* trans. John Bowden. Fortress Press.

Thomson, Robert W. 1999. *The Armenian History Attributed to Sebeos.* Liverpool University Press.

Thwaites, Reuben Gold, ed. 1900. *The Jesuit Relations and Allied Documents: Travels and Explorations of the Jesuit Missionaries in New France.* Vol. 68. Burrows Brothers.

Tigay, Jeffrey. 1986. *You Shall Have No Other Gods: Israelite Religion in the Light of Hebrew Inscriptions.* Scholars Press.

———. 1987. "Israelite Religion: The Onomastic and Epigraphic Evidence." In Miller et al., eds. (1987).

Tobin, Thomas H. 1992. "Logos." In Freedman, ed. (1992).

Traunecker, Claude. 2001. *The Gods of Egypt,* trans. David Lorton. Cornell University Press.

Trigger, Bruce G. 1993. *Early Civilizations*. The American University in Cairo Press.

Tuckett, C. M. 1992. "Q (Gospel Source)." In Freedman, ed. (1992).

Turcan, Robert. 1996. *The Cults of the Roman Empire*, trans. Antonia Nevill. Blackwell.

Turnbull, Colin M. 1965. *Wayward Servants: The Two Worlds of the African Pygmies*. Natural History Press.

Turner, George. 1831. *Nineteen Years in Polynesia*. John Snow.

Tyan, Emile. "Djihad." In Bearman et al., eds. (2003).

Tylor, Edward. 1866. "The Religion of Savages." *Fortnightly Review* 6:71–86.

———. 1871. *Primitive Culture*. Vol. 1. John Murray (from facsimile editing published by Gordon Press in 1974).

———. 1874. *Primitive Culture*. Vol. 2. Appleton.

Uffenheimer, Benjamin. 1986. "Myth and Reality in Ancient Israel." In Eisenstadt, ed. (1986).

Van Bakel, Martin A. 1991. "The Political Economy of an Early State: Hawaii and Samoa Compared." In Henri J.M. Claessen and Pieter van de Velde, eds. (1991), *Early State Economics*. Transaction Publishers.

van der Toorn, K., B. Becking, and P. W. van der Horst, eds. 1999. *Dictionary of Deities and Demons in the Bible DDD*. 2d ed. Brill Academic Publishers.

Van Selms, A. 1973. "Temporary Henotheism." In M. A. Beek et al., eds. (1973), *Symbolae biblicae et Mesopotamicae, Francisco Mario Theodoro de Liagre Bohl dedicatae*. E. J. Brill.

Vecsey, Christopher. 1983. *Traditional Ojibwa Religion and Its Historical Changes*. American Philosophical Society.

Walker, Christopher, and Michael Dick. 2001. *The Induction of the Cult Image in Ancient Mesopotamia*. Vol. 1. State Archives of Assyria Literary Texts, the Neo-Assyrian Text Corpus Project.

Watson, Adam. 1992. *The Evolution of International Society*. Routledge.

Watt, W. Montgomery. 1956. *Muhammad at Medina*. Oxford University Press.

———. 1964. *Muhammad: Prophet and Statesman*. Oxford University Press.

———. 2003. "Makka." In Bearman et al., eds. (2003).

———. 1974. "Islamic Conceptions of the Holy War." In Thomas Patrick Murphy, ed., *The Holy War*. Ohio State University Press.

Weinberg, Steven. 1979. *The First Three Minutes*. Bantam.

Welch, A. T. 2003. "Al-Kuran." In Bearman et al., eds. (2003).

Wente, Edward F., and John R. Baines. 1989. "Egypt: The New Kingdom." In *Encyclopedia Britannica*. 15th ed., vol. 18.

White, Leslie. 1959. *The Evolution of Culture*. McGraw-Hill.

Williamson, Robert W. 1933. *Religious and Cosmic Beliefs of Central Polynesia*. Vol. 1. Cambridge University Press.

———. 1937. *Religion and Social Organization in Central Polynesia*. Cambridge University Press.

Wilson, A. N. 1997. *Paul*. Norton.

Winston, David. 1985. *Logos and Mystical Theology in Philo of Alexandria*. Hebrew Union College Press.

Witt, R. E. 1997. *Isis in the Ancient World*. Johns Hopkins University Press.

Wright, Robert. 1994. *The Moral Animal: Evolutionary Psychology and Everyday Life*. Pantheon.

———. 2000. *Nonzero: The Logic of Human Destiny*. Pantheon.

Wyatt, N. 1999. "Astarte." In van der Toorn et al., eds. (1999).

Xella, P. 1999. "Resheph." In van der Toorn et al., eds. (1999).

Yoffe, Norman. 1995. "Political Economy in Early Mesopotamian States." *Annual Review of Anthropology* 24:281–311.

Zevit, Ziony. 2000. *The Religions of Ancient Israel*. Continuum.

Index

Reading Group Guide

THE EVOLUTION OF

GOD

by

ROBERT WRIGHT

A conversation with
Robert Wright

In The Moral Animal *you track the evolutionary psychology of such things as friendship, monogamy, and xenophobia, arguing that natural selection furnished us with basic moral intuitions but also with a tendency to deploy moral reasoning in a self-serving way. In* Nonzero, *you link Darwinian thought to game theory to suggest that human history has a moral direction and has led people to expand their conception of community, acknowledging the fundamental humanity of more and more people from more and more ethnic, religious, and national backgrounds. In* The Evolution of God *you tell a similar story from a religious perspective, proposing that the increasing goodness of God reflects the increasing goodness of our species. What prompted you to write this book and how has your notion of what a mature religion could look like changed? Is it still evolving?*

Religion is so important to so many people that it seems to me unlikely that we can forge a global community without its help. So I wanted to go back and see whether religion has shown the ability to help people expand their conception of community. And, happily, the answer is yes: I argue in the book that ever since their birth, Judaism, Christianity, and Islam have all proved benignly adaptive in that respect (notwithstanding their undeniable bad patches). In that sense they've all grown morally. Whether they will take the culminating step in their maturation—do the things necessary to forge a truly global community—is yet to be seen. But their evolution continues, and I'm hopeful.

You were born in Oklahoma and raised predominantly in Texas. What was your religious upbringing like? Did you attend church as a child?

My parents were Southern Baptists. They weren't fanatical, but they were devout, and going to a Southern Baptist church was a fairly intense experience, I guess, at least in the sense of filling me with a very potent sense of God's existence.

When did you begin to think critically about religion?

My parents accepted the literal creation story in Genesis. So once I started hearing about evolution—and, in particular, once I learned the theory of natural selection in tenth grade—I started to feel tension with my religious faith. Eventually, my religious faith had to recede.

Do you ever pray now? If so, what form does your prayer take?

I meditate, and occasionally my meditation morphs into a kind of prayer to become a better person, but so far as I can tell I'm just talking to myself—or, you might say, one part of me is talking to another part of me.

The Evolution of God *seems a welcome antidote to the spate of books by atheists such as Richard Dawkins, Christopher Hitchens, and Sam Harris, to name a few, that have become huge bestsellers in recent years. Do you believe that atheism has become its own form of fundamentalism? What do you think of these writers' work?*

They're smart guys, but I think that to varying degrees they commit the same mistakes: overestimating the amount of bad religion has done, underestimating the amount of good; and (therefore) thinking that the salvation of the world depends on the eradication of religious faith. One point of my book is that in fact the further evolution of religions can abet the salvation of the world—that is, can help usher in a time of world peace.

Do you think religions share certain core principles?

I think all religions are capable of fostering really beautiful values and really horrible values. Love, hate, heal, kill, and so on. Which values prevail depends on the circumstances in which believers find themselves, and this relationship between circumstance and scriptural interpretation is one thing I tried to illuminate in *The Evolution of God.*

You write often about the failure of the moral imagination, especially as it applies to the three monotheistic religions. What in your mind would it take to inspire these communities of religious people to be more imaginative?

By "moral imagination" I mean the capacity to put yourself in the shoes of other people, especially people in circumstances very different from your own. And I think the fate of the world depends on our ability to expand our moral imaginations. As for what forces would aid this process right now: I think the main thing is for people in the different faith communities to see (a) that people in other communities are fundamentally like themselves, driven by the same basic set of human needs and aspirations; and (b) that the people in the world's various communities are increasingly in the same boat; the world is becoming a pretty small place, and our fortunes are increasingly intertwined.

The Bible is a collection of books written by multiple people, whereas the entire text of the Qur'an is said to have been uttered by Muhammad. Do you think that this influences the ways in which these two texts are interpreted today?

Well, I think this sometimes leads people to judge the Qur'an unfairly. Comparing the Bible to the Qur'an is like comparing a library of great books collected over a millennium or more with a single book written within a couple of decades. And, actually, some of the "books" within the Bible—Psalms, for example—are themselves the work of many people working over many centuries. (Of course, Muslims believe the Qur'an emanated ultimately from God, not from Muhammad, and for that matter some Christians and Jews have comparable beliefs about the ultimate source of biblical scripture, but here I'm making the basic scholarly assumption that scriptures are the work of human beings.)

You talk about the scriptures of Christianity, Islam, and Judaism as maps of the "landscape of religious tolerance and intolerance." How can contemporary followers of these religious communities read their scriptures?

Well, they should understand that both the belligerent scriptures, espousing violence, and the benign scriptures, espousing tolerance and mutual understanding, were written under particular circumstances that were conducive to those respective themes. In a certain sense both themes were appropriate to their circumstances—at least, both themes grew naturally out of the perceptions that were prevalent at the time. And what I want to emphasize is that we're at a time in history when, if our perceptions of our situation are true, they will lead us to emphasize tolerance and understanding, because that's what's in our interest.

In a time when prejudice is as rampant as ever—and when religion appears, at least on the surface, to be the cause of this unrest—how can people incorporate your theories about religion into their daily lives?

I would encourage people who observe the so-called religious conflicts in the world to consider the possibility that religion isn't really the problem. In other words, underlying these conflicts are disputes or resentments or grievances that aren't themselves grounded in religion. The Israel-Palestine conflict is a good example. It started as an essentially secular dispute over land, and, as the dispute went unresolved, extremists on both sides started justifying their extremism in religious terms. One basic point of *The Evolution of God* is: religion isn't the *source* of the world's tensions; there are deeper causes, and if we address them, religion will adapt benignly in response.

Questions and topics for discussion

1. Near the beginning of *The Evolution of God,* Robert Wright states that he is a "materialist." What does he mean by this and can you explain what a materialist view of the scriptures might look like? In your opinion, can a materialist explain the history of religion?

2. Discuss the origins of religion from Wright's point of view. How do they alter the commonly perceived order of events?

3. Does it matter to you that the modern incarnation of a religion might be so dramatically different from what it was when it came into being? If so, why?

4. According to Wright, religion develops mainly in response to political and economic events. Discuss Wright's theory on the connection between the political power of a people and the god that they believe in.

5. What does Wright mean when he talks about the "moral imagination" of a people?

6. Discuss the different meanings of "salvation" in the three Abrahamic faiths. In Wright's view, what one thing does salvation require according to the prophets of all three faiths? What distinctions are made between "social salvation" and "personal salvation"?

7. What is the difference between a zero-sum versus a non-zero-sum view of the world? What is the relationship, according to Wright, between non-zero-sumness and globalization? Do you think that combining religion and economics could be problematic? Why or why not?

8. What, according to Wright, are "facts on the ground" and how do they influence how and why religions evolve?

9. Some people have been skeptical about Wright's claim that religious history seems to be going somewhere, as if guided by an invisible hand, and that Judaism, Christianity, and Islam (as well as other religions) appear to have a "moral direction"— and that the direction is on balance toward the good. Do you agree that the "invisible hand" metaphor accurately captures Wright's view? Do you agree with Wright's view?

10. Do you believe that religion has become more ethical over time and that morality within societies dominated by Abrahamic faiths (or, for that matter, morality within other societies) has increased? If so, do you believe that this increase came from faith and did it involve non-zero-sum logic? Is this, in your opinion, evidence for the existence of God?

11. At the end of the book Wright begins to wonder whether the evolution of "God," the concept, might provide evidence for the existence of God, the reality. Were you surprised by this line of thought?

12. Do you believe that there's room for religion and notions of divinity and higher purpose in a modern scientific world?

About the Author

ROBERT WRIGHT is the author of *Nonzero: The Logic of Human Destiny* (2000), *The Moral Animal: Evolutionary Psychology and Everyday Life* (1994), and *Three Scientists and Their Gods: Looking for Meaning in an Age of Information* (1988). He has taught philosophy at Princeton and religion at the University of Pennsylvania, and has been a contributor to *The New Yorker, The Atlantic,* the *New York Times Magazine, Slate, Time,* and *The New Republic.* He has won the National Magazine Award for Essay and Criticism, and his books have together sold hundreds of thousands of copies and been translated into more than a dozen languages. He is currently a Bernard Schwartz senior fellow at the New America Foundation.

The Ornament of the World

How Muslims, Jews, and Christians Created a
Culture of Tolerance in Medieval Spain

by María Rosa Menocal

Foreword by Harold Bloom

"An illuminating and even inspiring work.... The rich and remarkable landscape that we behold in *The Ornament of the World* dates all the way back to the so-called Dark Ages, but the book itself could not be more timely or more encouraging. María Rosa Menocal shows us a rare moment in history when Muslims, Christians, and Jews found a way to live with each other in peace and prosperity.... By showing us what was lost, Menocal reminds us of what might be."
—Jonathan Kirsch, *Los Angeles Times*

"Engaging and accessible.... This study of medieval Spain shows that a powerful Islamic society and its committed Christian opponents were once capable of contending in arms, for a mastery of rich territory, without losing their sense of mutual respect.... It is a valuable contribution." —Stephen Schwartz, *National Review*

"Menocal tells the story exceptionally well.... She successfully drives home an important lesson for a multicultural America fighting fanaticism externally and internally."
—Anne Bartlett, *Miami Herald*

"It is no exaggeration to say that what we presumptuously call 'Western' culture is owed in large measure to the Andalusian enlightenment.... This book partly restores to us a world we have lost."
—Christopher Hitchens, *The Nation*

Back Bay Books
Available wherever paperbacks are sold